Sacha Lord is synonymous with Manchester's nightlife. For over three decades, he has been at the centre of the city's transformation, bringing international music events and festivals to its streets as co-founder of Sankeys and The Warehouse Project. From 2018 until 2025 he was Night-Time Economy Advisor for Greater Manchester by Andy Burnham. He lives in south Manchester with his wife and young son.

Luke Bainbridge is a bestselling author and journalist from Manchester. He has written for the *Guardian* and *Observer* for 25 years and was deputy editor of the award-winning *Observer Music Monthly*. Just like Sacha, he was at the centre of many of the music events recounted in *Tales from the Dancefloor*. He lives in London with his two daughters.

TALES FROM THE DANCE FLOOR

SACHA LORD

with LUKE BAINBRIDGE

MANCHESTER / THE WAREHOUSE PROJECT
PARKLIFE / SANKEYS / THE HAÇIENDA

Harper North

HarperNorth
Windmill Green
24 Mount Street
Manchester M2 3NX

A division of

HarperCollins*Publishers*

1 London Bridge Street   Macken House, 39/40 Mayor Street Upper
London SE1 9GF   Dublin 1, D01 C9W8, Ireland

www.harpercollins.co.uk

First published by HarperNorth in 2024
This updated paperback edition published 2025

1 3 5 7 9 10 8 6 4 2

A catalogue record for this book is
available from the British Library

HB ISBN: 978-0-00-865631-7
PB ISBN: 978-0-00-865635-5

Printed and bound in Great Britain using 100% renewable
electricity by CPI Group (UK) Ltd, Croydon

To my mum, Sandra – I still haven't got
a proper job, but this seems to be working out OK …

And in memory of Pete Bainbridge, Luke's dad,
who passed away while we were finishing this book.

CONTENTS

CONTENTS

CONTENTS

PROLOGUE
A TALE OF TWO CITIES

'Right, fuckin' listen up … here's what's happening … we're going to give you this bag with 20,000 pounds in cash, and you're gonna put on a big night at the Academy for New Year's Eve. Fifteen-hundred tickets, we'll do the door and we'll split the cash fifty-fifty, and you better not fuck it up!'

The guy talking was one of Salford's biggest gangsters. Not someone to be messed with. I was twenty-three, scrawny, and so far out of my depth that I was drowning. I'd not long been promoting student nights and was living in a tiny bedsit, always having my phone cut off because I didn't have twenty pounds to pay the bill. They had bundled me into the back of a car and driven me round town to make me an offer I couldn't refuse, and I didn't understand, either. *Why me? I couldn't do this.*

'But who will we get to DJ?'

'You. You can DJ all night, then we don't have to pay anyone, and make more money.'

Me? 'I can't DJ!'

'The fuck you on about? You're Sasha, aren't you?! You played The Haçienda last month and it sold out!'

I saw a glimmer of light. A possible escape route out of an impossible situation.

'No, I'm not *that* Sasha. I'm not Sasha the DJ, I'm just Sacha, a shitty student promoter. You've got the wrong guy, sorry ...'

'Fuck's sake ...'

The car pulled over, and I was thrown out on to the pavement ...

Like most Mancunians my age, my life is a tale of two cities. Then and now. It has been the best of times, and the worst of times, often in the same week, sometimes the same night. It was a time of euphoric highs and crushing lows. The light and the shade. You don't get a town like this for nothing. Manchester really has been the making of me, and it has so much to answer for the person who I am today.

I've been shot at in a drive-by shooting, bundled into a car by gangsters and had death threats, which was not very acid house. I've been sued and broke, I've had to deal with an army of rats who were high on cocaine, had £130,000 stolen from me during an armed robbery, and have been targeted by a Romanian organised crime gang. Not Balearic, as we say in Manchester.

But I've also been lucky enough to have had some of the most incredible, life-affirming experiences, and to be in the eye of the storm of a musical and cultural revolution. I've gone on to meet many of my musical heroes and have thrown some of the biggest parties that the UK has even seen.

Over the past thirty years, my generation witnessed a musical revolution, as electronic music went from being a niche, underground music genre to arguably the biggest one in the world.

Along the way, I went from a chain-smoking student living hand to mouth, always in danger of having my phone cut off, a visit from the bailiffs or threatened by a gang, to running the biggest nightclub in the world, and the largest metropolitan festival in the country.

We've had some terrible incidents over the years, including tragic deaths at The Warehouse Project and Parklife, which is something you never really get over. No one should go for a night out and not come home again.

I am telling many of the stories in these pages for the very first time.

The Manchester I grew up in is very different to the city it is today. I think some people believe that the reinvention of Manchester started in 1996, after the Manchester bomb planted by the IRA, but the cultural revolution that started with acid house was already well underway before that event.

Manchester has always been a pop-culture city and the revolution of the city is absolutely rooted in that. It's a fundamental part of what makes this the most invigorating and essential place to live: Manchester is the engine room of British music. Even back in the nineteenth century, German immigrants in the city complained that the locals preferred to sing popular contemporary songs rather than listen to the purities of classical music. Manchester is always looking forward. London may have most of the business, but it's Manchester that, more than any other city in the UK, defines the musical direction of this country. I don't think we would have been able to throw the parties and raves in disused breweries, air-raid shelters, and train stations in any other city. The Warehouse Project in particular is inherently Mancunian. It could only happen here.

This is also a city where you can reinvent yourself. You can be who you want to be in Manchester. This is the city where

Morrissey met Marr, Jack met Vera, and Bobby met George and Denis. It's where Engels met Marx, and Rolls met Royce. It's a place where you can make things happen. It's a fascinating, inventive, groundbreaking city that is always moving and makes you feel part of that movement, not a bystander. It's a true city of the people, an egalitarian city, not one based on old money. There's a very little 'old money' in Manchester. This was the world's first industrial modern city, and the world's first post-industrial city. In the words of Tony Walsh's poem 'This is the Place': 'This is the place to do business then dance, where go-getters and go-setters know they have a chance'. That's always been the case, ever since the industrial revolution. Back in 1912, Sir Edward Abbot Parry wrote: 'Manchester is the place where people do things … "*Don't talk about what you are going to do, do it.*" That is the Manchester habit. And in the past through the manifestation of this quality the word Manchester became a synonym for energy and freedom and the right to do and to think without shackles.' The writer Anthony Burgess, admittedly biased having been born in the city's Harpurhey district, recalled in his autobiography *Little Wilson and Big God* how, for a Mancunian, a visit to London before the Second World War 'was an exercise in condescension. London was a day behind Manchester in the arts, in commercial cunning, in economic philosophy'. I'd still agree with that now.

I went from selling leather jackets on a market stall to promoting my very first student club nights. There's that old saying, 'You've got to see it, to be it'. Noel Gallagher says when he first heard 'Sally Cinnamon' by The Stone Roses, it was a real lightbulb moment. He just knew straight away: 'I can do that. I can write songs like that.' When I first started going to nightclubs I thought, *I can do this. I can't DJ or be the singer in the band on stage, but I know I can put the actual night on. I can be a promoter.*

I was just a normal kid growing up. I wasn't a tearaway. I'd never been in trouble or met anyone who was a member of a gang. The only gangsters I'd seen were in *Goodfellas*, so my first year putting on club nights in Manchester was a wake-up call. We'll get to that later, but there were some hairy moments. This city was lawless for a long time in the 1990s.

A lot of people are driven on by their childhoods, or their relationship with their parents, and I guess that I am too. I had a difficult relationship with my dad, who a lot of the time made me feel I'd never amount to much, and I think subconsciously that has pushed me on, to prove him wrong. I also watched him make a bit of a mess of his life and I was determined the same thing wouldn't happen to me.

I still get imposter syndrome, even though I'm not ashamed to say I've done all right for myself. From living in a grotty Salford bedsit, I now live in leafy South Manchester, and I've been lucky enough to hang out with iconic music heroes backstage. But through it all, there was always a nagging part of me that said, *You shouldn't be here. You shouldn't be running the biggest nightclub in the world, and one of the biggest festivals in the UK, and advising the Mayor of Greater Manchester … You should still be on the market stall flogging knock-off leather jackets!*

This is not a memoir, it's more my view of the rebirth of a city and a musical revolution over the past thirty years, and how I was lucky enough to be a part of that. Luck has played a huge part in shaping my story, although I've worked bloody hard as well. I think you need both of those to achieve anything. Some people work their bloody bollocks off all their life, but they don't get dealt much luck. Some people get dealt amazing luck but perhaps only realise with hindsight and don't put the effort in to make the most of it. I think I had two major slices of luck – the first one was to be born in Manchester, an incredible city to be who you want to be, where you can write your own story. The second was to be born when I was, to be around when the acid house explosion changed the face of nightlife for ever. Blessed was it in that dawn to be alive, but to be very young was heaven. Nostalgia can be a disease, and The Warehouse Project and Parklife were always about looking forward. We were always building for the future, but at the same time also absolutely aware we were building on foundations that were laid down in that period. I've been lucky enough to work with some amazing people, who have helped me along the way, not least my business partners in The Warehouse Project and Parklife, Sam Kandel and Rich McGinnis, but also many others who, though less visible, were and are absolutely key to the success of The Warehouse Project and Parklife.

I've worked with Sam Kandel since 2000, when we first reopened Sankeys. Sam was the one who first came up with the name and concept of The Warehouse Project.

Now felt like the right time to tell these stories for the first time. It's been thirty years since I put on my first night at The Haçienda, and twenty years since I persuaded Manchester City Council to let us hold the first Warehouse party in the country after the Criminal Justice Bill, which sowed the seed for The Warehouse Project. I think we've done a good job over the years of talking about what happens on stage at our events, but I've never really talked about what happens backstage before.

More than anything, this book is a love letter to Manchester, and to the dancefloor.

THEN

1990s

MANCHESTER, SO MUCH TO ANSWER FOR

THE BOY WITH THE THORN
IN HIS SIDE

If there's one area of Manchester that has been transformed over the past thirty years that I've been running club nights, it's the corridor that runs along the Northern fringes of the city centre, from Cheetham Hill to Ancoats. Most of the significant moments in my clubbing career have happened here, from Sankeys to the birth of The Warehouse Project. Thirty years ago, these were pretty much no-go areas at night. Whole areas of the city where people were really wary of venturing to after dark. When we took over Sankeys in Ancoats in 2000, it was still an urban wasteland all around us. There weren't any street lights and kids in balaclavas on BMXs were always riding around, looking for clubbers to mug. Ancoats now has a Michelin-starred restaurant and loft apartments that go for over a million quid. When we started out at Sankeys, you couldn't buy a pint of milk round there, let alone a Michelin-starred meal.

Cheetham Hill is one of the most historic areas of Manchester. It's where we first launched The Warehouse Project, in 2006, in the old Boddington's Brewery, next to Strangeways prison. But my links to Cheetham Hill go way further back than that. It's an area that has had several waves of immigration, from the Irish fleeing the Great Famine, to the Jewish population in the late nineteenth and twentieth century to migrants from Pakistan and the Caribbean in the 1950s and 1960s, and more recently from Africa and Asia. It's long been home to a lot of Manchester's rag trade, of which my family's history runs parallel with.

My dad's family had been in textiles for generations, my grandad's family originally came from Llandudno, then they moved to Southport. In the late 1930s, grandad somehow managed to secure a massive order from a Swedish company for black fabric. The order was so big that grandad and the business didn't have the money to buy the material up front, so he re-mortgaged his house and borrowed as much as he could from the bank and as many friends and family as possible. He leveraged himself up to the absolute eyeballs to pay for the fabric, and just about managed to do it, but then the order was cancelled at the last minute, which meant he was absolutely fucked. He had a warehouse full of black fabric that he couldn't shift and was about to lose the shirt off his back, go bankrupt, and face having to tell all his friends and family that he'd lost their money. Then the Second World War kicked off, and all of a sudden the British government needed to buy up as much black fabric as they could, to make blackout curtains, which rescued grandad's business. He bought the mill which is now home to a great little nightclub called Hidden that opened in 2015, and he didn't look back from then on.

The guy who opened Hidden, Anton Stevens, used to work for us at The Warehouse Project and is a friend. I actually helped him get planning for the club, as he was struggling a bit, so I rang a copper, another friend of mine, and arranged for him to go down there and help with it. I think a lot of people see The Warehouse Project as this big behemoth with a wall round it that doesn't care about other smaller venues, but that's not true at all. I will always help people at new venues like Anton at Hidden, or Shaun Ryder's son Oli Ryder, who also used to work for us at The Warehouse Project, and now has his own club night, Animal Crossing, and a venue called The Soap Factory, behind Victoria Station. The way I always saw it, they're not in competition with The Warehouse Project. On the contrary, they actually help WHP in a way, because they're almost like feeder clubs for us, for new up-and-coming DJs, and also helping develop new audiences.

When I went to the opening of Hidden, back in 2015, I knew it was in the building that used to be my grandad's old mill, but I wasn't quite prepared for the weird feelings of déjà vu I got in there. Even though it had been thirty years since it was in our family, there was still bits that I recognised, like the original wooden panelling, and it gave me chills down my spine. I remember someone seeing the look on my face and saying to me, 'Are you all right Sach?' as I was quite freaked out. It's called Downtex Mill now, but when our family owned the building it was called Fab Lord House, Fab for Fabric, and Lord for our family name. My grandad bought it after the Second World War, and I remember playing there a lot as a kid, climbing over the rolls of fabric. It was real hard work for the lads in the warehouse, because back in those days they had to spend all day wrapping orders of fabric in brown paper and then tie them with string. If they were using string like that all day, it would cut between their fingers, so to harden the skin on their hands they used to piss in a bucket when they got in every morning, and then whenever they stopped for a break or lunch, they would soak their hands in the bucket of their own piss to harden the skin up. Even as a child I thought that was absolutely disgusting. Safe to say it's not a work practice that would pass health and safety regulations these days!

In the mid-1960s, my dad, then in his twenties, took over the business and moved to Manchester where he had an apartment in Appleby Lodge – an old crescent of flats, which is funnily enough right opposite Platt Fields, where I would start Parklife festival forty years later.

At that time, my dad was knocking about with people like the bookmaker Selwyn Demmy and Malcolm Mooney, who were both best mates with George Best. All that gang used to hang out around the area down Bridge Street, off Deansgate, which was then called The Village – George Best had a boutique there and Malcolm Mooney's salon was there. The building that is now Crazy Pedro's used to be George Best's boutique. Selwyn was a right character, who lived in Appleby Lodge, like my dad, and had legendary after-parties at his flat. A big drinker, smoker, and womaniser, my dad was also a gambler, which is how he met that crowd. He was also pretty right wing in his thinking, and a Mason. I look back at who he was and how he lived his life with a bit of disgust really. I'm so far removed from who he was, and his interests, and everything he represented is completely opposed to how I live my life.

Selwyn Demmy also owned a club called Blinkers, where all their crowd used to hang out. My mum and dad actually met in Blinkers. But then I guess they were only ever going to meet in a boozer, because my dad spent most of his life in the bloody boozer.

My mum is from Worsley, which is technically in Salford, although if she was still alive my grandma would kill me if she read that. The worst day of my grandma's life was 1 April

1974 when Greater Manchester was created and all the local borders changed overnight, which meant that Worsley was now in Salford. She had been perfectly happy living on Green Acre Lane, behind the Bridgewater pub, in what had been Worsley, Lancashire. But then the borders changed, and her address became Worsley, Salford, and my grandma never got over that for some reason. She never accepted that she now lived in Salford and not Lancashire.

Our family wasn't musical at all when I was growing up. I can remember the first record I ever bought, in 1979. My dad gave me 50p and I bought 'Video Killed the Radio Star' by the Buggles, who included Trevor Horn, who went on to be the force behind ZTT and Frankie Goes to Hollywood. Like most young kids, I was into chart music like Duran Duran and Culture Club. I remember seeing Culture Club's infamous performance of 'Do You Really Want To Hurt Me?' on *Top of the Pops* in 1982, which was a huge cultural moment. I knew I couldn't mention to my dad that I liked Culture Club and Boy George because it was exactly the sort of thing he would have hated. Being a bit of a reactionary bigot, he would have poured scorn on Boy George, and on me. My dad was exactly the sort of *Daily Mail*-reading little Englander that the Tories try to appeal to with their fake culture wars these days. He would have probably voted for Brexit and absolutely hated the idea of anything 'woke'. His views were almost Nigel Farage-esque.

Boy George later fully embraced acid house when it exploded and he used to go to the early days of Danny Rampling's Shooom when it was still held in a basement fitness centre, and lots of the other really early acid house clubs. He then reinvented himself as a house DJ, after the first of many hiatuses from Culture Club. I've booked him a few times over the years, but I never had a chance to talk to him till recently, when I went to see Morrissey at Hammersmith Apollo. I was invited to some drinks in the green room before the gig and Boy George was there, too, so we got chatting and I told him I remembered that *Top of the Pops* performance as a kid, although I imagine he gets people telling him that every day of his life, as it was such an iconic moment. He was actually really nice, we chatted about him playing at Sankeys and I asked if he remembered playing my event at Granada Studios. He said he did, but I think he was just being kind. Before Morrissey walked on stage, they played 'Johnny Reggae' by The Piglets, and George stood up and started singing along. He also knew all the words throughout Morrissey's set and sang along.

I had a small record collection, mostly *Now That's What I Call Music* compilations, and it was one of those that got me in trouble with my mum one day. Like most schools, there used to be a few dog-eared porn magazines passed around between the kids, and I used to hide my small selection in one of my *Now ...* record sleeves, because I thought, *Mum will never look in there.* But my parents then brought my little brother his own record player for his birthday, and he didn't have any records of his own yet, so when I was out one day, he went into my room to borrow some of my records and found the magazines, which – brothers being brothers – he immediately showed my mum. When I got home, she was sat in the kitchen with them all laid out on the table in front of her, and wanted to know where I got them. She was furious and sent me to my room to wait for my dad to get back from work and speak to me. When he got home, Dad walked into my room trying to look stern, but I also noticed a slight smirk when he was telling me off. I actually think that was one of the rare moments in my childhood that he was quite pleased with me.

We were always being told not to touch my dad's stuff, and he had this old brown box suitcase that he stressed we were never to touch or look inside. Obviously, as a kid, if you're told never to look inside something, the first thing you do when your mum and dad go out is peek in it. So, one day when my brother and I were searching in the box, we found the weirdest things. There was this a little apron, and some weird medals, all of which were to do with the Masons, and then we also found these weird little packets. We had no idea what they were, as we were just young and naïve, so we kept one of them out, and asked my mum what they were. They were condoms, so she was obviously not best pleased. It was just another example to us of the mistrust between Mum and Dad.

I remember realising from about the age of eleven, that things weren't going too great with my parents. From as far back as I can remember, my mum and dad were always arguing. My dad would always be moving out for two weeks, and there would be a lot of shouting and screaming. It was really horrible for me and my brother. I remember as a kid going to bed crying quite a bit because I was so upset by it all. We had to move several times and were always moving into smaller houses. My dad had the family business handed to him, he never had to earn it, and he was a bit useless at managing it – squandering the money on drink, gambling, and women.

One of the last houses we moved into before my mum and dad split up sums up his lack of entrepreneurialism and nous to me. The house had a big garden and my dad applied for planning permission to build another house on the land, which was granted. Then, when Mum and Dad got divorced and had to sell the house, my dad forgot about the planning permission, which meant the people who'd just bought the house could pay off their mortgage by selling off half the garden. Dad had just given all that away by not thinking it through.

Mum didn't really work much when I was growing up. She did a bit of sewing and craft stuff, but it was more of a hobby than a business. But as my dad's business failed, my mum stepped up and turned that hobby into a fledgling interiors business, and she became the main breadwinner. Dad was losing money hand over fist and Mum was the one paying the bills. When my dad finally left us, he didn't leave my mum anything, not a penny. He didn't even give her any maintenance till the divorce was finalised. I was seventeen, living at home and doing my A levels, so it was quite a difficult time for me, but not a situation that I wasn't used to thanks to my parents screaming matches. Having failed it four times in Sale, I managed to pass my driving test on the fifth attempt, when someone told me it was easier if you did it in Wilmslow, as the roads were quieter and wider, so I did it there and passed. I had a red C-reg Peugeot, and I used to drive to school, and give my mates a lift there. Then one day a bailiff just turned up with a tow truck, and took my car away, as it wasn't in my name it was in my dad's; I had to tell my mates my car had been taken away, and I couldn't give them a lift anymore, and we were all back to taking the bus to school every day.

BELLIGERENT GHOULS RUN MANCHESTER SCHOOLS

I'm fully aware that Morrissey was referring to far less salubrious Mancunian education establishments than my first school, a preparatory in south Manchester, when he sang those words about 'belligerent ghouls' running Manchester schools in 'The Headmaster Ritual', the opening track from *Meat is Murder*. I'm also sure a few tiny violins will come out if I say my esteemed school could be quite tough, but the teachers there could actually be just as sadistic as any other school. We didn't have the cane, but we did regularly get smacked with a ruler to the legs. We had to wear shorts every day, even if it was minus five in winter, and would get slapped on the back of the legs if we did anything wrong. The first time it happened to me I was only seven years old, and it was from Mrs Jones, because I refused to drink my daily milk. At 11.15 a.m. we all had to go to the canteen and drink a small bottle of milk, but I hated milk then and still do now. It was the dinner ladies' first job every day to bring the crates of milk in, but if it was a warm day the milk had been sat in the sun for hours by then, making it curdle. I'd had enough one day, my stomach couldn't take it anymore and I refused to drink it. Mrs Jones told me to face the wall and said, 'If you move when the ruler hits you, then you will get it twice.' I was desperate for the toilet so when she did hit me, I did a little piss, and that just made her hit me again with the ruler. Who does that to a seven-year-old? It's just spiteful. The other thing she would do is march you to the toilets if you said a rude word and physically wash your mouth out with soap. I think kids nowadays think it's a myth that they did that, but she actually did it, with soap from the dispenser. Despite all that, I did OK at Prep School. I wasn't a standout pupil, but I was always in the top half of the class. There was one decent teacher there called Mrs Fallon, who spurred me on, and I did really well in her year.

The problem came after I left the prep school, when my parents desperately wanted me to get into Manchester Grammar School, which, looking back, was totally the wrong place for me. I don't blame my parents for that because they thought they were doing the right thing; they even paid for a private tutor to make sure I could get in. The tutor was called Mr Stockton, and he knew all the tricks to play the system to get into Manchester Grammar, that's what you paid him for. One of the things you had to do in the entrance exam is write an essay on something to show your standard of English, and Mr Stockton made me memorise a list of what he called 'a hundred colourful phrases', which I could then slip into any essay and get good marks. I can still remember the phrases today, stuff like 'the moon looked like an incandescent pearl' and 'the tree was twisted and gnarled like an old woman's hand'. It must have worked, because I wrote an essay about a walk in the woods, and slipped in as many of his colourful phrases as I could. I passed the entrance exam and got in. The only problem was I went from being one of the brightest in the class at my junior school to consistently being at the bottom of the class at Manchester Grammar, which gave my confidence a pretty big knock.

I was pretty strait-laced for most of my time at Manchester Grammar. I was the smartly turned-out kid in the blazer with a neat tie, and I even had one of those 1980s briefcases, the box-shaped ones with the gold combination locks on the top. It doesn't get more 1980s than that, really, but it's a weird school bag for a kid to have. Kids going to other schools would have Head or Nike bags, and I'd be getting on the 141 bus with my briefcase looking like a right nerd.

The only subject I really enjoyed at school was art. I used to spend a lot of the lunchtimes in the art room, and I really found solace in it. I just loved doing still lifes of pot plants and things, I found it very zen.

Even though I wasn't a top pupil, I was still a bit disappointed not to be made a prefect in all the time I was at Manchester Grammar. So, when the school got back in touch with me a few years ago, after The Warehouse Project and Parklife had become successful, to ask if I would go and give a talk to pupils, I said yes, but on one condition. That the headmaster stood up at the same time as me and made me a prefect in front of everyone. So, thirty years later, I finally got my prefect badge. My picture is up in the corridor alongside other alumni, like Sir Ben Kingsley.

I don't make a habit out of bearing grudges, but I will make an exception for some people. There was a kid in my year at Manchester Grammar School called Simon, who was a right little bastard, and he used to bully me. I got my revenge on him a few years later, when I was running my student night at Paradise Factory. He came down to the club one night trying to get in when I was on the door, but I recognised him straight away and made him queue up with all the other punters for ages and when he eventually got to the front of the queue I said, 'No, fuck off, you arsehole, you are *never* coming in here.'

The one good thing that came out of Manchester Grammar is that it was an early education in the traditional Mancunian art of blagging it. I knew the only way I could get through was by copying other people's homework and winging it. Blagging is a pretty essential skill for a club promoter, especially when you're starting out, and I guess I first learned that important skill at school.

Although there was a lot about Manchester Grammar School that I didn't enjoy at all, there was one teacher who was a real inspiration to me and who really did change my life. Mr McGinnis, my Art teacher. I don't just say that with the benefit of hindsight, sometimes you only realise later the people who have shaped your life, but I did actually really appreciate at the time how he changed my way of thinking, and opened doors in my mind that I didn't even know were there. I'm hugely grateful to him, because I'm fully aware that not every kid is lucky enough to have a teacher like him, and at that time I really needed his influence. He gave me something I wasn't getting at home.

Mr McGinnis knew what was going on at home with my mum and dad's divorce and, after meeting him at a parents' evening, he also hated my dad as much as I did. My parents had gone round all the teachers and when they sat in front of Mr McGinnis he told them, 'Sacha has actually had a really good year, and is showing some real promise in art.' But my dad just went, 'Yes, but art is pointless, isn't it? It doesn't mean anything. You're never going to get a job or earn any money through art. I don't even know why we're bothering to talk to you.'

So obviously Mr McGinnis hated my dad after that, quite rightly, and had some sympathy for me.

One day, Mr McGinnis made a comment to me about something James Anderton – Chief of Greater Manchester Police at that time – had just done, and how disgraceful it was. Anderton was a real oddball character, and very homophobic, coming out with statements about people with HIV 'swirling in a human cesspit of their own making'. He even had police boats with spotlights searching for gay men on the canals around what would later become the city's iconic Gay Village. He was friends with Cyril Smith and Margaret Thatcher, and often claimed he was doing 'God's work'. He even said that God talked to him directly. Hard to believe that a Chief of Police could come out with such nonsense, but he did, and was backed by Thatcher. He was a laughing-stock to most people and was nicknamed God's Cop. Happy Mondays even lampooned him in a song called 'God's Cop' on their 1990 album *Pills 'n' Thrills and Bellyaches*. I went home that night and made the mistake of mentioning to my dad that Mr McGinnis had said James Anderton was a disgrace, but of course my dad, being a right-wing bigot, thought James Anderton was completely in the right. 'You can tell that Mr McGinnis *he's* the one who is a disgrace!' he said, 'he's a good man, James Anderton.' Of course, my dad would be one of the few people who liked James Anderton. He probably met him through the Masons or something. Looking back, I was beginning to see that there were very different ways of looking at the world, and my dad and Mr McGinnis were definitely showing me two very different views.

One day in 1989, Mr McGinnis gave me a tape by a band called The Man from Delmonte. Although they were a Manchester band, I'd never heard of them but, then again, I'd never really listened to much outside the charts at that time. I loved it and it really opened my mind musically. There was

one particular track, 'M.I.C.H.A.E.L.', that was my favourite.
I loved the tape so much that when I heard they were playing
a gig, I bought tickets to go and see them at the Free Trade
Hall. It was my first ever gig and The Man from Delmonte
were the support act to some band I'd never even heard of. I
just watched them and left and didn't even bother to watch the
headliners, but in doing the research for this book, I found an
image of a ticket stub for the gig online, and realised that it
was actually The Fall who were headlining! So, I could have
seen them at my first gig as well, if I hadn't left.[1] That gig was
quite a turning point for me: after that I started listening to
more alternative music, and got into The Stone Roses, Happy
Mondays, and New Order. I stopped being the Manchester
Grammar kid carrying a briefcase around and started to hang
around places like Affleck's Palace to discover things for
myself.

I'm still in touch with Mr McGinnis now, and he said to me
once, 'It's OK to call me Steven now, Sacha.' But he'll always
be Mr McGinnis to me.

Around the same time in the late 1980s, I had a girlfriend called
Celia. We met at a summer camp called Camp Beaumont, at
Tabley House in Knutsford, and then started seeing each other
afterwards. Celia's family lived at the back of Mere Golf
Course, and Rick Astley was her neighbour. He was at the absolute peak of his fame then – 'Never Gonna Give You Up' had
been number one in twenty-five countries around the world –
and I was desperate to meet him. I would play football with
Celia's brother in their garden, and twice deliberately kicked his

---

[1] Many years later, when we first launched The Warehouse Project, I actually had to throw Mark E. Smith out one night as he was being a bit lairy.

football over the fence into Rick Astley's garden, so I could knock on the door to get it back and hopefully meet him, but both times he was out, and someone else answered. Gutted.

Celia was another person who really turned me on to alternative music, especially The Smiths. Celia was absolutely *obsessed* with The Smiths, and a huge Morrissey fan. At the time Morrissey lived with his mum in Hale Barns, a stone's throw from where I live now, and Celia would go round to Morrissey's mum's house on his birthday, knock on the door and give him a birthday card and a small gift of sorts. Morrissey was always really pleasant to her. His sister, Jacky, still lives in that same house now with her sons, Sam and Johnny. I presume she is the Jacky from Morrissey's 2017 album *Low in High School* on the track, 'Jacky's Only Happy When She's Up on the Stage'. And that was the same house that Smiths' band member, Mike Joyce, tried to have repossessed during the court case over band royalties. I've been a huge fan of The Smiths and Morrissey ever since, and Johnny Marr is one of my friends now, but I'm not a huge fan of Mike Joyce, after an incident on social media.

Around 2009, Mike Joyce started following me on Twitter. I didn't have many followers at the time, as Twitter was quite new, and I was like, *Fucking hell! One of The Smiths is following me!* I immediately followed him back, obviously, and the next day he sent me a DM saying, 'Any chance my daughter can come to The Warehouse Project this weekend?' I replied, 'Yes, of course! Send me her name and her mates' names and I'll make sure we really look after them.' His daughter and her friends came down to the club that weekend and, as promised, I made sure they were given VIP treatment. They had a great time. But first thing the following Monday morning, Mike Joyce unfollowed me. I couldn't believe it! I was fuming.

BIGMOUTH STRIKES AGAIN

I was offered a place to do Art Foundation at Manchester Metropolitan University and all I needed to get was two Es in my A levels, but I only managed to get one E (insert your own gag here) so they wouldn't have me. In a way, I'm lucky because that would have set me off down a different path and who knows how my life would have turned out. But I didn't feel lucky at the time.

My mum and dad finally split up, and when they were getting divorced my dad made me sign a document that his solicitor had prepared, to basically get him a more favourable divorce deal. I signed it under duress, even though I kind of knew then it was wrong, and it's one of the biggest regrets of my life, because it upset my mum so much that she and I didn't speak for nearly two years after that. I moved in with my dad and his Scouse girlfriend Jackie, in Dad's post-divorce bungalow.

That was a lost year for me, really. It felt like everyone was going off to university, some were going backpacking around Southeast Asia or Australia, and I was stuck living with my dad and working for him as a door-to-door salesman. Not quite the dream. As if that wasn't bad enough, if I wasn't home by 9 p.m., my dad would lock the door and I would have to sleep in my car on the drive. That happened on a regular basis.

As I've said, my dad had a terrible business sense. His latest idea was selling home-brew kits called Beer Bags. There was a bit of a home-brewing trend at the time, and they were basically weird hessian bags that you could brew your own beer in. But the bags didn't work, and the 'beer' that came out was disgusting, undrinkable stuff. I was the one who was given the short straw of going out and trying to flog them to factories and businesses around Manchester. I would explain how they worked, then leave them with a few, and come back a few days or a week later to collect, and the company would get a cut. It was a shit business idea, especially as they didn't work, so I never got any repeat custom. Later my dad decided to try and convert them into wine bags, and changed the stickers on the front of them, but if anything that was worse.

Dad had me on commission only, so I was going out all day, door-to-door, trying to sell his shit product, earning peanuts in return. My dad's curfew meant that, even if it was midwinter, if I got home a minute after nine, I'd have to sleep on the drive in my car, freezing, till he unlocked the door the next morning at eight and let me in for a shower. I'd then be sent straight back out on the road, selling those shitty home-brew kits.

It was a horrible eighteen months or so. This was 1990. Outside the world was changing and Manchester was the centre of the world, especially in youth culture. It was what the world was waiting for. Madchester and the acid house explosion was happening on my doorstep, but I was trapped in this shitty situation, traipsing round factories being treated like dirt by my dad. Rave on. Fuck me. I knew it was bad at the time, but looking back I can't quite believe I put up with it for so long.

Around the same time, he and Scouse Jackie had a party and invited about forty people around the house. I was told my job was to serve drinks to all his friends, which I did. But part of the way through the evening, after he had a few drinks inside him, and for no reason at all, Dad stopped the music and shouted at the top of his voice, 'WHY DID GOD GIVE ME SUCH A CUNT OF A SON?!'

After shouting this across the room, there was an embarrassed silence and I thought, *What the fuck?* As did most of his mates. A few chuckles and sniggers could be heard, but most people just looked down at their shoes, embarrassed, because it was such a horrible and weird thing to do and say to your own child.

Not long after that, he and Scouse Jackie decided to go on holiday for ten days. 'You're going to have to find your own accommodation while we're away, I'm not having you staying in my house on your own,' Dad told me.

Again, what the fuck? Who would do that to their own son? But I just said, 'Right, fine …'

'I've changed the alarm code as well,' he said, 'to make sure you can't get in the house while we're away. So don't even bother trying …'

Nice. Thanks Dad. Before they went away, I wrote down a list of twenty or so combinations that I thought someone a bit simple like my dad might use for an alarm code, dates of birth and other really obvious dates that could be easily remembered. The day they left, I hid around the corner and waited for them to go, then went back to the house and tried the numbers I'd written down. The third one on my list, my dad's birthdate, was right and deactivated the alarm, so I stayed in the house while they were away, and it was actually the only time I enjoyed being in that bungalow. I made sure I cleaned up properly before they came back. The whole house was spotless, and it looked like nothing had been moved. The perfect crime. Or so I thought. Unfortunately, I'd made one significant fuck-up: a forgotten pie in the microwave. I hadn't spotted it when I was doing my last check around the place and he discovered it, uneaten and cold, when he came home.

Dad stormed round to my mum's house, where I was staying, to collect some post or something, and in the street outside he confronted me about the pie. He gave me a load of shit then punched me square in the face before driving off. I never saw or spoke to my dad after that ever again.

Aside from when he punched me, which my mum still talks about to this day, my dad's abusive behaviour was more psychological than it was physical, which can often be worse and leaves unearthed scars. The way he behaved has undoubtedly had a lasting effect on our family, too.

It was 1992, when I was twenty and he was forty-five, that I last saw my dad. He died seven years later at the age of fifty-two – the same age that I am at the time of writing. At his funeral, my younger brother gave a speech, but I didn't want to say anything about him. Something told me I should be there though, so I just went and stood at the back.

I suspect if my dad had been around to see me make a success of myself with The Warehouse Project and Parklife he would have been proud, even if it were begrudgingly so. But, then again, I don't know because when he was still alive, and I started off promoting club nights, he thought it was an absolutely ridiculous idea. He thought what I was doing was utterly pointless and I was just totally wasting my life.

After that last incident with my dad, I moved back in with my mum for a few months and got a job at Flannels in

Altrincham, then I got my own place, a bedsit in Salford, near my grandparents. My mum thought it might be a good idea for me to be near them so that I was guaranteed a decent meal inside me. I could just walk across Worsley Green to my grandma's and get my tea, which I ended up doing most nights, because she was a great cook. It was mostly comfort food, but always really tasty – things like Spam hash, and meat and potato pie, but my favourite was her egg and chips, which she always did on Saturday. She made the best chips I've ever tasted, although her secret was to cook them in lard, so they weren't very healthy. My grandpa hated them as they were so unhealthy, and he was the opposite.[2]

My grandparents were great to me, and I wish they had been around for a few more years, to see what I managed to achieve.

---

[2] He was only small, but he went to the gym most nights to work out and once won the Mr Lancashire title in a bodybuilding contest!

THE HAÇIENDA MUST
BE BUILT

The first ever nightclub I ever stepped foot inside, when I was sixteen, was called De Villes and it was on Lloyd Street in Manchester city centre. There were actually two bars/clubs next to each other: De Villes, and one called Lazy Lils, and there was an interconnecting corridor between them, which had the worst sound bleed I've ever heard in all my life, but I just thought that was normal in those days. Lazy Lils was more of a late-night bar, and right in the middle of the floor was a bucking broncho, which just seems surreal now. Can you imagine someone putting a bucking broncho in a club nowadays? You wouldn't get it past health and safety for a start. Let's get everyone hammered and then stick them on the bucking broncho! Recipe for disaster.

The night I went was a Saturday, an indie night, and it was pretty rough. There was chicken wire around the DJ booth to stop things being thrown at the DJs. My mate Pete Armistead, for a joke, went up to the DJ and said, 'My mate says can you put some Bros on?' and pointed at me, and the DJ replied, 'Tell your mate if he doesn't fuck off now, I'll announce that to the club.' I later learnt that the DJ was Alan Maskell, who has owned 42nd Street nightclub for the past twenty years. Years later, when I realised it was him and told him the story, we laughed about it. De Villes was pretty incredible, and a bit of a baptism of fire for me. There was a fight every half hour and things used to properly kick off, but that didn't seem unusual at that time.

I also started to go to a few of the chrome-and-carpet type of nightclubs, mostly Discotheque Royales and Piccadilly 21, where you had to wear a tie to get in. Piccadilly 21 was a weird place; it even had a restaurant in there. I used to sometimes grab a plate of chips on my own halfway through the night, and sit alone, in my tie.

At school, people started to talk about where they were going out, and the cool kids were on about this place called The Haçienda. I was getting stressed at school, because most of the other students were quite focused, and had a plan to get in to a top university like Oxford, Cambridge or St Andrews, and what they would read there, while I still didn't have a clue what I wanted to do with my life. I had a sense that life was slipping away a bit, or that I was getting left behind. I think it was clear to me from the day I started Manchester Grammar that everyone else was more intelligent than me, and by the time I got to sixth form it was clear I wasn't going to university, but I didn't have a back-up plan, and had no idea what should do.

It was the late summer of 1989 when I started to hear about The Haçienda, it quickly became this mythical place that all my mates were talking about, and we decided to check it out one night. Despite everything we heard about the club and the music, the one memo we didn't get was about what to wear. At other clubs I'd been to, like Discotheque Royale and Piccadilly 21, dressing up was necessary for a guaranteed entry. It was still the dark ages, sartorially, where you wouldn't get in if you were wearing jeans or trainers. I thought, *If I'm going to The Haçienda tonight, then I'm going to get properly suited and booted so that I can get in.* I borrowed my dad's suit, my dad's shirt and my dad's tie. What an idiot. We turned up and started queuing, so preoccupied worrying about whether we were going to get in or not, that we didn't even notice at first that everyone else in the queue was dressed completely differently to us. You didn't need to dress smartly to ensure you got in The Haçienda, in fact if you did, you would stand out like a sore thumb. Most people were wearing loose baggy clothing, T-shirts and baggy jeans, sometimes even shorts. We eventually got to the front of the queue and the main bouncer took one look at me and just said, 'Fuck off!' I was absolutely gutted.

After we'd realised the error of our ways, we regrouped (and redressed) before heading back the next week.

That first night we walked into The Haçienda, we actually stopped dead-still, our mouths open, and almost started laughing at the scene in front of us. We had never seen anything like it. Everyone was dancing with their hands in the air, which I'd never seen anyone do before in my life. At the other clubs, the only time you'd dance was when you would kind of shuffle next to a girl you were trying to cop off with. This was something completely different. I'd never seen anyone dance with so much feeling and abandon. Everyone was totally lost in the moment. The weirdest thing was that within half an hour we were on the dancefloor doing the same thing: dancing with our hands in the air. We had no idea that everyone else in the club was on ecstasy – I don't think we'd even heard of ecstasy at that point – the energy and the mood was so infectious, that we just got caught up in it.

I was wearing an Armand Basi turtle neck wool jumper, so I was sweating my tits off, but I felt cool, and one guy even stopped me in the toilets and said, 'Hey Armand Basi, cool.' I'd seen the jumper in L'Homme, Richard Crème's shop opposite Russell & Bromley by St Ann's Square, which I first heard about when Prince was playing a gig in Manchester and the *Manchester Evening News* reported that the shop opened at midnight especially for Prince. My dad knew I wanted the Armand Basi jumper and incredibly he bought it me for my birthday, which was so unlike him. I later learned that it was a fake, and he'd bought it in some dodgy pub in Liverpool.

Most of the other DJs at the clubs we'd been to were mainly playing chart hits, and they were still announcing records and saying, 'Happy Birthday to Sharon!' The Haçienda was something else. Firstly, you didn't recognise any of the music, and it was just one long soundtrack all the night, because the DJs were mixing the records. It sounds ridiculous now, particularly from one of the founders of The Warehouse Project, but I'd never heard a DJ mix records before, and I don't think I was alone in that. Richard Hector-Jones, who went on to work for Bugged Out and as a music journalist, was working in the Eastern Bloc record shop at the time, and he remembers a woman coming into the shop and asking,

'Have you got that record they played at The Haçienda last night?'

'Which one?'

'Well, they only played one record and it lasted all night.'

Because there was no gap in the music, she actually thought it was just a single record that lasted all night! I wasn't quite that confused, but I'd certainly never heard anything like it before in my life. I'd also never seen the crowd facing the DJ, in worship almost. In the other clubs I'd been to, nobody ever paid much attention to the DJ, unless they were moaning to him to play something they liked – the idea that the DJs there were people to be respected or worshipped would have been ludicrous. But at The Haçienda it was different. The DJ seemed to be in control of the dancefloor and the crowd responded with him and followed him.

Unbeknown to me at the time, the DJ that night was Mike Pickering, who was one of the first DJs to start playing house music in late 1985 and early 1986, at his Nude night, with early proto-house records like J. M. Silk's 'Music Is The Key' and Dhar Braxton's 'Jump Back (Set Me Free)'. Mike tells the story that one night at The Haçienda a kid from Moss Side came up to the DJ booth and said, 'Check this out, Mike' and gave him a copy of Adonis' 'No Way Back', which he listened to in the headphones and then immediately stuck on. Mike was going to New York in the mid-1980s to visit Simon Topping, who used to be in a band called Quando Quango, and together they decided to make a Latin house record. They called themselves T-Coy and that record, 'Carino', is arguably the first British house record. It still sounds incredible today. Mike, of course, went on to start Deconstruction records and then form M-People (the M in M-People stands for Manchester). I knew absolutely *nothing* about any of this at the time, I didn't even know it was Mike DJing that night. Much later, Mike would be a huge help to us when we first started The Warehouse Project; he helped spread the word and helped bring some of the artists and agents on board. That meant a lot to us at the time, as it felt like a stamp of approval for The Warehouse Project.

Like most clubs back then, The Haçienda shut at two in the morning which always, always left you wanting more – desperate to come back and do it again. These days, we run nights till

4 a.m., sometimes 6 a.m., and though at times you can look out and it feels like it's beginning to drag on a bit, that never happened back then because the 2 a.m. deadline left you on a high. Don't get me wrong, we often have nights that finish at five and fly by, but sometimes you get the feeling it might have been better if it had ended an hour or two earlier. A few years later, The Haçienda did get their licence extended till three, but I remember Paul Cons, who used to run the queer night, Flesh, would still finish at two, his reasoning being that everybody would leave on a high together, which was a bit of a gamble, but I think it did pay off for Flesh. It always left people wanting more.

Everyone who falls in love with nightclubs, electronic music, the dancing and the energy has their own epiphany, their own moment when it all just clicks. And though I'm sure younger generations are bored of those of us banging on about The Haçienda, the energy in that place, when it was going off, was just something else, something indescribable. It changed your life. I only hope that The Warehouse Project has created a similar experience for others just like the one that me and my mates had on those formative nights out in The Haçienda.

There were often people there who were wearing amazing designer clothes, but there were also people in there wearing Joe Bloggs or Stolen From Ivor or second-hand clothes. People even wore shorts or bikini tops because it was so hot. Nobody cared what you were wearing. It didn't matter. Nobody was competing with, or comparing themselves to, anyone else. It felt like everyone was on the same vibe, all these different tribes merging to become one, and I'd never experienced anything like that feeling before in my entire life. Something changed in me that night. It was definitely a turning point in my life. A switch was flicked.

I knew I needed to be part of this.

I wasn't even sure what *this* was yet, let alone how I could become part of it. But I knew I wanted to be in it.

I WOULD GO OUT TONIGHT

The first inkling of the idea to do my own club night came to me in the unlikely venue of Yesterday's, a club in Alderley Edge. I had a mate called Arnie, who was a really nice lad. His family owned Texet in Cheetham Hill, which was a big electronic firm that sold calculators and stuff, so they were quite well off. For Arnie's 21st they hired Yesterday's on a Monday night. I think Arnie only invited about seventy or eighty people but word spread somehow and around 300 kids turned up, a lot of whom he didn't even really know. I remember it, like it was yesterday, no pun intended, when the idea hit me. I was stood there looking at all these people out there on a Monday night when the club wasn't usually open and thought, *I can do this. I could get this many people out on a midweek night. If I could persuade a club in a better location to give me a chance and let me put on a night then maybe there's something in this. I could charge everyone three pounds to get in and I could make it work.* I was still working in Flannels at the time, earning £20 a day, and I was also topping that up by running a stall at the weekends on Stanley Dock Market in Liverpool. I found a factory that had a load of Next leather jackets that were seconds, and I would buy the seconds off them really cheap. The leather jackets retailed at £140 and the seconds I bought only had a button missing or something, so I would get that replaced and then sell them on my market stall for £100. Even if I only sold two all weekend, that would earn me more money than working in the shop all week. But I didn't want to be getting up at 5 a.m. on a Sunday and drive over to Liverpool to sell leather jackets on a market stall in the freezing cold for the rest of my life. I desperately needed something else to do with my life, so I was excited by the idea of putting a club night on. Maybe this could be the start of something. Maybe this could be my way out.

I didn't have a pot to piss in, though. Not a bean to my name. The only way I could make the plan work was to find someone else to put the money up front. I talked to Arnie, who was in right away, and we started planning about where to hold the club nights. Not knowing anyone who went out in Cheshire, I didn't really have much pull on that scene – and everyone I knew went out in Manchester, so we needed to find somewhere in town. Being a bit bolshy, and probably setting our sights way too high, we thought about The Haçienda.

We managed to set up a meeting with Ang Matthews, who was The Haçienda's assistant manager at the time. We were over the moon just to have secured a meeting with her. We couldn't believe it. We thought we were proper little business-men. We were going to a meeting at *The Haçienda*, the most famous club in Manchester, to discuss hiring it. This was beyond our wildest dreams! We turned up at the meeting and it was all surprisingly straightforward. Ang suggested a Monday at the start of July, and we agreed a one-night hire fee for The Haçienda of £1,000 plus VAT.

Arnie and I thought we had done the deal of the century. We really did. We honestly came out of that meeting at The Haçienda walking on air. I thought I was the new Peter Stringfellow. But we'd actually been completely ripped off. They must have been high-fiving themselves in The Haçienda office the second that we walked out of there, saying 'What a pair of clowns!'

What they knew, and we didn't, was that it would be virtually impossible to get enough people through the door on a Monday night in July to cover that hire fee. Arnie and I thought we were home and dry. I think we thought, 'If you book The Haçienda, they will come', right? We soon realised just how wrong we were. In fact, we were fucked. The first absolute schoolboy error we made was, though we were planning a student night, and Manchester has one of the biggest student populations in Europe, we'd booked The Haçienda for the first Monday of the summer holidays, when all the students had fucked off home and weren't around. Idiots. We didn't pick the date, that was the date The Haçienda offered us, and now we realised why.

When we went back a few days later to collect the invoice we dealt with a guy called Jon Drape. That was the first time I'd ever met Jon, and I remember he had his hair in curtains, and was always sweeping it back behind his ears. Half of the lads in Manchester had curtains at that point, and I even had curtains myself at one stage. Jon was usually the one who answered the phone in their office in those days, and I remember he had quite a posh phone voice: '*Hell-o, Haçienda.*'

Little did I know that I would end up working so closely with Jon Drape years later, on The Warehouse Project, Kendal Calling, Parklife and many other projects, but we'll get to that later. I've still got the invoice from The Haçienda for that night, and it's framed on the wall of my office at home, signed by Jon Drape. An invoice for £1,000 plus VAT, which we paid.

Also in the office was Paul Mason, Bobby Langley was kicking about, and Rob Gretton. I never saw Tony Wilson in The Haçienda office, I didn't meet him till much later. I think a lot of people associate Tony Wilson, more than Rob Gretton or anyone else, with The Haçienda. Tony was a public figure. Even if you asked the staff at The Warehouse Project, 'Have you heard of Rob Gretton?' I doubt most of them would know who he was, but if I said 'Have you heard of Tony Wilson?' they'd say, 'Of course … Mr Manchester!'

But people in the know, in Manchester and the industry, know that Rob was the real driving force behind The Haçienda. Rob sadly passed away in 1999; Tony in 2007. Far too young, both of them. But they both left huge legacies in Manchester and in music. Their influence can't be overstated. We wouldn't have the Manchester we have today without Rob Gretton and Tony Wilson. They made us all believe that things were possible. That you didn't have to go far to achieve great things, you could do it on your own doorstep. In fact, it might be better if you did it here in Manchester, running things on your own terms, which you might not be able to in, say, London or New York. I'm pretty sure The Warehouse Project would not have been such a success if it was based in London. There's something inimitably Mancunian about The Warehouse Project.

Anyway, Arnie and I were in a bit of a hole, as we'd already paid up front for the club (well, Arnie had), so we *had* to fill it. We had to find a way of getting close to 700 people into The Haçienda on a quiet Monday night, when the students were away; so we came up with a bit of a scam, a bit of a blag. This was pre-internet days, pre-email, and hardly anyone had a mobile phone, so the biggest way to promote club nights was still flyers. Promoters would hand these out on the street, outside bars, outside other club nights, and also put piles of them in the coolest record shops, clothes shops, and hairdressers around town. Most of those shops would have a table near the door, or a windowsill, or somewhere you could leave flyers. Some of the places would be a bit discerning about what flyers they took – a really cool shop like Geese wouldn't take flyers for a cheesy student night. So, I came up with the idea of going round town, to all these cool places, and saying, 'Hi, we're from The Haçienda and management really want to say thank you for supporting us by allowing us to put flyers in here. We're having this huge party at The Haçienda, and everyone is going to be there – Take That, Manchester United players, *Coronation Street* stars, everyone. We can give you a couple of free guest lists and you can also give us as many names as you like for a £5 discount entry list.' A total lie. The management didn't know anything about it, it was just a blag to try and get as many people through the door. I didn't know any celebrities back then, although I did know Justin Orange, the identical twin brother of Jason Orange from Take That, so I made sure he came down. I thought if anyone moaned and said, 'I thought you said there was going to be loads of celebrities?' I'd say, 'Look, there's Jason Orange from Take That, what more do you want?'

A lot of people were pretty grateful and said, 'OK, cool, thanks', and gave us a list of names. I think we eventually ended up with 787 people through the door and we made about £700, so it was a success in the end.

The funny thing was we didn't go out and go crazy and celebrate. After the club closed at 2 a.m., we went back to Arnie's family's house in Cheadle, where his mum had stayed up and made us some samosas. That's how I celebrated my first ever successful club night: eating a samosa in my mate's mum's kitchen.

DODGIN' THE RAIN AND THE BULLETS

As far back as I can remember I never wanted to be a gangster. I was a bit of a nerdy kid from the mean streets of Altrincham who went to Manchester Grammar School, my idea of gangsters was the same as the next person. Gangsters were just people in films like *Goodfellas*. They may have seemed cool, slightly romantic figures if your only experience of them was watching Henry Hill or the Krays on the big screen. I had heard of the Quality Street Gang, as they were on the periphery of my dad's social circle. They were a wide loose collective of characters, a lot of them from Ancoats, and you certainly wouldn't mess with them, as their reputation proceeded them. They were proper old school heads, with nicknames like Jimmy the Weed and Jimmy Swords, and they were known and feared throughout town. People would do a sharp intake of breath if they walked into a bar or club and nudge each other. Jimmy the Weed ran The Brown Bull in Salford, where George Best and a lot of journalists and Granada staff, like Michael Parkinson, would drink, and it was famous for after-hours drinking. George Best once went round taking fish and chip orders at a lock-in, then popped out and got them for everyone. Best would even sleep in there sometimes. One of the other haunts was Phyllis's, a late-night-hotel-stroke-shebeen in Whalley Range run by Phyllis Lynott who described it as 'showbiz digs'. Phyllis was the mother of Thin Lizzy lead singer Phil Lynott and his song 'The Boys Are Back In Town' is about the Quality Street Gang and the other characters that would frequent his mum's later night 'showbiz digs'.

Although my dad wasn't close friends with the Quality Street Gang, they could often be found in the same drinking and gambling spots. My mum used to make me get the bus into town after school on Fridays so that I could go to a basement club called Drummonds on Peter Street to collect my dad and make sure he came home for the weekend. He was always surrounded by women and dodgy characters like the QSG.

When you have to face the reality of dealing with gangsters, though, there is nothing romantic about it, trust me.

The modern-day gang problem in Manchester really kicked off not long after acid house exploded at the end of the 1980s, and it was horrible for the best part of a decade – casting a long shadow over the city for most of the 1990s. The gangs were out of control and running the doors at most of the nightclubs. Everybody knew what was going on. The police knew, the authorities knew, the public knew. And anyone who worked in nightclubs sure as hell knew as they had to deal with it on a daily basis. Acid house had changed things so quickly that the police and authorities were just playing catch-up, and promoters like us were left to deal with it on our own. Everyone who worked in and around nightclubs in the 1990s will have stories about the gangs.

There was one bar in Manchester that was owned by someone who was connected to one of the gangs and it was common knowledge that they used to keep guns in the freezer. It seems ridiculous now but that's what Manchester was like at the time. I'm sure there's a criminal element and gang problem of some degree in most big cities around the world, especially in nocturnal businesses that involve large amounts of cash, but it's usually a bit more underground, a bit more hidden away. In Manchester, at that time, it was blatant. It was always there, bubbling away just under the surface. You didn't have to look hard to find it. Some press even started calling the city Gunchester, although no one on the streets actually called it that. Gio Goi, the Manchester clothing label even did a T-shirt with the slogan, 'Manchester – dodgin' the rain and the bullets', like it was something to be proud of.

It's no exaggeration to say the city was like the Wild West back then. It was lawless and out of control. Different gangs and gangsters were running large parts of the city, and often fighting each other over territories, and at times it seemed like they were untouchable.

When I look back now, I can't believe a lot of what happened. I don't know anybody who ran a club night in the 1990s in Manchester who wasn't threatened or intimated, many of them had guns pulled on them or had to pay protection money; quite often people were severely beaten up or kidnapped. Saying that now is really shocking, but what's more shocking, and frightening, is how normalised it was. Instances of pretty shocking, heavy violence were commonplace. You were always hearing that there had been a shoot out on the door of such and such a club, or some other story like that. The gangs themselves didn't make much attempt to keep it secret, either. A lot of the time it was brazen, and happened in full public view, which was almost a show of force from the gangs, to intimidate people. Because they knew they could get away with it at that time. It was almost like, 'What are you gonna do? Who are you going to tell? We can do what we want and nobody in this city can stop us.'

The worst gang violence at The Haçienda was before my time. Because of the gang violence, Greater Manchester Police had first tried to shut down the club in 1990, but Factory fought back by employing the legendary George Carman QC to fight its case and won a six-month reprieve. Not before Carman had to tell the rest of Factory to stop Tony Wilson from constantly shooting his mouth off, famously exclaiming: 'Gentlemen, shut that loudmouth up!'

Shortly after the reprieve, though, The Haçienda decided to close the doors voluntarily, after their new Head of Security was threatened by someone with an automatic gun. 'Someone who was turned away by a bouncer went back and got a machine gun,' recounted New Order's Bernard Sumner. 'He chased the bouncer through the club, cornered him by one of the fire escapes and pulled the trigger, but the gun jammed … the head doorman was chased out of the club by a kid holding an Uzi. The doorman ran out of the back door, jumped in a car, sped home to London and never came back. Poor bastard. That ended everything. The other doormen packed up and left too. Clearly we were fucked.'

DJ, Mike Pickering, even stopped his own sister and friends from coming to the club because he was worried for their safety. It had got to the stage where people were getting mugged at knifepoint in the toilets. It was lawless. One night, Pickering's management team from Deconstruction Records came down to see him DJ and after half an hour they ended up banging on the door of the DJ booth, saying, 'Fucking hell! Let us in here, we're not staying out there, it's horrible.'

On 30 January 1991, Tony Wilson called a press conference on The Haçienda dancefloor and announced the decision to close the club voluntarily:

The Haçienda is closing its doors as of today. It is with the greatest reluctance that for the moment we are turning the lights out on what is, for us, a most important place. We are forced into taking this drastic action in order to protect our employees, our members and our clients. We are quite simply sick and tired of dealing with instances of personal violence ... when we opened The Haçienda we never thought we'd have to deal with the sort of people we've had too. We hope, we must believe, we can reopen The Haçienda in a better climate. But till we are able to run the club in a safe manner, and in a way the owners believe will guarantee the role of The Haçienda at the heart of the city's community, it is with great sadness that we will shut our club.

Luke Bainbridge spoke to a lot of the people who were at the heart of that when he was writing his book about the history of acid house. People like Pickering, Graeme Park, Jon Da Silva, Paul Mason and Fiona Allen, who went on to be a comedian and one of the creators and stars of the Channel 4 comedy sketch show *Smack the Pony*, but back in the day worked at The Haçienda and sometimes did the door.

'Unfortunately, the mood in the club changed a lot quicker than most of the punters realised. Because I was working on the door myself and doormen got to know every little dodgy kid coming in there and what they were up to. Violence would escalate quite quickly, and almost every week I'd end up driving someone down to casualty because the ambulance and the police – how can I say this – took their time to turn up whenever we rang them. Either that, or they just happened to be rushed off their feet every time. One kid, a lovely, cheeky chappie, ventured onto someone else's patch and ended up getting stabbed in the leg, just missing a major artery. I was so used to it by that stage I remember taking off my belt to try and make a tourniquet, and as I was doing it I thought, "I only bought this belt today". That's how commonplace the violence had become, that you could have a thought like that while trying to stem the bleeding from a stab wound. The week before, I had seen the inside of someone's skull after they'd been glassed in the club.

Though most people at The Haçienda were still having a euphoric, great time, one night there was a bang and I looked up to see that there was a guy walking across the road towards the club with a gun. The doormen had scattered so I desperately started pressing the button that closed the shutter over the main door, and it was the slowest moment of my life as it came down. I was pleading with the shutter to hurry up and close: "Please, come on!". That's the reality of what went on at the time, and they're only just a few examples. People were either looking away not to see it, or they tried to forget it. But I'm not forgetting it, because it was horrible.'

The last straw for Mike Pickering was when he had a knife pulled on him the night of The Haçienda's birthday. He and David Morales were DJing that night. Pickering was upstairs, Morales was downstairs. He could tell Mike was a bit down at the start of the night and said to him, 'You've not got fed up with DJing have you?' And Mike just said to him, 'Between you and me there's a lot of trouble in here. A lot of gang trouble.'

The door to the main DJ booth at The Haçienda was like a stable door, it was in two halves. The top half of the door was open and some kid from Salford leaned over and grabbed

Pickering's beer. Pickering said, 'That's my beer ...' and the kid pulled a knife on him. Pickering just said, 'You know what, have the fucking beer,' and shut the door.

Meanwhile, downstairs, someone threw a bottle that smashed just behind Morales, and scattered broken glass over him and the decks. Pickering and Morales both walked out of the booths and bumped into each other at the front door. Pickering said, 'I told you, didn't I?' and Morales replied, 'Man, let's get the fuck out of here.'

They walked out of The Haçienda and Pickering, who had been one of the driving forces behind the club since it started, sadly never set foot in there again.

In 1994, long before the Lowry, the Imperial War Museum North, and the BBC and Media City transformed Salford Quays, I saw one of the gangs in action for the first time. I had just started promoting – it was right after the first night I'd done at The Haçienda – and there used to be a boat moored in Salford Quays called *The Flying Dutchman*, which had been converted into a bar by the owner, Jan. He lived on it, too, and had even converted the cockpit into a little bedroom. Jan must have been under pressure from gangs to pay some protection money, because I remember reading a quote from him in the *Manchester Evening News* saying he was going to stand up to any form of intimidation from gangs.

The boat had a bar down below and there were also some tables and chairs out on deck. I quite liked it and used to go there now and again for a drink. One evening, we were sat outside on the deck, when all of a sudden this souped-up Ford Escort screeched to a halt next to it, and a bunch of guys ran on board and just started smashing the bar up, smashing everything. Then they grabbed fire extinguishers and came up on deck and just started spraying everyone. It was horrible. People panicked and were desperately scrambling to get away from them, women were screaming, and a couple even jumped off the side of the boat into the dock.

I think Jan tried to keep *The Flying Dutchman* open for a little while after that, but the writing was on the wall really, and he eventually decided it wasn't worth it. He sold the boat to the street art and theatre company Walk the Plank, and Jon Drape from The Haçienda actually ended up living on there for a very short time at one stage.

Understandably some people just had enough of the club scene, and they got out. Andy and Mike Mckay were two brothers running clubs in Manchester, around the Gay Village, who inevitably had to deal with gangs, and one night in 1994 some gang members took Andy outside and doused him in petrol and threatened to set him alight. That was the final straw for Andy and Mike. They took the money they had made that night, booked one-way flights to Ibiza, and never came back, or looked back. They established a club called Manumission (with the 'Man' in Manumission referring to Manchester) and it became one of the biggest clubs in the world for the rest of the 1990s, infamous for its sex stage shows, where Mike and his wife Claire would have sex on stage each night, in front of thousands of punters. You wouldn't get away with that in Manchester on a wet Wednesday night. Manchester's loss was Ibiza's gain.

After our first Scandalous night at The Haçienda, I had got the promoting bug and was beginning to think I had found something I might be good at. We did two further nights at The Haçienda that year – a fresher's ball in September then a student Christmas party in December. That was when I began to realise the harsh reality of promoting club nights in Manchester in the 1990s was that you had no choice but to work with the gangs and people who ran the doors at the clubs. It was a nocturnal minefield and you needed to know who you were dealing with and how best to work with them and keep them on your side, because if you didn't have them onside you were fucked.

At that time, Damian Noonan ran the door at The Haçienda, and he had a fearsome reputation. Everyone knew who he was, including the punters, especially any punters who had unintentionally got on the wrong side of him. My fresher's ball event in September had sold out, and when I turned up on the night Damian asked me how many tickets I'd done. I told him it was completely sold out. 'OK, how many tickets have you got for me?'

'I don't have any. I had about fifty left over, but they're all at home.'

'Where do you live?'

'Chorlton.'

He called one of his guys over and said to him, 'You're in your car tonight, aren't you? Run Shrimpy back to his house in Chorlton, he needs to pick up some fucking tickets for me …'

Damian's nickname for me was 'Shrimpy' for some reason. I never had the balls to ask him why. I was living on Cromwell Road in Chorlton at the time, but I was bright enough to know I didn't want Damian and his crew knowing where I lived, so I got the bouncer to pull up on a road parallel to Cromwell Road, jumped out and ran down a random person's drive as if it was my house, then jumped over their back fence and into my garden, so they never knew where I lived.

Our next night at The Haçienda was the student Christmas party at the end of 1996. It sold out again, but this time I'd made sure to keep some tickets to give Damian to sell. I also roped in my old friend J-Boy to dress up as Father Christmas and rented him the outfit from a fancy-dress shop. As soon as Damian saw J-Boy dressed as Father Christmas he said, 'I'm having that suit at the end of the night. I'll use it for my kids on Christmas morning.' We thought he was joking, but at the end of the night he demanded J-Boy give him the suit.

'But it's only rented,' I tried to protest, 'I've got to return it on Monday.'

'I don't give a fuck.'

'What am I going to tell the fancy-dress shop?'

'Tell them Damian Noonan's got it.'

I wasn't going to argue with Damian. J-Boy had to take the Father Christmas suit off there and then and give it him. The thing was, he only had boxer shorts on underneath, so I had to drive him home in his underwear in December, freezing his bollocks off.

Not long after I started promoting, there was the incident I mentioned in the introduction where I was bundled into the back of a car by a couple of Manchester's biggest gangsters and made an offer that I couldn't understand, let alone refuse. They tried to give me a bag with £20,000 cash in and wanted me to put on a big night at the Academy for New Year's Eve. I knew I couldn't do that; I'd only just started promoting.

Damian had a fearsome reputation, and I was as scared of him as everyone else, but I also got on well with him on some level as well. I was having a bit of trouble with a rival student promoter called Paul Bennett at the time. He was a cheesy student promoter who was quite a bit older than me, a mature student in his early thirties, who lived in student halls. He had a massive team of students working for him and he was getting them to rip all my posters down and bin all my flyers, and it was really affecting my nights and losing me a lot of money. He was trying to just wipe me out completely. I tried various things to combat it, and I was at the end of my tether. I decided to phone Damian up and tell him I had a problem with this rival student promoter.

'Come round to my house tomorrow Shrimpy, I'll sort it.'

When I got to Damian's house, he had a huge baby pink leather suite and the biggest TV I've ever seen.

'Right, what's the problem Shrimpy?'

I explained the situation with this Paul.

'What do you know about this guy?'

'Not much. I know he lives in Dalton Ellis student halls, and he drives a dark blue BMW M3.'

'OK, give me his number …'

I gave Paul's number to Damian, and he rang him up.

'Is that Paul? … It's Damian Noonan here. I'm sat with Sacha; he's been telling me that there's a problem between you two. Well, if you've got a problem with Sacha, then that's a problem for me. If you don't leave him alone, I'm going to come and find you, smash you and your dark blue M3 through the doors of Dalton Ellis student halls, got it?'

I never heard from Paul again. Never spoke to him or saw him ever again. He obviously got the message, because he just disappeared.

There were running battles between various gangs and factions about running the doors of different nightclubs at the time, but I just tried to keep my distance from all of those battles. The key thing was not to let them know too much about you that they could use against you. I certainly didn't want anyone knowing where I lived, because then you always had the worry that they could turn up on your doorstep.

One of the problems in the 1990s was that clubbing was a purely cash business. *Everything* was run on cash. Punters paid cash for tickets, cash on the door, and cash over the bar. What gangs and criminals wanted more than anything was cash, and in particular, cash that can't be traced. Nightclubs back then were nocturnal businesses dealing with large amounts of untraceable cash, so they were obvious targets for gangs. Especially if they could control or take a cut of the lucrative drugs trade that was being done in a lot of those clubs.

Thankfully the past is a different country, gangs did things differently there. Nowadays things have completely changed since the dark days of the 1990s. The police and authorities have a much better handle on things than they had then, when they were simply playing catch up. These days we work hand in hand with the police, authorities, and council. But to be honest, one of the biggest things that has changed is there is hardly any cash changing hands anymore. Almost all payments are done by card or contactless now, so there simply isn't large amounts of untraceable cash around to be targeted. When I can think back to the amount of cash that went through some of our nights and events in the late 1990s and early 2000s, it's unbelievable.

Shaun Ryder from Happy Mondays thinks *The Wire* is very true to life in the way that gangs move on to legitimate businesses, or seemingly legit businesses, and quite a few of those gangsters from the 1990s and 2000s have done that. A lot of them are now dead, including most of the main figures whose names were enough to strike fear into anyone, but of those who are left, quite a lot of them have gone legit. They're not going round threatening people physically anymore; they're making money in other ways.

COME HOME

After my first successful nights at The Haçienda, I started looking around for another venue I could use on a regular basis. I thought I could do a weekly student night, but I wouldn't be able to fill The Haçienda each week. I needed an alternative and managed to get a meeting at Home.

Nobody talks about Home much anymore, or certainly not as much as they bang on about The Haçienda, but Home was a really important club in the early to mid-1990s. Home was launched by Tom Bloxham, who came to Manchester as a student, and first started out selling bootleg posters in Affleck's Palace. Tom went on to found Urban Splash, a ground-breaking property company who were one of the first to start turning Manchester's derelict old mills into loft apartments in the 1990s, and then across the country. Tom also went on to be the Chairman of Manchester International Festival and trustee of the Tate and Manchester United Foundation. He was already a really impressive character when I met him at Home, and you could tell he was going to play a big role in shaping the future of the city. He also stood out because he was quite a sharp dresser. While most of us were wearing baggy clothes and dressing down, Bloxham and Wilson were the only ones round town who were wearing Yohji Yamamoto suits.

Although house music was now pretty established, and the basis of most of the biggest club nights across Manchester and the country, student nights were slower to catch on.

By the time I started promoting student nights in 1994, students were more clued up, and getting bored of the still pretty formulaic nights that hadn't changed for years. You would get half an hour of 1970s music, and then half an hour of 1980s music and then a few more modern tracks like 'Jump Around' by House of Pain or maybe something by The Prodigy or Cypress Hill. I could probably list you fifteen of the songs that would always get played. To me it was pretty obvious that there was a big gap for someone (me) to do a student night that was more dance-music orientated. Even if it was the more accessible end of house music, and not something really underground. So, I started a night at Home with my friend Jonathan Newman, who I called J-Boy, and it started to do well almost immediately.

I was made to feel really welcome at Home. I was still living in the bedsit in Salford and Home became a bit of a home from home. The building at Ducie House had some really creative people working out of it. So What Arts, Simply Red's management team led by Elliot Rashman were in there, plus the *Jockey Slut* offices, led by John 'Johnno' Burgess and Paul Benney, who had just started doing a night called Bugged Out at Sankeys, and who I still work with at The Warehouse Project to this day. 808 State also had their office in there and they were really friendly and supportive, too. All of a sudden I felt that I was part of the Manchester music scene, albeit a very small cog in the machine at the time, but almost everyone made you feel welcome. The manager of Home was called Joe

Strong, who had been one of the original managers of Ministry of Sound. There was also a really lovely guy called Simon Calderbank who ran a night called Foundation, that was really successful there. There was a really good crowd at Home. The only person who looked down on me was Mick Hucknall, when he came in the office. He just seemed a bit arrogant and pretentious.

It was also at Home that I saw cocaine for the first time. The drug of choice for many people was changing, and that definitely brought about a change in the mood in clubs as well. From the collective euphoria of the early halcyon days of ecstasy and acid house, things had gone slightly darker. In the early 1990s cocaine wasn't very widespread, but by the mid- to late 1990s it seemed like it was everywhere. The collective mood of a club full of people on ecstasy is very different to the collective mood of a club full of people on cocaine. Particularly the cheap street gak that seemed to be everywhere at times.

At that time, I was just a one-man band, really, and would even go out and flyer all my nights and do everything myself. I didn't even have a computer, let alone a website or email. All I had was my basic Ericsson mobile. I would run everything from that one phone, and some weeks I couldn't even do that because it had been cut off because I hadn't paid the bill, because I was skint. I was still living a hand-to-mouth existence really.

When the student nights got established, Tom Bloxham asked me if I could get a bit more involved with the weekend nights. It was then than I became more exposed to the gang trouble they were having. There were two incidents in particular that stand out. The first one was when twenty guys from Salford walked up to the club all wearing balaclavas. They just went through the whole club, smashing the place up, and obviously scaring the life out of the punters; they just walked out, and nobody could do a thing. It was all because they wanted to run the door and if they weren't going to be given the door, then they were going to cause as much trouble as possible.

The other incident was when I got caught in the crossfire of a drive-by shooting and was very lucky to survive. I was running the guest list on a Saturday night, and I was stood outside by the bouncers, with the guest list on a clip board. We heard it before we saw it and looked up to see a car flying round the corner and a gunman leaning out and opening fire. The bouncers immediately realised what was happening and ran inside and shut the steel doors, but I must have been a bit frozen to the spot, like a rabbit caught in the headlights, and I was left on my own stood outside, still holding the fucking clipboard in my hand. Thankfully all the bullets somehow missed me, but you can still see the bullet marks clearly on the corner of Ducie House to this day. Every time I walk or drive past and see them it sends a shiver down my spine and takes me right back to that evening.

After the drive-by shooting on the Saturday evening, Tom Bloxham called and chaired a meeting on the Monday morning. Tom was pretty hands-on with the club at that stage, and while he was talking and discussing how we should handle it, I could see Joe Strong, the manager, writing something down on a piece of paper. I just thought he was taking notes, but when he'd finished writing he pushed the piece of paper across the table to Tom. In hindsight, I realise that it was a resignation letter. Joe said, 'Sorry, Tom, I've got a family to think of. I can't do this anymore, I'm off' and got up and left. That was the last time we ever saw him, and I've no idea what happened to him. He'd just had enough and walked away. He wasn't the only one.

I was still a kid at this stage. I was only twenty-three. A year ago, I'd been working in a clothes shop for twenty quid a day, and living at my mum's, and now I was having to deal with gangsters on an almost daily basis.

I remember Tom Bloxham telling one of the gangsters in Home one night, 'Listen, don't come in the club and threaten me. You know where my office is. I'm there every day from nine to six, so if you got a problem come and see me in there and we'll sort it out.'

The doors at Home were being run by Mickey Francis and his firm, who were known as Loc 19. They were old Manchester City hooligans, and one of them only had half an ear, because he'd lost the other half in a fight. At the time they were taxing me fifty pence for every person that came through the door on my nights. I charged £2.50 (£3 for non-students) and they took fifty pence off me for each person. It probably doesn't sound like much, but if I had 600 in attendance, I had to give Loc 19 £300 (about £700 in today's money), so they were probably taking half my profit.

Problem is, I would have good weeks and bad weeks, especially when the students were on holiday, but they didn't give a fuck if I'd had a bad week. They still wanted paying a decent amount on bad weeks, even if I didn't have the numbers. Some weeks I wouldn't make any money at all, I was literally putting the night on and doing all the work, just to hand over whatever I made straight to the gangs. One of my DJs at the time was a guy called Leaky Fresh, who was from Moss Side. He was a really lovely cool guy – tall and good-looking, with braids. Leaky had a really laid-back manner, and a way of charming women. He was a great DJ, too, and he'd actually been in the World DMC Championships in 1989, which is like the World Championships of DJing. At one stage, when I was having a few bad weeks, he could see what was going on, so decided to help me out, as it was no good for him if the nights became unworkable because he wouldn't get paid, either. Leaky called a meeting with one of the head doormen from Loc 19, a bloke called Warren, in his little record shop in town. There was a record store in the Corn Exchange downstairs near the entrance of Konspiracy called Underground Records run by two guys, but it had a small backroom where Leaky ran his own little shop from. Leaky managed to convince Warren to give me a few weeks grace from paying Loc 19, otherwise the night would be finished, and I would go bust. I was really grateful to Leaky for calling that meeting and trying to help me out, but I knew it was only a temporary reprieve. They would soon be demanding money again. Although I never considered leaving Manchester, as some people did, I knew I was going to have to leave Home.

PARADISE FACTORY

After I'd decided to leave Home, I found myself in Paradise.

Located on Charles Street, behind the old BBC building on Oxford Road (fifteen years before the BBC moved to Media City in Salford), Paradise Factory was located in the old Factory Records headquarters. At the heart of Factory's halcyon days in 1989, Factory famously bought the building and spent a fortune converting it into their new offices, including an infamous boardroom table, suspended from the ceiling. After Factory went bust in 1992, Peter Dalton and Carol Ainscow bought the building and set about converting it into a nightclub, which they called Paradise Factory, in a nod to the building's history. Carol and Peter's partnership had first made their name with the opening of Manto bar in the Gay Village in 1990. Before the arrival of Manto, the Gay Village was a rough collection of pubs based around the canals and red-light district, and had a pretty seedy reputation, not helped by the bigoted God Cop James Anderton, who had regularly targeted the village and came out with homophobic comments. Manto started the revolution of Gay Village, it was the architectural 'coming out' of the village. Unlike the old-school queer pubs like the New

Union, that kept their business hidden within, Manto was on full display, with floor to ceiling windows.

Peter and Carol were really important, pioneering figures in the development of Manchester in the early 1990s, and they could also be pretty formidable, particularly Carol, who sadly died in 2013, aged just fifty-five, after battling a brain tumour. Peter was a great supporter of mine in those early days, Carol perhaps less so. I was petrified of her.

I was still pretty naïve at the time, I was only twenty-three and had been putting on club nights for less than a year when I moved to Paradise Factory, and on my first night there I went up to the head doorman, Roy, to find out how much he was going to tax me.

'How much do you want off me?' I asked him.

'What you mean?' replied Roy, 'Aren't you paying the club a hire fee, like?'

'Well, yeah,' I said, 'but don't you want something off me as well?'

I had just presumed that was the norm after my dealings with the bouncers at Home. 'They used to take fifty pence a person off me at Home, and it was killing me some weeks, so can we do forty pence a person?'

Roy just looked at me.

'What … the doormen used to tax you on the door?

'Well, yeah.'

Roy just laughed. 'Nah, I won't do that. Just give us a drink at the end of the night if you've done well.'

I liked Roy and got on with him, and even used to give him £50 at the end of each night, which doesn't seem that generous now, but he was happy with that at the time.

Paradise Factory was great. I ended up working there for seven years, which is an eternity in clubbing years, and I loved it. I ran two nights there – Release and Shooting Stars. Release was the first one I started, and that ran from 1994 to 2001, so I had several generations of students through the doors. Its success, I think, was down to two things: first, we didn't patronise the students when it came to music policy – we didn't follow the formulaic approach of other nights going on in town that had a mixture of 1970s and 1980s classics, we played decent house music, even if it was the more accessible type of house music, rather than underground – and second, I was all over the promotion. There were roughly 60,000 students in Manchester at that time, and I did everything to make sure that every one of them knew about Release at Paradise Factory.

On the music side, most of the credit at my Paradise nights can go to one guy. I began to book a DJ who I honestly hand-on-heart believe is one of the most underrated DJs of his generation, certainly in Manchester and the UK, Dave Booth.

Dave had been a DJ in Manchester since way before I had started going out to clubs, in fact since I was at primary school. Dave started out DJing in the 1970s at a club called Pips, which was a hugely influential Manchester venue located near the old Corn Exchange, right by where the National Museum of Football is now. Joy Division did their first ever gig at Pips, and Dave was the DJ at that gig, so it doesn't get any more seminal than that. A generation later, he was also a tour DJ for The Stone Roses and played for them at a lot of their land-mark gigs, including Spike Island. He also played at many other clubs including Playpen, Isadora's, The Haçienda, and Garlands in Liverpool. Dave tragically passed away in 2020, although it was nice to see all the tributes that were paid to him from everyone including Peter Hook, Ian Brown and 808 State, and to know that he was really appreciated by people who mattered. Even though he never truly got the wider recognition he deserved, I've never seen anyone who could control a room and a dancefloor quite like Dave Booth could, and he certainly got the respect of everyone who was involved in Manchester's clubbing scene at the time.

The manager of Paradise Factory back then was a guy called Andy O'Dwyer, and although I wasn't being taxed by the bouncers, he *did* start taxing me.

At first, I didn't say anything about being taxed, as I thought I was pushing my luck working there anyway, so I just grudgingly accepted it, but after a while I got more and more pissed off with handing over £700 to Andy every week, so I complained about the situation to Peter. At this stage, I was making probably £500 or £600 a week, still just about getting by, but then I had costs to cover as well. (Andy was making more money than me most weeks!). Peter and Carol wanted proof that he was taxing me, so they asked me to phone him up and try and negotiate with him and record the conversation. I did that and when I played them back the recording, and they had proof of what had been going on, Andy was sacked.

I was still doing all my own promotion for most of the nights, standing outside clubs and bars, night after night, handing out flyers and talking to people and spreading the word. One night when I was out doing that, I met a girl called Elisa Marchionne.

Though she had grown up in Cheshire, Elisa was half Italian: her dad came from a small village called Carpineto, up in the hills of Pescara. Elisa was doing a course in window design in Italy, where her family was from, but was back home for the holidays. We went out on a date and quickly became an item, and then she started working with me on the nights, and we became a team, and I was no longer a one-man band. It was Elisa who really managed to get the student market nailed when it came to our promotion. She was the real driving force behind that, and she ended up with teams of students working for her, getting the message into all the student halls and unions. We even managed to borrow the keys to some of the halls, from one of the cleaners, in exchange for a bottle of whisky each week. We managed to leave flyers and posters actually inside the halls, where none of our rival promoters could get to, and they could never work out how we managed that.

Elisa and I ended up getting married in 2000, and although we later split up, we're still on good terms, and she is still part of The Warehouse Project and Parklife team.

One week, I decided to give away a car at Release, as a bit of a gimmick. I promoted it beforehand, and on the night everyone who came in was given a raffle ticket, and we announced the winner towards the end of the night. It was only an Orange Ford Escort, that I had bought through AutoTrader for £400 or something. Paradise Factory had these big service doors on the side of the building, so I just opened up those doors and drove the car onto the middle of the dancefloor and had it there all night till the raffle. It was all a bit tongue in cheek, just a silly gimmick. But what I hadn't thought through was that in those days everybody still smoked in clubs, and obviously the car was full of petrol. It was a huge fire risk – a health and safety nightmare. Peter Dalton didn't find out what I'd done till the morning after, and then he went fucking mental at me. He hit the fucking roof, and to be honest, he was right. It was pretty bloody stupid of me. But then, nobody else had said anything on the night either.

A similar thing happened at The Haçienda once, when they thought it would be a good idea to have a full-size ice cream van in the club. They drove it in through the service doors on

Whitworth Street West, but then a fire officer happened to turn up and just went, 'What on earth? That's full of petrol and people are smoking in here!', so they had to take it out immediately. Being The Haçienda, they pushed it outside, siphoned all the petrol out so it wasn't a fire risk, and then pushed it back in, to get round the fire officer.

One of the other battles I had with Peter Dalton at Paradise Factory, was when I had the idea of a foam party, but he kept saying, 'No, no, no. You're not doing a foam party. No way.' But I was desperate to do one, and kept pestering him, and in the end I just wore him down and he said, 'For god's sake! OK, you can do one foam party next week, but it's a one-off, Sacha, and don't ask me again after this!' We went ahead and did it, and it was a total sell out, and a huge success. It was a bit grubby, the Paradise Factory, to be fair. Most nightclubs and late-night bars are. Punters just can't tell usually because it's usually dark and loud when they're in there but trust me if you went in your regular nightclub during the daytime you would be shocked at how dirty it was, and how it stank of stale beer. The morning after that foam party, Peter rang me up first thing and said, 'You can do a foam party every week if you want … that's the cleanest the club has ever looked!'

Foam parties are not as easy as they seem. The first time The Haçienda had one, they hired in a foam machine and Paul Mason, the manager, was fixing it to the balcony and trying to get it to work. He managed to switch it on, but had it facing the wrong way, so the highly concentrated foam mixture shot straight into his long, curly hair. Poor Paul had to walk down Deansgate in the rain, back to his flat at St John's Gardens for a shower, with this trail of foam coming off his head behind him!

The other night I ran at Paradise Factory, called Shooting Stars, ran on Thursday nights and took its name from the Vic Reeves and Bob Mortimer TV show that was hugely popular at the time. The idea was that we would have a guest celebrity every week, the kind of celebrity that would appear on Vic and Bob's show, and the flyer would give a clue as to which celebrity was going to appear that week. We had all sorts of characters – from Timmy Mallett to Howard Marks to Katie Price to Margarita Pracatan, the Cuban singer who used to appear on Clive James's TV chat show. Timmy Mallet was great; he went round the club and was interacting with all the students. Katie Price, the notorious Page 3 model turned up pissed, and all she really did was get on the mic and say, 'Do I make your cock go hard?'

Bob Carolgees with Spit the Dog was a bit tricky. After we had agreed a fee, Bob's agent said, 'Do you want Spit to come as well, because there will be an extra fee for him?' Of course I wanted Spit! That's who I thought I had already booked. Who is Bob, without Spit?

I booked Howard Marks, the famous drug dealer, one night. His book *Mr Nice* had just been released and was a huge bestseller. The only problem with that night was that there had just been a huge drugs raid by the police on Paradise the weekend before, and after the raid, Peter Dalton rang me up and said, 'You're going to have to cancel Marks, we can't have him appearing at the club just after we've had a drug raid.' But I knew it was going to be a massive night, as Howard was so huge at the time, so I persuaded Peter to let us go ahead, and thankfully it passed without incident. The students absolutely loved him. Quite a few punters had brought ready-rolled spliffs for him to autograph, which he was happy to do, and he told a few stories about his exploits smuggling coke from South America, and they lapped it up.

After I'd been at Paradise Factory for a while, the door was taken over by a guy called Ratty from Wigan. Ratty seemed quite quiet when I first met him. He was in his late twenties, over six foot and built like a tank. He had short blond hair, and he was no stranger to a sunbed. All his crew were from Wigan and Preston, and had broad Lancashire accents. Although he seemed quite quiet, you definitely wouldn't want to get on the wrong side of him. After taking over from Roy, Ratty ran the door for quite a few years at Paradise Factory, till after I stopped doing nights there. He had to deal with people trying to intimidate him and take the door off him, but that was almost expected back then. One night I was walking down Charles Street to the club and the whole street was thick with smoke, and I couldn't work out where it was coming from till I got closer to the club, when I realised that a gang had firebombed Ratty's Mercedes convertible, and it was smouldering outside the club.

There was another particular incident when an Egyptian guy was trying to muscle in and take some of Ratty's doors from him. One night Ratty and his right-hand man decided to make matters clear to him and took him to the bridge over the canal on Charles Street, by Paradise Factory, and held him over it by his ankles, threatening him. Unfortunately, Ratty's right-hand man sneezed while he was holding him and dropped the poor guy in the river. He seemed to get the message.

GRANADA: FROM THE NORTH

After a couple of years at Paradise Factory, I was getting more ambitious, and increasingly feeling the need to do something bigger. I needed to. I had to. I really wanted to prove to myself, and to everyone else in Manchester, that I was capable of pulling off something bigger than student nights. But there was also a need to start making real money, because I was still living hand-to-mouth, week-to-week, getting my phone cut off now and again because I hadn't paid the bill and receiving the odd unwelcome visit from a bailiff about some other bill I hadn't paid. It was no way to live, and it was also reminding me of my life when I was a teenager when my dad was in financial trouble, and everything started getting repossessed. I had to find a way to make a gear change, to step things up a little.

I started looking around for a possible venue and came up with the idea of doing a night at the Granada TV Studios Tour. Back in the 1990s, Granada was still based in the city centre, at the bottom of Quay Street, near where the new Factory International building is now. It was the brainchild of Granada's David Plowright who had envisaged it as a 'Hollywood-on-the-Irwell' (the River Irwell runs alongside the site) and originally opened in 1988. The exterior was a replica New York street scene, which was supposed to look a bit like Times Square, with yellow cabs and huge neon signs. Inside there were various mock sets from past Granada productions including Baker Street from *The Adventures of Sherlock Holmes*, the giant room from *Return of the Antelope*; and then the main attraction for most people was the actual *Coronation Street* set that they used for filming. You could walk down the famous cobbles and even pop in and have a pint in a mock-up of the Rovers Return. In 1997, they added Skytrak, which was the world's first flying, solo roll-ercoaster: a single person was strapped in and suspended, in almost the same position as a hang glider would be, and then 'flew' round the theme park.

I thought it could be a great place to do a huge party, but when I initially approached Granada they weren't fully convinced about the idea and they also told me, 'Look, it's company policy that we only work with blue-chip companies.' At that stage my little operation was still more chips and gravy than blue chip, so I needed to bring someone else in to convince Granada to take a chance on the event.

I had already done a couple of nights at The Haçienda that were sponsored by Tim Cox, who owned a Häagen-Dazs fran-chised shop in St Ann's Arcade in Manchester. He only ran that one shop, he didn't really represent Häagen-Dazs or anything, but I thought if I brought him on board we could use the Häagen-Dazs name to get us in the door at Granada. I also misguidedly thought that Tim was loaded and might be able to help with cashflow. I subsequently learnt he was as skint as me, and his image was all a bit of a front. But Tim and I agreed to be partners on the first event with a fifty-fifty revenue split. Most importantly, badging it as a Häagen-Dazs event did the trick and got us in the door at Granada. They still had their reservations and I had to continually reassure them, but we were in the door and started to set plans in motion.

It was the first time the Granada Studios Tour had ever done an event like this. They had previously hosted a queer event, but that had been quite a bit smaller, nothing on the scale that I was planning. Rightly so, they had their concerns about protecting their brand and reputation, particularly about the risk of any stories in the press about drug use. Granada was a household name, a family name, the home of *Coronation Street*, and they didn't want that name being dragged through the mud or being attached to any controversy; they had their staff and security all over me and the event. We weren't really running a lot of the show, Granada were. We booked all the acts, promoted it, sold the tickets, and put the production in, but when it came down to the nuts and bolts of running the actual venue, the bars, and the security of the venue, Granada kept all that in house.

I was continually reassuring Granada that I had everything under control and all the preparation was going to plan, but to be honest, I was flying by the seat of my pants and making it up as I went along as I'd never run an event like this in my life.

I brought in Colin Sinclair to look after the production side of things for me. Colin owned a club called The Boardwalk on Little Peter Street, which had opened in 1986 and ran till 1999, and was a great club for most of the 1990s – Dave Haslam, having first made his name DJing at The Temperance Club on Thursday nights at The Haçienda, did a long running club night there on Saturdays called Yellow. Colin's dad owned the building that the Boardwalk was in and there were rehearsal rooms in the basement that everyone from Simply Red to Happy Mondays had used. Oasis had a rehearsal room in there for two years before they got signed, writing most of their first two albums in there.

I really liked Colin and got on with him. We used to have our planning meetings in Oliver Peyton's restaurant, Mash and Air, during the day. Colin got a guy called Andy Stratford to do all the heavy lifting and legwork on the production and put the PAs in (Colin wasn't the type to get his hands dirty) and he did a really good job.

As ever, we had some real issues with gangs around the event. Damian Noonan wanted to do the security but the Greater Manchester Police were totally against that. At that stage they were trying to get to grips with the gang issues. One of the problems was that Damian's door team had recently done an event at G-Mex, when the police knew they had basically let all their mates in, and there was blatant drug-dealing going on in the venue. I had to have a meeting with the council and police, and Damian sent along his right-hand man, but the police officer present said to him, 'Under no circumstances are you going to get to run the security at this event, and I'm instructing Granada now, to that effect.' It got really heated and I realised I was way in over my head at this point. I'm the type of guy who always makes sure I'm under the speed limit, and if a police car is behind me when I'm driving I start worrying even though I've done nothing wrong. But here I am, still only in my mid-twenties and caught in the middle of a stand-off between the gangsters and the authorities. Damian's representative just stood up, stared at the police officer and said, 'I'll be reporting back to Daddy.' All Damian's crew used to call him Daddy. He threw his business card on the table and said, 'There's my card, you will be calling me in a few days' and walked out. I was shitting it and said, 'Oh, my god, is that a threat?' And the police officer said, 'Yeah, they do this all the time.'

In the end, the door was run by Mark Logan from Showsec, who we still work with to this date – he is responsible for the security at The Warehouse Project and Parklife. The Granada Studios Tour was also the first time I realised why Dunbury Spring Water seemed to be strangely popular in licensed premises around Manchester. There was a member of Manchester City Council's Health and Safety team, who lived somewhere out near Buxton – famous for their spring water – and had a stream at the bottom of his garden. This guy's wife would spend all day bottling water from the stream, and then sticking the labels on they had printed that read 'Dunbury Spring Water', like a Northern version of that episode of *Only Fools and Horses* where Del Boy starts supplying restaurants with freshly bottled 'Peckham Spring' water. Although Del Boy wasn't a member of the council's Health and Safety team!

Two days before the event, this health and safety officer turned up at Granada Studios Tour, in his official capacity, to sign off my licence for the event. His opening gambit was something like, 'Good to meet you, now, what water are you selling?' It seemed a strange first question to ask.

'I've no idea,' I replied, 'we don't run the bars, Granada do ...'

'Oh, OK. But you will need water for all your production staff and artists, won't you?' He asked me, pointedly.

'Er, yeah, I guess so.'

'A couple of pallets should do it? ... It just so happens that I'm in my van today, and I've got a couple of pallets of Dunbury Spring Water with me. So, I can drop them off while I'm here, and give you an invoice?'

'Er, OK.'

'Great ... well, everything seems in order here, so I'm happy to sign off the licence.'

That's how it worked! If you went out in Manchester back in the 1990s and remember buying a bottle of Dunbury Spring Water from The Haçienda or one of my events, and thought, 'Dunbury Spring Water? I've never heard of that before?' now you know where it came from. If you ask any promoters or club managers from that time, they will laugh about that, and were quite possibly 'persuaded' by the Buxton resident that it might help get their licence signed off if they were to stock Dunbury Spring Water at their event. I can assure you, that would not happen these days.

I had brought in Ang Matthews from The Haçienda, and her boyfriend Billy Idle, to programme the event and book all the DJs. It was a step up from the talent I was used to booking. We'd gone from booking John Harlow, Ashton-under-Lyne's finest, to Jeremy Healy, Farley Jackmaster Funk, Boy George. I think we paid the headliners about £5,000 each, where I was used to paying DJs around £250.

A lot of DJs on the bill were people Ang and Billy knew already, like Jeremy Healy. One of the other headliners was Nigel Benn – the professional boxer – who for a short period back then had a second career as a DJ. He played in the Baker Street studios, where they filmed *The Adventures of Sherlock Holmes*, and even I will admit he wasn't great. I remember standing there and overhearing two lads in front of me talking and one of them asked the other, 'This is terrible, is he actually DJing with his gloves on?'

Jeremy Healy had also taken a booking in Swansea the same night, and we ended up doing a live link up from Granada to the venue in Swansea, and during his set, every now and then, he would hold up a sign that said, 'Hello Swansea'. I can't imagine it was the greatest experience for the poor crowd in Swansea, just watching that on a feed from Manchester!

Ticket sales for the event had been incredible, though. Capacity was 4,500 but I accidentally sold 5,200 tickets and took £150,000 on ticket sales. Overselling it really was accidental. I was selling tickets through various outlets around town, and even though I'd rang up and told them it was sold out, some of them carried on selling till I picked up the leftover tickets, as they wanted their cut. The problem was, the entrance at Granada had full-length turnstiles that automatically counted people in, so I had to find a way of getting the extra 700 people in without them being counted. In the end, when we had got 4,000 people through, I got Andy Strat to fuse the electronic turnstiles, so they stopped working and then all the punters had to come shuffling in through the manual gates. Granada were never the wiser and never knew exactly how many people we had in there.

The Skytrak rollercoaster was predictably a bit of a disaster on the evening. All these drunk punters were getting on it, and then flying around above the crowd like Superman, and inevitably half of them would be sick on the crowd below, so we had to close that down after less than an hour.

The crowd itself was quite a commercial crowd, quite mainstream. Much more Discotheque Royal than Warehouse Project. We actually had to throw out a couple of students that evening after we caught them having sex in Jack and Vera's backyard. They knew exactly where they were, and they must have been big *Corrie* punters. They'd deliberately gone to Jack and Vera's and were having sex next to Jack's pigeon shed. We saw it on CCTV and couldn't believe our eyes. *Next to Jack's pigeon shed?* You wouldn't have thought that was the sexiest place, would you? I can't remember exactly what they said when we kicked them out, but they weren't embarrassed at all, I think they were actually quite proud of what they'd achieved and thought it was definitely worth getting chucked out for. I doubt it's a tale they'll tell their grandchildren, though. Or maybe they will if they're massive *Coronation Street* fans too. No pigeons were harmed in the event.

This really was a turning point for me. It was the first time I had made any proper money, and I managed to pay off all my bills, and was still left with £10,000 in the bank. I was fluid. That might not seem like a fortune to some people, but I felt like a millionaire right there. It gave me belief that I had something to build on.

NEVER INVITE BOUNCERS TO A WEDDING

On reflection, it probably wasn't the wisest idea to invite a bunch of nightclub bouncers to my wedding at a genteel golf club in Cheshire. I mean, a bunch of big bouncers from Wigan that liked to party hard at a posh wedding in Cheshire – what could possibly go wrong?

It was August 2000, and I'd been working with Ratty and his boys for quite a while at Paradise Factory, and we'd just given them the door for Sankeys, so we were pretty friendly at the time.

Elisa's parents, Fiore and Lynn, were pretty well connected in Cheshire, and they invited a lot of the Hale and Bowden posh 'set'. They had a business selling high-end Italian furniture to the local ladies who lunch, and that was their circle. The wedding was quite a high-end affair at Mere Golf Club, which is really hoity-toity, and just near where Rick Astley and my first girlfriend lived. It was a mixture of posh Cheshire set, and then forty-eight Italians from Elisa's dad Fiore's home village of Carpineto. Most of Elisa's relatives didn't speak English, and were farmers from rural Italy, not the rough streets of Naples; so to come to a big city like Manchester was a bit of an eye-opener for them.

There was a weird mix of demographics there already but then, in the middle of that mix, there was the Paradise Factory table, with Ratty and his crew and Peter Dalton, and a few others. I noticed pretty early on that their table was getting rowdier and rowdier, which I should have expected really. They were clearly there to have a good time, let's put it that way.

It so happened that our wedding was the night before Captain's Day, which is like golf's FA Cup Final, and the biggest day of the venue's year – a huge annual showpiece event. So obviously everyone at the golf club will have been building up to Captain's Day for months, with extremely detailed preparations to make sure everything was perfect.

Just after the speeches, as it was getting dark and the party was about to get started, management came looking for me, and they were absolutely livid. Unfortunately, Ratty and his boys had stumbled across where the golf buggies were stored, god knows how, and had somehow hot-wired them. They were out on the golf course, speeding up and down the fairways and doing handbrake turns and donuts on the greens. 'We tried to stop them,' fumed the manager, 'but they just told us to fuck off.'

So, the night before the golf club's big showpiece event, Ratty and his mates had ripped up the turf on some of the greens. To say the manager was apoplectic is an understatement.

Unfortunately, things only got worse from there on. Fiore and Lynn had put up all of his Italian family in the Bowden Hotel and organised a coach to take them back there from the club. But Ratty found out that Elisa and I were staying at Mere Court, a small quaint country-house hotel on the outskirts of Knutsford. So Ratty and his crew gatecrashed the Italians' coach and told the coach driver in no uncertain terms that he was driving them to our hotel first. Apparently, they were singing songs and being really boisterous on the coach, and Fiore told me later that all the Italians were a bit intimidated.

After the coach driver dropped them off, Ratty and his crew were determined to carry on partying. It was now about one in the morning, and it was only a small quaint hotel, but Ratty and his crew were really going for it, and having a proper party, getting up to no good, being boisterous, and playing music too loudly. The first knock on the door came from some poor teenager who worked behind the bar, who had been sent up to tell the group to turn it down, but when Ratty answered the door and this kid saw this guy the size of a brick shithouse, he just looked and said, 'Er, it doesn't matter.' They must have sent up about three or four different staff to get the music turned down, and in the end they just gave up. I don't think the hotel dared to bar Ratty and friends the next morning, but I think we knew they would never be welcome back there.

Fiore's poor family from that little town were probably scarred for life, just like the greens on the golf course from the hijacked buggies!

FLYPOSTER WARS

When I initially met Dave Vincent in the late 1990s, I thought he was an arrogant little Cockney, with a big mouth and little manners. Which is exactly who he was back then, as I'm sure he would be the first to admit. But apart from being arrogant and annoying, he was also a bloody good promoter. (I'm sure he'd be the first to admit that too!)

Dave was a proper Cockney. He came from a rough estate in Stepney and had quite a tough upbringing. He and his mates had their fair share of brushes with the police as teenagers. I don't think Dave had seen much life outside of London, till he went to visit a mate of his called Avi, who was at university in Manchester, and it opened his eyes a bit. Dave went on to move to Manchester and became a mature student at UMIST. While he was a student he quickly fell into promoting club nights as well, and by the time I met him he was selling out big nights and had become one of my rival student promoters in Manchester. One of the things that helped Dave in the early days of the late 1990s, was that he knew quite a lot of the London DJs, especially in the growing garage scene, and he was one of the first to offer them gigs outside London. He started to do pretty well, and by the time I got to know him a bit better, around 1997, he had a night on called Colours at The Haçienda, which was regularly selling out and had a good reputation on the clubbing scene. He also promoted Ministry of Sounds nights there.

Dave, it's safe to say, was a character. He was larger than life, and you would always be hearing crazy stories about what he was up to. He was obsessed by Danny Tenaglia, and he was involved in one of the first mad stories I heard about Danny. Dave had booked Danny to play the Academy in Manchester, and he had to collect him from Sheffield first, because Danny had just been performing there. Dave, being obsessed, offered to drive over to Sheffield and pick him up himself. Snake Pass, as it is known locally, is a road that runs over the Pennines and Peak District from Sheffield to Manchester, and it's really exposed to the elements, so high in the peaks, and often gets closed off due to bad weather. That night it was snowing and visibility on the roads was awful, as Dave and his mate Jools were driving back over the top with Tenaglia, in Dave's little Clio. It was pitch black, and as they came round a blind bend, they hit a cow that was in the middle of the road. It was a large cow, and it ended up stuck across the bonnet of the Clio, and Dave and Jools had to jump out and drag the cow off the car before they could carry on. Tenaglia must have thought, *What the fuck have I got myself into?!* God knows what the poor cow thought too. I believe it was still alive when they dragged it off the bonnet, hopefully it survived to tell the tale.

Towards the end of the 1990s, Dave and I were in direct competition, and we would play dirty tricks on each other; anything we could do to try and get one up on each other. He had an office in Beehive Mill and now and again I would phone up his office and disguise my voice, I'd say something like, 'There's a group of us who were planning to come down to Colours this week, but is it true it's been cancelled?'

'No, why would you think it's been cancelled?'

'I've just seen your posters up in Chester and it's got a big 'cancelled' sticker across it.'

'What?!?'

Dave or one of his team would then fly out of his office in Beehive Mill and drive down to Chester, Stockport or Bury (I'd always choose a location which was a bit of a drive, to make it more of an inconvenience for them) to check on his posters, and they would lose a day's work and promoting. It was a pretty low trick, looking back, but he absolutely gave as good as he got back by pulling similar stunts on me, too. Most promoters would. Promoting was a dog-eat-dog world back then, so everyone was playing a little bit dirty. You had to. I knew for a fact that Dave or his team were tearing down my posters, and as soon as he was putting up posters, we would go around town pasting our posters over his. If I knew he was out in Bury that day, putting posters up, I'd go round after him and rip them down before the paste had even dried, or post mine over his.

It's hard for young kids and promoters nowadays to understand just how important flying and flypostering was back in the day, but before social media it was the main way of promoting your night. Email didn't even exist when I started promoting. Well, it maybe existed, but I didn't even have an email address and most of the punters I wanted to reach definitely didn't have one. I didn't have a website. I didn't even have a computer! I just ran everything through my mobile phone. That was my office. My mobile phone and my Filofax were the only office I used back then. I still use both. I must be one of the few people running nightclubs who is still using a Filofax in 2024, but it's just habit. I've got the same Filofax I had twenty years ago; I just buy a new diary insert each year.

These days almost all of our promotion for The Warehouse Project is done online and we have a full-time social media team in the office. The only time we would really do flypostering now is maybe at the start of the season, to announce the line-up. But back in the 1990s and early 2000s, there was no social media. Flyers and flypostering *was* our social media, and they were hugely important to nightclubs. There was almost a direct correlation between how many posters you managed to get up around town and how many paying punters you got through the door. Obviously which artists you booked also had a huge effect, but flypostering was almost as important. Didn't matter who you had booked, if you didn't paper the town then you wouldn't sell out. In the early days, me and Elisa would sometimes spend all day flyering, go home for tea, then back out till 2 a.m. in the freezing cold and rain putting up posters in the dark, dodging the police. After a while, I started flypostering during the day in a high-vis jacket, and the police would just drive past and assume I had permission as it was so brazen.

Most of the flypostering in and around Manchester was controlled by Kev and Vinny back then, who were real old-school characters. They weren't gangsters but they knew *everyone*. I really liked Kev and Vinny, but I didn't use them all the time, as I never wanted my poster to just be one in a row of twenty other posters, jostling for attention. I always wanted to find a way to stand out and use different sites. I did use them sometimes as there was kind of an unwritten rule that everyone would use Kev and Vinny at some stage, they were kings of the flypostering world in Manchester in the 1990s.

I always got on well with them and they even invited me shooting and horse racing with them. They were both really into shooting, and I don't mean clay pigeon shooting; they would go on proper old-school country shoots in Cheshire and come back with a brace of pheasants or grouse. Kev and Vinny lived amazing double lives. Monday to Friday they would be grafting the streets around Manchester, dealing with club promotors and sorting any problems out on the streets, dealing with some pretty rum characters ... then they would spend their weekend hanging out with Lords and toffs on their incredible rolling estates in Cheshire, shooting grouse. I never went shooting as it didn't appeal to me, and I have no idea how they got into that scene. Kev and Vinny are now retired, but their nephew Keith set up his own flyer and promotion company called Exposure in the 1990s and he's still running it now; everyone knows him as Keith Exposure or Minced Beef. Lovely lad and a big United fan.

Kev and Vinny had some rules they would stick to about not flypostering on glass windows and bus stops, but back then I didn't really give a fuck. I wouldn't dream of doing anything like this now, but I was still young and determined to make my nights work, no matter what, so I would flyposter everywhere. After he had left The Haçienda, Paul Mason moved in with his girlfriend, Jo, on the ground floor of Sally's Yard, one of Urban Splash's first developments, just off Oxford Road. He got up one morning, drew the curtains open, and it was still dark. He thought, *What the fuck?* and went outside to investigate, only to find out that someone had completely flypostered over the windows of their flat. He was absolutely fuming. To add insult to injury, he then got up on a ladder with some soapy water to try and remove the offending flyposter, and as he was up the ladder, a police car pulled up behind him and started to caution him for flypostering. 'It's my bloody flat!' said Paul, 'I'm trying to get the bleeding thing off, not stick it up!'[3]

Dave Vincent also didn't stick to fly-posting etiquette, and the tit for tat between us was getting a bit ridiculous, so one day he called me and said, 'Listen, why don't we have a chat and see if we can work together, because we can't go on like this, we're both spending half our time battling each other instead of trying to fill nightclubs!'

We arranged to meet at the bar Generation X, for a bit of a summit meeting, where we both agreed we were wasting a lot of time and money on competing with each other, and that we should try and find a way to work together instead. We had quite a lengthy talk about how we could move forward, then Dave suddenly looked at his watch and said, 'Shit, I'm gonna have to go, it's Patsy my girlfriend's birthday tomorrow and I've got stuff to organise.' I was like, 'Wow, that's a weird coincidence it's actually Elisa's birthday tomorrow as well.' Dave looked at me and said, 'When's your birthday?' I said '26th January' and Dave went white and said, 'Fackin' hell. That's my birthday too!'

Which was a bit of a weird coincidence, and we bonded a bit over that, and decided we were going to work together. Our birthdays were about the only thing we had in common, as Dave and I were very different characters. He was a wide boy Cockney, I was Manc. He'd wear the same clothes for days, while I tried to be a bit more groomed and even ironed my jeans each morning. I tried to be diplomatic, but he was a

---

[3] I never knew this story till Luke told me while we were writing this book, but I think that may well have been me who pasted a flyer over his window. Sorry, Paul.

bull in a china shop. I'm quite fussy about what I eat, and try to be healthy, he would just grab a greasy donner kebab at 4 a.m. I was always prompt; he was always late. Dave just wanted to throw the best party ever, I was more about making sure we could run a tight ship and a proper business. But despite all our differences, we did have a bit of respect for one other and thought we could each bring something different to the mix. Dave was running Colours and Ministry of Sound in Manchester and had great contacts with DJs, and pretty good relationships with a lot of the big names, but he was living in London. I had a lot more contacts than Dave on the ground in Manchester. We decided to pool our resources. For the first few months we were just scouting around, trying to find the right opportunity. We had a few good ideas and some pretty daft ones too, but still hadn't found the right thing.

Then one morning, Dave rang me up really excited, like a little kid saying, 'Look, I've not slept a wink, I've had this mental idea …'

'Go on …'

'Instead of doing nights together, why don't we open a night*club* together?'

'Because it would cost a fortune …'

'I don't mean build one. Hear me out. I've already spoken to Andy Spiro this morning … and we can go and have a look at Sankeys if you want …'

'Sankeys? … *Are you fucking mental?*'

2000s

STRANGEWAYS HERE WE COME

'THIS AREA IS MORE FUCKED UP THAN DETROIT!'

Sankeys originally opened its doors in the summer of 1994. It was set up by Rupert Campbell and Andy Spiro, inside Beehive Mill in Ancoats, and the name of the club came from the fact that the Mill had historically been used to manufacture soap. Rupert and Andy had been in a band together and were running Beehive Mill for the building owner, Joseph Steinright, turning it into a space for designers, small record labels, and other creatives. Beehive Mill was an outpost in an urban wasteland at the time, there was nothing else round there. They managed to convince Joseph to let them open a club inside the mill, a month before I first held my own club night, across town at The Haçienda in 1994. They had a tricky first few months, and nearly went bust within the first six months of opening their doors, but the turning point was when they gave the Friday night to Bugged Out, a club night run by the editors of *Jockey Slut*, John 'Johnno' Burgess and Paul Benney. Johnno and Paul didn't even have a name for the night at first. Johnno says Sankeys suggested the names 'Soap Opera' and 'Okey Dokey' to them, but they eventually chose the term 'Bugged Out', which they borrowed from a techno artist's description of his own music in *Jockey Slut*. Bugged Out was an overnight success, with the in-house residents James Holroyd and Rob Bright being joined by big guest names like Justin Robertson, Underground Resistance and Derrick May. Daft Punk even played some of their earliest shows there, before they took to wearing their helmets.

Ancoats in the early 1990s was unrecognisable to the place it is now. There can't be many places in the Western world that have changed as much over the last thirty years. In the mid-1990s it was still a desolate wasteland. That probably sounds overly dramatic to younger readers, but it really isn't. Desolate wasteland is being polite. Anyone who went to Sankeys back in the day will tell you what it was like and will have a war story or two about making the perilous half-mile journey from there, back to the city centre. There were no street lights and almost every building was derelict.

Historically, Ancoats had been Britain's first industrial suburb, when it was the centre of an industrial revolution. Manchester was the first modern city in the world, and Ancoats was its industrial heart, especially after the opening of Rochdale Canal in 1804, which saw huge mills springing up and dominating the area, and tightly packed housing for the workers. By 1815, Ancoats was the most populous area of Manchester, but also one of the poorest. L. S. Lowry would often visit Ancoats in his day job as a rent collector, and painted some of his famous street scenes there, as mentioned in the lyrics to 'Matchstick Men and Matchstick Cats and Dogs', the No.1 from 1978 by Michael and Brian: *He painted Salford's smoky tops/ On cardboard boxes from the shops/ And parts of Ancoats where I used to play'*.

It was written by the band's Michael Colman, who lived with his mother and siblings in Britain's last workhouse, in Ancoats, when he was growing up. One of Lowry's paintings of the area, *Ancoats Hospital Outpatient's Hall*, depicts the hall where Michael went to be treated after being mugged when he was only eight, and sadly lost his eye as a result. The Smiths also made a reference to the area, when Morrissey's pitched-up backing vocals on their 1986 single 'Bigmouth Strikes Again' were accredited to the *nom de plume* Ann Coates.

After Britain's cotton industry slumped in the 1930s, Ancoats never truly recovered, and by the 1960s slum clearances removed a lot of the housing, which left behind a barren wasteland. By the early 1990s, Ancoats was still empty. Once you crossed Great Ancoats Street, Manchester's very own 8 Mile (or half mile), there might as well have been a note on the map that said 'Here be monsters'. People who hadn't been to Sankeys before would be walking down the darkened streets saying, 'Where the fuck are we going?' Detroit is famously desolate, once the industrial heartland of America, but after the race riots in 1967 fuelled the 'white flight', the city's population halved, leaving swathes of the inner city derelict and abandoned. When the legendary Detroit-based DJ, Derrick May, was booked to play Bugged Out at Sankeys, he arrived, got out of the car, looked around him, shocked, and said. 'This area is more fucked up than Detroit!'

Fast forward to the present day, and Ancoats has loft apartments that go for over a million and a Michelin-starred restaurant, Mana. The set menu at Mana is £195 a head, and wine pairing is another £140 a head. £195 gets you 'A series of servings reflecting the season at the time of your visit. Produce at its peak is enhanced by methods of preservation from seasons past. Fermentation and fire are the widest pillars of our kitchen.' While we were writing this chapter of the book, Jay Rayner, the esteemed restaurant critic, was raving about the epicurean qualities of Ancoats in the *Observer*, describing it as 'a fast-developing district of boozy and edible promise, where the industrial past has been repurposed for the service industry present. You'll never want for a negroni or a chilli-spiked Gordal olive in Ancoats.' You couldn't buy a can of coke round there in the early Sankeys days, let alone a negroni, and if you got spiked it certainly wasn't with a chilli Gordal olive. Jay Rayner was reviewing the Edinburgh Castle, which back in the 1990s was a really rough pub, run by Jimmy Swords, one of the Quality Street Gang, but is now yet another great pull to the area.

In the years they were running Sankeys, Andy and Rupert were dogged by issues with gangs, like most clubs in Manchester at that time. Unfortunately for them, their time at Sankeys was probably the nadir of gangland trouble in Manchester. The gangs had permeated everything and, in the end, Sankeys, Home and The Haçienda all closed within a year of each other. Creativity in the city was being stifled by the presence of gangs and the Greater Manchester Police still didn't have a grip on the culture of the gangs, and there were also a few bad eggs in GMP at the time. Spiro tells a story about how they tried to work with the police to combat the gangs, but soon realised there were some old-school coppers who were more than willing to turn a blind eye to the crime. After he got increasingly frustrated by two CID officers, who came down to the club but refused to do something about a gang member who was in that night, he complained to their commanding officer, who he knew was concerned about the gang situation. The next day, Spiro was in his office, when the door was kicked open and the two CID officers stormed in, grabbed Spiro, and pinned him up against the wall, threatening him for going above their heads, and making threats about what they would do if it happened again.

It wasn't just nightclubs that were getting squeezed by the gangs either. Oliver Peyton, who is now one of the judges on the BBC's *Great British Menu*, decided to come to Manchester after his huge success in London with the Atlantic Bar and Grill. In 1996, he opened Mash and Air, a futuristic four-floor bar, restaurant and micro-brewery, on the edge of the Gay Village, which was way ahead of its time. Because it was the place to be seen after it opened, it soon attracted the attention of the gangs. Oliver and his sister Siobhan, who ran Mash and Air on a day-to-day basis, were pretty shocked with what they were faced with. Siobhan knew that Spiro and Sankeys had their issues with gangs and would sometimes ask Spiro for advice. One night she rang him up and said she had well-known gang members on one table in the restaurant, and a group of CID officers on another table. The gangsters actually sent over a bottle of champagne to the CID, who gratefully received it and waved their thanks. When the gangsters finished their meal, they simply got up and walked out without paying, in full view of the CID and there was nothing Sarah and her staff could do to stop them. When Sarah told Spiro this, he said, 'Are the CID still there? Put the champagne on their bill, they drank it.' She did that, but the CID refused to pay for it either, saying, 'No chance. We didn't order that champagne, the other table did, they just sent it over to us.'

There were so many incidents like that, making running a restaurant impossible, let alone a nightclub. In the end, in 2000, Oliver Peyton threw in the towel and went back to London.

The gang's grip on the area got too much for Rupert and Andy too, and it was a huge shame for Manchester and the UK clubbing scene in general when Sankeys closed. It might have only been open for four years, but it had left a strong legacy. I could absolutely see why it was so attractive to Dave, and why he was so excited about the idea of reopening it. But by the time he came to me with the idea, the club had laid dormant for two years.

To be honest, I wasn't sure that reopening Sankeys with Dave was a remotely feasible idea at first, or that we could get a licence to open the club either, but Elisa persuaded me that we should at least try. For the first few weeks I just went along with the idea to humour Dave. I thought it was such a mental idea that it would soon become apparent that it wouldn't work, and the whole plan would just go away. Instead, it became more and more real as time went on.

Dave had made some good connections with people who worked in the City and found three investors who were willing to put money into the club. They were city boys who had done well for themselves but also liked to party. Between them, they put £38,000 in, which was the entire budget of what we had to reopen Sankeys.

Originally, there were going to be three partners in the club – myself, Dave and John Hill, who used to run a club night called Golden. John was a really lovely guy from Stoke, and Golden was one of the top club nights in the country at the time. But John was fully aware of the gang problems that had plagued Sankeys during its first incarnation and, in the end, he got cold feet about coming in with us. He just didn't want all the stress (of which there is a lot) and risk hanging over his head and told us, 'I can't do this. It's too risky in my opinion. I'd still love to do Golden on Saturday nights, but I don't want to be involved in the running of the club.'

We had to go to Manchester Magistrates' Court to get the licence for Sankeys to reopen, and we really didn't have a clue till the day of the decision if we would get it and be able to reopen. In the end we did, but it was touch and go, and plenty of people couldn't believe we'd succeeded, including one of the magistrates who, after the licence had been approved, turned to his colleague, exasperated, and said, 'I cannot believe we're allowing Sankeys to open again!'

Daryl Butterworth, who at that time was Head of Licensing for Greater Manchester Police, was also in the Magistrates' Court that morning to hear the outcome. Afterwards, he came over to me and said, 'Listen Sacha, you will only *ever* see the blue lights *once*.'

What he meant was, at the first sign of trouble, the police would be called to Sankeys to shut us down.

WE'VE FOUND THE KEYS

Once word got out that Dave and I were reopening Sankeys, everyone in Manchester thought we were, not to put too fine a point on it, absolutely mental. All the trouble that the first Sankeys had gone through was well known throughout the city and the club was seen as a poisoned chalice. Everyone really missed Sankeys, but nobody thought it was feasible to reopen it, or wanted to take the risk of doing it themselves. The clubbing world were more excited about the news of the club reopening, but still thought we were a bit crazy to take it on.

Although we had some financial backing from our investors, £38,000 is not a lot of money to open a nightclub, even back then. We really were working on a shoestring. We hired everything and bought nothing. From the sound system and the lights to the glasses for the bar ... Everything was borrowed. Firstly, for cost reasons, we just didn't have the money to buy everything, and secondly because we didn't know how long the club was going to last, it made sense to hire things rather than invest in them. At least for the first few months, while we saw how things panned out.

Dave suggested we bring in a young promoter called Sam Kandel, who he had worked with previously on his club nights, as Promotions Manager for Sankeys. Like me, Sam had put on his first ever night at The Haçienda, but he was only fifteen at the time! He obviously hadn't let The Haçienda know exactly how young he was, or they turned a blind eye to it. Weirdly, Sam still has his first contract from them as well, like me, and it's also signed by Jon Drape, who we would both continue to work closely with in the future. Sam then worked with Dave for a couple of years while he was doing his A levels, helping out with promotion, before he went off to Birmingham University when he was eighteen. While most people chose their university on the strength of the course, or the reputation of the establishment, Sam chose Birmingham simply because he'd managed to secure the Friday-night slot at Bonds nightclub (also home to Miss Moneypenny's), so he could continue his promoting career while studying. Coincidentally, the week Sam graduated and left Birmingham, he ran into Dave outside Affleck's Palace in the Northern Quarter, after having not seen him for a couple of years. Dave told him about the plans for Sankeys and persuaded him to come join us as our Promotions Manager. I'd never met Sam before, which is odd because he grew up pretty near me in Altrincham, and although he was a few years younger than me, we immediately hit it off and became quite close pretty quickly. Sam had also been a regular at Sankeys in the early days, showing up there every Friday night for Bugged Out, and knew the club inside out, meaning he knew exactly what made it so special and what it would take to capture the magic once again. Sam was a brilliant addition to Sankeys, but I had no idea at that time that we would end up being business partners for almost two decades.

Although Sankeys had only been closed a couple of years, two years in clubbing years is a lifetime. It had really been missed, by Manchester and the whole clubbing world, becoming a bit of a mythical place, so we came up with the following tagline and built our promotion around that for the reopening: 'We've found the keys'. The 500 key-shaped invitations that were sent out to VIPs were embossed with gold.

The police warned us that if we brought any of the gangs in to work on the door that they would shut us down immediately, no questions. Things were beginning to change a little in Manchester already, and the police had a better handle on the gang situation, but some members of these gangs still wanted to run the doors at clubs, because if you run the door of the club, then you also run what goes on inside.

Everyone who knows me, and anyone who has been a regular at The Warehouse Project over the years, knows that I like to stand on the door at my own events as much as possible. That way I can see what the crowd is like as they come in, which gives you a sense of what kind of night it's going to be but is also good to keep an eye on numbers. Back in the day, I also used to do it to make sure that the bouncers and security weren't dicking about. But I was warned by police and my own security that it would be too dangerous to do that, at least for the first few months after Sankeys reopened, as I might be a target for the gangs who didn't get the door.

We worked bloody hard in the month leading up to the reopening, and by the final week we still had people working on site in the club. In the end, Dave and I took turns sleeping there, so that one of us could always be at the club, twenty-four hours a day. Just to make sure Sankeys was ready in time.

The night before the big launch, I was asleep in bed when I got a call from Greater Manchester Fire Rescue, telling me there had been a bad fire at the club and asking me to come down to assess the damage. I couldn't believe it. I jumped in my car and picked up Dave, from the flat he was renting around the corner from Sankeys, on the way. When we got there, we couldn't believe what we found. The electricity substation right behind the club had deliberately been blown up. One of the gangs, angry about not being given control of the door, was determined that if they couldn't run the door, then they weren't going to let Sankeys open at all. They had come down in the middle of the night, thrown a mattress over the steel fence surrounding the substation before pouring petrol over it and setting it ablaze. The whole substation was ruined. Unbelievable. Dave and I were so exhausted by this stage that when the guy from the fire service was explaining what had happened to us, we both just burst out laughing, and couldn't stop. The whole thing was surreal.

Obviously it was pretty scary that the gang had gone to such extremes, but it wasn't going to stop us. What the gang obviously didn't know is that Sankeys actually had its own generator. A hangover from when it had been a mill. So, although the substation had gone down, and the rest of Ancoats was pitched into darkness, Sankeys itself was absolutely fine, and we opened the next night as planned.

Because the rest of the area was still in complete blackout, Sankeys stood out even more as a beacon in the urban wilderness. We felt like we were in our own little bubble, having this full-on rave in the middle of an otherwise derelict dystopian landscape. Somehow, it made the opening night even more special.

Then reality set in. The atmosphere around the club and the office was really tense for the first few weeks. We were wary that at any time we might be targeted by gangs. For the first three months, one of my security team, a guy called Dave

Power, would pick me up from home at the start of the night and then drop me off at home again at the end of it. It was his idea of mitigating risk. It's not much fun having to look over your shoulder on the way home every night. Trust me.

We had to employ a General Manager to be the licence holder for Sankeys, as neither Dave nor I were allowed to hold the licence at the time, as neither of us had passed the exams. The first few people I asked were scared off by the trouble Sankeys had previously had and didn't fancy taking on that stress. But one guy who was up for it, and was another great addition to the team, was James Cassidy. I'd known James for a few years since I ran nights at Paradise Factory, when he was one of the bar managers there. He saw the opportunity to step up at Sankeys and grabbed it, and he became our GM licensee. James was great. He was about my age, a big Irish guy with a long ponytail and he didn't take any shit from anyone, including Dave, who could drive him crazy at the bar with all his hangers-on wanting free drinks. Dave used to call James 'Anthat' because James used to finish every sentence with '… and that.' At the end of every night, when the music stopped, James would stand in front of the DJ booth and shout to the whole club, 'Ladies … Gentleman … unless you're coming home with me … fuck off!'

One of the other legendary characters at Sankeys was Crazy Paul, who we inherited from the first incarnation of the club. Paul was in his sixties, but he looked like he was in his eighties, he had a huge head of white hair and a big white beard, and glasses, so he looked like some sort of mad professor. The kids at Sankeys loved him, especially the first time they saw him, they couldn't get over the fact that this guy who looked old enough to be their grandad was working there, and obviously as into the music as they were. Paul loved working the lights, he saw them as his little babies, he treated them like family. He also loved speed and would sometimes spend all day Sunday in the club, still up, going round singing to himself and taking the lights down individually and polishing them. He eventually fell out with Dave and I after we decided the lights needed an upgrade, and we replaced them without running it past Paul first. He went absolutely ballistic at us, you would have thought we had sold his own children, but to Paul that's what they were, and he never forgave us for that.

At the same time as we were reopening the club, I was also still running my student nights. I had no idea how Sankeys was going to pan out, so needed to make sure I had a back-up plan, just in case. So, Elisa more or less took over the day-to-day running of the student nights, while I focused on Sankeys. A week or two after the club reopened, I was at Discotheque Royale one night when I recognised their head of security and started chatting to him. He was asking me how it was going at Sankeys. He had a pretty fearsome reputation and was notorious for giving people a dead hard smack. Instead of punching people, he had this signature slap instead and I knew he was connected to one of the main gangs, so it was pretty obvious that he was trying to glean some information from me. I told him it was going fine, and we hadn't had any trouble, but that was probably because the police had set up surveillance on the club and had plain-clothed officers in the building opposite the club every night it was open, watching and documenting everything that happened at the club. It was complete bollocks. Although the police were genuinely keeping an eye on the club from a distance, they certainly didn't have any covert officers watching the door all night, but I thought if I put that out there as a rumour and word got back to the gangs, that might put them off if they were thinking about putting any more pressure on us.

ARE YOU TRIBAL?

Dave Vincent had been a regular at the original Tribal Gathering in the early 1990s, and it was an event that held mythical status for him. He told me about a time at Tribal Gathering where he had taken something that made him convinced that he was a giant. It was only when the drugs wore off that he realised he'd just pulled his tracky bottoms up too much. A very Dave anecdote.

In 1999, just before Dave and I started working together, he had bought the rights to the Tribal Gathering name, and really wanted to bring Tribal Gathering back. As the first step in achieving this, he came up with the concept of doing Tribal Sessions on Friday nights at Sankeys. It sounded great on paper, but after we reopened the club and launched Tribal Sessions, it was a real slog for the first few months. Tribal ran every Friday and the DJs Dave was booking were great, including people like Andy from Portishead, but we just couldn't get the interest, we couldn't get enough punters through the door – around 200, 300 at the most – and the place looked empty. As well as losing money, it just wasn't happening.

The tagline for that night was, 'Are you Tribal?' Unfortunately, the answer to that from most of Manchester, at first, was a big fat No. They definitely did not consider themselves Tribal.

At the turn of the Millennium, the Northern Quarter was just starting to change in a big way, and obviously it was right on our doorstep, a five-minute walk away (although that five minutes did involve you taking your life into your own hands). It should have been a decent potential market for us, but the Northern Quarter was pretty cliquey and, ironically, quite tribal. Just not in our sense. We felt like we were out on a limb a bit, and we thought maybe that was part of the problem and why the Friday night wasn't taking off as planned. Dave and I just weren't in with the cool crowd, and we decided we should make more of an effort to get 'in' with the Northern Quarter crew.

A bar called Cord had just opened, and a lot of the music scene had quickly coalesced around that, people like Luke Una (who lived above it), all the Fat City and Grand Central crew, plus all the Manchester music mafia that worked for record labels and promoters like Twisted Nerve, Ear to the Ground, Paper Recordings, plus people like Chris York from SJM concerts, Richard Hector-Jones, Rob Bright and James Holroyd from Bugged Out!, everyone who worked in key shops like Oi Polloi, Eastern Bloc, and Piccadilly Records, plus members of bands like Doves, Crazy Penis, Alpinestars, and Alfie. Cord was owned by Paul Astill (who years later would design The Warehouse Project office), Pete Orgrill, and Simon Cooper, and they had quite cleverly deliberately targeted that nascent Northern Quarter crowd when they opened, and they'd done a really good job of it. Not least by having a wall of tankards behind the bar, engraved with the names of all the people in the music scene they wanted to be regulars, and it worked.

Dave and I were definitely not part of that crowd. There was never going to be a tankard engraved with 'Sacha' or 'Dave' behind the Cord bar. It didn't bother us personally, but we did think it might help our Friday nights and the business if we made a bit more of an effort to get 'in' with that crowd. One night, we decided to go down to Cord to try and ingratiate ourselves. We walked in there and I immediately felt super self-conscious. I'm sure it wasn't quite like this in reality, but in my head when we walked in it was a bit like those scenes in Westerns where someone walks into a bar: the music, the balls on a snooker table roll silently before stopping dead, and smoke fills the air. I felt like everything went a bit quiet when we walked in, as if everyone in there was thinking, *What the fuck are they doing here?*

I walked up to the bar and ordered a Coke, and Dave in his loud cockney voice, said, 'Can I have an Advocaat and lemonade, please?' Once Dave said that I knew we weren't going to be accepted as part of the Cord crowd. We never went back after that night.

Back at the club, we called a Tribal Sessions summit meeting to discuss what we were going to do. Dave was determined to make it work somehow. 'We need to have one last go at making Tribal work, and give it everything,' he stressed. He went away and came back having booked Dave Clarke for the main room downstairs, and Bob Sinclar for the upstairs set. Sam went to town on promotion for that night, and I mean he *went to fucking town.* There was not a lamp-post, phone box or an electricity box in Manchester that wasn't plastered with a poster advertising 'Tribal Sessions with Dave Clarke and Bob Sinclar'. I can still remember the artwork for the poster now. It sold out, and it was a brilliant night, and we all had a huge Tribal sigh of relief. That was it then, we were away. Golden kept us going for the first six months, but when Tribal kicked off as well, it really felt like Sankeys was back in all its glory, where it belonged.

What became apparent, which was slightly annoying to me, was because Tribal was booking the 'cool' talent, that a snobbery emerged between the people who went to Tribal and those who went to Golden. On Saturday nights, Golden had DJs like Lisa Lashes and Judge Jules, and pulled in a different, largely female crowd, with girls in fluffy bras, that the Tribal crowd looked down on. It wound me up a bit because I loved Golden. Not necessarily because of the music, but because it was paying the bills. Tribal was losing a fortune to begin with. There was also a bigger bar spend at Golden nights, and there was a good reason for that.

As the night became successful, the Tribal crowd quite quickly became quite, well, I guess, 'tribal'. There was a really close group in the centre of it, and Dave became like their cult leader. His ego began to grow when Tribal Sessions really started to take off. I hadn't seen that side of him before. That clique of regulars started calling themselves The Tribalists and used to wear face paint and Native American tribal dress. You'd never get away with that now. There were about twenty Tribalists and they were a law unto themselves, and Dave let them get away with murder, they could do whatever they wanted. They were there every week, always on the guest list, never paying for entry or drinks.

We didn't have a dressing room, green room, or VIP area, so backstage was basically just the Sankeys office. I used to go into the office on a Monday morning and there would be remnants of powders all over my desk, empty drug wraps and other leftovers from the weekend's partying and it would more often than not be the Tribalists who were responsible, rather than the guest DJs and their entourages. I had constant run-ins with the Tribalists and I'm sure the dislike was mutual. They saw me as the boring fun police, pouring cold water on the party. I just wasn't 'Tribal', in their eyes. I didn't mind people partying, I mean it's a nightclub at the end of the day, but I also wanted to make sure Sankeys was successful as a business as well, not just an excuse to party. The Tribalists could be lawless, and I used to lose my rag with them, saying, 'At least clean the fucking desks when you're done.'

After they had finished at the club, the Tribal clique would head off to these after parties, which often went on till Monday morning. I never went, but I would hear stories about them playing weird games, like Hungry Hippo. I would ask, 'What's 'Hungry Hippo'? It turned out, this was a more druggy and less wholesome version of the children's game. It involved them all sitting about in a circle as one person sat in the middle of the group with their mouth open so that everyone else in the surrounding circle could try and throw pills into their mouth.

One night at Tribal Sessions, after we had closed, I was getting ready to leave at about 4 a.m., I was just waiting on James to give me all the figures, when I noticed what looked like a piece of steak in the middle of the dancefloor, and I thought, 'Who the fuck has brought a steak into the club?' But, as I walked over and looked more closely at it, I could see that it was actually a rat (or the remnants of what used to be a rat). Because Sankeys was in an old mill, we would often get the odd rat or two. We didn't have a vermin problem, but like every old building you would get a rat every now and again. This poor thing must have tried to make a run for it across the dancefloor at some stage in the night, possibly trying to escape the Tribalists, and it had got trampled on instead because it was a rammed night, the kids had just been dancing on this dead rat all night, pulverising the poor little bastard to pieces. The only way I could tell it had been a rat was when I looked closely enough to see the poor little fucker's tail. Thank fuck the Tribalists didn't see it – they would have probably taken it to their after party.

In 2001, Dave organised a big joint birthday party for his thirtieth and my twenty-ninth. Dave wanted it to be a gangsters and molls fancy-dress party, and he hired a barge for the night that set off from Castlefield. The second the barge set off, it became clear it was going to be a really debauched affair, which is not quite what I had in mind. After about half an hour, I'd had enough and asked them to pull over to the side of the canal, and me, Elisa, J-Boy and his wife got off. We scrambled up the bank and suddenly realised we were in the middle of Salford, dressed in 1930s fancy dress, but we managed to flag down a taxi, and decided to go back to Sankeys. When we got back there, we were in the courtyard outside, still in our comedy fancy dress outfits, when a gang of about thirty turned up, walked straight past the bouncers on the door into the courtyard. I was at the end of my tether at that point, and without thinking through the ramifications, I just walked up to them and said, 'Can you not just leave us alone? You're ruining the night for everyone.' One of them threatened to stab me, and on reflection I was pretty lucky that they didn't react, but thankfully they just left.

PUT ON THE RED LIGHT

Golden had a really great run; it had single-handedly kept Sankeys afloat in those early days. But by 2001, the numbers were starting to dwindle, and it felt like the night was running out of steam. The sands were shifting beneath its feet, and the music world was moving on a bit.

We knew we wanted to make a change and move slightly away from the trancey feel of Golden, so we looked for ideas for a new Saturday night, and at the start of 2002 we decided to go to the Miami Winter Music Conference for some inspiration, to see and meet new DJs and make some contacts in the industry.

The Winter Music Conference started in 1986, and by the 1990s the five-day blowout was a huge chemically enhanced *bonhomie* for the dance music industry, with thousands of DJs, producers, label execs, agents, and promoters, like us, converging on South Beach, from all over the world, hustling and partying hard. My perception of Miami was pretty limited to be honest, it was probably mostly based on *Miami Vice*, so the trip was a real eye-opener, swapping the mills and street lights of Ancoats for the pastel-coloured hotels and palm trees of Miami.

It goes without saying that it was a lot more glamorous than going out in Manchester. If you were going to Pacha in Miami you had to make a bit more of an effort than if you were just popping down to Cord bar or Sankeys. I'd never been to a club outside of Manchester before this trip, which people might find ridiculous. I'd never been to a club in Leeds, Liverpool, or Sheffield, let alone London, New York, or Ibiza. The only time I'd been to Ibiza was on holiday with my grandparents when I was a little kid. I've still not been since. To be honest, I never really saw the attraction. It always seemed like too much of a busman's holiday for me. I spent my whole life in clubs, I didn't want to then go on holiday to visit even more clubs.

When I walked into Pacha in Miami, I'd never seen so many ridiculously incredibly good-looking people in my entire life. It was more like being at a fashion show than a club. We were hanging out with people from the industry, like Charlie Chesters, Dave Beer, and other agents that we knew, and were invited to some amazing parties. Dave Vincent and I had always dressed very different. Like with many things in our lives, we had a different sartorial outlook. I was more clean-cut, while Dave had this baggy look going on, which I just didn't get. I'm sure he thought I dressed oddly as well. When we were in Miami, he spent the whole time in baggy shorts, white socks, and sandals. One night when we were going out, I couldn't help but say something.

'C'mon Dave, you need to make a bit of an effort ...'

'Nah, fack off, it's a London thing.'

'It's not a London thing ... it's a shit thing.'

Miami was pretty wild. Dave had brought two of his mates with him, Theo and Beans. I don't think Theo and Beans went to one club all week. Dave would come to meetings with me, and to the clubs to check them out too. But Theo and Beans? They just stayed in that suite all week.

While we were in Miami, we met up with a big agent who represented a lot of iconic music acts. He has calmed down a lot now, but back in the day he had a huge reputation as a bit of a party animal. We met in his hotel room, where he did a massive line, then called up the hotel reception and kicked off with them because he hadn't been able to withdraw money from the cash machine in the lobby. After a while, the staff on reception explained that the main problem was that the machine downstairs he had been trying to withdraw money from was actually a payphone, not a cash machine.

There was a Silver Diner across from our hotel and we ate there for every single meal. Breakfast, lunch, and dinner. Talk about Brits abroad. It's a bit embarrassing looking back now, but we weren't exactly epicureans back then. One night when we were in there with the agent, the waitress came to take our order.

'I'll have a cheeseburger please,' I said.

She looked at the agent and he said, 'Ketamineburger!'

The waitress just looked confused and said, 'Sorry?'

'Ketamineburger!' he roared.

'I'm not sure what you mean by a Ketamineburger, sir.'

'Just bring me a cheeseburger and I'll show you!' he replied.

When the poor waitress came back with his burger, the agent said, 'I'll show you how to make a Ketamineburger ...' and in front of her, he lifted the top bun off the burger, produced a little bag of ketamine from his pocket, sprinkled it on top, and sat the bun on top before taking a big bite, with a smile.

We all looked on in shock.

While we were over there, we went to see Danny Tenaglia do an incredible twenty-four-hour set at Space, which even by Miami standards, had a reputation for its marathon raves, running parties into the following morning and evening. We had to get there at the start of the set, and there was one track on loop for the first two hours, gradually getting louder and louder and louder, and when it eventually kicked in, the whole place went fucking mental. I've never seen a reaction like it. Next thing I know, the agent was at the side of the stage, wearing this lovely black cashmere jumper, and suddenly lifted up his jumper and set fire to all of his chest hairs. What the fuck?

Security rushed in and were patting him down to make sure they were OK. It was his party trick back then, apparently, to set all his chest hair on fire, and it wasn't the first time he'd done it.

This agent is still one of the biggest ones working in the UK today but is completely different to how he was twenty years ago back in Miami. Over the years we've booked loads of his artists for Parklife and The Warehouse Project. He has always been really good to us, and is really on it when it comes to the next big thing. In the very early days of Sankeys, he called us up, all excited and said, 'I've got this brilliant new band from New York, they're gonna be huge. Nobody's heard of them yet, but I've got them coming over to do a couple of early gigs and they'd be great for Sankeys, they're called Scissor Sisters, I'll send you a tape.' He sent this tape up to us, but we weren't keen on the music, and hated the name, so we didn't book them. After saying no initially, he even said that we could book them for just £500, which wouldn't have even covered the cost of their train from London. We even turned him down then. Scissor Sisters, of course, then exploded and went absolutely huge. We'd turned them down for £500 and, only a year later, Renaissance paid £1,000,000 to book them!

After we came back from Miami, we had the idea for our new Saturday night: Red Light. We wanted to sex things up a bit, get away from the trancey feel of Golden and – it sounds ridiculous on paper I know – but we wanted to bring a bit of Miami to Manchester. We couldn't bring the weather, but we could bring the soundtrack. Dave started booking DJs like Danny Tenaglia, Felix Da Housecat, Erick Morillo, Jacques le Cont and that second wave of Chicago house DJs like DJ Sneak, plus the best British DJs at that time like Xpress-2, who were absolutely fucking amazing.[4]

We came up with an idea for these provocative-looking, sexy flyers for Red Light. We used pixelated images of couples in various carnal positions, the most explicit of which was a man taking a woman from behind. When it was pixelated on the flyer, you could just about make out what was going on, so it was more suggestive than anything. But what we didn't realise was when we blew it up to huge poster size, from a distance it didn't look quite so pixelated after all, it looked a lot more graphic, bordering on pornographic. The posters went up all around Manchester, and possibly caused a few car crashes, or near misses, from goggle-eyed blokes who couldn't

---

[4] We had no idea at the time, but in 2020 Erick Morillo was arrested for assault and sexual battery. He was found dead at his Miami home on 1 September 2020, three days before his court case was due to start. After his death, nine other women came forward with accounts of being assaulted by him.

avert their gaze. They also ended up with me getting banned from my favourite Thai restaurant.

Kevin and Vinny were flypostering for us at the time, primarily targeting Sale and Altrincham more because they knew Sam and I lived there. It's the oldest trick in the flypostering game: make sure you've got a heavy presence near the club owner's home and office, and they'll presume you're doing a good job. There were more of these soft porn posters around Altrincham than anywhere else.

There is a great Thai restaurant in Altrincham called Phanthong, next to the market, which I really loved. It was owned by an elderly Thai couple who I got to know quite well, and they were really friendly to me. But that all changed one night when I went down there just after those Red Light posters had gone up around Altrincham. Chorchaba, the wife, had seen the posters all over Altrincham, and was really offended by them and absolutely furious with me. 'Sacha! Your posters are disgusting, they are *filth*! They should not be allowed. I am *disgusted* with you! Get out, *get out* of my restaurant!' she fumed.

I tried to reason with her and explain, but she was having none of it. The restaurant is still there now, and I think that I'm still barred.

We booked Danny Tenaglia to do a twelve-hour marathon set, which we were all super excited about. It felt like we had completed the Red Light circle, as seeing his marathon set in Miami had been one of the original inspirations for our very own slice of Miami in Ancoats. Dave was absolutely obsessed with Tenaglia. Obsessed. Dave was always in the DJ booth at Sankeys, he'd be in there all the time at Tribal nights and bring girls in there with him, or some of the Tribalists. The thing is, the DJ booth downstairs at Sankeys wasn't that big, so though some of the DJs didn't mind if they were in a party mood, some of the others, who took everything more seriously, used to get really fucked off about it if Dave and his crew were in there with them. Tenaglia's manager knew all about his antics, having dealt with him in the past, so he demanded a stool outside the door to the DJ booth, and he sat there for the whole twelve hours. Didn't move once. Just to make sure that Dave couldn't get anywhere near Tenaglia.

EASTENDERS *COMES TO SANKEYS*

One of the weirdest episodes at Sankeys was when *Eastenders* came to film an episode on location in 2002. I'm pretty sure it must also go down as one of the weirdest episodes of *Eastenders* in its history.

It was a one-off episode set in Manchester, which was a departure for *Eastenders* for a start. We were contacted by a location manager from the BBC who wanted to hire Sankeys to use as a one of the locations for the episode. We agreed a hire fee of about £7,000 for the week they were filming, but we didn't know anything about the plot before they started filming and had to sign an NDA (Non-Disclosure Agreement) so we couldn't even tell anyone that the BBC were filming there.

When it did go out on-air, the episode focused on the characters of Ricky and Bianca, who had been out of *Eastenders* for a few years by then and were returning for a special feature-length episode only. Bianca was living in Manchester and working for a character called Vince (played by Craig Charles) who ran a nightclub (played by Sankeys), but he was also a drug dealer. When the programme aired, everyone was intrigued to see what the episode would be like and how

Manchester would be portrayed when it first broadcast. Truth be told, it did feel a bit like the city was typecast a bit. Within the first five minutes, Luke Una was texting Luke Bainbridge saying, 'Raining and gangsters FFS!'

There was a really rough pub next door to Sankeys, run by an Irish guy in his sixties, called Shaun. He had a pretty unorthodox approach to running a pub, life, and interior decor. There was always scaffolding *inside* his pub. God knows why. He was forever ripping up floorboards and taking ceilings down, and the place always looked like a working building site. It just didn't look safe, which meant that hardly anyone ever went in there. Shaun also lived right above the pub, and we could see into his bedroom from the Sankeys office. He quite clearly had a penchant for ladies of the night, and we saw a few things from our office that I'd rather not have seen, let's put it that way.

When the *Eastenders* crew arrived on site, they mostly filmed in the evenings, so it looked moody and desolate. Once Shaun saw all the BBC trucks, he must have seen a possible pay day. He started blasting pro-IRA songs out from his pub, really loud, which was obviously interfering with the filming, meaning the BBC had to stop filming so that they could go and ask him to turn it down. He flat-out refused at first, so they had to plead and negotiate with him, and in the end I think they had to give him £1,000 to get him to turn his music off so they could finish filming without any more IRA background music. They had no choice. He probably spent it on more scaffolding and ladies of the night.

We weren't around for filming, so even though Craig Charles's character Vince was using my desk throughout the filming, I never got to meet him, although we did have a couple of incidents with him a few years later. When he played Kendal

Calling in 2011, he was booked to headline the Thursday night, then on the day of the gig he said he couldn't do it because the *Coronation Street* filming schedule had changed, and he was now filming first thing on Friday morning. I was sat in 'Event Control', which is really the command centre of an event while it is running, and I was listening to this conversation about getting Craig Charles a car back to Manchester. He had previously been caught in a tabloid sting, smoking a crack pipe in the back of a taxi while watching porn, so without even thinking I came out with, 'Make sure there's a crack pipe in there for him too!' There was a deathly silence and then I turned round and saw his management were sat there too. *Shit*. I had to apologise and explain to them I was only joking.

THE LEGEND RETURNS ...

After Tribal Sessions had really taken off and started to smash it, Dave pushed for us to do a Tribal Gathering Weekender. This was his baby. He'd always wanted to throw a party like this ever since he had been to the original Tribal Gathering parties, and he was determined to pull it off. The original Tribal Gathering didn't mean as much to us in the North, but to Dave, it was like the Holy Grail. I think in his eyes, the weekender was like the passing of the baton from the hallowed old guard to Dave, and he was now the new guardian of the Holy Grail.

Bugged Out had thrown a weekender in Prestatyn a couple of years earlier, which was already a legendary addition to the clubbing history books, although perhaps not for all the right reasons. Run by Bugged Out and Chris York from SJM, they had a great line-up, including the Chemical Brothers and other amazing Balearic offerings, like the Doves playing an acoustic set in the on-site pub on the Sunday to people who had been awake for days. I was quite keen on avoiding such tales of extreme hedonism, and actually making a profit from the event. Dave, as usual, just wanted to throw the ultimate party.

We chose to do it at Pontins in Southport, which had been the home of Southport Weekender since the early 1990s. The promo flyer we produced was a bit OTT, to say the least. It declared:

The Legend Returns TRIBAL GATHERING The Weekender 2002

Mountains they traversed, over oceans deep and wide, the Tribal legend returns, to bridge the dance divide.

Tribal Gathering, pioneers of the multi-arena dance festival, has not been seen on the event circuit since 1997. Just as the tribal movement was hailed as one of the world's fastest growing phenomena, suddenly, almost overnight, it strangely disappeared from the scene. After the legendary 1997 Kraftwerk show, the organisation that had long been regarded as the 'People's Party' was gone. As it left, cloaked in a veil of mystery, a dark corporate cloud descended on the scene.

Now in 2002 while 'super-clubs' continue to produce massive multi-arena festivals with 100 DJs and a million flyers, there now comes time for a new beginning. After five years in the wilderness, the Tribal legend finally returns with an intimate event for 4,000 people, encompassing all the things that first attracted us to dance music. Tribal Gathering is back with the unique creative experience to push the boundaries once again ...

We managed to get the front cover of Manchester's *City Life* for the event, which Luke Bainbridge was Editor of at the time, and Dave insisted we do a Tribal-themed photo shoot. It was Dave, me, and Greg Vickers, dressed in full Tribal gear, around a tepee, and managed to drag poor Grandmaster Flash and Justin Robertson into the photo shoot too. The facial expressions in the photo tell the whole story. Dave's face is contorted like he's snarling 'Come onnnnnn!', Greg and I just look a little bit unsure about the whole thing. Justin and Grandmaster Flash look like they would rather be anywhere else.

City Life interviewed a lot of the main DJs including Sasha, Justin, Flash, Erol Alkan, and Ashley Beedle. Grandmaster Flash had just DJed in front of the Queen at the closing ceremony of the Commonwealth Games – 'When the Queen invited me, I was very happy about it. I didn't understand it, but I came ... It was the biggest event ever played by a DJ. A billion and a half people. It should be in *The Guinness Book of Records*.' Sasha was very complimentary about Sankeys, saying: 'It's without doubt the best sound system in any nightclub in the country. I'd go as far as saying that the sound in the booth is the best I've ever heard when it comes to playing and mixing records. To my mind they have the most amazing crowd at the club since they reopened. And I love David Vincent. He always bends over backwards to make me feel welcome when I come to Sankeys.' Erol Alkan's Trash was the coolest club night in London at the time, but he was a bit of a wildcard for us at the time, as he wasn't the usual Tribal booking, it was a bit of a departure from our usual music policy. He's a brilliant DJ, and twenty years later he's still a regular at The Warehouse Project, especially on Bugged Out nights. When he was asked what his chalet would look like at the end of the weekend, he said, 'I'm actually notoriously tidy and tend to leave hotels in better shape than when I find them.' Sadly, that would not be the case with the Tribalists and a lot of the punters, who would take a more Balearic approach to chalet life.

The security we used for the events was a squad of ex-Marines that were recommended to us by Southport Soul Weekender, who had used them several times before and said they had kept everything in check, and they'd never had any trouble. The Marines took everything very seriously, as you'd expect. When I first turned up on site, they were doing exercise routines and were always shouting at each other. They had this one guy in charge, and when he barked an instruction, they'd all shout back 'SIR, YES, SIR!' like the recruits in Stanley Kubrick's *Full Metal Jacket*.

The marines were fully prepared for any eventuality, including watching for people jumping over the fence to get in under the cover of darkness. Everyone was searched on the way in, but because Southport was quite close to Liverpool you would have Scouse gangs sending people over the fence after dark as drugs mules, to avoid the searches on the way in. The Marines were wise to that and had come armed with night-vision goggles and would lie down in the grass, scouring the perimeter for Scouse drug mules clambering over the wall. It all seemed a little over the top to me.

Dave had wanted to be a comedian when he was younger and still loved being the centre of attention. He had come up with this spoof character called Ketaman and embraced it as an alter ego. I didn't quite get it myself, but I guess it was an in-joke among the Tribalists, and I wasn't part of their gang. He had this whole outfit with a cape and an eye mask and everything. In Dave's eyes, Ketaman was the Tribal superhero. He had first introduced him at Tribal at Sankeys, and I'd tried to persuade him it wasn't a good idea. If I was leaving slightly early, I'd pull him aside and say, 'Dave, I'm off now, please don't get Ketaman out.' But within twenty minutes of me leaving and driving home, I'd get a call from James Cassidy to say, 'Ketaman's out ...'

The thing was, Dave now decided he wanted to develop his alter ego and add additional characters for a comedy show at the Weekender. Alarm bells started ringing with me from the off, but once Dave had his heart set on something, there was nothing you could do to stop him. He brought in his friend Jules and a couple of the Tribalists to play other characters, and they were rehearsing in the Sankeys office in the week or two before the event. From what I could tell, Dave conceived it as a way of lampooning what he saw as the 'cocaine set' that he felt had ruined clubland, because in his mind the Tribalists were the keepers of the flame, the warriors keeping the true spirit of acid house alive. Some bollocks like that anyway. He had all these props made, including a huge credit card, and a 10ft-long £10 note. The thing about in-jokes is that they don't translate. To make things worse, Dave decided to put the show on just before Sasha's headline set. It was a recipe for disaster. When the time came, I was stood just to the side of the stage with a few other Mancunian heads, including Luke Una, Richard Hector-Jones, and Marc Rowlands. The room was absolutely rammed with a crowd desperate for Sasha to come on. Instead, Mad Mike and his cohorts came on and started this apocalyptic acid house cabaret. It was an absolute car crash. Imagine if Vic 'n' Bob did an acid house spoof of *The League of Gentlemen* and you're still nowhere near. The crowd started booing and I thought, *Oh god*. Luke was there and says it was one of the most bizarre, astonishing things he's ever seen, and he wasn't the only one. Anyone who was there will tell you how weird and misjudged it was. No one could believe it, and at the same time, no one could look away. The booing just got louder and louder. The kids were peaking and were desperate for Sasha to come on, they didn't want this car crash cabaret of in-jokes. In the end, the booing got so loud, that they had to cut the show short, and troop off with their Tribal tails between their legs. I did feel sorry for Dave, because he'd put so much effort into it, and no one likes to be booed off, but it was a doomed idea from the start.

The Tribalists had always been keen on their after-parties, and the promotional material that we put out for Tribal Gathering even encouraged it:

> The party will last for two nights and three days, over five rooms and four serious sessions. Not only that, but when the main room shuts down at 7 a.m. each morning, a thousand after parties explode into action in the chalets surrounding the main complex. This Tribal Village will become the home of the Tribalist community.

I'd not looked back at the flyer for the Tribal Gathering Weekender for the best part of twenty years till we started working on this book, but when I dug it out of storage and read that back I honestly couldn't believe what I was reading. Nowadays, on any event we run, there's detailed planning for the mass exit with security, police, and the relevant authorities on how we're going to manage the customer flow after the event, and make sure it's as peaceful as possible, and everyone gets home safely, with minimal disruption to the wider local community. But at Tribal Gathering Weekender, the promo was actively encouraging everyone to carry on partying after 7 a.m., and to 'explode' into the next day. Un-fucking-believable. No wonder it got out of control ...

As dawn broke, the head of the Marines came and woke me in my chalet, to tell me, in a sorry voice, that they had lost control of the site. I went outside into the dawn light and was faced with an acid house Armageddon. The hardcore Marines had well and truly lost their grip on the situation. You could hear parties from every block, people were lying around on the grass in various states of undress, others were throwing themselves out of top-floor windows, and in the middle of all this, my business partner Dave, was speeding round on a moped, dressed as Ketaman, firing rockets and fireworks at everyone. It was chaos.

The 'chalets' were two-storey accommodation blocks and, as expected, a lot of the kids went mental once they got back to their chalets and continued the partying. Music was blasting from every chalet. A few people trashed them, others threw mattresses out of windows. People started jumping, off their heads, out of the upstairs windows, onto the mattresses below. Of course, the Tribalists were right in the middle of all this, and even Greg Vickers, our resident DJ, got involved. He was one of the ones throwing himself out of the top-floor window, and actually ended up hurting himself quite badly. Who would have guessed that throwing yourself out of an upstairs window while off your head could be dangerous?

While all this was going on Dave, who on paper was supposedly one of the responsible people in charge, was charging about causing even more mayhem, still dressed in his Ketaman outfit, complete with flowing cape. He had somehow found a mini moped, and armed himself with a load of fireworks that he got passed security, and was speeding round the site on this moped, with his Ketaman mask on, and his cape flapping behind him, firing rockets and fireworks at the Marines, his own security team.

THE FIRST WAREHOUSE PARTY

In 2003, we decided to hold the first warehouse party in the UK since the much-criticised Criminal Justice Bill had been passed by John Major's government in 1994. We didn't know it at the time, but this was the event that sowed the seed of an idea that would eventually become The Warehouse Project. The original idea came from an insane one-off club night we went to at The Haçienda in March 2001. Not the real Haçienda, because that had been shut for four years by then, but a deconstructed-reconstructed Haçienda inside a warehouse in Ancoats, just around the corner from Sankeys.

In 2000, film director Michael Winterbottom was in Canada shooting *The Claim*, his adaptation of Thomas Hardy's *The Mayor of Casterbridge*, and got snowed in while doing a recce in a remote logging town. After getting frostbite, he decided he wanted to make his next film closer to home and decided, 'Let's do something about Manchester, Tony Wilson, The Haçienda and Factory Records'. He signed up Steve Coogan to play Tony Wilson and then brought in the brilliant Frank Cottrell-Boyce to write the script for what became *24 Hour Party People*.

Naturally, Winterbottom wanted to shoot some scenes for the film in The Haçienda. But in classic Factory timing, the original Haçienda had been knocked down just months before, reduced to rubble to be turned into flats, like every other building in Manchester back then. The developers of The Haçienda site even had the nerve to put a huge banner on the side of the new flats, which declared, 'Now the party's over, you can come home', which was sacrilege to some of the old congregation for whom it had been their church. One day, a famous Manchester DJ drunkenly pulled the banner down in a rage, took it back to his home and hung it from his sixth-floor flat.

By the time Winterbottom wanted to film some scenes for the film in the club, he'd never see The Haçienda. It didn't exist. So, it had to be rebuilt. Having made the decision to do that, the film crew were on the hunt for a suitable location somewhere in Manchester, and eventually came across a warehouse in Ancoats on Pollard Street, which was owned by Carol Ainscow, the property developer, who I knew and had already worked with because she owned Paradise Factory. Winterbottom decided the best way to film The Haçienda scenes would be to throw an actual club night in the rebuilt venue. Partly because they wanted to try and get it to look authentic and partly because the film crew fancied spending some of the budget on a huge fuck-off party. Luke was in and around the filming quite a lot, and even played a music journalist in the film, and he witnessed first-hand the cast and crew were partying impressively hard. More than once a member of the cast turned up to film a scene having not been to bed the night before. Let's just say there was a lot of method acting going on during the making of *24 Hour Party People*. Luke still has the original invite to the party on

Friday, 2 March 2001, which is Fac 451. The invite declares: '*What do you have to say to that? Yes, we will have to "build The Haçienda" for ourselves.*'

There were lots of rumours going around town before the party, about who would be DJing and what the venue would be like. Obviously it was the hottest ticket in town and there was much consternation about who had managed to get their hands on tickets and who hadn't. Those who had been the real regulars back in The Haçienda's heyday justly felt that they had more right than anyone to be there, but it had been a dozen or so years since the club's heydays, so they all looked a dozen years older (some of them looked a lot more than a dozen years older, thanks to their recreational habits) so that wouldn't have looked right on screen. Because the production team could only fit in so many people on set, they were never going to be able to please everyone. Somehow, they managed to keep the exact details of the night secret, so none of us knew quite what to expect when we turned up.

In fact, it was an incredible night. The production team had spoken to Ben Kelly, the original designer of The Haçienda, and got hold of the original plans for the club, recreating it exactly as it was during its prime in the 1980s. It was so weird. It was incredible. It was only the main room, so there were no stairs down to The Fifth Man and the Gay Traitor, and the door that led to the original toilets was in the right position, but it just led out to some portable toilets. Everyone spent the first half hour walking round pointing at stuff, saying, 'Wow, it looks just the same!' After the novelty wore off, people just got down to partying hard.

What was quite strange was that everybody fell into old habits, so you would see people you recognised dancing in the same places as they used to in the original Haçienda. As if that wasn't weird enough, you also had all the actors playing Tony Wilson, Joy Division, New Order and Happy Mondays walking around and partying. Half the real musicians, people like Bernard Sumner and Peter Hook from New Order, members of A Certain Ratio, Mani from The Stone Roses and the real-life Tony Wilson were also walking around. Not to mention Sean Harris, who played Ian Curtis, and looked just like him, which was a particularly spooky glitch in the Mancunian matrix, given the real Curtis had died two years before the original club was built, and never saw inside the actual Haçienda. Steve Coogan was in character as Tony Wilson and made a speech from the DJ booth for the film. I was stood outside when he arrived, and even though he was dressed as Wilson and not Alan Partridge, people started shouting 'A-Ha!' at him.[5]

Coogan's night was more bizarre than anyone's, and he partied hard too, as he later admitted in an interview with the *Guardian*: 'I got goosebumps when I walked into the re-created Haçienda. One of my first gigs was there in 1986, supporting my brother's band, the Mock Turtles. There was no legendary last night as depicted in the film. I got my climactic speech for that scene out of the way with a clear head, then took half an E. It was – what's the fashionable word – an immersive experience. We weren't particularly well behaved.'

That night was so wild, brilliant, and hallucinatory that for the rest of the weekend everyone who had been there was in a bit of a daze.

I was as blown away as everyone else, and over the weekend started to think about the amazing space, and how it seemed

---

[5] Coogan's memories of growing up watching Wilson on television had been partially his inspiration for Alan Partridge.

such a waste to use it for just one night. Wouldn't it be a great idea to hire the reconstructed club and throw some parties in there? Since I already had a relationship with the building's owner, it seemed like an absolute no-brainer. All the people who had been there for the film's one-night party and loved it, were just a tiny percentage of the tens of thousands of club-bers in Manchester and beyond who would love a unique chance to party in the deconstructed-reconstructed Haçienda. *Who wouldn't?* We began to get really excited about the possi-bilities and even started thinking about line-ups.

Unfortunately, by the time I managed to get hold of Carol the following week, to ask about hiring the set, she told me it had already been knocked down. I couldn't fucking believe it. They had flattened the whole set the day after filming. We'd never see the reconstructed Haçienda again. It didn't exist. It had been built, but then, for the second time in a year, The Haçienda had been knocked down.

Mutability is our tragedy, but it is also our hope, as Boethius the Roman philosopher (played by Christopher Eccleston) tells Coogan's Wilson in *24 Hour Party People*. After we had got over the initial shock of the film set being knocked down, we thought, *Well, why don't we do we throw a huge party there anyway?* It took a while to plan, but Carol was up for it in theory, and I verbally agreed a hire fee with her. Stupidly, I never confirmed it in writing, which would come back to haunt me. The council were less enthusiastic than Carol, and in the weeks leading up to the event I felt like they were trying to block us in every way possible.

When we started planning, we were almost looking back-wards for inspiration, in order to move forward. Not to The Haçienda, but to the original UK warehouse raves. We wanted to give a nod to the M25 orbital raves (that Orbital took their name from), and the Blackburn warehouse raves from the halcyon days of acid house. I was too young to have been to the Blackburn raves, and so was Sam, but Dave had been to some of the original orbital raves.

We decided from day one there would be no permanent structure in there. All the bars were on the back of trucks. We also had some nods to the original warehouse raves with the production, like sourcing a 'vintage' laser from the 1980s. We did what we could to recreate that vibe and that feel. The whole clubbing scene had got a bit shiny and glam, and we wanted to remind people of its roots.

When we first got on site there was a mammoth clean-up operation to be done. There were two old, battered Portakabins, which had possibly been used by the film crew and then left there. Pollard Street was just on the cusp of the red-light district, and the Portakabins had been adopted by the local sex workers who would take their clients there. Others used them to shoot up in. They were in a right state, so in the end we had to send the diggers in to crush them.

The week of the event, licensing came down and said we needed an extra fire exit in one of the huge walls, so we had to knock a huge hole in one of the walls. Unfortunately, there was an old persons' home a little way away, and the new hole meant that the sound would be travelling directly towards it. So, we had to source a truckload of hay bales from a farmer and build a wall of hay against the exterior wall to soak up the sound.

It was such a proud moment for me personally when we finally got the licence for the event, and I decided I wanted to thank the people at Manchester City Council who had helped it happen. I had given them a namecheck personally in the Tribal warehouse programme, so as soon as they arrived back from the printers, I drove round town and dropped a few off to the relevant people, saying, 'Thanks again, this is a great thing for Manchester, and we've given you a namecheck in the programme'. Unfortunately, I hadn't checked the programme fully, and it was only when I got home that night and was looking through it that I noticed Dave had inserted a full-page advert for a Ketaman DVD. Under the banner 'Special K presents ...' There was big picture of Dave, dressed as Ketaman, pretending to do a line through a traffic cone. I couldn't believe it. My blood ran cold. I'd personally dropped these programmes off to all the powers that be at Manchester City Council, with a full-page advert for Ketaman. I was really worried that they might think we were completely taking the piss out of them, and it could sabotage the event, and even be the end of my career. (Remarkably, no one at the council ever mentioned it, so maybe they didn't even see it.)

With three days to go, Carol rang me and asked me how it was going. I told her everything was fine and that we had sold out in advance. 'Great', Carol said, 'I need you to come and see me in my office.' I went over to see her at the old Daily Express Building on Great Ancoats Street, where her office was, with Daz Jameson, our Production Manager.

'So, you've sold out?' Carol said, 'How many tickets have you sold?' We had sold 12,000 tickets in advance, but I didn't like where this conversation was heading, so I decided to play it down a bit and said '8,000'.

Carol said, 'Right, I want another £10,000 in that case ...'
'What for?!'

'Let's call it 'inconvenience' ...'

I tried arguing and negotiating but Carol was ruthless, and I ended up having to agree to give her another £10,000. I had no choice; she held all the cards because we only had a verbal agreement, and we couldn't afford to lose the venue three days before the event. It was an expensive lesson. Even if you know someone and have worked with them for years, if you have agreed something, make sure you get that agreement in writing. Get it in black and white, otherwise you're leaving yourself open, and they can fuck you over.

There was no online banking then, so I couldn't just transfer her the money. I didn't have £10,000 in the bank to do that anyway. Everything was cash in those days, and that was what Carol wanted, so I had no choice but to somehow find ten grand in cash to give her that very same day. I drove off and went round Eastern Bloc, Piccadilly Records, and all the other places that were selling our tickets, collected the ticket money, and went back to Carol with a bag full of the cash.

The final issue before the event was the council again, when the licence officer came down to inspect the site on the day of opening. He looked around for a bit, asking a few questions before finally asking, 'Where are your sniffer dogs?'

We'd agreed that we would have sniffer dogs on the door, and he wanted to make sure we had them. I'd asked Ratty, our head of security, to organise them, so I rang him to see what was happening.

'Ratty, where are the sniffer dogs? Licensing are here and want to see them.'

'I'm just picking them up now, I'll be there in half an hour.'

He finally turned up nearly two hours later with the most unlikely-looking bunch of sniffer dogs you've ever seen. There were four of them and they all looked like they'd come last in the local village dog show (or were cast-offs from a *Beano* cartoon). One of them was a Pomeranian for god's sake. They didn't look like they could sniff out a juicy bone, let alone drugs. Bizarrely, and thankfully, somehow the licensing officer was happy when he saw them and signed off the licence. I later found out that

Ratty had completely forgotten to organise sniffer dogs, so he'd just got his bouncers to drive round Preston, where they lived, and just grab random dogs from people's gardens!

Dave had booked almost all of the artists, but we also brought in Rich McGinnis from Chibuku Shake Shake in Liverpool to book one of the rooms. That was the first time we'd ever worked with Rich, but he would later become a partner of The Warehouse Project and Parklife. I'm not sure what the artists were expecting before they turned up at the event. We had existing relationships with most of them by this stage, through Sankeys, but none of them had played an event like this before, as there hadn't been a proper warehouse party in the UK since the 1990s. The only artist who saw the venue before the event was DJ Sneak, who happened to have been playing Sankeys a couple of weeks before, and Sam drove him down to take a look. He stood in the middle of the empty warehouse, blown away. 'Shit man, this is so dope! Ya know what ... this shit is going to go down in history!' he told Sam.

We had coaches full of punters arriving from all over the country for the event, so it was busy from the minute the doors opened. The one young kid that sticks in my mind is this poor lad who was on a coach from Middlesbrough or somewhere, and within an hour or so of the doors opening, he'd gone to use a Portaloo, and his mates had pushed it over when he was in there. By the time he managed to get out he was covered in shit. One of our staff did try and clean him down a bit and then he had to just sit on the coach till 6 a.m. and wait for it to set back off again. Poor bastard.

I'd asked Tony Wilson to turn up and give a speech from the stage, as I thought it was a nice link back to the filming of *24 Hour Party People*, when Coogan gave a speech as Wilson. He turned up in this long raincoat and security didn't know who he was so, thinking he was a local homeless person, wouldn't let him in at first. They radioed through saying there was someone saying he was Tony Wilson on the front door, and I had to go down and get him in. He didn't stay long, Wilson was never one to hang around and party, but he seemed to enjoy it and appreciated what we had managed to pull off. We really appreciated him showing up, it was always like getting a blessing from Mr Manchester when he turned up at your events.

It was one of the most bizarre, wildest, and most brilliant events that we've ever put on. Anyone who was there that night felt the same: emotional, ecstatic, confused, and celebratory. Looking back, we really were out of our comfort zone in so many ways, and it's a miracle that we got away with it and eventually came out the other side.

Elisa was running the cash office, which was located in a room up some metal stairs – I presume it was the foreman's office back in those days, because from that room you could see the whole dancefloor, so the foreman would have been able to see the whole factory floor. We had a security guard at the bottom of the stairs, and one at the top, and we also had clear visibility of the stairs, so could see if anyone unauthorised was trying to come up. The cash was taken up there for Elisa to count, throughout the night. There were 12,000 people in there, spending cash all night. There were no card machines, so Elisa had to hand count £250,000 that evening. Quarter of a million. I remember her telling me that by halfway through the evening, her fingers were tingling, and she felt like she was losing the feeling in them.

Nowadays, particularly since the pandemic, almost all payments are cashless, which makes such a huge difference to big events. Back then, holding a large amount of cash was a

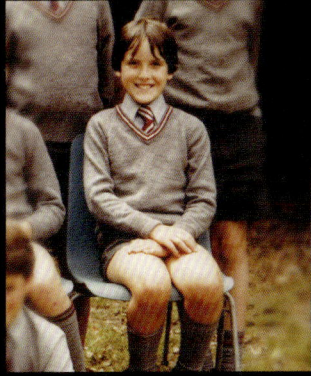

My very first photo shoot
for my school, 1981.
© Sacha Lord

Manchester Grammar School,
1983. Butter wouldn't melt.
© Sacha Lord

J.L.P. Concerts present

THE FALL

The Man From Delmonte
& The Sandmen
Thursday 13th July 1989
FREE TRADE HALL, PETER ST. MANCHESTER
DOORS OPEN 7.00pm
Tickets £5.50 advance

PLUS BOOKING

No 112

Ticket stub from
my very first gig.
I went to see
The Man From
Delmonte and
left before the
Fall came on.
© Belinda Mizrahi

student night flyers. None
of these will be found in The
Design Museum any time soon.
© Sacha Lord

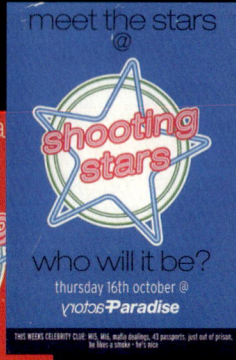

The return of Tribal Gathering in 2002.
Justin Robertson and Grandmaster Flash
don't exactly look thrilled to be there.
© Sacha Lord

Me and Mum in the Haçienda,
at one of my early student
gigs. Mum is holding a bottle
of Dunberry Spring Water
© Sacha Lord

Krysko, me and Dave Vincent (l-r) in the DJ booth at Sankeys. © Sacha Lord

Set times for a night during the inaugural Warehouse Project season in 2006. © Sebastian Matthes

WHP streaker during 2 Many DJs set. © Sebastian Matthes

The dancefloor at WHP, doing its day job. Store Street was a car park during the week, and we had two hours every Friday to turn it into the country's best nightclub. © Sebastian Matthes

When the lights went up, and everyone had gone home, we had to turn it back into a car park again. © Sebastian Matthes

Mark Ronson taking a well-earned break after his set at WHP in 2007. © Sebastian Matthes

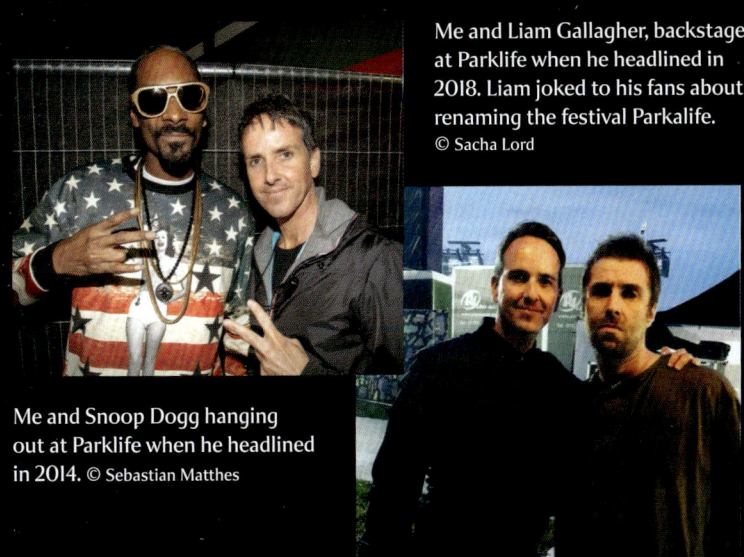

Me and Liam Gallagher, backstage at Parklife when he headlined in 2018. Liam joked to his fans about renaming the festival Parkalife.
© Sacha Lord

Me and Snoop Dogg hanging out at Parklife when he headlined in 2014. © Sebastian Matthes

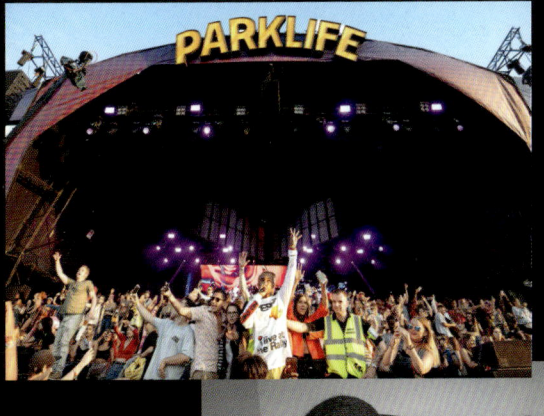

Pharell Williams at Parklife in 2018. There was a slight moment of panic in Event Control when this happened, as he hadn't warned us he was going to invite the audience up on stage.
© Rob Jones

Me (far left) and The Prodigy, taken a WHP, before the sad passing of the immensely lovely Keith Flint (next to me in the pic) in 2019.
© Sebastian Matthes

Goldie, in the
mix at WHP.
© Sebastian Matthes

Preparing for
the Haçienda
day as part of
United We
Stream, which
I launched during
lockdown in 2020.
© Sacha Lord

A drone shot of the return of Parklife after Covid, in 2021. It's possibly
my favourite photo of Parklife. © Parklife Festival

Me and Boy George, backstage at a Morrissey gig, Hammersmith, 2023.© Sacha Lord

The WHP family, on the last ever night at Store Street, including me Krysko (back, far right), then next to me, Kim O'Brien, my business partner Sam Kandel, and Rich McGinnis, with WHP photographer Sebastian Matthes crouching, far right, next to my ex-wife Elisa.
© Sebastian Matthes

This is just two random punters at WHP, but I've always loved this picture. Something about it captures the mood of WHP for me. © Sebastian Matthes

The main room at WHP, Mayfield Depot, 2023. © Rob Jones

Parklife is now the biggest metropolitan festival in the UK. © Parklife Festival

huge security risk, particularly with the gangs still knocking around. It would obviously be all used notes, and therefore totally untraceable, which made it even more attractive to anyone who might want to rob you. The more money you have on site in cash, and the longer you are holding it, the more chance you have of getting robbed. I decided one way of getting cash off site safely was to use some of it to pay all the DJs and suppliers on the night. It was all legit, everything still went through the books, we just asked all the DJs and suppliers to arrive with their invoices and then paid them there and being it was a simple security measure to reduce the risk of us drama at times ... gunpoint, though it wasn't completely without

We were using a PR guy from London for the event, a lovely guy, and he came up to me at one point in the evening and said, 'Here's my invoice, can I get paid?' and I said, 'Sure, no problem', and took him up to the cash office. We had two bouncers on the door, one outside, and one inside. I took the PR guy in, who gave Elisa his invoice, but she was counting out his payment when we suddenly all heard this huge sniff from behind us. We all looked round at the same time and the security guard who should have been guarding the inside of the door was doing a massive line of coke off the table. The PR guy looked at me and said, 'This *really* is fucking acid house, isn't it?'

I just said to the security guard, 'What the *fuck* are you doing?' and he just looked at me with this big shit-eating grin on his face.

When the party finished at six the following morning, I realised I'd made another error. The club night had started at 2 p.m. and run till 6 a.m. and at Sankeys we always booked the security to finish twenty minutes after doors closed, so I'd done the same with the Warehouse party, but the egress took slightly longer than expected, so by the time I was ready to leave, about 6.45 a.m., I was stood outside and all the security had long gone. Nowadays, Pollard Street is a really nice part of Ancoats, with great restaurants, bars, and coffee shops, and a brilliant artisan bakery called Pollen. Back then, there was nothing and taxis refused to pick up passengers from around there, because the drivers had been robbed at knife point so many times. So, I'm stood on a street corner in Ancoats with £100,000 in cash in a rucksack at 6.45 a.m., and all the security staff have fucked was off home, which is not a good situation to be in. There who used only myself, Elisa, and a guy called Charles Robert, who used to drive the DJs for us, so I told Charles I had all the cash on me, and he said he would drop me off on his way home.

Because it was a Sunday morning and a bank holiday, the banks didn't open till Tuesday morning. Forty-eight hours away. This meant I had to keep £100,000 in cash on me for two days. Elisa and I lived in Warburton, just on the edge of Partington at the time, and I knew if the wrong people knew were we lived we would be in trouble, as they could put two and two together and figure out we had the takings. Elisa and I spent the next two days with the curtains closed and the lights off; we didn't once let the rucksacks of cash leave our sight. We just sat on the couch with the curtains drawn wearing the rucksacks. I didn't even take if off when I went to the toilet. Elisa cooked dinner wearing hers. We were both bloody terrified of something happening.

On the Sunday evening, I got a call from Darren Jameson.

'Where are you?'

'I'm at home.'

'OK, meet me at Lymm services as soon as you can.'

'Why, what's wrong?'

While Darren and his crew were de-rigging and cleaning up the warehouse, they had found a box containing £5,000 in cash. I'd tried to contain the cash system as much as possible, and we had a system where people had to use tokens at the bar, so none of the bars took cash, but that meant there were boxes of tokens and cash flying back and forth between the upstairs office, and somehow one of the boxes had got mislaid and not made its way there. Fair play to Darren, we might not even have noticed that was missing if he hadn't told us.[6]

First thing Tuesday morning, I was waiting by the door to the bank for when it opened. I've never been so relieved to see a bank door open, never been so relieved to see any door open.

I often think back to that event with fucking fear because we were so so so out of our depths. We did not have a clue what we were doing. Why the gangsters didn't come and ruin it for others, I've just no idea. While no one was taken ill, it was a huge success.

Creamfields were very upset with us and wanted to make sure we didn't do it again on an August bank holiday, as Jim King told us he thought we took 5,000 tickets off them. Because of the financial success, too, it made us think differently about the benefits of doing big statement events like that versus the endless slog of managing weekly club nights.

People who were at that first warehouse party still mention it to me. With the benefit of hindsight, I think we all began to believe our own hype a little bit after that. It was a huge thing to pull that off when everyone said it wouldn't happen, we wouldn't sell enough tickets, issues with the council, and Carol taking an extra £10,000. Perhaps we became slightly arrogant and thought we'd done something really fucking special and

---

[6] I gave him a few hundred quid as a thank you.

possessed the Midas touch. Dave most definitely did. He went on a different trajectory after the Tribal Warehouse party.

We are often asked why we didn't do it again, but we couldn't do it again on that site, because that warehouse was torn down, to (you guessed it) build new flats. We looked at other places, but never found somewhere that could match up to that original warehouse because it was so special.

The other knock-on effect was because we had been focusing so much of our efforts on the Warehouse party, Sankeys suffered. Not just because our focus was elsewhere, but also because when you take 12,000 people out of your potential market of customers, like we did that weekend, it doesn't just affect that one weekend, it affects a couple of weekends either side. In a way, our success had taken away from other successes. Like I said earlier, we only needed a couple of bad weekends for Sankeys to really start suffering financially, and we'd taken the wind out of its sails for the best part of a month. It also affected the second Tribal Weekender, because there was no way that could live up to the Warehouse party, and it all felt a bit flat after that.

After the huge success of the Warehouse party, we wanted to do another one, but unfortunately the same warehouse wasn't available. After a lot of searching, we found the old Bauer Millet showroom behind G-Mex, that they were moving out of. Most people in Manchester know the Bauer Millet site. It was a garage showroom that sold high-end cars, but you weirdly never saw anyone in it. I'm a bit of a petrolhead, and I've bought a few silly cars over the years, but even I had never been in there. We did the deal with Laurence Millet in the showroom, and he was a pretty old-school car dealer. He was about sixty, always suited and booted, and wore a lot of gold about himself. Glasses, watch, bracelet, everything he wore was gold, and he had very strong aftershave. I've never met anyone wearing that much aftershave. He was a bit like a Mancunian version of Swiss Toni from *The Fast Show*. I'm sure renting his showroom to us to put on a party was very much like making love to a beautiful woman.

We put on a New Year's Day party for 1 January 2005, and I think we were one of the first to do that, to put on a New Year's *Day* rather than New Year's Eve party. It was also one of the first Haçienda reunion events. The club closed in 1997, so it had been shut for seven years by that stage, and we were the first to bring the resident DJs Mike Pickering and Graeme Park back together on a bill. That was the first time I properly met Mike Pickering, who would go on to be a really good friend of The Warehouse Project when it launched, and Graeme Park, who is lovely, and we still work with to this day. Peter Hook wasn't very happy when he saw the artwork for our event (this was before he started putting on his own Haçienda reunion events) and I had to go and meet him and pay him £5,000 so we could continue with the event.

That was also the first time I met 'The Lieutenant', when Jon Drape brought him in to work on the production side of the event. The Lieutenant is obviously not his real name, but he prefers to move in the shadows rather than court publicity, so he didn't want his real name in this book. The Lieutenant has been around in Manchester since the late 1980s. He's earned his acid house badges. He's definitely not a gangster but he's well connected around Manchester. The Lieutenant has worked with us ever since and is an integral part of The Warehouse Project. I would go as far as saying that for the best part of twenty years he was my eyes and ears on the ground.

Meanwhile, Sankeys was continuing to struggle a little. Especially throughout the summer months, when the students had gone home. We didn't realise it then, but looking back at it now, the Warehouse party was the beginning of the end for Sankeys. We just didn't see it through the strobe lights.

LEAVING SANKEYS

By the spring of 2006, I was getting increasingly demoralised by what was happening at Sankeys. It was very clear that Dave and I had, shall we say, very different priorities.

It had become blatantly obvious, to me at least, and it was affecting the business. He was living in London during the week but coming up to Manchester every weekend and partying heavily for forty-eight hours. Behind my back, and when I wasn't there, it had become a bit of a free for all. Dave was like a kid in a sweet shop. Actually, worse, he was the naughty kid that co-owned the sweet shop. He saw Sankeys as his own private playground, and he invited lots of other naughty kids to party there all weekend, every weekend, often at our expense. It was no way to run a business, in my eyes. From my perspective, it seemed like Dave wasn't really interested in running a business and just wanted to throw the best parties. It didn't seem as if the cost or practicalities mattered to him at all and I was still seen as one thing: the fun police.

It had all gone too far.

As I mentioned, after the success of the Tribal warehouse, I think we were all slightly guilty of getting ahead of ourselves and believed our own hype, but with Dave it was next level. He went off and decided to do a Tribal Gathering charity event on his own in Luton, which was supposed to raise money for Syria. He actually described himself as the 'Bob Geldof of dance music' at one stage, and he thought the event was going to make a huge difference. Unfortunately for Dave, he hadn't really got a proper organisational structure in place, the whole thing collapsed around him, and they had to pull the entire event at the last minute.

After the debacle of the Tribal Gathering charity event that never happened, Dave seemed to double down on his partying, and it was becoming really detrimental to the business. He bought a penthouse in central Manchester, five minutes' walk from Sankeys, and had a lap-dancing pole installed for his after-parties.

There were so many incidents where he went too far. Too many straws that broke the camel's back. When the super club Home (in Leicester Square, London) went bust, we bought their Phazon sound system from them for £78,000. When they'd opened, Home had made a huge fanfare about their specialist, state-of-the-art sound system, custom-built by a guy called Steve Dash, from New York. Steve had built the original Phazon system for Twilo nightclub in NYC, where Sasha and Digweed were residents in the 1990s, so this sound system was a huge deal, and when Home went out of business Dave was determined we would get it for Sankeys.

Stupidly, we hadn't bothered to measure it to make sure that it would fit into Sankeys before we bought it. Fortunately, when it was delivered, it just about fitted into the club, and I mean *just* about. The ceiling in Sankeys was much lower than Home, and when we finally managed to install it there was only a tiny gap between the system itself and the ceiling.

Because it was such a specialist system, we had to pay Steve Dash to come over from New York and install it. Steve was a pretty unique individual. When he arrived in Manchester to install the system, from what I could tell, Steve spent a week sitting in the middle of the dancefloor, listening to white noise, and making very tiny adjustments to the levels. I couldn't work out if he was taking the piss out of us.

Once Steve had spent that week setting up the sound system, he left us and went back to New York. You'd have thought everyone would've been quite protective of the fabled Phazon sound system that we'd just installed, but no. Not long after Steve had gone, I left the club one night at 3 a.m., and as soon as I'd left the building, some people went absolutely mental and threw a huge party on the dancefloor, flinging jelly and talcum powder about the place. Some of the powder got into the speakers and damaged the system, and we had to get *another* specialist in to fix it.

That was typical of the problems that Dave's partying was causing at the time. He was a brilliant promoter, and his knowledge was first rate, but his hedonism was affecting everything. We would have a promoters' meeting every Monday afternoon, and Dave, who had usually been partying all weekend and hadn't been to bed for seventy-two hours, would quite often fall asleep during the meeting, with his head down on the table. He and I had worked together really well for a good few years, but it's hard to maintain respect for someone if they put partying above business and fall asleep during important planning meetings. Especially if that person is supposed to be one of the leaders of the business. It would be like all the players turning up at Manchester United on a Monday morning to find Alex Ferguson or Roy Keane asleep when they should have been leading training or having a debrief on the weekend's game.

During the last eighteen months or so of my time at Sankeys, all the fun had gone out of it for me, and it became a slog really. As a business it was beginning to limp on hand-to-mouth, week-to-week, and I think we all realised that the clock was ticking. All of us apart from Dave, that is, who probably still had the blinkers on a bit.

I decided I wanted to get out of Sankeys. I *had* to. I couldn't handle Dave's behaviour anymore and our relationship had deteriorated so much that I was now at my wit's end. I rang Mike Chilman our main investor and said, 'We need to do something about Dave, he's out of control.'

I felt bad about going behind Dave's back to Mike, but I didn't know what else to do. Shortly after, Dave randomly bumped in to Mike in London, and Mike said, 'What's going on Dave? I've had Sacha on the phone blah blah blah ...' Dave hit the fucking roof at me going to Mike behind his back, and everything just went turbo. The following week, Mike called a meeting with Dave and I at the Lowry hotel in town, to try and sort things and clear the air, but it quickly became apparent that it wasn't going to be sorted and the air wasn't clearing. It seemed the only way out was for Dave to buy me out, or me to buy him out. We both agreed to go away and spend the weekend thinking about our options. I honestly think Dave thought that despite it all we would kiss and make up again the following week, but I'd had enough and on the Monday morning I said, 'Right, I'm off ... make me an offer.'

Dave was pretty shocked, but we agreed a deal with each other directly. He could buy my share of the business. As part of the deal, Dave didn't want me to set up another nightclub in Manchester in direct competition with Sankeys. After that, we went down the legal route. Dave had taken other advice and now thought the deal wasn't a fair price after all. After I had declared I was leaving, Sam Kandel and Kirsty Smith both decided they would leave at the same time because they had both had enough as well. We began to talk about what we might do next, and one of our first ideas was acquiring a few rundown properties and doing them up. We came up with the name 'Ugly Duckling Group' to reflect the idea of taking old buildings that were real dumps and transforming them into something special. We quickly realised that we didn't have the money to do anything of any sort of scale, so we would need to find something to finance the project.

Our initial idea was just to throw a handful of nights, which would give us enough capital to start the business properly. I thought between four and six parties would do it, but very quickly the idea started to snowball. The three months from September to Christmas were always the best part of the year at Sankeys, and the rest of the year was usually a struggle, so we thought, *Why don't we just find a warehouse that we can put parties on for those three months a year?*

It was actually Sam who came up with the name and concept for the project. He was living with Krysko at the time, and the two of them stayed up really late one night, putting the world to rights, and talking about ideas for our new warehouse project, when Sam suggested running it for the final three months of the year, and said, 'Why don't we just call it The Warehouse Project.' When he told us the next day, we loved the name, and began to put plans into action and I put some money in to get us started.

We found an image on Google of a random warehouse that looked really cool and moody. We had no idea where it was,

I'm not sure it was even in Manchester, but Sam and Rich added it to The Warehouse Project proposal they were sending out and taking to artists and their agents.

On my final night at Sankeys, Dave wasn't even there, which was a bit of a blow considering the years we'd spent building this together, but indicated how damaged our relationship was and what little respect he actually had for me. Dave was actually on a plane to South America, heading off to *find himself* deep in the rainforest.

Having frowned on Dave's hard partying at Sankeys with his acolytes, that final weekend I just didn't care. It was my last night at Sankeys, and it got pretty wild. The bar was a bit of a free for all. It was a Red Light night on a Saturday, and everyone knew it was my last night so I DJed at the end of the night. Well, I didn't DJ, I just selected ten of my favourite tracks and Krysko actually played them for me. New Order's 'Blue Monday', Prince's 'Controversy', and The Smiths' 'Panic'. Not very Red Light at all, but the crowd loved it. I've got a picture of me at the end of the night, with long hair, wearing a headband. Not a great look.

One of the people working at the club at the time was a guy called Wayne, who was also leaving. Dave had caused Wayne no end of headaches, and he wasn't Dave's biggest fan. So, we had a little backstage party afterwards, and Wayne asked if he could borrow the office I shared with Dave for a couple of minutes. I said, 'Yeah, if you really want.' I had no idea what he was going to do.

Dave's office 'chair' was a hollow cube, and Wayne just took a shit on the floor, and put Dave's cube over it. I never heard from Dave about that, he probably thought it was me who did it.

Dave and I were still having a legal ding-dong, going back and forth over our agreement after the relationship between us had broken down beyond repair. It was costing both of us an absolute fortune in legal fees. He hired lawyers, I hired lawyers, and the whole experience was just one big, horrible exercise, especially after we had built Sankeys together and were both proud of what we'd achieved.

Because neither of us were keen on dragging out the negotiations any further than they already had been – the only thing we *did* agree on! – we both agreed to walk away and head off to do our own things. Dave would continue with Sankeys, and I would embark on something new. Sometimes, you just have to know when enough is enough and call it quits as it's not always worth the hassle. In the end, we both agreed to walk away.

I'm not sure what we would have done otherwise. We would have probably opened The Warehouse Project but with me behind the scenes, rather than being the public face of it.

The Warehouse Project was the future. We knew it.

THIS CITY IS OURS: THE BIRTH OF THE WAREHOUSE PROJECT

Although I was hugely excited about our plans for The Warehouse Project, there was one slight issue that we needed to sort before it could all kick off: we didn't have a warehouse.

We had the *project* bit of The Warehouse Project, we knew what that was and that was all great, but we still didn't have an actual bricks and mortar *warehouse* to put the project in. While Sam and Rich were down in London, giving the big speech to all the agents and the wider industry, getting them all excited by showing them the picture of a random warehouse they had downloaded from the internet, it was my job to scour Manchester and find an actual warehouse that we could use. I looked all over the city, speaking to estate agents and developers, and even driving down random streets in deserted parts of town to find somewhere. There can't have been many empty warehouses in Manchester that I didn't take a look at.

Then one day, I read a story in the *Manchester Evening News* about Boddingtons Brewery closing down, and an idea began to take hold in my mind. The brewery was a Mancunian landmark, on the outskirts of the city centre, at the foot of Cheetham Hill, between Strangeways prison and the Arena. Boddingtons had been brewed on the site for over 250 years so the beer had long been one of the symbols of Manchester, and they played up to that image in the 1990s, calling themselves the 'Cream of Manchester' and running a famous TV advert with Manchester as Venice, starring Anne Chancellor (who shortly after being the face of Boddies went on to star in *Four Weddings and A Funeral*) who grabs a pint from a passing gondolier, sips it and declares, 'By 'eck, it's gorgeous!'

Shutting down the brewery and moving it out of Manchester and into Wales was a huge moment for the city, and more than symbolic for everyone who worked there. It was a proper old-school workforce and generations of families (mostly men, their fathers and grandfathers) had worked there, so it touched a nerve when you saw pictures of them leaving the brewery for the last time, carrying cardboard boxes with their personal effects away with them. The brewery was a huge site, right in the centre of Manchester, and it now lay there empty, and I thought we could turn it into a positive story for the city. It kind of played into the Ugly Duckling idea of giving something a new lease of life, and I thought maybe we can turn this sad moment into something different. It's the end of one thing, but the start of something new.

I didn't think about this connection at the time, but Luke pointed out that Factory Records decided on the name Factory because when they were planning their first club night in the summer of 1978, Manchester was in a post-industrial slump. There were 'Factory closing' signs all over the city at this point, and they wanted to buck that trend and have a 'Factory opening' one instead. I suppose there was a similar spirit in what we were thinking. We wanted to breathe life back into the nightlife of Manchester. OK, it was business, I won't shy away from admitting that. But we did also want to put something back.

I found out that the building was now owned by an old-school Iranian Jewish guy called Mr Hakim, and I went to see him and explained we wanted to put a few dance parties on in the building. I didn't really go into much detail, and I think in his mind they were going to be some sort of tea dances such as people threw in the 1950s. He was pretty traditional, and I decided the best policy was a 'need to know' basis, and not explain who Felix da Housecat and The Chemical Brothers were. We agreed to pay Mr Hakim £60,000 to rent the warehouse for the whole season.

We took over the old brewery site in June 2006 and had three months to clear out all the old machinery and turn it into a venue. It was a lot of work to do in that time span, and it didn't help when a group of travellers then moved onto the site, presumably because they could see the worth in stripping out some of the old scrap metal. Mr Hakim went down to bargain with them to get them to move off site, and I told him 'Whatever you do, don't pay them off ... if they won't leave, we need to get the authorities involved.'

But Mr Hakim wanted to tackle the situation head on and get it resolved, so he ended up paying them to move off site. Lo and behold, three days later, another bunch of travellers had moved on site, obviously being tipped off that there was money to be made, and they wanted paying off too. This time he went with my suggestion, and took the legal route, and we managed to get them moved on, but it meant we lost vital time to get the site ready.

Jon Drape was our Production Manager, as well as the person in charge of turning the Boddingtons site into a groundbreaking nightclub, the man who had to make sure we *could* organise a piss-up in a brewery, if you will pardon the pun. He did an incredible job in turning it round in a few short weeks, but we were all working blind a little bit. We didn't really know how the venue would work till it opened. We'd never done anything like this before, nobody had, really. Nobody had turned an industrial site like this into a nightclub. It was technically 'the two-warehouse project' for the first season, as we split the old brewery into two warehouses, one slightly larger than the other. The larger of the two was where the actual Boddies had been brewed for centuries, and was known as 'The Racking Hall', the other was the cold store where the kegs were stored, and we called that 'The Box'. Most of the events used both, but some more intimate events just used The Box.

That whole year was a baptism of fire for the entire team. I would never have admitted it at the time, but nearly twenty years later, I don't mind saying that there were points where it felt like the whole thing was hanging by a thread, and other times where it felt like a game of Whac-A-Mole. One problem would pop up, and by the time we had dealt with that, a different problem had jumped up somewhere else behind our backs. It was relentless.

Tony Wilson and Factory Records used to talk about 'praxis'. It's the idea that you do something because you want to do it, and only after you've done it do you realise why you did it, and what it meant. We had an idea of what The Warehouse Project was in our heads, and on paper, before we started that first season, but it was only by actually doing that first season that we found out what The Warehouse Project truly was, and what it could become; which bits worked, which bits didn't, who the crowd was, and what they would respond to. The kind of artists who would work in a space like that, and those that didn't translate as well.

When we first announced The Warehouse Project, we were pretty bolshy in our teaser campaign, which declared: *For twelve weeks, this city is ours ... Manchester is back.*

We didn't announce the location at first, as we wanted to maintain an air of mystique and keep people guessing. We also wanted to stress that it was only going to be here for twelve weeks, as we wanted to make sure people felt the urge to check it out before it disappeared.

When we finally put out the flyer with the line-up for our opening season, we revealed the location:

> *Things are starting to bubble, as the North prepares for twelve weeks of warehouse parties. With the venue now revealed as The Old Brewery, one of Manchester's most iconic landmarks, it's time to start spreading the word. Everybody from Manchester knows this legendary site, with its towering chimney peering out over the city. It was here that they made the legendary tonic for over 250 years ... Now, in 2006, and for three months only, we take a piece of the city's cherished history and catapult it into the twenty first century. We couldn't have asked for a more perfect backdrop for the first Warehouse Project.*
>
> *People have been asking why the project will only last for these three months. The truth is, it will be something that is here, and then gone very quickly. While it lasts it will be truly amazing, and nobody will even get the chance to get bored of it. The idea for the project was revealed several months ago, with the tag line 'For twelve weeks, this city is ours ... Manchester is back.'*

There were twenty-five events in that opening season, from the first night on 5 October till New Year's Eve. We booked Public Enemy to play the opening preview night, their first gig in Manchester for years, which was a big deal for us. The opening Saturday night was Mike Pickering presents 'Welcome to The Warehouse'. Seventeen years on since I had walked into The Haçienda and had my own moment on the road to Damascus, thanks to Mike Pickering (although I hadn't known at that moment who he was, or that he was the mythical figure in the DJ booth), now he was helping me to open the next step in Manchester's clubbing evolution. I don't remember dwelling on it too much that night though, I was too busy trying to get punters in from the chaos on Cheetham Hill Road. Pickering was joined on the bill with live DJ sets from Kasabian, Doves, Tom Findlay (of Groove Armada), The View, and Aim. I think that was Kasabian's first DJ set, Pickering had persuaded them to do it, as he had originally signed the band. It was a bit of a curveball for us but made for an interesting story. They didn't even want a fee, they just wanted paying in chips and gravy! Which, obviously, I was happy with. I would have even thrown in some mushy peas. Unfortunately, they had to pull out the night before, so they never did get their chips and gravy.

We had sold out the first few weeks before we even opened the doors, but we still didn't really know what to expect on that first night, especially as we hadn't established a proper queuing system yet. We did manage to correct that for the second week, but on the opening night it was a bit of a free for all, with 3,000 people in the streets, on Cheetham Hill Road. Right at the front of the queue was Pat Barrett, an ex-professional boxer who had a pretty big reputation around town, and owned a club in Collyhurst that was always kicking

off and was now running his own security firm. When I saw
him at the front of the queue, I began to wonder what we'd let
ourselves in for.

Because of the lack of a proper queueing system, it was a
real bun fight for the first couple of hours, and I was thinking,
*Jesus Christ, maybe everyone who was telling me not to do
this was right?* Two hours after the doors opened, when we
just about managed to get everyone in, my phone started
ringing. A withheld number. I ignored it at first, presuming it
was someone trying to blag a last-minute spot on the guest list.
But whoever it was kept ringing and ringing, and after about
the sixth or seventh time, I thought I'd better answer it in case
it was important.

It was the Governor from Strangeways Prison, which was
just next door to The Warehouse Project. I've no idea how he
got hold of my mobile number, but he was really annoyed.

'Is that Sacha? Right, can you tell me what time this bloody
party is going on till tonight?'

'It's a live gig tonight,' I told him, 'So we'll be finished by
1 a.m.'

'OK.'

'But we're open till 4 a.m. tomorrow as it's a club night ... '

'You're open again tomorrow???'

The Governor thought it was just a one-off event.
'Yes, till 4 a.m. tomorrow ... and we're open for the next
twelve weeks.'

'*Oh God!* You do realise the bass is coming out from your
roof and reverberating around the whole of Strangways?'

Strangeways was an old Victorian prison, and to be honest
none of the authorities had raised the prospect of sound
leaking out into the prison prior to us opening. But it was

clearly an issue. The Governor, to put it mildly, was not happy and remained so throughout the entire season.

The inmates, however, had a very different reaction! Within a week or two of The Warehouse Project being open, we started to get a few letters from Strangeways prisoners, on HM Prison-headed paper, saying stuff like, 'I could hear a bit of Annie Mac's set from my cell last night, and it sounded great, is there any chance you could send us a tape of her set?'

The Governor later went on record blaming us for a surge in drug taking within the prison, saying that drug abuse had rocketed during the period when The Warehouse Project was running.

Not long after I had that conversation with the Governor, a chafferer-driven Jaguar pulled up at the front door, and Mr Hakim got out of the back, puffing on a huge cigar. He looked around and took everything in, the type of clientele we had and how busy it was. He realised straight away that we'd pulled the wool over his eyes a little, but thankfully he didn't seem angry, he almost respected it. 'Sacha,' he said to me, slowly, in his very deep voice, 'you are a very *naughty* man.'

As a gesture, and a bit of a PR stunt, we invited all the workers who had been made redundant from Boddingtons to come down and check out what we had done with their old brewery one night and have a drink on us. Quite a few of them turned up, and we were shocked by just how much they could drink. *By 'eck!* To use Boddingtons old parlance. Quite a few of them had driven down, and we had to politely suggest that it might be better if they got a taxi home and came back for their cars in the morning, after they weren't six pints in.

Strangeways weren't the only people who had an issue with noise from The Warehouse Project that first year. Noise is a very difficult thing to control, it can leak out of the smallest, weirdest places, and it also travels in unpredictable directions. One of the biggest problems we had was with a block of high-rise flats in Salford, which was about a mile away. Somehow, the sound was leaking out of our roof, bouncing off the River Irwell and hitting this high rise a mile away. It sounded pretty unlikely when we first had complaints from there, but I went round there to check it out myself, and from the top of the high-rise you could hear the music almost as clearly as if you were on the dancefloor. We tried everything to mitigate it; we put in a second ceiling and insulated it with sound proofing, but the issue still remained.

After this, we then had the Environmental Health department after us because of the sound, and at one stage it really looked like they were going to close us down. I spoke to my lawyer, who told us that if they were going to serve us papers to shut us down, they could only serve them by hand to the Director. They had to physically hand *me* the papers, so I made sure I never gave them that opportunity. They used to park across the road from the venue every night and wait for me. Our Production Manager, Jon Drape, put a ladder over the back wall of the venue one night when we really thought they were going to try and serve me these papers, and I had my car waiting on the other side of the wall to make a quick getaway. We had this system set up where if they came into the venue to try and get to me, I'd run through the venue, up the ladder, over the wall, and drive off into the night. Somehow, we got away with it, and we managed to stay open for the whole twelve weeks.

On a couple of occasions, we had two nights running concurrently – one in The Racking Hall and one in The Box.

The most eventful of these was a Saturday night in October. In the more intimate Box, was The 3 Chairs Party, curated by Luke Una from Electric Chair, with Kenny Dixon Jr, Moody-mann, Theo Parrish, and Rick Wilhite, while Federation was in The Racking Hall – a pretty wild and no-holds-barred queer event. It's safe to say they attracted quite different crowds, with The 3 Chairs crowd being full of beardy crate-digging chin-stroking Northern Quarter types, and Federation, pulling the full-on, tops off gay crowd who were, they wouldn't be ashamed to admit, pretty promiscuous. There was only one set of toilets shared between The Racking Hall and The Box, and a few of the beardy 3 Chairs crowd saw some things in the shared toilets that night that opened their eyes a little and, to be honest, might have also made their eyes water a little!

We'd already finalised the line-up for New Year's Eve, when I got a call from Mike Pickering:

'Sach, can you do me a favour and put this new guy from Scotland I've got on your bill for New Year's Eve?'

'We're fully booked I'm afraid, Mike.'

'Can you just stick him on for an hour, early doors? As a favour to me? He's called Calvin Harris.'

Nobody had heard of Calvin Harris back then. Mike had just signed him to Sony, and his debut album *I Created Disco*, wasn't released till the following summer. As a favour to Mike, we juggled things around and put him on at 9 p.m. We didn't tell Calvin the doors didn't properly open till half an hour later, so he just thought it was quiet for the first half hour because it was early. We paid him £250 after his set, and then he presented his first-class train tickets to me to get reim-bursed. I had to tell him I'd never agreed to pay first class, and just gave him the standard train fare instead. The following year, Calvin had Top Ten hits and was writing songs with Kylie

Minogue. Then he had a smash No.1 with Dizzee Rascal with 'Dance wiv Me'. Calvin gets an eye-watering amount for a gig now, and travels everywhere by private jet. They don't stick him on before the doors open anymore!

Lots of the artists that we had booked that first year, went on to be regulars at The Warehouse Project for many seasons. Annie Mac played that first season, and she was brilliant. She's played every single Warehouse Project season since, bar one and always pulls a great crowd.

Within the first week of The Warehouse Project, we really knew that we were on to something; we knew we had stumbled on something with huge potential. But within a few weeks it also became abundantly clear that the old Boddingtons Brewery could not possibly work as a long-term home for us. Despite myriad problems with the site, the prison next door, and especially the merry dance with the Environmental Health department, we somehow crawled to the finish line, although it was very touch and go.

In just twelve weeks, it felt like The Warehouse Project had established itself as a significant player not just in Manchester, but nationwide. We had pulled it off and made people sit up and take notice, which felt great. However, as soon as that first season had finished, we were homeless again.

It was time to begin the search for a new home.

UNDER THE PAVING STONES, THE BEATS

I'd already looked at most of the empty warehouses in the city centre on my first recce, so I started thinking more creatively – thinking outside the warehouse box. One of the things I googled for ideas was 'air-raid shelters' and I came across mention of one under Piccadilly station, on Store Street. We went down to have a look and it turns out it was the biggest air-raid shelter in Manchester city centre during the Second World War. If you go through the entrance on London Road there is still an old sign on the wall that says: 'Warden's office'.

Inside was an amazing cavernous space created by the huge Victorian brick arches. The only problem was it was currently in use as a car park, which was a slight issue. Undeterred, I set out to find the owner of the building, and by an unbelievable stroke of luck discovered it was Mr Hakim. Although Hakim had called me a 'naughty boy' at the start of the first Warehouse season at the brewery, by the end he was really happy with us, and didn't want to lose us as tenants. We began to get quite excited about this new space. It wasn't a warehouse, it was a car park, and the 'Car Park Project' doesn't have the same ring about it, but I took Sam and Jon Drape to see it, and we all thought we could do something very special there.

I didn't realise at first, but this place was also a link back to the first ever Manchester warehouse scene. Around the corner on Fairfield Street, there was another doorway, leading to a smaller space, which held a few hundred people, and that was where those seminal warehouse parties were held in the mid-1980s. The first three parties were held in 1985 by a guy called Steve Adj; this was before acid house had properly hit Manchester. The Adj is a legendary figure. There's plenty of real characters around Manchester, and then there's people like The Adj, who are next level. He'd been there, done that, and got the T-shirt, twenty years before everyone else.

Back in 1985, The Adj had somehow managed to get hold of this warehouse space, and Ian Brown from The Stone Roses remembers The Adj ringing him up and saying, 'I've got this place behind Piccadilly train station and I'm thinking of throwing a party. I'm gonna call it The Flower Show and I want a band to play. Are you up for it?'

The Stone Roses were still pretty unknown then, but they'd already put out some of the songs that would make up their 1989 debut album, and there's a clip on YouTube of them playing 'I Wanna Be Adored' from that first warehouse party in 1985. The Adj went on to tour-manage the Roses and he was there throughout their most pivotal moments. It was The Adj who took them to throw paint over their old record company offices, and it was he who handed Ian Brown the inflatable globe as he went on stage at Spike Island.

Chris and Antony Donnelly, the brothers behind Gio Goi, then held an early acid house rave at this space in 1989 called Sweat It Out. There were only about 300 people there, but it was a much smaller scene then, so a lot of the important faces were present, including the Mondays and the Roses, and early Haçienda regulars. Chris and Antony built a rudimentary stage from scaffolding, and Mike Pickering and Jon Da Silva from The Haç DJed. Tony Wilson turned up with a video camera and shot some footage of it, which is on YouTube these days, including a clip of Shaun Ryder, who is trying to persuade Wilson to 'lend' him money to buy drugs. Wilson lapped it up because he loved anything anarchic. The police were totally unaware of what was happening, and didn't turn up till 9 a.m. the next morning, when Chris and Antony were sweeping up, to find a lone pile of water bottles. The police were like, 'What's going on here?' Chris said, 'We've just had a private party, officer, but as you can see there was no alcohol, and Tony Wilson from *Granada Reports* came down as well.' The police were like, 'OK, fine'. They didn't have a clue.

It was early 2007 when we first saw the location, and we decided to test the water to see if we could make it work as a venue before we made the jump and installed The Warehouse Project there. Initially, we put on three parties over the Easter weekend. We didn't want to connect those three events to The Warehouse Project, so we called them Beneath the Streets.

Somehow, we had to find a way to work around the fact that the place was still an operational car park Monday to Friday – a huge logistical challenge, to say the least. I arranged with Mr Hakim to get the keys to the space at 6 p.m. on Friday, when it closed as a car park, and hand the keys back at 5 a.m. on the Monday morning. That meant we only had four hours on Friday evening to turn a car park into a ground-breaking nightclub, between 6 p.m. when we got the keys, to 10 p.m. when the doors opened. Afterwards, we would then have to convert it back to a car park and leave no trace that a nightclub had been there by 5 a.m. on the Monday. We must have been mental to even consider it, but we didn't have many other alternative sites to consider. In fact, we didn't have any. But if anyone could turn a car park into a nightclub in four hours, it was Jon Drape and his team. It was a military operation. The production team would be waiting outside with everything on standby, and as soon as we got the keys, they would start loading production in. It was pretty hairy the first night, but the space worked really well. It went off. It was such a good night that within a couple of hours we knew we had found the new home of The Warehouse Project.

Though turning a car park into a nightclub in the space of a few hours was a nightmare, it also echoed those early warehouse raves, when the organisers would find an empty warehouse or space and convert it into a place to have a party the same night. Darren Partington from 808 State once told Luke: 'I didn't like it when acid house was badged the second Summer of Love and associated with Woodstock and hippies and all that. I hated that. For me it had fuck all to do with hippies. Me, Andy, and Eric spending Saturday afternoon sweeping out an industrial warehouse in the city centre and then installing a generator so we can have a huge party and have it right off that night – what the fuck has that got to do with middle-class hippies? Fuck the hippies – they had nothing on acid house.'

The Beneath the Streets weekend was sadly the last time I ever saw Tony Wilson. Wilson was good friends with Jon Drape, and he came down with his dog to check out the venue. He had already been diagnosed with cancer and I was shocked by how frail he was at this point; his suit was just hanging off him.

Despite his deteriorating health, Wilson was still in pretty good spirits and said how fantastic he thought the venue was.

It meant a lot to have him there, as it always felt like your event had been blessed by the spirit of Manchester's musical heritage when he came down.

On 10 August 2007, a few months later, he passed away. It's nearly twenty years ago now, but it's still hard to believe he's gone, his legacy is everywhere in Manchester. It was Tony, Rob, and Factory that made Manchester believe in itself again. No Tony Wilson, no Factory Records, no Haçienda, no Home, no Sankeys, no Warehouse Project, no Parklife.

The only mistake we made on those first three Beneath the Streets nights was the food. In those days, a condition of the licence was that you had to serve food. You don't have to now, that's changed, thankfully, but back then you had to have food available, even though no one was coming there to eat. So, we found a burger van – the type of van that lined the streets on the way to Old Trafford on match days – called Bob's Burgers. Pete Tong was the headliner that night, and we arranged for Bob to drive the van into the venue and set up in the first archway. It was a schoolboy error on our part. As the doors opened, Bob started cooking up his burgers and onions and stunk the whole place out. He also had this bright neon sign saying 'Bob's Burgers'. Sven Vath was the headliner that night, and I remember standing at the back of the venue and all you could see was the stage in front of you and then this big lit-up sign to the right stating Bob's Burgers. So, Bob had to go. We wanted to move him outside, but we didn't have the right pavement licence, so we just moved him to a quieter spot inside, and told him he wasn't allowed to fry anything, not burgers and certainly no onions, just boil the burgers and keep them warm so there wasn't any smell. The burgers were pretty grim, but like I said, no one comes to The Warehouse Project for a burger.

After the success of those first few Beneath the Streets nights, we knew we'd found our new home and we quickly pushed on with booking the winter season of 2007 for The Warehouse Project. Because of our good track record with the first twelve weeks of Warehouse nights, it was easier for Rich and Sam to book acts now. We announced the line-up and ticket sales flew; everything was looking great. The opening night featured Radio 1 live with Pete Tong from The Warehouse Project, which completely sold out of tickets weeks in advance. Everything seemed to be slotting into place. Or, at least, it did till a week before we were due to open.

One morning I got a phone call out of the blue from someone in the licensing department of the city council to say we had a problem. Our capacity was 1,800 and we had already sold that many tickets in advance. But after the latest site inspection, the council's fire officer declared that our capacity needed to be reduced to 1,200. A huge fucking problem. 'There has to be some confusion,' I said, 'we've already run the Beneath the Streets events at 1,800 capacity without any issues.' Sam and I arranged to meet the fire officer at the venue on the Monday morning to hopefully sort out the issue. When we got there, we walked around the venue and the fire officer explained that all our existing fire exits were on Store Street, so if there was actually a fire on Store Street we wouldn't be able to get 1,800 people out in time, so that's why he was insisting the capacity be reduced to 1,200 – unless we could create a fire exit on the other side of the venue, on the London Road side. 'It just isn't possible,' I explained. Because it was an old air-raid shelter, and the walls were 6ft thick, we couldn't just knock through to create a new fire exit. We didn't even own the venue anyway, it belonged to Mr Hakim.

'I didn't do the fire inspection for the events at Easter,' said the fire officer. 'I had no idea they were happening. If I had done, then there is no way I would have given you a licence for 1,800.'

'We've already sold 1,800 tickets for each night.'

'That's not my problem, I'm afraid. I'm issuing you with a Prohibition Notice for the venue.'

The notice he served to Sam and me basically meant that if we let just one more person in over 1,200-person limit, then we would go to prison, as it had been declared a danger to human life if we were to go over capacity.

We couldn't believe it and drove back to the office in shock. Sam, with his head in his hands, said, 'That's it. That's the end of The Warehouse Project.'

The only way out of the situation was to somehow knock through one of the 6ft walls to create an extra fire exit. And get it done in the next four days. The first thing I did was go with Kirsty to see Mr Hakim and explain the situation to him.

'Impossible,' said Mr Hakim. 'I don't even own that wall, Sacha. It belongs to Network Rail. And, have you not seen that there is a memorial on the other side of the it?'

'But if we don't put a new fire exit in, then we won't get the licence and we'll have to cancel the whole season.'

'What you ask is impossible, Sacha ...' Mr Hakim insisted.

Fuck. *That's it*, I thought. *The end.*

Driving back to the office, over the Mancunian Way, I was thinking we would have to call Radio 1 that afternoon and tell them the live broadcast was off; then we'd need to put a press release out and start the process of refunding all the tickets. I had no idea how much it was going to cost us.

Half an hour after I'd got back into the office though, I got a call from Mr Hakim.

'Sacha, come and see me by yourself. Come now.'

What now? I drove back to Mr Hakim's office alone. When I walked in, before I had a chance to say anything, Mr Hakim said: 'Whatever happens to that wall I don't know anything about it ...'

'What do you mean?'

'I mean, whatever happens to that wall, I don't know anything about it ...'

The penny began to drop for me. 'Do you mean ...?'

'I *mean* I'm not going to go down there this week and I don't know *anything* about whatever happens to that wall.'

That was all the encouragement I needed. I got back to the office as fast as I could. We needed to make a fire exit in a 6ft-thick wall and hope that Network Rail wouldn't notice. *How the fuck could we do this?* In the end we managed to find some builders in Salford who had a huge diamond-tipped drill. You may well wonder what a firm in Salford is doing with a diamond-tipped drill that can go through 6ft-thick walls. I decided not to ask too many questions. Take the Hakim approach. Whatever else they used that diamond-tipped drill for was on a need-to-know basis as far as I was concerned. Right then, we just needed a new fire exit.

Sam and I briefed the lads from the Salford firm. 'Right, this is the deal. We need to go through a 6ft-thick wall, that we don't own, on London Road, one of the busiest roads in Manchester, just below Piccadilly Station. We have to go through without anybody seeing what we're doing. Oh, and there's a memorial on the other side and we need to avoid damaging that.'

It was beginning to feel more and more like a bank job as we came up with the plan. We had three nights to get it done, so our idea was to wait for the car park to shut at 7 p.m. each night, then put up camo netting on the outside and start drilling from the inside, right through the night, till the car park reopened at 6 a.m. the next morning. Either Sam or I stayed up each night to keep an eye on the progress. Unbelievably, no one came to investigate what we were doing, or what the noise was, and towards the end of the third night, we broke through to London Road. We spent the next day tidying up the hole and turning it into a usable fire exit. The day after, the fire officer came back down; he could not believe we'd managed to do it. He was shaking his head in disbelief as he signed off the licence. We'd even managed to do it without disturbing the memorial. The new doorway had, still has, the two bronze pillars of the memorial either side. We nicknamed this new fire exit The Temple of Doom.

We still weren't in the clear, though. We were convinced it was just a matter of time before Network Rail noticed the new double doorway that had miraculously appeared on one of its walls.

Remarkably, sixteen years later, still nobody has ever noticed the new doorway. Every time I pass it, it reminds me how close we got to losing The Warehouse Project.

We never had to use the fire exit for the public in the end, because thankfully we never had a fire, but we did use it when there was ever any need for an ambulance, as it was the quickest way for the paramedics to reach anyone who fell ill in the club, so it definitely came in useful.

After a few weeks, Jon Drape and our production team had mastered the job of turning a car park into a nightclub in just a few short hours. They had it down to a fine art. Though there was always the odd issue to deal with. One night I got a call from Kim, our general manager, to say the car park had closed but there was still a car sat in the middle of what would soon be our dancefloor. Someone had forgotten the car park closed in the evening and not come back for their car in time. 'Don't worry,' I said, 'I'm sure they'll turn up soon.' Half an hour before doors opened I got another call to say the car was still there, and they were doing soundchecks and were ready to open. In the end, we had about five bouncers at each end of the car, and they just bounced it off the dancefloor. But just as they were doing that, this little bloke walked in carrying a plastic carrier bag, and shouted, 'My car!' and ran over. He didn't even ask what they were doing, I think he was in a bit of shock and just got in before driving away. To be fair to him, you don't expect to park your car and return three hours later to find that the car park has turned into a nightclub.

The other issue we didn't expect to face in that first season at Store Street was a battle with cocaine rats. A film came out recently called *Cocaine Bear*, a comedy based on the true story of a grizzly bear who discovers a drug dealer's stash that leads to comical consequences. Well, forget *Cocaine Bear*, we had Cocaine Rats, and a fucking army of them! And it wasn't a comedy; it was a nightmare. What would happen was that outside the club, in the smoking area, some customers would have dropped empty wraps or bags on the floor that had remnants of cocaine on them, and once the club was closed, the rats would come out and obviously be sniffing around and devouring anything that was on the floor, including all the discarded wraps. By the time The Lieutenant opened up the next morning for the cleaners, there was an army of rats on coke, ready to take on the world. It's the only time I've seen The Lieutenant scared in all the years I've known and worked with him. He's had to deal with organised-crime groups, gangsters, football hooligans, stag-dos, and all sorts. No problem.

But an army of coked-up rats? A step too far for The Lieutenant. In *Cocaine Bear*, there's one particular scene where a kid shouts, 'There's a bear, *and it's fucked!*' and that's exactly what The Lieutenant was like. 'There's an army of rats, and they're off their fucking tits! I'm not going anywhere near those nasty little fuckers!'

STORE STREET GOES FROM STRENGTH TO STRENGTH

After the first season of The Warehouse Project, Jon Drape and his production team had got the art of turning the car park into a nightclub within a few hours down to a fine art. Sam and Rich were doing an incredible job curating the line-ups, and it felt like The Warehouse Project was really making waves. It had quickly become the favourite venue in the country to play for many artists, because the atmosphere was so incredible, the space was so unique, and they knew they would be playing to a knowledgeable crowd.

Because it was an old air-raid shelter under Piccadilly Station, still operating as a car park during the week, and everything we had to install was temporary, there were always some logistical problems with the venue. In 2009 we had an issue with the smell from Portaloos being a bit overwhelming, and no matter what we did, we couldn't get rid of it completely. In the end we used to send Harry, who did our merch, over to Affleck's Palace every week to buy a huge pile of joss sticks. One particular Friday we had a big drum'n'bass night on, and we noticed that the whole venue stank of weed. It wasn't just the odd whiff, that you might get, if one or two punters have smuggled in a cheeky spliff, it was throughout the venue. We got security to go through the crowd and try and find the source of it, but they couldn't find anyone smoking weed anywhere. It was only after about an hour that Harry must have gone to light some more joss sticks to get rid of the smell and came back embarrassed to admit that he had accidentally bought 'cannabis flavour' joss sticks, and that's what the smell had been all along!

James Cassidy had been the first licensee at The Warehouse Project, but at the start of the second season, as we started at Store Street, he decided to leave, so Kim had to step up. She was still reasonably young then, but really did step up to the plate and became an integral part of The Warehouse Project ever since. She has been Operations Manager since 2008 and ran all the bar operations at Parklife and The Warehouse Project and that side of the business for sixteen years, until she decided she wanted a new challenge in 2024, and left for pastures new. Kim and her team must have trained thousands of bar staff over the years. There are so many people now running bars, restaurants, and venues in and around Manchester who got their first training under Kim O'Brien at The Warehouse Project.

One of the artists I remember being really blown away with in those early Store Street years was a female singer we had booked for just £500. She was called Florence, and I didn't know anything about her, I'd literally never heard of her, and she was only booked to go on quite early. I saw her warming up backstage, taking it incredibly seriously, going through all these strenuous vocal exercises. I remember thinking she had an amazing voice, but that she was going a bit over the top, *It's the Warehouse Project, it's not the Royal Albert Hall, love*. But then when she went on, she absolutely smashed it. Within a year of that, Florence and the Machine were pretty much the hottest act in the country and went on to headline Glastonbury.

In 2009, Annie Mac was doing a documentary on club culture and wanted to come and film some scenes at Store Street. She was filming outside the club, where there were about a thousand people queuing up waiting to get in. Annie had to do this scene where she walked down the queue and past the sniffer dogs, while talking to camera. Unfortunately, one of the sniffer dogs wasn't well at all, and as she walked past him, the dog did a projectile diarrhoea across the pavement. I've never seen anything like it. Fortunately, that was the only such incident we've ever had with sniffer dogs, they're usually pretty well behaved.

We generally got on well with other promoters, although Sam and I did get invited over for a 'discussion' with Cream once, when they were pretty unhappy with one of our bookings and thought we were stepping on their toes. Sam and I went over to their office in Liverpool, to meet James Barton and his brother Scott. We were there for an hour, and it was a bizarre meeting. Sam and I were fully expecting a robust discussion about bookings, but for the first fifty-six minutes it was just James telling us his views on the benefits of colonic irrigation, and then in the last few minutes he said that if we ever did a booking like that again he would open Cream in Manchester and it would be a full-on war with us. Everything was fine between us after that, and Scott and I still laugh about that meeting now.

We had some bitterly cold evenings at Store Street. There was a period in 2010 when it was quite regularly down to about -5 degrees some nights. The location of the entrance to the club under that railway bridge could also be a wind tunnel some nights, meaning the wind chill factor made it seem even colder. The Lieutenant swears it was actually -15 degrees down there one night. The other thing about being under the bridge, was there would often be water dripping down from somewhere, and when it was bitterly cold that water would freeze so quickly it would form stalactites, hanging above where the queue for The Warehouse Project would normally line up. Some of those stalactites looked like daggers of ice, so we would worry that the heat from the queue underneath would detach them, and they could fall onto the punters and possibly hurt someone. In the end, the unorthodox solution we came up with was to bring a football or two in, then The Lieutenant and the security guards would volley the balls as hard as they could up towards the stalactites, to try and break them off, and keep doing that until they were all gone.

One night when it was particularly cold, I sent The Lieutenant back to my house to pick up my patio heater. I don't know why I hadn't thought of that earlier. We stuck it outside the entrance and fired it up, and The Lieutenant, me, and a few of the police on duty that night were all huddled round it, warming up. After a while, there was a funny burning smell. 'Can you smell that?' we asked each other. 'What a weird smell? Smells like burning rubber or something …' The Lieutenant then went 'Shit, it's your fucking helmet!' One of the policemen had huddled too close to the patio heater, still wearing his helmet, and the top had melted and just folded in on itself. I'm not sure how he explained that to his superiors.

He wasn't the only police officer to lose his helmet at Store Street either. We ended up quite friendly with the police who regularly worked the door, and now and again I might take one of them to the side of the stage while the headliner was playing, so they could experience it. One night when David Guetta was playing, I was taking one of the officers to the side of the stage, and one of the punters at the front of the crowd grabbed his hat while he wasn't looking and just disappeared. By the time the officer turned round, the culprit and his hat were well gone.

David Guetta was one of the artists who would pull a slightly different crowd to The Warehouse Project; him and Swedish House Mafia in particular. They were a bit more mainstream than our usual bookings and would draw in more of an out-of-town crowd. We might have up to twenty coaches on some of those nights, from all over the country, especially northern cities like Liverpool, Leeds, and Newcastle. We had big digital screens in place at Store Street, and some of the artists would bring their own visuals, but lots of them were happy to use our in-house visuals. Guetta's team would use them to try and excite the crowd before he arrived. They would flash up messages before his set saying, 'David is ten minutes away' then 'David is five minutes away', then they had this countdown and with three minutes to go it would flash up 'David is in the building!'. It was pretty cheesy but it had the desired effect in getting the crowd worked up for his set.

Every night after the club closed, the staff would obviously do a sweep to make sure that everyone had left, but there was one Friday night when they missed someone. The cleaners came in on Saturday morning and started cleaning, when all of a sudden one of the Portaloo toilet doors opened and out fell this young girl, who they said didn't look older than about nineteen, wearing a tiny black dress. How she didn't freeze to death being in there all night, I don't know, but thankfully she was fine, and the cleaners helped get her a taxi home.

One morning, Kim came into the office looking like she'd seen a ghost. She had picked up the float for The Warehouse Project, which was about £10,000 in cash, then decided she needed to stop off in Didsbury and pop into a shop there. She parked her car and stupidly left her bag on the passenger seat that had the float in it. She was only in the shop ten minutes, but in that time, someone had smashed the window and grabbed the bag. I bet the thief couldn't believe their luck, when they found £10,000 in cash in there. That wasn't the only incident with Kim and a float either. We had to order the float a couple of days in advance and then Kim would pick it up from the HSBC on the corner of Oxford Street and Charles Street. She was in there one day picking it up, when she suddenly noticed her car rolling down the street, through the bank's full-height window. She'd forgotten to put the handbrake on. She ran outside to find her car had rolled down Charles Street and smashed into a police van full of officers. She started apologising and explaining she had just been to pick up the £10,000 from the bank and that's why she had parked right outside. They then questioned what she was doing with £10,000 in cash, so she explained it was for The Warehouse Project and that broke the ice, as one of the officers said, 'Ah, I DJed there once! Do you work with Sacha?' It turns out they were a bit of a DJ in their spare time, and they'd played an early slot at the first season of The Warehouse Project.

The police who work on The Warehouse Project always had a soft spot for Kim anyway. It was a running joke that we didn't think there's one police officer who has worked on The Warehouse Project who didn't ask Kim out at some stage, and that includes the married ones!

2010s

THERE IS A LIGHT
THAT NEVER GOES OUT

MAD FERRET: THE BIRTH OF PARKLIFE

In 2009, we were approached by the guys behind a student festival in Manchester called Mad Ferret, which took place at the end of the summer term in Platt Fields. There were originally five students behind the event – five ferrets – and despite not having much of a budget or experience they had managed to get to nearly 10,000 students, and book acts like Finlay Quaye, and The Streets. But they'd gone as far as they could with it. They had run up some debts and they didn't have the experience or knowledge or infrastructure to take the event any further. Like Kendal Calling, they had the bones of a good idea, the makings of what could be a decent festival, but things had escalated beyond their control and experience, and they desperately needed some investment to take it to the next level.

Mad Ferret was basically an end-of-year party, run for students by students. The concept wasn't bad, but the infrastructure and business side of the festival needed a lot of work. It felt like it was an event run by students, because that's what it was.

The first year of Mad Ferret hadn't really been on our radar. We were aware it was happening, but from what we had heard through the Mancunian grapevine it was logistically, meta-phorically, just about held together with Sellotape. Dave Vincent had just bought a double-decker bus at the time, which he used to encourage students to go to Sankeys and ferry them to and from the club. Let's just say it was a 'party bus'. The Mad Ferret production guys had only put basic fencing around their site, which was not very secure, and apparently Dave paid his driver to simply drive the Sankeys bus straight through the fencing, knocking it down, and then just parked, waiting to take students to Sankeys for an after party. An absolute piss-take.

By the second year of Mad Ferret, things had obviously gone seriously awry, because they rang me three days before the event, and they were desperate. They told me they needed £100,000 immediately or the event wouldn't go ahead. They were in a real mess and wanted me to lend them the money. I think it's fair to say I wasn't exactly 'mad for it'. 'Why would I lend you £100,000?' I said, as I didn't really know them at all. They tried to convince me by saying I could sit by the tills at the event and take back the first £100,000 they took. The whole thing seemed farcical, and they had obviously lost control of the business.

They also tried a few other people who ran event companies in Manchester, but since the Mad Ferret guys didn't really have any collateral, none of them were prepared to lend them the money, especially at such short notice. Eventually, they managed to convince Joel Wilkinson to bail them out. Joel started out with a small venue called Trof in Fallowfield, in the heart of Manchester's student land, then opened a second Trof in the Northern Quarter, along with The Deaf Institute (he later went on to open Albert Hall, Gorilla, and Diecast). Joel's house in Fallowfield literally overlooked Platt Fields, so maybe that influenced his decision to lend Mad Ferret the money, as he wanted the event to work.

So, the event went ahead, with Joel sat by the tills, pocketing the first £100,000, just as the Ferrets had suggested I did, and he got his money back, but loads of suppliers weren't paid. Out of the five original Ferrets, three of them disappeared, but two of them – Ben Paget and Jack Gutteridge – faced the music. Fair play to them, they could have walked away, too, but decided to face their portion of the bills.

By this time, I'd been running larger scale events for a decade and, impressed that Ben and Jack had wanted to pay the people they owed, I was pretty confident we could turn Mad Ferret into something much more professional with wider appeal. Sam and I met with Ben and Jack and worked out a deal to form a new company to turn the event into a proper festival. The new company comprised of me, Sam, Rich, Kirsty, Jon Drape, Steve Smith and David Norris from Ear to the Ground, Gareth Cooper, and the two Ferrets. We did have discussions with Joel about him being part of the new company as well but couldn't agree anything. Ben and Jack, the last Ferrets standing, are both really lovely guys, and are still shareholders in what became Parklife.[7]

We weren't keen on the Mad Ferret name at all, and we decided to rename it Parklife. Sam came up with the name, inspired by a festival in Australia, not the Blur song. The first actual Parklife was held in Platt Fields in the summer of 2010.

---

[7] I didn't find out this till quite a few years later, but it turns out Ben's full name is Benedict Dashiel Thomas Paget and he's the Earl of Uxbridge! His father is the Marquess of Anglesey, owns half of Anglesey, and at the coronation of King Charles in 2023, he carried the standard of Wales. A far cry from the 'broke student' vibe Ben gave out when we first met!

Ben and Jack, looked after the decor and all the fluffy stuff: the flags and all the creative dressing-up that turns a large expanse of grass like Platt Fields into a festival site. Jon Drape took over as Production Manager and made sure everything was running more professionally, while Sam and Rich took over the booking, and Kim took over the bars. One of the major costs of putting an event like Parklife on is the production, so it doesn't really make sense to build a site like that for just one day, so we decided to put a second day on, aimed at a slightly different crowd. If you look at most urban festival sites now, a lot of them do something similar. All Points East share their production in Victoria Park, East London with Field Day; The Mighty Hoopla share their production with Cross The Tracks and a few other events in Brockwell Park, South London. It just makes sense, you split the costs. We decided to book Ian Brown for the Friday night, for a more Mancunian crowd, and then Calvin Harris to headline the Saturday night for the more student-friendly Parklife crowd.

It was quite an eventful first year, to say the least. We had to deal with the local Rector, the biggest guest list in Manchester's history (including lots of wrong 'uns), and a gang stealing one of the bars (not the takings from the bar, but the actual bar itself), I ended up getting stalked by a weird policeman, and on top of all that, I had to sack my Mum.

One of the issues with Platt Fields was the Holy Trinity Platt Church, located within the park itself, which means there are restrictions on noise when there is a church service on. Jon Drape and I had to go and see the Rector, Steve James, to discuss the issue. Jon and I are quite lucky in that we work well together in those situations; the dual approach usually helps us get what we want. But the Rector was not for budging. We got our licence for the event, but on the condition that there was no audible music between 6 p.m. and 7 p.m., when there was a service on, which was obviously going to be an issue. It's just weird if the music suddenly goes dead for an hour in the middle of the festival, and who knew how the crowd would react.

We were lucky, that first year, though, and that was down to the good weather. When the weather is good, and you've got a beer in your hand, the sun on your face and your shades on, it's a lot more difficult to get annoyed about anything. Whereas if it's pissing down, you're cold and wet, your new trainers are getting trashed, there's nowhere to sit down because everywhere is wet, everywhere undercover is rammed, then you're going to be pissed off already. In the end, thanks to the weather, a lot of people didn't even realise that we had turned the sound off, they were too busy having a laugh and a beer and a buzz, and a fair few of those who were quite refreshed just kept on dancing, even though there was no music. It was like a huge silent disco. Nobody realised the sound had gone. As a festival organiser, the last thing you want is wet weather. Aside from all the production issues it creates, it also makes it hard to keep your crowd happy, and then you're in trouble. Young kids will put up with standing or dancing in the rain if they're watching some band or DJ they're really into, but if there's no band or DJ, then they're standing in the rain just to get wet on purpose. But though we were lucky that year, the following year would prove to be a different story.

The other institution that's located within Platt Fields is Manchester High School for Girls, an historic independent school that opened in 1874 and was the first girls' school in the north, and one of the first in the UK. We reached out to them to try and maintain a good relationship and offered to show some of their pupils around the site and explain how a festival runs. The school said that would be great, so the day before Parklife started, Jon and I took a group of fifteen-year-old girls around the site, happily explaining it all to them, till we got to the silent disco area, and I couldn't believe what I was seeing. Unbeknownst to me, the Mad Ferret decor team had decided to decorate the silent disco area with huge wooden phalluses. Jon and I were both speechless. We had no idea they'd done this. The girls just giggled, but the look on the teacher's face was priceless as they surveyed this field full of 6ft wooden cocks and balls.

The first summer of Parklife was also the centenary of Platt Fields Park, so we had arranged with Manchester City Council to commemorate the date by planting a tree and having a little ceremony on the first day, when Ian Brown was headlining. Ian had kindly agreed to be there for a photo opportunity with some of the Parklife team and members of the council. Unfortunately, Ian, as you might expect, has what you might call a flexible approach to timekeeping, so I wasn't that surprised when he didn't turn up on time for the photo call. We had the council and everyone else waiting so I kept ringing John Ward, AKA Little John/LJ as everyone calls him, to see where they were.[8] Every time I rang LJ he kept stalling, saying, 'We've been held up, we'll be another ten mins.' In the end they turned up an hour and a half late. 'What happened? Where you've been?' I said to LJ. Ian Brown overheard me and said, 'Oh, we stopped off for a Buzz Rocks on the way!' Buzz Rocks is a famous Caribbean takeaway not far from Platt Fields in Hulme, started

---

[8] Little John (LJ) used to work at The Haçienda, and he has tour-managed Ian Brown, been his right-hand man, for years, going round the world several times with The Stone Roses when they reformed.

by Basil 'Buzzrock' Anderson, who got his name because: 'They used to say that I would make my dumplings so tight. Tight like rocks!' So, Ian had kept the city council and the police waiting for an hour and a half, but at least he's got his jerk chicken, rice and peas, and fried dumpling!

We got the photo done in the end, with Ian Brown, me, Kirsty, Eamonn O'Rourke from the City Council, and a couple of Greater Manchester Police, one of whom was a copper called Michael Waters, who would later behave very oddly towards me. Eamonn O'Rourke and the council were happy, and they got their picture in the *Manchester Evening News*. Unfortunately, not long after the tree was planted, Dr Loos, who supplies the Portaloos for our festival, were a bit careless on site, and one of their Portaloos fell off the back of their truck and flattened the commemorative tree. I don't think anyone has noticed yet.

The other issue with Ian Brown is that he wanted a guest list of 1,000 people, the biggest guest list in Manchester's history. As if that wasn't enough, they didn't supply it in advance, as we always request, and it wasn't even one list – LJ handed me various scraps of paper on which 1,000 names were scribbled in pencil. They weren't in alphabetical order or anything and we had to try and make sense of it all. It was a nightmare. The first thing that was apparent was these names were a who's who of all the people you *don't* want at your gigs. Or at least people whose reputation precedes them. Luckily enough, Kim had Leroy Richardson running one of our bars, and Leroy knew all the characters, so he could look after them, and make sure they were happy and there was no trouble. Leroy was the original bar manager at The Haçienda, he started on day one there in 1982, and was there till it closed fifteen years later. Leroy is one of a select few people in Manchester, like The

Adge and The Lieutenant, who are invaluable, as they know most of Manchester, and of all the dynamics or politics between different groups that we need to be aware of. Because they have been around and seen everything, they also have respect from people, who know they're stand-up guys.

That 1,000 people on Ian Brown's guest list cost us quite a bit of money. I think people who are not involved in events think that sticking people on the guest list doesn't cost the organisers anything, but it absolutely does. Firstly, you've got the lost tickets sales – a ticket for Parklife is now £129.50 so if you've got 1,000 people on the guest list that's £129,500 of lost tickets sales, if those people would otherwise have paid for a ticket. But there's also the extra production you have to put in for the increased numbers. You still have to provide toilets, security and all the necessary infrastructure for those extra guests, even though they haven't paid, and Jon Drape reckons that costs us at least £50,000 at Parklife every year, on top of other costs.

As the crowd were leaving after Ian Brown's headline set, I was stood on the observation point, which is a raised platform that the GMP officers use to survey the crowd and spot any issues. We were watching the crowds leaving, when one of the police officers said to me, 'Is that the bar moving?'

He was pointing at a Red Bull caravan that had been turned into a bar.

'Nah, how can it be moving ... Hold on, you're right it is.'

I couldn't believe what I was seeing. As the crowd were moving slowly out, the bar was moving with them. I know Red Bull gives you wings, but bloody hell. It turns out that a gang from Salford had literally lifted it up and were walking out with it, complete with all the stock, fridges, and till. The police decided it was better to just let them walk off with it, than start an altercation while we had thousands of people trying to leave the site.

That first year of Parklife, we'd booked Grandmaster Flash, the legendary New York DJ, who must have forgiven us by now from the Tribal Gathering photo shoot with the tepee.

We put him up in the St John Hotel, which was the newest and best hotel in Manchester at the time, and shortly before his set I sent Jon Caine, our driver, to go and pick him up. When he was round the corner from the hotel, Jon rang Flash's room and said, 'Hi Flash, it's your driver here, I'll be at the hotel in two minutes, if you could come down when you're ready.'

'Have you got security for me?' asked Flash.

'Er, no ... '

'I'm not coming down till you get me some security, man. I just looked out the window and there's too many fans waiting outside, I'm gonna get mobbed!'

'What do you mean you're not coming out? You're due on in forty-five minutes.'

Jon had no idea what Flash was going on about, but when he turned the corner to the hotel, he saw that there were hundreds of young girls outside. Jon quickly realised that Take That, who were headlining the Etihad stadium were also staying in the same hotel as Flash. Poor Flash had no idea, he'd probably never even heard of Take That, and he presumed all the fans were for him. Jon rang up to Flash's room and assured him that he wasn't going to have a problem with being mobbed. When he came down to get into Jon's car, the Take That fans didn't give him a second glance.

Despite all the incidents we had to deal with, the first Parklife was a real success.

We've had police on the doors of our events since the first Warehouse Project in 2006, when we thought that if we were going to start a big rave in Cheetham Hill, it might be wise to have police on the door. I've always got on pretty well with them, and in all those years, we've only had one dodgy copper, and that was the first year of Parklife. He was a PC called Michael Waters; I got on reasonably well with him, and I can't remember why, but he had my mobile number, though that's not unusual since lots of people working on the event would have my number. The Tuesday after Parklife he said, 'I've got something for you' and said he'd come down to my office and drop it off. He walked in and dumped a huge back holdall with 'GMP' on the side on my desk.

'There you go, that's a gift for you …'

'What is it?'

'I've nicked it from the station for you …'

I opened the holdall and there was a full riot gear outfit, including a helmet. *What the fuck? Why would I want this?* He thought I would love it, but I just thought it was a really odd thing to do and felt really uncomfortable about having it. I did take it, but I didn't know what the fuck I was going to do with it. It's still in my office now. Not long after that, he texted me and said, 'Me and my mate have got United season tickets, and he's going through a heavy divorce and needs the money, do you want to take on his season ticket?' I was a big United fan, and I didn't have a season ticket at the time, so I thought, *Why not?* and took it on. The thing was, it was in the middle of The Warehouse Project season, so most weekends I wasn't getting to bed till 6 a.m. and sleeping most of the day, so I never went to a game for the first few months. After The

Warehouse Project season finished on New Year's Eve, United were at home to Liverpool in the FA Cup on 9 January, so I said to him, 'Can I use the tickets for the Liverpool game?' but he said, 'No, sorry I'm going to that one.' I thought, *You cheeky bastard, I've not been to a game all season*. So, I kind of fell out with him after that, and stopped answering his calls and texts, and that's when he went a bit weird. I started getting offside texts from him saying stuff like, 'You've just arrived at the Trafford Centre' and it was obvious that he was tracking my car via the police's ANPR (Automatic Number Plate Recognition) system, which is pretty dodgy behaviour, and surely illegal. I don't know where he is now, but I think he's still in the police force. Hopefully not abusing the ANPR system to follow other members of the public around.

On top of all the other issues we had at the first Parklife, I also had to sack my mum. She was working in the cash office for us, helping count the money as it came in from the box office and the bars and everywhere else. For some reason, she had a box of cash under her desk, waiting to be counted, and she kicked her shoes off, put her feet in it, and took a picture with her phone. How do I know this? Because she posted the bloody picture on social media, with the caption, 'Using Sacha's money to keep my feet warm!' I couldn't believe it! At any event back then, or now, you want to keep the cash side of the operation as quiet as possible, otherwise you're asking for trouble. So, I had to tell her, 'Mum, you can't do this', and in the end decided it would be better if she wasn't involved. Well, she decided and I agreed.

SINK HOLES AND THE MISSING £250,000 IN CASH

Having been blessed with good weather for the first year of Parklife, we were cursed with wet weather for the second. The bill included Chase & Status, Mark Ronson, 2ManyDJs, Skrillex, DJ Shadow, Annie Mac, and a whole host of other artists. There was definitely a bit more of a Warehouse Project influence coming in, and it wasn't so completely focused on the student market. We had sold a lot more tickets than the first year and knew early on that the weather wasn't going to be great, so unlike the first year, an hour without music was going to be a big problem.

Before any major event like a festival, there is what is called a SAG meeting, which stands for Safety Advisory Group, which is attended by representatives from all the relevant authorities. For Parklife, this meant the festival organisers, police, City Council, Environmental Health, NHS, licensing for taxis, Transport for Greater Manchester, and Head of Parks. We hold the first SAG meeting three months before the event, and then have one a month up to the week before the event, when we have them daily, to raise and tackle any looming concerns. During the event itself we then had them twice a day, so that every department could give an update and flag any potential issues that might arise. There will also be a representative from all those authorities in what we call Event Control. The 'silent hour' we got away with in the first year was obviously a potential issue, especially when we could see from the weather forecast that it was going to be wet. Discussing it in the SAG meeting in the week before the festival I asked the police: 'What happens if it kicks off in one arena during the hour that sound has been turned off, what would you do?'

'Well, we'd have to assess the situation, but we may make the decision to turn the music back on in the arena where the incident was.'

'But you can't just turn the music back on in that one arena,' I explained, 'because then all 20,000 punters will be trying to get into one arena, which only holds 3,000 people.'

'Yeah, that's a good point. Well, we'd just have to assess the situation at the time ... '

I knew we needed to do something, so Sam and I came up with a plan. It was our idea, so I won't blame Jon Drape or anyone else. We just thought, if we've got 20,000 people in the rain and we turn the music off, there will be a riot. It will boot right off. So, what we did was round up a few mates, and mates of mates, put them all on the guest list, and instructed them to stage fights almost as soon as the music went off at 6 p.m.. It was co-ordinated, so that just after 6 p.m., these little groups started two staged kick-offs in different parts of the festival site. Security then radioed through about the incidents to Event Control, where I was and where the police were, keeping an eye on everything. I said to the police, 'We need to do something, there's a danger of this escalating ...' knowing full well that there was little chance of it escalating, as they were just manufactured scuffles. In the end, the police made the decision to turn the music back on after only eleven minutes. So, most of the punters there probably didn't realise it had stopped. It was a little underhand, I'll admit, but it also did possibly stop some trouble. Some of the people who were in the SAG meeting and Event Control that year are still part of the SAG meetings for Parklife now, and they never knew I did that, so apologies to them. The first they'll know about it is if they're reading this book. If you are one of them, I can assure you that year was a one-off, and I've never pulled a stunt like that since!

The weather also caused us other huge problems that year. First, we had a temporary bridge that collapsed. Jon Drape and his production team decided to build one over the stream in the middle of the park, to ease the flow of festival-goers around the site. Unfortunately, the weather was so bad that within a couple of hours of the site opening, the bridge was beginning to sink, and in the end, we had to cordon it off and stop using it.

As if that wasn't bad enough, a sink hole then suddenly appeared in the middle of the main field. A bloody sink hole! It was about 8ft wide, and it was so deep that you couldn't see the bottom of it. We had no option but to fence it off, and then have a ring of security staff stand around the sink hole for the rest of the weekend to make sure there was no incidents. 'Students lost down sinkhole' was not a headline we wanted in the *Manchester Evening News*.

I think that was the worst year we have ever had with weather at Parklife, and it's fair to say Jon Drape and his team had their work cut out, constantly firefighting and dealing with various issues.

If you go to a festival as a punter and it's wet, you're exhausted by the time you get home and everything you're wearing is soaked. As an organiser of a wet festival, you come home feeling like you've been at war.

A few days after that second year of Parklife, just when I felt I had finally recovered, I got a phone call which almost sent me straight back under. I was walking through the Arndale centre with Kim, on the way to buy some running trainers, when my phone rang. I can picture exactly where we were in the Arndale because the call stopped me in my tracks. I could not believe what I was hearing. It was my bank manager at HSBC.

'Hello Mr Lord, I don't want to worry you, but I'm afraid we think G4S have lost £250,000 of your money.'

'What?!'

'Like I said, I don't want you to worry you unduly, but it seems they have misplaced a quarter of a million in cash somewhere.'

'You don't want to worry me unduly? What the fuck? They've lost £250,000 of our money! How can they lose a quarter of a million in cash?!'

I felt sick.

'This does happen occasionally, and it usually turns up.'

'What do you mean, it usually turns up? It's not even our cash. That's money that we need to pay all our suppliers. We've got to pay all the production crew, the PA and lighting, the staging …'

When I put the phone down, I was in shock. *How the fuck do you lose a quarter of a million in cash?* Funnily enough, this was around the time when G4S were in the news quite a lot because they had lost a few prisoners. But this wasn't 'funnily enough' to me. We couldn't take this hit, we couldn't just lose a quarter of a million pounds, this could be enough to sink our business. I spent the next three days on the phone every hour, to my bank and to G4S, chasing them to see if there was any news yet. I couldn't sleep.

After three of the longest days of my life, G4S finally rang and said they had found the money, 'it had been dropped in one of our warehouses in Salford'. That was seriously their explanation. Where do you start with that? What sort of operation are you running that you can be so blasé about losing a quarter of a million pounds in cash of a customer's money, when that person is paying you specifically to guard their money? You literally had one job. Also, I thought, just how much money is floating around in the G4S system and warehouses, that they can lose track of this much cash, and it doesn't even seem like a big deal? It goes without saying, that I was just relieved that they finally found it. If they hadn't then that was another moment that could have been the end of Parklife and The Warehouse Project. The first thing we did was pay all the suppliers and crew from Parklife.

After that, I finally managed to get a decent night's sleep for the first time in days.

I vowed never to use G4S again, and we never have.

THE ANNUS HORRIBILIS *PROJECT*

More than a decade on, I still find it hard to get my head around the extreme events that happened after we made the decision to move The Warehouse Project to Victoria Warehouse. By the end of the 2011 season, having done four years at Store Street, it felt like we had outgrown the venue. By now, The Warehouse Project was firmly established, both with the crowd and the industry, and we desperately needed more space. We had been thinking of moving for a while, but as ever with The Warehouse Project, the bigger we got the harder it was to find a suitable new venue. Especially as the redevelopment of Manchester continued apace. Thirty years ago, we could have had our pick of warehouses in the city centre, but with its reinvention we were competing with property developers.

One morning I got a call from a guy I know called John Rennie, who is a bit of a character around town, and has owned various businesses. He said he'd seen a space owned by a family called the Cohens that he thought would be great for The Warehouse Project, and did I want to go and have a look? Always interested in looking at potential new spaces, I went to check it out. I saw straight away that it had huge potential. It was a vast warehouse (The Warehouse Project would actually be back in a Warehouse!) on the Old Trafford side of Salford Quays. When it was built in 1932, during the heyday of industry in Trafford Park and Salford Quays, the vast building had been a storage facility for the Liverpool Warehousing Company. Later, in the 1980s, it suffered a huge fire and had been derelict till the Cohens took it over. I remember it as a disused warehouse when I used to go and watch United as a kid, because there was a huge Trafford Park-themed mural by Walter Kershaw on the side of it featuring Manchester United players and references to the area's industrial heritage. Walter Kershaw was a Rochdale-born artist who's known as the first British graffiti artist but is, in fact, a muralist. His colourful murals were dotted around Northern mill towns in the 1970s and 1980s, often on the gable ends of terraced houses. The one on the side of the Victoria Warehouse was his largest ever mural, it must have been 80ft high.

I met the Cohens, and at first I was reasonably impressed with them. They seemed like serious business people. And over the course of several meetings, we agreed a deal to move The Warehouse Project to Victoria Warehouse. It was a great idea in theory. We desperately needed to grow, and moving there allowed us to more than double in capacity, going from 2,000 capacity to 5,000 capacity. On paper it looked like a great move for us. But unfortunately, it turned into a nightmare.

I should make it clear that Victoria Warehouse is now run by a different operator, who have nothing to do with the ones we had to deal with. The new operators do a great job with Victoria Warehouse and it's now a really successful venue, but back when we first went there it was a different story. Chalk and cheese.

Looking back now, a decade or so later, I can safely say that those two years at Victoria Warehouse were the worst years of my professional and adult life. My business partner in the Warehouse Project Sam would say the same, as would Kim, Jon Drape and all of those close to the business.

We had the horrible experiences of the death of poor Souvik Pal, who somehow ended up dead in the nearby Bridgewater canal, after visiting The Warehouse Project earlier in the evening of New Year's Eve 2012, and also the death of Nick Bonnie, a thirty-year-old charity worker, who died after a night out at The Warehouse Project on Saturday, 28 September 2013. They were both tragic events, and it was the first time we'd ever had to deal with the deaths of people who had been to The Warehouse Project. It's something their families will obviously never get over, and it also left an indelible mark on everyone in our business. Nobody should go for a night out and not come home again.

There were also a succession of horrible things going on behind the scenes, most of which the public and Warehouse regulars had no idea about, and still don't to this day. Most of these things I'm going to talk about here for the first time. There was a co-ordinated campaign to close the club down, an armed robbery in which our staff had machetes pulled on them – we also lost £130,000 – and we were separately targeted by a Romanian organised crime group. And there was much, much more. Most of these stories have never been told before.

Before those awful events, though, the building needed a lot of work to make it ready for The Warehouse Project – and even at that stage, alarm bells were starting to ring about the Cohens. For a start, they had no experience of running a venue like The Warehouse Project, and they just didn't listen to us when we suggested where the toilets should go. In our minds the Cohens were just the landlords, whereas we were the ones who should be running the venue because we had the expertise. It became very clear early on that these boundaries were somewhat blurred in the eyes of the Cohens.

The opening night was an indication of what was to come. We ended up with the fire brigade on site all night – never a great look – because there was an issue with the recently installed fire alarm. There were also some major issues with the flow of people into the building. One of the main acts came off at midnight, and hundreds of people who were watching them then tried to get out to the smoking area. But it had just started pissing down outside, so those hundreds of people desperately tried to come the other way. The Lieutenant says that's one of the few times he's been really scared about a crowd at The Warehouse Project, as it was obvious the layout was wrong and couldn't cope. Fortunately, no one was injured and after that night we made some adjustments to make sure it didn't happen again, but there was also a rumour spreading that someone in the crowd had a knife, and though thankfully that rumour proved to be false, it caused some panic. It was just a hugely stressful opening night, and a portent of things to come. Even though most people were blissfully unaware of the problems, and the shows were doing really well, selling out, behind the scenes there were all sorts of issues.

That very first night at Victoria Warehouse, The Lieutenant and I were stood outside, as we usually do, but with the owner's son stood next to us. Right next to us, just watching us, noting everything. The next week, he turned up again, and again stood next to us, but he was dressed exactly the same as me. I've always dressed very much in the same way – I have a kind of uniform, especially for The Warehouse – and at that time it was black converse with white toes, black jeans, black T-shirt and a three-quarter length black bubble jacket with a fur collar. The owner's son was dressed *exactly* like me: black converse with white toes, black jeans, black T-shirt and a three-quarter length black bubble jacket with a fur collar. The Lieutenant just whispered to me, 'He's come dressed as you … what the fucking fuck?'

During that first season, it became increasingly clear that the Cohens, who were getting excited about the numbers coming through the doors, were trying to find out more and more about the way our business worked. For example, I turned up one night and they had installed an electronic counter on the door, to track the number of people we had in each night. In pulling stunts like that, they basically destroyed any remaining trust in the business relationship we had with the Cohens, and because of that we realised that the Victoria Warehouse couldn't be the long-term home for The Warehouse Project. We would have to start looking, *again*, for a new home.

One of the other problems we had at Victoria Warehouse, is when we started getting high numbers of mobile phones stolen. You might get one or two stolen, but all of a sudden we were getting up to fifty phones a night stolen from customers. We couldn't work out what was happening. One night it happened again, so we decided to shut the front door and put a system in place to search everyone on the way out. The Lieutenant was stood by the door just observing and saw a guy come out and clock the searches and panic, this guy went behind a burger van and was about to try and climb over the wall to get out, when The Lieutenant, in his own words, 'smashed him from behind, and he went down like a sack of spuds'. The police searched the guy and found forty-three mobile phones down his trousers. Turns out he was part of a Romanian organised crime group who were not just targeting us, but lots of other venues across Manchester like the Arena and the Apollo. Apparently they could get hundreds for each phone back in Romania, so it was a really lucrative business.

That New Year's Eve, in 2012, we had reports of a customer missing. This had happened to us before, as it has with all large-scale events. I'm sure a lot of people reading this book will recall being out in a big group and having one of their mates disappear; but there's usually an explanation for it – they've peaked a bit too early, and have taken themselves home, or perhaps they got lucky and ended up back at some new friend's house, unaware that everyone is wondering where they are. That sadly wasn't the case with Souvik Pal. The nineteen-year-old Manchester Metropolitan University student came to The Warehouse Project event on New Year's Eve with his friends. At one stage he became separated from them and, after charging at a member of staff to try and get past the one-way system, he was asked to leave the club. His flatmate reported him missing the next morning, and the last confirmed sighting of Souvik was on our CCTV camera at 11 p.m. Shortly after that, two people were caught on another nearby CCTV camera, and one of them appeared to be trying to climb a fence next to the Bridgewater Canal. Police frogmen searched the canal in the days after he went missing, but didn't find anything, and it was only three weeks later when they went back into the canal that they sadly found Souvik's body. The inquest and the post-mortem showed no injuries, and the cause of his death was given as drowning, so the Trafford Coroner, Joanne Kearsley, recorded an open verdict. It was just tragic.

Our second Easter at Victoria Warehouse we did another three events over the bank holiday weekend. Good Friday, Easter Saturday and Easter Sunday. They all sold out, so we did really well. I was at home resting on Easter Monday morning, when I got a call to say there had been an armed robbery. At 10 a.m., we had staff in the cash office – an office lady, who was working for us, Jason Argyle, and Scott, who still works for us now. They were cashing up after the weekend, preparing for the security guards to collect the cash, who were due to turn up at 11.30 a.m., when suddenly a gang burst in, armed with crowbars and knives, and threatened them into opening the safe. Thankfully, none of the staff were injured, but they were obviously all traumatised.

It was pretty obvious, because the armed gang knew exactly where the cash office was and what time to come on Easter Monday when there were three days' worth of takings bagged up and waiting to be collected by the security van, that it was an inside job at some level. We didn't suspect any of the people who were working that day, but I knew someone connected to The Warehouse Project must have supplied information to the gang, which put us in a horrible situation because we started to look at everyone who worked there in a different light.

I got down to the warehouse as soon as I got the call, and obviously all the staff were in shock. The local police that day were pretty useless. I'll never forget being sat in Victoria Warehouse talking to the police, as two lads on mountain bikes and wearing balaclavas just rode nonchalantly past the entrance to the building, almost as if they were laughing at us. I said to the police, 'Aren't you going to go and speak to them?' They said, 'We can't stop and search people for wearing balaclavas.' I said, 'Don't you think it's a bit weird that we've just had an armed robbery and lost £130,000 in cash, and only an hour later, two lads wearing balaclavas are slowing down on bikes, to see what is going on here?'

GMP is a different beast nowadays, and we have a really good working relationship with them, particularly since the new Chief Constable Stephen Watson took over. But back then they never found out any information on who was behind the armed robbery, but we did manage to find out something ourselves quite a while later, on the underground Mancunian grapevine. An associate of The Lieutenant's was doing a short stint in Strangeways and overheard someone boasting that a connection of theirs had done over The Warehouse Project. We had never told anyone there had been an armed robbery, so only a handful of people inside our business and the police who handled the case knew it had even happened. Along with whoever had done the robbery, of course.

The associate of The Lieutenant rang him up and said, 'You've not had an armed robbery at The Warehouse Project, have you?' And that's how we found out who was responsible. We drew a few connections, and by process of elimination we were pretty sure it was one of the bouncers who had supplied the inside information. Needless to say, he didn't work for us after we worked that out. Kirsty Smith found the whole experience at Victoria Warehouse so traumatic, that she decided to leave the business, and Sam and I bought her out.

While we were still reeling from Souvik Pal's death and the armed robbery, the Cohens were also making life very difficult for us. They had upped the rental for our second season, which made it harder for us to make the venue work for The Warehouse Project. We didn't immediately sign the contract, and then David Cohen just stopped taking our calls. We had already announced the new season of The Warehouse Project and put it on sale, but we couldn't get hold of the landlord to confirm the venue. It got to within two weeks of the opening night of that season, and we still didn't know for definite if we had the venue confirmed. I think the Cohens just wanted to make us sweat. In their eyes, it would make us realise how much we needed them, and they would regain some power over us. In the end, Sam and I went for a meeting with Bowlers, another venue just down the road, to make sure we had a back-up plan in place. The very next morning, David Cohen rang me back for the first time in weeks.

Sam and I went and met with the Cohens at their hotel, but at this stage I didn't trust them at all, so I took a recording device with me to record the conversation. I think they must have known we would try and record the conversation as they sat us under a speaker that was blaring out music, so when I listened back to the recording later all you could really hear was the music. We managed to agree a deal for the imminent season of The Warehouse Project, which involved us giving them a million-pound guarantee for the season, but I think it was clear to both sides that this relationship had run its course. It certainly was to me, anyway.

In the early hours of Saturday, 28 September 2013, we then had another tragic incident at The Warehouse Project. Nick Bonnie, a thirty-year-old charity worker, collapsed and was treated by our on-site medics. He was transferred to hospital but tragically later died.

On some nights, I would leave before the event ended, as I wasn't hands-on responsible for anything, so I had actually left the building when Nick was taken to hospital. The first I knew about it was when I turned on Sky News first thing the next morning and saw it there. One of the first calls I got that morning was from a police officer who we worked with called Simon

Collister, who said the Head of GMP Trafford, Mark Roberts, wanted to see me. Kim and I went together to meet him at the station, and he just wanted to reconfirm the facts, as we knew them, and speak to us face-to-face, as it was obviously a terrible incident. Roberts could tell we were shaken up but was really reassuring and said to us that from what he could tell, we had done everything we could, and nothing wrong. He warned us that the press would be all over us, and there were already some journalists outside the police station, so he let us leave through the back door to avoid them. It just so happened that it was the Tory party conference in Manchester that weekend, so as soon as the news broke, several politicians predictably jumped on it to try and score a few points, but it did also mean that there was more national press than normal in the city that weekend.

The Warehouse Project was due to open again the following night, and there was never any suggestion from the police or the authorities that it shouldn't, although Sam and I did discuss among ourselves whether it was the right thing to do. A death like that affects everyone involved in the business, from the bar staff to security, and we didn't have a dedicated HR department to support all staff members, so it was up to us as management to deal with it as best we could and Kim, in particular, was in the thick of it. It's very hard to know exactly what the right decision is to make at times like those, but once you are running large scale events – football matches, theatre productions, shopping centres even, not just live concerts and nightclubs – you're going to have to face incidents where people get injured. Anywhere that has a large footfall is going to have to deal with incidents at some stage. In the end, Sam and I decided to open the following night but with increased safety and security, though that caused a bit of backlash from customers because it took some people hours to get in due to the increased level of searches on the door and there was also a lot of press and TV outside, filming people as they went in. But rather that and know that we'd done everything we could to keep people safe.

We later found out that Nick had worked for The Prince's Trust and his mum, Pauline, worked for a Stroud dog support charity called The Nelson's Trust. I never met her or Nick's dad, Andy, personally, but they seemed to handle the whole situation brilliantly, or as well as any parent can handle the tragic death of their child, and they never ever put blame on The Warehouse Project. They put out a statement saying, 'Nick Bonnie lost his life tragically, senselessly and needlessly in a nightclub in Manchester on a 'lads' weekend. This has devastated the lives of [his family and friends]. Everyone who knew Nick was aware he loved life, lived it to the max and in making one stupid mistake he has cost himself his life. We hope that after reading this, we may have gone some way in helping anyone/everyone in the realisation that drinking, and the use of any illicit drugs, are a killer with consequences that will devastate lives for ever.'

Andy and Pauline may not have blamed us, but as that season went on there seemed to be intense public pushback against The Warehouse Project. We've never had anything like that sort of concerted campaign to muddy our name before or since, and at first, I had no idea who was behind it, or where it was coming from.

Then, one night at The Warehouse Project, I was stood with Jon Drape at 2 a.m. when my phone rang. It was a guy I knew called Graeme Bell who owned a few venues in the Gay Village and had been in business with The Lieutenant at one stage. Graeme was very distressed and upset and said to me, 'Sacha, I've been really bad. You've always looked after me, but I've done something really, really bad. I need to meet you.'

I had no idea what he was talking about, but I was really worried by the sound of his voice. I could tell it was something serious, he sounded in a right state.

'Graeme, what's going on? What's happened? You're panicking me a bit …'

I arranged to meet him the next day at the Four Seasons hotel, but at the last minute I switched the location to the Bowdon Hotel, as I'd become so paranoid after everything we had been through in the preceding months. Sam, Jon Drape, The Lieutenant, and I met Graeme in the bar of the Bowden Hotel, and he looked half the man he used to be. His hands were shaking so much that The Lieutenant got him a glass of white wine. When he told us what had been going on I could not believe it. Graeme said, 'I've been paid £500 a week by your landlord to create this campaign against The Warehouse Project …'

We sat there as he explained exactly what had been going on and handed over all his emails, which backed up everything he was saying. It was all there in black and white. It seemed the Cohens thought they could get rid of us and basically run The Warehouse Project themselves under a different name, that seemed to be what their idea was. It goes without saying that was never going to happen.

I tried to help poor Graeme as best I could, as did The Lieutenant and Jon. We got him away from Manchester and rented him a place in Glasgow, away from all the stress, in the hopes that he might be able to rebuild his life – Graeme had been a really successful entrepreneur at one stage. Tragically, though, his worries and demons must have got too much for him, and a few months later he took his own life. That hit all of us really hard, as Graeme really had been such a force of nature, before things started to escalate out of his control.

Without a doubt, those two years at Victoria Warehouse were the most traumatic of my lifetime. It was horrible and it all really affected me for a long time. Kim and I had become an item in 2011, but we had decided it would be best to keep it under wraps as it might not look too professional to some people. It came about because we were the only two on The Warehouse Project that weren't really into going to after-parties at the time. We didn't want to go partying after working all night at The Warehouse Project, but at the same time, you need to wind down for a couple of hours before you can sleep, so I started to invite Kim around to my house for a picnic after The Warehouse Project. I know that sounds a bit weird, a picnic at 5 a.m., but that's what we used to do. Scotch eggs, cocktail sausages, mini pizzas, and a few dips! We were together for a few years, and I thought we'd done quite well to keep it on a need-to-know basis, till I was working on this book, and I said to Luke, 'You probably don't know this, but Kim and I were together at one stage …' and he rolled his eyes and replied, 'Sacha, *everybody* knew.'[9]

We were obviously a lot more stressed and affected by it all than we thought, and one day Kim just decided she'd had enough. She was round at my house and told me she was looking for another job. She was so integral to the running of The Warehouse Project at that point that when she said she was leaving it triggered a panic attack in me. I'd never had a panic attack before, so I didn't know what was happening to me. I thought I was dying. Kim was really concerned and rang an ambulance. Two paramedics turned up and I think they

---

[9] I guess the fact that we used to always go on holiday at the same time was a bit of a giveaway. Although we're not together now, we're still best friends.

thought I was overreacting: 'You're not dying, it's OK, calm down, you're just having a panic attack.' If you've ever had a full-on panic attack, you'll know it's a really scary experience. Once the paramedics found out we ran The Warehouse Project, they seemed more concerned about getting on the guest list for the following weekend than my condition! They told me to just chill out for the rest of the day and have some comfort food, whatever my favourite food was. So, Kim ordered me a Chinese takeaway and we watched *Nanny McPhee* and tried to calm down.

As I mentioned, earlier, it's now run by completely different operators, one of the most respected in the country. It couldn't be more different. But back then, we just had to get out. After the last night at Victoria Warehouse, we made sure we got everything out of the building. All the production, the lot. It took a few days, and then it was time to make a couple of calls. On 6 January, I picked up Sam and together we called everyone who we knew had been involved in the campaign against The Warehouse Project. We had proof of what they had all done in the emails that Graeme had given us. When I spoke to David Cohen, I told him, 'Just so you know, Graeme Bell has been working with us since the beginning of December and has passed us every email with details of what has been going on.'

There was silence at the other end of the phone. But it was a silence that, to me, spoke volumes.

All we wanted at that stage was to move on and get The Warehouse Project back to what it is supposed to be. I don't think I will ever feel more relief than I did in the early hours of New Year's Day, after the last event of that Warehouse Project season. I drove home at 5 a.m., almost shell-shocked, walked into my house, fell to my knees and burst out crying. I was literally on my knees, sobbing.

I've never felt relief like it.

I didn't know where The Warehouse Project was going to go at that stage, but I knew we would be back.

Most importantly, I knew the nightmare of the past two years was over.

WE'RE GONNA NEED A BIGGER PARK

By the third year of Parklife, Platt Fields was bursting at the seams. It was no longer a student event, it had crossed over and become a mainstream event, attracting young people from all walks of life, not just from all over Manchester and the satellite towns, but from further afield. We had managed to get to 32,000 by doing everything we could to increase the capacity. To be fair to Manchester City Council and the rest of the authorities, they were as helpful as they could be. Everyone could see that Parklife was becoming a really important part of Manchester's calendar, and they wanted to support us as much as they could. It really was beginning to feel that Parklife was too big for Platt Fields though. Parklife had become too-big-for-this-park-life.

One person who certainly thought she was too big for Platt Fields was Kelis. She turned up with a slight cold and a huge attitude. She made a huge scene and refused to go on till we got a doctor to give her a B12 injection. She threw a big hissy fit, acting like she was the main act, even though she wasn't. The mighty De La Soul were.

I was reminded of Kelis's hissy fit a few years later in 2015, when Grace Jones was one of our headliners at Parklife, after we moved to Heaton Park. When Grace Jones arrived in Manchester, flying in from Australia, she really was ill, and she'd just got off a twenty-four-hour flight. But Grace was an absolute trooper and argued that the kids have bought the tickets to see her perform, so she was determined to do that. I was so impressed by her attitude. What's more, Grace was sixty-seven at the time, more than twice Kelis's age, which makes it all the more impressive.

In the end, Kelis ended up going on late after all her shenanigans, which was problematic. Every festival has a curfew, an agreed time with the authorities when the music has to stop, and if you go past that curfew then you get a huge fine. So, you have to stick to stage times at a festival. Letting one act over-run their stage time then has a knock-on effect on all the other acts, particularly the headline act, who'll potentially have to play a shorter set. And when you have more than one stage you also try and 'flip-flop' the stages, which means that the 'changeover' periods between acts are at different times on different stages, to make sure there are always acts on stage at any time in the festival. If one act goes over, then that knocks everything out of kilter. We had warned Kelis before she went on that we couldn't let her eat into De La Soul's stage time, but she ignored us and carried on playing. In that situation the first thing we would do is probably speak to the act's tour manager and try and get them to get their act to finish. If that doesn't work, the last resort is to pull the plug on the act. And it really is the last resort, because it's not a good look.

In the end, we had to pull the plug on Kelis, and she was absolutely furious with us. It was like her debut single 'Caught Out Here' when she screams 'I hate you so much right now'. She got in her driver's car and was still ranting as he drove off, calling us 'the most unprofessional promoters she's ever worked with', and that wasn't the worst thing she said. It's the only time we've had to pull the plug on any artist at Parklife, but it was the right thing to do, and most festivals have had to do it at least once.

A few years before our incident with Kelis, I was watching Glastonbury 2009 on television, and they pulled the plug on N*E*R*D* on the Pyramid Stage on the Friday afternoon. Pharrell Williams was as furious about it as Kelis was at Parklife (funnily enough, Pharrell and The Neptunes had produced Kelis's early hits) but if you don't get artists to stick to stage times at festivals then it becomes chaos. We've only ever run over our curfew once at Parklife and that was a few years later at Heaton Park, when we had an incident with Frank Ocean, and we managed to get round the hefty fine on that occasion due to an incident on the Metrolink, but more of that later.

It was obvious after the 2012 event that Platt Fields was now too small for Parklife. We literally couldn't get any more people in. We were in discussion with Manchester City Council, who came to us and said, 'Look, if you want to expand it, why don't you think about moving it to another park?'

The thing is, at that stage, we still thought Manchester's huge student population was the key to Parklife, and Platt Fields was right on their doorstep. We weren't convinced how many of those students would travel to the other side of the city to a different location. Wythenshawe Park was the only park (at a push) in walking distance of the student areas and could hold 50,000. The problem we uncovered was that there was an ancient covenant on Wythenshawe Park. It turns out that the estate had been owned by the Tatton family till 1926, when the Hall and 250 acres of land were bought by Sir Ernest

Simon and his wife Shena Simon. Ernest Simon was an industrialist and had been Lord Mayor of Manchester – he was later one of the sponsors of the construction of Jodrell Bank. His wife Shena was a politician, as well as a feminist and writer – the Shena Simon campus of Manchester College is name after her. The covenant dated back to when they donated Wythenshawe Park to the residents of Manchester, and basically said the residents had a say on what did and what didn't go on in the park, which meant that if just one resident objected to an event, it couldn't go ahead. It was annoying as I remember there being a party in the park back in 1994, an event called Pollen, run by a guy called Rollo, but nobody must have clocked the covenant at that point.

It was Vicky Rosen at Manchester City Council, who has since retired, who first suggested we look at Heaton Park. She said, 'Look, The Stone Roses and Oasis have both done huge gigs there, and they've had 80,000 people, without major issues. We'll give you loads of free transport, loads of free advertising, you can use all the council boards around town.'

Factory records had put on a smaller festival at Heaton Park in 1991, called Cities in the Park, but – apart from the Oasis and The Stone Roses gigs – the last time a huge crowd had gathered there was for Pope John Paul II in 1982, when an estimated 200,000, including a then ten-year-old Liam Gallagher with his mum, Peggy, turned up to see him speak. 'Last time I was here I came to see the Pope,' Liam told the crowd, when Oasis were playing there in the early 1990s, 'he was all right, but he didn't have many tunes.'

We had some major reservations about moving to Heaton Park, the biggest being that we didn't think Manchester's students would travel that far. There's a bit of a North-South divide in the city, and the majority of the 60,000 students live in South Manchester, in an area based around the Wilmslow Road corridor of Fallowfield, Withington, and Rusholme. I'd say 90 per cent of students who come to Manchester never venture north of Victoria station, and rarely leave the Wilmslow Road corridor. Parklife was going to have to change all that if we moved to Heaton Park and take the students out of their comfort zone.

PARKLIFE MOVES NORTH

It was a huge decision to move Parklife to Heaton Park, but after Wythenshawe Park was ruled out, it was the only real option if we wanted to grow the festival and cope with the increased demand for tickets. Heaton Park is huge, it's the biggest park in Greater Manchester and it's also the biggest municipal park in all of Europe. It has a long and rich history including hosting the Heaton Races – the early horse races held there from 1827 to 1838, after which they moved to Aintree, where the Grand National is held today. The park was also an army base in the Second World War, and after the war, prefab housing estates were built there for Manchester residents who had been displaced by the war. Mark E. Smith of The Fall spent his early years growing up in the park, living in one of those prefab houses.

Heaton Park had undergone a huge renovation in the late 1990s, and was also served by the Metrolink, the tram-rail service that would help get people to and from Parklife. The council were key in the move. To be fair to Manchester City Council, their events strategy over recent years has been really forward thinking. Much more forward thinking than other UK cities.

While other cities like Liverpool would bid for one-off events like hosting the Eurovision Song Contest or Capital of Culture or such events, Manchester decided that it actually wanted to create and support its own unique landmark events that were part of the fabric of the city, such as Parklife or Manchester International Festival. Events that Manchester *owned*, and would return year after year, and support the economy and drive tourism.

The council agreed a 50,000 capacity for the first year of Parklife, with a plan in place for it to increase to an 80,000 capacity if everything went well in the first couple of years. Oasis and The Stone Roses had already held huge gigs there, so we knew the park could cope, but we were still very nervous about the move. It was a big step up from the 32,000 we'd had at Platt Fields. There was a big demand for more tickets, but we just didn't know if all the audience would make the jump with us to Heaton Park.

There were a few reservations from local residents, it has to be said, but there had also been reservations about the Oasis and The Stone Roses gigs that were held there. Whenever you put a gig or a festival on in a public space there is always a small number of local residents who object. I do understand. I do get that its disruptive, but on the other hand, it does bring in millions of pounds to the local economy (£12 million a year now) and it is for only one week a year.

With Greater Manchester Police, we had meetings with the residents before we moved there, and we continue to have annual residents' meetings, but some of them can get quite testy. One particular, feisty, attendee actually tried to punch Jon Drape at a meeting once, and GMP had to step in and calm things down. I do like to think we got most of the local residents on board in the end, and like I say, we did appreciate that it's disruptive for them.

Obviously, in the first year, we had no idea how the move to Heaton Park would go, but since Parklife was established there we have done everything we can to consider and respect the local community, such as the huge Jewish population there, who we work closely with.

The Jewish community have their own technical boundary, called an Eruv, which if you had no idea what it was, just looks like a wire – a power cable, or a telephone wire – strung across an area. But it is hugely important and sacred to the Jewish community, basically expanding the area in which practising Jews are allowed to do activities on the Shabbat – the Saturday – such as carrying things, that they would not normally be allowed to do outside their home on that day. The Eruv for Crumpsall and Prestwich crosses that side of Heaton Park, and as we put additional entrances in that side of the park for the festival, it has to be delicately handled, working with the local Rabbi, to make sure the Eruv remains intact. We give the Rabbi one of our site buggies to help him get around each year, although I must say, he doesn't stick to the strict speed restrictions on site! All the site crew are safely adhering to the speed restrictions backstage, and then you'll see this speeding Rabbi go shooting past! He's very pleasant, though, and always gives our site manager a bottle of whiskey to say thanks. It makes sense all round to maintain good relationships with your neighbours.

There are plenty of local residents who completely embrace Parklife and lots of them have decided to use it as a money-making opportunity – from Airbnb-ing their spare bedrooms, to putting printers in their front gardens and charging people a fiver to print off tickets. Asian families might sell homemade samosas from their front gardens, and a few people with decent-sized back gardens have really gone for it and turned them into 'glamping sites', putting up bell tents or tepees and installing toilets and hot showers. Some of them manage to charge about £300 a night!

The first year, Sam and Rich managed to pull together a great bill, including Plan B, Example, and Professor Green – who were pretty much the biggest artists in their field in the UK at the time. Other artists included Rita Ora, Maccabees, Disclosure, Iggy Azalea, Rudimental, Erol Alkan, Horrors, Temper Trap, Shy FX, Joker, Benga, Todd Terje, Toddla T, Julio Bashmore, and Cyril Hahn. Example loved Parklife so much he decided to hang around and partied so long into the night that he missed his gig the following day. There were some incredible performances, but it was Disclosure who stole the show, they were amazing that year, and their performance was one of the greatest Parklife moments to date. It felt like it was a tipping point for Disclosure as they were just exploding at the time as their song 'Latch' with Sam Smith had been huge. It was a real 'glad I was there' moment, anyone who was at the first Parklife at Heaton Park will tell you that.

We put a lot of effort and money into turning the park into a proper festival site, too. As well as a big wheel and various other rides, we even bought in a log flume! I think we might be the only festival in the world to have one on site. The day before the event, we did the final walk around with Greater Manchester Police, who couldn't believe we had a log flume, and loved it. They insisted it needed to be tested, and all took their hats off and gave it a go, which was a brilliant comedy moment. Sadly, I don't think anyone took a picture. We had the flume for the first two years, but unfortunately it took up a lot of space, and as the festival grew we had to get rid of it.

My business partner Sam hated the rides, mainly because of the terrible music they generally blast out, and I can totally see his point. Sam and Rich and their team carefully curate a brilliant bill of cutting-edge musical talent, meticulous planning the changeovers between the acts, and balancing what is on the other stages at the same time, and then when you walk around the site you get snatches of this terrible Happy Hardcore or Bounce music blasting from dodgy speakers on some of the fairground rides.

We also had a big Nando's stall, which was hugely popular and rammed all day. They had a DJ set up there and Rudimental ended up playing a secret set on the stall, which went down a storm. The other thing that happened there was that, unbeknown to us, the actress Maisie Williams, Arya from *Game of Thrones*, had come to Parklife just as a normal punter. Maisie was at the Nando's stall when someone spotted her, and word quickly got round that she was at the festival. The kids lost it, and she was getting mobbed. Security had to rescue her and bring her backstage for her own safety and sanity.

Anyone who has ever run a festival will tell you that you never know what you're going to come up against each day. You try and predict the issues, but there will always be something that crops up. I certainly didn't predict the issue we would have with The Lieutenant on the first day of Parklife at Heaton Park. As I drove on site that morning, one of The Lieutenant's crew ran up to my car, holding out his phone, and said, 'It's The Lieutenant, he needs to speak to you now.'

I could tell by his expression that this was not good news. I took the phone and heard The Lieutenant's voice on the other end of the line, who told me he'd been arrested and was in a cell in central Manchester. Probably best not to go into finer details too much here but, suffice to say, The Lieutenant had been stopped by the police and they found something in his car that shouldn't have been there, so he had been taken into custody. It was obvious straight away that it was pretty serious.

The Lieutenant used to sometimes call me 'Daddy'. In jest. Or at least I hope it was in jest. He had used his one phone call to reach Daddy. I reassured him I'd do whatever I could to help him, but it was the last thing I needed on the opening day of the biggest event I had ever run: one of my right-hand men being arrested and banged up. With hindsight, maybe someone else would have reacted differently, and blown their top at him for making such a mistake, but my knee-jerk reaction was *The Lieutenant's in trouble, he needs my help*. I got on to my solicitors right away and had them arrange to send one of their top barristers down. That done, we had to just get on with running the show, without The Lieutenant.

The case ended up going to court a few months later and The Lieutenant was so convinced that he was going to be sent down to spend some time at Her Majesty's Pleasure and wouldn't be coming home for a while, that he took a little bag containing his toothbrush and a few other personal items with him to court. Fortunately, the brief I'd arranged for him had done a brilliant job, not only in defending his case but also by pulling in some character references, including from high-profile Manchester musicians, and, perhaps more importantly, a couple of police officers. We had all spent so many long, cold nights with the police on the door of The Warehouse Project, that we'd got to know each other well – we'd even been to the football together. So, a couple of those officers were prepared to vouch for The Lieutenant. In the end, The Lieutenant got off with a suspended sentence and was, in his words, 'A very lucky boy'. But there was no group celebration on the steps of the courts, like in *Goodfellas*, where they all clap the young

Henry Hill on the back and say, 'Hey, you broke your cherry!' I'm pretty sure The Lieutenant's cherry had been broken a few years prior to that anyway, to be honest. He's been around that block and got the T-shirt. It did strengthen the working relationship between me and The Lieutenant though. He knows, without question, that I've got his back, and he has proved to me on several occasions that he's got mine.

In the end, our worries about moving Parklife north to Heaton Park were unfounded. We were helped by the weather, which was a lot sunnier than the previous years, but moving to this new location proved to be a brilliant decision. It had made Parklife more of a destination festival, and it meant we could now be much more ambitious for the following years.

YOU DON'T GET A TOWN LIKE THIS FOR NOTHING

The month after the first Parklife at Heaton Park, we put on New Order for the first time, at Jodrell Bank in Cheshire – Jodrell Bank Centre for Astrophysics, to give it its full name – a pretty cosmic place for Mancunians. The centre is part of the University of Manchester and was established by astronomer Bernard Lovell after the Second World War. It's dominated by the huge Lovell Telescope, the world's largest steerable telescope when it was built in 1957, and still the third largest in the world today. Many Mancunian musicians have been fascinated by the telescope, not least Doves, who used a picture of the telescope on the cover of their first record 'Space Face', back when they were called Sub Sub, and later used it to bounce a guitar riff off the moon. It doesn't get more prog rock than bouncing a guitar riff off the moon. In 2010, Luke Bainbridge got Doves to do an acoustic performance for the *Guardian* at the Jodrell centre, and shortly after that we began to put on gigs there.

For New Order nowadays, Jodrell Bank is actually more of a local gig than Manchester, as Bernard Sumner lives round the corner in Alderley Edge, and Steve Morris and Gillian

Gilbert live on a farm just outside Macclesfield. Steve has lived in the area all his life and once told Luke that his earliest memories of visiting Jodrell Bank were when he was a kid and used to go to the farmers' market there with his mum and dad in the late 1960s.

A few days before New Order's gig, we got told that the band wanted to arrive by helicopter. I couldn't understand why they needed a helicopter when they all lived a stone's throw away from Jodrell Bank. It's literally on the doorstep. But if the headline act wants to arrive by helicopter, you need to make it happen.

The only issue was that the nearest available helicopter was at Barton Aerodrome, which is half an hour's drive away in Eccles, Salford. So, we ended up driving the band to Salford, to fly them back in a helicopter, which seemed slightly self-defeating! The relationship between the band and Hooky – Peter Hook, New Order's original bassist – was a bit strained at the time, and he also lived near Jodrell Bank. I had a sneaking suspicion that it was more to do with Hooky being able to hear them arrive in a helicopter.

Another issue was that because the band had only requested the helicopter the week of the gig, we had no landing space organised for it at Jodrell Bank. A slight oversight! Jon Drape realised twenty minutes before they landed and had to send security out into the farmer's field next door to tread the long grass down in to a 'H' shape.

At the gig itself, Johnny Marr warmed up for them and I think I'm right in saying it was the last time the legendary Joe Moss, who'd managed both The Smiths and Johnny, saw him play. Joe sadly passed away a few years later. Bernard Sumner came on during Johnny's set, and they performed 'Getting Away with It' by Electronic – the band they'd formed together in 1988 – which was pretty special.

New Order were on fantastic form and played songs they rarely play live, like 'World', and five Joy Division songs, including 'Ceremony', which Bernard Sumner introduced, deadpan, as 'The song we wrote as Joy Division, before our singer inconveniently died.' We projected the band's visuals onto the 76-metre dish of the Lovell telescope, which felt like a futuristic celebration of electronic music legacy, and the band seemed to love it. 'Thank you to Jodrell Bank', yelled Bernard at one stage, 'it's a stately institution – just like us!'

A few years later, in the winter of 2015, we booked New Order to play Store Street, and that felt like another defining moment. Bearing in mind the band's legendary status, the pivotal role they have played in dance music and clubbing culture, both in Manchester and internationally, to have them play The Warehouse Project at Store Street was like booking electronic music royalty.

Because it was a live gig, we actually undersold it by 200 tickets, partly because we knew New Order would have a reasonably sized guest list, as it was a hometown gig, which they did – though not an Ian Brown-sized guest list, but we were still within capacity. Within half an hour of the doors opening, however, Sam and I knew we had a problem. New Order's crowd is different to the normal Warehouse Project crowd, not just in age and demographic, but in its actual physical size. The Warehouse Project usually attracts skinny, eighteen- to twenty-five-year-old students who don't wear bulky clothing as they are there to dance all night; and even if it's cold outside in the Mancunian winter, it won't be cold inside. But a sizeable number of the New Order crowd at those Store Street gigs was considerably bulkier than your normal Warehouse Project punter, all wearing big jackets, too, which meant they were taking up nearly twice the space of our usual crowd. Even though we were officially just under capacity, it felt over full. Not dangerous, but definitely uncomfortable.

We got through the two shows, but a lot of people were unhappy or angry with us because they thought it was too packed and busy. I remember the poet, Mike Garry, leaving quite upset, as did a few other people. Even though the gigs themselves were fantastic, as you don't often get the chance to see New Order in a space like Store Street, it was a lesson learnt for us – and apologies to anyone who was at that gig who wasn't able to enjoy it properly. We've never made that mistake again.

Because a few people had put in official complaints about the gig being overly busy, the licensing department was all over us and I was dragged in to speak to the fire officer that week. Kim and I were completely upfront about it and explained the whole situation and said that we had actually been *under* our official capacity, but we had underestimated the effect that the different demographic would have. I had an inkling they would want to come down and double-check on us, and sure enough, the following weekend a Greater Manchester Fire and Rescue vehicle turned up. One of the big bosses wanted to have a walk around and check out Store Street for himself. Fortunately for us, the show that he came down to, Jungle, was the only night of that whole season that hadn't sold brilliantly well, so he could see there was actually plenty of free space, not too lively or shoulder to shoulder, and it didn't feel packed or remotely uncomfortable. I think he was quite surprised at how civilised it all was and couldn't understand what all the fuss and complaints had been about. To our relief, he left saying everything was perfectly fine.

New Order at Store Street was really special, but perhaps even more special was when we put the band on at Heaton Park in

2021. New Order created a video montage of their career and Manchester over the last forty years, which showed on the big screens just before they went on stage. It feels special to have promoted New Order's biggest ever headline show, but really it's testament to the staying power of the band and their incredible career. Not many artists can say they played their biggest gig by far in their fourth decade as a band.

SNOOP, YOUR MUM, AND AITCH

In 2014, we booked Snoop Dogg as one of our headliners for Parklife – which felt like a real step up. Snoop was our first real global superstar and it felt like a statement booking, like Parklife was putting its flag in the ground as one of the major festivals in the country.

Our social-media team are always looking for innovative and interesting ways to engage with the audience and reach new people, and at the time they were experimenting with some new software which allowed us to send a text to everyone on the Parklife database, but change the name of who the text was received from. When it popped up on your phone it would look like you had received a text from 'David Beckham' or 'Ronaldo' even though they obviously weren't in your address book. We tried this first with a message from Snoop Dogg, that just popped up in people's phones with the message – 'It's Parklife, biatch!' – and a link to buy tickets, which actually ended up going viral.

A couple of months later, I was driving from home into work one morning, when my phone suddenly starting pinging like mental with notifications. I didn't know what was going on, so pulled over to have a look. At the time we were giving a big promotional push to some of the Parklife after-parties and unbeknown to me, our social media team had decided to use the same text technology that we had used with Snoop to send out a message to the Parklife punters that came up as if it was a text from 'Mum'. It simply said 'Some of the Parklife after-parties have already sold out. If you're going, make sure you're home for breakfast!'

It was meant purely as a light-hearted way of engaging with our Parklife audience, but it backfired horribly. Some people just saw it for what it was, but others, who'd recently lost their mum, were estranged from their mum, or perhaps never even knew their mum, were terribly upset. Some of them were quite vocal about it, including Sir Ian McKellen's nephew, who lived in Chorlton and had been to Parklife a couple of times previously. Sometimes you have to admit you've misjudged something and got it wrong, even if there was no intent to upset anyone.

Quite a few people complained to the press or made official complaints. In the end we were fined £70,000 by the ICO (Information Commissioner's Office, the independent authority set up to 'uphold information rights in the public interest'). The ICO's reason for fining us was because 'the identity of the person behind the text' we sent to customers was 'disguised or concealed'. Steve Eckersley, Head of ICO enforcement, said: 'This was a poorly thought-out piece of marketing that didn't appear to even try to follow the rules or consider the impact that their actions would have on the privacy of individuals. It made some people very upset in an attempt to sell tickets to a club night. The fine sends a clear message that using this type of marketing is unacceptable.'

We put out a message saying: 'The communication was intended as a fun way of engaging festival-goers. However, the festival acknowledges that this was not an appropriate theme for everyone. The Parklife Weekender wants to apologise for any offence caused by the SMS marketing message sent to their customers earlier this year.'

We've all sent texts that we regret afterwards, though most of us don't get fined £70,000 for doing so!

We just wanted to draw a line under it, so we paid the fine straight away. I even managed to get a 20 per cent reduction for paying it immediately, and we haven't used the technology since.

That same year, 2014, we also began to have real problems with people jumping the fence. Parklife had become such a huge event that it's inevitable that we were going to attract some fence jumpers. There are so many trees in Heaton Park that one of the ways to try and get in free to the festival was to climb one of the trees whose branches overhung the festival perimeter fence. We would obviously try and put the fence away from any trees, but that's not always possible in Heaton Park, where there are so many trees. There is one specific tree on the edge of the festival site that had a TPO (Tree Protection Order) – an order made by a local planning authority to protect certain trees that are deemed to be of specific merit. In our case it meant that this tree was protected, and we couldn't do anything to it. We couldn't damage the tree, cut any of its branches or anything. Frustratingly, the tree had quite large branches, which extended over the perimeter fence, and in that first year of Parklife it was used by quite a few fence jumpers to get into the festival without paying, which really pissed me off. So, for the second year of Parklife, we decided to adjust the site map of the festival so that the police compound was below the tree, inside the festival fence. Any fence jumpers who used that tree and thought they had made it into the festival – congratulating themselves on jibbing into Parklife – got a bit of a shock when they jumped down.[10] The looks on their faces were priceless as they realised they had simply jumped into the police compound, and were quickly apprehended by GMP.

Nowadays, only about ten manage to fence-jump into the festival, but in the first year or two we might have had about forty to fifty people doing it, including one of our recent headliners, Aitch, who boasted that he'd done it when he was younger. Aitch is from nearby Moston, and we booked him to headline in 2023, which was announced just before that year's Brit awards. Aitch proudly told the press on the red carpet that it was beyond his wildest dreams to headline a festival that he used to have to jump the fence to get into.

Back to 2014, and the moment Snoop Dog came on for his headline slot was unforgettable. I can remember exactly where I was: standing with Sam at the side of the stage. As Snoop came on stage to a crowd of 50,000, we looked at each other and were like 'Woah, we've created a festival.' That moment felt like a huge leap – Parklife was now a major event, not just a little student festival. Moments like that don't come very often, believe it or not. Usually, everyone working on an event – and that includes me, Sam, Jon, Kim, and The Lieutenant – is usually too busy making sure everything is going to plan to

---

[10] 'Jib' is Mancunian for getting in for free. A group of Manchester United fans who pride themselves on getting the train to away games without paying, call themselves 'The Inter City Jibbers'

register big triumphs. We very rarely get to stand back and enjoy our success as it happens.

Sadly, that special moment coincided with a tragic event in the audience that neither Sam nor I knew anything about at the time. Just before Snoop Dogg came on stage, there was an altercation in the crowd as someone was hitting a girl on the head with a blow-up doll. The girl's boyfriend, Robert Hart, then intervened and asked them to stop, but the person obviously didn't appreciate that and punched him. Robert was nearly knocked out and collapsed. The medics arrived on scene and Robert seemed to be fine at first, apart from a small bruise above his eye. The medics later said he was alert and talking and didn't meet the criteria of a major trauma. But any head injury or chest pain incident at a festival is treated with standard procedure and that person is taken to hospital to be checked out. Because the medics found Robert Hart was alert and talking, he was sent to North Manchester hospital rather than Salford Royal, which specialises in brain and head injuries. What happened after that we only found out at the inquest. A CT scan was carried out on Robert at the hospital and sent digitally to Salford Royal, but a wrong interpretation of his brain scan led to a delay in his transfer to Salford Royal. That delay was fatal, and tragically Robert died four days later.

Everyone connected with the festival was devastated. I spoke to his girlfriend to pass on our condolences, and she kindly said she didn't blame Parklife. We were keen to find the person responsible, though, and after speaking to his girlfriend and the police we announced a £20,000 reward for any information leading to an arrest. GMP ran a massive public campaign to try and find the individual who attacked Robert, and when the person responsible still hadn't been found by the time of the following year's Parklife, GMP handed out leaflets to everyone to try and trigger memories, but again no one came forward. All we know is the person had a Scouse accent. The police were pretty adamant that whoever attacked Robert must have had protection around them, to keep everyone quiet.

RETURN TO STORE STREET

After two pretty traumatic years behind the scenes at Victoria Warehouse, it was a huge relief to all of us when The Warehouse Project returned to our spiritual home at Store Street in 2014. It's impossible to describe how heavy a weight it felt had been lifted off our shoulders. Not just for Sam and me, but for everyone who worked with us and for us, from the production staff to security. Thankfully, most of the punters had no idea what had gone on behind the scenes at Victoria Warehouse, as obviously we had done everything we could to make sure it didn't affect the experience of those coming to The Warehouse Project for an incredible night out. But those two years really had taken a toll on everyone who worked behind the scenes.

Moving back to our spiritual home at Store Street, we felt like we were waking from a nightmare. Joni Mitchell lamented in her song, 'Big Yellow Taxi', 'they paved paradise, and put up a parking lot'. Sorry Joni, but we could not have been happier to be going back to a parking lot, that *was* paradise for us after Victoria Warehouse. Or as The Lieutenant said, 'It felt like coming home after the worst shitty holiday you've ever had.'

The Warehouse Project was now too big for Store Street, we were more than halving our capacity by going back there, so the initial idea was only to return for one year, while we found a new permanent home in time for our 10th anniversary. As Sam said at the time, when we announced the line-up, '2014 is about The Warehouse Project going back to its roots. Smaller capacity, more intimate — an opportunity to revisit our spiritual home for one year only before we take the next step … before we get to that, one year only back beneath the streets.'

In the end, we ended up staying there for four seasons, and they were arguably the most joyous seasons we've ever had at The Warehouse Project. The atmosphere was incredible every week. We were back in a space which we knew so well. The crowd was also a little different as almost every show would sell out really quickly, which meant that you really had a hardcore crowd of dedicated music lovers. The bigger your events get, it stands to reason that the crowd is diluted a little and you need to have broader appeal, which has its pros and cons. But when we were back at Store Street with a smaller capacity, almost every night felt like a crowd of real dedicated music lovers, because you had to be pretty dedicated to get a ticket for most shows as they would sell out so quickly.

It was still a difficult space to work with, the logistical problems were still there as there's a lot of restrictions on the Store Street space – not just the capacity, which means there were some artists we couldn't book because the numbers wouldn't stand up, but also on a production level. The relatively low ceilings create a great atmosphere and help it feel intimate and underground – if it wasn't for the police on the front door it would feel like an illegal rave – but they are also restrictive in terms of the show you can put on: the size of screens and all sorts of other production issues for artists. After every season at

Store Street, we would sit down and say, 'Right, what can we do to make the experience better next season?' I didn't just mean the line-up: we were always trying to improve the sound, the lights, even the toilets, or the customer experience of getting in.

We had so many highlights in those seasons back at Store Street. In the first season alone, some of the nights that stand out were three-hour sets from the Chemical Brothers, the late great Andrew Weatherall and Bicep on the same night, a special Bugged Out twentieth anniversary night, and a night curated by Jon Hopkins and Jamie XX.

It wasn't just the punters that loved Store Street, for many of the DJs and artists it was also the favourite place to play, because of the atmosphere and the fact they knew we had such a knowledgeable and up-for-it crowd. Many DJs said that playing The Warehouse Project was one of the highlights of their year, and for some of them the partying when they got to Manchester was one of their highlights of the year as well. There was a time when we used to put some of our headline acts up in a hotel with suites in the Northern Quarter called The Light. One particular night, our headline DJ was booked into the penthouse suite, which had a hot tub on the balcony. It was known as the Simon Cowell suite, as he used to stay there when he was filming *Britain's Got Talent* in Manchester. Our headline DJ finished his set and decided he wanted to carry on the party back at his suite and invited some of the female bar staff back. It all got quite debauched and out of hand, and the DJ ended up in the hot tub with some of our bar staff. Simon Cowell might not have been staying there that night, but unfortunately, according to hotel management, someone from the show was, and they heard the commotion outside. When they looked out of the window they must have been pretty shocked at what they saw, as allegedly they reported it to the management, and The Warehouse Project was then banned from The Light.

Store Street was also the first time we had Elrow at The Warehouse Project, which was an incredible night for everyone. Well, everyone but our cleaners. On the nights when we used confetti canons at The Warehouse Project, we would probably use 5 kilos of confetti. Elrow absolutely went to town and came fully armed with 75 kilos of the stuff, *fifteen times* what we would normally use. Their show was amazing and memorable for everyone there, but it was memorable for the cleaners for another reason. Customers literally had to wade out of knee-high confetti on the floor on their way out. The cleaners took one look at the state of the venue and resigned *en masse*. We were still finding remnants of confetti from that night for a year later.

The Warehouse Project is not really a celeb hangout, and we never wanted it to be. We never had a proper VIP area for celebs, which probably puts off any of them who are not really coming for the music, which is fine by us. Although we never had a VIP area, there's been a couple of times when we've had to make sure someone didn't get mobbed or hassled. Gary Lineker has been down a few times, as we have a mutual friend called Jonathan Downey, and he's always been really friendly and down to earth. He came to see Groove Armada, and I took him up to the lighting desk as it's the best view in the house, and he loved it, but when the lights went up, the crowd spotted him and started chanting 'There's only one Gary Lineker', so we had to escort him out as we didn't want him to be hassled and it was also stopping the crowd from leaving.

The Warehouse Project has always been about looking forward, but we did usually have one Haçienda night a year. It was our nod to the clubbing heritage of Manchester and recognition that we're standing on the shoulders of giants. The

Haçienda nights have quite a different demographic to the usual Warehouse Project nights though. It's twenty-six years since The Haçienda closed now, so obviously anyone who was old enough to go there when it was still open is now probably in their fifties. If you were eighteen the day The Haçienda closed, you're now forty-four for fuck's sake, that makes me feel old. On Haçienda nights we quite often got families coming together, dad and son, mum and daughter, all partying together. I can't imagine partying and dancing all night with my mum. We sometimes even had three generations partying together at the Hac nights – gran, mum and daughter, all off their tits together. Or grandad, dad and son coming in together, which is slightly embarrassing on the door when you see either the granddad or dad gets stopped when security finds a wrap of coke on them. The two other things that stand out on Haç nights are it's pretty much the only night where quite a few people want to pay cash on the bar. Every other night the punters use contactless to pay, but quite a few of the Hac punters carry cash, so we had to organise a float especially. We also needed to order extra ear plugs, because we got more punters going to welfare asking if they've got any earplugs.

Store Street was a forgotten bit of Manchester before The Warehouse Project first moved there. An unloved side street under Piccadilly. Not many people know that Manchester Piccadilly station was originally called Store Street. The actual station name was Store Street when it opened in 1842, it was renamed Manchester London Road in 1847, and only became Manchester Piccadilly in 1960. I didn't know that before starting work on this book! But in the last few decades before we moved there, Store Street had almost fallen off the map. Taxi drivers didn't even know where it was when The Warehouse

Project first opened there. I think the club put Store Street back on the map. It's still a car park during the day, and the car park attendant told me that he often gets people taking selfies outside or walking in and taking a video clip of it. Although we may have put Store Street back on the map, we may have made it harder for some people to find it, as we took the two Victorian street signs down for posterity when we left. They were 25ft up on the wall, but I got The Lieutenant to go up a ladder and remove them. I had one in my house and Sam had the other in his. A bit naughty to nick the street signs, but Store Street had been such a huge part of our lives that we wanted something to remember it by.

Laurent Garnier played the final ever set at The Warehouse Project at Store Street and as he dropped his seminal track 'The Man With The Red Face', it was one of those really emotional special moments, looking around at all the faces in the crowd, where everyone in the building was connected, on the same wavelength and in the same moment, and it felt like the perfect soundtrack to end that chapter of The Warehouse Project.

GRACE JONES AND THE STOLEN POLICE BUGGY

Mancunians don't generally look too reverently at many other cities, but the nightlife and clubbing culture of New York has had a huge influence on Manchester. It was New Order's wild nights out on their early trips to New York, being shown around clubs like Danceteria, The Fun House, and smaller places like Better Days, by people like the legendary New York producer Arthur Baker, that inspired the group, Rob Gretton, and Tony Wilson to think 'Why hasn't Manchester got any clubs like this?' and then come home and build The Haçienda. Personally, I've always been obsessed with Studio 54 and its reputation for excess and debauchery, the impossibly glamourous clientele, and photographs that remain of it. I don't think I've ever seen any image of Studio 54 that didn't look incredible. Grace Jones – the first black supermodel – always looked amazing, iconic, pictured there – so you can imagine how excited I was when we booked her as one of the headliners of Parklife in 2015.

Grace was flying in from Australia for Parklife and her team sent a message to say that she was really under the weather. She was staying at The Lowry – the five-star hotel in central

Manchester favoured by most popstars and by Manchester United at that time.

I'd never watched Grace Jones live in concert before, and when you see her for the first time it really is something else. She ended up performing topless, apart from tribal make-up, and did an incredible seven-minute version of 'Slave to the Rhythm', while hula-hooping. It was an amazing set by anyone's standards, but for a nearly seventy-year-old with a fever it was staggering. When Grace finally walked off the main stage at the end, she literally collapsed in her dressing room. I don't think any other artist has ever given their all at Parklife like she did that night. She left it all out there on the stage.

I rarely ask artists for selfies, or to meet them, but Grace was such a living legend and I was so blown away by her performance I just wanted to say hello and thank you. Her manager said, she's exhausted so won't want to do any photos, but she'd like to invite you into her dressing room. When I walked into the dressing room she was only wearing men's boxer shorts and a white see-through T-shirt. On her rider, she had demanded vintage champagne, brandy, and very specific rare oysters and a particular kind of oyster knife. She suggested I sit down and have a glass of brandy, and I didn't have the nerve to tell her I never ever drank when I was working. I felt like a little boy, and just couldn't say no to Grace Jones, and I also thought it might calm my nerves a little. It's still the only time I've ever drunk at any of my events.

I've dealt with gangsters, having guns pulled on me – and death threats – but I don't think I've ever felt more intimidated than I did by Grace Jones in her dressing room that time. I've heard so many legendary and possibly apocryphal tales about her, and her fierce reputation preceded her. She stared at me really intensely, while cracking open her rock oysters and then slurping them, which in itself was pretty unnerving, while I just stumbled over my words and tried to think of something intelligent and interesting to say to her, the Grace Jones. We ended up having a nice chat and laughing about her infamous appearance on the Russell Harty show, when she attacked him because she thought he was turning his back on her.

The footballer Micah Richards was still playing for Manchester City at the time, and he came to Parklife that year, and was one of the first big Premier League players to come down to the festival. He is a really, really lovely guy, he's just everything that you want and expect Micah Richards to be. Larger than life, physically and personality wise, with that huge laugh. He did have some mates with him who were not as entertaining. In fact, one of them was a bit of a dick, who, when another mate of theirs went to use a Portaloo backstage, pushed over the Portaloo with his mate stuck inside. I've never understood why people think that is such a hilarious thing to do.

That year at Parklife, we also very nearly had a serious medical incident with poppers, or amyl nitrite, which are legal in the UK, and give people a short euphoric high when they sniff them. We sell them at Parklife, through individual vendors around the site. I was in Event Control when we got word that we had five very poorly customers within the space of half an hour. They had all individually necked a bottle of poppers, which is a really weird thing to do, but also very dangerous, and were being treated by medics. I thought everyone knew that you're supposed to just have a quick sniff of poppers, and certainly never drink them, but it turns out there was a young member of staff selling them that day who didn't know what they were. He obviously hadn't been listening properly when he was briefed, and thought they were energy shots. You can buy energy shots in garages and other places that look a little similar to poppers bottles. Anyway, obviously most of the people buying them off this young lad knew what they were, but a handful must have asked, 'What is it?' and when he told them they were energy shots, they'd bought some, and just downed them. That could have been very serious, but fortunately the medics were able to deal with it really quickly, and everyone affected was fine in the end.

That was also the year that Greater Manchester Police managed to have their buggy stolen, embarrassingly for them. We have dozens of buggies on site at Parklife, and they are all assigned to different departments or individuals who need them. GMP had their own buggy with 'GMP' on the front. At one stage, two police officers had gone to North Gate, the busiest entrance to the whole festival, to collect all the drug confiscations. When customers are searched on their way into the festival, any small amount of drugs found, which are obviously just for personal use, are confiscated. As we have 80,000 people on site, all those small confiscations can mount up, and over the weekend we probably confiscate drugs with a total street value of anywhere between £40,000 and £50,000.

That day, for some reason, having picked up the big bag of drug confiscations from the main entry gate, the police then parked their buggy outside the police command area, with the confiscated drugs just sitting on the back of the buggy, and nipped inside to grab some paperwork. When they came out, the buggy was gone, and so were the drugs. I was in Event Control with Gold Command, who are the head of police on the event, when these two shame-faced officers came in and had to confess that they had lost the police buggy and around £30,000 of confiscated drugs. Gold Command were not best pleased, to put it mildly. We had to put a call out on the site radio to all the production staff, asking if anyone had seen GMP's buggy.

What a lot of people don't realise is that the buggies we use at Parklife don't have unique keys, one key will work any buggy. It turns out that someone had taken one of the cleaner's buggies, so the cleaner had simply taken GMP's buggy, not realising that it belonged to the police. They'd gone off round the site blissfully unaware that they had £30,000 worth of drugs just sat on the back seat, which anyone could have grabbed. Fortunately, the cleaner was quickly tracked down, and the drugs were returned to the police, but I don't think those two police officers will be leaving their buggy unattended ever again.

LIVE NATION AND
THE PARKLIFE FOUNTAIN

In January 2016, I was in Rome for a short holiday with Kim after that year's Warehouse Project season. I always used to try and take a break to recharge my batteries at that time of year because The Warehouse Project was so draining, but the Rome trip that year didn't turn out to be very relaxing.

First, I woke up to the news on 10 January that David Bowie had died. I've always been a huge fan of his, and I thought the way he released his final album *Blackstar*, on his 69th birthday, two days before he died, was incredible; with all the hidden messages and meaning in the music, artwork, and videos. I particularly loved the cover artwork of Blackstar, which had a deconstructed star spelling out 'B.O.W.I.E.'[11]

The other thing that happened when I was in Rome was I got a call to say that Live Nation were interested in buying 50 per cent of Parklife and The Warehouse Project. We did a call with Live Nation on 22 January, and it all sounded really promising, so then myself, Sam, Rich, and Simon Moran went

---

[11] I even got a tattoo of it on the inside of my foot, which is still the only tattoo I've ever had.

down to London and met with Denis Desmond from Live Nation for lunch at the Pollen St Social Club. We got on really well, he clearly knew our business well, and knew what Live Nation could bring to the table. Denis suggested that we come up with a figure of what we wanted for 50 per cent of the business. Sam, Rich, and I bought some cans of gin and tonic from Marks & Spencer, got back on the train to Manchester and sat round a table on the train: we came up with a figure. It was a lifechanging amount of money and we had no idea what Live Nation would say in response; half of me thought they might have laughed at the figure. But they didn't. They came back within forty-eight hours and agreed on the figure, on condition the deal was completed within twenty-eight days. That was twenty-eight of the most stressful days of my life. There was no reason for the deal to not go ahead, but till it was finalised, I was nervous that for some reason it would all fall through. It was like the stress of buying a house, times a thousand. You know when you're stuck in limbo – you've had your offer accepted on a house that you really want, but then you're left in limbo for weeks or months waiting for the paperwork and the solicitors to pull their finger out. John Rennie, who owns quite a few bars in Manchester, had given me a jeroboam of vodka for Christmas, which is a huge three-litre bottle. That vodka helped me through those weeks.

With any deal there's always some last-minute things that need to be sorted. One of the issues was the 'S building' on Station Approach, above Store Street, that used to be owned by the NHS, had been turned into a hotel, and they were kicking off about the sound from The Warehouse Project. In the end we had to do a deal with them to book out the whole first four floors of the hotel for every night The Warehouse Project was on, which was eighty-four bloody rooms. They charged us £130 a room, which is nearly £11,000 each night, which is a big hit to take. Obviously, we needed some rooms for DJs and crew, but we didn't need anything like eighty-four rooms, and we ended up re-selling them to Warehouse Project punters where we could.

The other issue was Network Rail needed to put a huge new generator into the Store Street site, which was more or less in front of the main entrance. It didn't look great aesthetically, but the real issue is that it would reduce our capacity by 600, from 1,800 down to 1,200. This would basically mean The Warehouse Project wasn't financially viable, which would jeopardise its future and mean the whole deal with Live Nation was off. It was an incredibly stressful time, but thankfully our Health and Safety Officer Mike Atkinson, with the help of Kim, came to the rescue, not for the first or last time. Mike is a lovely bloke and has been our Health and Safety Officer since we launched The Warehouse Project back in 2006, another long-term member of The Warehouse Project family. Mike found a new fire company who managed to find some more space by restructuring the layout of The Warehouse Project. I'm not sure how he and they did it, but he undoubtedly saved The Warehouse Project, and the Live Nation deal.

On the day that the deal was to go through, all the shareholders came together at Pannone, our solicitors on Deansgate. Their offices are in the church at the end of Deansgate, opposite Atlas bar, which actually used to be recording studios owned by Pete Waterman. Everyone from Kylie Minogue to the Manchester United team have recorded in there. One of the Pannone's staff wheeled a trolley into the room with champagne on it, but I said, 'Nobody is touching a drop till the deal is completed.' It was supposed to go through in the afternoon, but it didn't actually go through till two hours before midnight.

By that stage, the feeling was almost extraordinary relief, rather than celebration.

We did receive some criticism for doing that deal, as I knew we would, with people accusing us of selling out or cashing in. I won't deny that I, and the other shareholders, did well out of the deal, but it wasn't just about us cashing in. It was also imperative we did that deal to give The Warehouse Project and Parklife financial security, and allowed us to build, and grow both businesses. As I've talked about, there were several times before we did that deal that we had come perilously close to losing The Warehouse Project.

The Live Nation deal gave us greater security. We had no idea that Covid was going to hit us when we did that deal, for instance, but if we hadn't gone into partnership with Live Nation, I honestly don't think The Warehouse Project and Parklife would have survived the pandemic.

Predictably, the first Parklife after we did a deal, there was an incident that meant the festival nearly didn't happen that year, which would not have been a great thing for us to have to tell Live Nation. Neither Manchester City Council nor North West Water had told us that there were two water main pipes running under Heaton Park that served over 200,000 homes, about half of North Manchester. Jon Drape and his production crew had a map with all the various drainage pipes and utilities marked on it, but these two water mains weren't on there. The week leading up to the festival, one of the Big Top contractors arrived to start erecting one of the huge Big Tops, drove a steel tent pin down into the ground, and fractured one of the Victorian cast iron pipes. There was a huge fountain of water. I have never seen anything like it. It was like the Bellagio Fountains, or the sort of comedy water fountain you see in a cartoon. Which is the last thing you want in the middle of your festival site, three days before opening. Jon Drape and the production crew were straight on it, and called out United Utilities, who were a bit useless at first. They kept sending more and more senior people, but all they seemed to do is look at this huge fountain of water and stroke their chin. One guy suggested they would have to get a collar custom-made to fit over the gap, and that could take ten days. *What are you talking about?* I thought, *Ten days? We've got a huge festival here in THREE days!*

Thankfully another guy arrived, who was more of a problem solver, and he just said to Jon, 'Have you got a digger? Let's have a look at what we're dealing with here.'

One of the production crew used a digger to expose the pipe and found out that the hole was actually only about 5 inches wide, but this huge fountain was coming out of it. This latest United Utilities guy, who was pretty no-nonsense, just said, 'Let's just try and plug it with a fence post.'

Which seemed a ridiculous idea, and no one thought it would work. But, against the odds, it did. They hammered a fence post into the hole and remarkably it stopped the fountain of water. The site crew quickly filled the earth back in over the top, and unbelievably it held. So, to this day, half of the people of North Manchester have got a fence post to thank for their supply of water. And we have a fence post to thank for not having to pull Parklife that year, which would have been a nightmare.

That Parklife was also the second year running that Greater Manchester Police had their buggy taken. Not by the cleaners this time, but by two punters from the festival. It went viral on social media, because the two guys stupidly posted pictures of them speeding round Heaton Park, outside the festival site, on it. Thankfully, GMP had not left the drugs amnesty bag on the buggy that time. The police eventually found the buggy abandoned in Prestwich. They've never had their buggy stolen since, but a few officers got a bit of a bollocking that year, and I imagine they make pretty sure they don't just leave it lying around unmanned nowadays.

THE ARENA BOMB AND THE MANCUNIAN RESPONSE

On Monday, 22 May 2017, I was at home having a chilled evening, when I started hearing reports on social media of an explosion at Manchester Arena – at that evening's Ariana Grande concert. My very first reaction was that maybe a speaker had blown or something, I didn't immediately presume it was something serious. The last thing I suspected was that it would be terrorist attack. Nobody did. As I've mentioned previously, when you're planning a huge gig or event you always have SAG (Safety Advisory Group) meetings with all the relevant authorities beforehand, to run through planning for various possible scenarios. The authorities want to make sure arrangements are in place for worse-case scenarios. But up till that horrific night at Manchester Arena, we had never been asked to have a specific plan for a terrorist attack. Sadly, such plans are now vital.

As the news rolled out that night, it quite quickly became apparent that what had happened at the arena was really serious. We later learned that as the concert ended and people started leaving, Islamic extremist Salman Abedi had detonated a nail bomb in his backpack in the arena foyer, killing twenty-two people and himself, injuring 1,017 others. It was the most serious act of terrorism and first suicide bombing in the country since the 7/7 bombings in London in July 2005. And though Manchester had already been victim to an IRA bombing in 1996 – the biggest bomb the IRA had ever exploded on the British mainland – that caused huge damage to the city centre, thankfully nobody had been killed in that attack.

There were so many shocking things about the incident. Obviously, the loss of so many innocent lives, and the severe injuries to many others, but also that Abedi seemed to have deliberately targeted young people and children having fun at a concert. That felt like a first in this country, and it made it all the more shocking. The fact that Abedi had grown up in Manchester and had gone to school here, quite possibly with some of those injured or connected to people who'd died in the attack.

What was absolutely incredible, and still astonishes me to this day, was the response to the arena attack from Manchester as a city. Completely united. Parklife was the first large scale event in Manchester's calendar after the arena attack – just under three weeks later. First thing on the morning of 23 May, when the arena attack was all over the international news, and Mancunians and the rest of the country were still reeling, I got a call from Greater Manchester Police. It was Ronnie Neilson, the Head of Licencing for GMP, and he told me he had been asked to ring Parklife on behalf of the council. 'This is a message from the top,' Ronnie told me. 'It's business as usual. We're not cancelling any events. We're not bowing down to terrorism.' It was an amazing response really, and just showed the determination of Manchester to stand proud and defiant in response.

In the following days, there were incredible scenes across the city, from the thousands of people at the vigils in Albert Square outside Manchester Town Hall, to the one in St Ann's Square, a week after the event, where after the minute's silence one woman started singing 'Don't Look Back in Anger' and the crowd joined in. Nobody living in Manchester will forget how the city came together after the tragic incident, and I know I've never witnessed anything like that in my fifty years of living in this city.

The music industry also put on a united front. Just two weeks after the bombing, Ariana Grande, Simon Moran (SJM Concerts), Melvin Benn (Live Nation), and the American music executive Scooter Braun put on a benefit concert called One Love Manchester at Old Trafford Cricket Ground. Ariana Grande, along with Simon, Melvin, and Scooter basically opened up their black books and called on everybody, from Justin Bieber to Pharrell Williams, Katy Perry and Miley Cyrus to Chris Martin and Liam Gallagher to Take That. I was at the One Love gig, and it was amazing. The atmosphere was incredible, and, I'll be honest, it's probably the most starstruck I've ever been. I was backstage in the dressing rooms, and *everyone* was there; Pharrell Williams even opened the door for me. But even though there were all these global icons present, there was one moment that stopped everyone in their tracks. The door opened and in walked Liam Gallagher, in this bright orange cagoule. Liam's got such a presence that all these other iconic music artists just stopped and stared.

The whole One Love Manchester concert was broadcast on BBC One and BBC radio, it was televised in thirty-eight countries around the world, and raised nearly £20 million for the British Red Cross.

As incredible as One Love was, it was very much a global response to the attack, and I decided we should have a more personal, *Mancunian* response, a week later, at Parklife.

Andy Burnham had only been appointed Mayor of Greater Manchester a few weeks previously, and I'd never met him, but I contacted his office and asked him to make a speech from the main stage at Parklife, and we also invited representatives from Manchester City Council. But most of all, I really wanted to invite representatives of the first responders, paramedics, police, and fire on stage, as they were the real heroes of the event. It was a hugely emotional moment.

The mood was understandably very nervy backstage on the morning of Parklife and in the days leading up to it. We turned up at that show half expecting something to happen. We'd had countless SAG meetings and other high-level meetings with the police and authorities to prepare. The police had put a large number of security measures in place that we knew of – including roadblocks and a ban on any drones – and we were told if anything was spotted flying about Heaton Park it would be shot down by the police. But there were a few extra security measures even we weren't told about. Such as none of us knew till the day that police marksmen were stationed in the trees around Heaton Park. Thankfully, the day went off without any incident, but it was without doubt the most nervous any of us have ever been before an event.

As if we hadn't had enough stress to deal with that weekend, there was then an incident with Frank Ocean's headline set. He's an incredible artist, and we were made up to have him headlining, but he's also pretty particular and specific about his stage show. He'd already cancelled his appearance at that year's Primavera festival in Barcelona, citing 'production delays beyond his control', and had done the same at another couple of shows, so we were nervous before he turned up, in case there was a repeat of that. Frank had asked for a specific stage, which we had to build for him, and also had a huge light show, using LED screens at the back of the stage. As most people know, huge LED screens are actually made up of lots of tiny screens and there was one tiny screen in the bottom left that wasn't working and Frank Ocean refused to go on till it was fixed. He was due to go on just before it was dark, but I think he wanted to find an excuse to not go on till it was dark because, remarkably, coincidentally, as soon as it got dark, the screen magically started working again. Funny that. He went on twenty-two minutes late, but since he was the headliner closing the whole festival, his management insisted he did his full set as Frank wasn't prepared to cut it short. This meant he would be finishing at 11.22, which meant we would be in breach of our licence and would get a huge fine. We had no option but to agree, though, and figure out how we would deal with it afterwards.

Ten minutes after Frank had gone on stage, and still wondering how we were going to resolve going over time, I was back in Event Control when we got word that the Metrolink was down. There had been an incident at Victoria Station: two homeless people had a fight and one of them had pushed the other one on to the tramline, which was horrible. Metrolink had been shut down while the incident was dealt with, and it was going to be at least twenty minutes before it was up and running again. I was stood with Jon Drape, the police and all the other authorities, all of whom were unaware of the other issue we had with Frank Ocean. 'Look,' I said, 'If the Metrolink isn't going to be running by the time the festival finishes, then we need to stay open for a little while longer, for safety reasons, otherwise we're going to have tens of thousands of kids starting to walk back to Manchester city centre, which is a health and safety nightmare.'

Egress is one of the most delicate parts of organising a festival, making sure that everyone gets off site safely, so there was truth in what I was saying, but there was also the ulterior motive of avoiding a penalty for breaching our licence. Fortunately, the authorities agreed, and allowed us to extend the licence by thirty minutes. Even so, it was a stressful end to what was probably the most draining and emotional Parklife we've ever had.

LIAM AND PARKALIFE

After being reminded of his incredible presence and how he stood out even among all the other stars at the One Love Manchester concert the previous summer, we booked Liam Gallagher to headline Parklife in 2018. It was his biggest ever solo hometown gig. Liam was having one of his regular rows with his brother Noel at the time and kept referring to him in interviews and on social media as a 'potato' and 'Mr Potato Head'. Noel had also just released a record which included a French female musician playing 'scissors', which Liam couldn't get his head around at all. When Noel then performed on *Later with Jools Holland*, with the French woman playing scissors, Liam found it hilarious. He put a tweet out asking fans to 'peel some spuds' at his next gig.

I decided to have a bit of fun with it and put out a press release saying that we'd had to ban potato peelers from Parklife after announcing Liam as the headliner. *Manchester Evening News* picked up on a story and ran with it, including a quote from me saying we'd been 'blown away at how many people have asked to bring in potato peelers for Liam's main stage performance'. 'Let's not forget', said the *Manchester*

Evening News article, in all seriousness, 'they're sharp implements which is not ideal in a crowded situation.' The MEN then quoted me on whether people could bring potato peelers to Parklife: 'In case you're wondering – the answer is most definitely no.'

Of course, not one person had asked to bring in a potato peeler, it was just a joke, but the *Evening News* were happy to run with it.

Liam joked with his fans online about the name of Parklife, as obviously Blur had a huge hit with a song of the same name back in the 1990s (although our festival is definitely *not* named after the Blur song!). Liam tweeted 'Rite up for this festival in Manchester … not sure about the name though', then followed that up by tweeting 'Stick an A in the middle of the K and the L and we're there PARKALIFE sounds better already', so we temporarily changed the name of the festival on our social media accounts to Parkalife. We normally have about three to five 'headliners' at Parklife, so people rarely buy a ticket to see one act, they're buying into the festival, but with Liam Gallagher, there was definitely a large contingent who had come to see him, and they weren't disappointed, he put on an incredible performance.

The other jokey news story at that year's Parklife was The Piccadilly Rats on the main stage. The Piccadilly Rats were a band of street buskers, who used to play in and around Piccadilly Gardens in Manchester and had become infamous for their appearance, and rough and ready cover versions. The drummer and bass player would wear rat masks when they were playing, which is how they got their name. In early February of 2018, the lead singer had tweeted me saying, 'Hi Sacha can you get us a five-minute slot on the main PARKLIFE 2018 stage we don't want paying! Just need a few butties and a bottle of dandelion and burdock for Tommy 😎👍🎸🐀🥔❤️🍺'. I then jokingly tweeted from the official Parklife account, saying: 'Thinking of getting these local legends involved this year what do we reckon?' with a video of them busking. I went downstairs to the toilet and by the time I came back it had already gone viral. After seeing that reaction, I thought, why not? I got in touch with The Rats and agreed to put them on first on the main stage. There was only about fifty people there to watch them when they performed at 1 p.m., and The Rats got absolutely hammered backstage. We found one of them comatose in one of the dressing rooms. The hilarious thing was, they were making a film about The Piccadilly Rats at the time, so they filmed their performance, but when I saw the finished film, they had cut their performance with shots of Liam Gallagher's audience for his headline slot, so it looked like 70,000 people were going crazy to The Piccadilly Rats!

Sadly, the following April, one of The Rats, seventy-seven-year-old Ray Boddington, died after he was hit by a tram near the Arndale centre. One of the other Rats got in touch with me after he died, to say that they couldn't afford a gravestone for him, and asking for my help, so I gave them £500 to pay for the headstone. The only thing was, they got back in touch the following week to say they needed an extra few hundred quid to pay for the engraving!

Like having Liam Gallagher to headline, when Sam and Rich booked Cardi B as the main act at Parklife the following year, we knew lots of the audience would have booked tickets specifically to see her, as she doesn't play that often in the UK. So, when she pulled out of a few of her other gigs the month before Parklife, we started to get nervous. The reason she gave for cancelling the gigs was because her breasts hadn't healed after having plastic surgery, which was a new one on me. She posted on Instagram, saying, 'You know I hate cancelling shows because I love money. I'm a money addict and I get paid a lot of money. A lot of money for these shows, like I'm cancelling millions of dollars in shows. But like health is wealth, so I have to do what I have to do ... My breasts gotta fucking heal and it is what it is.'

We were still being told she would make Parklife, but then in the end she pulled out just days before the event, which was a massive pain in the tits for us, as well as for her. It's really not a great look to lose your headliner on the week of the event, and we were really nervous about how the audience would react, but when the news went out there was a bit of a backlash, but it was more against her than towards Parklife. We rejigged the schedule and Rich persuaded Mark Ronson to DJ in the Cardi B slot. It was really good of Mark to agree to do that last minute, but it didn't really work well on the day, as only a small audience turned out for him, and Mark was really pissed off with us. He's really good friends with Rich, so Mark took most of his frustration out on him. They're still good friends to this day, but I'm not sure Mark has ever totally forgiven him for the Cardi B episode.

At that year's Parklife, we also had one of the most bizarre medical issues we've ever had. A young lad, who can't have been more than twenty, presented himself at the medics' tent within the first hour of the doors opening. He was really worried and came completely clean about what the issue was. He had put fifty ecstasy pills in a balloon and stuck them up his bum, in order to get past security on the gate. The problem was the balloon had gone too far up inside him, and he couldn't get it out. The medics were obviously really worried, because if the balloon had popped inside him then he would have died. The poor lad spent two hours bent over, with medics prodding gently further up his bum. They managed to get the balloon out in the end, but as soon as they did, the poor bugger (no pun intended) was arrested by the police for possession of drugs. We honestly think he wasn't an actual dealer; he was just the mule for his group of friends and carrying the drugs for them. It was a bum deal, in more ways than one, and he won't be doing that again in a hurry.

KING OF THE NORTH

After he appeared at Parklife in 2017, I kept in touch with Andy Burnham and his office, and Kevin Lee, who is the Director of the Mayor's Office, and Gareth Williams, in particular. I met with them a couple of times, and I think in retrospect they were trying to suss me out at first.

When it had been first announced that Greater Manchester would be getting a Mayor, I had followed all the candidates' campaigns, went to all the hustings and listened to their ideas. I also asked all of them if they would support the idea of something like a night-time economy taskforce. In my mind, I was imagining some sort of committee of people who represented that sector of society and industry. All of the candidates said they would support that idea, apart from Shneur Odze, the UKIP candidate. He was the only one that said he wasn't interested. But then he was a man who had quite particular and peculiar interests. He was quite an odd character, to put it mildly. He was friends with Nigel Farage and was a strictly Orthodox Jew who was married with four kids, and refused to shake hands with female political opponents on religious grounds. It was then later reported through social media and the press that he allegedly was pretty kinky on the side.

The reason I had come up with the idea of a night-time economy taskforce, was that over the previous decade or so, as Parklife and The Warehouse Project had grown and become bigger players in the night-time economy, I'd become increasingly pissed off that there was no unifying voice for us. By night-time economy I don't just mean nightclubs and bars, I mean restaurants, theatres, festivals, cinemas, and all of the wider entertainment industry. Then you also have the shift workers, and NHS and emergency services who work through the night. There didn't seem to be a voice for this huge sector. In Greater Manchester alone, that sector employs 494,000 people, nearly half a million people, which is nearly a fifth of the population, and they didn't seem to have a voice. Westminster just seemed so far out of touch with that whole sector of society, how they live their lives and what their concerns and worries are. Especially the incumbent Tory government (at the time of writing) who are so far out of touch with most working people's lives it's a joke. I've spent my whole adult life working in the night-time economy, so I know from bitter experience that decisions are continually made by those in power that are completely ill-informed about how the industry works and how people actually live their lives.

I was already part of the Night-Time Industries Association, and we had assembled our own Night-Time Commission, with members including BBC Radio 6 Music DJ, Mary Anne Hobbs, and Clint Boon, Inspiral Carpets keyboardist and DJ, to discuss and formulate policies that would make Manchester stronger and safer after dark; campaigning for a late-running Metrolink and other public transport services. London, Berlin, and Amsterdam already had a 'night czar' or similar role, and I thought Manchester really needed a similar champion to help it become a proper twenty-four-hour city.

After Andy Burnham became Mayor of Greater Manchester, and after he appeared on stage at Parklife, we continued these discussions for about six months. In the end, Andy asked me to take the chalice and become Manchester's first Night-Time Economy Advisor. Andy held a press conference and announced my appointment at the Clarence pub in Bury on 6 June 2018.

Burnham said: 'By appointing a Night-Time Economy Advisor and panel, I want us to build on our strong reputation to make it even better – for residents, visitors, and those who work in the sector. Sacha brings with him a wealth of experience. He's a real Greater Manchester success story and I'm thrilled that he's joining us as our first-ever Night-Time Economy Advisor.'

I got on like a house on fire with Andy immediately, and I have loved working closely with him over the past five years. In a time when we're saddled with the most out-of-touch government in living memory, Andy is a complete breath of fresh air. He's unbelievably passionate and hard-working, and his ideas and policies are based on solid foundations and are not grandstanding or the populism nonsense we see from Westminster at the moment. They are serious well thought through ideas that tackle the real issues that people face.

Not long after we had started working together, we went to do a talk with female students at Manchester University. As we came out, Andy and I walked back to the office together. On our walk, he stopped at one point and pointed across the road and said, 'Do you know the significance of that church?'

I didn't. 'I thought you were a Smiths fan?!' said Andy, 'That's the Holy Name church from 'Vicar in a Tutu'!'[12]

Andy has been brilliant for Greater Manchester. The three biggest things that he's done for Greater Manchester are – firstly, tackle rough sleeping. Secondly, take back public control of public transport, which has really resonated. Thirdly, apprenticeships – to stress that it's not just about going to university, and university doesn't suit everyone, so we need to have other routes in place.

Personally, he's also had a big effect on me. He's made me look at life slightly differently. Some of the things he's said to me have really stuck. I remember when he was talking to me about dealing with a particular tricky individual in government, and he said, 'Sacha, it's easier to work with people sometimes, if you want to get results.' That really stuck with me, as it's not always the approach I've taken in life, but he's absolutely right. Due to the difficult relationship with my dad, and then spending most of my career battling other promoters, a lot of my life has been spent in battle against other people, without probably realising it, and that's likely influenced my outlook and psyche. Working with Andy has helped me see that sometimes it's better to work with people than just battle against them the whole time. I'm at the stage of my life now where I thankfully don't have to worry about paying the leccy bill next week, whereas a lot of other people do, sadly. I hope

---

[12] The opening line of 'Vicar in a Tutu' is 'I was minding my business, lifting some lead off the roof of The Holy Name Church'. I had no idea it was that church, and Andy's knowledge impressed me.

that I've become a bit more relaxed and open in my views about things.

Andy has definitely been a huge influence in helping me to see life through a different lens, and I'd go as far as to say he's been as formative an influence as my old art teacher Mr McGinnis was, back in the day.

SPIKED, COVID, AND UNITED WE STREAM

In early March 2020, we had a few Warehouse Project shows in the Depot, including Michael Bibi. My wife, Demi, and I had been for dinner one night, and afterwards we thought we would swing by The Warehouse Project and see what was happening. I never usually hang out around the DJ booth when I'm working, but that particular night I got us a couple of drinks and we were stood by the DJ booth watching Bibi perform. I was drinking Grey Goose and lemonade, and we only stayed for a couple of drinks, but by the time I left I was staggering all over the place. The Lieutenant was there, working, and he had to put his arm around me and help Demi pour me into a taxi. I don't really remember anything about the taxi journey home, or anything really from when I left the venue till the following morning. When I woke up the next day, Demi looked really worried, and said to me, 'Do you remember what happened last night?' I had no idea. Demi went back through the night before with me. She said when I got home, I went upstairs and was projectile vomiting everywhere and then collapsed in the bathroom, landed on our glass bathroom scales and smashed them, and hit my head on the wall with such force that it went through the plasterboard. Demi had managed to get me to bed and clean everything up, but she was obviously really worried. We tried to piece together what had happened, because I hadn't had much to drink, and remembered I had put my drink down by the side of the booth, while we stood there, so we could only conclude it had been spiked. Over the next few days, I tried to carry on as normal, but whenever I lay down the room started to spin, so I went to Wythenshawe hospital and got checked out. They couldn't find anything wrong with me, and I have no idea if I was purposely spiked, or I'd just picked up a drink meant for someone else. If it wasn't meant for me, then maybe it was meant for one of the Warehouse punters, and although it was a horrific experience for me, I'd rather it was me than some poor unsuspecting female customer.

We haven't had a specific problem with people being spiked, but there was a bit of a flurry of national media stories about drink spiking a couple of years ago, not at The Warehouse Project, but just generally, and after that people were more vigilant about it. We were the first club in the UK to introduce the on-site spiking test, which looks a bit like a pregnancy test, and the medics can tell immediately whether you've been spiked or not, so we did test a lot of people, but never had anyone test positive for being spiked.

It was while I was at the hospital after being spiked, that I saw a Portacabin outside with a sign on it that said 'COVID TESTING'. I remember thinking, *That seems a bit over the top*. Little did I know what was about to hit us. But then it's pretty clear from what has come out since, that the Prime Minister didn't really have a clue about the magnitude of what was about to unfold, either. Two weeks later, he was forced to announce to the country that we had to go into lockdown.

Like every other business owner, I was completely in the dark about how this might pan out. We had no idea if lockdown was going to be for a couple of weeks, or a couple of months. No one had any idea at that point that lockdowns would continue on and off, for eighteen months and that the long tail effect of Covid, on people's health, the economy, and hundreds of thousands of businesses, would last for years. There was no direct guidance or contact from the government at all, either to me as a business owner, or as Night-Time Economy Advisor. Throughout that time, I got constant calls and emails from people and business owners who were desperate for more information, but I was just as much in the dark as everyone else. The first we heard of any coming lockdown or change to the tier system was when we read it in the press or on BBC News like everyone else. I was fielding constant calls from people who were desperate, whose businesses were going under, and there was nothing useful I could tell them.

The constant chopping and changing of guidance was an absolute joke. Matt Lucas, the comedian, summed it up with a bumbling impression of Johnson that went viral, saying, 'Go to work, don't got to work, don't use public transport, if you can use public transport, go to work …' In the end people didn't know if they were coming or going, or allowed to come and go, or what to believe. The pandemic was a first, none of us had experienced anything like that before in our lives, so I think much of the country initially had sympathy and patience for the government, because we knew it was a first for them, too, but their dreadful mishandling of it, soon erased all that goodwill.

In 2020, during the first summer of lockdown, there were two huge illegal raves in Manchester, one for 2,000 people and one for 6,000 people. The Mayor's office was concerned that more needed to be done to entertain people, to try and keep them in their houses and stick to the guidance, particularly young people. Andy Burnham rang me up and said, 'Sacha, I've been thinking about this. You're the promoter, can you find a way to entertain everybody? To try and keep them occupied and in their houses? Just put your thinking cap on.'

I started to investigate and found that in Berlin they were already streaming techno sets from a closed nightclub and calling it United We Stream. You could watch it for free, but you could also donate a few Euros if you wanted. It was the bones of a good idea, so I thought we could do something similar, but we'd do it on steroids. I rang Andy Burnham back and said, 'Andy, this is what we're going to do, an online stream called United We Stream, and we'll take charity donations. I need your backing on this, and your help to find a venue, and to allow artists to be allowed to travel there so they can be part of it.' I'm pretty convinced Andy didn't understand what I was talking about, and in fact he later openly admitted he didn't know what I meant, but he agreed to help. He arranged for us to use The Met theatre in Bury, they gave us the keys, and everything was filmed and streamed from there. Andy's office gave me a letter for all the artists involved in the filming for the stream, so that they could prove to the police that they were allowed to travel, in case they got pulled over by them. I knew we'd put something really good together, but I had no idea how it was going to go, because I'd never done anything like that before. My whole career has been about getting people out of the house and into a nightclub, not encouraging them to stay at home. But the response was mental.

In the end we did ten weeks of streamed shows, and had twenty million viewers in total, raising £612,000, which was distributed to freelancers and local charities across Greater Manchester. The biggest show we did was the all-day Haçienda party in the second week, which was really special. The stream went down when it started, at 2 p.m., because so many people were trying to watch it, which was a bit hairy, and I had Andy Burnham on the phone asking what was happening, but we got it back up quickly, and it was a huge hit. I was getting sent videos of neighbours dancing next to each other in their gardens and messages from everyone from Angela Rayner, 'This is amazing!' to Gary Lineker, 'This is unbelievable!' As the day went on, and I had a few drinks, my ego got the better of me, and I put my 'I love Manchester' T-shirt on and put some clips out on social media asking people to donate money, as if I was some acid-house Bob Geldof or something! Demi had to rein me in a bit.

I'm still immensely proud of not only what we pulled off, but how much the money raised helped freelancers and artists who really needed it. Neither London nor any other city in the country did anything like that to support their artists. The Mayor's office took all the requests for support, and they distributed all the money. I didn't have any part of that, and everything was confidential, but I do know there were some well-known names who received support. It all hit home just how bad the pandemic had hit our sector.

As the months went on, it was clear there was something very wrong going on with the handling of the pandemic. I felt the hospitality industry and the night-time economy were really hung out to dry by the government. They didn't receive the support that other sectors did and were particularly messed about by the chopping and changing of the rules when it came to tiers, and absolutely ridiculous things like the 'Scotch egg rule', which said you could only have a drink if it was accompanied by a substantial meal. After me and my team asked the government to disclose their Equality Impact Assessment Report to us, they asked me to sign a non-disclosure agreement. After this I accused them on social media of 'employing a bullying tactic to try to delay our case'. I thought the Scotch egg rule was particularly discriminatory as the majority of 'wet-led' pubs (ones that don't offer food) were in lower income areas, which meant people in Altrincham and Didsbury could go for a pint in their local upmarket gastro pub, but people in more deprived areas couldn't go to their local as it wasn't allowed to open because it didn't serve food. I felt so strongly about it that I ended up taking Matt Hancock in his capacity as Health Secretary to court, over the 10 p.m. closing rule and the Scotch egg rule. I personally brought the court case forward, and paid for it myself, but Andy Burnham's office were right behind me. In the end the government dropped the 'substantial meal' policy, but I didn't see it as me winning, I absolutely saw it, as I said at the time, as a 'landmark victory for the hospitality industry', which had endured some of the toughest restrictions of any sector since the beginning of the pandemic. I've got the court papers from 'Sacha Lord vs Matt Hancock' framed in my downstairs loo, and it gives me a little smile every time I go to take a piss.

Three years on, during the Covid enquiry in December 2023, Andy Burnham was called to give evidence and he made it abundantly clear that the government minutes showed that Tier 3 was imposed on Manchester as a 'punishment beating' for his defiance. He referred to a minute from the government's Covid-O committee, which was responsible for Covid operational matters, that said, 'Lancashire should have a lighter set of measures imposed than Greater Manchester since they had shown a greater willingness to co-operate. Tougher measures should be imposed on Greater Manchester that day'.

As Andy told the committee: 'Because we stood up for people in our city region who would otherwise have really struggled had they gone into that lockdown without the funds to help them, because we took that stand they decided to make an example of us. It's unbelievable for me now to look at evidence saying they knew it didn't work, they knew Tier 3 didn't work. They knew that, but they were still going to impose it on us without enough financial support.'

It was absolutely shocking, and I said so at the time. As Night-Time Economy Advisor, I thought I should stand up for the sector. I've done a huge amount of press, organised by my brilliant publicist Nina Sawetz. Andy and I were out one night in Manchester and bumped into Nihal Arthanayake, the great presenter from BBC Radio 5 Live, who is a regular at The Warehouse Project, and Nihal was joking that Andy and I were 'like The Kray Twins' the way we stood up to the government during that time. I'm fully aware that you're going to get online abuse once you stick your head above the parapet on an issue like that, but I didn't expect to get physically attacked for being outspoken. Demi and I were out one night in a place called One Central in Altrincham. It's a place that opened during the pandemic, it was outdoors with lots of good street-food traders, and DJs. Morrissey's nephews Alex and Jay, who I know, used to DJ there, so Demi and I used to pop down with Pickle, our dog, quite often. This one evening, Demi and I were sat down at a picnic bench, and I went off to the toilet. When I came back there were two blokes sat on the bench with her, but I didn't think much of it, as it's the sort of place where people share benches. I sat down and was just chatting with Demi, when a couple of minutes later, one of those lads suddenly stood up behind me and he just started raining punches down on the top of my head. I couldn't move away easily, as my legs were trapped in a bit by the bench legs, so all I could do was just put my hands up to protect my head.

It's the first time I've been randomly attacked like that, and it does shake you up. I didn't leave the house much for a couple of weeks. In the end, Andy Burnham was having some drinks at Freight Island to thank everyone who helped him in his leadership campaign, and he rang me up and said, 'Look, Sacha, I think you should come down, it will do you good to get out.' But even then, at an event like that, in a place owned by my friends, I still felt wary when I went to the toilet, I was thinking, *I could get jumped again here.*

I'm fine now, but it took me a while to get over it. If you're campaigning for something nowadays, you've got to accept you're going to get some abuse online, that comes with the territory, but there's no excuse for physically attacking someone.

When I later saw the CCTV of me being attacked, I couldn't believe Demi's reaction. She was sat opposite me, holding our dog Pickle under her arm, but as soon as this guy started raining down punches on my head, Demi launched herself over the table, and punched this guy full-on in the face, while still holding Pickle under her other arm. She absolutely flew at this guy. I've never seen her look more Scottish!

I first met Demi in 2017, in the gym in Hale Country Club. We starting seeing each other and she started staying over at my house on the weekends, and then you know how it happens. The toothbrush appears in the bathroom, and then it's 'Is it alright if I put some of my stuff in this cabinet?' We've now been together for seven years, and got married in April 2022 in a beautiful place in Capri, Italy. If you've never been to Capri, I can't recommend it highly enough. Get to Naples and then it's a forty-minute ferry from there. As soon as you set foot off the ferry it's like they've pressed pause on Italy in a glorious 1970s summer.

The wedding itself was held on a cliff edge (no symbolism intended!) and our wedding car was a tiny 1960s Fiat, which looked stunning, but it was a bit of a squeeze in the back for Demi and me!

Manchester Evening News ran a story on our wedding and predictably some guy commented underneath, slagging me off: 'You're supposed to be supporting Manchester's hospitality trade! You should be getting married here, not supporting Capri's hospitality trade!' I'm never going to reply to any online comments like that, but I was pleased to see someone else respond to him, saying, 'It's his wedding day FFS, give the guy a break!'

Demi is an incredible woman. She has been my rock over the last seven years – she gets me. We recently launched the Sacha Lord Foundation, which aims to support kids like me, who are a little bit lost after leaving school, and not sure what they want to do, to get into the entertainment and hospitality industry. Demi is going to head up the foundation. I know I can rely on her, and she also absolutely keeps me completely grounded. There's no danger of me getting above myself on Demi's watch. When I was invited on *Question Time* in January 2020 it was a big moment for me, so I recorded it so I could watch it back. A few weeks later, I went to rewatch it and Demi had recorded over it with *At Home with the Kardashians*! I was like, 'What the fuck, Demi?' She couldn't understand why I was so bothered: 'You've already watched it about seven times for fuck's sake!' That was me told.

One other example of how she keeps my feet on the ground: after Parklife in 2023, I was driving home in the early hours of the morning and I was absolutely done in. Not only is it a really long day, it's also difficult to describe the pressure of being ultimately responsible for the welfare of over 120,000 young people across two days, which doesn't really let up until you know that they are all off site and have got home safely.

I was driving home, absolutely exhausted, when Demi texted me: 'Are you on your way home yet?'

'Yes,' I replied, 'I'm shattered.'

'It's bin day tomorrow,' she replied, 'Can you make sure you put the bins out when you get home.'

NOW

THE DEPOT, HOMOBLOC, AND FUTURE DESTINATIONS

The Warehouse Project is now eighteen years old, so if you were born on the day we first opened its doors, then this coming season you will be legally old enough to come in. That blows my mind. Time moves fast on the dancefloor.

In 2018, we left Store Street for the final time, and moved to Depot Mayfield, a huge 10,000-capacity venue in a historic former railway station, only two minutes' walk from Store Street. We had tried to move to Mayfield previously, when we were having our *annus horriblis* at Victoria Warehouse, but it didn't work out.

The first sign we got that we may be be able to reignite the idea was when Manchester International Festival (MIF) used Mayfield for a couple of shows. They asked us to help run a couple of shows with them, including a ground-breaking collaboration between Massive Attack, the documentary maker Adam Curtis, United Visual Artists, Punchdrunk, and Es Devlin in 2013, and then some shows that Mary Anne Hobbs curated in 2017. As we were working with MIF, I asked them if they thought there was an opportunity to do more shows in the space, and they thought there was.

The site was run by a combination of Manchester City Council, Transport for Greater Manchester, and a developer called Richard Upton. Shortly after that conversation, Broadwick Venues, who also run The Printworks, and Drumsheds in London, took over Mayfield. We already had a working relationship with Broadwick, not least as Jon Drape is one of its directors – as is Gareth Cooper, one of the shareholders of Parklife – so we managed to do a deal with them to move The Warehouse Project to the Depot.

There was a lot of nervousness about moving away from Store Street again, because it really is The Warehouse Project's spiritual home, and the last time we had left Store Street precipitated the worst two years of my life. But after we had been back there three years, it had got to the stage where we really had refined the experience as much as possible, and there was nothing left we could do. We were bursting at the seams, and had outgrown the place, so the time had come to reluctantly close the door on that chapter of The Warehouse Project.

We were still nervous about the move, though. Either it was going to work, or it wasn't. If not, that would be the end of The Warehouse Project. We knew there would be a backlash from a minority that we had gone too big, but there is always a backlash from a minority when you make a change, and to be honest, if what you really want is a sweaty basement for 200 people then you are probably not going to come to The Warehouse Project anyway. The Warehouse Project is a coming together of tribes, and it's all about the communal, collective experience, it's not a niche basement rave.

Moving to Mayfield allowed us to collaborate more, so The Warehouse Project <u>now didn't</u> curate every single night, we also collaborated with other people on nights like Homobloc and XXL.

The opening night of the Depot, Sam and Rich booked Aphex Twin – the pioneer of experimental techno – to headline, which was a bit of a statement: we might be moving to a much bigger space, but The Warehouse Project would still be booking the most credible and challenging artists in electronic music. Aphex Twin brought his own VJ with him to do his show, and there was one point halfway through the show where the screens started showing a succession of famous Mancunian faces, from Johnny Marr to Eric Cantona to Frank Sidebottom, and then, slap bang in this procession of heads, the face of Fred Talbot – the weatherman, who a couple of years previously had been disgraced – flashed up. I never found out if that was some weird bad-taste joke on Aphex Twin's behalf, or a mistake, but thankfully not many other people seemed to notice it.

Everything had to be scaled up when we moved to the Depot. Not just the production and the staff. When you start dealing with 10,000 people each night then you need to start thinking about counterterrorism measures, putting in place concrete blocks to stop any vehicle attacks and things like that. Everything moves to the next level. The security at The Warehouse Project is now as robust as any venue in Europe, but we also try and streamline it as much as possible for the customer. Along with the usual security staff, we have eight knife arches (metal detectors) and sniffer dogs, but also paramedics on the front door, keeping an eye out for anyone who might not be feeling too well. Once you're inside we have twelve 'roaming angels', who walk around the venue all night checking on people and making sure they're OK. If they do find someone who looks a bit the worse for wear, they will take them to welfare and maybe just give them a cup of tea, biscuits, and a chat, if that's all they need. But of course, the medics are always there if they need them. I don't think any other venue in the UK goes as far as we do when it comes to looking after customers.

We have that many staff now that there's also a security operation for them. There are sniffer dogs and searches on the staff entrance – even I get searched when I come in each night – there's no exceptions. Because it's now a bigger operation, we've been targeted by organised criminal gangs. One of the most brazen was the time when Kim caught a guy working behind our bar with his own PDQ (card payment) machine. Most customers pay by card now, and this guy had got a job working on the bar and bought his own card machine in, so when he served a customer drinks, he just presented his own card machine to them instead of ours. By the time we clocked it and stopped him, he had already done £11,000 on the one card machine in a week!

The Warehouse Project has a much wider catchment area now. Of the 10,000 people partying each evening, it's probably 50 per cent Mancunians, 20 per cent from across the North, and then the last 30 per cent national and international ravers. On some nights like Homobloc, people come from all over Europe.

Homobloc, run by Luke Una, is now one of the key shows of The Warehouse Project season. I first met Luke Unabomber over twenty years ago, when he was running the club night The Electric Chair with his partner, Justin Unabomber, and was one of the Cord crew, that cool Northern Quarter crowd that I wasn't part of, but I always got on well with him. He's a brilliant force of nature; one of the most gregarious characters in the nocturnal underbelly of Manchester.

When we used to book him to DJ at Sankeys, twenty years ago, he would turn up with a shopping trolley with his boxes of records, and the bouncers would have to help him in with them. He would wheel the shopping trolley all the way to Sankeys from his flat in the Northern Quarter!

Luke had curated a night with us at the first Warehouse Project at Boddingtons, and we'd always been talking about doing something bigger. We had various meetings about doing an Electric Chair festival over the years, but it never happened.

During Covid, Luke became an Instagram celebrity with his off-the-wall posts. He DJed for us for United We Stream during the pandemic, and I remember him turning up at an empty Bury Met theatre and he had this little puppet with him, and he put his puppet in the front seat of the auditorium to watch him DJ. It was off camera, so it wasn't for anyone else's benefit, just for his own benefit, so he could DJ to this puppet. When we moved to the Depot, Luke came to us with the idea for Homobloc. He'd been running Homoelectric for twenty years, but it was normally for just a few hundred people not 10,000, so it was a huge step up. But we really thought there was a market there for a huge LGBTQ+ warehouse party. Nobody had done anything remotely like it before, but we really thought there was an opportunity to do something special. Luke says that the night before tickets went on sale, he thought, *What have I done? 10,000 people? As if!* Even people on the LGBTQ+ scene were saying to Luke, 'You're off your head, you're never gonna get 10,000 people!'

But Luke had been banging on about this idea he had for a promo for Homobloc with this drag queen called Cheddar Gorgeous, and the first time I saw the finished promo clip I knew the event was going to smash it. The first Homobloc sold out within twenty-four hours, but we still didn't know what sort of crowd to expect. Luke remembers that, 'Seconds before we opened, I felt like Eddie the Eagle going down the ski slope – you're going into the unknown but it's too late to go back. I had no idea if the crowd would work, or if we'd get some knobheads ruining it for everyone. But the first three people through the door were this amazing older dude who looked like Gandalf, his daughter and her friend who was trans. As soon as they walked in, I knew it was going to be great.'

Homobloc doesn't really feel like any other Warehouse Project night, and we left Luke and his team to get on with the creative side of it to keep it that way. It's Luke's night really, his vision, and WHP provide the support to make it happen. The attention to detail that goes into trying to encompass everybody from that scene is phenomenal. We even brought specialists in to train security and bar staff, just for that one night, on how to address people, to make sure no one was offended. I thought it would be a good idea if all the bouncers on the front door wore glitter face paint, and they were surprisingly up for it! It reminded me of when Bowie persuaded his band The Spiders from Mars to wear glam make-up, although our lot were more like The Bouncers from Wigan, all saying, 'Ey up, pass us t'glitter, you daft bugger.' Kim also got all her bar staff to wear glitter face paint.

There are about 200 performers each year at Homobloc, not just the artists and DJs, but a whole host of other perfor-mance artists who make Homobloc unique. There's a huge backstage area for them all, and at the first Homobloc I wandered through it and people were walking around naked with their various bits hanging out. I've seen a few things in my time, especially at Paradise Factory back in the day, but it was still a bit of an eye opener. Homobloc is wilder than other

Warehouse nights. If you've never been to anything like it before, it is pretty debauched, all the staff are given a heads up, as there might be an eighteen-year-old student working on the bar who comes from a tiny village in Wales and has lived a bit of a sheltered life. It does get pretty wild. I didn't witness this happen, but I did see a tweet the morning after Homobloc last year, where one of the artists talked about achieving 'lifetime goals' when they rimmed their best mate *on stage*.

You don't get that at a Coldplay gig.

THE RETURN AND FUTURE OF PARKLIFE

The pandemic meant that we were forced to cancel Parklife in 2020. We returned in 2021 but had to push the date back to later that year, due to Covid restrictions. When we confirmed the date, Saturday, 11 September, we were a little unsure about the move to late summer, but what no one could have predicted was that it would clash with Ronaldo's second debut for Manchester United! Rod Stewart was also performing at the Etihad stadium the same day, so town was absolutely heaving.

The whole of Manchester was even more rammed than usual. Luke remembers walking out of Piccadilly station, and it was the busiest he'd ever seen it. Thousands of people pouring out of the station, United fans singing 'Viva Ronaldo' and kids dressed for Parklife.

Because it was the second year of Covid, we had to make a lot of changes on site, including taking the roof off the Hanger, so it was open air. We also bought 25,000 Covid tests for punters to use, although we ended up using hardly any of them, so we donated all the leftover ones to the NHS.

Ronaldo scored twice for United that day. He didn't come down to Parklife afterwards to celebrate, but then he's never been much of a party animal, he's more of a machine, and he rarely drinks. A few of his teammates came down, though. Marcus Rashford came with Jesse Lingard (who had also scored that day); Darren Fletcher was also there with his family, who were lovely, and Paul Pogba arrived separately. Pogba is good mates with the Nigerian rapper Burna Boy who'd watched him at Old Trafford that afternoon, so Burna Boy returned the favour and invited Pogba to Parklife. Wearing a United shirt, with Pogba's name on the back, Burna Boy got Pogba up on stage with him, and the crowd went absolutely mental. Pogba obviously loved being on stage, as being up there once with Burna Boy wasn't enough: he also later jumped up on stage with D-Block Europe, too. Burna Boy's management hadn't told us he was going to the United game, otherwise we would have been a bit nervous about him making it across town to Parklife in time for his stage appearance. I still don't quite know how they managed it.

Pogba had arrived in a black Mercedes-Benz Viano, with an official Man United driver, and he left before the roads closed for egress. Nowadays, the police shut all the roads around Heaton Park at 9.30 p.m. and they don't open again till 12.30 a.m. It's to make egress as safe and painless as possible, so we can get everyone off site safely. Pogba might have got the memo, but Rashford and Lingard unfortunately didn't, or they forgot. I'm normally the first out when the police reopen the roads, and as I was sat in my car waiting, Rashford and Lingard were sat in Rashford's car next to me. I thought to myself, *There's no way if Alex Ferguson was still in charge at United, he would want his footballers out past midnight at a festival, a couple of days before a Champions League game.*

That thought came back to haunt me when I was watching United away at Young Boys in the Champions League two days later. In the last minute of added time, Lingard misplaced a back pass and Siebatcheau reacted quickest to slot home a winner and cause euphoria in the Swiss capital. My first thought was, *Fucking hell, if the manager knew he was at Parklife till the early hours of Monday morning, he'd do his nut.* I felt like it was my fault!

Mind you, when United players want to come down to Parklife they normally get Mary-Jane Dalton, who was Richard Arnold's executive assistant, to ring up and arrange it for them, so the manager would probably go even more mental if he knew it was someone in the club getting them on the guest list.

That same year of Parklife, there was talk of Drake turning up as a special guest. Drake had been at Wireless festival in London the night before, and rumoured to be coming to Parklife, which would have been incredible. We'd heard the rumour, like everyone else, but hadn't had any contact from Drake's people, although that didn't necessarily mean it wasn't going to happen last minute, so we were half expecting the call.

Early evening, I was walking backstage and saw a fleet of black Rolls Royces arrive through the artist gate, and my first thought was, *Ah, so Drake has turned up*, which was going to be a huge moment for Parklife. But it wasn't Drake, it was the Kamani family, the family behind BooHoo. I've no idea how they managed to get their Rolls Royces back stage, but I can only assume they rocked up at the artist entrance and the security on the gate thought, *Well it must be someone special, even if they don't have the right vehicle access passes, because they're in a fleet of five black Rolls Royces.*

We later heard that after he had appeared at Wireless, Drake had a party back at the Rosewood Hotel, a lovely luxury hotel where I sometimes stay. Some gangs turned up and tried to infiltrate the party, and when they weren't allowed in, they shot at the hotel windows. I don't think that ever came out or was reported in the media, but apparently Drake just thought, 'Fuck this' and went back to America, so he never made it to Parklife.

Parklife can't get any bigger at Heaton Park. It's now 80,000 capacity and we get over 200,000 people registering for tickets, but there really is no more space to use. It takes over 1,000 people to build the festival site, with the first person starting work three weeks before the show, and the last person leaving two weeks after the show.[13]

Even by Parklife standards, 2023 was a bit of a crazy year. Sometimes it happens like that, it will have been all smooth in the lead up to the festival and then it goes crazy. We had Aitch headlining, which we knew was going to be massive, alongside The 1975, another local act. Just after we announced Aitch, he appeared at The Brit awards and (along with his story about fence jumping the festival when he was younger)

---

[13] Parklife also has 1,200 security staff and stewards, 1,000 bar staff and 200 police. There is 5 miles of perimeter fence, 1,000 toilets and over two acres of marquees. Over the weekend the food concessions serve 10,800 pizzas, 3,100 burritos, 3,600 gyros and 31,000 portions of chips. Over 300 kilos of leftover food is donated to the food charity Open Kitchen MCR after the show.

he said some really nice things about being asked to headline Parklife, describing it as a 'real, genuine bucket list kind of thing'.

Other headliners on the stages included Fred again, Fisher, the Prodigy, Mercury Prize-winner Little Simz, Self Esteem, Raye, The Wu Tang Clan, and Nas.

In the week leading up to Parklife 2023, Angela Rayner, Deputy Leader of the Opposition, who I get on with really well, messaged me to say she wanted to come down with her son, so I said yes, of course. Angela said, 'Fisher is playing. I *love* Fisher, is there any chance we can meet him?' I said 'Yes of course, I can arrange that.' I arranged to meet Angela at half past eight on Sunday evening in the backstage hospitality area, and I then drove her over to the Artist Village on the other side of the site to meet Fisher. When we got there, Fisher was FaceTiming Jack Grealish, who was in the middle of his lost forty-eight hours partying after Man City won the European Cup. Grealish and Fisher were mates and Grealish was asking Fisher if he could come down to Parklife when their plane landed back in Liverpool. Obviously, I said yes, but then when the City plane landed in Liverpool, the players – including Grealish, Kyle Walker, Foden, and a couple of others – clocked a private jet sat on the tarmac, and they were like, 'Shall we just hire that and go to Ibiza?' Apparently, City had hired out a Chinese restaurant in Manchester City centre and only three players turned up because all the rest had flew off to Ibiza.

Jack Grealish didn't make it down to Parklife, unsurprisingly. I've met some real party animals in my life and anyone reading this book will know people who can go out and party really hard. But Jack Grealish has to be up there. It's quite refreshing in this day and age to have a footballer who has a bit of personality and likes to party, as most of them are really square. Jack might not have made it to Parklife, but he has become a bit of a regular at The Warehouse Project. He always turns up in a bucket hat to try and avoid getting mobbed, but then hangs at the stage where the crowd can see him anyway. He's also danced on stage with Fisher.

Angela Rayner asked me to take a picture of her with Fisher, and then she sent it to ex-New Zealand Prime Minister Jacinda Ardern, who was clearly a Fisher fan, too. Angela and Fisher obviously got on, because as he closed the Hangar stage, she was dancing on stage and he shouted on the mic to the audience, 'This is the future Prime Minister!' It was a pretty bonkers Parklife moment and at that stage I thought I'd better leave them to it.

A couple of weeks later, Angela Rayner was on holiday out in Ibiza, and I had got her on the guest list for CamelPhat and Fisher, and the *Daily Mail* did a piece on her partying in Ibiza, although they only got the information from her Instagram account.

Parklife is at capacity, but we could still add an extra date on the Friday, like when we did New Order or The Courteeners. But a decade after we first looked at moving Parklife to Wythenshawe Park, we finally started to do shows there, after managing to work around the covenant. We're now hoping to do three large shows there every August bank holiday. The first one we did, in 2023, was with Noel Gallagher, which was great. In 2024, the two headliners will be New Order and Blossoms. The New Order show will be their second biggest Manchester gig ever, after the Heaton Park gig we did in 2021, which means we have promoted the band's two biggest ever Manchester gigs.

Andy Burnham came down to the Noel Gallagher gig. I introduced him to Noel backstage and they had a big old chat, and it turns out they've got a family connection: a cousin of Andy's does Noel's PR. Noel then dedicated a song to Burnham during his set, but he mustn't have been reading his setlist properly, and fucked it up. 'Dedicating this to Andy Burnham' he declared, and then played 'The Importance of Being Idle'. Everyone was like 'WTF?' 'Got the songs in the wrong order,' Noel apologised after the song 'didn't mean to say he was a lazy cunt. It was supposed to be this one,' and then he played 'Masterplan'.

The Warehouse Project is now settled at Depot, but it will still keep moving forward. In 2023, we did our first overseas Warehouse Project seasons, in Rotterdam and Antwerp. For years, we've had countless offers to take it to other venues, including different festivals, but it's never felt true to The Warehouse Project. It wouldn't feel right to just curate a tent at a festival and slap 'The Warehouse Project' name on it, when it needs to be in a bricks and mortar space, ideally a warehouse.

The first text I got when we announced The Warehouse Project Rotterdam was from Mike Pickering, the first DJ I'd ever seen at The Haçienda, three decades previously. 'Genius' he said, 'Brilliant to not go with the obvious choice of Amsterdam. Rotterdam is amazing.' I'd forgotten that Mike had lived in Rotterdam at the start of the 1980s, before he came back home to launch The Haçienda. The spaces in Rotterdam and Antwerp are similar to the Depot, huge industrial spaces but with a smaller capacity of 4,000, and we work in collaboration with local promoters out there. It's always tricky to gauge how many people actually get The Warehouse Project outside of the UK, but Rotterdam and Antwerp have shown that they really do, and that there is a huge appetite for it.

Otherwise, we spent quite a lot of time and effort looking at venues in New York, but never found exactly the right space. London is always on the radar. The fact that WHP hasn't done London or New York yet, proves how difficult it is to find the perfect venue, and that Manchester is The Warehouse Project's natural home.

I might have stepped back, but I have no doubt that the future is bright for The Warehouse Project, as it keeps pushing boundaries and pushing forward. In ten years' time, it could be in twenty cities across Europe. And not just restricted to Europe. It could well be in the US, Australia and further afield.

But one thing's for sure, it was Manchester that made The Warehouse Project. At times I've questioned myself and the decisions we've made over the years, but one thing has never been in question. Manchester is in The Warehouse Project's DNA, and its home will always be in Manchester.

This couldn't have happened anywhere else.

EPILOGUE

AFTER THE PARTY?

There's been two huge changes in my life since this book first appeared. The first is I have become a dad for the first time, the second is I have left the Warehouse Project and Parklife.

My son Lowen was born on 28 October 2024. I think I made it clear in the early chapters of this book that my dad was far from a great father figure. So, I did have a slight concern when I found out I was going to become a father myself. Would my dad's behaviour shape the sort of dad I would be? Demi worried a bit too, since I'd told her enough horror stories about my dad. But hopefully the fact that, unlike him, I'm not a womaniser, gambler or alcoholic, puts me in good stead.

We found out Demi was pregnant when we were having a posh weekend in London at Claridge's. We had an inkling but we were booked in for dinner at The Clove Club in Shoreditch that evening, so we decided not to do a test until the morning. The Clove Club has two Michelin stars so I presumed it would be a suited and booted affair, but when we turned up I was massively over dressed and felt like a schoolteacher or estate agent. Neither of us slept well that night and we ended up getting up at half five to do the test. Positive. We were both stunned and we just lay in bed until a reasonable hour to phone our mums and tell them the news. I have a double espresso every day for breakfast, and it must have been super strong that morning because with the combination of the baby news and the coffee I was bouncing off the walls. I actually had to go and have a run round Hyde Park to try and calm myself down.

Demi came up with the name Lowen. We both liked the name Rowan for a girl, and Demi just played around with it. Apparently it's Cornish for joy or happy, which is nice. Granted, the only Cornish connection I have is that I quite like pasties but the alliteration worked – plus my favourite Bowie album is *Low* and Morrissey made an album in 2017 called *Low In High School*.

That weekend happened to be the exact moment I was also finalising the sale of my shares in WHP and Parklife to Live Nation. The deal was first agreed three years ago, but we still needed to finalise the agreement. At the end of March 2024, we were on the way back from a visit to Dunfermline to see Demi's family when I got a call to say that Live Nation wanted to complete that day. By the time I'd driven home from Tebay Services, the deal was done and the money was in my account.

I opened a bottle of good champagne I had been saving for the occasion, but to be honest it took me a while to get my head around the fact that I was leaving the WHP and Parklife, even though it had been planned for three years. You can't just switch off. I actually own the building that the WHP office is based in and for the first few weeks I was still going into my office every day, and working on my Night Time Economy Advisor role, for Andy Burnham. It was almost like muscle memory, getting up and driving into town every day, just as I had done for the previous sixteen years. Then one day I had a moment of clarity and thought, 'What am I doing?' and since then I've worked from my home office.

My other focus in spring 2024 was the launch of this book. I was (and am) really proud of it. I felt I had something to prove after only getting a 'U' in English Literature all those years ago at school, so I wanted to make sure the book got the attention I felt it deserved and threw everything at it. I'm a promoter, that's what I've done all my life, and so I promoted the hell out of the book. I used all my contacts to get posters and electronic billboards up all around Manchester and I even had cupcakes made with the book cover on and distributed them to key bookshops around Manchester.

When I finally got the first finished copy of the book in my hands it felt completely surreal. In the end, the book got to No. 2 in the *Sunday Times* chart, which everyone told me was an incredible achievement, but I was slightly gutted to only just miss out on the top slot. If you'd said to any of my teachers at school 'one of your pupils is going to be a *Sunday Times* bestselling author', I don't think any of them would have picked me.

Parklife 2024 was my last one, and the whole weekend felt weird to me. I was at once part of it but also not, if you see what I mean. I was no longer the one pulling the strings, and I felt I was just there to say goodbye. I love Parklife and the WHP and they have been the defining features of my working life so far, but even when you're at the best party you should always know when it's the right time to go home. This just feels like the right time to leave the party for me. As I write this, I'm 53 and it's time for younger people to lead the party.

I've had a lot of people ask me what I'm going to do next. The immediate answer is to take some time off. I've not stopped working since I left school, and I feel I've earned the right to recharge my batteries. I also want to fully embrace being a dad for the first time. So, I decided to take a full year off, which I'm well aware is a luxury not many people can afford. I'm already six months into that as I write this, and I'm getting more and more energy to get back and focus on the next thing. I've really enjoyed the work I've done with Andy Burnham, and that's the future direction I want to go in. That's my next chapter. I'd really like to take what I do in Greater Manchester to a national level. I get a lot of people approaching me from different cities around the country, asking me if I can help them, and I think that's the next logical step for me. Someone I really admire is James Timpson, and I commend the way he's now stepped back from Timpson and taken up a role advising the government on prisons. I can see myself making a similar step.

One thing I won't be doing is launching another festival or nightclub. The nocturnal landscape has changed dramatically since we launched the Warehouse Project in 2006, and I think it's much riskier and harder to launch and run a nightclub or a festival now, than it was back then.

I still get imposter syndrome, every day, which I'm pretty sure is rooted in my teenage years, my relationship with my dad, and that moment when everyone I knew went off to university and I didn't have a clue what I was going to do with my life. I went on to be the co-founder of the biggest nightclub in the world, the biggest metropolitan festival in Europe, a *Sunday Times* bestselling author, Greater Manchester's first

Night Time Economy Adviser to the Mayor, and a dad … but there's not a day that goes by that I don't expect a knock on the door from someone telling me it was all a huge mistake, and I need to go back to flogging leather jackets on the market stall.

Sacha
Hale, December 2024

A MAP OF MANCHESTER LOCATIONS

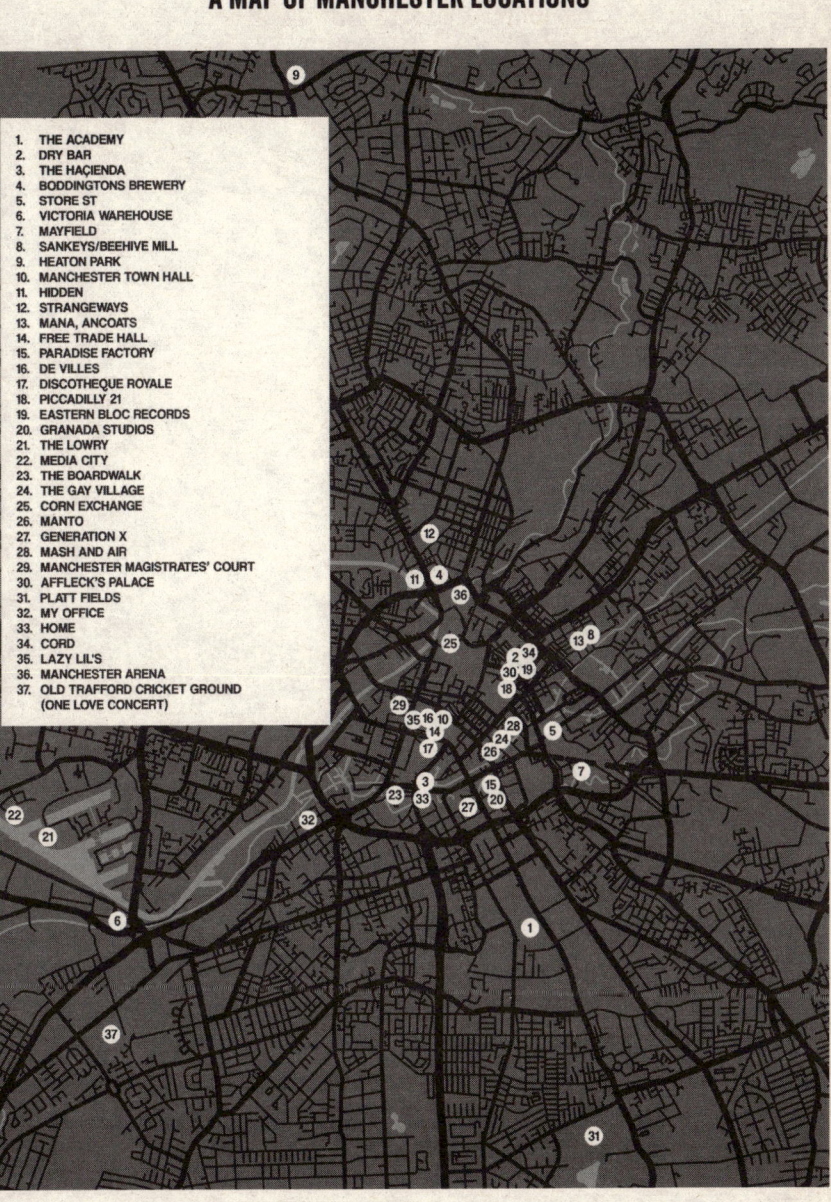

1. THE ACADEMY
2. DRY BAR
3. THE HAÇIENDA
4. BODDINGTONS BREWERY
5. STORE ST
6. VICTORIA WAREHOUSE
7. MAYFIELD
8. SANKEYS/BEEHIVE MILL
9. HEATON PARK
10. MANCHESTER TOWN HALL
11. HIDDEN
12. STRANGEWAYS
13. MANA, ANCOATS
14. FREE TRADE HALL
15. PARADISE FACTORY
16. DE VILLES
17. DISCOTHEQUE ROYALE
18. PICCADILLY 21
19. EASTERN BLOC RECORDS
20. GRANADA STUDIOS
21. THE LOWRY
22. MEDIA CITY
23. THE BOARDWALK
24. THE GAY VILLAGE
25. CORN EXCHANGE
26. MANTO
27. GENERATION X
28. MASH AND AIR
29. MANCHESTER MAGISTRATES' COURT
30. AFFLECK'S PALACE
31. PLATT FIELDS
32. MY OFFICE
33. HOME
34. CORD
35. LAZY LIL'S
36. MANCHESTER ARENA
37. OLD TRAFFORD CRICKET GROUND
    (ONE LOVE CONCERT)

TRACKS THAT MADE THE DECADE

1990s

1. 'Groove Is In The Heart' – Deee-Lite
2. 'Missing (Todd Terry Club Mix)' – Everything But The Girl
3. 'Can You Feel It? (In-House Dub)' – Todd Terry presents CLS
4. 'Bingo Bango (Latin Bango Mix)' – Basement Jaxx
5. 'Higher State of Consciousness' – Wink
6. 'Plastic Dreams (Def Mix)' – Jay Dee
7. 'U Don't Know Me' – Armand Van Helden feat. Duane Harden
8. 'Move Your Body (Club Mix)' – Xpansions
9. 'Playing With Knives' – Bizarre Inc.
10. 'Deep Inside' – Hardrive
11. 'Born Slippy' – Underworld

2000s

1. 'Shades of Jae' – Moodymann

2. 'The Revival' – Braxton Holmes ft. Mark Grant

3. 'The Way' – Global Communications

4. 'Fix My Sink' –DJ Sneak

5. 'I'm So Crazy' – Par-T-One

6. 'I'm A Disco Dancer' – Christopher Just

7. 'Hazin & Phazin' – Harry Romero

8. 'Where Ya At' – Derrick Carter

9. 'You Can't Hide From' – DJ Sneak

10. 'Boogie' – Stacy Kidd

11. 'It's Yours' – Jon Cutler

12. 'Play the Game' – Kenny Hawkes

13. 'Tub' – Grant Phabao

14. 'Indo Silver' – Bucky (Redlight Edit)

15. 'Lazy' – X-Press 2 feat. David Byrne

2010s

1. 'Tribesmen' – Solardo
2. 'Glue' – Bicep
3. '(It Goes Like) Nanana' – Peggy Gou
4. 'Kids' – MGMT
5. 'Get Up' – Eats Everything
6. 'Eat Sleep Rave Repeat' – Fatboy Slim feat. Beardyman (Calvin Harris Remix)
7. 'White Noise' – Disclosure feat. AlunaGeorge
8. 'Move your Body' – Marshall Jefferson x Solardo
9. 'Forget' – Patrick Topping
10. 'Hungry for the Power' – Azari & III (Jamie Jones Ridge Street Remix)
11. 'Pjanno' – Eric Prydz
12. 'Losing It' – Fisher
13. 'Cola' – CamelPhat, Elderbrook
14. 'Around' – Solomun, Noir, Haze
15. 'Jack' – Breach

ACKNOWLEDGEMENTS

I've been lucky enough to work with some amazing people over the years, not least my business partners in The Warehouse Project and Parklife, Sam Kandel and Rich McGinnis, but also many others who, though less visible, are absolutely key to the success of The Warehouse Project and Parklife.

I've worked with Sam Kandel since 2000, when we first reopened Sankeys. Sam has been a massive part of The Warehouse Project, and he and Rich McGinnis have booked the majority of the acts for both The Warehouse Project and Parklife, since we first started out. Rich started off booking acts for Chibuku Shake Shake in Liverpool, and we first brought him in to work with us on the Tribal Warehouse in 2004, and he and Sam now share responsibility for booking talent for The Warehouse Project and Parklife, supported by the staff in our office.

Jon Drape has been essential in helping to building The Warehouse Project and Parklife. He is the man who can get *anything* done in Manchester, from getting streets cordoned off to turning a park into a festival site overnight, and we could not have done it without him and his huge arm of brilliant production staff and specialists.

I first met Kim O'Brien at Sankeys, when she was one of the regulars who partied well into the early hours of the morning. Since she joined The Warehouse Project she was an absolutely integral member of the team until she decided, in 2024, that the time was right for a new challenge, and left for pastures new.

My beautiful wife, Demi, who has to put up with so much… and sadly for her, will have to put up with it for many more years to come. Thank you for all your support and words of encouragement.

Huge thanks to my oldest friend and best man Jonathan Newman, who was also Father Christmas in the Haçienda, all those years ago (sorry Damian stole your outfit).

To my mum, Sandra, thank you for everything.

Elisa was a driving force behind the student nights we promoted together, and continues to work for The Warehoue Project and Parklife to this day.

Huge thanks to my oldest friend and best man Jonathan Newman, who was also Father Christmas in the Haçienda, all those years ago (sorry Damian stole your outfit). Krysko started DJing for us just after we took over Sankeys and quickly became part of the family. He has Djed for us ever since, playing every Warehouse season and every Parklife.

The Lieutenant is not a man to court publicity, but he is my eyes and ears on the ground at The Warehouse Project and Parklife. My equivalent of the Wolf in *Pulp Fiction*. An acid house firefighter.

Dave Vincent is another person who I should mention here, even though we disagreed at times, he was (and still is) such a brilliant promoter and a huge part of my early success in this industry.

The list of people who I've worked with and who have helped me over the years, but aren't mentioned in the book, is extensive. I've tried to remember everyone but, undoubtedly, I will have missed many off who should be here.

Nina Sawetz, my publicist, who I know I drive mad. I would highly recommend her, but not if that means all her time won't be focused on me!

Great Influence: Amy, Ash, Claudia and Megan.

Manchester Grammar School: Mr Bohl, Mr Brown, Mr Davidson, Mr McGinnis, Mr Simpson, Mr Thorpe.

Student nights: Jason Argyle, Brian Cheetham, Si Frater, Jon Harlow, Ann McGrath, Shaun Wilson.

Live Nation: Scott Barton, Melvin Benn, Rory Brett, Jim Campling, Ian Coburn, Andy Copping, Matt Corbin, Raye Cosbert, Daniel Cuffe, Denis Desmond, Jo Dipple, Stuart Douglas, Geoff Ellis, Selina Emeny, Gary Ezard, Diane Fallow, Ele Hill, Paul Latham, Lynn Lavelle, Katie Moore, Andrea Myers, Nethelli Ordish, David Pepper, Peter Taylor, Jana Watkins.

SJM concerts: Rob Ballentine, Simon Moran, Conrad Murray, Randy, Chris York.

Accountant: David Shapiro

PR: Gemma Gore, Lisa Morton, Angie Towse, Tania Von Pear.

NTIA: Mike and Silvana Kill

Andy Burnham's Office: Karen Chambers, Amy Davies, Gill Doyle, Marie France, Joe Heyes, Kevin Lee, Michelle Waugh, Tom Whitney, Gareth Williams, John Wrathmell,

Greater Manchester Leaders and Councillors: Carl Austin, Bev Craig, Paul Dennett, Sean Fielding, Kate Green, Joe Heyes, Pat Karney, Alison Mackenzie Folan, Eamon O'Brien, Mike Parrott, Lucy Powell, Luther Rahman, Rebecca Never Becky, Tom Ross, Arooj Shah, Jeff Smith, Fraser Swift.

Ticketmaster: Andrew Parsons, Sarah Slater.

Kendal Calling: Ben Robinson, Andy Smith.

Hideout: Steve Allison, Wilf Prophecy

Mustard Media: Ed, Oli, Rob and Sian Bennett.

United We Stream: Marie Claire Daly, Colin and everyone at Badger and Coomes, James Monaghan, Vic from the Bury

Met, Gareth Williams; every single artist and DJ who donated their time to both raise funds and raise everyone's spirits.

Sankeys: Darren Bisby, Bucky, Jason Furmidge, Greg Lord, Colin Oldham, Crazy Paul, Tidy, Greg Vickers.

Aitch, Bicep, Ian Brown, Blessed Madonna, Shaun Ryder for support on the book.

Industry allies: Steve Alton, Emma Maclarkin, Kate Nichols.

Wythenshawe FC: Carl Barratt, John Cotton, Chris Howard, Martin Howe, James Melville, Pete, Shane, Steve, all the teams and all the fans.

People who try to make me look good: Emma, Olivia Hammond, Dr Rosh, Abby Whittle.

My wife Demi's crew: mother-in-law Donna Mackenzie, Rhoddy Mackenzie, sisters-in-law Mia and Millie, Gary and Laura Stenhouse, Munroe and Wren, Carol, Paul, Tracey, Wendy, Arlene and everyone at The Bruce.

Primary Security: Thanks to all our labour partners and providers.

Harry Bayford, Lola Cameron, Charlie Lothman, Shamsun Khatun, Anil Patel, Dan Perry, Danny Tracey, Mark Turnbull, Lizzie Williams, Daniel Wolfendale.

Gemma and everyone at W.E.L.S.A.F.E

The Loop and MANDRAKE.

Printer: Kevin, Mike Lynch and Vinny Posters.

GMP: Martin Aylett, Andy Brookes, Paul Cocker, Shakey Dave, Dave Henshall, Andy Owen, Sarah Pickstone, Dave Smith, Phil Spurgeon.

All of our photographers, but especially Jody, Pippa and Sebastian.

Designer: Paul Hemmingfield for all of his work with Sankeys and early Warehouse materials.

WHP designer (and huge help with designs for the book): Katie Hamill.

Artist Driver: Jon Caine

All current office team, including Mark Abbott, Abi, Ashleigh, Kirsty Batchelor, Sophie Bee, Caolon, James Crossan (Croissant) Chelsea, Damo and all the artist liaison team, Daphne, Edite, George, Martin Goodwin, Katie Hamill (thanks for the map on p.292), Jess, Charlie Lothman, JP Mackey, James McGraw, Joe Redmore, Rod, Shamsun, Emma Zillman.

Bars/Office: Aaron the baker, Rachel Barber, Tom Booth, Will Bosworth, Simon Bryne, Joe Burke, cleaners Hannah and Anthony, Laura Connerty, Harry Feigen, Jonny Heyes, Tasha Hulme, Matt Lang, Chris Legh, Bruce Lerman, Scott O'Connor, Dan Pirie, Andre Proverbs, Frankie Rushden, Abbie Stein, Warwick Tams, Vicky Valdez. Every single member of bar staff who has worked at any of our events.

Christine Cort, David the tout, Farris, Rick Gordon, Matt the builder, Moussa, Will Orchard, Ollie Ryder, Lee Stone, Luke Walsh, Alex Poots, James Pyrah.

Fabric: Cameron Leslie/Keith Reilly

Cream: James and Scott Barton

Flyer crew: Sophie Eustace, Lewis Harrison, Raushan Kumar, Lucia Midda, George Mossman, Dave and Shauna, Colin and Yvonne, Yasmine, all the Toms, especially Tom Stalker.

Mike Parrott, the man who lets events happen in Manchester!

All the production staff involved in The Warehouse Project and Parklife, including Meg Ah-Tow, Jason Argyle, Cordi Ashwell, Mike Atkinson, James Brown, Max Cairnes Steve Collinge Jim Gee, Jon Green, Ben Johnstone, Alex Knight, Charlie Lister, Dr Loo, Will McHugh, The mighty Bruce Mitchell, Sheena Platt, Louise Renn, Sarah Rowland, Tom Sheals Barrett, Tom Sabin, Sausage Fingers, Stev.

DBN Audile, including Rob Ashworth, Rob Leach, Stephen Page and Peter Robinson.

Nat Lea at Depot, Broadwick. Clodagh Buckely and Steven Gilholme at TFGM, Mark Logan at Showsec.

A huge, huge thank you to Bucky, Graeme Park and Solardo, who have created sets to accompany each decade of the book.

I've never been one for self-analysis or therapy, so it's only through the process of writing this book with my co-author Luke Bainbridge that I started to reflect on some of the events that shaped my life. After some of the early sessions I had the best night's sleep I'd had in years, so I guess a weight must have been lifted! Luke helped paint the background to my story and Manchester, drawing the links from L.S. Lowry to Sankeys, God's Cop to Heaton Park, including plenty of things I hadn't even realised myself, like the fact that The Warehouse Project wouldn't exist if film director Michael Winterbottom hadn't got snowed in while doing a recce in a remote logging town in rural Canada. I first met Luke back in 1995, when he was a young writer for *City Life* (Manchester's answer to *Time Out*) and he came to one of my early nights at The Haçienda. He was there on the dancefloor to document Manchester's change in the late 1990s and 2000s, before moving to the *Observer* to launch *Observer Music Monthly*, the biggest music magazine this country has ever had. Over the years, he's been to most of the events mentioned in this book, so he was the perfect person to work on it with me.

Thanks to everyone at HarperNorth for believing in the book and the story and for helping it become a *Sunday Times* bestseller.

Harper
North

Book Credits

HarperNorth would like to thank the following staff and contributors for their involvement in making this book a reality:

Sarah Allen-Sutter
Fionnuala Barrett
Samuel Birkett
Peter Borcsok
Laura Braggs
Ciara Briggs
Katie Buckley
Sarah Burke
Matthew Burne
Alan Cracknell
Jonathan de Peyer
Anna Derkacz
Tom Dunstan
Kate Elton
Sarah Emsley
Simon Gerratt
Monica Green
Natassa Hadjinicolaou
Emma Hatlen
Jo Ireson

Megan Jones
Jean-Marie Kelly
Taslima Khatun
Holly Kyte
Rachel McCarron
Ben McConnell
Alice Murphy-Pyle
Adam Murray
Genevieve Pegg
Amanda Percival
Florence Shepherd
Colleen Simpson
Eleanor Slater
Hilary Stein
Emma Sullivan
Emily Thomas
Katrina Troy
Daisy Watt
Ben Wright

For more unmissable reads,
sign up to the HarperNorth newsletter at
www.harpernorth.co.uk

or find us on Twitter at
@HarperNorthUK

Harper
North

RISING
FROM
FLAMES
AND
STARLIGHT

AVA THORNE

For anyone who loved with their entire heart and has had that love twisted into something ugly. I see you, I am you, and I love you. It never made you weak, it made you stronger than they can ever imagine.

Trigger Warnings

This book contains themes and elements that some may find difficult. These include blood, gore, violence, on-page descriptions of death and killing, torture, cursing, sex with explicit descriptions.

This book contains reference to sex trafficking by a loved one and on page sexual assault of a main character.

Please read at your own discretion.

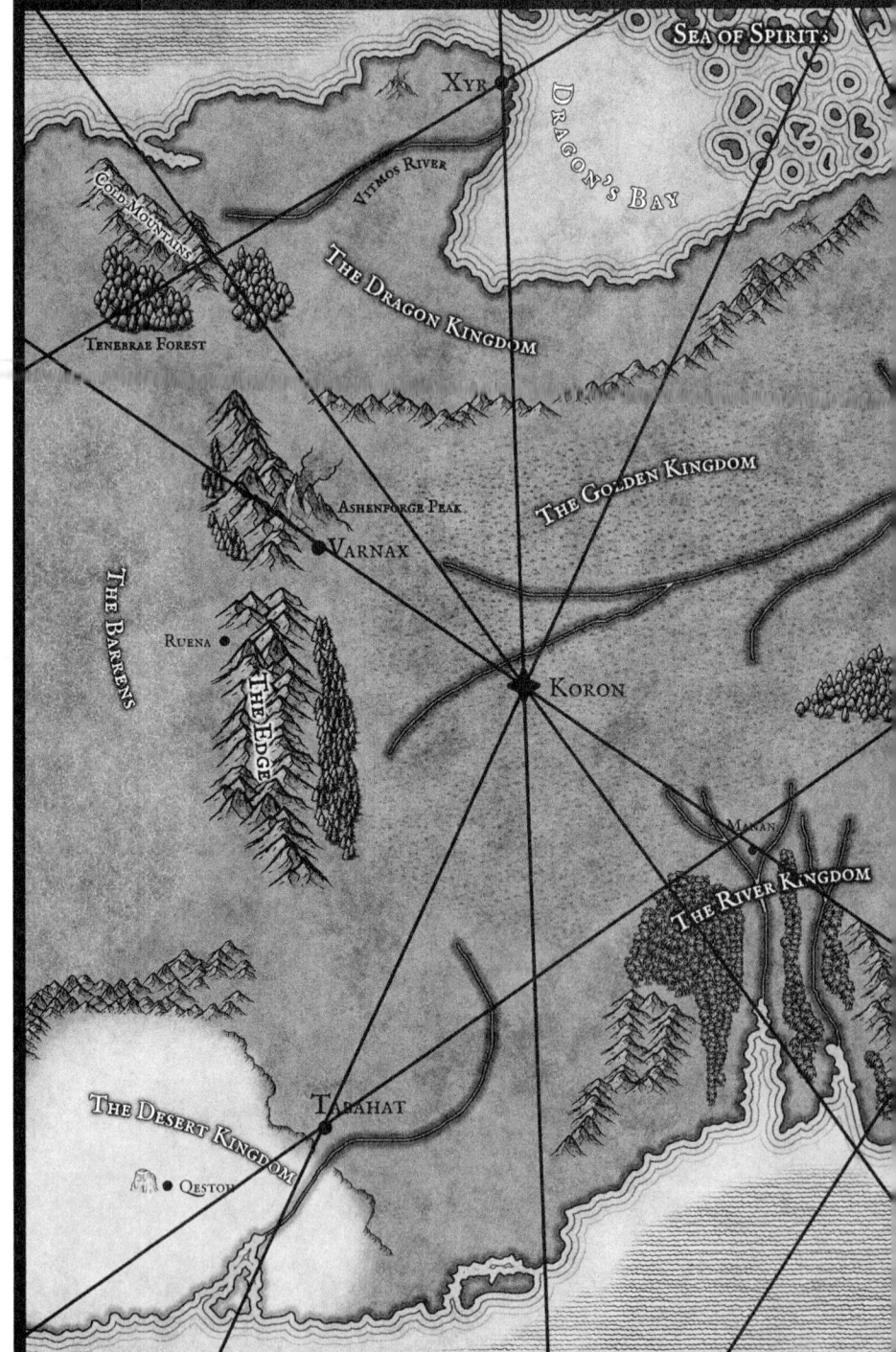

THE SHADOWED SEA

THE CONTINENT OF ADIMOS

Haverfalls

VARDA RIVER

Metlin

N

THE SEA KINGDOM

THE CERULEUN SEA

VATH

OETH

THE PEARL KINGDOM

KOSTAH

NIATA

Summary of Book One

The Great Prophecy of the Third Age foretells the World Breaker, who is destined to destroy the magic of the world, and is born of dragonfire. The Great Hero must face the World Breaker, and restore magic.

Fae Princess Tori Khato accompanies her beloved twin brother Jun, who is in a melancholic mood. She tries to cheer him up by teasing him and offering to take his place at court for the day. Tori has always protected Jun, who is a kind and gentle soul, while she was always the fighter. At court with her father, it becomes obvious that her parents don't value her opinion, or her presence. After an altercation with her father, she leaves in a foul mood.

This is quickly interrupted as her home is invaded by an unknown army. Tori rushes through the palace looking for her brother, and helps many of the human servants escape along the way. Her escape is thwarted by an unknown assailant. She awakens to the Fae King Abraxas threatening her father and his court. She attempts to attack him, but is interrupted by the

Great Hero himself, Emperor Hadeon. She thinks she is saved, until it becomes obvious that Hadeon is no hero and is behind the entire invasion. He takes her brother Jun as his captive, and casts Tori off to Abraxas.

Abraxas journeys with Tori back to his home, with her fighting him every step of the way. Her only thoughts are of rescuing Jun and returning home, but trapped on a ship with an entire army, she doesn't have many opportunities. At the insistence of Commander Avlyn, Tori joins the daily training of the soldiers, and it quickly revealed that she has trained for decades with a sword. She gains rapport with the soldiers, but this is lost when their ship is attacked by an ancient Leviathan, whom Tori frees. All the ancient beasts are believed extinct, but that is obviously not the case.

Abraxas confronts Tori for her reckless behavior, but the encounter quickly becomes heated, both Tori and Abraxas refusing to back down. Tori attempts to stab the King with his own dagger, which only draws him to her more. Luckily, or unluckily, they are interrupted before anything more can happen. Tori cannot deny her attraction to Abraxas, despite her seething hatred.

They arrive in Xyr, Abraxas' home, and Tori is surprised to find a city full of life, not one oppressed by a tyrant as Abraxas' reputation would suggest. But she is quickly whisked away to the castle, where she meets her handmaid, Ciara. She, like most everyone else on her journey, meets Tori with kindness that she quickly rejects. Abraxas tries to return to the order of his life, searching for an ancient diadem, but finds himself constantly interrupted by thoughts of the Princess. He approaches her to make a bargain. If she draws information out of a particularly tight-lipped guest, he will allow her to continue her sword training. Tori cannot refuse. She uses the charms of seduction she learned during her life at court to acquire the information, despite Abraxas' continued jealous interruptions.

Tori returns to training with the soldiers, and quickly finds herself at ease with them. They are impressed by her skill with a sword, and after a few duels, all the messiness with the Leviathan is forgotten. She grows close to one soldier in particular, Kaleos, who takes her under his wing. She even ends up dueling Abraxas himself. She holds herself back until he allows her a true bladed sword. Tori reveals her true skill fighting in a duel wielding style, and defeats Abraxas, but hesitates before killing him.

Tori trains during the day, and plans her escape at night, but she's lost in an entirely new land, with no allies. Until one night she overhears a secret conversation between Abraxas and Avlyn, revealing a somber but venerable side to the king. She confronts him, but a mysterious force connects their minds, and Tori and the king exchange memories. She sees the memories of a man haunted by his past, and he sees the same in her, including a memory where Tori attempts to take her own life after abuse from her father. Before the pair can actually have an emotional connection, Hadeon arrives with Jun in tow, captured in a powerful enslavement enchantment that allows Hadeon to control Jun, and to control his magic. Tori always knew Jun's singing was special, but she never imagined it was due to the magic coursing through him. Hadeon confronts Tori, and demands she reveal her magic as well. Tori insists she has no magic, but manages to land a solid punch on Hadeon before Abraxas can drag her away. He locks her in her room, insisting it's for her own protection.

This drives Tori over the edge, and the next day she makes her great escape. But it all goes wrong, and she is nearly killed falling from a sea cliff.

Abraxas cares for Tori as she heals from the injury that is life threatening even for a fae, and he realizes how much he cares for her, and how his own actions are what drove her to her desperate escape attempt. They grow closer as she recovers, even if she never truly heals. The injuries to her left arm were so severe she can no longer move it properly, and she mourns her ability to fight.

As 'punishment' for her escape attempt, Abraxas insists that Tori accompany him to a local festival. The hedonism and energy of the night lead to Tori and Abraxas sharing a dance that puts both on dangerous ground. When they return to the castle, Abraxas once again insists that Tori remain locked in her room, despite the continued festivities at the palace. Tori sneaks out, and discovers that the debauchery earlier in the night was only the beginning, as she stumbles upon an exhibitionist party, where she is confronted by Abraxas. They share a passionate kiss, but are interrupted before it can go any further. Tori can't sleep, and makes her way to Abraxas' chambers. They share a night of intimacy, but it seems to drive Tori only deeper into her dark thoughts, and she finds herself taking a sleeping potion to quell the noise of her mind, something she swore she wouldn't do again.

Tori and Abraxas continue to provoke each other even as it becomes obvious that Abraxas' feelings for Tori are more than a sexual tryst. But Tori cannot accept her own feelings, until Tori is taken captive along with Kaleos by an unknown group. Kaleos is stabbed, and Tori is injured as she fights their way out. At the last moment, Abraxas arrives, wielding his sword and magic to save her. After this, their encounters change. Abraxas longs to reveal his feelings to Tori, but he knows it would drive her away. When Tori leaves him no choice after demanding more sleeping potion, Abraxas reveals himself, but also his long-standing hatred for Hadeon that drives him. He releases Tori from her imprisonment. After Tori finally accepts the feelings she has, she returns to Abraxas who has lost control of his magic in anguish. She calms him, and he invites her on his quest to find a lost enchanted diadem.

The two journey to the Tenebrae Forest despite Avlyn's strong protests against. They find themselves trapped in the forest that has magically surrounded them. After another encounter with a mythic beast, the forest reveals itself to be sentient, and quite angry at all of fae kind. Abraxas talks to the forest, and wins its trust, allowing them to travel to the ruins of an ancient castle. There, Tori befriends a baby giant spider that leads them to the diadem, but it provokes the ire of the ghosts of the ruins. Tori cannot fight them without magic, and Abraxas has been weakened. As the end draws near, Tori embraces Abraxas which allows the magic of the earth to rip through her body and power Abraxas, allowing their escape.

As Abraxas and Tori work through what their encounter in the forest could mean, Hadeon visits them again, notably lacking Jun. Tori learns that Jun is dying due to Hadeon's imprisonment. After Tori convince Hadeon that Tori is completely controlled by Abraxas, they travel to the capital. They use the enchanted diadem to break Jun's imprisonment, but he does not awaken. They also use it in an attempt to break Hadeon's control on his own magic, but their plans are thwarted by Ciara, who has been a spy for Hadeon the entire time. Hadeon captures Tori, and attempts to use her as leverage against Abraxas. Abraxas attacks Hadeon, and Tori and Avlyn fight off defending soldiers. But they are quickly overpowered by Hadeon and his forces. When all seems lost, Abraxas reveals that the World Breaker wasn't the last dragon, but he is. He shifts and they escape Hadeon, but the use of so much magic puts him into a sleep like death. Tori and Avlyn try to determine the location that Abraxas delivered them to, to find an ancient fae seer who informs Tori that the last dragon is not the World Breaker, but she is, and the only way to save Abraxas is to fulfill her destiny and destroy the world she knows.

A full Glossary can be found at the end of the book.

Part 1

Chapter 1

Abraxas

9 months ago

The mist I conjured had worked beautifully, not that we really needed the advantage against Niata. They had been caught completely unaware. The Long Peace made them compliant—*Fools*. But perhaps it was a blessing. It would allow us to hit their primary defenses with minimal casualties.

I shouted at Commander Avlyn, but it was unnecessary. Avlyn had been running the army for decades while I sat on the throne and strategized. I trusted them implicitly.

The last of the troops departed the boat, and I followed. I stepped off the gangplank to the rocky shore, and it was as if the world had tilted on its axis, the sky becoming the sea. The moment I touched the land of the Pearl Kingdom, a substantial force wrapped itself around my heart, around my very soul. I could feel it sinking through me, like a golden tidal wave that removed everything that I was and replaced it with something else. Someone else. *Her.*

I saw her in flashes. A hand gripping the cliffs around the beach, pulling herself up. A scroll full of scribbles and doodles, a tutor looking on in disappointment. A pair of swords dancing against an opponent who was quickly disarmed. Human children ran around her skirts as a soft laugh echoed from her lips.

I clutched my chest and fell to my knees. My breath caught, and I coughed, trying to force air into my lungs. "Abraxas, what's wrong?" Avlyn ran to me, putting a hand on my shoulder. I let them help me up before pushing them off.

"Nothing. I need you to lead the army today."

Their face still held concern, but they rolled their eyes. "Wasn't that already the plan?"

"Yes, but I will rejoin you later." Their face showed confusion, but they nodded and returned to the front of the ranks.

I didn't know where I was going, but my body did. It was as if she were a siren luring me in. I ran to her. My mind kept showing me more images. Younglings running through the rainforest, chasing after each other with sticks. She sneaked through the kitchens at night, gathering up sweet rolls. A book opened before her, illuminated by the moon through a window.

I passed through the main gates of the castle complex, which weren't even closed before my troops blew through them. I turned my back to a secluded alcove to get my bearings, but my mind had caught up with me. *This can't be happening.*

Centuries ago, I had given up the hope that I could have a mate. There were no dragons left; I would have felt them. No clutches of eggs were hidden anywhere, and even if there had been, no one was left to care for them. Any that would have been hidden away would have perished by now. And certainly, my mind wasn't showing me images of a dragon but of what appeared to be a fae female.

From the sea, a great volley of Emperor Hadeon's lightning projectiles fired at the castle. With a crash that shook the very earth, one of the castle's main towers was struck. Another image came to me, but this one felt more vivid. She was being pulled away from a window that overlooked the collapsed tower that I was now viewing from outside. *There you are.*

I moved. But the images were coming faster now, uncontrolled. It was as if the magic that connected us had been pent up for too long. Some were indecipherable, while others were manageable. Dancing feet swept across a floor. She hugged her knees and cried in a dark room. A handsome half-fae male was laughing. A moment later, that same man was grinning as he gripped her breast, and she rode him into oblivion.

My feet stopped as rage burned me from the inside out. Centuries had passed since I had allowed the beast inside me to awaken, but now he threatened to overpower me completely. I gripped the wall, trying to regain control, my fingers piercing the stone. An unsuspecting group of Niatan soldiers appeared before me. How unfortunate for them.

Even I could barely keep up with my movements. In under a breath, half of them were already dead on the floor. The rest struggled to draw their swords and fall into defensive positions, but they were already far too late. Two more breaths and they were all dead.

Blood ran down the edge of my sword, dripping like the ticking of a clock. The beast inside me was satiated, at least for the moment. I had to keep moving. Another vision came. A room overturned, and a voice whispering, *"The tunnel in the kitchens."*

Avlyn surprised me by placing their hand on my shoulder again. "Your Highness, there has been little resistance. We have favored capture over bloodshed." They looked over my shoulder at the very dead cohort at my feet but kept a stony face. "We have located the prince. I'm sure the king and queen won't be far behind. We haven't yet found the princess. What are our next steps?"

"The kitchens. Bring your cohort and meet me there." The

confusion showed on their face, but again, they did not question me. They raised their hand and waved the cohort forward.

It was simple to find the kitchens. The floorplan of the building had seared itself into my mind. Half of the entryway had already collapsed, and we filed in. The building was quiet, as if holding its breath, waiting for the next move. We made our way to the back when a unit of soldiers clad in silver mail charged us from a side hall.

I didn't have time for this. I needed to find her. Now. I cut through the men in front of me, clearing a path when I felt her. That golden thread pulled taut, and my head snapped up. She was the most beautiful creature I had ever seen. Her magenta robes were incredibly fine, embroidered with the white peacock of the royal family. They were covered in dust and disheveled, revealing the warm skin of her shoulder. I followed the perfect line of her long neck to slate eyes that blazed with rage. For a moment, she held my gaze, and I swear the entire world stood still. But then she ran away, and the beast inside me yearned to give chase.

I was lost to him, my sword cleaving through every man in my way; my feet moved of their own accord. I could feel it, her fear; it would be delicious on her skin. How satisfying would it feel to sink my talons and fangs into her, claiming her over and over again until the only sound from her lips was my own name. *She was mine.*

I whipped around a corner and saw her duck behind a hidden wall panel. I approached, ready to rip it straight off the wall, when that golden thread around my heart pulsed. It wasn't gentle either. It gripped so hard I fell to my knees again; my body froze.

I tried to catch my breath and get my heart beating again when I heard a voice through the panel. "Princess Tori, what are you—"

My suspicions were confirmed, and it wasn't good news. She was the very princess I had been sent here to capture. My mate, whom I had waited centuries for and given up hope for, was the very person my greatest adversary wished to sink his claws into.

Avlyn and the cohort rounded the corner. "Your Majesty, why have you come back this way?"

"Commander, take the troops and find the king and queen. I'll finish up here."

Avlyn couldn't hold themselves back anymore. "Abraxas, what's going on? This erratic behavior isn't like you. What about the princess?"

My teeth ground together at the very mention of her. "I'll take care of her. You follow my orders, Commander."

They nodded and led the rest out. I circled around the hallways, listening, when a loud crash came from behind a door. I listened, and I could hear her directing the human servants. But then the roof shook violently, and I threw open the door and reached out with my magic. It wasn't elegant, but I pulled her from under the collapsing rubble at the last moment. She pushed herself up, and I couldn't resist her any longer.

"There you are, Princess. I've been waiting for you." Waiting lifetimes, waiting even when I had given up all hope. My soul, which I had thought long gone, had just been in a deep slumber, dreaming of this moment when it would finally be completed.

Her eyes filled with unmitigated hatred as she beheld me. The anger she held found a focal point, and I knew that if I gave her half a chance, she would destroy me. But the ceiling snapped again, and the entire building came down. I threw my magic out like a net, trying to stop her from being crushed. It half worked, and after the rubble had settled, she lay unconscious but alive.

I pulled the bricks and beams away and gathered her up in

my arms. Her breathing was steady, even as blood dripped from her head and her body was bruised. She seemed so breakable like this, almost calm and serene. But as I held her, listening to the beautiful sound of her strong heart, I knew mine wouldn't survive it.

None of this made any sense. She was fae, and while I had pretended to be one for so long, I had almost forgotten that's not what I was. Fae didn't have mates; only dragons did, and she was no dragon. I pulled out my dagger and held it to her throat. She was breakable and weak. If I let her live, that's what I would become as well. I could end this all here. Just remember it as a cruel dream, fate laughing at me one more time.

Fate had taken my mother and father along with every other dragon in this world. It has taken my people and, in the process, my soul. It had taken my magic, the only thing I still had that reminded me of what I once was, and with that, it had taken the sky from me. Now, it dangled this last piece of hope in front of me, distracting me from the revenge I had let shape me for these last centuries. I tensed my muscles to pull that blade through her skin and feel her warm blood as the life left her. But I recalled that fire in her eyes, her fearlessness, and I knew I was only fooling myself.

"You will be my undoing, won't you, Princess?"

The dream was always the same. If I dreamed of anything else, I don't remember it. But this one haunts me whether I'm awake or asleep.

That great dragon stared down at me, laughing at my weakness. His lips curled back in a snarl as his tongue lashed out to taste my fear and shame. His teeth descended like knives for my throat, and all I wished was that he would finally end me.

· · · • • · · • • · · ·

535 YEARS AGO

I heard the deep rumbling of the sky, like thunder but more deadly, and ran out of my parents' bed to hide in the cupboard— a child's foolishness. My parents hadn't even woken up.

Smoke curled in under the seam beneath the cupboard door, and the deep red light of the flames danced between the slats of wood that were shoddily nailed together. That great, terrible rumbling filled the sky, and my body shook uncontrollably.

"Mama? Papa?"

"Hadeon, where are you?!" The panic in my mother's voice was the only memory I had of her.

A scream pierced the burning night air as the ceiling over my parents' room collapsed in a crash. I can't remember their faces. It was like the flames of that night had singed them from my memory, but I will always remember that scream. It was quiet except for the snapping of wood under the relentless attack of the fire.

"Mama!" I shoved my shoulder into the door, and it flew open. Flames consumed everything. The cupboard was the only part of the house still standing. Even at such a young age, I knew they were gone. But I was stupid and tried to dig into the smoldering ruins as the skin on my hand sizzled away.

"*Mama!*" My call had been more of a wail than a cry, and I heard the sizzling of my tears dropping into the embers.

Another beam snapped, and something hit me across the face so hard I blacked out. When I came to, I knew nothing but pain. I was stuck beneath flaming rubble, and I could feel every inch of my skin burning away.

I screamed and pushed to escape, every part of my soul longing to live, but my body would not respond. I thrashed and wailed, but it was useless. I was too small, too weak to help anyone, even myself.

Then, that great rumbling was just above me, and the flames flattened to the ground as a great burst of wind consumed what remained of my home.

One enormous, taloned claw cleared the rubble on top of me with a great snap. Deep ochre eyes set into iridescent maroon scales peered directly into my soul as the chilled night air whipped over my destroyed skin, creating a new level of pain.

The dragon opened his massive jaw, and a long, forked tongue flicked out as if to taste the air. I saw his throat and heart glow a deep blood red as he summoned his dragonfire.

My body froze as his jaws moved to encompass me, his teeth scraping grooves into the flesh of my arms. I was beyond panic, beyond reason. I was dead and witnessing the end.

Then a soft screech broke the sky, and the dragon's head snapped up as a smaller dark shadow passed overhead.

Malech flapped his wings and took off, never giving me a second thought. My view of the sky was clear now, and the stars mocked me with their twinkling. How dare they look so peaceful as I lay there dying? My body lay scorched and frozen until I was nothing but pain and blackness.

5 DAYS AGO

I awoke to the smell of burning fabric. My magic had lashed out in my sleep, singeing and almost destroying my room. It had reduced the bed to ash; long, creeping veins of burned wood had scorched the floor and walls.

Pain lingered as my flesh knit itself back together. The irony was not lost on me that my magic mimicked the feeling of being burned alive.

I sighed and pulled myself from the wreckage of my bedchamber. The next room was undamaged, and I dressed myself. The slaves knew what to do. I had the tongues cut from their mouths so no one would know my nightly turbulence.

I finished dressing just as a soft knock resounded on my door. "Enter."

Pallas stepped inside, her eyes cast downward. She was clad

in just a simple silk nightgown, but despite her plain attire, she was a vision as her long golden-brown hair caressed her breasts. I had her for centuries now, and I hated to admit how much she still affected me. I pulled her into my lap and saw her eyes widen in shock for just a moment.

"Your Eminence?"

"So formal this morning, Pallas." I twirled the ends of her long hair around my fingers. The soft curls caressed my skin, and I pulled them aside to place a kiss on her neck. She let a small sigh escape as she pressed against me, running her fingers through my hair. I tugged my head back to capture her lips with my own and ran my fingers down her back, sinking them into every inch of her soft flesh. She pulled back with a smile.

She was certainly the most beautiful woman in all of Adimos, her hair lustrous, her lips soft and plump, and every inch of her body shaped to perfection. But her blue eyes were always dull, like the sky just about to be overtaken by a storm. She was a thousand leagues away even though she sat with me.

"You asked to know as soon as Abraxas and his pet were near; they should be in the city within the hour." She watched my face as she delivered the news, and she didn't flinch as a small amount of my power lashed out and swept through her.

Yes, Abraxas had requested a visit to my court. It had been decades since he had last been to my kingdom. I knew he was up to something, and I was racked with anticipation. I just returned from my trip to Xyr, so it was particularly suspect. Finally, a little fun. Part of me wanted to believe he wanted to simply show off that little princess he had tamed, to finally accept his place as an esteemed member of my court, but I knew better.

I stood, and Pallas slid off my legs elegantly. I gripped the back of her head, pulling her to my chest.

"Be wary of the princess, Hadeon. She is not as docile as she seems." The words were muffled as Pallas spoke against my flesh, and I gripped her tighter.

"I'm not concerned with the actions of a little girl like her. It's obvious now she's useless with no power of her own." It wasn't entirely true. She would serve her purpose. Abraxas had become far too attached to the pathetic thing; I would need to correct that.

"Hadeon..." Pallas' voice shook. "Jun still hasn't awoken. If we could just..."

I snapped her head back so hard her neck audibly cracked, and the corners of her mouth flinched with pain. "I told you, if he can't bother to keep himself alive, he's of no use to me."

Her lips tightened. "But his gift of voice, we've just scratched the surface. There is so much more he could do for you."

I pulled her hair tighter, and she didn't continue. Pallas had grown attached to Jun in the last few months. At first, I had allowed it in the hopes it would bring the boy more swiftly under my compliance. But I still needed to collar him, and Pallas had been defying me more often, more than she had in centuries. She would need to be reminded of her place.

"If the boy's magic is strong enough to be of use, he will survive. Now, go prepare yourself for our esteemed guests." She bowed her head and nodded, not meeting my gaze. Just as she reached the door, I called out to her again. "Oh, Pallas, my love. Lord Plagis won't be able to attend tonight's festivities. He has requested that you come and entertain him beforehand. Would you make sure he is *well* taken care of?"

She hid it well, but a shudder ran through her body. *Good.*

"Of course, your Eminence." She bowed her head again and left.

I walked to my window, and in the distance, I could make

out the dark shape of Abraxas and his soldiers approaching Koron.

"What fun are we going to have tonight, old friend?"

Chapter 3

Tori

The hard scales of his side pressed into my face. The edges and peaks of the scales left divots in my skin as they embossed me while I slept. My hand traced them over and over, a distraction from the truth that Abraxas still slept. I had fallen asleep listening to his heartbeat, the only sign he was still alive. But I could feel it getting weaker, my heart along with it.

Avlyn and I hadn't spoken since our encounter with the Seer. The silence weighed heavy as Avlyn just sat down next to the spring on our return, mimicking Pallas' earlier position. I found her asleep next to Jun, pinkies wrapped together, her chin tucked into his shoulder.

How many times had he and I lain like that, hidden in the forest, watching the stars pass over us? Tears rose in my eyes, and I turned away. I didn't know their relationship, but Pallas had shown me she cared for my brother. I should have been happy that he had someone there for him, even though I knew it should have been me.

I let those tears fall as I pressed myself into Abraxas. It was like trying to cuddle a boulder, but I had fallen asleep all the same. Now I was awake, and I couldn't bear it. Those familiar dark tendrils crept into my mind, and I longed to be nothing. If I was nothing, I wouldn't worry about Jun. I wouldn't worry about what we would find beyond this cave. I wouldn't worry about how I was the one who had to save Abraxas, and I had absolutely no idea how.

I slammed my fist into Abraxas' side. My knuckles split open, the pain scorching up my arm. But it wasn't enough. The worry remained.

"I know nothing, Abraxas. You, Avlyn, and that damn Seer didn't tell me anything. How am I supposed to help you?" I slammed my fist into him again. It changed nothing. That great wallowing pit of despair opened in my stomach, and I was ready to jump right in.

But then I heard shuffling behind me and a masculine moan. I launched away from the beast and was at Jun's side in two strides. Pallas had awoken as well, and her eyes were full of worry. Jun moaned again, and I saw his eyes flutter.

"Jun..." My voice came out a hoarse rasp. "Jun, wake up."

His eyes opened, but they were unfocused. They darted around wildly as he tried to focus on my face.

"Pallas?" That substantial weight gripped my chest, and I struggled to breathe like someone had clamped a pillow over my face.

"I'm here, Jun." She pushed herself in front of me. "We are together." Perhaps the Tori of yesterday would have struck her, shoved her away from my brother. But he had asked for her, not me. She was his comfort, and that great wallowing pit inside me only seemed to grow wider.

She helped him sit up, and I did all I could to keep my tears contained when Jun looked at me.

"Tori? Is that really you?" He sat up, his eyes shining, and all I could see was the little boy I always needed to protect. "How did you—?" He started coughing so roughly that he doubled over again. I ran to the pool and cupped my hands together. Water filled them, and I carefully carried it back to him.

The water still contained that ethereal blue glow as I held it to his lips, and he gulped it down.

"He needs more," Pallas slung the command while her gaze pierced me. At that, a bit of the old Tori surfaced. I could feel my skin prickling with indignation, but she was right, so I fetched more.

After Jun drank it all, his coughing subsided, and his eyes seemed more focused. "What happened?" he asked. Pallas and I exchanged another set of slightly less hostile glances. But before we could answer, his hand came up to his neck and rested where the collar had been.

"Is it over?" He looked at Pallas, not me. His eyes were still unfocused.

"Yes." She held his face in both her hands, and then he collapsed into her, sobbing. She held him tight, her arms stroking his back as he continued to cry. "It's alright, you're alright."

I hadn't known it was possible to feel emptier, but I did. As Jun continued to sob, I walked to the edge of the pool and just stared at the glowing light of it, willing my mind to be as mercifully blank.

"Caught some dinner." I jumped nearly a foot in the air as Avlyn appeared beside me. I hadn't even noticed them leave. They held up three small rodents by their tails. I raised an eyebrow at them.

"Oh, too good for squirrels now, Princess? Don't worry, I'll eat your share." As if on cue, my stomach let out a loud growl. I would not be passing up my share.

15

"Quite the hodgepodge of creatures living in this place. I thought it might be best to give you and your brother some space." They glanced over to where Pallas and Jun were whispering to each other and frowned. "Not quite the reunion you expected?"

I said nothing, but I knew Avlyn could read everything on my face and in my swollen eyes.

They locked their arm around my shoulders gently. "Come on, help me make a fire."

I gathered sticks and kindling from nearby, but everything was damp and wouldn't light. "We could use some help over here," Avlyn shouted over their shoulder to where the dragon slept. Nothing. They shrugged and went back to trying to light the fire with their flint.

I saw Pallas lead Jun over to the edge of the pool. He knelt and cupped more water in his hands to drink. Pallas did the same.

My eyes stung again, and I turned away. I pushed my fingers into the grass and earth below me. I might have been useless to Jun for too long, but I could do something.

I allowed my breathing to settle, even though errant sobs still attempted to sneak through. However, the wild magic of this place was itching to be unleashed, so I didn't require any additional focus. I reached just below the surface of the earth and felt the warm sensation of energy. I closed my eyes and remembered the feeling of my skin sizzling under Abraxas' flames, the heat and ash that burned away all that stood before it. I reached along that invisible golden thread that tied me to Abraxas, and in my mind, I saw it turn emerald green. I quickly opened my eyes and focused on the kindling, and one tiny green flame erupted.

"Oi! Warning next time," Avlyn yelled, then bent over and blew on the rising smoke, trying to get the spark to catch. After a few more breaths, the green shifted to orange, and a tinder caught in the kindling. I helped set more branches on top when they signaled, and soon, we had a stable fire going. Avlyn set to work skinning the squirrels with their dagger.

"So, it seems you aren't completely useless." Pallas crouched down near the fire, but she kept her eyes fixed on mine. Fuck her.

"I doubt you mentioned this, but I was the one who got that collar off of Jun." My voice shook, and I dug my nails deeper into the dirt to stop myself from lashing out at her. "And you didn't get him out of there. We did."

"Only because I took you to him. What would you have done if I hadn't? Just leave him behind again?"

I jumped up, and she did the same.

"You don't know me, Pallas. I would have never left Jun! Never!"

"Oh, really? Before Hadeon collared him, he kept saying you would come for him. Kept saying you wouldn't let anything separate you. I wanted to believe you would; that he had someone out there who loved him enough to do that. But you never came." I froze. She had me cornered. "Then I find you had been too busy fucking yourself into a queenship to rescue the brother who needed you."

"Fuck you. Like you're one to talk. How long have you been with Hadeon now, centuries? What was it again? *'Tied to him for all eternity?'* Give me a fucking break."

"You think I had a choice?" Pallas whispered it like a curse.

"I don't see a collar around your neck." I reveled in the way her jaw clenched at that.

"Ladies, why don't we all just calm down?" Avlyn had their hands up, calling for a truce. We both rounded on them so fast that they took a step back. "Gods, commander of an army at war, and I'm in more danger trapped with you two." They sat back down, focusing on cooking again.

I took a breath. Then another. Finally, I asked, "How did you know about the necklace?"

Pallas paused, some of that hatred leaving her face. But it quickly returned. "How did you light that fire just now?"

We both sat there, unwilling to yield, until I saw Jun fall next to the edge of the pool.

"Jun!" Pallas and I screamed in unison. We both darted over to him, but I was faster. I wrapped him up in my arms, and he moaned weakly. I ran my hand over his forehead, and he felt clammy.

"He's still weak. He needs time to recover," Pallas said as she placed her hands on his chest.

"Some food would likely help." I held her stare until finally she gave in and turned back to the campfire.

"Jun, I don't know how, but we are going to get through this, alright?" I whispered in his ear.

He mumbled, "Tori, if we keep sneaking out, Father will catch us. I don't want you to get in trouble." He was confused, and I just held him tighter.

"You're the one in trouble now, Jun. But I'm here like I should have always been." I laid a soft kiss on his forehead, and his sweat mixed with my tears, leaving a salty taste in my mouth. Pallas returned with the small, cooked body of one squirrel on a stick. She pulled a small piece of meat off and blew on it.

I propped Jun up against my chest, and Pallas gently placed the food in his mouth. I was worried he wouldn't eat it, but his hunger won out, and he chewed it rapidly and opened his mouth again. Pallas continued to tear off small pieces and cool them before giving them to him. We sat like that for quite a while in silence.

Per usual, I was the first one to break it. "Thank you, Pallas."

She had been reaching out to Jun, and I saw her hand falter. "Thank you for taking care of him when I couldn't." It was clear she cared for him, and as much as it pained me, I owed her a great deal.

Pallas flattened her lips but nodded to me. We fed Jun the rest of the meat in silence.

Chapter 4

Tori

After eating, Jun dozed off, and I begrudgingly left him with Pallas. She leaned against a nearby rock and let his head lay in her lap while gently stroking his hair.

I returned to Avlyn and scarfed down my share of the meal. It wasn't particularly good; the meat was stringy and dried out from the smoke of the fire, but I ate every morsel.

I was licking the grease from my fingers when Avlyn said, "What's the plan, Princess?"

I threw my stick into the fire and wiped my fingers on my ruined dress. "Why are you asking me? You're the commander. What was the next step of the plan?"

"This was never damn well in the plan, and you know it." They crossed their arms over their chest.

"Do I? I didn't know the army was going to invade. I clearly wasn't privy to you and Abraxas' schemes." The tears were rising again, and I was already so tired of it.

Avlyn's face softened. "That's protocol. Knowing could have compromised your role. It wasn't because we didn't trust you."

"But you don't trust me. You've said as much, many times in

20

fact." I raised my knees up and wrapped my arms around them, tucking my head into my arms so that I could hide my shame. Tears fell, and I just felt numb all over.

Avlyn put their hand on my shoulder, but I didn't raise my face. "Tori, I saw you fight for him, for us. I know you can be trusted, and I'm sorry I didn't before." They sighed heavily. "He means everything to me, too."

Yes, Avlyn was mourning, too. Abraxas had kept his secrets, and now we didn't know if we would ever get him back.

"I think I got so pissed off when you tried to escape, when you got hurt, because of how he reacted. I hadn't seen him like that in centuries since the years after Malech's defeat. It was like he was completely gone, dead, even if his body was still moving. I knew then how he felt about you, but I hated how you made him hurt like that again, even if that wasn't really fair."

My heart stuttered. I'd been asleep, so I hadn't seen it. Kaleos had mentioned something to me, but I'd been so blind then, unwilling to see the truth of his feelings and my own.

Avlyn continued, "The only thing that brought him back all those centuries ago was anger, his desire for vengeance. I 'spose I can see why now. All his family killed; his entire species gone... except for him. At the time, I thought he killed his father. I thought that's what was eating him up. I didn't understand why he had done it, but I was young then, never questioned him. I never did later, either... maybe if I had..."

I looked up. "It's my fault we failed, Avlyn. I froze up in the dungeon. He had my... my mother strung up, and I froze. I let them capture me."

Avlyn's eyes were kind. "It was a long shot anyway, Princess. I don't blame you."

"You didn't make it seem like a long shot when we were planning."

"Not a great idea to tell your troops the odds aren't in their

21

favor. It doesn't build morale. Besides, you weren't the only one to blame for the situation."

My lips pulled tight, and I said nothing, not wanting to think about Ciara. Avlyn seemed of the same mind.

"It's always the beautiful ones you need to watch out for." Their eyes darted over to Pallas.

"It's too much. I can't carry this all on my own. I don't know how to save him, and if I really am…" We didn't speak of it, like saying it would make it true. "…if I really am the World Breaker, maybe it's best if I don't. Maybe I should just stay here with him until the end."

They furrowed their eyebrows. "No way in hell I'm letting that happen. As far as I'm concerned, what that old crone said changes nothing. She said it herself. Prophecies aren't straightforward things, so let's not try to pretend we understand something greater than ourselves. All we can do now is move forward."

Their honey-colored eyes were strong, and I felt that tiny spark of hope in my chest. "How can you be so sure this is the right thing, Avlyn?"

"Oh, I'm not, but I promised Abraxas that I would keep you safe, so that's what I'm going to do."

My fingers shook, but my anxiety seemed to ebb a small amount.

IN THE CAVE, MY SENSE OF TIME WAS DISTORTED, BUT THE last rays of the sun could be seen through an opening in the rock ceiling. Avlyn and I decided that at first light, they would try to hunt for some more breakfast, and we would start our journey out of this place.

"Best get some more rest while you can, Princess. We don't know what we will find," Avlyn said, and with that, they rolled over and went straight to sleep. Being able to sleep anywhere was an old soldier's trick, one that I was often jealous of.

I walked over to Jun. Pallas had dozed off, but as my footsteps approached, she snapped awake. It seemed she had a soldier's habits as well. She wrapped her hand defensively over Jun's forehead and the other over his chest.

"May I sit with him for a bit?" I hated to ask, the words tasting like ash on my mouth. Who was she to keep me from my brother? But maybe after all of this, I really was tired of fighting.

Once again, for several moments, we stood at an impasse, her eyes set in stony resolve. But then she slowly shifted her legs out from underneath Jun and held his head so I could slide my thigh underneath. She walked away, and I didn't really care where she went.

I stroked Jun's sweaty forehead, pulling his long bangs out of his face. I had known him with long hair for over two hundred years, so it still felt so foreign to me. In fact, everything about him felt foreign to me, as if the person sleeping on my lap wasn't the brother I knew but a stranger with a familiar face.

"Jun, do you remember that song I used to make you sing to me? You said it was too dramatic, but you knew I loved it. I wish you would sing it to me now." He kept sleeping, but his heartbeat was strong, and his breathing was deep. I could be happy about that. I ran my fingers through his hair.

In Niata, physical affection between family members was rare. The light squeeze of my arm was all I remembered from my mother, and my father's touch was never kind. But Jun and I had always been drawn together. My parents had expressly forbidden our touching even as young children. I knew the reason. Queen Soraya and her brother-husband King Soractes had been in front of everyone's minds. My parents wanted to keep any unsightly rumors about Jun and me at bay, but it had been no use.

When we grew older, our nighttime excursions always centered on causing some mischief, but they had started just as a way for us to lie in each other's arms and talk about every single thought on our mind. I had always known it hadn't been something sordid but something precious that existed between us. And here he was, laying with me just like when we were younglings, but everything had changed.

I wasn't a talented singer, but I tried my best.

In a land of sun's embrace, where warmth ignites the sky,
A land of ancient stories, where legends never die.
Beneath the blazing constellations, dreams take flight,
Guided by the flames burning through the night.

My pitch was off, but that had never bothered Jun. I stroked his head again when I saw his eyelids shift like he was in a deep dream, and his lips opened. The voice that emerged was weak, hoarse.

In the realm of icy whispers, where frost paints the scene,
A land of hidden secrets, where mysteries convene.

With each word he sang, the surrounding land shimmered. The wisps that danced over the spring leaped across the grass and danced around us. Beneath me, the warm earth and plants seemed to grip me in a soft embrace. As Jun kept singing, I calmed my breath. I felt it then, the same feeling I had always had with him, but through a new lens. His voice spilled over me like warm honey, and I followed that sensation deep into the earth.

It wasn't hard to find. The magic of the earth was writhing to get free here, and it latched to me immediately. I pressed on Jun's forehead and felt the power spilling into him. His mind felt like it hid in a deep shadow, but I could feel him trying to get out. I let the magic burn away those shadows. They fought me and clung to him, but as every small piece burnt away, his voice became clearer, and the song soared.

Underneath the shimmering tapestry of night's embrace,
Two worlds collide, each with its own unique grace.

I placed my hand over his heart, the magic flowing beneath my palms, and his slate-colored eyes popped open. For the first time since we had been taken from Niata, they were clear, and I could really see him. I felt the magic of his voice entwining with the magic of the earth, and tears leaked from my eyes as we finished the song together.

And as the stars entwine in a cosmic dance,
Both worlds find a common thread, a second chance.
Two souls, once apart, now dare to intertwine,
In the tapestry of fate, their destinies align.

Our last note rang out into the cave, echoing off the walls. The silence left behind was almost deafening. But slowly, the cave came alive again, and the sound of water trickling and the rustling of leaves resumed. But I barely noticed as I watched Jun. He slowly sat up, running his hands through his hair.

He turned to me. "Tori? You're here?"

"Yes, Jun. I'm here." He reached out his hand and gripped my face like he didn't believe it was true. Tears welled in his eyes. He leaned in, his forehead pressed against mine. I reached out to embrace him but saw his body flinch. I thought of Pallas, how she had only touched their pinkies together. I slowly reached out to his hand and looped our smallest fingers together. "I'm here, Jun, and I won't ever let you go again."

For a moment, he just breathed, and then he started laughing. A hysterical laugh that would normally have me worried, but instead, my own crazed laugh bubbled up in my throat. What an image we must have painted. Pure manic laughter huddled in the grass at the edge of a magic lake. But I didn't care. He was here, and he was awake. We kept laughing, and I didn't let go.

After Jun and I had laughed until we couldn't make any more sound, Pallas reappeared.

"Pallas, you are safe, too?" Jun had tried to stand to embrace her, but his legs wobbled, and I caught him under his arm. Pallas knelt but did not touch him. She said nothing, just held Jun's gaze gently with her eyes. I saw the shimmer of tears, but she quickly blinked them away.

"Jun..." She didn't complete her thought.

"It's alright, Pallas, I know. I'm glad you are here." Even now, my stomach churned with jealousy at their closeness, but I did my best to control that. Jun could have found people to befriend, maybe even more. Gods knew I had. I turned back to Abraxas, his form unchanged. Jun, whether it had been truly him or just my memory of him, had helped me find the strength to be with Abraxas. The least I could do was not be openly hostile to Pallas. Well, at least I could try.

Chapter 5

Tori

"So, this is him?" Jun gently reached out and stroked the scales on Abraxas' side.

"Yes, turns out the Dragon King is actually a dragon." I placed my hand next to his.

"That's not what I mean, and you know it." My brother shot me a scowl, and I couldn't help but laugh. How often had I given that same look to Abraxas? Hell, to everyone? The laughter died quickly.

"How could you know about us, Jun? You had that collar long before we... well... before we were anything." I was unable to imagine what being controlled in such a way would have been like, so I didn't want to push and make him relive it so soon.

As I feared, the dark circles under his eyes seemed to grow, and his face grew pale, but he linked his finger to mine, and it was steady.

"The collar... it made everything like a dream. When I obeyed Hadeon, it was like being drunk on ambrosia, out of control, but nothing hurt. But when I disobeyed... there was nothing but pain."

I remembered the throne room and the small look of defiance in his eyes. What had that cost him? He squeezed my finger tighter.

"And you fought back. You disobeyed."

His free hand went to his neck, rubbing where the collar had been. "Not as much as I wanted. I was never as strong as you were, Tori. In that strange reality, sometimes I even convinced myself I could hear your voice telling me to fight back. But it hurt too much, and eventually, I just stopped."

I squeezed his finger back. "You know I was only strong because I had you, Jun. No one could have fought off an enchantment like that. I'll tell you what we had to do to get it off you another time." I gave him a small smile, hoping to lighten his mood, but it didn't work. His face grew even more grim.

"He wanted to do the same to you. I heard him. He even had the collar made... Pallas told me, but she promised she wouldn't let that happen."

He looked over his shoulder at the woman, who was dozing by the fire that still flickered from our dinner. A bit of his smile returned.

"Is she a..." It didn't feel right to say "lover," even though I very much wanted to know. But his skin grew even paler as his forehead became sweaty. My heart stopped. I hadn't let myself think about how Hadeon had called Jun his lover, not that anyone controlled like he was could ever be that. The thought filled me with so much rage that I could feel it shaking the earth beneath my feet. That wasn't fair to Jun. He was the one who had suffered, and my outrage didn't help him.

I wanted to loop my arm over his shoulders and hold him tight, but I resisted. "I'm sorry I asked. We don't have to talk about it. If you want to, when you're ready, we can. But for now, perhaps a bit more rest? We are going to try to get out of here tomorrow."

Jun didn't speak again but nodded and made his way to lie down next to Pallas. They didn't touch, but she rolled over, so their pinkies were intertwined as they lay side by side.

I needed rest as well. I could feel the exhaustion of everything weighing on me. But instead of approaching the fire, I simply pressed my back against Abraxas' hard side and slid down so I was cradled in the crook of his arm.

"Good night, my Dragon King."

THE OCEAN OF MY MIND EBBED CALMLY. BUT IT GLOWED that mystic blue of the wild spring. I landed on the shore, but I was also in the cavern, the ocean becoming the spring that glowed softly. I knew it wasn't real since I couldn't focus on anything, and my surroundings shifted with my thoughts. So, a dream then? I sat where I had fallen asleep, but there was no fire, and no one lay around it. I leaned back into the hard scales of Abraxas' side, only to find a cool, soft body instead.

Abraxas wrapped his arms around me and whispered in my ear, "It's good to see you, little bird."

I spun around, and there he was, just as I remembered him. Just a fae man, his ears pointed and his smile wicked. His long silver-white hair ran down over his bare shoulders, and I saw the scars from our fight with the Nalle across his chest.

He raised his hand up and cupped my face. "Aren't you happy to see me too, Tori?"

I punched him right in the face.

He let out a pained groan, but I didn't stop. I slammed him down, but he snagged my wrists and flipped on top of me.

"YOU ASSHOLE!" I rammed my feet into his stomach,

and he flew back as I scrambled up. I lunged at him again, but he easily blocked me, sending my arms off to the side. His viridian eyes twinkled, and it only pissed me off more. "You absolute asshole! Why didn't you tell me? You said we had no secrets, and now... now..."

He blocked my blows, and I could hear an occasional muffled groan when one landed, but he was laughing now. "I'm dying, Tori. Be gentle with me."

I slammed my fist into his chest, and tears streamed from my eyes. "You can't, you liar. You can't die." I collapsed, my face pressed to the skin of his chest, sobbing. He wrapped his arms around me and gently stroked my hair.

"I wanted to tell you, my little bird, every single day. It was forbidden. No dragon has ever revealed our ability to shift, not once in all of written history. I couldn't tell you, even if you are my..." he trailed off.

"Say it," I commanded.

He sighed. "Even if you are my mate."

"You lied to me about that, too. How long did you know?" I lay on his chest for a while, listening to his heartbeat. It was weak, so weak.

"I knew from the moment I set foot in Niata you were my mate. Whatever magic it is that connects us, it must have been bound by the sea and the salt water. But once I touched that land, I knew you were meant to be mine."

That stirred something in me, a deep hurt. He was dying, and I didn't know what to do, but still, I found new ways for pain to cut me.

"So, what? All I've felt was a lie? This was all because of some mystical connection we had no control over."

He laughed, really laughed then. "The connection may have drawn me to you, and yes, I convinced Hadeon to let me take you to Xyr because of it. But do not think I didn't regret that choice many times over."

I pushed up off of him. Was he really saying what I thought he was?

He raised his hand and gently pushed a stray hair back behind my ear. "For a time, I hated you. I hated how weak you made me. I hated how my every waking thought was consumed by you. I hated how when you were near, I couldn't control myself. You possessed me, mind and soul. I hated how I would have done anything, *anything*, for you to smile at me."

He hit me with that grin that pulled at my heart, and his eyes sparkled. "Because I saw you, Tori. I really saw you, the ferocious, caring, and uncontainable force that you are. How could I not have hated you completely and fallen madly in love with you?" His words soothed my aching heart. "I fell in love with you the moment you held your sword to my throat with that perfect ass planted on my chest, and let me tell you, that had nothing to do with this bond. You were so filled with life and fire, and it reminded me what I was truly fighting for before hatred turned my heart to stone."

He squeezed me tight, and I lay my head back down on his chest. "I love you, too, Abraxas." I let myself linger there with those words finally shared between us, and I imagined his heartbeat grew a bit stronger.

"No more lies, Abraxas," I sighed. "Or maybe it doesn't matter. I don't even know if this is real or if it really is just a dream."

He gripped my face softly, running his thumb over my lips. "Does this feel real?"

I shivered. "Yes."

He leaned in. "And what about this?" His lips traced over the sensitive skin of my neck, trailing small kisses up and down.

"Yes."

His hands came up, gentle at first, caressing around my waist. His fingers trailed lightly over my skin; the sensation was almost unbearable as he traveled over my ribs. But then his thumb traced the curve under my breast, and I felt my nipples peak.

"Is this really the time for this, Abraxas?" I was still mad at him, but that feeling was quickly melting away into something much more primal.

"I can think of no better time, my little bird." He didn't have to say the rest. This might be the last time. My eyes pricked with tears, and I refused to accept it. I found his lips with mine. He tasted real, and the warmth of his lips and tongue pushed away the chill that still gripped my heart. I weaved my fingers through the long silver locks of his hair, pulling him even tighter to me.

His hand encompassed my breast, and he teased me by tracing around my nipple gently but never giving me that pressure I craved. I growled at him, and he chuckled, "Impatient princess."

I traced my hands over the planes of his chest, letting my fingers caress every line of him and running along the scar that wrapped around his ribs. I placed my lips on the pulse that beat under the skin of his neck. I pushed my hips into him. His responding hardness had my own arousal growing, and I ground down harder until I had him whimpering beneath me.

The world seemed to swirl. I could still see him, but I could feel the damp warmth of the cave as well, the grass pressing against my face. "I think I'm waking up."

He growled and grabbed me by the back of my neck, spinning us and pinning me under him. "I'm not letting you go yet, Tori." Our mouths crashed together, and our hands moved with a new desperation. The real world faded away, and I just focused on him, forcing myself to only feel his weight and the smooth sensation of his skin.

We ripped off the rest of our clothes, and I felt the velvet hardness of him press against my cunt, my arousal coating him. He ground into me, his teeth scraping over the skin of my shoulders. I lifted my hips to him, and we fit together perfectly.

I felt his hands move up the inside of my arms until his fingers were tracing the grooves of my palm. Then he tightly wove his fingers through mine, holding me to the ground as he thrust into me. Each meeting of our hips brought me one step closer to the edge, that beautiful golden light threading between us. He released one hand to run it down my side, over my hip, and down my thigh. He pulled my knee up along his side, and he shifted himself deeper inside me. The new position had him hitting that place that had me seeing stars.

"Abraxas..." that delicious tension was building in me, but I could feel the world swirling again, trying to rip one more thing away from me. I closed my eyes, trying to stay in that place, when his lips met mine.

"Tori, my love, look at me." I opened my eyes, and his face was so beautiful. His skin was flushed with effort and arousal; his soft lips parted as he moaned. I kissed them, swallowing the sound.

"Stay with me, Abraxas." I ran my fingers through his hair, down his back, feeling the muscles pulse with each agonizing thrust. He tightened the grip of his fingers on mine in time with the drive of his hips.

"Until the sky burns, Tori." He held my hip tight, his fingers commanding the skin and flesh beneath them, as he slid into me with relentless force, and I was lost. That golden light that lived between us became the stars in the sky, and I was floating in my body, my climax weaving itself into every muscle and nerve. I moaned his name over and over, and I felt him shudder along with me. Before we could come down together and I could revel in the feeling of him in my arms, he was gone.

Chapter 6

Hadeon

My muscles quaked, spasming as they tried to heal themselves from overuse in the field. Dirt from digging clung to my nail beds, and my palms were inflamed, where the skin had torn off from lifting stone blocks to build the new wing of the dragon temple. Bolts of pain sliced through me as I hauled myself back to the rotten hole I slept in. The chains at my ankles clacked against the stone floor as my feet dragged across their abrasive surface.

The torches of the temple cast shadows like ghosts upon the wall, their eyes following me. The hiss of the pitch was their laughter at the weak creature I had become. My pathetic refuge was carved in the back of the great stone dragon statue, hidden under his tail. It was fitting because I was worth less than the shit left behind by one of these monsters.

After my village had burned down, raiders came through to claim anything that wasn't destroyed. I was one of those things. They tossed my burnt body in the back of the wagon, and the next thing I knew, I was sold to the priests at a nearby temple to the old gods, like some pathetic human child.

I made my way behind the statue and collapsed from exhaustion. I barely felt the lice and fleas burrowing into my hair and flesh as sweet darkness took me.

Then, a rough hand was pulling me out of my alcove. The pads of his fingers seemed to find their way to the same bruises. There was nowhere I could go, nowhere that was safe, nowhere that was just mine.

"You're filthy, boy. Unfit for this holy place. Come with me." I knew what that meant.

The priest dragged me to the altar underneath that great stone dragon's maw. Bowls of tepid water sat out from the day's rituals, and he grabbed a stained rag, dragging its coarse fibers over my skin.

He pulled off the scrap of fabric that was my clothes, so I stood naked in that great hall. The priest's eyes glazed over with hunger, and I knew it wouldn't be long now. But I didn't fight him as the rag wrapped around me. He had left the pokers in the urns of embers on the altar, a reminder of the pain I had received over and over when I had fought him before. And I was just so tired; my body was already broken. I just hoped it would be over soon.

He laid me down on the frigid stone of that altar, and I floated away from my body. It wasn't me this was happening to. I let my mind drift anywhere else. Above me, the torchlight swayed over that great dragon statue, and he came alive. His eyes glowed ochre, and his tongue lashed. His deep, menacing growl struck into the deepest part of me, his hot, disgusting breath on my neck, my face, my lips. I felt his teeth bite into my skin over and over. That deep red flame surrounded me until I could see nothing but its endless depths. *Beautiful boy, how I love to devour you.*

THE DARK RED FLAME FOLLOWED ME INTO MY WAKING consciousness. It seeped through my closed eyelids and snapped them open. No, it wasn't me who was the prisoner anymore, but *him*. I had defeated him, and now his heart glowed; that deep, blood-red crimson trapped within the layers of enchantment bound him to me. My nails cut into the stone bench I lay upon. His power was *mine*; his life was *mine*. I was the Great Hero, the savior, but still, I felt I could hear his deep growl inside of me, and the hairs on the back of my neck rose. Lightning crackled over my skin, and I thought about reaching out and destroying us both.

"Ah, Your Eminence, you've awakened!" Leather-clad feet approached, and I slowly raised my aching body off the stone slab.

"Plagis, why am I down here?" I grabbed my aching head and propped my elbows on my knees. The red light of the dragon's heart caused every exposed inch of my skin to itch.

"It seemed prudent to place you as close to the heart as possible to speed up your recovery."

Slowly, the memories came back to me. The girl sitting on my lap as I tempted Abraxas. He barely resisted the trap. It had all backfired on me as his army arrived at my borders. His magic clashed with mine with a strength I hadn't felt in centuries. It still hadn't been enough.

"Where is he now?"

When I first saw his true form, I couldn't believe it. The great empty pit of denial that comes when a tragedy too large for the mind to comprehend unfolds before your very eyes. Then the anger came. How had I not known? How many times had I looked into those emerald eyes over the centuries? The truth had been right in front of me, and I had not seen it.

"He was last seen flying north. Sources have him flying out into the Sea of Spirits."

I shook out my limbs, still stiff from the recovery. Did Abraxas know how close he had come to overpowering me? Did he know I had laid under the fiery artifact, closer to death than I had come to since I first gained my powers? I stripped off the flimsy white robe I had been dressed in, surveying the large burns that ran over my chest. I'd used every healer I could find to rid myself of a similar scar after facing the World Breaker, but here it sat again, reignited. A fate I could never escape.

The wound was still fresh enough that it stung as the surrounding skin pulled with my movement. I ran my fingers over the raw surface, savoring the pain that laced through me.

"Your Eminence?" Plagis lingered behind me.

"Send every scout we have to the islands. I want him found immediately."

"Sir, with the Dragon Army's invasion, it would be prudent not to—"

I lashed out and struck him across the face with both my hand and power. He crumpled to the floor immediately.

"I want him found. Now."

"Of course, sire." Plagis clutched his cheek as he rose from the ground. "I will see it done." He scampered from the room, and I was alone with the heart.

I turned to face it. The dragon's heart floated in the center of the room, its fire still beating as if the magnificent beast merely slumbered. Glyphs danced along enchanted circles, glowing the same deep red as the magic and my blood. They orbited the heart in all directions, binding it to me.

For a moment, the maroon flames flashed a vivid green in

my mind. Abraxas, how I desired him and how he resisted me. But no longer. He would be bound to me, just like his father. He would be *mine*.

Chapter 7

Tori

I woke to the pale light of morning streaming into the cave. Despite the humid air, I shivered. I tried to fall back asleep and will my mind back to him, but it was too late. The day had claimed me in its cruel clutches.

I placed my hands on his side, the chill of him penetrating into the skin of my palms. I reached down into the earth, finding the magic easily. I guided it through my body and willed it into him with every fiber of my being. I helped Jun; maybe I could help him. It was futile. The magic wouldn't cross over into him. The shadow of death clung to him and prevented my efforts. It differed from the shadows of Jun's mind. These were darker than the void that had formed everything, something no light, no life could cross.

Before, the magic had felt like a river, a flow that molded and changed within my body. I shaped that amorphous power into a hard and sharp sword. I struck that dark barrier over and over, but nothing changed. My fingers shook with the effort, and I could feel my knees give way as more of my energy was drained. My heartbeat grew dangerously slow, but still, I fought, ruthlessly striking that magical barrier.

That was until a rough hand landed on my shoulder. "Careful, Princess." It was Avlyn. "No point in killing yourself before we can figure this whole thing out. Leave him be. I have some breakfast for you."

I finally pulled my palms off the dragon's side, and Avlyn supported me as I wobbled over to the fire.

Breakfast was squirrel, again. I knew better than to complain. Pallas sat in silence, sharing hers with Jun. He made a bit of a face as she pulled pieces off for him but didn't protest. I noticed Pallas ate very little of their shared squirrel.

Avlyn had scarfed theirs down in about three bites. I nibbled at mine and gave half to Pallas. As I held it out, she characteristically said nothing but slowly took the squirrel from my hand with a small nod.

"Sorry I couldn't catch more, but they were getting wise to my trap," Avlyn mouthed around their last bite.

"Thank you for hunting for us, Commander," Pallas murmured, and Avlyn's eyes went wide in surprise.

"Um, yeah, of course," they mumbled. "And you can just call me Avlyn." They busied themselves with cleaning their greasy hands on their trousers and stood.

"Well, I suppose this is as good a time as any. Let's head out. We've only got one bladder for water, and it's full. But keep your eyes peeled for water sources as we travel." Avlyn scratched their head. "It's been quite some time since I've traveled in a group that was all fae, so we might push ourselves quite a bit."

I was about to protest when Pallas did it for me. "Jun is still recovering; we won't be able to push him."

A small frown curved at the corner of Avlyn's lips, but they nodded. "We can take turns helping him as needed as well. Alright, troops, let's head out."

I saw Pallas roll her eyes at that, but she didn't complain as she stood and helped Jun do the same. She slung his arm over her shoulders, supporting him as they followed Avlyn. I brought up the rear.

I felt very naked without a weapon, but the only one Avlyn had hung on to in our escape was a single dagger, which they held. They led us back to the tunnel we had previously found. We made slow progress through the growth of the cavern, Jun occasionally tripping on roots and Pallas needing to assist him. She struggled as well, wearing heeled shoes that were appropriate for court but not for adventuring through rough terrain. On another day, I might have found the situation hilarious, watching Pallas' face scrunch up in disdain as her heel sunk into the muddy earth. She looked an awful mess, her luscious hair tangled horribly, her beautiful gown covered in soot and dirt, and her makeup was smudged. She more resembled a farm girl than a lady of the highest court. I was sure I looked no better, but I knew it would affect her more than me.

I wasn't laughing today. Instead, my gut clenched at our horrendously slow pace, and I wondered just how long she would last out here.

Chapter 8

Pallas

I stood up from the dying fire as Commander Avlyn put out the last of the embers. Extending my hand to Jun, I helped him stand. He was still unsteady, so I gently slung his arm over my shoulders, letting him use me for support.

I felt Princess Tori giving me a pointed stare, but I ignored her. I didn't trust her. If she really cared for her brother as much as she said, she would have come for him sooner. She would have tried harder. The Dragon Kingdom always had its secrets, and it seemed she fit in perfectly. I don't know how she helped Jun or started that fire when she had no magic of her own. Hadeon would have known if she had. She could keep her secrets. The only thing that mattered to me now was getting Jun safely out of here.

I followed the commander as they led us deeper into the forest of the cavern. The ground was permeated with roots, rocks, and other obstacles, and my poor Jun kept faltering. I found that I wasn't much help either. The shoes I wore were some of my finest, the short heels perfect for dancing at court.

They were not built for the thick mud of wherever the hell we were.

After about the fifth time a heel sunk so deep into the mud I had to stop and wrench it out, I finally released a curse of frustration. I ripped the shoes off my feet and tossed them as far as I could into the brush. Commander Avlyn turned around, giving me a curious glance, but I heard Tori shifting behind me and turned to see her offering her own shoes to me.

"I'm fine." I didn't need help, least of all from her.

Her eyes practically hit the back of her skull. "Oh, I'm sorry, I didn't realize you were so used to walking barefoot on rocky terrain. Maybe it was the haughty attitude or the fine clothes that confused me." What a bitch.

"I said I'm fine."

"Look, you will injure yourself, and it won't bother me one bit to leave you behind, so take the damn shoes."

"Tori..." Jun looked at his sister with soft eyes, and it drove a spike into my heart; she didn't deserve his kindness. But I had no doubt she would leave me the first chance she was given. I wasn't about to make it easy on her. I held my hand out and took the shoes, slipping them onto my feet. They were made of leather with a firm sole, likely making them ideal for sword fighting. I pulled the laces tight; they fit well enough.

I stood and gave her a quick nod before following the commander. They still gave me that concerned look, so I narrowed my eyes in annoyance. They gave a small chuckle, and I thought I heard them mumble something about "birds and feathers."

The commander guided us to a small tunnel that led out of the cave. The deeper we went, the darker it became until everything was pitch black, slowing our progression even more. This would be the perfect place for a predator to ambush us, I assumed, not that I had much firsthand experience with hunting. I let my hand trace along the wall to keep my bearings. It was wet and unnervingly smooth like thousands of hands had polished it by tracing over the surface as I did now. That thought was very discomforting.

Unsurprisingly, the princess couldn't keep her mouth shut and started babbling to the commander about something. They quipped back and forth at each other. I just ignored it all, trying to focus on placing one foot in front of the other, but their talking was incessant and grated on my ears. I gritted my teeth, and Jun looked at me with concern. It seemed my reaction didn't go unnoticed by Tori, either.

"Let's switch. I can help him for a bit." She lifted his arm from over my shoulder. I was about to protest, but Jun leaned on her readily. Having his weight off me was much more relieving than I wanted to admit, so I said nothing.

The surrounding air was rapidly growing cold, and soon, without Jun's body against me, I began shivering. My dress was torn to shreds. It had been one of my finest. I would have mourned it had I not been shivering so fiercely. An icy blast came down the tunnel, and I clasped my arms around myself. Where were we? It was summer on the continent, so very few places felt this cold. We could be in the Ashen Mountains, but since the king brought us here, it seemed more likely we were far north in the Dragon Kingdom.

"Let me know if you need someone to cuddle up with, my lady." The commander had snuck up beside me without my notice, and I jumped at their proximity and flirtation.

I couldn't see their face in the dark, but their voice sounded apologetic as they said, "Sorry, old habits die hard. It's getting quite cold. We might not have a choice soon."

I didn't respond. I'd found throughout my life that my responses never mattered. Everyone had already decided on their actions without my consent. So why bother wasting the energy? I shivered violently at the cold as we kept walking, and I expected the commander to wrap me up in their arms at any moment. I knew what would happen. There would be a not-so-subtle caress of a finger over the curve of my breast as they pressed their hips into the curve of my backside. I lost count of the times I dealt with that and much, much more. But the commander's advances never came.

We kept walking, and the temperature kept dropping. My teeth were chattering so loud the sound echoed off the tunnel walls.

The commander surprised me again by speaking very close to my ear. "Look, I understand this isn't ideal. But if you keep this up much longer, your body could start shutting down, or you might just rattle those teeth right out of your skull. So, my lady, can I touch you?"

My feet froze, but not from the cold. I couldn't remember the last time someone asked before touching me. I'd been Hadeon's plaything for so long. Had I really forgotten I deserved that basic decency?

"Yes, Commander."

"Call me Avlyn."

Their arms were muscular and unbelievably warm as they wrapped around me from behind, pressing their whole body against my back. It was glorious, but the embrace was very restricted and professional. They were just stopping me from going into shock.

"What's the holdup?" Tori and Jun had caught up to us.

"Nothing." The commander shifted away, and a tiny whimper fled my lips as the cold air whipped between us. I felt them hesitate, then wrap their arm around my side so that we could walk together, still touching. They gently pushed me forward, and we continued our descent.

"Thank you, Avlyn."

"Ah, she speaks!" A chuckle fled their lips. "But don't mention it. History would show that I am way too lenient for beautiful women with bad attitudes."

"You better not be talking about me!" Tori called back over her shoulder. Avlyn laughed again. The sound sent a warmth through my heart that had nothing to do with their body heat. They leaned close to whisper in my ear, the warm air of their breath ghosting over the pointed tip. "Like I said, very bad attitudes."

We walked until even the commander was barely keeping me warm. When I noticed I could just make out the elegant lines of their face. That meant...

"Daylight ahead!" called the princess. Avlyn quickened our pace, and a few moments later, we reached the end of our tunnel. The icy wind whipped me even harder, and I looked out over a small beach nested against sheer rock cliffs. The ocean that beat the shore was a dark, menacing grey, and I couldn't see much beyond our small landing because of the thick mist.

"The Sea of Spirits," the commander whispered. I pushed myself deeper into their side as my shivers resumed. They wrapped their arm around me tighter.

"How can you be sure?" I asked.

"My lady, I would know this ocean were I blind and deaf." I didn't have time to ask why before Tori and Jun came up beside us.

"Nowhere to go," Jun commented.

"I wouldn't be so sure," Tori gently responded. "I was always quite the climber, you remember."

Jun huffed, "Yes, but I never was. Besides, have you climbed since..." He trailed off, looking at her arm. Her dress was more torn up than mine, and I saw a massive scar running around her left bicep. She clasped it reflexively under his gaze.

In the palace, I pulled her by that arm, and she had winced.

At the time, I thought she was just being dramatic, but now something like guilt stirred in my stomach.

"I'll be alright; we have little choice anyway." She kept rubbing her arm as she spoke.

"Ok, you two, stay here or in the tunnel to avoid most of the wind. Tori, you come with me." The commander released me from their hold. I wasn't as gentle as I should have been getting Jun next to me in the tunnel's entrance, but I was desperate to stay warm.

We sat shivering together, and he undid his coat to wrap us under it. We sat in silence, watching the commander and princess dart around the small beach, examining the cliff walls and who knew what else. Tori's talkativeness had rubbed off on Jun.

"You can trust her, you know." His voice was barely above a whisper.

"How quickly you have forgiven her."

He sighed. "She's my sister, Pallas."

"That means nothing."

He looked at me with sad eyes filled with pity. I glanced away so I didn't have to see it. He sighed again. "It means something to me."

I leaned my head onto his shoulders, and we didn't say anymore. We knew we never had to speak of it. This silence was especially loud. I had grown used to Jun's singing; it always lifted my broken heart. Jun's magic was incredible. In all my research with my father, voice-channeling magic was some of the rarest, even before magic disappeared. Most required external facilities to control their magic, whether that be glyphs, enchanted instruments, or even magical tattoos.

Jun had never been trained. He learned to control it himself. He'd even told me it had been easy, natural, although he hadn't even known that was what he was doing at first.

That's why Hadeon had been so desperate to claim him. He'd spent the last five hundred years killing or capturing anyone with even the slightest hint of magic. So, when rumors came from the Pearl Kingdom of a twin with a magic voice, he hadn't been subtle in his invasion.

I'd been so relieved to see him go, knowing that I'd have a few weeks of peace; I hadn't spared a single thought for the people who wouldn't survive it. As long as I survived, that's what mattered. Then I met Jun.

8 MONTHS AGO

The gardens were barren in the middle of winter. Nothing remained but the frozen earth and a few dried vines; the leaves barely held on in the crisp breeze. In the spring, the palace gardens would have this place looking like something out of a dream. Flowers of every color blossomed between stands of the golden ambrosia flower that fueled everything in this empire. No one was out here during the winter. It was a perfect hiding spot.

I'd worn a thick fur coat to keep out the winter chill. The soft white fur had come off a mountain cat from the Ashen Mountains. There was nothing magical about it, but there were so few left that the coat was worth more than what most people in the outer ring made in a year. I let the dirt touch the hem as I sat on the edge of the derelict garden bed, trailing my fingers through the dead soil.

"Pallas, my love, I have someone for you to meet." My whole body tensed as the bottom of my stomach dropped out. He was back. I'd seen his entourage coming up the main road of the city. I'd grown stupid in his absence, bold.

I clenched the coat's lapels in my fist, hoping it looked like I was trying to stay warm and not hiding my flushed skin. Hopefully, my swollen lips would be mistaken for chapped in the dry winter air, and the chilly breeze would sweep away the scent of ash and rose.

I lifted off the ice-cold stone and turned to greet Hadeon. He wore his typical elegantly embroidered purple coat with golden threads that glistened in the afternoon sun. The straight collar nearly reached his sharp jawline. By his side was a boy, but not truly a boy, for he had the body of a tall, slender man and a low voice to match. His angular face was clean-shaven and handsome, complimented well by his long dark hair that was pulled back into a tight bun. His deep slate eyes shone with innocence reserved for the very young. Hadeon had his arm around him, and the boy tried to shift away unsuccessfully. I saw him flinch each time Hadeon's body shifted, and I knew what that meant.

"Pallas, this is Prince Jun Khato of the Pearl Kingdom. I have a feeling we will all become very close soon." Hadeon grinned that terrible grin I knew all too well. He looked at the boy as if he wished to devour him, which he surely would. A horrible part of me was grateful for it. Maybe this new toy would distract Hadeon away from me, and I could have a bit more peace. How many toys had Hadeon played with and discarded over the years, but I remained? I didn't care what happened to them.

But then Jun looked up at me, giving me the softest smile I had ever seen. It was hesitant and beautiful, a shy smile many hadn't seen.

"It's nice to meet you, Lady Pallas."

For centuries, I'd hardened my heart. I wasn't meant for

much in this life and most days, all I clung to was the idea of survival and the hope that I might somehow outlive this situation. I had long ago given up the thought of escape or happiness. I belonged to Hadeon, and I wasn't worth anything without that possession. But maybe these last weeks without him had allowed a fatal flaw in the armor to crack open.

One look from those kind grey eyes and my heart split. He did not know what was coming or what Hadeon would put him through. I did. I had long ago given up on myself, but the thought of this boy going through what I had scraped open wounds I thought long plastered over.

"It's nice to meet you too, Prince Jun."

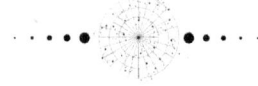

"WHAT'S THAT?" JUN SNAPPED ME OUT OF MY MUSINGS, pointing out at the sea. I squinted. Through the mist, I could just make out a ship. I waved my arms and tried to hop up and signal them, but Jun held me back with surprising strength. His face was like stone.

I looked again and saw the purple sail of the ship materialize through the fog. The flaming crown etched in gold seemed to burn as the wind whipped the sails. Hadeon's soldiers. My saviors and my nemesis. I was at a crossroads, unsure which path I would take. Would I choose my abuser or Tori's? Despite centuries of pain, a part of me still longed to run back to Hadeon, to face his wrath, if only because I understood that path. I knew what would come. With the commander and Tori, everything was uncertain. Jun's grip shook around my hand. I had a choice to make.

Chapter 9

Tori

A vlyn and I were trying out a crack in the cliff to see if we could traverse it until the sight of Pallas waving her arms in my peripheral caught my attention. I snapped around to see what she was looking at, and my stomach sank at the sight of the Court of Flames vessel.

I slid down the cliff to Avlyn's side, and they pulled the dagger out of their belt.

"Don't love our odds with one dagger between us." I tried to make it sound lighthearted but failed.

Avlyn's lips were set in a thin line. "I'm more concerned about her," they were looking at Pallas, who had stopped trying to signal the ship, but it was too late. It was headed straight for us. "She's an unknown. I don't like unknowns."

"We can't let them find Abraxas. He is defenseless." I balled my hands into fists; they felt hollow without a sword.

Avlyn nodded their head in agreement. It looked like fighting was our only option. "Got any good ideas, Princess?"

"No, but I do have a stupid one."

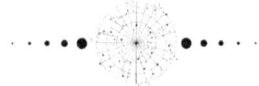

THE SHIP HAD NEARLY REACHED THE SHORE BY THE TIME I made it back to Pallas and Jun.

"What are we going to do, Tori?" My brother was shaking, and not from the cold.

I knelt down in front of him but looked only at Pallas. "Jun says I can trust you. Prove it. Help us."

She was silent; we didn't have time for this. I was about to turn back to Avlyn when I heard Jun whisper, "I can't go back there, Pallas." I practically saw her resolve at his words.

"It's stupid to trust me. I could easily turn on you. Those are my men out there." She wasn't wrong. That's what made this a stupid idea. But she had helped us, helped me, already. I didn't understand her motives, but I thought back to when we were at that party in Xyr. For just a moment, I had seen her shell crack. Perhaps that was the person for whom Jun cared so deeply.

"I have a feeling those men don't belong to anyone but Hadeon. And the truth is, you don't." Something flashed so fast through her expression that I almost missed it. I stood and reached my hand out to her. "I'm asking. Help us."

She reached out her hand, but I gripped her forearm the way I did every other soldier to help her rise. She met my eyes and nodded.

"Good. Besides, if you betray us, I'll make sure you don't leave this beach alive."

A SMALL BOAT WAS LAUNCHED TO THE SHORE WITH SIX fully armored soldiers, not good odds. I had to hope they weren't all fae. Who knew how many were still on the ship? I would worry about that later.

I held Pallas in front of me, my arm locked around her neck. Avlyn held Jun, dagger pressed to his throat.

"A little tight, Tori," she mumbled.

"I have to make it believable, Pallas." She grunted at that.

The soldiers disembarked, and one moved ahead of the others. Undoubtedly, he was the leader. He removed his helmet, revealing a shaved head. His long fae ears were clearly visible. *Fuck.*

He raised an eyebrow. "What's the meaning of this?"

Avlyn, their dagger still pressed against Jun's throat, sneered, "A bit of leverage, soldier. You wouldn't want harm to befall the prince, would you?"

The soldiers exchanged glances as their hands gripped the hilts of their weapons. I tightened my hold on Pallas until I felt her wheeze; I tried not to enjoy it. "We want safe passage back to the ship." I moved to the side.

The leader's eyes followed me, and he stepped away from the others, who kept their eyes on Avlyn. "You think you are getting off this beach alive?" he chuckled.

I glared at him. "We can make this easy or very, very messy. Your call."

He walked towards me again until we were only a sword's distance apart. Pallas was my only shield from his blade. He laughed again, and all the soldiers drew their weapons. We were outnumbered, so we had to play dirty.

Pallas slammed her elbow into my gut much harder than I thought she could. I released my grip, and she ran. "Help me! Save me!" The group all turned to track her, and it was just enough. I closed the distance between the enemy and me, cracking my fist against his bare cheek. He staggered, and I tried to wrestle the sword from his grip.

"Now, Jun!" I screamed.

A single, clear note rang out over the beach, echoing off the cove's walls. Everyone was caught in his song except for me. I pulled the sword from the leader's hand. Jun's voice broke, and with it, the spell was lifted. With my next breath, I sliced the fae's neck before he could recover. I had counted on more time. Avlyn was outnumbered.

Jun coughed in Avlyn's arms as the soldiers ran at them. Pallas threw herself onto the back of one, pulling him down. It was stupid, but I didn't have time to worry about her or be grateful. There was shouting coming from the boat. Avlyn threw Jun aside and blocked a strike as best they could with the small dagger. I closed the distance between us, striking the nearest soldier right at the seam of his armor at the back of the knee. It was not a lethal hit, but it was enough to incapacitate.

We engaged the three standing men as best we could. Avlyn still had armor, so they used their body to block me, but I heard them grunt as the enemies' blades found their mark.

The soldier Pallas tackled hit her, and I cringed as she fell. She caught herself like someone trained in combat. *Or someone trained in pain,* the thought ran through my mind.

Hitting the ground running, she dashed towards the ocean's edge with the soldier giving chase. There was no escape, and she stumbled on the wet sand. Pallas' legs were kicked out from under her, and she crumpled. I was too far away; I wouldn't make it in time. The soldier raised his sword. Her eyes widened. I had seen that look before, the fear laced with acceptance that there was no way out. She closed her eyes, but a great wave suddenly crashed over the man, knocking him to the ground. Before he could get his bearings and rise back up, Avlyn closed the distance and skewered him.

I danced through the soldiers, landing strikes where I could on any exposed portion of their bodies. I grabbed the sword of the man whose knee I had struck and tossed it at Avlyn with my bad arm; pain radiated throughout my muscles. The sword flew too far to the left.

Avlyn scrambled for the weapon, and a soldier raised a blade overhead. I ran into his body at full speed, knocking both of us over in a mess of limbs and swords. He rolled onto me, his armor cutting into my very unprotected body, and slammed his fist into my face until I tasted blood, scrambling for my sword, and grabbed it from the sandy beach.

I struck the side of the soldier's helmet with the pommel. It shocked him enough to free myself and avoid another swing. Avlyn struck the man's back, and he went still. Avlyn helped me up, and I had just a second to see that we were very fucked. Three injured soldiers remained, but each drew their sword and took a fighting stance. Three more small boats were being lowered from the main ship, all full of reinforcements.

Avlyn stepped in front of me, their sword at the ready. "I have these fuckers. Help Jun. Without him, we won't stand a chance."

I dashed to my brother's side as Avlyn's swords clashed with their opponents. Pallas had her hand on his back as he continued to cough.

"Tori, I'm sorry. I can't. It's like he still has me. The pain..." he coughed again; this time, it came out more ragged.

I placed my hand over his heart and stared into his dark slate eyes. It was like looking in a mirror. "It's always been you and me against the world. We do this together, Jun."

I reached into the earth with my mind. The magic was waiting for me. But an even stronger pull came to me from the sea. The magic there was deep, primordial, and much more vicious. I pulled at just a thread and felt it sink into Jun.

Immediately, his coughing stopped. I felt the shadow that still lay over his throat and sent the magic there to wash away the ghost of his collar. The ocean's power snapped it up in one great wave.

But more shadows remained. I analyzed his body with the magic, and when I reached his heart, pain laced through my soul at what I found. Shadows were etched into every nook. With every beat, his heart strained against their control. They had made themselves at home. This was not something I could wash away without destroying Jun. I didn't think any magic could.

I pulled the ocean's magic back, trying to turn it from a vicious thing into a soft caress. It was impossible. The sea didn't want to be contained. So, I let it go, and instead reached for that same feeling inside my own heart. I pulled a small amount of my own life out, just a thread, but it left me weak. I wrapped it gently around Jun's heart. It didn't remove the shadows or even touch them, but I hoped it would make them easier to bear.

He opened his mouth, and a pure note escaped. Even I was entranced by its beauty. The soldiers on the beach fell to their knees, awe plastered on their faces. We had unlocked something, and Avlyn, Pallas, and I were still free. Avlyn, ever the soldier, didn't hesitate to end our enemies.

I finally took a breath, but it was stolen almost immediately. The soldiers on the boats still approached, unfazed.

"They plugged their ears; I watched them do it," Pallas said.

"And that would work? This is magic we're talking about." Avlyn was panting, but they still held their fighting stance.

"It seems so," I responded, gently releasing Jun. His face was pale as he stopped singing.

"What do we do now?" Pallas asked in a strained voice. A tiny smile crossed her lips. "Don't tell me I chose the losing side."

"Not the most appropriate time to reveal a sense of humor, Pallas."

"Seems like it might be the last chance I have."

I placed a hand on Avlyn's shoulder. "What about your magic? They are still on the water."

"I don't think splashing them is going to do much," they said with a huff.

"Everyone's so funny when they are about to die. I'll channel for you, just like Jun."

Avlyn gave another grunt but didn't object. I placed my hands on them and reached for the magic again. The ocean seemed even more vicious and hungry. Its depths expanded beyond what I could fathom, and its dark heart pulsed, but a vast, dark shadow was coming straight for us. I could feel it extending tendrils, reaching for the surface. For a moment, I felt a huge yellow eye looking back at me.

"Any day now, Princess." Avlyn tightened their grip on their sword as the first boat reached the beach.

The shadow arrived, and a great tentacle shot from the water, grabbing hold of the small boat and flinging it into the air. The soldiers' screams were cut short when their armor pulled them under the roiling surface. The sea looked like it was boiling as more tentacles writhed in the depths.

Before they could react, the remaining boats were crushed in the Leviathan's arms. Wood splintered, and the men aboard were pulled violently under.

There was shouting coming from the main ship, but the Leviathan wrapped itself around the vessel in a heartbeat. Its limbs climbed the sides like the hands of death itself, impervious to the swords and spears on deck. The attempt to harm the creature was futile as each tentacle wrapped around a soldier and pulled him into the grasp of the ocean.

The very last soldier tried to stand his ground, evading a

large tentacle with his sword, but fell victim to a smaller one wrapped around his leg. As he was lifted over the ship's railing, his screams echoed across the crashing waves, laced with fear only prey can feel. The sea parted, and the great jaws of the Leviathan emerged, row after row of hideous fangs that descended into an endless black pit. It dropped the soldier, and the crunch of metal was audible as the Leviathan swallowed him whole.

All of us on the beach were stock still. It had only taken the space of five breaths to destroy all the small boats and the soldiers. Content, the Leviathan sank beneath the waves.

I reached out with my mind once again.

Now we are even, little beast. The voice that rang in my mind sounded deeper and colder than the most unknown trenches of the sea. I felt the Leviathan sink back into a world of silence and darkness.

Thank you. Despite my call, there was no reply.

Chapter 10

Hadeon

525 years ago

I lay on the stone altar long after the priest had finished. The great dragon's maw lay open above. *Do it. Eat me, you beast. Kill me.* I prayed to him, but now he was just a statue, unmoving. *Please.* But tonight, no prayers would be answered.

A hand tugged at my arm, and I flinched. But it was an old hand, wrinkled and etched with the marks of time. I turned my head, and the harsh stone scraped along my skull. Her face was even more wrinkled, and she had a messy halo of golden-brown hair streaked with white.

"Come on, young one. Let's get you to bed."

They all knew. Every single person in that temple knew what that monster was doing to him, but they said nothing, did nothing. Except for her. The Seer.

She was half-fae, positively ancient, and fragile. But she would crawl out from her room, her own personal hell, and hold me as I fell asleep weeping each night. But she could not fight them. She was a prisoner to that temple, just as I was.

Seers were not chained, but the herbs they gave them for

their visions infected their blood, and they couldn't live without them. The pain of the withdrawal was said to be one of the worst things a human or fae could bear, death being the sweet release at the end.

I sometime still wonder if she had made the whole thing up, her attempt to free me. It hadn't freed me. I'd just gotten a bigger prison.

I remember the moon had shone full through the tall windows cut out of the temple walls. The main room was filled with worshipers, prostrating themselves and leaving offerings for those terrible dragon gods who had bestowed life upon us and who continued to deny me the sweet release of death. I hid away in a corner concealed by shadows, my shame and weakness as my only companions.

A hymn had just ended, the last note still hung in the air when a crash cut through the reverent atmosphere like a blade. The curtains pulled back, and smoke billowed from the stone doorway of the Seer's chambers. The air was scented with blood and the herbs she craved, that were both her gift and her damnation. She lurched out of the doorway as if her legs and arms weren't attached to her body properly. Her eyes glowed like the moon above.

The room was silent as each worshipper held their breath. It was believed that the most potent time to recite a prophecy was on the full moon. Even without that, magic had already faded enough that even a prophecy from the Seer of some minor temple was worth more than gold.

She raised one gnarled, ancient finger and pointed to where I lay hidden. "He's the one who will face the World Breaker. The Great Hero is his demise."

For a moment, the entire world had held still. And then there was the flood. Hands grabbed me from every direction. I was pushed and pulled into the crowd. All I saw was that stone dragon's face and heard his menacing laughter as I was dragged away.

Present Day

"We've lost three ships out in the Sea of Spirits." Luxos twirled a dagger between his fingers lazily while he leaned against the wall of my room. "None have returned with any information on the Dragon."

"Perhaps you should look less pleased about delivering me this unpleasant news, Commander," I said, pressing down on the head of the woman who had my cock in her mouth. She hesitated when she heard Luxos' voice, and that wouldn't do.

Luxos continued his casual ministrations to the blade in his hand. "I told that old fool Plagis sending ships out there was a fool's errand. No one outside the Dragon Kingdom can navigate those waters, not without some sort of guide."

The woman gagged loudly as I pressed her down again, and I let out an aggravated sigh, pushing her so she collapsed to the ground. "Get out of my sight." I waved her away as I stuffed my cock back into my pants. She had the good sense to look afraid as she scrambled out of the room, glancing at Luxos as she left. If she was looking for pity, she received none. He only gave her a disgusted look as she passed by.

"So, what would you suggest, Commander?"

"With Abraxas gone, we should push his forces back. They are divided and lack a leader. This is the time to strike."

Luxos knew as well as I that Abraxas' army was larger than

mine. I'd gotten lax these last few centuries, allowing him to run almost all military operations. I saw now how he'd been pushing his advantage all this time, and I felt my skin crawling with my power as anger built in me.

Luxos didn't flinch as bolts of lightning struck out across the room. He threw up a wall of shadows, blocking a bolt that came too close. That was something I liked about the commander, his restrained control. The attack fizzled out against his dark shield, and when it dropped, he was wiping lint off his shoulder.

"Even divided, we stand to lose too many of our forces to a direct assault."

He gave a wicked grin. "Let me see what I can do inside the kingdom. Perhaps we can keep to the shadows."

I raised an eyebrow at him. "Has something changed? You could never enter the kingdom before."

Luxos rolled up his sleeve, revealing dark glyphs snaked around his forearm. The ink still glimmered, and blood leaked from the edges of the tattoo. "Just had the new Huldu ink these. They feel potent. In fact, everything has felt more potent ever since..."

He was wise not to finish that sentence. But I knew, for I had felt it, too. Ever since the spring, I'd felt it. The whispers of it on the wind, the echoes of it beneath my feet. But after Abraxas had changed, there was no denying it. Magic. Magic as it had been before I'd killed Malech, and every last drop had dried up. I couldn't quite reach it, but it was there, just below the surface. Ever since he and that girl had slipped through my fingers.

"I expect results, Commander."

"Of course, Your Eminence." He exited the room, and I called to the storm in my heart. As it had for the last five hundred years, I felt the great stream of magic it called to, linked to the dragon's heart locked away below my feet.

I sent the bolt out of my hand and into the armoire across my room. The lightning fanned across the wood in an erratic pattern. The entire thing disintegrated.

Let them come. Let them all come. The magic of this world belonged to me, and I would destroy any who tried to claim it.

Chapter 11

Tori

The Leviathan had considerately left the ship remarkably intact. It was flawless except for a few broken boards and ominously empty living quarters still scattered with the soldiers' personal effects. Avlyn quickly took the helm and began shouting words at Jun, Pallas, and myself. Some of them I even understood.

"Pallas has an excuse, but you two grew up on an island. How do you not know how to sail?" Avlyn questioned us as they bustled around the ship, tying knots and moving the sails.

"We grew up as royalty. I had people to sail for me." I crossed my arms over my chest.

"That is the most spoiled princessy thing I have ever heard you say. Although I remember our journey to Xyr, so maybe I can figure out why you never enjoyed sailing." Avlyn huffed a laugh.

Even just the jostling of the ship as we prepared to sail had my stomach lurching. I kept near the railing.

Pallas kept glancing at the dark water below; the color was drained from her face.

"It's not coming back. You can relax," I tried to reassure her.

"How can you be so sure?"

"Because it told me."

Pallas and Jun exchanged a glance at that. "I thought Tori didn't have any magic?" My brother directed the question at Pallas.

"She doesn't."

"I'm standing right here, thank you very much. What would you know about my magic?"

Her eyes returned to that dead stare; the color washed out of them. "Hadeon wanted Jun's and your powers. Twins are always born with more magic, or at least they were. He thought maybe your powers just hadn't emerged yet and went to great lengths to get it out of you."

I remembered my dance with Hadeon and Luxos stabbing Kaleos in that derelict temple. "So, he figured abusing me would awaken it?"

"That's what happened to him." I didn't like what her words implied. They hung in the air a few more moments before she continued, "So, he thought it would work on you as well. But it didn't, so he assumed you were powerless. But you obviously aren't." She looked me up and down.

Jun came over to me and held my hand. "Do you have magic, Tori?"

My eyes were locked on Pallas. "You've sided with us. But you must trust us as well. You obviously know Hadeon well, maybe better than anyone. What are you to him?"

She didn't move. That dead gaze I'd seen in Xyr locked into her eyes.

"Have I sided with you? Or am I just doing my best to survive? You stole me away from my life, Princess. I owe you nothing."

I gritted my teeth. Why was she being so difficult? She

already helped us once, and I didn't have time for her waffling. "Well, if you are so keen on being my enemy, perhaps I'll treat you like one." I grabbed her upper arm, pulling her away from the railing. Her eyes snapped to mine and lost that dull shade. I saw it again, that fierce hunter's look. Good. I shoved her so she crashed into the railing; she flailed to not fall over.

"Tori, stop." Jun's voice cracked, but I didn't stop.

I pulled vicious and hungry power from the ocean beneath our boat. I let it fill me until my body practically vibrated with it. "Does this look like no power to you, Pallas?" I stalked closer, and her eyes grew wide.

I saw deep below the fear that she was a cornered and beaten animal that had been subjected to repeated abuse. But deep down, she remained a predator. I wanted her to fight.

So, she did, but not in the way I expected. "You're just like him."

Immediately, my power fled. And like the predator she was, she saw my hesitation and weakness and struck.

"Use your power to control me, Princess. Chain me, imprison me, but don't for one moment pretend you aren't just like them, like every fae who has ever wielded power for their own selfish gains."

Jun was whimpering, looking between us. "Pallas, Tori, please don't—"

"I don't want to control you, Pallas."

"Then you must accept that I will not help you."

I wanted to rip her stupid, beautiful hair out of her head. I felt rage swirling within my gut like flames, eager to engulf her in them. But Jun was practically vibrating with fear, and I couldn't bear it one moment more. I spun around and walked as far away from Pallas as I could on that small ship.

MIST WAS ALL I COULD SEE IN ANY DIRECTION. IT shrouded everything, making our path forward indiscernible. But somehow, Avlyn continued to guide the boat. Rocks would rise out of the sea, but they had already altered the course long before we could see them.

I clung to the railing, letting the frozen spray from below drench me. It seemed to help calm the fire that danced through my veins. I looked out at the ocean below, tried to find my breath and calm my racing heart. The sun was fading into the horizon like the sea was swallowing it whole. I stared into its fading red light, that deep crimson glow. As it finally disappeared beneath the waves, I thought I saw a flash of green light, vivid and other-worldly, and my heart squeezed tight. I tried to call to Abraxas' flames again, but my mind was still reeling. My chest ached, and I gave up.

Darkness fell on the ship, and I finally turned away from the railing. Pallas was nowhere to be seen.

Avlyn stood at the helm of the ship. I offered to take over, but they claimed they wanted to make it to Xyr in one piece, so they responded with a "no, thank you."

"We aren't too far now, Princess. I can stay awake tonight; tomorrow, we should be back home. You get some rest."

Rest, that sounded like a good idea. It seemed calm, but sleep was beyond my grasp. I lay on the deck of the ship, looking up at the starry sky through the riggings, when Jun came and lay down next to me.

"I guess we both can't sleep, huh?"

"I've done enough sleeping for a lifetime." His response was so humorless it broke my heart. I thought of those deep shadows I had seen. I wanted to rid him of them, to rip them out. But I knew that wasn't possible.

I lifted his arm and laid my head on his chest, as we had done countless times before. But it didn't feel the same as it once did, and I doubted it ever would again. As I lay my head down, I felt him flinch as my touch sparked fear.

I moved to lie beside him, close but not touching. We were silent for a few moments when I felt his pinky intertwine with mine.

Despite living together for two hundred years, in just a few months, so much had changed between us. I listened to his heartbeat and felt the squeeze of his finger. For the moment, that was enough.

"Who is she to you, Jun?"

I wanted to wait, wanted to let him heal slowly and come to me in his own time, but it had become very apparent just how crucial Pallas' knowledge would be.

I turned to watch his short bangs flutter in the sea breeze. Jun's lips pressed together, and I waited until it felt like the minutes had stretched on for the lifetime of our world.

"She... she was the one who was there for me."

My heart broke again. It should have been me, but I hadn't been there. Perhaps Jun would one day forgive me for that, but I don't know if I could forgive myself.

"I failed you. I should have protected you and kept us together at any cost. But I swear on the old gods, I won't let that happen again."

Despite the heaviness of the day, I thought I saw a small twinkle of starlight in his eyes. "You know, oaths like that mean something different now that I know you've got an old god at your side."

That tightness in my chest grew stronger. I didn't have him.

I knew I needed to leave to save him, but it still felt like I was leaving a part of myself behind. A single tear rolled down my cheek, and the silence stretched between Jun and me again. It was so unnatural; I wasn't sure what I hated more.

The stars twinkled overhead, and the great milky river stretched over the black dome of the sky, gleaming on the moonless night. It was called *Maiak* in the old language, which meant Final Crossing, for all souls had to travel the river of stars to pass from our world to whatever lay beyond.

"I read somewhere that the stars grew lonely in their eternity, so they created dragons to share the sky with. They gathered up the ashes of a dying star, and from that, the first dragons were born." I didn't want Jun to stop talking, so I said nothing. "Even though they were killed only a few centuries before we were born, they never seemed real to me. Just another story, something ridiculous the elders believed. I never dreamed I'd see one; I never dreamed a lot of things..."

He trailed off, and I could feel the deep sadness in his heart right along with my own. Jun wasn't a fighter. He had always been a creator. Creating amazing art and moving music to bring beauty into the world.

We were two different people, but I had no doubt the gods had designed us to complement each other. I couldn't stand that I had been designed to protect him and wasn't there when he needed it most.

"I don't know what the future holds, Jun. But I promise you this, and not on any god, but on my soul, we will face it together. I can't promise you any more than that, but I will stay by your side, no matter what."

He moved just a slight bit closer to me. "I never blamed you for not being there, Tori. I always knew you would come for me. Sometimes I just wish..."

I gave his pinky the slightest squeeze for courage. He sighed.

"I just wish that I didn't need you. That I could have saved myself. You've always been so strong and fearless. I wish I could be like that."

I'd never heard him voice anything like this, that he wished to be like me. How many nights had I cried myself to sleep as a youngling, wishing I could have been like him? Graceful, beloved, kind, and soft. Not hardened and brutal. Not cast aside for not fitting the mold I was destined for. How trapped we had both been.

"I'm not fearless, Jun. I'm afraid all the time."

"But still, you fight on." He didn't meet my gaze.

"Can't think too hard if you don't stop moving," I quipped. He didn't laugh.

"Tori, what I went through, those few months, it nearly killed me. Pallas has been with him for nearly five hundred years. Try to be gentle with her."

I thought about that beast I had seen within her, caged and beaten. Scared and hurting in a way that I couldn't truly understand. But I also thought about her standing at Hadeon's side. She was stone-faced, unyielding as he had collared Jun and hurt him.

"She doesn't look like a victim to me."

"I bet many people would have said the same about you," he remarked. I had nothing to say to that. "I never stood up against father for you, and yet you loved me."

"That's different."

"Is it?" Again, I had nothing to say. "I trust her, Tori. You can trust her, too." At that, Jun rolled on his side, pressing his forehead against my shoulder. It was the lightest touch, but it was enough. The ship bobbed on the waves and lulled me closer to sleep.

"Do you love her, Jun?" He was already asleep. I kissed the top of his head gently and let the ship's rocking finish its job.

Chapter 12

Tori

The stars in the sky swirled around me, and I found myself back in the cave we left behind. Abraxas was his fae self, sitting by the edge of the glowing spring.

"Why do I never see you as your true self? You always appear as a fae to me?" I sat down beside him, leaning my head against his shoulder. Immediately, his hand ran up my spine and through my hair. He gripped me gently, pulling me close enough to place a chaste kiss on the top of my head.

"I wouldn't want to scare you, Tori."

I laughed at that and leaned into him when I felt the scrape of claws against my scalp. I jerked away to see that wicked smile on his face and long onyx talons that extended from his finger-tips. That mischievous gleam twinkled in his eyes as the claws slowly faded back into his hands.

"You keep surprising me, Abraxas. What's next? Do you have a tail hidden away?"

"Of course I do. It's impossible to maintain your balance flying without one."

Flying. Of course, he had flown free above the clouds,

amongst the stars that had birthed his people. Memories of his younger self rose to greet me, the ones I'd seen so long ago. His arms outstretched, running towards the edge of a cliff, nothing but the unadulterated joy of freedom rushing through his veins.

"What is it like to fly?" I asked him.

He laced his now claw-free fingers through my own. "Nothing compares. Leaving everything behind and riding the wind, it's like nothing holds you back." I saw the awe on his face fade away. "It was the worst part of being trapped in this fae body. The sky had been taken away from me."

I placed my hand on his chest, letting it rest just over his heart. "Can you show me?"

He didn't respond but placed his hand over mine. I felt the weak thrum of his heart, and the golden light of our bond leaked from his chest, surrounding our hands. Much like it had all those nights ago, I felt our minds connect. Before, the bond needed to beat the connection into us, but now it was soft and warm, inviting me into his memories.

Once again, I was a young Abraxas, standing on the cliffs above Xyr. I looked to my father, King Amaros. Long dark brown hair whipped around a face that was all harsh angles and stern eyes. But as he raised his hand to point out over the cliffs and to the sea of the Bay of Dragons, that same mischievous smirk I loved so much cracked the severe expression, revealing shining white teeth. Excitement fluttered in my heart, and I turned and dashed out towards the edge of the cliff, running at full speed.

The edge came closer and closer, but I did not slow. I placed my foot at the very edge before I launched myself over. The earth fell away, and my stomach rose into my throat. But then a great surge of magic, hot and unrestricted, flooded through my body, and I changed. My fingers grew long, the nails stretching and thickening into onyx talons. My skin fell away to reveal obsidian scales that directed the wind around my body perfectly. My back was shot through with pain, but I hardly noticed, knowing the reward it would bring. Great wings sprung out from beneath my scales, and I opened them wide to catch the air and stop my descent. My entire form grew larger, but it didn't feel strange. If anything, it made me realize how unnatural and compressed my fae form felt.

When I wore it for extended periods, the ache of that restraint just became a part of living—a dull ache that one could almost ignore, like the page that has bent so many times it falls into compliance. But when it was released, and I could be whole again, it always surprised me how truly light I could feel.

Soaring over the bay and out into the Sea of Spirits. I kept to the mist as best I could. I didn't want to scare any fisherman out for an evening haul. But the further out I flew, the more my caution gave way to exuberance. I read the wind, riding its currents while curling my magic through it, shaping it to my needs. I could feel the vortexes created as they passed over waves and rocks, warning me of their presence long before I could see them. But I always liked to see how close I could get before turning away at the last second.

When I first learned to fly, I crashed into more rocks than I could count. But after mastering my body and the wind, I could have a little fun. As I darted between the labyrinth of islands, I tucked my wings in and dove at breakneck speed down towards the water's surface, using the flair of my tail to push into a spin. Only when I felt the spray of the saltwater on my scales did I spread my wings wide, pulling up at the last moment. I repeated this over and over until the muscles in my back ached.

A disturbance in the air told me I wasn't alone anymore, and I saw my father's form fly overhead. His great, deep maroon scales gleamed in the ochre light of the fading sun, his eyes an almost perfect match for the glowing orb that was sinking beneath the ocean's waves. He flashed his golden teeth at me and then, with a might that I only hoped to possess when I was finally full-grown, pumped his great wings and rose into the air beyond my sight. Despite my fatigue, I followed suit, muscles straining in protest as I used my entire body to surge upward until we were both above the clouds.

The sun finally dipped below the sea, and the purple of the horizon faded into the inky black of night as the stars came out to greet us.

The memory faded from my mind, but I was left with Abraxas' joyful feeling in his heart—something so pure and innocent—the joy that can only be felt by the young, before the weight of the world, has crushed that beautiful and precious innocence from them.

I didn't have the words to describe how I felt after seeing that. I was grateful that he had shared it with me, profoundly happy that he had those memories, and miserable that all of that had been ripped away from him. I squeezed myself into his body, taking him into a deep embrace, hoping that he would understand. He wrapped his arms around me, and I felt he did.

"So, you were trapped in this body? How?"

That sly but sad smile returned to his face. "A prison of my own making, in a way. When my father was killed, he was the last great conduit. In my dragon form, I was too. But I was in fae form when he died. Transforming from dragon to fae is the hardest thing I ever had to learn and takes a great deal of magic. In fae form, I can no more conduct magic than any other." He gave a soft chuckle. "Well, any other fae that isn't you." I thought of the feeling of magic in his memory. It was so raw and undiluted, a great mountain waterfall that made everything I had felt thus far feel like nothing more than a small forest creek. A deep part of me was jealous that he had lived when power flowed unrestrained like that.

"When he died, the last true well of magic on this earth died with him. I had to make a choice. Use the magic of his death to change myself one last time or stay and protect my people and deal with the aftermath of the attack on Xyr. I still wonder if it was the right choice..." He trailed off, his gaze hard and distant.

I squeezed his fingers between my own. "You chose hope. You could have changed, and what would you have done? Fought Hadeon, tried for revenge to whatever end? Instead, you stayed with the people who needed you. You rebuilt Xyr."

"You exalt me. I'm not sure that's what I was thinking, but it was the path I took." He paused again. "But it meant that I couldn't transform. I knew that if I did, well, I assumed I wouldn't survive long. My life force would be... is... tapped out."

He finally turned to look at me. "Our bond has let me hang on to life longer than I expected."

This asshole. "Who were you to make that choice, to kill yourself for some heroic gesture? We could have still fought our way out... somehow..." I knew it wasn't true. We had been surrounded, but I couldn't stand that I'd failed him so completely. I couldn't stand how much failure I'd caused in such a short time. Tears leaked from my eyes at my own self-pity, and Abraxas gently wiped them away.

"It wasn't your fault, Tori."

"Don't lie to me, Abraxas. I failed to find Hadeon's weakness. I failed to undo his power. And from the sound of it, I also caused your whole plan to crumble with my impatience. It is all my fault. And now..." He held me to his chest again as the tears flowed freely now, sobs breaking up my speech. "Now I've almost lost you."

"The blame is mine, Tori. Avlyn was right. Once I had you, I became reckless like a child. I was so happy in a way I thought I would never be again. I wasn't thinking clearly. I wanted everything with you, to experience everything I waited a millennium for. I should have held off on everything, but I could never deny you."

"If we waited, I would have lost Jun."

He placed another soft kiss on my temple. "How is he now?"

"He's like a stranger. He's alive, and I can be grateful for that, but I feel like I don't know him or what he needs. My brother, my twin, and I don't know him."

"Give it time, little bird. Knowing Hadeon..." He didn't have to say anything. I had seen the dark shadows around Jun's heart, so similar to the ones that had kept my magic away from Abraxas. Death's hand had Jun in its clutches as well.

I let the threads of magic twirl around my fingers. I wished I could burn it away, all of it. The shadows around Jun's heart, the shadows holding Abraxas prisoner. I was so fucking tired of feeling helpless. I focused on that, and the magic between my fingers shifted from that soft blue to vivid green and burned hot.

Abraxas chuckled, "Not bad, Princess." He snatched the flames right out of my hand, letting them dance between his fingers. "It's real dragonfire, too. I don't think any fae has ever achieved that."

"How can you tell?"

"Telling you that would be like trying to explain how we know to breathe. It's just something I know." He let the flames jump up out of his hand, and they disappeared. "I wish I could have taught you more, told you about everything. If I had told you about my father's heart, maybe things would have been different."

I raised an eyebrow at him.

He sighed again. "That is Hadeon's great treasure. Somehow, he has taken control of my father's heart. That is what allows Hadeon to still wield magic."

"He's using your father's heart? A dragon's heart... so, he's using it to pull magic from the earth, like some sort of corrupted conduit."

I thought about what the old Seer had said in the cave about this revelation, my own powers as a conduit, and the feeling of pure magic in his memory. Something, an idea, perhaps a solution, danced in my mind, just beyond my grasp. I could almost see the pieces of the puzzle falling into place, but something was still missing.

"Show me, Abraxas. Show me your true form. I don't understand this dream we are in, but let's use it to our advantage."

To my surprise, he pulled away. Something I hadn't seen often flashed across his face. Fear. "I don't want to hurt you, Tori."

"I have never been afraid of you."

"You don't know what you are asking. I had to work for centuries to learn to control my actions. Locked in a fae body, it was easier, but dragons aren't civilized. They are the embodiment of nature. Nature is vicious, brutal, and deadly. And you are my mate; who knows what I would do to you unleashed?"

I pressed my hand into his chest, hard. "We are in a dream; how could you hurt me here? What's a better place to find out what you would do?"

That deep fire flashed in his eyes, and before I could react, I was on my back, his hands holding my wrists down. "Is that what you want, little bird? To see me become nothing but rage and lust, to tear into your soft skin with my claws, my fangs? To devour you completely?"

He sank his teeth into the flesh of my neck, and I felt a sharp prick as he broke the skin. A hiss escaped me. He pulled back, the red of my blood coating his lips and his teeth. They had elongated into sharp fangs.

"I'm yours, Abraxas. I'm your mate, so show me what that means. I want to see you lose the control you have been holding onto so tightly." The fire in his eyes grew brighter at my words, and I knew I almost had him.

"You would have me undone without a semblance of my humanity?" His breath on my skin was hot... burning. His irises had lost their green, only that molten gold remained, his pupils elongated into slits. He pressed himself between my legs, and the heat of him traveled straight into the depths of my belly, my heat rising to meet it.

"Completely."

His control snapped. Our lips slammed together, and I felt a sharp pain as my tongue was sliced open on the tip of one of his fangs. But he pulled me in deeper, and I reveled in the taste of him that merged with the hot, metallic taste of my blood.

I scratched my nails down the flesh of his back. A moment later, I felt the hot sting of his talons tracing over my hips as he pressed harder against me. Whatever clothing I had been wearing was shredded under his ministrations. We released our kiss, and he drew his lips down my neck and across my chest. His tongue darted out over my aching skin, and I was so lost in the sensation of it that I didn't notice the unique change for a long moment. When I looked down to watch him lavish the peaked flesh of my nipple, I saw it was forked. He ran each part around the hard bud, trapping it, before pulling it into his mouth and teasing me with his fangs again.

My back arched as I tried to get closer to him, needing even more of the harsh sensation that danced on the edge of pleasure and pain. He was careful, as he ever was, to keep me on the side of pleasure.

"You're holding back, Abraxas."

He chuckled against my skin; the vibration was tantalizing. "Be careful what you wish for, Princess." I couldn't help the scream that escaped me as his teeth broke the skin of my breast. I never wanted it to end.

"I said I would devour you, Tori, and I have every intention of showing you how a god claims his mate."

And then he was transformed. Great black horns emerged from underneath his silver hair. His eyes burned even brighter, and the white of the sclera was replaced with deep black. His pale skin was pulled back on his temples and hands to reveal the obsidian scales beneath. I was entranced, but he refused to let himself change completely, hovering on his own edge between humanity and beast. He traced that strong, elongated tongue down my stomach, spreading my thighs with those clawed hands. I fell open for him immediately.

His tongue traced up and down through me before pushing deep inside. I bucked my hips involuntarily. "Oh fuck, Abraxas." Words were lost to me as I felt it twist, creating a sensation unlike anything I'd felt before. Without thinking, I grabbed onto his horns and pulled him deeper into me.

"You always were such a needy thing," he chuckled, licking my arousal off his lips; it coated almost the entire bottom half of his face. "Play nice with these," he gestured to his horns.

I moaned as he dove back between my thighs. I squirmed to get closer as he fucked me with his tongue. Each thrust was relentless and a tease as he stopped his momentum to circle my clit. It was a deep, unbearable pressure; each pass brought me closer to that perfect ecstasy. I was so close now that I barely felt his claws sink into the flesh of my hips.

"Abraxas, I'm going to..." He thrust into me with abandon, hitting every single sensitive part of my swollen cunt. I caressed his horns gently this time, and heard him moan against my flesh. The sound and vibrations sent me over the edge. As the limitless golden light of release danced before my eyes, he lapped up every last drop of my arousal like I was the most delicious thing in the world.

My legs were shaking as I came down from my orgasm, but

he didn't give me a moment of reprieve before he rose up on his knees and grabbed my legs, pulling me around him.

He was a vision straight from the hells. His pale, smooth skin gave way to dark scales; his arms and legs were almost completely covered. A second, smaller set of horns hugged his temples, and his wild silver hair matched the glow of his eyes. His talons sank deeper into the flesh of my ass as he pulled me onto his hard length. My core still spasmed with the last after-shocks of his tongue.

As he sank deep, we groaned in ecstasy. I squeezed my eyes shut, overcome by the sensation.

"Don't you close your eyes now, Tori." His claws wrapped around my neck and jaw. "You wanted to see your mate. Well, here I am." Wind ruffled my hair, and an audible whoosh had my eyes snapping open. His leathery black wings were spread wide behind him, blocking out almost all the light. The only illumination was the deep glow of his eyes and the tendrils of emerald fire spreading beneath the skin of his chest.

I saw the god he truly was, beyond anything a mere fae like me was designed to comprehend. He pulled me to him, again and again, each thrust growing harder, untamed as his moans transformed into something between a deep growl and a purr that shook the very earth beneath me. His body grew larger than what should have been possible. Still lodged deep inside my cunt, his cock swelled, stretching me beyond anything I had experienced before.

"Abraxas, Abraxas..." I couldn't think of anything to say other than his name as another orgasm tore through my body, making me completely limp and defenseless. I looked at him for a moment of tenderness but found nothing. The man I knew was gone; only the beast remained.

"Abraxas, wait..."

He did not. He was ravenous. His long tongue tugged over

my skin, capturing the blood that still dripped from my hips and breast. That emerald fire leaked from his mouth, and his cock pounded into me. My skin became sweaty as the air grew unbearably hot. His claws sunk into my skin without caution as his tongue raked my body, capturing my blood, my sweat, my tears.

A voice, deep and ancient, rumbled from inside of him. *You're mine.* I tried to call out to him one last time, but my throat was scorched as emerald fire consumed me.

Chapter 13

Pallas

I awoke to the sound of Jun's strained voice. "Tori, wake up!" He was shaking her by the shoulders when I ran over.

She looked horrible. She was sweating profusely, and her face was twisted in pain. She was moaning and clutching her arms, chest, and face. Her nails bit into her skin like she was trying to claw it off.

"**WAKE UP**!" Jun screamed at her, but the force of it knocked me backward, and the entire ship shook with its power. Tori's eyes flew open, and for a moment, they glowed an eerie green before fading back into their normal deep grey.

Jun doubled over, coughing, and both Tori and I were immediately at his side. But the princess' hands were shaking as she tried to steady Jun.

"I'm...fine..." he croaked; his voice was rough as if he had been screaming for hours.

"What the hell was that?!" Avlyn swung down from the rigging overhead, landing with surprising grace for someone their size.

"Words of Power." I hadn't really meant to say it out loud.

I'd always suspected that Jun might use them to concentrate his voice into something even more powerful. But Hadeon had tried too hard to control Jun, and that had stifled his magical development. Perhaps with the collar gone, he could finally discover the true limits of his ability.

But as I looked to see Avlyn's reaction, I saw they weren't looking at Jun or me, but at Tori, who was still sickly blanched. Her skin was clammy with deep circles set under her eyes. But she was still trying to comfort Jun the best she could without touching him.

Avlyn walked over to her. "Are you alright?" They reached down to touch her shoulder, and she flinched.

"I'm fine." She leaned away, putting space between them. "I just need a moment. Pallas, is Jun alright?" She was asking me?

"Yes, he just isn't used to using his power this way." But he would learn, and I would help him. I hadn't been able to save him, but this I could do.

Tori gave the slightest nod of her head before bolting to the railing of the ship, and she heaved the contents of her stomach over the edge. Avlyn followed her. As Jun stopped coughing, I heard Tori mumbling, "I'm fine, just seasick." *Liar.*

The sun had just breached the sky, its pale rays barely making it through the thick mist of the sea. Jun had settled down with a jug of water, and Avlyn leaped up to the upper deck, taking back over at the helm. I watched as their muscular legs bounded up the stairs but froze when they turned around, locking eyes with me. Their face looked so soft despite the high cheekbones and defined jaw. They were so at ease sailing these open waters and so different from the warrior I had seen on the beach. The warrior who had saved my life. I felt my heart race as their amber-colored eyes held my gaze for a moment before I dropped my chin to look away.

I slowly shuffled over to Tori, who had her forehead

resting on the back of her hands on the railing of the ship. She stayed hunched over, but I didn't think she was going to vomit again.

"What happened in your dream?"

Her head shot up; her eyes were piercing despite the unease that still lay beneath them.

"Nothing." She always gave herself away.

"Obviously not." Her gaze hardened, but the ship rolled underneath us as Avlyn shifted our course, and Tori turned green before she leaned over the railing and vomited again.

I reached out and gently pulled her hair back, trying to ignore the clenching of my stomach at the sound of her expulsion. Eventually, she stopped and rested her forehead on her hands again.

"I really hate boats," she mumbled.

For a few more waves, we stood there in silence, but for once, I was the one to break it.

"Dreams are one place that magic still lives most vividly in our world. But it's a fickle magic. Most dreams can mean absolutely nothing. But some... some can mean everything."

"How do I tell the difference?" she asked without raising her head.

I didn't answer her question. "What did you see?"

"I thought you weren't going to help me, Pallas." She was right. I was about to pull away when she spoke again. "I've been dreaming of Abraxas. But I know it's more than a dream. It's like I'm connecting to him, talking to him even though he's not with me."

I knew the feeling all too well. Hadeon haunted my dreams and often even my waking hours. Tori hadn't explained, but I had my suspicions about her connection with Abraxas. She had summoned his dragonfire in the cave. They were linked in a way outside of her control. How horrible to be unable to escape his grasp, even in sleep. Hadeon had been terrible to me, but Abraxas was a monster.

I set my hand gingerly on her back and whispered to her so the commander wouldn't overhear. "He's gone, Princess. We've left him behind. You never have to be with him again."

Her head shot up, anger filling her eyes, but they softened again as she beheld me. "I love him, Pallas."

"I saw what he did to you at those parties. Both in Xyr and Koron. The way he treated you. That's not love, Tori." *I would know.*

"It was all an act. We wanted it to look that way. That was part of the plan. But I love him, Pallas, and he loves me. I have no doubt of that."

I observed her. How often had I convinced myself of the same thing? For centuries I had. But there was something in her eyes, something so true I couldn't ignore it. Could it be that somehow, she and Abraxas had...?

"What was your dream about?" I asked again.

Shame crossed her face. "He... killed me. Alright, I know how that sounds! Don't make that face. I can see you don't believe me, but I think I can show you." She held her hand out to me, palm turned upward. I didn't move. She didn't close the gap but begged, "Please, let me show you." I didn't respond and saw the frustration in her eyes.

"Pallas, you can help us. It's clear you have more knowledge about Hadeon than almost anyone. And you seem to know a great deal about magic as well. Please help us. Please do some good with your knowledge."

Some good. The memory rose from the bowels of my mind where I had stored it away. Jun's screams, his desperate pleading. How he clawed at the collar as it snapped around his neck. How his eyes darted to me before they dulled into obedience. Me standing there, doing nothing. Doing absolutely nothing.

"And what you are doing is right?" I asked. "What, because you love Abraxas? Love is a fickle thing that comes and goes like the wind. It blinds you to the truth right in front of your eyes. A vacant thing that fills you with hope only to tear it away one small piece at a time until you have nothing left of yourself." I had said too much, revealed too much. I saw it in Tori's eyes.

"Pallas, let me show you." She held up her hand again. The frustration was gone from her face, and I saw the hints of pity below.

The deep part of me that was dark and sharp, all claws and teeth, tore at my heart. It was nothing but rage and hurt, seething with jealousy. *Don't look*, it said. *Don't let her show you the happiness you can never have.* But she didn't force me, and her eyes looked so much like Jun's at that moment. The animal was subdued, as it always was for him. I nodded to her.

She closed the gap between us, and her palm landed on my chest. A golden light flooded from her, mixing with the beams of the morning sun. I felt warm and safe in a way that I hadn't in centuries. I felt the kiss of a lover who desired nothing more than my joy and laughter. I felt the arms of a mother who held me to her heart as she sang me to sleep. I felt the embrace of a friend who knew me better than I knew myself. It was the rising sun and evening twilight and the dance of the stars and light of the moon. It was the endless sky and sleeping earth.

Tears streamed down my face, tears I hadn't let flow in years. I fell to my knees and clutched my face in my palms. It wasn't fair that she got to feel this when I had suffered so long. Yet, I was so grateful to her for sharing it with me, even for this brief moment. She released her hand, but still, the feeling lingered like the warmth that clings to stone after the sun has faded. I felt her arms around me, and I leaned into her and sobbed. She stroked my hair and cooed at me.

Then I felt another pair of arms. "It's alright, Pallas." Jun was touching me in a way I hadn't dared hope for in months. That golden light seemed to glow in my heart just a bit longer.

THE COMMANDER WAS SHOUTING ORDERS AT TORI, AND ALL she did was shout back snarky retorts, but the sails got pulled, eventually. In the distance, I could see the dark shore of the Dragon Kingdom emerging from the mist. Our boat bobbed in place, the sails stowed, but the commander assured us we wouldn't have to wait long.

They were correct. The sun had barely moved in the sky when a huge, dark vessel approached us. It didn't approach from the shore as it had been patrolling the bay. As the ship neared, I could see countless Dragon Army soldiers, clad in their pitch-black armor, lining the edge of the ship along with the sailors. Many had long bows drawn back so that the silver heads of arrows flashed in the morning light. They were all trained on us.

I could feel the fear in my chest growing as they approached. For how many people had this been the very last thing they saw before their untimely demise? The air grew colder around me, and I shivered.

The commander strode to the railing of our much smaller ship boldly, hands on their hips and shoulders spread wide.

"I'm glad to see you bastards can keep up the patrol schedules without me to beat them into you," they called out to the opposing army.

A rustle went through the ranks, and someone from the ship shouted, "Commander?"

"Who the hell else would it be, sailing in from the islands like this? Now get us to shore!" I could see bodies on the ship moving about, trying to haul over a plank to connect the vessels. Out of the corner of my eye, I saw a great dark shape swoop down from the upper deck, holding on to a single rope. He slammed down onto the deck of our boat, armor rattling, and the entire deck threatened to crack beneath him. He was as tall as the commander, and even more broad. He stood to his full height, and I couldn't help but shrink back as his hand came to rest on the hilt of his sword.

He reached up to take off his helmet. A sea of shiny chestnut waves tumbled out from below, revealing a handsome, strong face.

"Commander, is that really you?" He approached Avlyn cautiously, but that caution faded away quickly. "Is she with..."

The giant was struck from the side by the princess. For a moment, I thought she intended to fight him, but I saw she had wrapped him in an aggressive hug instead.

"I'm here, Kaleos. You won't be rid of me that easy!" Kaleos' armor strained as he returned the princess's embrace tenfold. I heard her groan as he squeezed the breath from her lungs.

"Hey, mind the bones, Kaleos!" But the man didn't let her go. A plank had been set between the two ships, and quickly, more bodies joined the crushing embrace. The exuberant shouting nearly deafened me.

I backed away from the joyous group, and that creature in my belly hissed with jealousy, clawing at my ribs in anger. I felt soft fingers lace with mine and looked up to see Jun smiling.

"It seems like she finally found it after all these centuries," he whispered.

"What?" I asked.

"Home."

Chapter 14

Tori

The last time I was in the Dragon Kingdom, I hated the place. The second time around, I couldn't believe how much I had missed it. As we passed through the gate to the Obsidian Keep, I couldn't help but feel exuberance. But it was tempered by our journey through the city. The outer wall was lined with soldiers, and spiked obstacles had been placed all over the surrounding fields. Kaleos had informed me that no attack had come to the city yet, but it was likely inevitable.

The bulk of the Dragon Army held beyond the Reach Mountains that separated the Dragon and Golden Kingdom. Hadeon's forces had recovered from the initial attack quickly, and they hadn't made progress to the capital.

I sat around the massive table in one of the council rooms. It had been carved from an ancient oak into a map of Adimos, and the officers placed various figures and flags all over it, denoting victories and losses, allies and, to a far greater extent, enemies.

"Have Queens Itzayana and Xareni sent their troops from the south?" Avlyn asked as they gestured frantically across the table.

"They have, but they aren't engaging as much as we need. I understand the hesitation, but the more they hold back, the worse it will be for them." The speaker was Commander Tulis, who I met at Tenebrae Forest.

"Can we send a cohort to him to help reinforce the troops?" Avlyn asked.

"Yes, but it will take weeks for them to arrive."

"Can we split the group already near Ashenforge?"

"In theory, yes, but our troops are already spread thin..."

They continued to debate their strategy, and I did my best to fade into the tapestries on the wall. I wasn't exactly sure why I was here. I was well trained in fighting, and to some extent, battlefield tactics because of my training with the Dragon Army. But I was no commander. I didn't know how to orchestrate an entire army. Avlyn had insisted I come.

They were clearly skilled at this, but who they really needed was Abraxas, and I was no substitute for him.

"...don't you agree, Princess Tori?" I snapped my head up. Avlyn had asked me something.

"I'm not sure it's my place to..."

They gave me an angry look, then turned back around. The other leaders barely spared me a glance. *They know you're a failure.*

After a bit more debate, the others filed out, and I slowly raised out of my chair, ready to be done with this. Avlyn slammed the door closed and rounded on me.

"What the hell was that? For the first time in your entire life, you haven't had something to say, huh?"

I pushed back from them, my defenses rising. "Avlyn, it's not my place to interfere. I don't know how to command an army."

"I wasn't asking you to plan, just to support me!" Their voice broke in exasperation.

I was confused. "You are the leader of this army. Why would you need my support?"

They shook their head, tracing their fingers over the bridge of their nose just the way Abraxas did, and my heart twinged. "Abraxas isn't here, Tori. I always had his support. I'm asking these men to fight a war when their king is gone. Last they heard, he turned into a dragon and flew away. You might see how that could shake someone's loyalty. I need you to be that powerful rallying point for us, for the kingdom."

A few moments of silence passed between us until I could finally voice what I needed to say. "I'm not the queen."

Avlyn didn't hesitate like I did. "As far as I'm concerned, you are. Maybe not officially, but this is war, and what's official is less important than warts on a hobgoblin's back. I need you to step up, Tori, for me and this kingdom."

Isn't that what I always wanted? To finally have respect, to enact change, to protect my people? I balled my fist, angry at myself for being scared now that the opportunity presented itself. A harsh whisper in my head echoed, *you'll never be good enough; you'll never deserve this.*

A soft golden light tried to wrap itself around my heart to soothe me. But the waves of my mind churned with fear, and the light wasn't strong enough. I could feel myself being pulled under. *You've failed. You failed Abraxas. You failed Avlyn. You failed Jun. You've failed everyone, and they can all see it.*

I sprung up from my chair. "It can't be me, Avlyn. I'll get Abraxas back, I'll do... something... but not this."

"Tori..." Avlyn's voice was soft, but I spun away from them and bolted out of the room.

91

I trudged to the wing of the castle where my old room was. I had sent Jun and Pallas there earlier to get cleaned up, and some well-needed rest, but the servants had recommended they stay elsewhere. Apparently, the wing had been mostly abandoned since we left. I now saw why.

Great webs spread all over the hallways, making them impassable. One path down a deep tunnel in the web could have been traversed, but every survival instinct in me fought that. Instead, I plucked one thread of the web and called out softly, "Spinner?"

The web shifted rapidly as a harsh chittering sound emerged from the back of the hallway, hidden in darkness. But I saw his eight great legs moving against the small pockets of light penetrating his fortress, and a few moments later, he was hanging from the roof in front of me.

He was much larger than the last time I saw him, as tall as the hounds used for hunting in the forest, and with his legs, much wider.

"My, how you've grown!" He popped his front legs up excitedly and waggled from side to side. A happy squeal escaped him as he hopped down to the floor in front of me, his landing perfectly silent.

I reached out and pet his head, but he ran his front legs over my body, searching my pockets and sleeves. My heart twinged. "And here I thought you missed me. I'm sorry, boy, but I don't have it."

He let out an annoyed hiss at that and crossed his front legs in such a human expression that I couldn't help but crack a smile. It vanished quickly.

"I lost it. It's..." The tears I held back started to fall. "...it's all my fault." Spinner spun around and nuzzled his head into my hand. I gave him a few scratches, but then he started spinning and clicking in a way that sounded very annoyed.

"Buddy, I don't know what you are trying to tell me." I didn't think it was possible for spiders to roll their eyes, but eight pupils rolled around before Spinner took off back into his nest.

I sighed and rose back up, wiping the tears away. Then I heard Spinner returning. In his mandibles, he held something long and pointy.

He dropped my sword in front of me. I pulled it from its scabbard and pressed the mechanism that released it into two separate swords. When Abraxas first gifted them to me, I could barely lift them with my left arm. Now, while a dull ache lingered—and likely always would—I spun the off-hand weapon easily. I'd grown stronger.

Spinner nodded his head at me vigorously.

"Clever spider."

Outside Jun and Pallas' room, I found Kaleos and Raula standing guard.

"I would think you have better things to do than stand guard over our two guests."

"So, the consorts of the fae, who we are currently fighting a war against, are our guests?" Kaleos asked. His face was contorted in a scowl, and I hated to see it.

Raula's deep voice chimed in, "Forgive him. His lover is in

there, and he's nervous." She cracked a wicked grin, her long tusks making it almost menacing, as Kaleos blushed a deep shade of crimson.

"He's not my..." But he knew he wouldn't get anywhere with us, so he just huffed and crossed his arms.

I patted his thick arm as I walked past. "Don't forget, I was once a guest here as well, and I turned out alright, didn't I?"

Shame shot across his face, and he released his tense stance. "You're right, I'm..." he started, but I gave his arm a squeeze to tell him he didn't have to say more.

I pushed open the doors to see Oryx fussing over Jun. For a moment I worried for my brother, but saw that Oryx wasn't touching him, just respectfully directing Jun to move and adjust his hair or clothes to the side as needed. I shouldn't have doubted. Oryx always knew what to do.

Besides, with Pallas standing watch over them like a hawk, I knew I had nothing to worry about. She had been given new clothes; they were simple and elegant, although I wouldn't say modest. But she wore them with ease, the soft blue of the outer dress highlighting her eyes and soft skin.

Seeing her dressed like that reminded me of someone I had blocked from my thoughts. Now, I couldn't help but think of Ciara's gentle hands as she helped me when I first arrived here.

Perhaps I should have felt rage at her memory, at her betrayal. All I felt was sadness. My first friend. I lost her to Hadeon long before her death. He had sunk his claws into her, just like he had to Jun. Just as he had to Pallas. I wouldn't let that happen again.

"How is everything, Oryx?"

"Both Jun and Pallas are in good health. Their bodies should recover quickly from their... ordeal." He was always tactful, but I understood his meaning. Their fae bodies had recovered quickly, but not all scars were visible.

"Thank you."

He nodded his head and exited the room. I looked at the pair. Jun sat on the edge of the bed, looking at his lap. Pallas stood with her arms crossed, staring at me, but I ignored her.

Jun's robe was still pulled down from where Oryx had examined him. I moved to pull it back up, but he flinched away immediately. Stupid. I had to be more careful with him.

"Sorry," my brother mumbled, still not looking up. The exam had been hard on him. I knew the tactic of placing one's mind away from the situation to cope, but I'd never seen it with Jun.

"Don't apologize." I knelt down in front of him. "May I take a look?" He didn't meet my gaze but nodded. I reached out with my magic. The shadows around his heart writhed as if they were content with his misery. They were spreading towards his throat and mind again. I called on the magic of the earth, but the shadows just twisted around it, snuffing out its light.

Something in me knew what to do. Jun and I were linked in a way that even Abraxas and I were not. The very depth of my soul was tied to his, and it called out to him.

Deep in my heart, there was a well of soft white light. It felt similar to the earth's magic, but it wasn't the same. The magic of the earth flowed like water, ancient and untethered. This light felt like life and merriment and running through a palace court-yard chasing a brother as we were both breathless with laughter. I pulled out one tiny spark of that light, guiding it into Jun. The reaching shadows burned away.

I panted, finding it hard to catch my breath, and my heart stuttered. Jun sat up a bit straighter and looked at me. "Thank you, Tori. I feel better. Your magic is amazing." He gave me a sleepy smile. It was all I wanted. I heard Pallas huff in the corner, but I ignored her again.

"Let's get you tucked into bed." I winked at him, and he

rolled his eyes. But he let me gently reach forward and pull up his robe. My heart stopped again when I did; it had nothing to do with magic.

Etched all over Jun's back was an erratic latticework of scars. They weren't bold, but a fae scarring was almost impossible. My arm and my back were the only scars I bore after years of battle. I had no doubt who had done this to Jun.

I felt every inch of my skin heat with dragonfire, but I pushed those thoughts away beneath the ocean of my mind as much as I could. It wouldn't do to draw Jun's attention to this now. I pulled up his robe and helped him move back into the bed. I tucked the covers around him in an exaggerated motion that had him huffing in what I would count as a laugh. I wanted to kiss his forehead but held back.

"Tori, a moment." I looked at Pallas, confused.

"Do you want to be tucked in, too?"

At that, she rolled her eyes at me. I decided whatever she was about to say wasn't worth it. I gave Jun one last smile and left.

My feet lead me everywhere in the palace but to his bedroom. Our bedroom. My eyes ached with weariness, but I could still feel his dragonfire as it tore through me, and his phantom claws pulled me to shreds. I knew sleep would not find me, no matter where I lay my head.

For not the first time in my life, it seemed sleep and I were enemies.

Chapter 15

Pallas

Jun let me pet his hair as he fell asleep. He hadn't let me do that in ages. After his breath leveled out into the steady, deep rhythm of unconsciousness, I tried to roll over and sleep, too. I ended up just staring at the dark ceiling for what felt like an eternity before gently rolling out of bed.

I slipped on one of those stupid night robes that were so loved in the Dragon Kingdom and headed for the door. It wasn't locked, but the brute and the orcess I had seen before stood outside.

The brute turned to me. "Can't sleep?"

I closed the door behind me, so we didn't disturb Jun, but also to show I wasn't going back in.

"No, I was hoping to take a walk." Was I a guest, as Tori had said, or just a prisoner? The brute and the orcess exchanged glances, but he said, "Alright, but I'll accompany you so you don't lose your way."

Right. He was more tactful than the other soldiers I had dealt with, but he was still just a soldier. I walked down the hall without another word, and he scrambled after me. We walked in silence for quite a while. Much longer than the princess would have held out, but eventually, the quiet was too much.

"So, it's Pallas, right? How did you end up here?"

I raised my eyebrows at him. Was he really asking me that?

Color rose in his cheeks. "Right, sorry... not a great question... how about... are you liking it here?"

I said nothing, and his face grew redder with each passing breath. It was almost... adorable. He was darker than an autumn plum when we both heard footsteps and saw the princess herself rounding the corner.

"Oh, thank the gods...." I heard him murmur.

"Couldn't sleep?" She crossed her arms over her chest, looking at me. I said nothing but nodded. "Well then, perhaps we can sleeplessly wander together. Kaleos, you and Raula get some rest. I'll see you in the morning."

The brute gave her a salute and immediately turned on his heels and fled. Tori still had her arms crossed as she looked me up and down. I hated how it made my skin crawl.

"Well, let's wander," she said. She gestured for me to lead the way, and I did. Fewer than five breaths had passed, and I knew she was about to speak, so I cut her off.

"You're playing a dangerous game."

She raised her eyebrows at me.

"What you did for Jun earlier."

Her face only grew more confused. "I just used my magic to heal him. Is that so wrong?" she asked.

"You don't have fae magic, Tori. That was your life force."

She frowned and put her hand over her heart. "Yes, it felt like... it felt like a part of me."

I shook my head. "It won't end well if you keep that up. It was the first lesson all magical adepts learned. Never use your life force to fuel magic, lest you overexert and, well... die."

She looked at me a long time before answering. "It's the only way I can help Jun. It's the only thing I have that works against whatever is clinging to his heart."

I knew all too well what she meant. I may not have magic, but only a fool wouldn't see what Jun carried. "That may be true, but it's too risky."

"Any risk is worth it for Jun."

"Do you think he would agree with you?" She said nothing. "We will find a way to help him, but this isn't the way."

"Suddenly so attached to me, Pallas?"

I couldn't stop a laugh from escaping. "Not a bit, Princess. But... Jun wouldn't survive losing you again. Not right now." She knew I was right. Logic always prevailed, even in those who seemed to ignore it, like Tori.

She sighed, "Alright, but we need to find another way."

I had nothing more to say, so we walked another two hallways before she let out a loud yawn. "I don't think I've ever been so tired in my life."

"And yet you aren't sleeping... are you afraid of dreaming?" I asked.

She jolted at my bold question, and I saw her hackles rise, but then she released a sigh. "Yes." It was all she said.

"You could take a sleeping potion, you know, prevent dreams."

"No." There was no hesitation in her voice. I remembered the information Hadeon had been given about her attempt on her life in her youth. She was not so afraid of her dreams to risk it.

"There are other potions, medicinal mushrooms that calm the mind. Perhaps that could help?"

She gave me a quizzical look, then nodded. "Yes, Abraxas mentioned Oryx was working on something. I will consult with him." Her gaze glazed over in thought for a few moments before her eyes jumped back to mine.

"Thank you. It seems you have quite a wealth of knowledge on medical herbs, runes, and ancient magics. Where did you learn all this?"

"My mother was Runya Morvavare." Tori's eyes widened. My mother's fame as the age's greatest enchantress preceded her even after all these centuries.

"I didn't know Runya had a daughter."

"Most don't." Before Tori could give me another pitying look, I barreled on, "She was an academic to her core. While some youths were spent playing and sword fighting, my mother had me spend hours studying every book she gathered for the Golden Kingdom library. All those lessons stuck."

She gave me a searching look as if she didn't quite buy my story. But she let it drop. I didn't need to tell her that for the first few decades, Hadeon had hardly let me out of his chambers. Only the kindness of slaves bringing me books to read had kept me sane. And my mother had amassed the greatest collection of tomes on magic in her time as the library's keeper in Koron before her death.

We walked a bit more in silence before she asked, "And you, Pallas? We've had a trying few days. What keeps you awake?"

"I've never slept well." The look she gave me was far too piteous for my liking, so I added, "Besides, I have heard there is a giant spider who roams these halls. Not the most comforting tale."

A wicked grin crossed her face. "Would you like to meet him?"

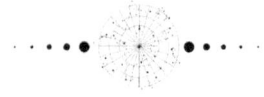

I WILL ADMIT, THE SPIDER HAD BEEN SURPRISINGLY affable. He gave me a cute spin as a greeting and brought me what Tori assured was a mouse wrapped up in his silk. It seemed awfully large to be a mouse, but I didn't question it. I pet his head as I would have one of the palace cats, and he purred in a similar but unnerving way.

After, Tori walked me back to my room. The two soldiers were gone. She didn't warn me to stay or lock the door, but I was sure there were eyes on me, nonetheless.

Jun slept peacefully, but I knew I wasn't ready for sleep yet. A small collection of books lay on a small shelf in the room. I grabbed one and a small candle. Sitting by the window, a glance outside revealed the flaming blue-green lights so famous in this region in the night sky above. I had never seen them before, and even I had to admit, they were enchanting. I was swept away in their soft, graceful beauty until the smell of ashy rose filled my nose. It was paired with something metallic, like smoke or even blood. It was a smell I had become well acquainted with over the past century.

"Hello, Shadow Walker. I thought you couldn't enter this city, let alone the palace?"

Commander Luxos stepped out of the shadows that clung to the corner of the room. "Well, with our beloved Dragon King gone, his warding has weakened."

Luxos' long, dark hair was pulled back, and the long white scar over his left eye was accentuated by the pale light of the moon. He wore the dark leather armor I was so used to seeing him in. Sweat coated his brow, and I could tell it had taken quite a bit of effort to enter the kingdom.

"It's time to go, Pallas. Our master awaits." He extended his hand to me and glanced at Jun on the bed. I didn't move.

"There is no way for him to know you could make it here

now. It's never been possible before. There would be no punishment for you not bringing us back."

He frowned. "Don't make this difficult. I've already risked my life for you." A twinkle lit his eye. "The reward for that had been much sweeter."

Yes, Luxos had been Hadeon's loyal dog for almost three centuries, but how many things had changed in the past few months? I was ordered to *serve* the commander numerous times before, but when Hadeon had traveled to Niutu, it had been the first time I'd slept with him for myself.

After that first stolen night, I had often found myself in Luxos' embrace. In his chambers, the gardens, or even in a vacant hallway. His expression told me he knew exactly what I was remembering. He shot me a smile that I was sure had caused the undergarments of many a courtier to disappear in a hurry, but I just scowled at him.

He frowned. "Don't tell me you prefer the company of that spoiled brat?"

I assumed he was referring to the princess. She had escaped his clutches twice, and I realized I was impressed. I couldn't think of another soul who had escaped from Luxos and his shadow troops. The man had killed two new recruits after his botched attempt to draw out Tori's power, testing them too hard after losing his best men. Perhaps I hadn't given her enough credit.

I looked into his dark eyes but said nothing.

"Pallas..." he growled at me, taking a step forward.

"Luxos?" I hit him with my bedroom eyes and batted my lashes. He froze, and the slightest color rose on his cheeks. But he shook his head and regained his composure.

"I would hate to have to force you."

"Haven't you already done just that?" It was foolish to provoke him, but maybe being around the princess had emboldened me. Anger flashed through his eyes. He stalked forward to grab me. I flung myself out of the chair, tumbling to the floor. As long as he couldn't touch me, he couldn't take me. He scrambled after me, and I flung my book at his face. It hit him square in the nose with a thud. He snarled and lunged, his hand mere inches away. We both froze as a groan came from the bed.

"Pallas, what...?" Jun's eyes locked on my assailant, and his face went white. I saw the panic creep into his eyes as he scrambled to cover himself with the linens. "**STOP!**" The word shook the room, and I felt my entire body seize up. I couldn't have moved if my life depended on it. Luxos' was also caught in Jun's spell. He groaned, trying to extend his arm just a bit further to grab me.

Then the door slammed open, and Tori came barging in. Her eyes immediately locked on Luxos, and they filled with hatred. "Look who's caught this time, Commander." She unsheathed her sword and raised it above her head. She ran at him, and his eyes bulged. Just as her sword fell, that ashy rose smell flared, and the light in the room warped as Luxos wrapped himself in shadows. Tori's sword cut through the darkness but hit nothing as the man disappeared.

She had swung so hard that the sword embedded in the wooden floor. She wrenched it out and spun around, searching the corners for the shadow walker.

"He's gone." Of that, I had no doubt. Tori gave me a look full of distrust.

"You sure about that, beautiful?" Commander Avlyn's voice came from the doorway. They were giving me the same distrustful look the princess was.

"Luxos never stays for a fight he can't win," I remarked. They both stared at me some more until even I was unsettled. But then, some soft sobs came from the bed, and Tori immediately turned to Jun.

"He was here... he was here... how did he get here?"

Tori sat with him, one hand cautiously patting his back as she made soothing noises. I moved to join her, but Avlyn blocked my path.

"I was wondering the same thing," they said, staring directly into my eyes.

"I don't know." I wasn't sure why I lied, but Avlyn saw right through it.

"Don't lie to me." They pushed me back against the wall, their forearm pressed into my collarbone. "Tell me what you know."

"Take it somewhere else!" Tori shouted. Both Avlyn and I turned to look at Jun. He was heaving great sobs, barely able to breathe as panic set in. Tears streamed from his eyes as he doubled over, trying to claw beneath the covers. He was speaking incoherently, and Tori kept mumbling, "You're safe. You're safe. You're safe."

She looked at me with pleading eyes. "What do I do?" I felt Avlyn's grip loosen, and I went to Jun. "What do I do, Pallas?"

I didn't have the words to tell her there was nothing she could do.

[AUTHOR'S NOTE: THIS NEXT SCENE CONTAINS ON PAGE SA. Please protect your mental health and do not read if you aren't comfortable. Skip to the next chapter break.]

Hadeon hadn't even waited until the evening of Jun's arrival to destroy him. A servant summoned me to Hadeon's bedchamber. I walked in to see him pressing Jun's face down into the pillows as he mercilessly thrust into him from behind. I had walked into similar scenes many times, but never before had bile risen in my throat. I had to use every ounce of my defenses to hide it. The pillows muffled Jun's soft wails, and my nails cut into the palm of my hands.

"Pallas, my love, would you help me make our guest more comfortable?" That charming smile he wore so well was all teeth, and he grabbed the bun on the back of Jun's head to lift him out of the pillows to make space for me underneath him.

Jun's face was a mess of tears and spit. I did all I could not to look as I slid my dress off and climbed onto the bed. As I drew closer, I saw his back was covered in fresh burns that fractured out like veins from when Hadeon had inflicted another type of pain. How similar they were to the scars on my back, but mine had always healed over. Hadeon had known better than to leave permanent marks.

He didn't show the same caution with his new prize. The scars that would remain would be Hadeon's unique, permanent fingerprint on Jun, forever.

I slid myself underneath his body. Internally, I debated sliding in stomach down so that I wouldn't have to look at him, but the crack in my heart didn't let me. I faced him and gently wrapped my legs around his hips. Jun was hard, but it wasn't of his own volition; it was just a reaction to the electric stimulation Hadeon loved to administer.

I gently grasped his wet face, but he refused to look at me. I heard him mumble, "I'm sorry, I'm sorry." Repeatedly. My heart cracked open even more. None of this was his fault, and yet, this was the first apology I had heard in centuries.

I knew better than to try and comfort him with empty words, so I kissed the trails of tears under his eyes, hoping he would understand that he wasn't hurting me. But Hadeon grew impatient and shifted his hips forward, forcing Jun into me. He whimpered pathetically.

I participated in countless debaucheries with Hadeon throughout my life, but I never felt as vile as I did at that moment. I continued to kiss Jun's face, hoping he knew it would be over soon.

"Come now, Pallas, you can do better than that." Before I could stop myself, I looked at Hadeon. The contempt must have shown on my face because, for a moment, that perfect charming grin faltered and turned ugly. He said nothing; just let his power snake over Jun's body. Violet light flashed until it arched into me. Jun screamed and gritted his teeth. I could feel him shaking even more violently as new tears streamed down his cheeks.

I was damned either way, but one path at least would end this torment. I moved my hips in time with Hadeon, the two of us violating Jun in tandem. My master grinned again and picked up his pace, slamming down as hard as he could. It forced all of Jun's weight onto my body, but I did all I could to keep moving.

"I'm sorry..." Jun was sobbing into my ear. "I don't want to but..." I felt his body tense. I needed him to stop apologizing, so I gently snared his lips with mine. His body quaked, and Hadeon groaned as Jun squeezed around him. We continued to kiss as Hadeon found his satisfaction and released us both.

He crawled off the bed and left without another word, leaving Jun sobbing on top of me. I gently rolled him onto his side and extracted myself to find a bowl of warm water and a few clothes. I cleaned between my legs before soaking another towel in the warm water and approaching the shivering man on the bed.

I touched the cloth gently to his lower back, and he flinched away with a violent force.

"It's alright. I'm not going to hurt you. I promise." Already, I lied. I was sure I would hurt him again. But he let me run the warm towel over his skin, cleaning up the blood and everything else that coated his legs.

"I'm sorry. I'm sorry... I've never..." I could barely understand him as his chest heaved with sobs.

"I know. I know. It's alright." I found the salve I stashed in almost every one of Hadeon's chambers and worked it between my fingers until it was pliant and rubbed it on the burns. "It's going to be alright." *Such a fucking liar.*

"PALLAS, WHAT DO I DO?"

Tori was looking at me with grey eyes brimming with tears, just like Jun had. Like I had any power what's-so-fucking-ever to do anything. That feral, cornered beast inside me lashed out, trying to survive the pain that cut straight through my heart.

"You should have fucking been there, Princess! You should have saved him. You should have protected him because I *couldn't!*"

I expected her to lash out at me. I wanted her to. I deserved it, every piece of her ire and each punishment she could ever bestow on me. I deserved it and so much more. Instead, I saw the tears fall from her eyes as she looked away. I felt the hum of her power again, and she wrapped Jun in it. She gave a piece of herself to him, and it only reinforced how pathetic I was. I had stood by and done nothing for him, worse than nothing. I had inflicted pain on him to avoid my own, like a coward. I wished she would just end this all.

"Time to go, my lady." I felt Avlyn gently grab my shoulder and steer me out of the room. I let my feet shuffle on the floor but didn't fight it. Finally, I'd get locked in the dungeons, just like I deserved. Finally, I could stop pretending like I had any worth. It filled me with vacant relief.

After a few minutes of silence, Avlyn led me into not a dungeon cell but a small room with a table at the center, likely used for meetings. They sat me in a chair and pulled another out to straddle it, arms crossed over the back, facing me.

"How did he get into the castle?"

I blinked at them. "What?"

Avlyn lifted one hand and rubbed their eyebrows with their thumb and forefinger. "Pallas, please, don't make this difficult. How did Luxos get into the castle?" They paused, then added, "And how did he get out?"

I finally met their gaze. "You saw. He's a shadow walker."

They let out a long exhale accompanied by an elongated *fuuuccccckkkk*. "Just one godsdamned thing after another, isn't it? I assume Abraxas' wards are fading?"

I nodded, and they scrubbed their hands over their face. "Guess that's what I get for giving him so much shit for maintaining them over the centuries. It would have been easy for you to leave with him. Why didn't you?"

I didn't answer. It wasn't a difficult question; the answer was deceptively simple. *I didn't want to go.* Even thinking it somehow felt like a betrayal. But a betrayal to whom?

The commander and I held each other's stare until a small squeak of the door opening broke the silence. I heard the pattering of eight small feet as Spinner pushed himself up against my legs, looking for scratches.

Avlyn looked down at the beast and sighed. "He's getting way too big; he seems to like you." I reached down and scratched the beast's head until he emitted those unnerving clicks of satisfaction.

Avlyn sighed again and rose out of their chair. "Alright then, well, time to go."

"Straight to the dungeons, I assume."

"No, I have something much worse planned for you..." Avlyn's face didn't match their threatening words as a slight smile played on their lips. My stomach bottomed out anyway. I deserved this punishment, but I was still a coward, and my hands shook as I gripped my dress on top of my thighs.

"You're going to help me restore the wards," Avlyn finished with a flourish.

"Is that...punishment?" I asked.

"I'll let you be the judge of that once I show you where we have to go."

"Why?"

Avlyn gave me a quizzical look. "You said yourself that they need to be restored. No time like the present."

"No, I mean, why me? I'm the consort of the man you've declared war against. I could sabotage them."

"I doubt you could make them worse than they currently are, besides..." Avlyn held my gaze with theirs, and it felt like they were peering right into my soul. "Are you going to sabotage them?"

"No..." I said slowly.

"Well, there you have it."

"Commander, that's stupid. I could be lying."

"You're not." Avlyn headed for the door. "Come along, my lady. We're going to have to get you a new outfit."

Chapter 16

Hadeon

E verything had moved quickly after that old seer had spoken. Magic was already fading, so even a prophecy from the seer of some minor temple was worth more than gold.

King Obion of the Golden Kingdom was informed immediately and claimed me. I was hauled to his palace, and he stared down at me like I was some gutter rat who had run over his fine carpets. It wasn't far from the truth. His lips pulled tight to show his glowing white teeth as he snarled, "This pathetic boy, he's the Great Hero?"

I couldn't even look up at him as he spoke, so all I remember was that dirt that was caked beneath my fingernails, so at odds with the fine rug I clutched in them.

"Take him to the dungeon. If he is worth something, he will show his merit."

From one prison to another. The pain was different than in the temple, but it was still pain. The king had his men torture me. I'd still been a youngling then, and my magic hadn't emerged. The king wasn't interested in waiting.

Time blurred in the dungeons under the Golden Palace.

Was it day or night? I never knew. All I knew was when there was pain and when there was not.

When my body was finally sound again, they dragged me out into a dusty ring. Sand coated the floor, which was already pockmarked with black blood stains from the previous occupants. They threw me forward, and I landed hands first in the sand, coughing as the dust stung my eyes. Stone walls encircled the area, and above them rose several rows of seating, like I had been laid out on some great stage.

They were empty except for King Obion and a few attendants. There was an older fae with dark short hair that was beginning to show white at the temples. Next to him was a thin and rigid woman who held a tablet in one arm and a quill in the other. As I looked up at them, she scratched something on the tablet like I was some experiment meant to be observed.

I struggled to stand and saw the king raise his hand. At his gesture, great wooden doors beneath him swung open, and three full-grown and enormous fae strode forward. They were clearly warriors, wearing plate armor. They held no weapons; they didn't need them.

I knew what was coming, but some part of me still dared to hope I was misreading the situation. As the first man's fist collided with my jaw, white light shot across my vision as the pain radiated through my face and neck. I fell to my knees, but they didn't stop. Feet collided with my ribs, and a hand pulled me back to stand just for another fist to collide with my nose. There was a sharp crack followed by pain, and blood gushed down my face.

I knew that my fae body could withstand quite the beating, and these men seemed determined to push it to the limit. I knew nothing but pain, and my vision tunneled. My mind fled my body to protect itself, and as red clouded my vision and the torches of the arena danced, I could hear that dragon's laughter. *Pathetic, worthless, delicious.*

"Enough." The king's voice rang over the arena, and the blows stopped, but the pain lingered. Rough hands grabbed me under my arms and dragged me out of the light and into the darkness.

I was tossed away and collided with the wet stone floor of my cell. Blood clouded my vision, and I could taste it running down my throat. My head spun as I lay there, willing my body to stop healing and just let me die.

That's when I saw her. I had thought it was the seer, at first. She had the same golden-brown hair. But she was young, younger than me, with striking blue eyes that shone like the sky I hadn't seen in weeks. She must have been a dream. She was far too beautiful to be real. Perhaps the gods could be merciful if this was the last thing I was to see.

Pain shot through me as she touched a cool rag to my beaten face, and I winced. She frowned delicately when she saw my pain and moved with increased gentleness.

"I'm sorry." It was all she said. She had nothing to be sorry for. She was a vision from the gods themselves. What could she ever have to apologize for?

She continued to clean my wounds. By the time she finished, I had almost completely healed. My head still pounded, but I sat up. She leaned away from me, and I reached out my hand and grabbed her.

"You're real?"

I saw a deep sadness rise in her eyes. "Yes, I'm real. My name is Pallas."

PRESENT DAY

"Any news from Commander Luxos?" I asked.

"He returned, claiming that he still could not enter the city. It seems the prince remains in their possession," Plagis said.

"Pallas as well, then?" I asked.

The man's face hardened. "Yes, the woman remains with them as well. Sire, if I may... she is the only person left who still knows about your origins. Perhaps it is best if Luxos... removes her for us."

"No."

"Your Eminence, should she ever—"

"I said no, Plagis. We have had this discussion before. Pallas is mine. She will not betray me. She wouldn't dare. Don't make me say it again." He bowed differentially, knowing better than to argue, but I saw his twisted mind working.

I thought of Pallas, her soft skin, her flowing hair. I thought of the nights we'd spent wrapped in each other's arms, her soft moans and whimpers. Her laughter was a melody, and her smile was more beautiful than the breaking of the dawn. I loved her for it and hated how she had always shined brighter than me.

I thought of her anguished cries and how, over the centuries, I'd broken her down. She was still beautiful perfection. But inside, she was broken and ragged. She was mine, completely, no longer a glowing sun but a collapsed star. Slaves were common, but to own someone as I did her bordered on divine. I possess her mind, body, and soul. I had ruined her, my first glorious conquest. I was sure I would eventually grow tired of her and her obedience. But that was my prerogative, not Plagis'.

He backed out of the room but froze when I spoke again. "Remember, there are two people left who know my origins. I would hope that I can instill enough loyalty that no harm should need to come to either of them." Plagis nodded, and I knew he understood.

Chapter 17

Pallas

I had been alive for over five hundred years, of course I had worn pants before. But I never realized how much the fine dresses worn to court had become a part of the armor I wrapped around myself until Avlyn had thrown a pair of simple linen trousers at me.

I changed into them, and a simple shift tied closed at the neck by a single cotton string. I pulled it out to tie my hair away from my face. The neckline was open slightly, making the curves of my breasts more visible. It was not much armor, but enough for the moment. Spinner joined me in the room, and I gave a small spin. "How do I look?"

The creature chirped, and the sound seemed positive.

I opened the door and presented myself to Avlyn. Their gaze dipped for a fraction of a breath before they bid me to follow them. The spider and I were led deep into the castle, and I thought maybe they reconsidered just taking me to the dungeons when we halted. I peered around Avlyn and almost missed the low hole in the wall hidden away in a dark alcove.

"Where exactly are we going, Commander?" I asked as Avlyn ducked down to look inside the narrow passageway.

"To the foundation of the castle; that's where the wards are."

"Are they tied into the ley lines?"

Avlyn gave me a quizzical look over their shoulder. "Yes, how did you know that?"

"I know a lot of things, Commander."

"Clearly, but most people think ley lines are a myth."

"Much knowledge is lost with time. Many humans believe that dragons are just a story told by their ancestors. I've seen too much in my life to discount such mysteries so quickly. Besides..." I didn't continue the thought.

When Avlyn realized I would not continue, they turned back to the passage. "It's a tight fit and a long way. Let me know if you need a break, ok?"

"I can handle myself, Commander." I said, crossing my arms.

They let out a small laugh. "I have no doubt about that." They waved towards the passage. "Now... ladies first."

All my bravado fled as I looked at the very narrow, very dark hole. Spinner pressed past my leg and headed down the tunnel without hesitation. I had no choice but to follow suit.

I crouched down; my legs bent so much that my ass almost touched the ground as I awkwardly waddled down the passage. The little light disappeared as Avlyn ducked into the tunnel behind me.

"Are we going to travel the entire way in the dark?" I asked.

"Keep a hand on the wall; in a few minutes, you'll be able to see again," Avlyn responded.

The journey in my bent position was hard enough that I didn't argue. My fingers traced the roughhewn wall, and I kept moving forward. Slowly, my eyes adjusted, and I saw that tiny tendrils of moss and dim blue mushrooms clung to the corners of the tunnel. They each had a soft glow that provided a little light, but my fae vision adjusted. There was only one way to go, anyway.

After what felt like an eternity, my back ached from crouching, and I wasn't paying much attention anymore. My foot slipped on a small rock, and I fell flat on my ass. My pride was wounded more than anything, but I heard Avlyn say, "Careful, my lady. I don't want to have to drag you out of here."

In the dark, I saw the shadow of Spinner approach us, and he pressed his head into my hand as he tried to crawl into my lap.

"You're getting too big for this, spider." He ignored me and almost pushed my body all the way over.

"Maybe a brief rest couldn't hurt?" Avlyn suggested, giving me an out for my aching back.

"Anything to delay my night in the dungeon."

Even in the dim, I saw the commander frown.

"What, no dungeon? You lot really are terrible kidnappers."

They frowned. "Would you prefer that?"

I had to stop myself from responding yes, but Avlyn saw the answer on my face anyway.

They crouched down low, so we were eye to eye. "That would be easier, wouldn't it? It would put us on familiar ground. Me, threatening to chain you up and commenting on how much I'd like seeing you that way." They hit me with an apologetic smile. "I can't do that to you, Pallas."

"Why? Is it no fun to break what's already broken?"

I hated the sadness that crossed their face. "You're not broken, Pallas. That much is obvious to me."

"Why?"

Their shoulders slumped, and they leaned back against the tunnel wall, their head scraping against the ceiling. "I've been a soldier all my life. I've seen more battles than I care to remember. On the battlefield, a person is stripped down to their base self. Fear and a primal drive completely take over the mind. That's why we train as much as we do, so our movements are done on memory, not conscious thought. If you overthink on the battlefield, you die." They sighed. "On the beach, I saw a glimpse of the real you. You were scared and had no idea how to fight, but you fought anyway." They gave me a soft smile. "No broken person would throw themselves at the enemy to protect the one they care for. You've just been caged so long that freedom chafes. It grates against you in the worst way with the unending possibilities of choice."

I had nothing of value to say, no way to accurately respond to words my very soul knew were true. Nevertheless, Avlyn looked at me with such misplaced kindness that I had to say something. "Wise words from a brute."

They smiled. "What can I say? I'm a very multifaceted person." Their grin was infectious, so much so the corner of my mouth twitched without my consent. "You may not believe me, but I promise you are safe here, Pallas. You're safe with me. I won't let you come to harm."

"It's hard for me to believe you when you've trapped me in an endless stone tunnel with a man-eating spider." I heard Spinner hiss angrily from up ahead at my comment.

Avlyn laughed. "No one larger than a cat has gone missing at his pincers, as far as I know. But as he gets bigger, we will have to keep him well-fed." Spinner chirped happily at that.

I stood up in the enclave we entered. The stone walls were smooth, like the space inside of a bubble that solidified at the base of the castle. The light blue glow from the mush-rooms dimly lit the space. On the far wall, a circle of glyphs glowed a very faint emerald green. I approached and ran my hand over the spell. The markings had been carved directly into the stone; a permanent spell that needed to be recharged with magic every few years.

Avlyn approached me and set a gentle hand on my shoulder. "So, what's the plan, my lady?"

I spun around. "You don't know what to do?" I asked incredulously.

They shrugged. "Not really. Magic was never my thing. It was already half dead when I was born. I figured, why waste the time learning it?"

"I take back what I said before. You're nothing but a brute."

They smiled mischievously. "Never denied it, gorgeous. Now..." Grabbing my shoulders, they spun me back around. "... let's see just how much you know."

I huffed in irritation but couldn't resist running my fingers over the glyphs for locking, for pulling, warding, and many others. "This spell taps into the ley line that runs under the castle. It uses the mana, or wild magic of the earth, that travels along it to create a protective barrier against other magical attacks. I'm surprised Abraxas maintained it all these years."

"I think you know exactly who this barrier was kept in place for." Yes, I did. Avlyn ran their finger over the glyphs, and the faint green light shuddered under their fingers. "I guess, as a bonus, it kept our shadow-walking friend out until now, as well. So how do we fix it?"

"It needs to receive a direct injection of animavigo to act as a catalyst for the spell to pull from the ley line," I disclosed.

Avlyn's face was blank. "Maybe try explaining it like I'm a brute?"

I laughed, not a soft, elegant laugh, but one that gripped me so tightly my stomach clenched. I couldn't find my breath again. When I finally recovered, Avlyn was smiling again.

"Glad I amuse you so much, my lady."

"Sorry, your face was just... anyway... where to start? Animavigo is the term academics use for what is commonly called magic. It is the energy that dwells within every mortal living thing's heart. For animals and plants, it's just a drop. For fae and some humans, that well is deeper. Magic users of old could call on this energy and manifest it into the world. Everyone's manifestation was unique, a mirror of their soul. Like the king's flames, Jun's voice..." I paused. "...your control of water."

Avlyn didn't balk but rubbed their chin in thought. "This is why I never learned about magic. Too complicated. If everyone has these wells of energy, this animavigo, why did magic die off?"

"That's the great mystery, isn't it? We don't know. We don't know why we stopped being able to tap into this power. Well, at least most people did." I eyed them again, but they ignored me.

"And how is that different from the great beasts?" Avlyn inquired.

"Beasts, like the dragons, don't have a well. It's more like a channel, a direct connection to the mana of the earth. The only limit to what they could do was what the earth would provide. A fae can't call on more energy than their heart can contain without risking their life. But a dragon or..." I trailed off, and Avlyn's eyes grew serious. We were both thinking about the princess. "...luckily, aside from dragons, none seemed very interested in using this power directly."

Avlyn turned back to the wall. "So, what are we doing here?"

"This spell calls upon the mana of the earth so that it can run continuously without interference. It can do this because the castle has been tied into a ley line, one of the earth's channels of power. But it needs... a spark, let's say. Something to get the flow started. That's where you come in."

"Me?" They looked perplexed.

"Yes, you. You still have access to your magic; we need that for the spark."

Their face twisted into a deep frown. "Can't you just say some magic words or something?"

I crossed my arms. "No, I cannot." I motioned to the glyph before pushing Avlyn forward.

They placed a hand on the glyph and furrowed their eyebrows. I waited patiently for a few minutes, but nothing happened.

"Everything alright?"

"Look, I told you, I don't know what I'm doing." Something like shame passed over Avlyn's face.

Moving closer, I gently touched their back, letting my other hand land on top of theirs on the glyph circle. "Your magic manifests as water, right? Think about what that feels like. Visualize the flow from your heart to your fingertips."

"I was never one for all this mindfulness shit." Avlyn's frustration cut through their normally calm voice.

I took a deep breath. "Close your eyes. Now, breathe with me. Focus on my voice. Imagine the blood flowing through your body and how the current moves and keeps you alive. Follow that stream to your heart; let it settle there. Do you see the light? Let it flow to your fingertips." Avlyn's breath steadied, and the glyphs' fading green light shifted to a warm, deep amber.

Avlyn opened their eyes. "Whoa! Did it work?"

"It did indeed." I couldn't keep the grin from my face, and they returned it in earnest. "It looks perfect."

"What, my face?" Avlyn pointed to themselves, and their contagious grin grew more mischievous.

Before I could think about it, my hand flew out and smacked them on the chest.

"Whoa, easy there hellcat," Avlyn laughed. "Glad to see you've still got some energy, as we still have three more of these to go!" They pointed to an even smaller tunnel I hadn't noticed.

I groaned; my back twinged at just the thought of stooping over again. Suddenly, the dungeons really didn't seem so bad.

As we finally crawled out of the last tunnel back into the castle proper, I saw the sun cresting the horizon through the floor-to-ceiling windows lining the hall we entered. I was exhausted and covered in dust and sweat, but somehow, I felt satisfied. The satisfaction of a task earned through hard work. For a moment, I basked in the feeling, forgetting just how worthless I was.

"Well, that's a job well done. Looks like we won't have any more late-night visitors. Well, except for the ones we invite, that is." Avlyn winked at me, and I turned away to hide the blush that rose up on my face. *What was I, a youngling again?*

"Sorry that you won't be able to foist me off onto someone else so easily now, Commander." I said still unable to face them.

"Pallas..." Avlyn placed their finger under my chin and, ever so gently, turned my face to look at them. "Like I said before, I won't let any harm come to you. Of any kind."

I couldn't stand their kind gaze. "Why?" *I'm your enemy. I'm worthless. I'm nothing.*

"That's what I do. I protect those who need protecting." Their smile was soft; it cut straight through the crack in my heart that seemed to be eroding like earth after a rainstorm.

"Have a thing for rescuing damsels in distress, huh?"

They laughed, "You can only rescue someone who wants to be rescued. Do you want to be rescued, Pallas?"

I didn't answer because I didn't know the answer.

Avlyn gave me that soft smile again. "When you figure it out, let me know, and I'll be first in line." They took my hand and placed a soft kiss on my knuckles before heading down the hall, leaving me with my head spinning.

Chapter 18

Tori

I woke up next to Jun. My eyes ached from fretful sleep. I had used a small bit of magic to calm him, but it felt too similar to the sleeping potions for me to use it more heavily. He had tossed and turned all night, but at every fitful awakening, I assured him he was safe with me.

Now that morning broke, he seemed to have finally reached a deep sleep. I cautiously crawled out of bed and closed all the curtains in the room to keep it dark. Pallas was passed out in a scrunched position on the cramped couch. She woke up easily when I approached.

"He seems to be sleeping now. Can you stay with him?" She nodded before silently crawling into bed with him.

I grabbed my sword and left the room; my body ached as I wandered without thinking. My feet led me to the beach. The crisp morning air was filled with the cacophony of shouting from training soldiers. My heart steadied. This was what my mind and body understood. I ran to join the back of the ranks, falling into the routine, but I couldn't find the stillness I craved, even as sweat built on my brow. My thoughts ran amok.

We broke for water. It had been too long since I trained; I was entirely unprepared for Kaleos when he landed a slap on my back.

"Look who decided to finally put in some work today," he laughed as I choked on the water. I sputtered, and his charming smile only grew.

"I've been a bit preoccupied, Kaleos," I explained, trying to wipe my face on my sleeve.

"Don't I know it? Perhaps it's time for a little distraction?" He waggled his eyebrows. "Come on, I know what will cheer you up." He tossed a blunted sword at me with an arrogant smile. His mood was infectious.

"Just you? I'll need more of a challenge than that." I winked at him.

"There she is, that cocky asshole I love. Square up, Princess. I can tell you're rusty; you've lost all the definition in your arms."

I took a casual swipe at him. "Not all of us spend half the day flexing in a mirror, Kaleos." I was grinning as we circled each other, taking casual swipes. As the cold sea air whipped my skin, I focused my breathing and found that place of deep peace inside my mind. That's when we really began to spar.

It felt amazing. If only for a few moments, everything else fell away. My doubts and worries were gone. There was just me, my sword, and the sand beneath my feet. Our swords clashed, sending sparks flying through the air. Kaleos spun and quickly dodged my counterattack by ducking and swiping my legs out from underneath me. The feeling of the air being knocked from my lungs was exquisite.

"Hey, didn't I teach you that move?" I laughed.

Kaleos extended his hand with a smug grin, helping me back to my feet. "You did, but it seems like you forgot your own lesson, Princess."

I brushed the sand off my clothes, still catching my breath. "I wonder, are you showing off for someone?" I scanned the beach for a head of red hair.

He snorted, sheathing his sword. "Just keeping you on your toes, Tori. Besides, if I don't challenge you, who will? None of these cowards would." He waved to where Noki and Raula had gathered to watch us. Raula shot him a rude gesture.

I punched Kaleos lightly on the arm. "Pretty sure there's a long list, but I appreciate the effort." My hand naturally fell to the sword Abraxas had gifted me, pulling it from its sheath, its two halves locked together. I still hadn't used it as two blades yet.

I unlocked them, twirling one in each hand. My left arm ached as I swung the weapon back and forth. Pain radiated from the scar wrapped around my bicep. I sighed, about to set the blade down, when I felt mana creep up my body and wrap itself around the old wound. It didn't heal, but some of the ache was pulled away into the earth below. I swung the blade again, and while the discomfort lingered, it was manageable. I looked back up at Kaleos.

He gave me his signature wide grin. "Guess I'm in trouble now. Try not to stab me this time, Princess." He grabbed a bladed weapon and took a fighting stance.

"No promises." I held each of the twin blades firmly. Their golden guards wrapped around my hands like my bond with Abraxas was wrapped around my heart. The pain in my arm throbbed, but it also said, *show them how strong you've become.*

I spun fast, my blades whirling through the air at Kaleos. Sparks flew as the crash of steel echoed over the beach. Whoops and hollers came from the watching soldiers, but it all passed me by. All I saw was Kaleos and his sword, as we met again and again. No matter what else happened, this I could do.

The minutes ticked by. Kaleos was still one of the best

swordsmen I knew, but my fae blood gave me the advantage of superior stamina. He started to slow down, and I used it, deflecting one of his too-wide strikes and pushing past his defenses. I rammed my shoulder into his chest, and he fell flat on his ass, my sword at his throat.

"Who's out of shape now, Lieutenant?" He grinned up at me from the sand.

"Hey! I need him in one piece!"

I reached a hand down to help Kaleos up as Oryx sprinted over to check his lover for injuries.

"Oh, do you now?" I waggled my eyebrows at them, and they both blushed.

Kaleos assured Oryx that he was alright as the healer continued to fuss like a mother hen.

Behind me, I heard whooping from the castle. I looked over to see Avlyn on one of the lower balconies with their fist in the air. Next to them stood Commander Talius, his arms crossed and gaze fixed on me.

I turned back to the troops. Oryx was still fretting over Kaleos' leg and the long cut that ran around his thigh. My blades were so sharp that I must have cut him without even noticing.

"I'm sorry! I guess I am always hurting you."

He waved his hand. "It's nothing. I'm really fine. This one just likes to fuss." Oryx gave him a stern look, which he smartly conceded to.

I placed my hand on his leg and reached down for mana. I brought up tendrils and wrapped them around Kaleos, but nothing happened. I frowned. Pulling harder, I focused on sending the energy into his body, and still, nothing. I let out a frustrated hiss.

"Everything alright, Your Highness?" Oryx put a soft hand on my shoulder.

Immediately, I was surrounded by whispers like the beach

had been crammed full of bodies. Oryx perked up, and I knew he heard it, too.

The wind whipped around us, and the voices rose. I looked at the cliffs and saw the green grass that shifted in the ocean breeze.

Spring is coming. Spring is coming. Spring is coming.

The words were layered over themselves a thousand times, each blade whispering individually and a part of the greater whole.

Oryx frowned at me. I understood why; it was late summer, nearly fall in the northern climate.

"Something lost in translation?" I suggested.

He shrugged. "I doubt the grass is well versed in common."

"Talking to the plants again?" Kaleos asked, making Oryx grin. He took his hand off my shoulder, and the whispers fell away.

I didn't understand this power I had, but it was time to test it.

Chapter 19

Tori

I reached down into that deep well beneath my feet. On the beach, I could once again feel the warm magic of the earth and the harsh, cold depths of the magic of the ocean. They seemed to clash where they met, much like the waves breaking against the shore. I focused on pulling energy from each of them. They didn't want to play. The great reservoir ignored me. I was no more than any other speck of dust.

I ground my teeth and tried to pull harder. Nothing. I was getting pissed off. Sweat formed on my brow, and I slammed my palms into the black sand of the beach. I reached out with my mind, burrowing my fingers in like I could dig my way to that power. But I couldn't draw it into me. I hissed in frustration.

"Take it easy now, Princess. No one learned how to channel the magic of the earth overnight," Avlyn laughed as they approached me. They moved to set their hand on my shoulder, "Come on, let's—" The power exploded.

As soon as their hand touched my shoulder, it was like when lightning connected to the earth. Immediately, the power I had been tugging at flooded over me and jumped to Avlyn through their touch. It was too much; I had been pulling too hard with nowhere for the magic to go. I felt the ground beneath us shake and rip, and my mind was overtaken by that deep, unending power.

It tried to wash all that I was away, but the golden light of my bond with Abraxas clung to my soul, preventing it from being washed away in the tide. It gave me just enough time to focus and hold onto myself. I focused on the beating of my heart and that deep golden bond, and I survived the onslaught. Seconds, or maybe hours, passed. But the flood of magic ebbed, and I could breathe again. I found myself lying flat on my back on the ground. I pushed up, and my temple throbbed, and black stole into my vision as the blood rushed out of my head. All I could see was a blinding blue light.

I held it in my hands. Was I blind? Why couldn't I see? I realized I was peering into a great chasm that had opened in the ground. The beach had cracked open like the shell of an egg, and from the depths, that eerie blue light of wild magic glowed. I scrambled back from the edge when I heard my name.

"Um, Tori..." I spun around to see Avlyn sitting on the beach beside me. They were naked, attempting to cover their small breasts as I stared at them, even though that was not what I was looking at. In place of their legs was a long, copper-colored tail, covered in small, pointed scales that shimmered like the waves of the sea. Small fins sprouted along the side, with two long, beautifully translucent fins on the end. They reminded me of stained-glass windows, each panel a slightly different shade that shimmered in the noonday sun.

I moved my gaze back up to Avlyn's, and we just stared at each other. "I guess you were right about your heritage." That was all I could think to say.

"You think this is fucking funny, Princess!? I'm a godsdamn fish! Change me back!" Their tail flopped about helplessly as they gestured frantically. I was still too dumbfounded to think when I heard footsteps approaching rapidly.

"What the hell happened? Are you al—" Kaleos and the cohort had run around the great gash in the earth and joined us, but they stopped short to stare at the commander. I couldn't blame them.

Avlyn's cheeks turned a deep maroon as they shouted, "Would you all stop fucking staring and help me?"

"You want us to toss you into the ocean, boss?" Kaleos asked.

"No, I do not want to get fucking tossed in the ocean. Get me my legs back!" With one hand still clamped over their chest, they tried to drag themselves across the sand with the other but made little progress.

"Kaleos, would you be a dear and fetch Pallas and Jun from the castle for me?"

A short while later, Kaleos returned with the others. Noki and I moved Avlyn partially into the water despite their protests. They sat there, fins and fingers drifting through the ocean waves, looking out at the Bay of Dragons. They hadn't spoken in some time, and we hadn't pushed.

Pallas and Jun both looked at the massive glowing rift in the beach.

"Did you do this?" my brother asked.

"I think so, but that's not the half of it." I pointed to Avlyn in the waves and saw Pallas' eyebrows shoot up.

"Can I talk to them?" Pallas asked me.

"Go ahead, it's your funeral." She rolled her eyes at me and approached Avlyn. She squatted near the commander, and I couldn't hear their discussion over the waves. The cohort still stood nearby, shifting uneasily, unsure what to do. I had tried to get them to leave the beach, but they refused. Jun continued to observe the light emanating from below the earth, and then he turned to me.

"World Breaker indeed," he said, with that old sarcastic glint in his eye. I was so happy to see it that I didn't even linger on what his words meant. Before we could discuss it further, Pallas stomped back over.

"Tell me what happened."

I tried to explain to her everything I had felt.

She raised her hand to her chin for a while, deep in thought, before blurting out, "Tori, I don't think you have any magic."

I was dumbfounded. "What? I mean... seriously, what? Do you see what has happened here?"

She looked at me, still rubbing her chin. "I think you are a conduit like you assumed, but it's different than the dragons. You can truly only conduct magic; you need someone to conduct it to. That's why when Avlyn touched you, the magic was unleashed."

I started to argue reflexively but held back. I thought about all the times I conducted magic before. With Abraxas, with Jun, with Oryx in the forest... I had always needed to be in contact with them. The only exception was the small flame I produced in the cave, but even then, I needed my bond to Abraxas.

"When was the first time you conducted magic, Tori?" Pallas asked.

"It was in Tenebrae Forest with Abraxas and Oryx. I touched them, and the magic channeled through me."

"And was this after you accepted your mating bond?"

"What do you mean? I didn't know I was his mate until he changed."

Pallas shook her head. "You didn't understand what it was, but that doesn't mean you hadn't accepted it."

I thought back to the night he let me go. He told me he loved me, in not so many words, by setting me free. I eventually returned to him, no longer afraid or resisting my heart. That golden magic had finally connected us. I hadn't known what it was, but Pallas was right. I had accepted it.

"Yes, I had. Just before we left for the forest."

Pallas sighed, "So you had his heart."

"What are you talking about?"

She finally looked at me again. "It's complicated." I gave her a withering look. "I'll explain later, but I think we should focus on the commander right now."

I looked back at Avlyn, who still sat in the soft waves; their bright tail was so at odds with the black sand beneath them. I nodded. Pallas squatted beside them, and Jun and I kneeled in the sand next to her.

"Alright. Tori, you are going to channel into Avlyn again. This isn't their natural form, and they seem willing to change back so—"

"So fucking willing! Can we do this?" Avlyn's face was tight with fear, so I reached out to put a comforting hand on their shoulder. Pallas did the same, which surprised me.

"So it should be, in theory, easy to return to their natural state. Jun will help." I felt him shrink into himself.

"It will be just like we practiced in Koron, Jun," Pallas encouraged softly.

He was shaking. "I can't..."

"It's alright. You don't have to," I reassured him, but I heard an almost imperceptible whimper from Avlyn at my words. I was caught like, well, a fish in a net and tugged in two directions.

"I can do this. I changed them without Jun; I can change them back." I gave Pallas a stern look, but she didn't flinch.

"To undo this will require fine control and precision with the magic. You don't have that, Tori. You're lucky Avlyn didn't explode." Another soft whimper came from the commander. "You're a sledgehammer when we need a quill." She looked at Jun. "You can do this."

He continued to shake. I wanted nothing more than to throw myself on top of my brother to shield and hide him away. All I saw was the little boy who needed my protection more than anything.

I wish I was more like you, Tori. What had my protection done for him? Had I ever really been able to keep him safe? We were brother and sister, twins bonded in more than blood. I had always been his protector, but maybe I had done more harm than good.

I placed a tentative hand on his shoulder. If I loved him, I could let him stand beside me. "She's right. I believe in you."

His eyes shone as he shook his head. "I can't sing, not anymore." My heart clenched to hear him voice those words, even if I knew they were true.

Pallas shook her head. "You don't need to. Just like on the boat and the other night, let Tori channel the magic. You just need to tell Avlyn what to do." She nodded at me, and I focused. Very gently, I pulled magic from the earth. Jun may not have been able to sing, but I remembered his song. I let the magic twirl through my heart; its thumping became the beat, and the magic's motion was the melody. I sent it to Jun and let it settle in his throat.

For a few moments, all I heard was the beating of our hearts, and then, in a voice both incredibly soft and infinitely piercing, Jun commanded, "**TRANSFORM.**"

I could feel more power being pulled through me like his word had fractured a dam. My heart raced, and I worried we would both be swept away. But Pallas was right; it was different from before. Jun's personal magic, combined with the magic of the earth, guided the power with a gentle hand. Turquoise light surrounded Avlyn's tail, swirling gently like the caress of a lover. Scales receded back into dark skin as their legs gradually split into two. The flow of magic slowed like a stream flowing into a pond and finally stopped completely. Avlyn sat naked but completely fae on the beach once more. Pallas shrugged the cloak off her shoulders, draping it around the commander.

We held our breath as Avlyn wiggled their toes. But the silence was broken violently with their loud yelp, "I'm me again!" They swung their arms around Pallas, pulling her into a tight embrace. She grunted awkwardly, and Avlyn immediately released her. Both refused to look at the other, and I was just going to ignore that for now.

I turned to Jun. "You always were the one with more finesse." I smiled, and it grew when I saw it mirrored on his face. I dared a small peek at his heart, and the shadows seemed to be just a bit weaker.

Chapter 20

Pallas

I wandered down to the barracks, looking for the commander. I wasn't exactly sure what had brought me there. I'd known of Avlyn for many years; their presence at the Dragon King's side was a constant. I never had much contact with Abraxas. I had always feared him, but he wasn't here. Avlyn was, and they were not at all what I had expected.

I slowly made my way down the halls deep within the castle. There were no windows this low, but torches lit the roughhewn surfaces, and soldiers milled about, chatting and roughhousing. A few gave me passing looks, but no one stopped me. I wasn't entirely sure where I was going or why I was even headed there. *You know why.* Yes, I'd seen that look on Avlyn's face, the fear in their heart that their body did not belong to them. I knew that feeling well, and it drew me.

I turned a corner and saw the brute Kaleos leaning against a wall. He stood up straight when he saw me. "My lady, can I help you?"

"Yes, I was looking for Commander Avlyn."

He turned to look at the door across the hall. "The

commander is in there, but they are with Oryx, and... well, they aren't receiving visitors."

I wasn't surprised. Tori had been mumbling in the library about Avlyn refusing to see her. Luckily, I didn't think this brute would be too hard to get past.

"I need to see them; I'm checking on any lingering effects of magic." An easy lie.

His eyebrows shot up. "Oh, yes... well, then... go in, I guess." Too easy. I strode past him and pushed open the wooden door.

The commander had their own private room. It wasn't large, but the stone floor had been covered in rugs, and a few comfortable—if unrefined—chairs sat around a low table where cards and dice were strewn. The commander sat on the bed, with the red-headed healer checking on them.

Avlyn's amber eyes moved to me as I entered the room. They looked much more suspicious than the brute had. Oryx stood up and went to the door, giving me a friendly smile before leaving without a word. The commander and I were alone.

"What do you want?" they asked. Their voice was strained, and they still held themselves rigidly. Their hands ran over their legs, still fearful that they might disappear at any second. It would have been easy to snap back at them, but I hadn't come here to be antagonistic.

"I wanted to see how you were doing."

"Just fine, thanks. Now, if that's all..." Avlyn gestured to the door. I ignored them.

"I need to see if you have any magic lingering from your change."

Avlyn's eyes narrowed, but they did not stop me as I approached. I was lying, but only partially. I could sense residual magic. It wasn't a gift, just a skill from growing up in my mother's labs, always surrounded by magic. I knew what it felt like. It left a sweet taste on my tongue and made the hair on my arms stand on end. That's how I knew something had changed about Tori's necklace that night in Koron. I wasn't sure what its magic was; the glamour on it had been expertly woven, but I could still sense it.

I sat on the bed beside the commander and slowly moved my hand to hover over their legs. I wasn't surprised to find no residual magic. Whatever Tori and Jun had been able to do together was seamless. Regardless, I didn't stop my hand and found myself leaning in closer. The room was quiet, with no sound except for our breathing. I could still smell how the salt air clung to them.

Avlyn placed their hand on top of mine, gently pushing it down so that my palm landed on their thigh. I looked up and saw that their face was very close. Were they...

"Do you feel anything? Am I going to change back?" No, they weren't being forward. They were terrified.

I gave their thigh a gentle squeeze and let it linger. "No. I don't sense anything. You don't have to worry."

Avlyn let out a long breath, and the tension left their shoulders as they leaned forward to hold their face in their hands. I instinctively started rubbing their back.

"I haven't seen magic in five hundred years, and I've already had enough."

I continued my ministrations. "But that's not true, Avlyn. You have clung to your magic all this time."

They huffed, "More like it clung to me. You saw; I was never any good with it. I preferred to ignore it when I could." They laughed, "Although it did help me save the princess's life once."

"And mine as well." Avlyn sat up straight and finally turned their face towards me. Their full lips pressed together tightly, and I leaned into them more. "You never wanted to use it? You never wanted to see what you could do?"

For a long time, they said nothing as their gaze never

wavered from mine. I felt their leg shift under my hand like they finally realized I'd left it there.

"It always called to me... the sea. When I used my magic, that call was almost impossible to deny. And when I changed, it was all I could think about. I ached to dive beneath the waves and just disappear into the depths."

"Why didn't you? You may not have the chance again."

Their jaw clenched. "I would have never come back," they stated simply. "I can't do that now. I have to stay here and fight for Abraxas, for Tori."

"But you want to go."

"I didn't until today, and I hate that a feeling I had no control over or desire for pulled deep in my gut. Have you ever wanted something with every fiber of your being that you knew you couldn't have?"

A dark shadow crossed my heart, and Avlyn must have seen it on my face because their expression softened. "I'm sorry. I'm just rambling." They placed their hand on my shoulder. "I feel better now. Away from the ocean, inside these walls, I know I'm not likely to start flopping around at any moment. Thank you, Pallas." They hit me with a warm smile, and I stared deep into their honey-colored eyes. My stomach squeezed at the rapt attention and adoration they were showing me.

"Actually, I came here to thank you, Commander."

They had saved my life. I assumed their motives were the same as anyone else who had helped me. They hadn't initiated anything, but that's how some people were. The commander was attractive, so it was no hardship to give it to them. If I was being honest, I wanted it, too. I squeezed their thigh tighter and pressed my chest against theirs. My eyelids fell closed.

Immediately, the commander's hand held me back by my shoulder. My eyes opened in shock. "You don't have to do that, Pallas." Avlyn's face was stern but not unkind.

I didn't understand the emotions that darted through me at the rejection, but I felt my lips twitch.

Their eyes widened. "It's not that I'm not... I did say I had quite a weakness for beautiful women," they stammered, and a deep blush rose onto their dark cheeks. "It's just... after what you've been through..." Their eyes widened more and their whole face was red. "You should get settled here before... well..." They were floundering, and my pride was wounded enough that I stood rapidly and made my exit.

As I opened the room, I surprised myself by calling back, "I'm glad to see you smile again, Commander." *What the hell was that?* As I closed the door, I heard Avlyn flop down on the bed with an aggravated huff.

I stepped outside and found Lieutenant Kaleos with his arm around Oryx. The healer's red freckles were almost hidden by the deep blush on his cheeks as the brute pulled him close and planted a soft kiss on his forehead. Seeing him be so gentle with another was really cutting into my image of him as a brute. I continued to stare until Oryx noticed me and gently pushed out of his lover's arms. He reached up and scratched the back of his head sheepishly, sending me a soft grin that I didn't reciprocate. "What did you find? Will the commander be alright?"

I shot him a confused look. "You examined them, don't you know?"

He shook his head. "I'm versed in physical healing. I use herbs, plants, and the gifts of our world to help people with some knowledge of anatomy. But magic... I've read about the healing that used to be possible when magic still flowed. How I wish I could have seen that! But that's not possible anymore..."

All three of us lingered on his last sentence. The barracks grew quieter, and I knew all the soldiers were listening to us now. How could they not after what they had seen on the beach this morning?

"It's not possible, right, my lady?" All their eyes were on me. What was I supposed to say? I was barely able to handle my own situation, trapped in this castle far away from my home. *Trapped? Really?* Yes, trapped. I was trapped but able to freely wander the palace and the city and able to see Jun any time I wanted. I was trapped because my body didn't understand that it didn't have to be afraid of being touched by anyone and everyone. It was hard to believe that there might be people who helped me without expecting my body as a reward. *The freedom chaffs.*

It was all a trick; it had to be. The princess was just waiting for me to slip up and try to escape so she could kill me without remorse. Avlyn was just luring me in with kindness. It had worked, and I had practically thrown myself into their arms. I'm sure, in the end, they would be the same as all the others and use me for their own pleasure, nothing more. And all the soldiers were still fucking staring at me. I turned down the hall and walked away, not saying a word.

I RETURNED TO THE LIBRARY AND FOUND THE TWINS huddled over the same tomes I had left them with. The stares of the soldiers seemed to follow me back here, and I couldn't stand it any longer.

"Why are you letting me wander freely? What's your plan, Tori?" She looked up at me and let out a small laugh. "It's not funny."

Her face grew more serious. "No, it's not. I was just remembering when I asked Abraxas the same thing." She stood and walked over to me, Jun following behind her. "You're free,

Pallas. You aren't a prisoner here." That little smile crossed her lips again. "If you want to leave, you can leave."

I was shocked into stillness. "Letting me go is a terrible idea."

"Is it? You've already had my life in your hands multiple times, and you haven't harmed me. And despite how you feel about me and this kingdom, I know you would never harm Jun. Besides, I really don't think you are going to leave."

I crossed my arms and felt anger stir in my stomach. "You don't know me, Princess."

She started to respond, but Jun interrupted her. "Pallas, do you really want to leave?" His eyes shined with tears. He knew he would have to choose between me and her if I did. I knew who he would pick. After everything we had been through, he would pick her. He should pick her after all I had done, after all the ways I had hurt him. It tore at my heart, and I was too weak to face it.

I sighed, "No, I don't."

He smiled, and the heaviness lifted. He lit up my whole life. Besides, where else would I go?

I sighed and leaned over the tomes they had open on the table. "Did you find anything?"

Tori flipped a page, then flopped back and pulled a piece of dried meat out of a bag, tearing at it with her teeth. I cringed, thinking about the oils on her fingers smearing the pages of these precious tomes.

"You'd think the library of the Dragon Kingdom might have some actual books with useful information about dragons, but no." Tori held the dried meat in one hand as she flipped through the pages. Jun leaned over and took a massive bite out of the piece. "Hey!"

Tori tried to jerk the food back, but her brother held on tightly and grinned around the meat in his teeth. The princess struggled with him gently, but it quickly escalated as he reached to grab the rest of her snacks.

"Get your own!" She pushed the side of his face, trying to move him away.

"Yours are better," he laughed around the stolen bite. He flung his whole weight onto her as they continued their tussle.

It was so stupid, the stupidest thing I had ever seen, but my heart seemed to glow. I think Tori realized how physical Jun was letting her be, and a small smile lit up her eyes as she wrestled the food from her twin's grip, triumphantly shoving the entire piece in her mouth.

The prince held his hands up in defeat as his sister nearly choked on her prize. He turned to me. "We haven't been able to find much in these books. What did you want to tell us on the beach? About Tori not having magic."

My study of magic had always been my greatest value; even Hadeon had seen that. If I could use it to keep Jun safe, I would.

"Jun knows this, Tori, but my mother was the one who built the enchantment around Malech's heart for Hadeon. Well, I should say she built it for King Obion, but that's irrelevant now. They discovered that a dragon's heart is the key to its conduit magic. The enchantment around it not only keeps it safe but also binds the heart to Hadeon, conducting magic directly to him. That is how he has been able to keep his magic strong after all these centuries. It's quite an elaborate enchantment, actually, the most elaborate one that has ever existed. It was truly a work of artistry that my mother created, combining the newest theorems on spatial control with ancient rites on power transference in a way..." I cut myself off as Tori's eyes started glazing over, but Jun was grinning.

"What?" *Pallas, would you stop with your droning on and on; it's tedious.* Hadeon's words rang in my head, and I hated how they made me shrink into myself.

"I love when you get so excited about enchantments. Your face always lights up," Jun said, still smiling.

He was too good for me. Those very enchantments had been what bound him to Hadeon, but he smiled at me. I saw the pain in his heart, as I'm sure his sister did, but he soothed the ache in mine I long thought was permanent. Of course, I would never leave him. I had failed him before; I would not do that again.

I saw Tori's fist clench on the piece of paper she was holding. "So, we were right. We need to break that enchantment, and then Hadeon will be powerless."

"No, he will still have his fae magic, a magic that was strong enough to defeat Malech."

"And that is different from what I have?"

"When you channel, what does it feel like?"

She pressed her lips together. "Like a flow... a river of power. It's like I'm trying to guide water with just my bare hands."

"You're able to control mana, at least a small amount. You can guide the very magic of the earth; that's something no fae has ever been able to do."

"Then what was magic before?" Tori inquired.

"Fae used to be born with a small well of their own power; *Animavita* or fae magic. Each was unique, something that resonated with the fae's soul. Jun's voice is an example, and Hadeon's lightning is another. They can manifest their magic until that well runs dry. It will replenish with time, but it is a slow process."

"The amount of power each fae had was different; some had more than others, while other folks, such as the Huldu, were especially gifted. Even some humans had it, but the fae tried to hide that fact. It was actually weakest among the royal lines." I gave a soft chuckle. "Except for the Corignus line... which now makes more sense." The small humor I found left me. "As you can imagine, the fae kings weren't so happy about not having their own power."

Tori's face darkened. "No, I can't imagine they were. Something that anyone could have; power they weren't able to control and horde."

"But Hadeon is royal, and his power was legendary before he even defeated Malech, "Jun interjected.

Hadeon isn't royal. I didn't say it. Every day I spent away from him, I realized more and more the abuse that I suffered under him. Nevertheless, I still couldn't bring myself to say his greatest shame.

Luckily, neither twin questioned it further. "So, the royals found another way. Enchantments, correct?"

I nodded. "Enchantments were originally developed by magi to enhance their magic and allow them to expand what they could do with more precise control. But then it was discovered they could guide mana. They act as a way for fae to tap into the earth's power. A small spark of animavita is all that is needed to activate them, and then a trade is made for the power."

"A trade?"

I nodded. "A fae with magic can offer up a small amount of their power, but one can also use—"

"Their lifeforce." Tori locked eyes with me. "Wouldn't there still be a limit on how much power one could use until the extent of one's lifeforce is up?"

"I never said that only the enchanter's lifeforce could be used."

A terrible realization dawned on her face. "The great beasts. They were hunted to power fae magic."

"Yes. Nothing could compare to the power released at their death. King Obion's entire kingdom was built on the souls of more beasts than can be counted. The more that were killed, the greater the price became until the earth no longer responded to our enchantments' call."

"But some still remain?"

"Yes. With enough fae magic, one doesn't need mana to power an enchantment. Hadeon can power every enchantment he has ever needed with just his own power. Abraxas was doing the same here, if to a lesser extent."

Tori nodded. "I understand the earth withholding its power, but what about fae magic? Why has that also disappeared?"

"That is... the great mystery. My mother spent the last decades of her life trying to discern why mana stopped responding and animavita faded. She never found an answer."

"But you have an idea." The princess didn't pose it as a question. "Say what you are thinking, Pallas."

"I have never been a mother, but I can imagine if I saw my children being killed for the selfish gains of the fae. I would fight back, too."

"Do you think that's the reason why magic started to fade?"

I shrugged my shoulders. "Just a theory."

Both twins held my gaze a bit longer before the princess shook her head. "We are getting off track. Why did you say I don't have any magic?"

"Well, much like Hadeon, aren't you also bound to a dragon's heart?"

The room was quiet for a very long time. "That seems quite... literal."

I shrugged. "Mother always said that magic had the most depraved sense of humor."

"So, I can conduct because I am bound to a dragon's heart. But dragons had magic of their own, why don't I?"

"The same reason many of us don't, I would assume. You will need to have contact with someone who has innate fae magic to channel, someone who hasn't lost that ability."

"And I was really looking forward to blowing something up." She leaned back in her chair and sighed.

"Even when magic still flowed freely, most magi needed glyphs or other guidance to use their powers, an anchor to hold and guide the magic. Hadeon, your brother... they are special exceptions."

"And Luxos?" Tori raised a brow at me.

"Luxos is able to wield magic, but he needs extensive glyph tattooing to wield it as he does now." Tori's eyebrows rose even higher in a silent question, but I didn't take the bait.

Jun interjected, "What about Tori's fire?"

I paused with my fingers on my chin. "I have been wondering that myself. I assume it is shared between you and Abraxas through your bond. So little is known about dragon magic; it is difficult to say." Tori's hand came to rest on her chest, and a disturbing thought struck me. "This also means that if something should happen to Abraxas, your powers will disappear."

Her face grew cold. "I won't let that happen." She looked at the book in front of her again before slamming it closed. "None of this matters if I can't figure out how to help him. I don't even know how much longer I can wait."

"Maybe it's time you talked to him again."

Her forehead creased. "I don't know if that will be possible, even in the dreams."

"You're afraid?"

She stiffened defensively. "He was out of control. I don't know how I could even get him to listen."

"Well... I've been thinking about that and have a few ideas." I pulled a few pieces of blank paper towards me and sketched out a glyphic pattern, explaining to her what it would do. "This should allow you to manipulate the dreaming environment to whatever you desire. It was used for... well, I'm sure you can imagine."

A wicked grin crossed her face. "It's always the quiet ones you should be the most worried about."

I blushed. "I never used it for that! I never had magic of my own, so I couldn't activate enchantments anyway."

"But you still learned so much about them?"

"I enjoyed the challenge, which was good since I didn't have much choice." I remembered the harsh biting of my mother's rod across the back of my hands and rubbed them absentmindedly. "Besides, it will be good practice for your channeling." She nodded.

Before Tori went to bed that night, I painted the glyphs on her forehead. I felt her conducting mana and the glyphs glowed a soft white. "Sweet dreams, Princess."

Chapter 21

Abraxas

Time was irrelevant in this place between life and death. The stars swirled above and below me, but they didn't matter because all my light was gone. Tori hadn't returned, and I didn't blame her. I had lost control. I had hurt her. I had killed her.

For over five hundred years, I controlled myself and turned my heart to ice. I had been the honorable general and fae king. I played Hadeon's lap dog, his loyal servant despite the beast inside me calling for his violent death whenever he was near. But I tamed it, controlled it.

With one perfect smile, Tori completely destroyed that control. It was like the gods had made her just to test me, to break me. She was my mate, so, in truth, they had. Dragons were not soft creatures. We raged with the deep fires of the earth, and violence followed our every step. I had been given a delicate creature as the guardian of my heart.

I chuckled. I knew she would hate that. And yes, by fae standards, she was fierce and unbreakable. But she quickly came apart under my claws. Oh, how delicious her ecstasy and fear were.

I sighed. I understood why she stayed away, but every piece of me that still clung to this life yearned for her. I hoped to see her just one more time before the end.

I leaned into the void of nothing that surrounded me. I searched for what seemed like years in this empty place, but I found nothing. There was no beginning and no end to it. Well, that's not true; there was an end, a great wallowing black hole that sucked even the meager light of the stars into it. It called to me relentlessly. No matter how far I flew, it stayed with me, inviting me to that final resting place. But the tiny golden glow at my heart clung to me, guiding me away.

Time stretched beyond measure. The past and the present swirled together in an inescapable mosaic.

I saw my mother, golden and beautiful. Her scales sparkled like late evening sunlight caught in a warm rain. Her heart's fire was white, tinged with just the smallest hint of blue, and reminded me of the clouds she loved to chase me through when I was just a fledgling. My father had taught me strength and precision in the air, but it had been my mother who taught me how to fly. She who had loved me enough that when I stepped off that cliff for the very first time, I knew she would always be there to catch me.

I remember her white, golden-sheened hair tickling my face when she would lean over and hold me close, reading me poetry by the fire in her room. I remembered the sweet sound of her floating laughter after I drew an unflattering portrait of King Obion, who had come visiting and put her in a foul mood. She wrapped me up in her arms, kissing me all over my face until I squirmed and wiggled out of her embrace. She planted one more kiss on the back of my head and called me *Verstak*, which she had told me meant "my mischievous one." One of my aunts later told me it more closely translated to "little shit," but it warmed my fading heart all the same.

I remembered my father, a beast of few words, whether dragon or fae. He'd been a force of nature and had flown with me out into the kingdom until I had learned every nook and cranny. But the land was always changing, and I always needed to keep a watchful eye. I also needed to watch and protect the humans and fae who lived in our lands. As a young, exuberant youth, I hadn't understood. *They are so small, father, their lives so short. Why should we care for them?*

He had laughed at me then. *When you live as long as we do, my son, you forget. You forget the beauty in a sunset, for you have seen thousands. You forget the magic woven into a song because you have heard so many. These mortals live with such abandon because of their fragility. That is more precious than all the gold in the land. One life is perfect, no matter how long or short. They gift us far more than we could ever gift them. We must protect them.* I hadn't understood him then, but he hadn't let me forget it, and with time, I had learned the beauty that was each precious life.

Then they all lay before me—destroyed. My mother was first. Everything about the scene was wrong. How softly the setting sun reflected off her, the field of white flowers she lay blowing gently in the calm spring breeze. The perfect open sky. How could these things exist while she lay dead? Thick rivulets of dark red blood cascaded from the bolt lodged in my mother's side, piercing straight under her front leg, perfectly lodging into her heart. An unbelievably lucky shot, or truly, a perfectly unlucky one. I had never seen my father cry, but the sounds he made shook the very earth, and he lost himself. His deep red fire scorched the flowers and the surrounding forest. He clawed at my mother's dead body as if he could somehow force the blood back into her. But her heartfire had been extinguished. I dared not approach him. I was still not yet fully grown, and I knew that he would destroy me unknowingly if I came between them.

My mother had died that day, but I had lost my father as well. He walked beside me for another two hundred years, but only as a ghost. I slept at the edge of the field, waiting for him. But as the stars twirled overhead, without saying a word, my father bolted into the sky, heading southwest. It was the direction of the closest town. I took off after him, but at that age, I couldn't catch him. I managed to save a few lives that day before he took them all, but I had lost him that day, too.

He had forbidden my transforming near the end of the War of Magic. I had been young enough that they had managed to keep my existence as a dragon a secret from the world. They had never even given me a dragon name. Abraxas was the bastardized fae translation of what my mother had wanted to name me, but she had never told me.

And so, I was stuck in my bastardized form, weak and bound to the ground as Hadeon's troops flooded the streets of Xyr. I had just been another commander then, following my father's orders, or so I thought. Once the army entered the city, every other cohort turned their weapons on the outsiders, and blood ran in the streets.

Protect our people. It had been the last thing my father had said to me. And yet, he led them straight into a slaughter. I felt the great clash of magic between Hadeon and my father outside the city walls, and I longed to go to him in my true body and fight at his side. But as my people spilled out onto the body-strewn streets and screams filled the air, I knew that I couldn't.

We had finally gotten everything under control when I felt it. The earth shook beneath my feet, and the wind kicked up to gale forces. Everything had pulled away, like the tide receding before a tsunami. I fell to my knees on those saturated streets and knew the truth. My father was dead. The last bits of magic that lingered on this earth were swelling, but they would be lost soon. My father's death channeled them one last time.

The beast in my chest roared for freedom. I could feel my skin pulling back, my scales emerging. It would be the last time, and I wasn't as strong as my father. I likely wouldn't kill Hadeon. The part of me that was dragon screamed for me to fight, destroy, and devour. My skull split as horns began to burst forth when a hand grabbed my shoulder.

"Prince Abraxas, Prince Hadeon has turned the rest of his army on the city. No one can locate the King; what do we do?" A young Avlyn looked at me with such need and pure desperation. The part of me that was dragon said *fight*. The part of me that was still a man said *protect*.

I made the choice that would shape everything. "Gather everyone you can at the front gate. I'll be there shortly."

Avlyn fled, and I grabbed the closest male body I could find. The man had been stabbed in the back, all too fitting. The best glamours were rooted in truth. Magic was almost gone now; I could feel it slipping through my fingers like sand on the beach. I had just enough. I wrote the glyphs for the glamour in blood and watched as the body in front of me changed to look like my father's. I carried him to the front gates of our city.

"Open the gates," I called to the soldiers up top.

"But sir—"

"I said open the *fucking* gates."

The reinforced wood cracked open to reveal a sea of soldiers clad in gold. I strode out onto the field, stepping over corpses and the crows who feasted on them. I carried the body in my arms, its long dark hair blowing in the wind as more blood dripped from its open wound.

When I was close enough for them to see, I dropped the body. "King Amaros is dead. I am King of this land now."

The sea of gold parted, and he emerged astride a horse. He

pulled off his helmet, and mahogany tresses flew in the wind. He was covered in deep red blood, my father's blood. My rage flared, and I called to my magic, my heart's fire. Nothing answered. There was nothing but a great resounding emptiness as my father's spirit drifted away on the wind.

Prince Hadeon approached me, looking down on the body at my feet. A smirk crossed his face that I could have ripped off if he was only closer.

"And how did he get that wound in his back?"

"You have defeated the World Breaker, and the King who defied you is dead. Let us end this now, Prince Hadeon."

Hadeon's grin only grew wider. He lifted his hand to me, and I saw the end. At least I would go with my father, at least I would see my mother again. I wouldn't be alone any longer. I should have been concerned about how much I welcomed the death he threatened me with. The blow never came. Hadeon's face twisted, and I saw what looked like fear in his eyes. I knew then that his magic was gone, too. My hand went to my sword, but Hadeon waved to his troops and rode off before I could even breathe.

The golden light of my vision twisted, no longer a horrible searing memory but something soft and loving. I knew she was coming. The light was growing, and a semi-corporeal world surrounded me. I found her waiting. My heart galloped in my chest, both with excitement and dread. I longed for her with everything I was, but what would I say to her now? No apology would be sufficient.

I wasn't the only one who hesitated. The world around me seemed unwilling to form, as if Tori wasn't ready to dream of me yet. I felt my body shift back into its fae form, but still, she would not come.

Out of the darkness came the metallic glow of stars solidifying into heavy metal chains that wrapped around me. Their cold steel slithered over my skin, tightening to an edge of pain. I fought them, but it was far too late. She bent my legs and bound my thighs to my calves, so I had to sit balanced on my knees and toes. My arms were locked behind my back, also chained together. She wrapped my chest and torso until I was completely immobile. An eternity stretched on, and then she stepped forward, her face lit only by the light of the stars. She stood before me, that strong, defiant woman I knew so well, and in an instant, my control was gone again.

It had been smart for her to bind me. I snarled and tried to free myself. My controlled mind watched my actions as if from a distance, as my body became that feral animal again, desperate for her. My horns and wings sprouted, clamped under the chain's tight embrace. I couldn't shift further. My fire glowed in my heart, and how I wished to consume her in it.

I saw her smirk at me. "I knew you would be naughty again."

I snarled louder. "You know if you wanted me in chains, Princess, you only had to ask."

"Yes, we may have to try this sometime later." She gave me a heated smirk, but then her face grew serious. "We need to talk, Abraxas."

I was the last dragon in this world, a god by all measures, and those words struck fear into my heart. She was my heart, my soul. I had hurt her, maimed her. I would always be a part of her, but... I couldn't blame her if she wanted nothing to do with me ever again. And she was fae. They were such fickle creatures with no sense of loyalty or commitment. She was my mate, but what did it mean for a fae to be mated to a dragon? She was my everything. Would she say the same for me?

The weight and sadness cooled the fire in my heart to nothing more than embers. The beast receded, and the man returned.

"My love, what I did—"

She pressed a finger to my lips. "Now is not the time. You can grovel for me later. I need your help. I need to know how to save you, Abraxas."

"My love, if I knew that, I would have told you already."

She huffed out an aggravated sound. "Alive for over a thousand years, and you have no ideas?"

I shook my head. "I was bound by the laws of fae magic in my body. I needed to trade for the power to transform, and there was only one method the earth would accept."

"Your life force."

I nodded. "Yes, I needed every last drop of it to change. I could conduct again, but it only bought me enough time to reach this island. As soon as we landed, the earth claimed its price. My life is gone, Tori; only my connection to you allows me to linger."

"Then how do I restore it? It's not too late. You are still here!" She was desperate, and I couldn't bear to see it.

"Little bird, I knew from the moment I first saw you that you would be my ruin. That I would never survive this. But do not think that for one moment I have regretted it."

"No!" She yanked the chains that held me. "I will not accept this. I will not let you die." She grabbed my face roughly and pulled me into a deep kiss, and she was nothing but delicious heat in this icy cold place.

She pulled away, her face wet with tears. "Don't you dare stop fighting, Abraxas."

"For you, my love, I would fight until there was nothing left of this world. Until all had turned to ash and dust. I will not give up, not until the void claims me, but—" I shook my head. I felt it creeping around me. That deep, endless cold and darkness.

She felt it, too, and it clawed at me as if she would latch her very being to mine. Death waited for no one.

"My little bird, I'm a creature of fire and flames, but I've never seen anything burn as bright as you. Don't let anything dim that light. Remember, *Morka Tempeli*. Death is the beginning. I have been blessed by the gods to have this time with you, but that time is up, my love. I will wait for you beyond the stars."

She floated away from me, and I could see her screaming my name, but there was no sound. The deep shadows of the void wrapped themselves around me. I was nothing, but a tiny golden light remained. *Not yet.*

Not yet, but soon.

Chapter 22

Tori

I woke up in a cold sweat. I ripped at the sheets on my bed, trying to crawl back to him. Panic set in, and my breath came in frantic spurts. He couldn't be gone.

I clawed at my chest as if I could rip out my own heart and give it to him. And yes, deep down, I still felt it. Our bond was barely more than a spark, but it was still there. He wasn't gone. Not yet, but I was running out of time.

I grabbed the closest pillow and screamed into it. I screamed until my throat ached. I got up from my bed and paced my room endlessly. *Think Tori! Think!* Unsurprisingly, nothing came. I paced to the window overlooking the Bay of Dragons. Stars still lingered above the rising sun, and the ocean's mist swirled up violently in the harsh wind of an approaching storm.

The mist swirled in erratic eddies, and it brought me back to Tenebrae Forest. The way the wind picked up after the death of the Nalle and the magic that allowed us to commune with the forest.

Morka Tempeli. Abraxas' words to me. I had seen it, many times. Our world churned in a great cycle. A tree fell in the forest, but from its corpse, mushrooms would grow. Animals would find their home, and new life began again. Death was not the end as we sentient creatures so feared, but just the beginning of something new. When our souls passed beyond the stars, did they stay there or return to live again?

Rain pounded the windowsill, and the sea mist obscured my vision. I felt like I could still see that island where Abraxas lay; deep within the earth he was concealed by. *Like he was waiting to hatch from an egg.* I chuckled at my own stupid joke. It was easier than thinking about how Abraxas HAD been born from an egg. I recalled the feel of his scales under my palms, his onyx claws that carried me through the sky, and the sheer size of him.

He was not like me; he was not fae. And yet, I could feel the connection of our hearts even now. I had clung to that feeling, but doubt snuck its way in for the first time. How could I be his mate? I was strong, a fae trained in battle who could easily overpower almost any enemy. Almost. Compared to him, I was nothing. A speck, an insect crawling on the ground. How could I be the one to save him?

Our souls knew one another, and it seems that the soul was not bound by the body that it inhabited.

The door behind me cracked open, and slate-grey eyes peered at me. "Are you alright, sister?" Jun asked. "Pallas told me about her dream manipulation spell. Did it work?"

I nodded. "It seems that with the right anchor, I can use some magic. The runes guided the *mana* in the way I needed."

"What about those flames you've been calling?"

"I have an anchor for those, too." An anchor whose tether could snap at any moment. I pulled the green flames to my fingertips. I held it away from my body, but I could still feel minor burns forming on the tips of my fingers. Fae weren't meant to play with dragonfire. I winced as I lost focus, and the flames licked the side of my finger.

Jun frowned. "Does it hurt you?"

"If I'm not careful, yes. It is fire."

"Well, I just thought... I guess I really just assumed it wouldn't."

I flicked the flames away. "Abraxas said it was dragonfire. He is immune, but I'm just fae. I can burn."

"Do you really think you are just fae, Tori?"

I looked at him, eyebrow raised. "I mean, you were there when I was born, Jun, just the same as you."

He shook his head. "Exactly, Tori. We were born twins. One soul split into two bodies. The old babas used to say, one soul was too much for a single fae body to handle."

"Do you think we are... something else?"

He shrugged. "Maybe we'll never know. But I always felt like I didn't belong, and I know you felt the same. We were born into bodies, into a life that we didn't fit, and that mold almost broke us."

"Jun..." I moved to hold him but stopped before he flinched. Instead, I wrapped my pinky finger in his.

"If the soul was split, then we aren't what we used to be."

"No." He looked out the window, and the rain cast moving shadows on his face. "We are something new."

A soul returned to this world but split apart and molded into something new, something different. The cycle turned, but somehow, everything was changed. I looked at my brother, the only constant I had in my entire life. The cycle of the world stopped for no one, and now we were different as well.

"Jun, when I went to Koron, I fought my way through the basements, looking for Hadeon's enchantment. I killed men. More than I even thought to count. I had a goal in mind; I had to save you and end Hadeon. I never once doubted; I never stopped to think if it was wrong."

He squeezed my pinkie. "It wasn't the first time you killed."
He had held my hair as I puked my guts out after my first patrol.

"Yes, but it was the easiest." A long pause stretched out between us. "I've been thinking..."

"Never a good thing," Jun jested, trying to lighten the mood. My serious face silenced him.

"An exchange, that's what Pallas said. Fae needed to exchange something with the earth to call on mana. That's what I need to do to get Abraxas back. Just my power as a conduit isn't enough. I need it and fae magic. What would I be willing to give? Would I destroy a home or perhaps a piece of beautiful art? That would be simple. What about a life? One life for another. After killing so many, it would be easy. What if it wasn't enough? How far would I go? Ten lives? A whole city? A whole world?" Jun just stared at me, and tears streamed down my face.

"You have a piece of my soul, and so does he. Is there anything I wouldn't destroy to have you both safe with me?"

"Tori..." He reached out, but I didn't stop.

"World Breaker. Am I meant to destroy it all? Is that the cost of having those I love?"

There was a long silence before my brother finally spoke. "Would that be so bad?"

"Jun?"

The shadows of the rain on the window continued to stream down his face, almost hiding his tears. His hand shook against mine, but something lit in his eyes. Something I had only ever seen in mine—anger.

Where had that boy I knew so well gone? The one who had simply smiled shyly at his bullies and tried to avoid conflict. The one who would sing me to sleep in the garden, soothing my bruises from all the fights I had gotten into to defend him.

Now, he wouldn't sing; that beautiful music from his heart was wreathed in shadow.

"They all knew Tori. Every last fae noble in Koron knew what Hadeon was doing to me, what he would do. But they didn't care. Every last one of them treats anyone they deem lesser as slaves, as chattel. Life has no value to them. I didn't understand why you hated them in Niata. But now... I see."

His dark gaze finally fell on me. "If life has so little meaning to them, perhaps they don't deserve theirs."

"They aren't all like that." The words surprised me. I knew that it was true. Lady Bogata, Lady Lovinia, and all the others I saw caring for the people of Xyr. I wanted him to see it, too. I wanted his kind heart to win out over the pain that strangled it.

"Does the kindness of a few excuse the wickedness of the many?"

"I don't know."

We stood in silence for some time, the only sound was the rain pelting the glass of the window, mirroring the tears on my cheeks. I had failed to protect Jun, and the anger I always protected myself in clung to him. I didn't know if he could survive it.

My mind drifted, trying to protect itself from those dark thoughts. It drifted to Abraxas again, alone and almost dead in that cave. I wondered if the forest there would talk to him like they had in Tenebrae, a comfort in the darkness.

My whole body stiffened.

"What is it?" Jun asked.

"I know what I have to do."

Chapter 23

Tori

I entered the war room, and it was in chaos. The commanders were all bickering with each other. Avlyn was especially heated in a discussion with Commander Talius. I listened for a few moments.

"We cannot accept this offer. He would never hold to it." Avlyn gestured frantically to something that lay on the table. I approached, and Talius turned to me, annoyance flashing in his eyes before he turned back to Avlyn.

"We are stretched thin as it is. We may not be able to stop a direct attack on the city. This could save thousands of lives."

Avlyn huffed, and I saw a scroll laid out across the table. The imperial seal was stamped at the bottom.

"What—"

"Hadeon wants us to surrender. If we surrender Xyr, surrender the whole damn kingdom, he says he will spare our citizens." Avlyn crossed their arms. "I'd rather die first."

"And you may just get your wish, Commander. You remember what happened last time," Talius retorted.

"Hadeon will never spare the kingdom. He won't uphold this bargain," I interjected.

Talius turned to me with nothing but disdain in his voice. "I'm sorry; what is she doing here?"

"Princess Tori is here to—" Avlyn started, but Talius raised a hand.

"I would hope she can speak for herself." He turned to me with nothing friendly in his gaze.

"Talius, I respect your desire to protect the citizens of this kingdom. That is my desire as well. But you cannot believe that Hadeon will stay his hand. He doesn't care about anything but maintaining his power. Anything that threatens that, he destroys."

"Oh? So, what would you have us do, Princess Tori? Stand, fight, and all die slaughtered on the Golden Army's blades?" Talius bore down on me, but I did not yield.

"Do you think so little of your own army? We have the advantage, and Xyr is not defenseless. If we can prepare for an assault, we could hold out."

"Hold out for what?" His harsh blue eyes felt like they were cutting into my very soul.

I felt doubt starting to crawl its way into my heart. I shook my head. "Hold out until reinforcements arrive. The River Queens, have they—" But Talius waved his hand again and turned back to the table, examining the figures laid out on the map.

I thought he was going to answer me when he said, "Just because you shared Abraxas' bed doesn't mean that your opinion is welcome here. If that was a criterion, we would need a much larger council chamber." I nearly stumbled back in surprise. Hurt and anger seethed in my belly. So, this is how he wanted to play.

Talius and I were the same height, but he still managed to

sneer down his nose at me. Avlyn moved to intercede, but I raised my hand, and they stilled. "The enemy is at our gates. We must stand united."

"United? Behind you?"

"No, beside me. I have fought alongside your armies and trained with them. I may not be royalty of this court, but I am fae royalty, raised in the art of diplomacy and strategy. And—"

"A princess whose own kingdom rejected her for the role. What a mockery of Abraxas' rule."

Every muscle in my body spasmed, itching to lash out, to strike Talius. I tightened my jaw, and did not move, did not react. Those words rose up in my head again, *you'll never be good enough,* but I cast them into the emerald flames in my heart and incinerated them.

"You may not trust me, Talius, but I will not let the people of this kingdom suffer because of your stubbornness."

"You have no authority here." Several of the other commanders started trying to join us. Many supported Talius, but a few stood in my defense. They didn't matter. Talius was the one I had to convince. I opened my mouth, but he cut me off. "This kingdom deserves better than a princess playing at being a general, at being queen." The last word was spat out like a slur.

"I am no general, and I am no queen. I am the mate of your king, so you will honor me."

There was a long pause as many of the commanders glanced at each other. Finally, one I knew as Pixso spoke, "So it's true, he really is..."

They all looked at me, silent. I guess I had their attention now.

"Yes, Abraxas is a dragon. The last dragon."

"Why has he not returned?" Talius asked. I felt it in the smallest tremor of his voice, fear and... betrayal.

Avlyn flattened their lips, but these commanders deserved

the truth. They served this kingdom loyally, and they should be shown the respect they deserved. The commander might not have agreed, but secrets are what got us into this mess in the first place.

"Abraxas retook his Dragon form in Koron at great personal cost. Right now, we do not know when he will return... if he will return." The room was suddenly deafening with the commanders' shouts, each upset for different reasons.

I slammed my fists onto the table, and silence fell again. "He is not lost to us yet. I will do everything in my power to get him back. Until then, you will stay the course. We will help our allies and defeat our enemies. But most importantly, we will protect those to whom we owe our allegiance, the people of this kingdom."

There was still some rumbling in the room, but I had enough. I tugged on the golden bond between me and Abraxas until it blazed green, and I threw a flame onto the table, incinerating the letter from the capital. Every eye, even Avlyn's, snapped to the blaze as the paper crumbled into nothing but floating embers.

"We will not yield," my voice boomed, mana still flowing through me. "Hadeon will not take one more good thing from this world. I will protect Xyr, protect this kingdom until my dying breath. So, will you stand with me or not?"

Talius approached without saying a word. He stood tall and proud. We may have been the same height, but his formal armor gave him bulk I didn't have. I stood my ground, planting my feet in a fighting stance. I didn't bring my hand to my sword; this was never going to work if we came to blows. I held his stare, and he did not blink.

His piercing blue eyes were fierce, unrelenting. Suddenly, he dropped to one knee. "Please forgive my harsh words, Your Majesty. I remember Tenebrae. I didn't enter with you, but all my men told me the same thing on their escape. You fought for them with valor and cunning. I had to see you would not yield. We face an enemy we cannot defeat if we show even a moment of weakness."

He slowly removed his sword from its sheath and held it aloft, the handle in one hand, the blade in the other, over his head. He bowed his chin. "My sword is yours; my life is yours; do with it what you will."

I dared a glance at Avlyn, and their eyes were sparkling. "Rise, Commander Talius. I have no desire to see you kneel." He sheathed his sword, and I gripped his forearm just as I would with any of the soldiers to help him rise. It surprised him for a moment, but I saw a grin flash across his face.

"I am a warrior, not a general. I will need all of you to win this fight. I do not need you to kneel, just to fight at my side, as you would have done Abraxas. Can you do that for me?"

Talius slammed his fist into the armor of his chest. "Until the sky burns, Your Majesty."

The sound of the remaining leaders slamming their fists to their chests was deafening, and they all shouted as one, "Until the sky burns." Avlyn's voice rang just a moment longer, and they sent me an approving wink from the back of the crowd.

W hat could barely be called fights continued. I would be beaten to within an inch of death and left in my cell to recover. After beating me with fists seemed to no longer satisfy the king, they brought clubs and maces to bludgeon me. The torture was endless, and I never understood the purpose. Surely, my pain could not amuse the king so much that he continued this process. He and the woman were always conferring as I was dragged away, neither seeming pleased.

For the first time in my life, my thoughts were not directed at willing my body to give in and die. Instead, something unfamiliar blossomed in my heart. After every beating, my ethereal visitor would come. Her hands would touch me with a gentleness that I had never known as she tended my wounds. I couldn't speak. My jaw was often broken, so she regaled me with stories.

Some were fantastical, of legendary heroes and unspeakable evils, but mostly, she spoke of her life, and I had never found anything so beautiful.

"You won't believe what Mother did to me today, Hadeon. She scolded me for taking the *Tome of Arendil* out into the garden, saying the book might become damaged. As if I can't care for a book properly. The weather was so gorgeous; how could I be expected to complete my studies inside? The best place to read is the garden under the great oak tree. I cannot wait to show it to you."

She lied to me like this often. The sweetest, purest lies telling me that someday my pain might end, and I would know more than darkness. Sometimes, I let myself believe her. She ran her hand gently over my forehead while my head lay in her lap.

"I wouldn't know; I never learned to read," I managed to croak out.

Her eyebrows shot up. "Well then, I must teach you! Reading is invaluable. Perhaps I can even bring you some books down here..." She continued on and on, but the words didn't matter. All that mattered was her sweet voice and the warmth of her hands on me.

THEY APPROACHED ME WITH SWORDS, AND I HAD NO DOUBT this would be our last dance. I'd bleed out before my body could heal. A few weeks back, I might have welcomed it, but something soft clung to my scarred heart. It was a soft laugh and a vision of an oak tree swaying in the morning sun.

The men approached me slowly, more hesitantly than normal. They knew this was the last time, so maybe they were showing me the only kindness they could by delaying the moment. All it did was let dread creep into my heart. I didn't want to die! Was this fate's final cruelty? I had been blessed with a fae's long life only to have it cut short at twenty years. I had been ready to die when fate had sent me *her* to give me hope, so that a deep, razor-sharp dread could claim me just before my end.

I was back in that burning house, and I was afraid. I was scared of Death as he descended on me, and there was no way out. Flames licked at me, devoured me, and I could hear my mother calling my name.

"Hadeon!" No, that wasn't my mother.

I looked up at the stands, and the king stood with Plagis and the woman as he always did. But clinging to the woman's robe, there she was—golden and perfect, with tears streaming down her face.

"Hadeon, run!" Pallas shouted. The older woman slapped a hand over her mouth as the king looked on in annoyance. She didn't fight, only looked at me with pleading eyes as her tears sending rivets of the arena's dust down her face.

No one had ever cried for me before. I stared at her and felt her gentle hands on me. I imagined her soft lips touching mine, as I had every day since she had first saved me from the dark. She had driven it away and filled my heart in a way I had never known before. Even at that moment, I could feel it, like a storm rising inside of me. As tears fell from her like rain, my heart filled with the clouds, thunder, and lightning of a tempest.

Pain slashed across my ribs as the first man struck me with his sword. I fell to my knees and looked up, but all I saw was her.

"Pallas..." I whispered her name, my final prayer for when the gods finally answered. Another man stabbed me through my stomach, and as he pulled the sword back out, a storm erupted. Lightning, uncontrolled and hotter than the sun, flared from my heart. All three men in the arena were incinerated, the smell of the burnt flesh was hot in my nostrils. The storm didn't stop. I heard stone crack as my power laced through the walls of the stadium. Wind and dust blinded me. I fell on one hand, the other clutching my stomach, trying to stem the flow of hot blood.

Lightning flared, and my vision went black. The last thing I heard was that beautiful voice calling my name.

I DRIFTED IN AND OUT OF CONSCIOUSNESS LIKE WAVES IN A storm. Sometimes, I heard voices so diffused they hardly seemed human. Other times, I felt a warm hand pressed against my face, calming me in the dark.

Eventually, shapes solidified, and I found myself lying not in a dungeon but a fine room. The voices around me became clear, and I kept my eyes closed to listen.

"What was your final analysis, Runya?" That was the voice of the king.

"The power he presented was remarkable. Even before the magic began fading, we hadn't seen someone at his level in centuries. He rivals the power Prince Abraxas held two hundred years ago."

"So, the prophecy, it was correct?"

"We can never be certain, but given what I have seen... I would say he is the best chance we have."

"Then it's time he learns how to be a prince. Let me know when he wakes," the king ordered, and I heard the door close as he left.

The bed beside me sank down, and my eyes snapped open. The older woman I had seen, Runya, sat next to me. Up close, she looked so similar to Pallas that my heart stuttered. But this woman wasn't Pallas. Her eyes were deep and pitiless, and the hand that touched my face was icy and harsh.

She pinched my face in her hand, forcing me to look at her. "You have a lot to live up to, Great Hero. I hope you are up to the task." Her grip was surprisingly strong, and my jaw ached. I felt that tempest rising in my heart again, and I felt the crackle of static over my skin. Her hand snapped back, and for a moment, I saw fear flash through her eyes, and something about that felt better than anything else in my life ever had.

The door flew open again, and a soft voice called out my name. "Hadeon!" A moment later, Pallas' kind face appeared over me. "You're alright! Mother, tell me he's alright." Tears clung to her eyes as she reached for my hand.

Runya, Pallas' mother, stood. "He will be more than alright. You may remain with him until the king returns." She left the room without looking back.

Pallas immediately sat on the bed and laced her fingers through mine. She gently stroked my cheek, and for the first time, I reached out and touched her back. I ran my hand over her hair, so soft and smooth under my callused fingers. I stroked her jaw, and a blush rose on her cheeks.

"Hadeon—"I didn't let her finish before I grabbed the back of her neck and pulled her down to my lips. She let out the most adorable little squeak, but after a brief hesitation, her lips softened on mine. For a moment, that was enough. We were both enough as the world stood still.

Then the tempest in my heart rose again, and I pulled her to me more tightly. I pressed my tongue through the barrier of her lips, and I felt her stiffen but did not stop. The tempest rose and I felt the hairs on my arms stand when she let out a small cry and pulled away.

"You... shocked me," she murmured, rubbing her lips with the back of her hand.

"Sorry." I knew it was the right thing to say.

She smiled softly, and I knew all was forgiven. "It's alright, you've been through so much. Oh, I have so much to show you, Hadeon!" She continued on and on, but I didn't hear it. I just clutched her hand in mine, unwilling to let go. I finally had something of my own.

Chapter 25

Pallas

The soldiers were gathering in the front of the castle, forming long, perfect rows that slowly exited through the wooden gates underneath the stone dragon carvings. I watched them, a silent apparition from where I stood high up on a balcony. I looked past the castle walls and out towards the city of Xyr. Despite the army moving through it, people milled about happily, some coming up to the soldiers as they passed and waving. Children ran through the lines as they expertly moved around them as if this was a common occurrence.

The sun shone brightly, and the storm that had threatened the skies earlier passed the city by. A soft breeze rolled up from the sea, and hints of summer could be felt despite how cool Xyr always remained. The mists that seemed to shroud this place were nowhere to be seen.

Below, a young human woman stuffed lavender flowers into a passing soldier's hand before leaning in to kiss him on the cheek, tears streaming down her face. He embraced her swiftly, planting a soft kiss on the top of her head before rejoining his ranks.

The lull of the summer sun had me in a daze, and my mind convinced me I could smell those flowers on the breeze that ruffled my hair.

The sunshine I missed more desperately than I realized soaked into my skin, a high more beautiful than any glass of ambrosia. I leaned against the stone railing of the balcony, my head tilted back, exposing myself to as much of that warm, golden light as I could.

My mind wandered, and I drifted back to a summer from so long ago, it felt like a different life.

5 1 5 YEARS AGO

The warm summer breeze wafted the gentle scent of ambrosia across the blossoming garden. Hadeon's long mahogany hair fluttered in the breeze as he lay with his head in my lap. The warm light of the sun lit up his tan skin until he glowed almost golden, just like the flowers around us. Just like the kingdom that would one day be his. We had both been so young then, barely twenty-five, nothing more than children in the life of a fae. I always thought it was destiny speaking to me that I had found a lover almost the exact same age.

I swept a stray piece of hair behind his long ear, and he blessed me with his perfect smile. He reached up and ran his hand under my jaw and behind my head, gently pulling me in for a soft kiss. I wished to stay in that moment forever.

"Do you have to go?"

His perfect smile became marred with doubt. "I'm the Great Hero. Father has me training every day. I have to fight the World Breaker. It's what I was meant for. He says it won't be long now before the war begins. The dragons have already been causing disturbances."

"What if something happens to you? I don't think I could—"

"Pallas." He sat up, his hand still behind my neck, holding my face close to his own. "I'm the most powerful fae in Adimos. No dragon can stop me; no one can."

I couldn't meet his eyes. Something always shimmered in them when he talked about the World Breaker. Something that I hated, a darkness that I could pretend didn't exist in the light of the summer sun.

"What about when it's over and your destiny is fulfilled?"

"Ha! Well then, we will drink, party, and celebrate the return of magic! I'll be a hero, the Great Hero."

When I looked at him, I still saw that broken boy I'd nursed in the dungeons. We never discussed the truth that he was not Obion's son and what the king had done to him. I had tried, but that darkness flared in him whenever it was mentioned. I'd been so young. So young and cowardly, and so desperately in love.

"We could go away. Just leave it all behind, the prophecy and this place. Just you and me." I couldn't meet his eyes as I said it, a coward, through and through.

I still didn't look at him, so he pulled on my neck until our noses touched.

"And give all this up? This place will be all mine someday, and I'll be the king. It's as much my destiny as any prophecy." He pushed my head back until I was forced to meet his gaze. "And then, I'll make you my queen."

Before I could respond, he locked me in a deep kiss, pushing me down onto the warm grass beneath us. He still held me gently then, treating my body with reverence as he pulled my pleasure from me. "Soon magic will return, and everything will be as it should be. And you, Pallas? You'll be mine? By my side, always?"

"Always, Hadeon."

He pulled me into another deep kiss, and his fingers unlaced the bodice of my dress. He ran his lips down my neck, his light breath was unbearable on my heated skin. He continued to trail kisses across my skin until his lips caressed the curve of my breast, and his teeth scraped along the tender surface. I shivered and my nipples peaked, hard against the warm air. I felt him murmur, "How I love to devour you." Our sweet moans entwined with the warm breeze, and I thought about how very blessed I was to be getting everything I ever wanted.

THE WARM SUMMER SUN OF XYR HELPED CLEAR THE TEARS that fell from my cheeks. Five hundred years had passed since then, and I was still that idiotic girl.

Footsteps sounded on the balcony behind me, and I quickly wiped the tears away. I turned from the sun to see Commander Avlyn with a broad smile lighting up their face.

"I've been sent to fetch you, my lady." They met my eyes, and that smile faltered. "Is everything alright?"

I pulled on that mask I knew so well, hardening my features. I don't know why I found it more difficult to do recently. "I'm just fine, Commander. When the princess summons me, who am I to ignore it?"

That worried look didn't leave Avlyn's face. "If you would rather remain at the castle... I don't know what we are going to face out there."

"What? And give up this chance to distract you in a dangerous situation? Not a chance, Commander."

A smile tugged and Avlyn's lips. "Careful now, Pallas, or I just might think you are starting to like me."

"Looks like someone has been sipping on the princess' mushroom tea," I said flatly.

At that, Avlyn laughed loudly and without restraint. Tears formed in their eyes, and they wiped them away with the back of their hand.

"It wasn't that funny."

"Maybe not, but I'm just happy to see you relaxing for half a second and acting like a real fae, not some stone statue."

I looked away as shame filled me.

"Aw fuck, Pallas I didn't mean it like that..."

"It's alright, Commander, it's what I deserve." I pulled the stone mask back on.

"Hey... don't do that." Avlyn gently placed a hand on my arm, but I flinched away as if they had struck me.

I saw the hurt in their eyes. It latched inside of me like tar sticking to my ribs, and no matter what I did, I couldn't get rid of it. So, I turned to face the balcony again.

"I'll see you on the boat then." Avlyn said as I heard them leaving the balcony.

"It was me." Their retreating footsteps stopped. "I made the collar; I made the collar that was on Jun." The tears flowed again, and for the first time in centuries, I didn't try to hide them. "It nearly killed him, and it was all my fault."

Avlyn didn't flee from my shame or try and quiet me. Instead, they grasped my hand in theirs. "And why did you make that collar, Pallas?" I didn't answer but they knew anyway. "The only one to blame here is Hadeon and his thirst for power." They gently ran their finger over my cheek, wiping away the tears that still fell. "You don't have to hold on to that guilt. It's a heavy burden, even for someone as strong as you."

I wanted to argue. *I'm not strong. I'm weak and cowardly. Why can't you see what's right in front of you?* But Avlyn's gaze was so warm, warmer than the sun that reflected off their dark, rich skin. All I could say was, "It's not just the collar. I've done so much, so many unforgivable things..."

Their warm, calloused hand stayed on my cheek. "Well, I'm just a stupid brute, so I can't tell you what will become of all those sins in your past. But I can ask you, what do you want to do with your future? It's yours now, Pallas, ready for you to shape into whatever you want. Don't spend so long looking backward that you forget to move forward." They gave me a gentle smile.

I sniffled, "That was quite poetic."

The smile grew bigger. "My mentor always had a big soft spot for poetry." They finally dropped their hands away, and I had to use all my will not to lean into them.

"Come find me in the entrance hall when you are ready to take that first step." They strode away and I was left alone again.

7 MONTHS AGO

"Don't collar him Hadeon. It will mute his magic. He won't be able to—" Hadeon raised a hand to silence me. His other held the collar.

He caressed the golden metal and flipped it over to examine the glyphs inside. He set it on the table before flicking a dagger out of his belt and pricking his finger. A single drop of crimson blood welled up, and he smeared it over the embedded clear crystal at the throat of the collar. Purple lightning flashed as he activated the spell with his magic. The crystal hummed and turned violet.

"Please, I'm begging you, please. I haven't asked you for anything. Please just let him be. I'll give you anything."

Hadeon turned away from the desk and finally looked at me. His expression changed to one I hadn't seen in decades. His eyes grew soft, and his mouth turned down in the smallest frown. He reached out with a gentle hand, running it over my hair and slowly under my jaw to grasp my cheek. He pulled me into his chest, and I felt him breathe in the scent of my hair.

"Oh, Pallas." He gave me a gentle kiss on the top of my head, and I felt my body relax. He was going to listen; he really was.

"What the fuck could *you* possibly offer *me* of any value?"

My calm shattered like ice, but before I could push away, he gripped me with all his strength and sent lightning through me.

It had been years since he made me scream with his magic. I had been a fool; even after everything, I let myself believe that this time would be different. Maybe this time I would see that boy I had held in my arms on that golden balcony so long ago when we were both just younglings.

This time, I screamed and screamed. Deep inside, claws lashed and tore me to pieces for the very last time. His lips slammed into mine as his tongue shoved its way into my mouth. He smothered me as his power destroyed me down to my very core. I thought I would pass out when he finally released my mouth and bit down on my earlobe until I knew it bled.

"You're mine, Pallas. You will always be mine. Don't ever forget that again."

He released another jolt of power so intense that my legs and arms seized up, and he released me. I collapsed in a boneless heap on the floor.

He left without another word, and tears flowed down my

cheeks silently. The cold stone floor seemed a relief for my burning skin. Deep inside me that feral creature raked her claws over my stomach and my heart. She curled up and purred words that I hadn't even dared to think for nearly five centuries. *I'm not yours. Not anymore.*

Part 2

Chapter 26

Hadeon

482 years ago

The shouting of the crowd was so loud it deafened me. I heard nothing, only a faint ringing. I saw nothing, not the waving arms filled with bushels of greens and red berries, not the smiling faces, only a blank, never-ending light. We had rushed back to Koron to complete the enchantment that would tie Malech's heart to me, and I could think of nothing else. Only that and the way my father's frown etched ever deeper as my name was chanted by the crowd over and over.

My magic was gone. I tried numerous times on the journey to summon it. It was like calling out into a gaping canyon; all that came back was a faint echo of myself. I needed this to work; I needed my power.

I saw my father's face laced with disappointment and could practically feel the stone walls of the dungeons surrounding me again. *Weak, powerless, pathetic.* No! The dragon was dead. I had killed him with my own hands and rent him apart with my power. This would work. I would allow for nothing else.

In the depths of the castle, Runya scampered about, making last-minute adjustments to her glyphs. I felt nothing as she sliced open my arm with a blade, spilling my blood into a wide-brimmed bowl. I saw her face twist as the runes on the bowl didn't react.

My father and Plagis stood motionless behind me. I felt the king's eyes boring into my back, and I didn't dare look.

Runya dipped her fingers into my blood and flicked it about, reciting memorized incantations. Malech's heart sat in the center of the floor, its slow beat seeming to die with each passing second.

"Faster, Runya." My father's voice was deep, and even I shivered at his tone. Runya, to her credit, didn't falter, but I saw the sweat beading on the back of her neck. She finished her incantation, then came and stood beside me. The room was quieter than a grave as we watched absolutely nothing happen. The heartbeat slowed, and the heartfire died before my very eyes, and absolutely nothing happened.

I heard my father shift behind me, but I feared death less than what he was about to say. I spun on Runya and grabbed her neck with both my hands.

"You said this would work! What did you do wrong?!" I pressed too hard for her to respond; she was already purple from the lack of air. The bowl of my blood clattered to the floor, red running along the seams between the stone tiles. She scratched at my hands with her nails, but I felt nothing. *This was not happening.*

Then her eyes lit up with that deep maroon fire, and a wicked grin crossed her face. A long-forked tongue darted out as she hissed, *You're nothing without me, boy.*

I dropped her instantly, and she hit the ground hard. Her face was fae, my hallucination had gone. The red light remained, covering everything.

"Your Majesty..." Plagis gasped. I spun and saw that the heart had reignited and was slowly rising off the ground. The runes peeled from the floor, along with drops of my blood. They began to spin fast around the heart until I couldn't see anything but a blinding light. Power flooded out of the heart. The burns on my skin ignited anew, but I felt lightning and something more surge through me. The tide was so strong I thought I might never escape, but then the light dimmed, and the runes slowed. They spun calmly, like the moon circling the earth.

What had been cold and empty inside of me was filled beyond overflowing. Lightning snaked over my skin in a way I couldn't stop, the power sought an exit in its excess. I shot a bolt across the room, and Runya's worktable exploded.

It had cost me nothing. I didn't feel weakened, even with the loss of blood and fresh wounds. I felt stronger than ever.

I turned around to see my father. He flexed his fingers, searching his palms as if he expected something. He gave a small sigh, then turned his attention to me with a warm smile I had never seen before.

"My son. I've never been prouder." He embraced me for the first time. It was simultaneously uncomfortable and perfect. I couldn't help but rest my head against his shoulder, even for just a moment. I was powerful, more powerful than I had dreamed. My father pulled away from me. "My son, my heir." For the first time, I believed him. I collapsed into his arms again.

He let out a small laugh. "You have saved our world, and just in time. I have a surprise for you." The warmth left his eyes as he turned to Runya, who was still coughing on the floor. "Finish the enchantment so that only we can enter here." Runya didn't respond, but she didn't have to. She had no choice.

My father nodded to Plagis, his eyes darting to the coughing woman for just a moment. The man gave a confirming nod as I was led out of the room. I never saw Pallas' mother again.

PRESENT DAY

I didn't hear Luxos enter the room. I never did. That's why he was still alive despite his failures. He had his value.

"Your Eminence, my spies tell me the princess is leaving Xyr. She is taking a cohort out into the Sea of Spirits."

I turned to Luxos, and he needed no other command.

"We are tracking her, and my troops stand ready for an attack. She keeps the prince with her at all times."

"And Pallas?"

"Still her prisoner. The princess never lets her leave her side. As I have said, I believe she thinks Pallas can be used as a bargaining chip."

I laughed, "Foolish girl. But nonetheless, should the opportunity present itself, return her to me, Luxos."

"Of course, Your Eminence."

"And you know what to do with the dragon?"

"Yes, Plagis informed me of the details."

"Good." I waved my hand as a dismissal.

Luxos nodded, and I felt the magic of his shadows wrapping around him.

"Oh, and Commander..." Luxos froze. "...don't come back empty-handed again."

Chapter 27

Tori

The beach was exactly as I remembered; Avlyn had steered us true. The small cove was much calmer than the surrounding sea, and we moored as close to the beach as possible. After everyone had settled, I made my way to the back of the cove and found the small opening we had emerged from before. Jun pressed against my side, lacing his fingers through mine. I felt my heartbeat slow down. He was with me; they were all with me.

The sun was setting. Our journey had taken longer than expected due to the rough seas. I wouldn't be waiting. The soldiers lit torches, most staying on the beach as reinforcements. I looked at the huddling masses to see Kaleos striding towards me with the rest of my cohort.

We headed down the tunnel. It was perfectly round and smooth, just as I remembered. I let my fingers trace over the eerily flawless surface to help guide me in the dim light. It hadn't taken us more than half an hour to escape the cavern, so I expected a short journey.

I was wrong. Not five hundred feet from the entrance, the

way forward was blocked. A perpendicular path cut through the tunnel, heading in a new direction. Whatever had created this new tunnel had pushed up enough rock that our original way forward was blocked.

Kaleos let out a whistle at my side. "Do I want to know what made this?" Whatever it was, it bore a perfectly round, smooth tunnel through almost solid rock. I shivered and stepped down into the new opening. I pried at the rock that blocked my path. It was compacted, but I could pull away a few smaller pieces.

Kaleos stepped up beside me and did the same. "Let's get a crew of men in here tonight; we could probably have this cleared by the morning if it's not too thick."

My stomach churned again. Another day of waiting. I didn't have time for this. I could feel the weakness of our bond; it was stretched thin to the point of snapping.

"Yes, get the men in here. I will head down this way and see what I can find."

"Like hell you are, Princess," Avlyn's voice chimed behind me. "Whatever made this, nature or creature, is still about. I won't have you wandering around making yourself a snack. Back to camp with you."

I made to argue, but Avlyn shook their head and gave me a look that said, *back to camp.* I grunted but pushed past them out of the tunnel.

THE SOLDIERS ON THE BEACH HAD SET UP A FEW TENTS TO protect themselves from the wind and huddled between them around a fire. Noki and Raula patrolled the borders of the camp on guard duty. I waved to them, ducked inside a tent, and was unsurprised to find Pallas and Jun huddled together. Jun was reading, and Pallas listlessly poked at some coals that were placed in a hole to keep the tent warm.

Jun popped his head up from the pallet and gave me a concerned look. "Back already?"

"Unexpected delays," I muttered, flopping down next to them.

Pallas frowned. "We don't have time for this, especially with your bond in the state it is."

"Yes, *thank you*, Pallas. I hadn't considered that at all." I dropped my head into my hands, willing the tears away. I felt an arm around my shoulder. I thought Avlyn had come in without me noticing, but I looked up to find Pallas next to me.

"Sorry..." she mumbled. I was too shocked to say anything.

Jun sat up straighter than an arrow. "What was that?"

"What was what?"

"You didn't hear—" He jolted again, hearing something none of the rest of us were privy to. "Tori, someone's in danger." Jun stood and went to the flap of the tent. I followed.

When Pallas rose, I snapped, "Stay here." To my surprise, she listened, sitting down with a hand on Spinner's back.

I followed Jun to the edge of light created by the campfire. Our elongated shadows were all I could see against the twilight blackness of the beach. Jun peered off towards the ocean, squinting to try and see anything. I looked around and saw a single torch bobbing in the opposite direction. I called out to Noki, who ran over to us.

"You see anything out there?" Noki shook his head.

"Did you hear anything?" Noki raised his eyebrow at Jun's question.

"No, nothing out of the ordinary; all is quiet." He looked over Jun's shoulder, and a frown crossed his face. "Where is Raula?"

We all spun, and I scanned the beach for any sign of her torch but saw nothing. I felt Jun stiffen, and he pointed out into the dark.

"There, we have to go now!"

I gripped his hand in mine and nodded to Noki. Without saying a word, we all took off at a sprint for the ocean.

When we neared the waves, Noki's torch illuminated Raula's back. She stood calf-deep in the swell, and her deep, raspy voice was mumbling a word I didn't understand. *"Faruk, Faruk."*

"Raula, what are you—" I moved to grab her when Noki's hand came down on my shoulder. He was shaking violently and pointed to the surf.

Barely visible under the reflections of the torch light on the churning waves was a pair of glowing red eyes. They hid just below the surface, fixed on Raula. She took another step forward and I tried to stop her. But she was an orc and stronger than me. Noki and I yanked at her, but it was hopeless.

"Raula, stop it! *Raula!*"

She didn't hear me; her eyes were fixed on whatever it was that haunted beneath the waves. "I'm coming. *Faruk.* I'll be home soon." Her face looked serene, not an ounce of fear to be seen, as she walked further into the waves.

"For fuck's sake." Noki kept tugging at Raula, but I let go and drew my sword, raising it above whatever was hiding away.

Its hellish gaze snapped to me, and I saw the water break as it rose out of the surf. Long glistening tendrils of hair clung to an elongated, horse-like face. Its skin was pitch black and glossy, like oil spread over the surface of the water. A huge mouth full of sharpened teeth grinned at me, and I swung. Its face shifted, and I froze.

The black tendrils of hair turned to a shimmering silver, and the smile turned mischievous and filled with gleaming white teeth. Red glowing eyes turned emerald green, crinkling at the corners as they stared at me. I froze mid-swing.

"Abraxas?"

"Yes, my love. It's me. Come with me; let's go home." He held out a beautiful, strong hand. He smiled in that devastating way. "Come to me, my love." I dropped my sword and reached out for his extended hand. Every fiber of my being begged me to run to him, but each movement was an effort like someone was holding me back.

"Yes, just a bit further, Princess. Then we can be together again." Something was wrong; I knew it. My legs were unbelievably cold, and I could hear... something. *This isn't right.* But all I could see was his face and how I wished to hold him in my arms as tears streamed down my cheeks. *Please, please, just let me make it in time.*

My fingers finally touched his, and his grin spread into something wicked, expanding across his face until it split unnaturally. His teeth grew into needles, and his eyes turned back into those glowing red orbs. I tried to lurch away, but he had me tight within his grasp, and I couldn't breathe.

Chapter 28

Pallas

I stroked the spider's back absentmindedly, listening to Tori's receding footsteps. "At least I've got you for company." I scratched the creature behind his eyes, and he chittered happily. Despite the panic I'd seen on Jun's face, I couldn't help but be comforted by the little creature.

I found him sneaking into our room numerous times over the past few weeks, always depositing some sort of wrapped gift at my feet. I never opened them, but he didn't seem to mind. He curled up at my feet as I read by the fire on nights that sleep couldn't find me. It had become our secret routine of sorts.

"Interesting pet you've found there." I lurched around to face the familiar voice. Spinner tensed under my hand and launched at the intruder, hissing. He leapt at Luxos' face but froze in midair as shadows surrounded him.

"Nice try, bug," Luxos laughed cruelly. Spinner squealed as solid shadows pulled his legs in all directions, his eyes spinning in pain.

"Stop it!" I yelled. Luxos tossed Spinner aside as the shadow walker closed the distance between us.

His hand clamped over my mouth, and he leaned in so his lips grazed the point of my ear. "Quiet now, Pallas. I wouldn't want someone to overhear us."

I bit down on his hand hard.

He hissed and pushed me away. "Learning tricks from that bitch now, huh?"

I ran over to Spinner, who lay still against the side of the tent. *How did magic spiders breathe?* When I touched him, he opened his eyes and gave a sad chitter.

Luxos stalked towards me, and I didn't think before grabbing the flaming hot iron out of the coals.

He gritted his teeth. "This is your last chance to come quietly. I won't be leaving without you again."

I brandished the iron as if I had any idea what I was doing. "I told you; I'm not going back." When I first said that, it was to convince myself. But with each passing day of peace and autonomy, the conviction became stronger, like a wound I finally stopped reopening over and over again.

The man snarled. The flap of the tent opened again. Avlyn stepped through, their hand on their weapon the instant they spotted Luxos.

"Fucking hells, Pallas, let's go." He said, hand extended.

"No!"

"It seems the lady isn't interested, Shadow Walker." Avlyn held their sword towards Luxos, but didn't move. Anger flashed in Luxos' eyes, and Avlyn smirked. "Oh, was that a secret?"

A blood-curdling scream sounded across the camp, making Avlyn's smirk turn into a snarl. "What the hell did you do?"

"Oh, not me, Commander. At least, not yet. Your little princess has been playing with forces that should be left alone and has awoken some things best left sleeping. Don't worry. Me and mine will join the fun shortly." Luxos gave a dramatic bow and disappeared into the shadows.

"Fuck! Pallas, come with me." I looked down at Spinner, who gave me a reassuring chirp before I set him on the pallet and followed Avlyn. Another scream came from the ocean.

"Gods-fuckin-damnit." Avlyn grabbed my hand and waved their sword towards their troops. We sprinted to the beach, and slowly, the torches illuminated our surroundings. All I could see was the churning of waves in the darkness. Their crashing drowned out any sound as their white caps blotched orange from the reflection of the torches.

That's when I saw it, a head popping out of the waves before being pulled back under. My mind immediately went to the Leviathan and its tentacles. I grabbed Avlyn's arm to stop them as they waded into the surf.

"It's too late." I wasn't wrong; the head did not resurface again. Avlyn struggled against my grip for a moment but gave in with a loud, aggravated snarl.

"LET GO!" Jun's voice rang over the cove, and I heard the clank of numerous swords and weapons dropping to the ground at his command. Avlyn sprinted towards his voice.

Our torchlight broke over Jun, and another soldier, pulling a struggling Tori out of the waves. She was soaking wet, but to my surprise, she seemed to be struggling *against* Jun.

"Let me go. He needs me. He needs me!" She was kicking her legs as the two men tried to drag her.

The orcess swooped in and tugged the princess up. "It's not real. *It's not real!*"

Tori held Raula's gaze for a moment, and her face softened when she was pulled back under the waves.

Raula, Jun, and Noki grabbed her. Tori rose out of the water and screamed as she was stretched like a rope in some twisted game of tug-of-war. I ran to help but stopped dead in my tracks when out of the water rose a horse-like creature. It was all wrong with a dark, shaggy mane, glowing red eyes, and sharp, vicious teeth that were sunk into Tori's calf. Blood ran down her leg and mixed with the salt water.

Avlyn didn't hesitate to raise their sword. It lodged into the side of the horse thing, who barely seemed to notice. Avlyn struggled to pull their sword out as the creature took steady steps back into the sea, pulling everyone with them. I couldn't just stand there. I could tug on Tori, but any more force, and her leg might just rip off.

Think Pallas, what would she do? Something stupid. So that's what I did. I grabbed the biggest rock I could from the surf and launched it at the side of the creature's head.

The creature lurched backward, and Jun slipped, letting go of Tori as everyone else was pulled forward again. I grabbed him, helping him up. In the torchlight, his eyes glowed with something I had never seen in him before. Anger.

He stood up tall and grabbed Tori again before staring down the creature. My world stood still as I felt him concentrate his power. He then shouted so loud my ears nearly gave out. **"BURN!"**

Chapter 29

Tori

My leg felt like it was about to split, and all I could think about was the image of this ugly thing swimming away with my foot in its mouth as some grizzly prize. The harder everyone tugged, the more I felt the tendons and sinew of my leg give way under those razor-sharp teeth. But then, through the pain, I felt something soft.

Without a single word or look, I understood Jun's request. I pulled up a tiny thread of magic for him. It was all I could manage with my mind so stretched with pain, but it was enough.

"**BURN**!" Immediately, flames sprouted all over the creature, and it released my leg. I splashed down into the wave, the saltwater stinging my exposed flesh. Hands dragged me onto the shore, and the creature let out a wail that sounded like the cry of a woman who had lost everything. It dove beneath the waves and did not resurface.

Raula and Noki pulled me to shore, and more faces than I could comprehend stared down at me.

"Is my leg still there?" My dulled mind didn't know what else to ask.

"Yep, nobody's snack today, Princess," Avlyn quipped. I leaned back into the strong hands that carried me and heard them shout a few more commands before unconsciousness took me.

I AWOKE IN A TENT WITH JUN STROKING MY HAIR GENTLY. My leg throbbed, but the pain had lessened. I heard Oryx directing someone to wrap my leg, but all I saw was my brother's face stretched tight with worry.

I smiled. "You saved me."

There was a small glimmer in the corner of his eye. "We are strongest together."

I gave him a broad grin. "That was a pretty flashy move."

His smile started to mirror mine. "I just thought, what would Tori do?"

I laughed but then hissed as Oryx tightened something on my leg. Spinner was wrapping my leg in his silk, creating a softly shimmering cast.

The healer nodded at the spider before turning to me. "Your leg will be alright; it's just going to take longer to heal due to... well, you know how wounds from beasts are."

I sat up. "Just another scar to add to the collection." It was the same leg the Leviathan had grabbed. I ran my hand over the scar on my neck and the one on my shoulder. I was quite the grizzly display at this point.

Avlyn pushed aside the tent flap, and Pallas followed.

"Everything alright out there?" I asked.

The commander nodded. "We are staying away from the

water's edge; patrols are in groups of three now. I'm bolstering our defenses for the attack."

"Attack? What attack?"

Avlyn raised their eyebrows and shot a look at Pallas. "Commander Luxos somehow managed to track us here. He threatened an attack on the beach."

My eyes locked with Pallas, and comprehension dawned on her face. "No, not on the beach..." she whispered.

I tried to keep my mind calm, my heart still, and my breathing steady. In an instant, the great ocean that was my mind evaporated. It vaporized into nothing but mist, and all that remained was flames.

Chapter 30

Pallas

Tori's face went blank. I had expected her to panic or yell orders, anything. Instead, her face grew cold and blank, like the statues in the gardens of Koron. She rose from the pallet, making Spinner slide off her lap, and walked out of the tent without saying a word. Avlyn spun to follow her; Jun and I scurried after them.

The princess walked slowly but deliberately towards the tunnel opening tucked into the rock walls. She didn't say a word, which was the most unnerving part. I had never heard such silence from her, and I knew it was wrapped around a force unspeakably dangerous.

Avlyn kept trying to grab her, telling her to wait for more troops. She did not stop or slow; she just kept walking. Her gaze remained fixed on the rocky mountain where the cave containing Abraxas lay hidden.

"The tunnel isn't clear yet, Princess; we will need to—" Avlyn tried to say, but Tori just kept walking. Jun looked at me in dismay, but we both just followed behind like lost puppies.

We reached the cave, and a small group of soldiers were working on the blocked path with pickaxes and shovels.

"Move." It was all that Tori said, and it wasn't even loud, but it echoed unnaturally, shaping the sound into something deeper and hostile. The soldiers didn't need to be told twice. They scrambled away from the wall, and I grabbed Jun's hand and pulled him a few steps back. Avlyn seemed torn but decided to join us in our retreat.

Tori placed a hand over her heart, and then I felt a surge of magic more powerful than anything I had felt in centuries. Green fire erupted from her hands, and she shot at the rock wall with such force that even as I slammed my eyes shut, I was blinded. The tunnel shook with a deafening quake, and the wall exploded.

My ears rang, and no matter how much I blinked, I couldn't see. Slowly, the tunnel came back into focus, lit with an eerie green glow as the dragonfire continued to circle Tori's arms and hands. The rock had been blasted to nearly nothing, and I could see a faint glow where some of the rock was freshly melted by the power of her rage. She slowly turned her head back to us, and her eyes were completely green, glowing like the fire that danced on her fingertips.

"Stay here." She turned back to walk down the tunnel.

Avlyn started to object, but Jun got there first. "You don't need to do this alone, Tori."

She hesitated, and I saw the stone-cold exterior crack. The flames at her command flared, and she set her resolve.

"I know what I have to do. I have to destroy it all. I won't be able to if you are there. Stay here. Stay with Pallas. Protect the beach." A slight grin lifted the corners of her mouth. "And I won't be alone. The commander and I have a score to settle."

With that, she walked down the tunnel, and darkness

surrounded us. Jun made to follow her, but both Avlyn and I grabbed his shoulders.

"Not this time, Nightingale." Jun scrunched his nose at Avlyn's new nickname for him. They laughed, "Let's see how effective those powers of yours are against boats, shall we?"

Chapter 31

Tori

I walked down the tunnel until the humid air of the cave hit me. I shed my coat and drew my sword. The cavern was lit by the soft glow of the wild magic spring, and I let my flames go out for the time being. The place was much louder than I remembered. Water seemed to drip from every surface, and the forest groaned with life. The sound of countless scuttling insects was broken only by the occasional shuffle of something bigger, and the leaves rustled in a breeze that didn't exist.

I didn't need to understand it to know what it said. *I'm alive,* it whispered. I would deal with it later. I needed to find Luxos, and it was all too easy for him to remain hidden here.

Luckily, today he wasn't hiding from me. As I approached Abraxas, I saw a dark figure standing before him, sword drawn. He didn't move to attack Abraxas, not yet. He was half turned so I could see his profile outlined by the dim light.

"Took you long enough, Princess. I thought this was going to be too easy."

I continued to close the distance. The leather on the pommel of my sword cut into my fingers as I gripped it tight. "If you lay a single finger on him, you won't live long enough to regret it."

"You know," he said, ignoring me, "I never thought I'd get to slay a dragon. Hadeon got to have all the fun there. It almost seems unfair. He's half-dead already, but I never much cared for a fair fight." He raised his sword, and I broke into a sprint. As the blade swung down, I extended my own just in time to block him. Sparks flew as steel met steel, and I shoved him back with all my strength. He skidded to a halt, and a cruel grin spread across his face.

"Keep your filthy hands off my mate, Luxos."

His grin only grew. "Time for us to finally play, Princess." He didn't hesitate to lunge at me. I parried the blow and countered him with enough force to cut him in half. As my blade was about to connect, he disappeared. My swing hit nothing, and I stumbled. As I struggled to regain my balance, he appeared behind me, and pain lanced across my back as he sliced me open.

"Fuck!" I gritted my teeth and swung around, but he vanished again and reappeared to kick my knees in from behind. My fingers were torn open as I caught myself on the rocky ground.

"That all you've got? How disappointing." He raised his sword up for the finishing blow, but I spun on my knees and kicked at his legs. Well, I tried, but he jumped away. At least my head was still attached to my shoulders.

He materialized a safe distance from me and laid his weapon on his shoulder. His finger waggled at me. "Tsk, tsk, Princess. You'll have to be faster than that." He was just toying with me.

I charged at him, and we continued this one-sided dance. I would swing, and he would shadow walk. I got better at predicting his position, so I could block his strikes, but twisting and turning to keep up with him was exhausting. He was laughing and hardly breaking a sweat. I wouldn't be able to keep this up, and I would make a fatal mistake. He landed another blow across my ribs, and my blood spilled over the forest floor.

I heard a familiar chitter, and from the edge of the trees, a faint glimmer caught my eye. I continued to dodge and strike at Luxos, guiding him slowly toward the forest. Strike, dodge, strike, dodge. His eyes laughed with malice, but we were almost there. The laughter fled as he stepped into the web Spinner had created between two trees. He tugged at his arms, only entangling himself further.

"Fucking bug," Luxos gritted, and I swung my sword. His shadows enveloped him and he disappeared again, but much of the web went with him. When he reappeared, he tripped as the cut silks wrapped around him, ensnaring him. A very satisfied chirp sounded behind me.

"Looks like I've finally managed to get you all tied up, Commander. Don't you look pretty like that?" It was his turn to snarl as I charged at full speed. He disappeared again but didn't immediately reappear.

I searched. But he was nowhere to be seen. There was no way he had run away again. I strained my ears to listen for any sound when I heard the slink of metal as it ran over a hard surface.

I spun and saw him standing on top of Abraxas, cutting himself free. We locked eyes, and that horrible smirk returned. "No more time for games, Princess. Too bad, it was starting to get fun."

I darted towards him, to stop him, when I was gripped on all sides. Dark shadows slunk up from the ground and grabbed my arms and legs. Ghostly hands gripped my flesh with icy strength. I struggled against them, but they did not yield, and I couldn't raise my sword to them, if that would even work.

Luxos smiled with too many teeth as he raised his sword above his head, straight over Abraxas' heart. "Say goodbye to the last dragon, gorgeous."

I pulled as much mana from the earth as I could and concentrated it at my heart. My whole body shook with rage as dragonfire raced through my very veins. I thought about Pallas' advice to Jun about controlling the magic, guiding it with a subtle hand.

Fuck that.

Blue light, pure mana, wrapped itself over Luxos' arms and sword. His eyes widened in shock, and it was his turn to be held immobile. I let the dragonfire in my blood free and it wreathed me like wings. Not a dragon's wings, but something made of ash and pure starlight.

"What the fuck are you?" Luxos screamed, pulling at my tethers as his shadows writhed and screeched as they were burned away.

In a voice that wasn't entirely my own, I said, "The beginning of all things and your end."

Dragonfire erupted from me like a meteor. Raging emerald flames flew straight at Luxos and wrapped around him. His screams merged with the crackling flames as they seared his flesh. I ran towards Abraxas, ready to deliver the final strike, but Luxos disappeared again. Whether he had been consumed by flames or managed to save himself, I didn't care. I ran my hands over Abraxas' side where the dragonfire had hit him. The area was warmer, but no marks marred him. He really was fireproof.

I sighed in relief and lay my forehead on his haunch. My relief was short-lived. The hand of death surrounded him. Its dark shadows were strong. I lit up my hands with dragonfire, but they didn't cower. If anything, they seemed to laugh at me, hissing and stretching over Abraxas. There was no more time to wait.

"Spinner," I said, as the little spider had crawled up next to me. "It's time for you to go." He gave me an angry chitter. I snapped, as I had once seen Abraxas do, and a single flame of green dragonfire appeared above my pointer finger.

"If one candle can burn away the dark, I wonder what an entire forest fire can do?" The green light reflected in all eight of Spinner's eyes, and I thought I felt him shiver.

"Well, you've certainly come a long way," a weathered voice rang out behind me. I spun and the fire flashed in my palm, burning my flesh. I hissed as the light fell over an ancient, toothless face.

"You? Have you come to stop me?"

The old crone chuckled. "Quite the opposite, my dear. I've come to give you our blessing."

"*Our* blessing?"

The old crone gave me that wicked, toothless smile.

"Were you ever truly the seer?"

"Oh, she came here long ago. And when her body joined us, her spirit lingered, unwilling to cross the star bridge until she could earn her forgiveness. She is us, as we are her. She taught us much, and we gave her peace. She taught us that fae only seem to listen to their own kind, so it was best we approach you as her. Together we have become more, something new. Not unlike you... and your brother."

"What do you—" I started, but the crone raised her hand.

"No time for that now. We have waited for you for over a thousand years, but now we have no time. Make haste, World Breaker."

"You know what I intend to do. You will be destroyed."

The crone nodded.

"Just like that? I don't understand."

"Those who are young never do. Perhaps when you have lived for millennia, you will feel the same. For something to be reborn, something must die. This is the way of all things." I nodded. Her toothless grin spread. "Not just us, little beast. The small creature you are now, she will die as well, but you will also be reborn."

"What will I become?"

"That is up to you." Her eyes crinkled, showing the slightest hint of kindness. "But that is not the right question to ask."

"Will I miss her? The girl that I was?"

The crone truly smiled. "Yes, in a deep aching way that will never settle. You won't be given the time to mourn her. You will steal that time in the small hours of the morning and in the moments between the work that must come. But she must die if all is to change."

"I understand."

"No, you do not. No one can until they have gone through it. But you must do it, anyway. And the time has come. No more delays, little beast. May She guide you into what you will become. Correct the imbalance, World Breaker." She stepped back into the shadows, and I held up a hand of dragonfire. She was nowhere to be seen.

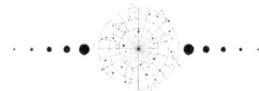

I SENT SPINNER OUT, AND MANY OF THE CREATURES THAT lingered here followed him. Their sacrifice wasn't needed. The cave was quiet. There was only the much too slow rhythmic breathing of Abraxas. I grasped his snout in my hands, running my fingers over the ridges of his scales. My nails met their hard surface, and I tapped softly. I ran my hands over the slits of his nostrils, so that he might know I was there.

I pressed my whole torso against the long line of his face so that my head lay between his closed eyes. "It's time, my Dragon

King. No turning back now." I gave him one more gentle squeeze, but he didn't move. I walked to the edge of the forest, where the trees and underbrush obscured everything.

I placed my hand against the bark of the nearest tree, feeling the rough texture under my fingertips. It wasn't dissimilar to the feeling of Abraxas' scales. I placed my forehead against the tree and whispered, "Thank you," one last time.

I closed my eyes and reached down into the earth. It had become almost second nature to me now. It flowed readily into the surrounding forest, soaked up by every root and leaf. It was life itself. It didn't feel any different from when I channeled to a fae or a human; it was just as precious and unique. I hesitated. Who was I to trade this life for another? Abraxas was mine, and more precious to me than anything in this world, but I was just a woman. Just another living on this world, like the men and women around me. Who was I to defy Death himself?

The magic of the earth curled through the forest, and every leaf and stem turned to me. Great swirls of blue light rose from the spring and filled the cave. It wove itself together until Life herself appeared before me. She was beautiful and larger than Abraxas. Her perfect, snow-white wings scraped the roof of the cave. Her eyes glowed a beautiful deep blue like a flawless sapphire plucked from the heart of the deepest mine. Her heart-fire glowed the same deep blue, and as she released a breath, every flower in the cave blossomed to life.

Life and Death. The very first dragons, the very first gods of the fae. Was she merely a vision, or had she risen from the depths of the earth to stop me? My fists clenched, and my resolve was set. I would fight them both if that's what it took to get Abraxas back. But as I called some of the earth's power into me, some of her power, she gave me a sad, soft look.

"It's time, Tori."

I held her gaze one more moment before she dissolved back

into the light streaming throughout the forest. Each tree was illuminated in her soft blue glow. I reached back for Abraxas with my mind and found the tiniest ember of emerald fire. I cradled it and pulled it along the fragile tether of our bond. It was just an ember, a spark. But the tiniest sparks are all it takes to light the mightiest fires, so that's what I did.

The tree under my hand erupted in emerald flame. I watched the embers leap to consume tree after tree until the heat was unbearable. I released my grip and turned back to Abraxas. The magic didn't need my guidance anymore, and in another minute, the entire forest would be up in flames.

I sat down in the crook of Abraxas' arm and placed my hand as close as I could to his heart. Sweat beaded on my brow and the back of my neck. The cave was doing its job, holding the heat from the fire in. I was in the heart of the forge, and hopefully, I could craft something new from it.

I reached out to Abraxas, feeling the shadows that were ready to strike, ready to consume him. As the fire roared behind me, I could feel them quake. It made them desperate to claw at him. But I would never let them. They should tremble in fear.

I pulled from the heat of the cave, the rampant destruction of the forest. Death was the beginning, and as the forest burned, the magic of life sprung forth.

Just as I had learned to summon the mana of the earth, I felt the lifeforce of the forest swirling around me. My heart felt like it was trying to claw itself out of my chest, but I slowed my breath and tugged at those threads that wove our world together. Mana from below, life from above, and they intertwined into something new and powerful in my heart. Threads pulled and lashed, trying to tangle into an irreversible knot, but my heart continued to beat, and I guided them. It felt... natural, as if I had always known how. And the threads of mana and life formed into a perfect tapestry of white light, like a newborn star.

I channeled that light through me and into those shadows, burning them away. They shrieked an otherworldly sound. No wait, that was me. As the magic ripped through my insides, my flesh burned away.

The fire overtook us, but I was not fireproof. All I saw was green light, and the pain was beyond reckoning. I watched as my flesh sizzled away into nothing. But as fast as it disintegrated, I saw it healing, the torn edges glowing with white light. I would heal just for it to be burned away again. The cycle was endless, with no respite. But still I clung to him. I focused and pulled more and more mana from the earth and life from the flames. I healed and I burned, but I did not stop.

My legs shook as my tears sizzled and evaporated from my eyes before they were even born. My vision tunneled into a white blur as the pain swept me away.

Chapter 32

Abraxas

A trickle of heat stirred me. Heat? In this gods-forsaken frozen wasteland? That great endless chaos was close now. I could feel it already sucking me in. Was this the last bit of comfort I would receive before the end?

A flash of light, blinding in the endless darkness, came between me and that great pit. Tori stepped through, golden, glowing, and warm. She lay her hands on me, and I was nothing but a man in the presence of a goddess.

"It's time, Abraxas."

I had waited so long, but I still hesitated. "What have you done, my love?"

She smiled at me softly. "I broke the world to get back to you." I could feel it. What had started as a warm breeze was now a molten flow, fighting back the shadows that clung to me. She held my face in both her hands and kissed me tenderly, as if I might fall apart under her touch. "It's time to wake up, Abraxas."

I shook my head, "Tori, I haven't been the beast for centuries. I don't know what will happen if I awaken."

"When you awaken," she corrected me.

"Tori," I reached out and clutched her cheek, "I could hurt you. More than that. It won't be a dream any longer."

"You could try." Her vicious smile set me aflame. "You would have to catch me first."

"Careful, little bird or you might get burned."

"I've always liked to play with fire, Abraxas." She slammed her hand to my chest, and dragonfire enveloped us both, but nothing shone as bright as her.

Chapter 33

Tori

My eyes snapped open, and the fire still burned around us. The vines that had embraced Abraxas for so long lit up and blew away as embers on the wind. Malachite flames enveloped us both. The earth beneath my feet shattered. The spring at the center of the cave bubbled. Still, the shadows clung to him. They dug in their claws and fangs, unwilling to give up.

"He's mine!" I dove deeper into the earth until I reached the molten core. The cave floor gave way, and blue light spilled out of the earth. Chunks fell away, but still, I clung to him. Underneath that light, magma rose. The lifeblood of our world consumed everything left of the forest. It took on a life of its own and spilled over the broken floor towards Abraxas. The shadows saw their end approach and tried to flee, but I destroyed every last one. I killed them with green flames, blue mana, and the white light of my heart. I burned, and they burned until there was nothing but light and silence.

"Wake up, my love." I placed a soft kiss on the end of Abraxas' snout.

A great beat, like a colossal drum, sounded through the cave.

Beneath the obsidian scales of his chest, his heartbeat grew stronger. Between his scales, his viridian green dragonfire glowed, and I saw its power swell as if he was absorbing all the magic around him. I channeled all that fire, life, and light through our bond. It rushed into him until nothing but a vacuum was left around us. The molten rock cooled, and the flames extinguished as every last drop of power was absorbed into Abraxas' glowing heart.

An eternity passed in complete silence as I waited, and the entire world held its breath.

His eye snapped open. They glowed like the sun with barely any green to be seen. He stretched his great wings so they almost reached the roof of the cave. His jaw opened in a massive yawn as his tongue lolled out of his mouth. His enormous tail swished from side to side, smashing over the freshly formed rocks, obliterating them to rubble. My heart didn't beat.

He inhaled deeply, and those monstrous eyes snapped to me, their elongated pupils focused on their prey. They dilated until his eyes were entirely black. I could feel all that magic burning him up. He was like a man who had overindulged in the earth's pleasures; his mind wasn't his own.

I heard his voice not with my ears but with my mind and body as it vibrated through me. *Run, little bird.*

A great shriek shook rocks from the ceiling, and I dove under his chest as dragonfire enveloped where I had been standing. He struggled to find me as I used his body as my shield, but he swiped massive claws underneath him, and it took all my training to dodge them. I slid into the dirt to avoid another, trying to place my hands over his heart. He was moving now, and I had to keep pace to not get trampled. I changed strategies. I darted out beneath his tail as he tried to locate me. His tail smashed more of the terrain as he went. He spun his head towards me, jaws wide open.

I waited as long as possible before launching myself up, one foot boosting me off his nose. He snapped his jaws closed and threw his head back, throwing me into the air. I tumbled and landed on one of his great spines; it pierced through my forearm.

Fuck. That was not elegant, but it held me in place as I avoided more snaps from his jaws. I slammed my free hand into his back just above his heart. I remembered his vision of changing, the flow and raw power he needed.

The earth was tapped dry; only a trickle of mana remained. It was enough. He screamed again, and I felt him shifting, shrinking in on himself.

The spine in my arm shrank, and I pulled free, willing just the tiniest flow of power over the wound to numb the pain while my body did the rest.

I landed on top of him, but he wasn't fully fae. There was no more magic for the earth to give, so his transformation wasn't complete. He appeared like he did in my dream; his black wings were splayed under me, and scales covered most of his body. His long black horns caught the deep amber light of the smoldering forest where they erupted from his silver hair.

He pushed up off the ground with clawed hands, and I slid off him.

"Abraxas?"

He rose slowly, his great wings towering over him. He clutched his face in his clawed hands and then pulled them away, examining the long black talons.

"Abraxas?" I reached out to clutch his shoulder. He turned to me, his face soft and confused.

"Tori?" His soft gaze fell to my hand, and he reached out to touch me. Then, his claws clamped around my forearm to lift me straight up in the air. I hissed as I dangled, and he gave me that wicked smile that tore me up inside.

"I thought I told you to run." I kicked him straight in the gut, and he dropped me. I ran as soon as my feet hit the rocky ground.

I sprinted as fast as my legs could carry me. I ran through what remained of the vegetation of the grotto, crashing into burnt branches and feeling the singe of embers on the soles of my feet. I knew I left a trail of blood for him to follow. My heart pounded, and it felt like someone had slid a dagger between my ribs, but I willed my feet forward.

I darted behind the smoldering remains of a tree to catch my breath. "Come out, little bird. You can't hide from me." I heard him with just a moment to spare. I ducked down as his claws crashed through the burned trunk, causing it to explode. I rolled away and kept running but dared to look back. That long, slitted pupil tracked me from glowing, golden eyes as I tried to dart away. He lunged, and the anticipation fueled me. I knew I had to make him work just a little bit harder.

In truth, I had been afraid. I'd avoided him in my dreams, fearing what might happen again. This fire had not only saved him, but it had changed me. He had been reborn, but it had burned away the small creature that I had once been. I'd channeled more power than any fae before me and brought him back from the edge of death. Just as his mind had been addled by the power, I was sure mine had as well. I rode that high. If he was the last god, then I had become the last goddess, and a goddess feared no one.

I had felt power flow through me, the power of life itself, and it had felt sublime. Better than any fae had any right to feel. There had been pain, but Abraxas had long ago shown me that pleasure and pain were intimately connected. I ran from him now, but only so my reward would be even sweeter when he caught me.

I ran, and he pursued. We both changed into something wild. Something that had never been chained to civil behaviors and niceties. Something that was free to act without fear of embarrassment or reprimand. Something outside of control. Something that was both ancient and new. When he finally caught me, nothing was left but the feral creatures that lived inside us.

He slammed into my back, knocking me to the ground. I threw my hands out to prevent my face from being smashed, and I scrambled for purchase. He grabbed onto my ankles and calves to haul me to him. I freed one leg and slammed it into his side as I rolled over. I launched at him, hands outstretched, knocking him onto his back with his wings pinned beneath him. I attempted to pin his wrists down as he struggled. His eyes still burned that golden yellow, a beacon.

They flared as he pushed off his wings, the force knocked me onto my back as he climbed on top of me. The bite of the rocks against my back mirrored the sensation of his claws raking down my front. What little remained of my burned clothes were shredded away. Small red lines bubbled under his touch, but I hardly felt them as my body ached for him.

I pulled him to me, raking my fae nails down his back, and a sound between a howl and moan escaped from him. He slammed his mouth onto mine, ferociously devouring me. Our teeth and tongues clashed in a battle for our lives. I bit down on his lip, and he hissed, pulling away to latch onto my breasts. His teeth scraped over the new skin. I had to check that I wasn't still alight with dragonfire, for every inch of my skin felt raw and scorched. His touch amplified the sensation, creating a perfect mix of pain and long-lingering pleasure.

He dragged his elongated tongue over my nipples before running it across my throat. "Are you ready to have me as I truly am, my mate?" he murmured in my ear, his teeth lightly closing on the pointed tip.

He chuckled, and the vibrations only ignited deep arousal in my belly. His erection pressed against me, hard and pulsing. There was more than I was used to. I looked down between us and saw why. He was still the beast, somewhere between fae and dragon and all that came with that. What had once been a sizeable but very normal fae cock was now something... different. Two long, hard cocks, each a deep shade of pink and ribbed from the pointed tip to the base, rubbed against my lower stomach.

I was sure my face showed my surprise, and Abraxas leaned in, grabbing the back of my neck with his clawed hand. His free hand snaked up my thigh until those onyx claws slid through my folds to move against my clit.

"You're drenched, little bird, but will that be enough?"

"You're mine, Abraxas. Give me all of you. I want everything."

His fangs flashed in the dying light of the cave as he carefully pressed his talons against the most sensitive part of me. I bucked my hips and grabbed his lengths with both of my hands. He hissed as I tightened my hold, feeling their new texture and shape. The ridges slid across my palms, and my stomach contracted as I thought about what they would feel like inside of me. I continued to pump them until they leaked all over my stomach, and Abraxas' claws cut into the ground beside me.

He looked at me, and I saw some green return to his eyes. "Tori..."

I snared his lips in a kiss before promising, "I want everything."

I felt the bottom side of his shaft slide up against my clit, gathering my wetness. I shifted my hips so his lower cock was placed at my entrance, and he gave a feral moan that said he couldn't resist anymore. I watched him shift his hips back before pressing forward, stretching me around his cock. Before he was even halfway inside, he was pressing against the very end of me, the pressure was equally unbearable and undeniable.

"You're doing so well, Princess. Look at me." His gold eyes were rimmed with green as he held my gaze. He pulled and pushed back in, settling a little bit deeper. Each of his ridges pushed against my opening, causing the muscles to spasm.

With every thrust, he pushed in another inch until the base of his second cock pressed against me. The hard length slid against my swollen clit with each movement.

His talons grabbed my jaw and turned me so his mouth could leave a trail of kisses and bites on my neck and shoulders. He pressed his body into mine harder, and I realized he was seeking more pressure on his top cock. I could feel it leaking more liquid onto my stomach as his pace increased. My legs thrashed as my muscles tightened.

I reached between us and fisted his cock. He froze for a moment, and I whimpered, "Fuck, don't stop."

He immediately resumed, even harder than before. He thrust into my cunt and fingers. The added tightness had his claws sinking into the ground by my head and flames licking my neck as he panted, trying so hard to be gentle.

I felt so incredibly full. My vision went hazy as my climax approached. "Don't fucking stop."

Chapter 34

Abraxas

Mine. Mine. Mine.

There was nothing but her—the scent of her and feel of her and the taste of her. Unlike before, there was no fear. She burned like a star as her tightness and warmth wrapped around me; I had to do everything I could to keep from devouring her.

Everything. If there was a fae in this world who could handle me as I was, it would be her, my mate. But...

She saw my hesitation, and her eyes hardened. She released my upper cock and grabbed the back of my neck, pulling me down so our faces were inches apart. I saw my flames lick her skin, but she pulled me into a deep kiss, swallowing them all.

I could never deny her. I moved faster, and she clenched around me. She arched her back and moaned my name in such a sweet orison that I nearly lost myself again. She was incendiary, and I was the flame. *Claim. Devour. Burn.*

"Come for me, Princess." She obeyed my command, and her nails raked my chest as she squeezed down on me as she rode the waves of her pleasure. Her face flushed a beautiful red, and her eyes rolled back. In that moment of weakness and surrender, I couldn't contain myself any longer.

I pulled out of her only to slam my top cock in a single stroke, her sweet cunt swallowing me all the way to the base. The bottom cock was enveloped between the beautiful curves of her ass and pressed against the tight entrance I so longed to claim.

I shifted to my knees and pulled her hips up as she rocked against me. I slid my fingers through the arousal that leaked out of her, coating them completely. I pulled at that tight entrance gently, then slowly slid one finger in, pressing until she relaxed enough to add another. Her eyes rolled nearly into the back of her head. I moved one of her legs to my shoulder, and she mirrored the other. I continued to work her as I slid my cock out of her, both now slick and ready. I removed my fingers and leaned into her thighs so that her hips shifted to the perfect angle, both of my cock heads pressed against her.

"Ready?" I let my teeth rake over the calf on my shoulder. Careful, I had to be so careful, or I would destroy her. My fangs broke skin, and a single, beautiful stream of red trailed down her leg. Her eyes were filled with that desire and defiance that had me undone, and she gave me a perfect smirk.

"Everything." She pulled me down into another kiss, and she sucked my tongue into her mouth, claiming me as I claimed her.

The hand on the back of my neck clenched harder as I moved inside her, but she took me without hesitation.

"You like that, don't you? So eager."

Every sound she made as I pushed further was the sweetest song until all of me was pressed completely into her.

"Abraxas, it's so much..."

"I know, little bird, I know. But look how fucking beautiful you look with me filling you completely." Every single inch of her belonged to me.

"You're mine, and I'm going to fill you over and over until there is no room for anything but me inside of you, inside of your soul."

"Yes!" she screamed, and another orgasm washed over her. She was so full of me that every single muscle in her body spasmed and relaxed until she was nearly limp in my arms. I wasn't done with her.

I bent her nearly in half, pressing her down into the ground, each thrust breaking the fragile surface beneath us. I didn't have long now, the feeling of her was so tight and perfect that I knew the gods had made her just for me.

I traced my lips over her ear. "You're mine, little bird, say it."

"Possessive reptile." She smiled at me. I twisted her hair in my hand, snapping her head back so that her elegant, long neck was fully exposed. I saw the bite mark I had left on her so long ago. She hadn't been mine then, but now she was, and I would never let go again.

I sank my fangs into her, and her hot blood tasted better than heaven. She moaned against me, so lost in pleasure that the pain only added to it. I pulled back to see the mark I knew would stay with her forever. She gave me that perfect smile. "I'm yours, Abraxas. And you are mine."

My climax bathed me in golden light, reaching over every inch of my skin, from the tips of my horns to the ends of my toes. Every wave sent more of me into her until I could feel it leaking out around me.

"Until you break this world apart, Princess."

I LAY IN THE ASHES OF THE CAVE, THE SMOLDERING EMBERS of the forest warm against my skin. After an eternity of the cold stars, nothing felt as divine as their infernal heat. Well, almost nothing.

I lifted up on my elbows to watch as Tori plunged herself into what remained of the spring. Its edges swirled with debris and ash, and the water was no longer glowing. I heard her gasp as she breached the surface, flipping her hair away from her face. The side of her head over her right ear was burned, and the hair there was gone. It only helped to accentuate the sharp line of her jaw, the beautiful curve of her lips, and the long line of her neck. She rose up out of the water slowly with liquid clinging to her, highlighting the curve of her breasts and the muscles that shaped over her hip leading down to that perfect patch of hair between her legs.

She was a vision. I had to remind myself I had not died, and this was not my heaven. The gods had deemed to bless me with her in this life, even though she was clearly meant for something greater than this world. She saw me staring and smiled; the universe split itself open in awe of her. Her steps were silent as small puffs of ash swirled around her feet.

"My goddess, what has this humble mortal done to deserve your divine presence?"

She knelt down beside me and rolled her eyes. "By all accounts, you are the god here, Abraxas."

"Do not let such heresies cross those perfect lips, my love." I laced my fingers with hers and pulled her close so her wet body slid against my chest. I gently kissed her. "I can only hope that this loyal servant can worship you in the ways that you deserve. I would lay my life at the altar of your power if you so desired."

"Dramatic reptile." She smiled at me again, the stars aligned, and she pulled me into a deep kiss that was the beginning and the end of everything.

She held me close, and I let my fingers slowly trace the curve of her lower back. I trailed kisses down her neck until I came to the beautiful mark I had left on her. I snaked my tongue over her sweet skin, and she shivered.

She ran her hands through my hair until she grazed the base of my horns. It was my turn to tremble. She traced up its length, feeling every groove and bump until she came to the very tip. She pressed it into the soft pad of her finger and pulled it back; a small drop of red blood welled up in the small cut.

I grasped her palm gently before pulling that digit into my mouth, not wanting to waste a single drop of her. She laughed. "Good thing I can feel some of the mana returning to the earth here. I'd need it to fight you off again."

I continued to lavish her finger for a moment more. "I have told you before, my love. No matter how hard you fight, you will never be rid of me. I would chase you to the very ends of this earth."

"Dramatic," she said again, but it was with a soft smile as she leaned in to press her lips to mine. When she pulled back, it had changed into something much more wicked.

"How would you feel about being a bit more dramatic?" I felt the power of the earth swell into me again through her in a way that I hadn't felt in five hundred years. It was raw and unrestrained and tasted of her. I couldn't help but mirror her wicked grin.

Chapter 35

Pallas

W e clustered on the frigid beach, a tight circle with fires every ten feet to keep the dark at bay. Even with their warm light, the stars above seemed to burn brighter, like they were lying in wait, just like us. The great river soared across the center of the sky, reminding me of how very small I was.

The group was subdued. Some tried to sleep, but most just watched the sky and the island. Not an hour before, I thought we were seeing another aurora, but instead, the top of the island glowed that acidic green I was becoming all too familiar with. Jun huddled close to me as the flames reached to the sky like the volcano that slept beneath these lands had awoken.

"She is going to be alright." It wasn't a question. His voice was the strongest I had heard in some time. In our past life, he would have sung me a song to express his feelings. I knew that wouldn't happen now. It might not ever happen again.

He might never sing for me, but I could sing for him. My mother had been a woman of scholarship and academia. She hadn't cared much for the softer things in life, but I always remembered the songs she sang to me as a youngling before bed.

In the land where mist and magic sleep,
Where dreams and stars their secrets keep,
Close your eyes, my precious one,
This gentle night has just begun.

In the moonlit glow, you softly lay,
Safe and warm till break of day,
Stars above will watch and keep,
As you drift into peaceful sleep.

Wisps dance in silver light,
Sprinkling dreams throughout the night,
Whispering tales of lands unseen,
Where joy and wonder reign supreme.

Sleep now, child, in dreams so sweet,
In the world where magic and your soul meet,
Rest your head and close your eyes,
As stars sing you their soft lullabies.

Jun smiled at me, and it reached his eyes in a way I hadn't seen in so long. He laced his fingers through my own, and I was about to lean into his shoulder when the earth beneath us shook. A sonorous roar rolled like thunder over the beach, and everyone scrambled to their feet. The top of the island no longer shone bright green; it was lit by a low, pulsing red glow of embers. Even from that dim illumination, we all saw the massive shadow that streaked toward the sky. The surrounding soldiers grabbed their weapons and scrambled to formation as the hulking monster circled in the air above us, just out of sight.

Green flames shattered the darkness, and everyone froze as the dragon descended from the sky. Jun and I clung to each other as the wind from his massive wings nearly knocked us off our feet. Embers flew from the fires as the flames were almost extinguished. Tents toppled, and the earth shook as his feet collided with the earth. A few soldiers readied their weapons while others pushed them down. His golden eyes burned bright against the darkness of the night, and the whole world held its breath.

Slowly, Avlyn walked forward toward that face that was larger than them. The dragon tracked their movement, his forked tongue lashing out and tasting the air around the commander. They stood with unnerving stillness until their hand flew to their weapon. I saw the streak of movement that had alarmed them as the princess, completely nude, flung herself down from the back of the dragon's neck, sword in hand. She walked forward and placed her hand on the dragon's snout. He leaned into her, his eyes closing in contentment before he began to shrink. Dragonfire wrapped around them both. Its green light was so bright in the depth of the night I had to look away. I still felt it. The great rush of magic made my skin tingle and my eyes water. It was primordial and powerful, rivaling what I had felt from Hadeon. When I looked back, the beast was gone, and only the man remained, smiling at the princess as if no one else in the world existed but her.

Avlyn's fist crashed into the armor on their chest. "All hail, Dragon King Abraxas and Princess Tori." A mighty roar went through the crowd as shields and armor were smacked together. Jun and I approached; Jun flung his arms around his sister before offering her his coat. She embraced him tightly in return.

Abraxas said to Avlyn, "You miss me, Commander?"

"One of these days, I'm just going to kill you myself, asshole."

WITH BOTH THE KING AND PRINCESS CLOTHED, WE huddled around the fire. Their hands were intertwined, and they couldn't keep their eyes off one another. It was insufferable, but something about it caused a smile to twist at the corner of my mouth. Jun saw my distaste, and I could read the amusement on his face, but he squeezed my hand gently. I didn't fight it.

Tori finally pulled her gaze from Abraxas and asked Avlyn, "So, what happened out here? Luxos' troops?"

They shook their head. "Nothing. Quieter than the inside of Kaleos' head out here."

The brute made a rude gesture at the commander, but Tori frowned, her gaze falling on me.

"He made his threats. Did he lie?"

"Tori, I'm not some walking crystal ball; I don't—" She kept her gaze fixed on me, unwavering. "No, he didn't lie."

Her head turned to scan the ocean beyond our small refuge. The dawn was beginning to break and though the mist was thick, no ships could be seen. Her body stiffened.

Abraxas looked at her. "My love?"

"It's not here he planned to attack. He knew Avlyn, and I would be gone, distracted. Our forces divided."

Both Avlyn and Abraxas jumped up. "Xyr," the commander whispered. "It will take us at least a day to return. If he was smart, the attack is already underway."

"He is smart," I said, trying to ignore the hurt look in Avlyn's eye.

Abraxas and Tori locked eyes. "Looks like it's time to fly, my love."

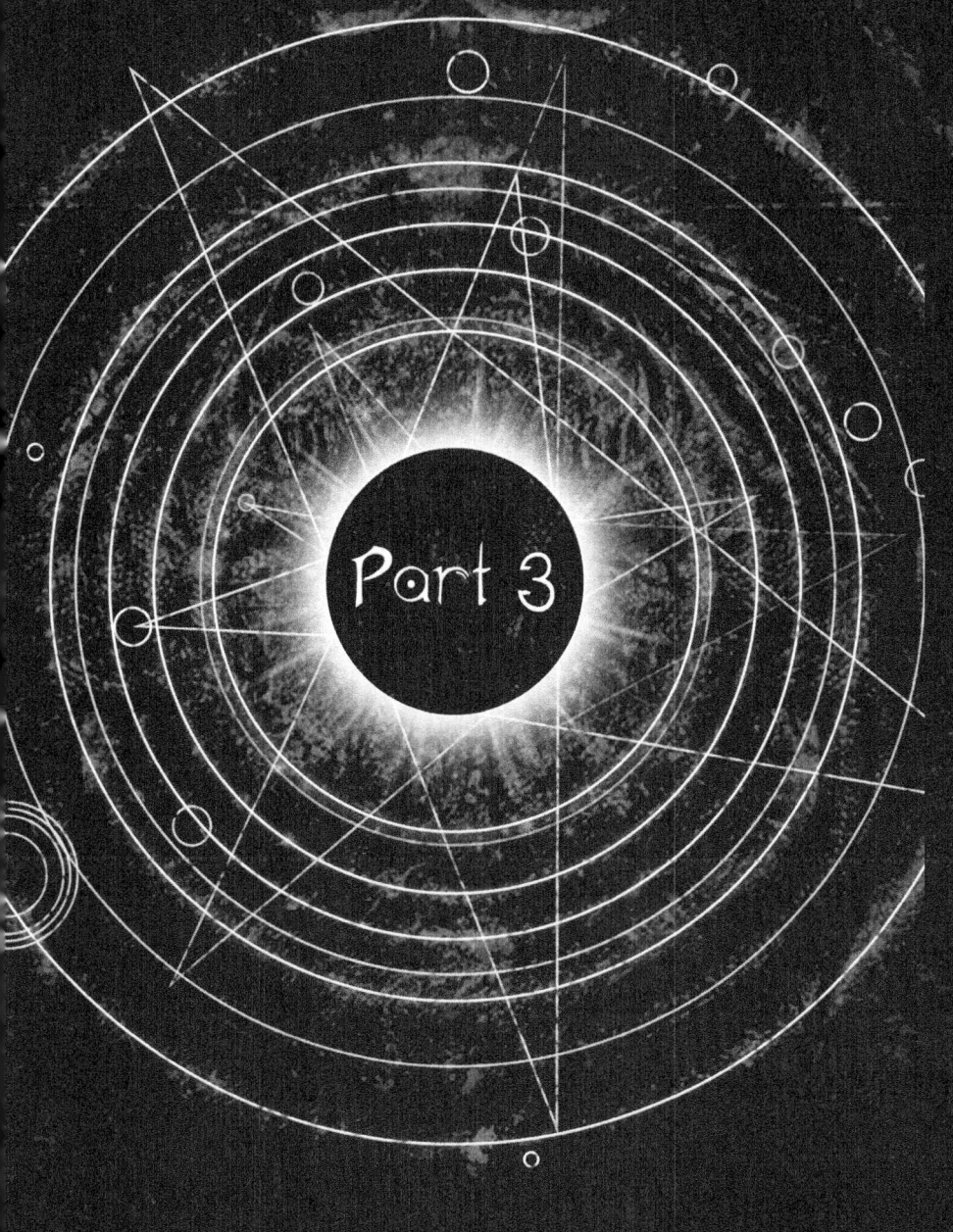

Part 3

Chapter 36

Tori

Jun clung to my back; his arms wrapped so tightly around my stomach that I could barely breathe. The wind whipped my hair into my eyes and mouth as I tried to shout at him, but I couldn't even hear myself as the sky flew past us. Instead, I gripped his hand in mine, squeezing tight. He had demanded to come with me, and I couldn't refuse. I wondered if he was regretting that now.

Under my thighs, Abraxas' scales rolled as his wings beat the air. I flattened myself against his back, avoiding the spines. Every muscle in my body ached from clinging to him, but the cost of letting go was death.

I would catch you, Princess. Abraxas spoke to me without words. Whether it was our minds or souls that spoke, I wasn't sure.

It is our minds. Long ago, dragons devised this method of communicating with the fae.

Stop that! Can you always read my thoughts now?

Only when you are letting them run rampant, as you are now.

So, knowing me, always.

Underneath me, a deep chuckle rumbled through Abraxas' chest. Jun let out a small squeak, and I squeezed his hand again. The laugh died quickly. I didn't have to hear his thoughts to know why.

We will get there in time.

Yes, and then what? My people will see a dragon descending on them, just as one did five hundred years ago. More fear, more death.

The scales of his neck were warm as I stroked them. *You saved Xyr then; you will save it now.*

I surrendered. That is no salvation.

Do you think the survivors of that day would agree with you? He didn't answer me. I lay my head down to hear the beating of his heart under the rush of the wind.

The surrounding clouds broke, and the warmth of the sun on my skin was blissful. My momentary relief was broken when I looked down at my city. Smoke billowed from every quarter. I couldn't hear it yet, but I could see our soldiers clashing with the enemy in the streets. Citizens fled in every direction.

I felt Abraxas' massive jaw clench. *It's just like five hundred years ago. What will the beast inside me do when it finally smells all that blood?*

I gripped down onto his neck with my hand. *It will be different this time. This time, we fight together.*

He turned his head, his golden eye landing on me. *Yes, we fight together.*

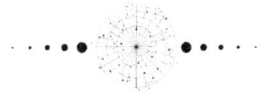

HE DESCENDED FROM THE HEAVENS LIKE THE GOD OF OLD that he was. The great plaza of Xyr was filled with bodies running in every direction; shouting and screams filled the air. But as Abraxas broke through the clouds, an unnatural silence fell as every head turned towards the sky; swords and spears were held aloft but unmoving.

Time to be a bit dramatic, I heard Abraxas say.

I clutched onto Jun's hand tighter. Abraxas tucked in his wings, and we dove from the sky; the wind was so fast that I felt it might rend the skin from my flesh. Then, in an instant, he spread his wings wide; they stretched nearly over the entire plaza. My legs shifted as he pulled in a great breath, and his heart glowed. A roar so deep it resounded in my whole body filled the plaza as dragonfire filled the sky.

There was only one place to land where our people wouldn't be crushed underneath him. The stone statue of the dragon at the center of the plaza I had once thought enormous was now nothing but a tiny, pale imitation of the real thing. As Abraxas' claws gripped it to find purchase, it crumbled beneath him. Jun and I jolted as the statue gave way, but Abraxas was unphased as he finally landed on the stone floor.

Faces looked up at us, both friend and foe. No one moved. No one dared. The wind swept up in a flurry, and a voice was carried to me on that harsh breeze.

"Princess Tori!" I saw the source; Lady Bogata, accompanied by a group of Dragon Army soldiers and Commander Talius. Her shout broke the spell on the plaza, and the soldiers of the Golden Army moved forward. My brother and I launched ourselves off Abraxas' back. I pushed him behind me and swung my sword to engage one of the soldiers fighting nearby. He looked at me for only a moment before he was crushed under a giant claw. I looked back at Abraxas.

I can handle myself, you know.

He nodded. *Get to Lady Bogata.*

I gripped Jun's hand to pull him after me as I fought my way through, but to my surprise, he stepped in front of me and shouted, "**MOVE.**"

The soldiers in our way parted like a giant invisible hand had swept them to the side, and we dashed through. A few errant swords came at us, but I blocked them and quickly dispatched their wielders.

We made it across the plaza quickly, and Talius and his men parted to let us enter their circle of protection.

"That was quite an entrance, Your Highness. I assume that is our king behind you?" Lady Bogata's face held the shadow of a smile, but it was lost amongst the dirt and exhaustion.

"Yes. But for now, I need a battle report." Talius had shifted himself inside the circle to talk with me.

"Your Majesty, the enemy was spotted early due to our patrols. But their numbers overwhelmed us, and they were able to enter the city. They have been using it to their advantage, engaging civilians to divide our forces." Lady Bogata's mouth twitched at the honorific he gave me but said nothing.

Anger roiled in my chest until I could feel the dragonfire licking at my fingertips. "Which districts have been taken, and which are still safe?"

"The market and gardens district have been overrun. We are evacuating the seaside district up to the mist district and the castle."

"I've had every noble in the mist district open their homes to those fleeing inward. But we can't keep our gates open much longer," Lady Bogata inserted. I felt Jun shift with surprise next to me.

"What's your next move, Commander?" I asked.

"Clear the sea district and secure the perimeter of the mist district before launching our attempt to push the enemy out."

"What do you need for that?"

"To gather our scattered cohorts to the mist district's three bridges, and maybe a miracle." He turned to look back at the plaza where Abraxas spun wildly, launching multiple soldiers into the air at once. "Luckily, it looks like you brought one." Under his helmet, I saw his teeth flash. "Your orders, Your Majesty?"

No time to hesitate now. "I'll head to the garden district and get as many out as I can. Commander, you head to the market district and do the same. Do not engage unless absolutely necessary. Gather troops and retreat towards the bridges. Lady Bogata, you head to the main bridge and keep the mist district open as long as possible; save as many as you can."

She nodded, and I noticed the broken piece of wood she held like a club. Blood coated the tip.

"Jun you—"

"I will go with Lady Bogata to hold the bridge." I didn't want him out of my sight, not again, not with so many enemies around us.

"Jun..."

"Go save who you can, Tori." He looked over at Lady Bogata. "Maybe they aren't all bad after all." Something passed between the two, and she nodded.

"I would say I would protect him with my life, Princess, but seeing what you can do, my Prince, I doubt you need me."

Jun's face was still stern, but he nodded again, and they headed out with half of the soldiers following behind.

Talius eyed the remaining troops. "I can send a dozen with you, Your Majesty. You can't go alone."

"Oh, I won't be alone." We all turned towards Abraxas.

The plaza was now almost completely cleared of enemy soldiers; many were lying dead or dying on the ground, covered in blood and burns.

One more lay trapped under Abraxas' claw, screaming and trying to free himself. Abraxas slowly lowered his jaws before snapping the man's neck; the screaming abruptly stopped.

How'd that taste? I inquired, half joking.

Delicious. He snaked his long tongue over his teeth and lips, licking up the remaining blood. A very primal fear gripped its fist around my stomach as he stalked forward. He was too big and powerful. Compared to him, I was tiny.

His eyes glowed with so much rage as blood dripped from his fangs. I felt the soldiers shaking, their armor rattled as they looked up at the monstrosity straight from nightmares. I was afraid, but I was also his mate, and he would yield to me.

Change back.

What?

That's an order. I placed my hand on his snout and let the mana flow through me. The wind kicked up to a gale again, and slowly, his scales receded, and he shrunk until only the fae stood before me. His eyes still shimmered that deep, violent gold.

The surrounding soldiers stood straighter, but I could still sense their hesitation. Talius stepped forward, passing Abraxas his sword. "Y-your Maje-sty." Abraxas gripped the weapon, and the soldiers all took a step back as he swung it violently before him, as if remembering how to move. He was still the beast. I could see it. He wouldn't care who ended up on the other side of that blade like this, lost to the violence and rage inside of himself.

I stepped closer and whispered in his ear, "Let's go save our people." I saw the beast hesitate. His face softened, but his grip on the sword was still harsh, and those eyes remained.

"Stay with me, Abraxas?" The green returned to his eyes. I reached my hand out to cup his cheek.

"Until the sky burns, Tori."

Chapter 37

Pallas

The ship buzzed with nervous energy as the soldiers bustled about, readying for our landing and the battle ahead.

I couldn't stand it. I was only getting in the way. I wasn't a warrior or a soldier. I had read my fair share of literature, histories, and battle strategies, but even that fled my mind as the troops sharpened weapons and helped each other don their armor. They moved fluidly and in sync, despite the frantic energy, like a hive of bees, except for me. I was the invader who disrupted the lines of communication and flow.

I finally fled to the front of the ship, hiding just inside the railing on the prow. I watched as the bow cut through the waves like a sword. Up ahead, the early morning sun was still caught in the mist over the ocean. The whole boat swerved to the side violently, and I was flung against the railing. After I recovered, I saw a huge rock island in the mist where our boat had been headed. Avlyn wouldn't have been able to see it, but now I understood that sight wasn't the only thing they used to guide them on the sea.

After hours curled up, my legs grew stiff, and I was drenched from the mist and sea spray. The cold clung to me, and I needed to move or risk freezing to the front of the ship. I hobbled through the throngs of soldiers, and they moved around me like the water at the front of the boat. I made it to the stairs that led to the deck, where Avlyn gripped the massive steering wheel.

I looked up, and our eyes locked before I could avert my gaze. Half of me wished they would ignore me, and the other half longed for them to come down. I wasn't sure which was winning that fight. A moment later, I heard them shout, and their boots clattered down the stairs. My stomach did a little flip, and the creature in my gut seemed to give a satisfied and smug purr.

"Are you alright, my lady?" The commander leaned down to look deeply into my face, and I could feel the blush rising. My creature purred louder.

"I'm fine, just got a bit chilled." They nodded and reached out for my shoulder before pulling back abruptly.

"No wonder! You're soaking wet. Here." They pulled a small cloth out of their belt. They gently pushed the long bangs that clung to my cheeks behind my ear. They gathered my hair and wrung out the mass with the cloth before draping it over my shoulders and gently wiping my face with a corner.

They gave a soft smile. "I know inside the hull is rank from all the bodies, but it will be warmer and drier."

Their hand lingered on my face as we talked. It was so warm, so inviting, and that creature in my stomach seemed to have taken over my mind.

"I'd rather just have someone to help keep me warm. I do recall you were quite good at it." I gave Avlyn my own soft smile.

I felt their hand twitch, and a moment of insecurity passed

over their face before that smile returned, no longer warm but hot.

"I live to serve my lady. Anytime you need a warm body, I am always available."

"You didn't seem interested before." That smile faded again, and the creature inside me hissed, *Stop pushing them away!* But how could I? When they looked at me like I might be worth something...

I went to move, but Avlyn's fingers gripped my cheek tighter, not letting me. "That was before I saw you... before I saw you attack a Nykur that had frozen an orc stiff."

"Well, Raula wasn't really frozen; she was actually caught in the Nykur's enchantment. It's an old magic that calls on a victim's greatest desire, similar to the nauthiz glyph used by fae magus. It makes what a person desires most appear right in front of them." There was that look again. Avlyn's eyes wouldn't let me go, and I wanted to sink right into them.

"I love it when you get all academic. It makes me almost wish I hadn't skipped my history lessons."

"Maybe you just needed a better teacher?"

"Nah... I had good teachers. I just didn't want to sit and listen to them. It's not the same with you. I could listen to you all day." Their hand flexed the smallest amount, and the ship under us swayed. Our faces were getting closer, just a little bit more...

"Commander!" A voice from the upper deck broke the spell. I saw Avlyn grit their teeth and turn to the soldier. "Land in sight, and it's not looking good."

Avlyn gave me one more long glance before bolting up the stairs. I heard them curse under their breath, and I ran back to the railing of the ship.

The dark beach of Xyr was in sight, but smoke rose over the city above. We were too far to see anything else, but I swore the wind carried cries of anguish out to me. I gripped the railing until the wood cut into my palms.

We nearly reached the dock when I felt a firm hand on my shoulder again. "Nearly there, my lady. I'm going to hide you in the lighthouse until the fighting concludes." I had never seen Avlyn look so serious.

"And what if it should *conclude* in a loss for the Dragon Army?" I asked.

Their face grew even more stern. "There is a ladder down the back of the tower. If you see the enemy approach, take it and head into the countryside. There is a small settlement a two-day walk to the southeast. It's so small that it hasn't been mapped. It will probably be spared."

"Why can't I just stay on the boat?"

"They will burn them as soon as they reach the docks." It was said so matter-of-factly, with no emotion. A soldier's truth, a commander's truth.

"Take me with you," I requested.

Avlyn's face finally softened. "Pallas, this is war. I won't be able to watch over you. I need to lead. I need to fight."

"I don't expect you to babysit me. Just..." What did I expect? Of course, I couldn't go with them.

They squeezed my shoulder again. "This is the safest place I can put you."

"Won't you just promise me that you'll come back for me?"

"I don't make promises that I can't keep, my lady."

My heart squeezed in my chest in a way I hadn't felt in centuries. I wanted to scream. I wanted to grab them and not let go. It was so unlike me, and that was terrifying.

My thoughts were disrupted by the harsh sway of the boat as it hit the dock. Avlyn's face returned to that stone-cold warrior's mask.

"Stay at my side as we disembark."

As the troops lined themselves up in formation to storm the city, Avlyn led me up the three-story tower. On the upper level next to the light used to guide ships sat a small tele scope attached to the railing. Avlyn swiveled it towards the city.

"Keep an eye out for any approaching enemy soldiers. If they approach, don't wait. Flee to the countryside. Do you understand?"

"Yes," I agreed, but the commander heard the lie.

"Do not wait for me, Pallas. It's too dangerous. Promise me that you won't."

"Avlyn..."

"Promise me." Their gaze was unyielding. but so was mine.

"I will, if you promise me that you will fight with everything you have to get back to me."

"Of course I will, Pallas. I—"

I grabbed their face and pulled them into a deep kiss. They gave a small yelp of surprise that was muffled by my lips before they surrendered, pulling me into a tight embrace. I could have stayed there forever, but instead, I only lingered one heartbeat more before pushing them away. Their mouth hung open in awe.

"Now go and retake your city."

Avlyn shook their head, regaining their senses, before smiling and turning to leave.

"Commander..." They turned their head back to me. "Don't die," I ordered with a smile.

Avlyn returned it and gave a dramatic bow. "I live to serve, my lady." With that, they took a step backward off the edge of the building. I scrambled over to the railing and saw them land gracefully on top of a canvas booth before bounding off down the street after their cohort.

Chapter 38

Pallas

I monitored the cohort's progress through the sea district through the small telescope. They moved mostly unmolested as they cleared houses and guided citizens toward the castle. I let out a sigh of relief. It seemed the Golden Army had not made it that far into the city.

I sat back down, hidden behind the stone railing of the tower's roof. I looked up at the massive mirror that lived on an equally large set of gears beneath it, allowing it to turn and shine across the bay, guiding ships to safety. At its heart was a brazier filled with long-spent coals that had once been its light source. It clearly hadn't been lit in some time. The darkness was another protection from foreign ships in the bay.

The noonday sun glinted off the top of the mirror through the hole in the wooden roof that allowed the smoke to vent. It wasn't really all that interesting, but I was becoming quite bored waiting at the top of this tower. I let out a small chuckle. Is this how the princesses in the stories felt, bored out of their minds, waiting for their prince to return?

Your prince, huh? The voice in my head sounded a great deal like Tori's, and I could just see her smug look as she said it.

Shut it, I retorted to no one, but a smile crept onto my face, nonetheless.

I had resorted to the ancient pastime of naming the clouds in the sky when a terrible sound broke my boredom. The cacophonous medley of dozens of armored soldiers marching towards the docks.

I pressed myself to the ground and slowly crawled towards a sheltered crack in the railing to peer over. Rows of soldiers clad in gold swarmed the docks and, just as Avlyn had said, headed straight for the boats. They carried torches and rolled barrels of what I assumed was pitch, their armor clanking like a tide of death.

Their movements faltered as their steps halted. They tugged at their feet, trying to move as the soldiers behind them almost trampled them. I looked at the ground, and in the glare of the noonday sun, I could see a silvery, near invisible web coating the dock's surface.

Then, a great roar sounded from the belly of the ships, and dozens of Dragon Army soldiers sprang forth from beneath tarps and below the decks. They swarmed the golden soldiers, and swords clashed with violent delight.

I ducked below my railing, trying to calm my errant heart. I couldn't block out the sounds of screams, of men dying. Which men, I didn't know. All I knew was that blood was being spilled, and it would never be able to be put back. I covered my ears and crouched down.

Coward, the voice inside me purred.

I'm no soldier. I was never meant for this.

So, you will just let them die, those who have fought to defend you when you least deserved it?

Shut up. I clawed at my chest like I could pull that voice right out of me, and she just purred harder. What was I supposed to do?

I crawled over to the far railing again to look through the scope without popping my head up. The cohort in the city was being overwhelmed. They'd been pushed back against the city wall with no way toward the castle. The Golden Army only had a slight advantage. They had the higher ground but not overwhelming numbers. I saw Avlyn lead another charge, gaining nothing. All they needed was something small, something to turn the tide. I had never been in a battle, but years of listening to Hadeon's men drone on and on about their victories told me that even the smallest action could change the course of a fight. I leaned back against the lighthouse lantern, looking up at the sky.

It was the clearest day I had seen in all my time in Xyr. It was like the sun had come out to fight as well. I hid under the shade of the small roof that covered the lantern.

What could I possibly do?

The voice inside me didn't answer. She was never there when I needed her. Tears welled in my eyes, and a different voice rose in my head instead. The voice of my mother.

Pallas, I raised you to be a woman with at least half a brain. Would you use it for once? She'd been scolding me for failing to properly translate the late scholar Eustemas' work on glyphic moderation of enchantments. She hadn't meant it as encouragement. But today, nearly five hundred years later, it sparked an idea.

I looked up at the great mirror behind the lantern in the lighthouse and then up at the sun above me. There was no way I could do this without being seen by the soldiers below. Hell, I didn't even know if I could do it at all. But I was done being a coward. The little voice inside me purred.

I wasn't strong like Avlyn or Tori, but I was still fae. I grabbed the wheel underneath the lantern and pushed it with all my strength. It barely budged. I let out an aggravated growl, throwing my shoulder against the wheel. It did nothing but send a deep, aching throb through me.

A dark shadow crawled over the edge of the tower. I threw myself down, looking for anything I could use to defend myself when it was on me. A friendly chittering sound came from Spinner as he ran his mandibles through my hair.

"Don't scare me like that!" He gave a small, dejected chirp before looking over at the mirror.

"Help me?" He chirped again and seemed to flex his legs before pressing his body into the other side of the wheel while I pushed from the front.

Slowly, the mirror turned, the ancient gears gave a terrible screech as we moved them. They gave way, and the mirror faced the city.

I heard a great crash at the bottom of the tower, and my body froze up.

"My lady, are you alright?" I dared glance down with Spinner. Lieutenant Kaleos and Raula were staring up at me. Shining golden armor littered the ground behind them with pools of red spreading beneath them. I decided to not look too closely.

"Yes. I'm alright, come up here and help me!"

They looked at each other, wary.

"My lady, we are to see you out of the city and join the others." *Godsdammit, Avlyn.*

"If you want to turn the tide of this fight, you will get up here and help me."

They looked at each other again, and then Raula yanked the door to the tower off its hinges before disappearing inside. I heard their feet pounding up the stairs. As they emerged from below, I bellowed, "Help me get the roof off this thing!"

"My lady, what ar—" Kaleos started, and I saw him shudder

as he looked at Spinner. The creature gave a menacing chitter, and the poor man went pale.

"Don't tease him, Spinner. I need their help." Could spiders pout? If so, he did.

They hesitated for one moment more before Kaleos drew his sword and swung it through the wooden column supporting the roof. It just happened to be the one furthest away from Spinner. Raula did the same. They knocked out all of them until Raula had to stop the whole thing from coming down on our heads and tossed it off the side of the tower with a loud crash.

I climbed up on top of the wheel, holding the mirror, and grabbed the top edge. The sun was directly overhead, which was about the best I could ask for. I yanked with all my strength, and it didn't budge.

"Help me!"

"We'll warp the mirror," Kaleos commented, dumbfounded. Raula's face lit up with a tusky grin.

"That's the idea, Lieutenant."

The mirror was made of metal, and slowly, ever so slowly, I felt it give under our strength, bending back so that the sun could fall directly on its surface.

"Stop!" I ran over to the scope. The Golden Army was pushing Avlyn back again. "Raula, move it right, no, the other right." She did as I ordered, and I saw the beam of sunlight cut across the buildings above the enemy.

"Shit, we need to go a little lower." I heard Kaleos groan as he shifted the mirror again, but the beam moved down, and the full power of the noon sun hit the soldiers' faces. I saw them stagger.

"We have to sweep it." There were more groans, but Kaleos and Raula moved the mirror back and forth. The golden soldiers would throw their hands up, trying to prevent themselves from being blinded, and then stagger when the light was moved away. It wasn't much, but it was enough.

I saw Avlyn lead the charge of soldiers forward and press their advantage. Soon, they had the golden soldiers on the defense, and more of them fell until they were overwhelmed.

A strong hand came down on my shoulder. "Pretty clever, *dijurk.*"

"What does that mean?"

She laughed, "A kind translation would be, 'one who is studious.'"

"And is it meant to be a kind translation?"

She smiled, exposing her tusks fully. It was mildly terrifying. "Today, it certainly is."

"We need to get you to safety, my lady," Kaleos said.

I ignored him, looking through the telescope again. "It looks like everyone is gathering in the castle and mist district. We need to head there."

"My lady, we were given specific orders to—"

I clicked my fingers and Spinner scrambled up behind him, giving an adorably ferocious hiss. The man blanched.

"Gods, I don't know why I even bother," he groaned.

Raula laughed and slapped his back. "Let's get going, Lieutenant."

Chapter 39

Abraxas

My fae heart pounded, and my lungs burned as Tori and I sprinted through the city's streets and alleys, Tori at my side. It was like we had fought together for centuries, our movements so in sync. Our subconsciouses connected through the bond, and we moved as one. No one could stand in our way. We cut down soldier after soldier, fighting our way through the city to the garden district.

It was so similar to how I had run with Avlyn through the streets five hundred years ago that I could almost laugh at the irony. This time, I had my mate at my side, and instead of being filled with despair and dread, hope clung to my heart.

Steel struck against steel. I cleaved my great sword through foe after foe as Tori split her blade into two parts and danced with a speed unmatched by any of my finest warriors. Emerald green dragonfire flowed between us, scorching obstacles or men outside our swords' reach.

We encountered small groups of soldiers that were separated from their cohorts and a few battered citizens. Whenever we found one of our people, we sent them off towards the mist district. Not many were still alive, and the flames of anger licked at my heart.

We rounded a corner to the main street running down the market district. A large home I knew well was surrounded by a dozen enemy soldiers trying to ram down the door. It was obvious civilians had barricaded themselves inside. No words needed to be spoken between Tori and me as we descended upon them.

Dragonfire, viridian and incendiary claimed half of them. Their screams rent the air, but Tori didn't hesitate to strike down one right after the other. I followed close behind. Soon, the entire host lay shattered at our feet. Tori's brow was drenched with sweat. She used the back of her hand to wipe her hair off her face, but it only managed to leave a streak of blood behind. I'd never seen anything more beautiful.

"It's getting harder to call the mana. I have used too much calling on your dragonfire. If we're not careful, there won't be enough if you have to shift again." I nodded at her. I hadn't used this much magic in centuries. She placed her hands on her knees, trying to catch her breath.

"Luckily, someone I know took down the Dragon King with her swords alone."

She looked up and gave me a flirtatious smile. "I heard his skills in swordsmanship have been exaggerated, anyway." She winked at me, and I snarled, ready to show her exactly what I could do. There was a crash behind the locked manor doors. The sound was like being drenched in cold water.

"This is your king. We must evacuate to the mist district. Come out now and we can escort you." Voices sounded behind the heavy front doors. I heard crashing from the level above, and a face looked down at me from a window.

"It's really him! Open the doors." The face disappeared. Groaning sounded from behind the entrance as the occupants moved whatever they had used to barricade the doors. The minutes seemed to drag on, and Tori kept spinning around, watching the streets for our enemy. Despite the distant sounds of fighting, the market district was now eerily silent. Dead.

Finally, the door opened, and Lord Nalux stood before us, sweeping into a deep bow. "Your Majesty, we thought..." He shook his head. "I gathered as many as I could when the army breached the walls, but I don't think we could have held much longer. Thank you."

I looked over his shoulder and saw dozens of people from all races gathered in his foyer. I clamped a hand on his shoulder. "You always were a good man, Nalux. It is I who must thank you."

"Of course, Your Majesty." Nalux gave me that beautiful smile I had always adored when I felt a tug down our bond. It was very small, but it felt like... jealousy. I looked over to Tori's pointedly neutral face.

Despite everything that was going on, I gave a small chuckle. "Now is not the time. We must make for the mist district. We will accompany you."

A small shape darted out from the crowd and wrapped around my legs. I faltered as Emilia buried her face into my filthy coat. "King A-a-abraxas, have you seen my pa?" The poor girl was sobbing so hard. I barely understood her.

I looked up at Tori, who was looking at the girl with tears in her eyes. We both looked over the wall near the outside of the city and saw smoke rising from the hills that would have been the farmsteads owned by Bronn. Emilia's five siblings gathered around me, the smallest clinging to Tori. Lord Nalux shook his head. "They came running in from the countryside when the fighting started... alone." Any humor I had found vanished.

Tori's voice shook. "I told Commander Talius to bring all the outlying citizens in days ago." Nalux shook his head again.

"Many did, but many did not wish to leave their homes, their livelihoods out undefended." Tears rolled down Tori's face, the guilt eating away at her.

"Save those tears for later, my love. For now, let us save who we can." She hardened her face and hoisted one of the small children on her hip. They wrapped their arms around her, burying their faces in her shoulders. She turned to Nalux.

"We move now."

"We have many injured," he said.

She didn't hesitate to push her way into the manor and started shouting orders. She set the children to the side and started pulling down tapestries and tearing apart furniture to build transportation.

She was beautiful and efficient, making groups and assigning leaders. If Lord Eltis had any objections to Tori tearing his house apart, he was smart enough not to voice them. I moved to join her when the tiny arms around my waist squeezed tighter.

I knelt down to look the girl in the eye. "Emilia, as I told the princess, there will be a time later for tears. All the tears you need. But for now, I need you to be brave. Your siblings need you to be brave."

Her breath caught in her throat. "I can't—"

"You can, Emilia. Your king is here to protect you." Her shoulders heaved a few more times as her small voice murmured, "She really is a princess, isn't she?" She looked at Tori, who waved frantically before ripping a bookshelf apart with her bare hands. "She's not what I thought a princess would be like."

"No, she certainly isn't."

Only a few minutes later, we were on the move. Our pace was glacial at best, with so many injured being dragged and the strides of so many tiny legs. Tori had one small child in each arm and a slightly larger one clinging to her back. We passed through the city, knocking on doors and pulling as many citizens along with us as we could until our entourage numbered over one hundred.

The sound of distant fighting echoed through the streets, the clash of swords on armor rang off the stone walls. Nothing was close, at least that I could sense. I could smell the fear dripping off the humans and fae alike, and the beast inside me reveled in it.

I shook my head, trying to clear the smell and taste of blood from my mouth. I needed to protect them. My father had failed, but I would not. I could not, with my mate by my side.

The streets were choked with dust, and it clung to her face. Clear tracks of sweat washed away the grime from her temples. She caught me staring and her eyes softened until the child on her back started to slip and she had to hoist him back up.

The street we traversed widened, and the buildings fell away as we neared the largest bridge to the mist district. The Vitmos River separated the southern city from the castle. Some of the older children dashed forward at the sight. They ran up the road and across the bridge until they were swept up in the crowd that waited just beyond the last open gate.

The sight of safety reinvigorated the crowd, and feet started shuffling faster. Tori and I were nearly knocked down, but the crowd continued to push, and the mass of bodies grew unruly as the mob took over.

Tori clutched her riders closer and started to run, trying to stay ahead of the wave of bodies. I followed by her side until a glint of gold caught the corner of my eye. I heard the release of a bow and drew my sword just in time to slash the black arrow in half before it pierced through my mate's skull. She stumbled, and shouts surrounded us. Golden-armored soldiers materialized from the shadows as if conjured by some dark spell. The sudden clang of steel rang out, a harsh counterpoint to the panicked cries around us.

"Run!" Tori screamed at the children, launching them down the road as she scrambled to pull her sword from its sheath. The surrounding mob descended into chaos as my citizens fled for the castle. I heard screams as the people on the edges fell under the swords of the nearest soldiers.

Tori released her sword into its two halves and charged towards the nearest assailant, striking him first on the back of his knee and then his neck.

I turned to do the same when the sky darkened as a volley of arrows rained down on us from the soldiers hidden on the nearby roofs. I threw up a curtain of fire over the entire street and watched as the arrows disintegrated into ash. There were too many for the power I had in my fae form, and I couldn't destroy them all. Horrible squelches and screams surrounded me as a few hit their marks, bursting through chests and limbs. Tori grabbed a nearby man and ducked with him under an awning just in time.

I fought my way over to her, my sword drenched in blood. Centuries of rage flowed through me as I cut down one man after another, and nothing stood in my way until she was at my side again.

She did the same, her blades singing as they met those of her adversaries. Tori's movements were precise, each strike parrying with grace before countering with lethal efficiency. Soon, we were back-to-back.

Down the street to the south, more soldiers approached, their armor clanked menacingly as they advanced with swords and spears at the ready.

Tori and I locked eyes, and no words were needed. She placed her hand over my heart, but then her face grew tight. "Abraxas, wait,,,"

There was no time to hesitate. I pulled the mana of the earth through her, but it was not the power flow I expected. The power stuttered, and the transformation was sluggish, the energy scarce. It pulled the last of my remaining magic to shift. Scales replaced skin, and my bones reformed and expanded into the massive frame of a dragon. My roar echoed off the buildings, a sound of both triumph and desperation.

In this form, I could channel the mana, and I saw why Tori had hesitated. I felt a disturbing void. The earth beneath my feet, once a vibrant source of my power, now seemed drained, as if the magic had been leached from the soil.

There is barely any mana left. How did this happen?
Fight now. Discuss later.

Tori nodded and spun, her swords clashing with those of a man nearly twice her size.

What had been chaos in the streets before was now pure panic. The sight of a dragon in the midst of the city sowed chaos among Hadeon's soldiers. Some fled, while others regrouped and attacked with renewed vigor.

A roar amplified in my chest and a fiery bout of flame erupted from my jaws, sweeping across the advancing troops. The air blistered with heat; the screams of our enemies briefly overpowered the din of battle.

More continued to come, and I needed to conserve what

little mana was left, especially if I wanted to be able to change back. Luckily, I still had my fangs.

I crashed through the approaching cohort, knocking bodies to the ground and trampling them as they tried to strike me. Most of their blows bounced off, but every now and then, pain would lance through my legs as a blade found its mark and a scale was pried loose. But each soon met his death as my jaws clamped around them and ripped them to shreds. The taste of blood was leaching into my very soul, and I could feel the madness of violence rising. I had to be careful. I spun quickly, making men fly and buildings crumble as my tail smashed everything in its path.

"Abraxas!" Tori called. She had gotten most of the citizens who were still alive to the bridge, but another barrage of arrows had been sent skyward toward where they ran unprotected.

To me.

She ran to me without hesitation. I flapped my wings once, and the wind threw the nearest soldiers back as she launched herself off a nearby toppled market stand and onto my back. She clung to me as I beat my wings again and we took off into the sky.

Together.

In this form, I could channel mana, just like her. We both drew from the limited pool that was left. I called it into my heart, and she wrapped it around herself as she pulled dragon-fire from me. My wings beat as we rose into the air after the volley of arrows. Together, we shot fire over the bridge and incinerated all of them before they could fall. Together, we were enough, and not a single arrow escaped. I watched as the last of the civilians ran through the mist district gate.

Our foes were prepared, and I was now a much larger target. A volley of dark-tipped arrows arced through the sky again, and we had no mana left to give. They flew true, striking my vulnerable wings. The pain was wicked, and I lost control, crashing against a nearby building, which crumbled under my weight.

Tori, are you alright?

She had already thrown herself off me and darted forward, slashing at a soldier who aimed a spear at my bowed head. Her blade met his with a shower of sparks, and with a quick twist, she disarmed him, driving her sword through his armor.

More were coming. The archers from the ruined building were pushing out of the rubble, and like this, I was too big of a target. I pushed myself up, my wings dragging as crimson blood soaked the streets and ruined buildings around me.

We can't stay here, Abraxas.

Another set of arrows flew and ripped through my wings. I let out another bellow that shook the stones in the street. My long tongue snaked out and wrapped around Tori's waist. She gave a surprised yelp but didn't fight as I barreled forward, knocking down another building as I made my way towards the bridge. I had cleared it halfway when another set of arrows flew, but I would not let the pain slow me.

As I crested the center of the bridge, shouts met me from the gate. I saw Avlyn and Jun waving frantically at us. I leaped; my ruined wings were barely able to help me glide the remaining distance as more arrows rained down. The gate wasn't large enough for me, and I needed to change forms to prevent taking the entire thing down with me.

Luckily, changing back into my fae form took significantly less power than the other way, and I pulled the last of what the earth had to give, letting myself shrink. I pulled my wings in around Tori and I as we flew through the gate. We landed with a smack on the stones just inside the threshold. My horns and wings disappeared as I dripped blood all over my mate.

"Abraxas!" Her warm hands were on my face as she rolled

me over. I could feel the wounds on my arms and legs struggling to heal, the wounds that had once been on my wings.

I looked up into her eyes and she was covered in blood, but it was mine.

"Looks like we'll live just a little bit longer."

Chapter 40

Tori

My cohort stood around me. Kaleos was on my left, and Raula and Noki had my back. We looked down from the top of the gate above the closed portcullis. Abraxas' wounds were still unhealed, his blood soaking the hastily placed wraps on his arms and legs. If the pain bothered him, he didn't let it show. His face was locked down with determination. I tried to mimic his resolve.

My legs shook, and my arm throbbed. I placed the two halves of my sword back into one. I wasn't as strong of a fighter, but I knew my left arm would give out if I kept dual wielding the blades.

I shook my left arm violently, willing it to obey my commands, but I couldn't overcome the fatigue with will alone. Jun stood to my left, and I saw his eyes dart to the limb at the movement. His usual calm demeanor was replaced by an intensity that made my skin prickle. "They're nearly here," I whispered, more to myself than to anyone else.

The sun dipped below the horizon, painting the sky in shades of bruised purple and deep blues. The distant clash of metal sounded like the relentless drumming of fate, an ominous beat that heralded the opponent we had yet to best. Beside me, Abraxas stood like a statue, his jaw set, his hand resting on the hilt of his sword. His eyes were fixed on the advancing Golden Army, their armor reflecting the last dying light of the day like a river of molten gold—an ironically beautiful sight.

They hadn't attempted to cross the bridge yet, taking the time to regroup before making the assault on the gates. "We will hold them off," Abraxas replied without looking at me, his voice a low rumble.

"For how long, Your Majesty?" Avlyn spoke behind us.

"Until none are left standing or until I no longer draw breath," he replied. My chest tightened. I tried to draw power from the earth, but it had nothing to give. It certainly wasn't enough for Abraxas to transform. It would be my sword I would need to rely on.

The sound of armored footsteps sprung to life, and that great golden mass moved towards us. I heard hundreds of bow strings pull back from the parapet above.

"Loose!" a lieutenant on the wall called, and now our arrows were the ones to blot out the sun. The Golden Army raised enormous shields overhead; our arrows bounced off the gleaming metal harmlessly. This is what they must have been waiting for.

I heard Abraxas' grip on his sword tighten. I kept my sword at the ready but reached down our bond and gave a gentle squeeze. His eyes softened, and he returned it. On my left, Jun shifted.

"Jun, perhaps you should go back and join Pallas. It's not safe up—"

"You are out of magic, aren't you? You and Abraxas both."

My eyebrows shot up. I nodded.

"I'm not."

"Jun, it's too dangerous. Please, stay with Pallas, keep her safe."

He looked at me, and his face was unreadable, but he turned around and headed away from the front lines. I let out a long sigh of relief.

The Golden Army had passed the midway point of the bridge, descending on us. Their shields continued to block any arrows that flew at them, and down the center of their ranks, they carried an enormous battering ram. Our portcullis was reinforced with iron, but it wouldn't last long against this. Their numbers had dwindled. If they broke through, we would likely be able to drive them back eventually, but at what cost? How many innocent lives would be lost before that happened?

I felt another tug at my heart, and I looked at Abraxas again.

"Until the world breaks, my love," I vowed. He gave me the smallest of grins.

"Together."

Archers from the back of the golden ranks let loose their arrows. We ducked behind the parapets. It was mostly a distraction, but one that could turn deadly quick. I ducked down behind the stone wall when my brother came up beside me again.

"Jun, get down!" I tried to grab him, but he moved out of my reach with methodical purpose. He stepped up onto the outer wall and I looked on with horror.

"Stop." It wasn't even loud, but his power resounded through the air as every arrow froze in place. I held my breath as they slowly clattered down. The army did not stop; the footfalls resonated through the arches of the bridge.

"Jun, what are you doing?"

He looked down at me with shadowed eyes. "Trust me, Tori," he said with a strange command that held no magic but had me entranced, nonetheless. His eyes closed, and the gate below us shook as the ram made its first strike against the gate. His eyes flashed open, glowing a bright white and his voice carried an ancient power. It resonated around us, vibrating through the very air. "**BREAK.**"

Jun's words, strange and melodious, seemed to seep into the stone of the bridge itself. Cracks webbed across its surface, spreading like wildfire, and the entire structure shuddered under the weight of the charging soldiers.

The bridge gave way with a roar that drowned out the cries of the Golden Army. Stone, metal, and men fell into the river below, a horrifying descent that ended in silence far beneath us. Many were crushed beneath the falling debris; many others were dragged under the water by the weight of their armor. A few souls managed to float or find dry refuge when tendrils of water rose up behind them, forcing its way into their mouths and lungs and pulling them under the surface. I turned to see Avlyn sweating with exertion.

As the dust settled, those members of the Golden Army who hadn't fallen with the bridge stood frozen in shock on the opposite side of the now impassable chasm. Jun coughed and I heard him whisper, "Run." It floated across the freshly rendered ravine on the wind, and the few souls who remained fled the city.

I was so stunned I nearly missed Jun's eyes rolling into the back of his head as he swayed dangerously. Luckily, Abraxas grabbed him, cradling his body gently in his arms. I pushed back the hair from his face, which had lost all color.

"Jun!"

He gave a soft grin, and I heard Abraxas chuckle, "You did well."

Chapter 41

Hadeon

482 years ago

The little creature wailed in its mother's arms as she lay in bed. The king's whore, whoever she was, fretted over him, cooing and rubbing her nose on his cheek. All I could do was watch in disgust. This tiny, pathetic thing was nothing. But my father looked on with something in his eyes that I had never seen. In that tiny thing, he saw his own flesh, his own blood, his own soul.

"You see, Hadeon, we've done it. We have the Dragon's heart, and now no one can stand against us. This world will be ours for us and your family. Nothing is in your way." He waved to the beasts on the bed. He looked at me, and I finally saw it. It was greed. I was just a youngling again, chained up. And he was dead, that Dragon was dead. I held his heart, but still he laughed at me.

I felt my power surging inside my body, and I couldn't control it. I didn't want to. They were all small; they were all weak. I was the Great Hero, the one who was prophesized, and they were nothing. "You're right, father. Nothing is in my way." I released, lightning flew from every point on my body, and enveloped the room. My father was immediately incinerated. A look of shock was the last thing that was etched on his face as it burned away in ribbons. I didn't even look at the woman and babe. I only heard a faint shriek and smelled the burning of flesh. I let everything release until the walls shook and nothing existed but the crackle of my power.

It faded, and I was left in the scorched room. I stepped over my father's destroyed body without a second look. They would come for me, and I would kill them all.

They must have been close because I hadn't even left the room before the door flung open and Plagis flew in with a trio of guards. I raised my power again to cut through them.

But Plagis spoke first. "Oh, what a great tragedy, Your Majesty." I paused. I was not the king.

The advisor held my gaze. "What a great tragedy to have befallen the Great Hero. His own family, murdered by rebels from the Pearl Kingdom, in their own home."

I quelled my power. Even an imbecile would have known this was my doing, but Plagis was no fool.

"Your Majesty, we must make haste. The people will want to see that their future emperor can take swift action against such an offense." He led me down the hall and motioned for the guards to close the door. Yes, Plagis was no fool.

"I'll make sure that is taken care of, Your Eminence. You won't have to think on it again. But I have heard that the new Dragon King has arrived in the city, ready to swear fealty. What a powerful tool to have against those Pearl Kingdom rebels, yes?"

PRESENT DAY

Plagis had been wise to send a slave with his note of the defeat in Xyr. I stepped over his charred body as I rushed to a lower wing of the palace. My magic struck out as I walked, cutting swaths through priceless tapestries and ornaments.

The halls quickly emptied of any souls who valued their lives as I headed toward my goal.

I reached the healer's wing and flung open the door to the main recovery area. Two healers fussed over Luxos until they heard my approach and scattered like cockroaches. What little color was left in Luxos fled him as I stood over his bed. His entire torso and the side of his face were heavily bandaged, and I could smell the putrid liquids leaking from his wounds.

"You have one chance to explain this failure, Commander."

Luxos gritted his teeth as he tried to sit up but ultimately failed. "The bitch had magic." Now, that was interesting. "The healers said it was dragonfire."

The scar across my own chest seemed to heat at that. "That's not possible."

"I can assure you, Your Eminence, that it very much is," Luxos groaned as he tried to move again. I saw a yellowish-orange stain blossom on one of his bandages. "She called herself his mate." Yes, Abraxas had said the same.

"Then you have failed me on numerous counts, Luxos." He froze, no longer moaning and adjusting to his wounds. I felt his shadows lingering just out of sight, but I knew he wasn't foolish enough to use them. He had learned better long ago.

I leaned over and gripped his jaw, and he hissed as I touched the burn on his face. His shadows rose but did not strike.

"You failed to discover the princess' powers. You have failed to bring me the dragon's heart or, at the very least, vanquish him. You have failed to win me his city, and now..." I let my magic lace over his open wounds until his shadows squirmed and I could hear them squeal. "...you have failed to bring me the greatest treasure I could imagine. The mate of the last dragon, a fragile and weak little girl." I sent lightning through him. He wouldn't scream, but his shadows flailed, revealing his agony.

"Tell me why I shouldn't kill you now."

"I can still get-t them for you." He could barely talk through his clenched teeth.

"And how will you do that after so many failures?"

"The same as before. Take those they care about. They'll come right to you."

I let my magic recede and released Luxos. He lay panting and sweating on the bed. His bandages were now coated in blood. I stood. "This is your last chance, Commander. Do not fail me again."

Chapter 42

Tori

"I want his head on a spike. I want his blood in the streets. I want—"

Abraxas wrapped his arms around me from behind, holding me tight. "I know, my love. But remember what happened last time we rushed things? We need a plan."

I grumbled, but he was right. It didn't settle the twitching of my fingers. How they longed to wrap themselves around Hadeon's neck.

I looked out over the throne room and the entrance hall. We brought as many of the wounded in as we could. All the palace healers dashed between the makeshift cots we managed to erect, but many of the wounded simply lay on the ground with nothing but a thin cloth between them and the stone. More and more people were being carried in by our soldiers by the minute. Our people lay broken and scattered around me, and I could feel dragonfire licking at my heart and fingertips.

"Easy, little bird." Abraxas slipped his hand into mine and pulled the flames away before snuffing them out. "Our vengeance will be swift. But as you told me, for now, we must focus on those in need." He placed his hand on my back, and I took a deep breath, calming myself. I let the flames inside me sink into that deep cerulean ocean.

"We're running out of space in here, Abraxas." Avlyn jogged up to us with Oryx following close behind.

"Have we triaged the most heavily wounded inside?" he asked.

Oryx shook his head. "We have done our best, but too many keep coming from the city."

Abraxas frowned. "Commander, have the eastern cohort break down the market stalls. See if we can get more cover in the courtyard. Oryx, keep a tight rotation going, but make sure none of your healers are getting overworked. It wouldn't do to have more in need of care." The healer nodded and turned to follow Avlyn before seeming to remember something. He spun back around and pressed an object into my hand.

"For your brother." He gave me a quick smile before running back out the main doors. I looked down, and for a moment, my heart stopped as the milky liquid shimmered within the glass vial. But the liquid was a soft gold, not that translucent white I knew. I clenched my fingers around it. I wasn't sure what it was, but I trusted Oryx.

"Go find him, I'll manage this for now," Abraxas said. I nodded and gave him a swift kiss on the cheek before running out into the courtyard.

I found Jun quickly in the crowd. He was ladling water out of a bucket to the gathered refugees. As I approached, he looked up. "To... ri..." he said; my name was a barely discernible wheeze. He turned his head and coughed. He sounded like he had been screaming for days.

"Jun, maybe you should sit down." He shook his head and tapped his throat, indicating he couldn't speak anymore.

"Oryx gave this to me. Do you know what it is?" I held up

the golden vial, and his smile grew wider. He snatched the potion from my hand, uncorking it and downing it before I could take a breath. He let out a relieved sigh.

"Well, I guess you knew what it was."

"For my throat." His voice was still hoarse, but he spoke without coughing. "Pallas helped him develop it."

"I'm sure she did. And where is our humble inventor of war instruments?" Raula had already told me all about the light-house. Jun shrugged his shoulders.

I helped my brother ladle the water. When there was a small break in the line, I turned to him. "What you did on the bridge was very impressive." He turned towards me, about to speak, but I cut him off. "But it was reckless. You could have died! You are still learning how to control your powers."

His mouth snapped shut, and his face froze. More refugees came by, and Jun busied himself with helping them. But after the fifth cup had been filled, he muttered, "Hypocritical of you to call me reckless."

"I know what can happen in battle. I've had them happen to me. I can't have that happening to you."

"I saved you all." Jun's face was... angry. It was an emotion so foreign on him I didn't know what to do.

"Jun, I—"

A cheerful laugh pulled our attention back to the line of awaiting patrons.

"I can't believe they have the Hero of the Bridge out here slinging water," Kaleos called loudly.

"I just wanted to be helpful." Jun asserted, not meeting his gaze.

"Well, you certainly were. I don't know where we would be if those fuckers had gotten through the gate. I'd say you were much more than helpful. Between you and your sister, I've racked up quite the life debt to the royals of Niata." Kaleos gave my brother that broad, flirtatious smile, but he didn't see the twinge of fear that rose up in Jun's eyes. I saw him raise his hand to slap Jun on the back, as he always did to me. I dove in between them, knocking Kaleos' arm aside.

"Oh... I... uh..." The soldier's smile vanished, and Jun simply looked away, but the silence stretched to the point of pain between us all.

"Well, thank you again, Your Highness. Once this is all over, we will properly celebrate your victory." Kaleos gave a formal bow and ran away.

"Victory, huh?" Jun said, to no one.

I sighed and slid my pinky into Jun's. "Kaleos means well."

"You all do." That was all he said.

Chapter 43

Pallas

After Kaleos, Raula, and I rejoined the main forces in the mist district, an executively minded noblewoman directed me to the castle to help with the wounded already there. Jun had assured me that he would follow. He had not.

I mulled over what I had heard happened at the bridge while I gently bandaged the arm of a soldier who had just received stitches from a healer. I tried to focus on it, but the work was too simple to draw my thoughts away from Jun and, surprisingly, more so, Avlyn.

As if my thoughts had summoned them, I heard their voice echoing off the stone walls of the castle entrance hall.

I turned my head to see the commander striding towards me. My stomach did a near-painful flip, and I tried to busy myself with the wrapping in front of me even more. They came up to my side and placed a hand on my shoulder. I slowly turned to see them beaming at me.

"Who knew we were hiding such a military force in the guest wing of the castle? I heard all about what you did on the tower. Perhaps I should have you working with our weapons development scholars?" They gave me their broad smile.

"I've done enough harm in this world. I don't need to make the tools to do more."

Avlyn's cheerful grin faltered. "Pallas, I was just—"

Jun and Tori came sweeping into the room, and I let out a sigh of relief. I was sure the princess would easily dominate the conversation, so I didn't have to face Avlyn after what had transpired on the tower. To my surprise, they wouldn't look at each other, and each turned to a different side of the room, engaging with a different healer. My palms started sweating again as the commander still looked at me expectantly.

The soldiers around me all straightened up, Avlyn included. They sprang to attention, and I wasn't surprised to see Abraxas sweeping into the room. I was surprised to see him heading straight towards me. My stomach clenched tight as he nodded his head in a polite acknowledgment before he said, "My lady, there is much we need to discuss."

450 YEARS AGO

"Your Eminence, your gown tonight is absolutely stunning." The courtiers around me had flitted about like birds, twittering and vying for my attention. They had still held me in respect then and considered me Hadeon's fiancé, not just his consort. I was the future empress, and they all wanted my favor.

I only had eyes for him. He shone like the sun, his long mahogany hair was styled to perfection, and his violet and gold jacket only made his eyes all the more beautiful. He held my arm in his and smiled at me. "She is absolutely gorgeous, is she not? The Golden Kingdom's greatest treasure. Now, you will all have to excuse me as I steal her away from you for a dance."

He pulled me away from the crowd and into the center of the palace's ballroom. The band immediately struck up a lively tune just for us, and he swept me away. I had taught him these dances, and he faltered, but I was good at covering it up. After his third misstep, his face grew sour, and my stomach clenched. I could feel his mood shift.

"I told you to wear the turquoise gown tonight, Pallas. Are you trying to embarrass me?" I felt the hand on my lower back tighten.

"No, my love. I just thought this one would match tonight's theme better," I explained quietly.

His eyes narrowed. "I'm sure you did, but it's hideous. I never want to see it again."

"Of course, my love."

"And refer to me as 'Your Eminence.' For gods' sake, I swear your mind is slipping."

I did everything I could to hide the tears rising in my eyes. "Of course, my—Your Eminence."

He scoffed, "You've become so sensitive, Pallas." He swept me around the floor until a great knocking came from the main entry.

"Finally," he mumbled, dragging me over towards them. "Try to at least be partially presentable, won't you Pallas?" I steeled my face as the doors opened to reveal the dark group waiting on the other side.

King Abraxas had arrived, his traditional dark armor only adding to the air of hostility around him. He was surrounded by beautiful fae women and men, all clad in practically nothing at all, as was the Dragon Kingdom's style. They quickly scattered all over the ballroom, like ants taking over the carcass of a slain beast. All the courtiers seemed to shrink away in fear, except for the few who looked on with devious lust in their eyes. I'd come to learn which types of nobles enjoyed Abraxas' visits the best.

The king approached Hadeon in a way much more brazen than any other would dare. I looked to see how Hadeon would take this insult and was surprised to find the smallest smile gracing his lips.

"My loyal general. I am honored by your presence." Abraxas pulled off his dragon maw helmet and tossed it to the dark-skinned soldier next to him without a second thought.

"The matter in Oeth has been taken care of. You won't have any more trouble from them." Abraxas said the words as if he was talking about the weather, but I had overheard the reports. Blood had run in the streets with over a thousand dead.

I shivered. What type of man took life so casually? His silver hair shimmered in the late evening light of the ballroom, but when I looked at him, all I saw was darkness.

"I expected nothing less from you," Hadeon praised. Abraxas twitched the corner of his mouth at my lover, and I felt him stiffen beside me.

They continued to chat idly, but my attention was caught on one of Abraxas' courtiers nearby. Her dress was nothing more than a transparent black swath of fabric draped over one shoulder. Her peaked nipples were very clearly the center of attention of everyone around her, and she reveled in it. That attention wasn't enough.

She draped herself over Abraxas' shoulder. I couldn't avert my eyes as he ran his hand around her exposed waist, his fingers moving slowly as he leaned into her hair and whispered something in her ear that had her giggling and blushing. Did he have no shame? But as I watched his fingers dip under the edges of the woman's skirts, I felt heat rising in my cheeks and was very aware of how Hadeon was not touching me.

Abraxas locked eyes with me before I could look away, and

he gave me a very knowing smirk that only made me blush harder. He turned his attention back to Hadeon and the other courtiers.

"You know, King Abraxas..." Commander Dagius interjected. "...some would say that you used unnecessary force in Oeth."

"Some would not know what sort of sacrifices are needed to maintain peace." Abraxas didn't even look at the man as he spoke; instead he pressed his face into the crook of his courtier's neck, his lips dancing over her skin as she emitted a soft moan.

Dagius turned bright red. "I suppose it's my own fault for expecting honorable behavior from a man who committed patricide."

It happened faster than I could see. There was a flash, and Dagius' face went slack. Red bubbled up over his throat as his head slid off his shoulders. His wife screamed, and she was covered in a fountain of blood. Abraxas calmly re-sheathed his sword and turned away as if the conversation bored him, dragging the courtier with as she turned deathly pale. He released her and grabbed Hadeon to lead him away. I stumbled after them, my legs barely connected to my mind. "Golden Kingdom parties have always been such a bore." This man was a monster.

He slung his arm around Hadeon's shoulder and pulled him in close. Much too close. Hadeon's eyes twinkled, and a horrible realization struck me. He was looking at Abraxas in a way he had once only reserved for me.

Abraxas leaned close to Hadeon's ear, and in a voice so deep and soft I barely heard it, he whispered, "If you'd lend me a few of your staff to assist, I could show you a real party."

PRESENT DAY

I sat across from Abraxas in what I assumed was his study. He sat leaning back in his chair, his legs crossed as he toyed with a quill between his fingers. He looked every bit the Dragon King I had known for centuries. Was this the man Tori loved so dearly? It seemed impossible. I clenched my fingers on the edge of the chair beneath me.

"It occurs to me that in the five hundred years we have known each other, Pallas, we haven't had much of a chance to talk."

"There never was anything for us to talk about, Abraxas."

I saw him mull over my use of his name in his mind, but he continued, ignoring it. "Well, I would say that situation has changed, hasn't it?"

I didn't answer. His lips curled up into that dark smile that made me wonder if I would have my head at the end of this conversation.

"I heard about your little stunt with the Golden Army," he continued, his tone dripping with disdain. "But let's not pretend it was out of the goodness of your heart. We both know better than that."

"Do not presume to know me. You know absolutely nothing about me." I felt the chair under my hands crack as my nails dug into the wood.

His smirk only grew. "What game are you playing, Pallas?"

"I'm not playing any games, Abraxas."

"Do not pretend to be the simpering courtier with me. Others may see you as nothing more than a beautiful face, but I see you. Everything's a game to you, isn't it? You've always had a knack for finding the winning move."

"What the hell are you talking about?"

"Five hundred years I've seen you sit by the side of the most powerful man in Adimos. Five hundred years you have clung to him. And then the moment the world shifts, I find you here, now somehow heavily embedded in my court. Do you not find that interesting?"

My heart raced, and I felt my breath coming in increasingly shallow breaths. Me, cling to Hadeon? It was both entirely false and painfully true. Hadeon had claimed me, but I had never tried to let go. Not until now.

Abraxas stood, and I felt the room grow darker. He didn't shift forms, but he still seemed to take up more space, and all the air was sucked from the room. I couldn't breathe.

"So, tell me, why have you come here?"

I could barely get the words out, but I managed. "My reasons are my own, none of your business." The creature deep in my gut hissed.

"Oh, but that's where you're wrong; it very much is my business. Especially where my mate and her brother are concerned. Especially when you are the daughter of Runya Morvavare, who created the enchantment that holds my father's heart."

He walked slowly across the room, his hand rested on the back of my chair, pushing it back.

"I'm not afraid of you." It came out as a squeak, a pathetic attempt at boldness. *Weak. You've always been so weak for these men. Stand up!* But I couldn't. I couldn't move. I was always frozen.

His smirk was an arrogant one. "Oh, then maybe you are a fool. Would you like me to remind you who I am?"

My heart was beating so fast I thought it might give out. I

could feel sweat cling to my neck as green flames danced around him.

"**BACK!**"

Abraxas slid across the room, and my chair slammed onto the floor. He shook his head and grinned as Jun put his body between us. Jun's power had been growing ever since his collar had come off. By the gods, he'd just decimated the mist district bridge. Abraxas looked unbothered as if the command had been nothing more than a gentle spring breeze. He smiled.

"It seems you are in good spirits, Prince." I heard Jun growl, a sound I'd never heard from him before. The king's smile dropped, but it wasn't because of Jun.

"Abraxas!" Tori stormed into the room; her face full of menace. "What the hell are you doing?"

I didn't hear how he responded. I couldn't hear anything over the ringing in my ears. I couldn't breathe. I couldn't breathe.

"Pallas, you're alright." It was Jun, and he held my hands, kneeling in front of me.

"Take her to your room." Tori's voice was filled with rage, but it wasn't aimed at me. I felt Jun gently guide me, and all I did was focus on putting one foot in front of the other.

Chapter 44

Hadeon

179 years ago

I remembered the day I saw the man Abraxas truly was. The memory was very clear. He had bent the knee to me, but his loyalty had been untested. I may have been a new ruler then, but I was no fool. Words meant nothing without action behind them.

The settlement was small and already half dead from the war. Even in its withered state, I could still feel the cold sweat creeping up my neck as I looked upon the stone temple to the old dragon gods that lay at its center. Those walls held my blood and my greatest shame. They couldn't stand any longer. Why not deal with two problems at once?

I led my horse up to the edge of the rise that looked over the town with Abraxas close behind me. His black stallion pulled up alongside mine, and he pulled off his helmet, his long hair fluttering in the gentle fall breeze.

"This is why you have summoned me and a full cohort out to the middle of nowhere? Some defenseless town?" His face twisted in disgust, and he refused to meet my gaze.

"This town is home to traitors against my new empire. It must be dealt with."

Finally, Abraxas turned to me, and I could see the hatred burning in his eyes. How he despised me and how I reveled in seeing him bend, nonetheless. "What intelligence do you have on the traitors? Where are they located? We can engage without unnecessary casualties if—"

"Oh, no. You misunderstand me, General. This entire settlement is condemned. I want you to raze it to the ground."

I saw that hatred light into a burning flame in his eyes, and just as in the throne room, a part of me wished he would act on it. He wouldn't survive it, but what a glorious ending that would be.

"You can't truly mean—"

"Are you unwilling to fulfill my command, General Abraxas?"

His grip tightened on the sword at his hip, and I felt a great surge of power in my heart as I pulled on my own magic. It was different from the magic before Malech's death; it was rawer. But I'd master it, just like I would master the man before me. I watched as the loathing in him burned even brighter before it was snuffed out, and his hand fell.

"Of course not, Your Eminence." He lifted his hand and signaled to his army, and they took off down the hill.

He kicked his horse to ride to the front of the ranks when I called to him. "Remember, General, every single one." He didn't turn back or acknowledge me, but I knew he had heard.

I watched as the townsfolk who had been performing their daily duties stopped in their tracks. Their eyes widened in fear as that great dark army descended on them. Many fled back into their houses while a few men approached the oncoming horde and Abraxas. I couldn't hear what they said, but it was irrelevant. He lifted his great sword above his head and cut through theirs. Troops spread out into the village. Screams filled the air as cottage roofs were set ablaze in Abraxas' emerald flames. People who fled from the burning buildings were slaughtered. All the while, Abraxas moved through the scene without faltering, and I swore I saw his eyes were blazing with something much deeper than hatred.

He moved like no one I had ever seen. He may have only had a fraction of the magic he once wielded, but he was still a sight to behold. The flames of the town seemed to call to him, and he bent them to his will. His sword moved through body after body as if cutting through softened butter at a midsummer picnic. Absolutely nothing stood in his way as he called the flames to him and set them spiraling into the ancient temple. Stone melted in on itself, and the entire building collapsed with a thundering crash. He was a power unlike anything I had seen besides myself. My fingers tightened on the leather of my reigns thinking about it.

What it would feel like to press myself against someone who could stand against me, our naked power unleashed. What might it feel like to feel him succumb to me, to surrender? His power my equal but his soul mine to devour.

As the walls came down and the dust settled, that terrible and great dragon statue emerged from the haze. Abraxas stood before it, unmoving. I made to call out, to taunt him, but he summoned his pure emerald flames and shot them at the beast. The old gold exploded into nothing but dust.

Chapter 45

Tori

"What the hell were you thinking?" Abraxas was still across the room from me, where Jun had pushed him back. He approached in two long strides; his arm looped around my waist and pulled my body tight against him.

"I like it when you're angry like this," he said, and I swore I saw his forked tongue dart out between his teeth as he leaned in and surrounded me.

"Abraxas, this is serious."

"Oh, it certainly is going to be..." His lips pressed into the skin of my neck as his fangs left trails of harsh sensation behind them. I shoved him back, and his face lost that glimmer of amusement.

"Are you truly so concerned with my treatment of her?"

"Pallas is the most valuable piece we have against Hadeon. She knows him; she knows about the enchantment around your father's heart."

"I know that, little bird. Why do you think I brought her in here? Gods, I didn't even hurt her."

"You think intimidation would work? Abraxas, she's delicate. You need to be gentler with her."

"Is that what you wish? For me to be soft-hearted and gentle? I fear you will be sorely disappointed, my love."

"Do you think I fell in love with the Dragon King for his gentle demeanor? No, but I also have never known you to be cruel. And what you just did to Pallas, that was cruel."

"Then I'm afraid you don't know me well at all." He started to caress my face.

I slapped his hand away. "Don't give me that. I know you, Abraxas. I know your very soul. Pallas has been Hadeon's prisoner for centuries. You, of all people, would understand that."

The corner of his lip curved down as his face pulled on the cold mask I hated more than anything. "She didn't look like a prisoner to me. What do you really know of her, Tori?"

"I know enough. The scars are there if you know where to look. Every woman does."

Abraxas stiffened. "I never considered that she, too, wore a mask; that she fought for survival..."

"Obviously, you didn't. And now look what you've done! All the trust I have built with her, destroyed in an afternoon."

"And you think she is worthy of your trust?"

"If she hadn't been here, Avlyn would be a fish somewhere in the Sea of Spirits."

His face went slack. "What?" He shook his head, regaining his composure. "My love, you have always been more trusting than is advisable. Remember Ciara? Remember how it cost us nearly everything? Pallas has had centuries in Hadeon's court. Do you really think she doesn't work to fulfill her own goals?"

"I think she has been fighting to just survive. We were finally making progress."

"You give too much of yourself too easily, Princess. You are too trusting. If you're not careful, it will be your undoing."

"You didn't seem to mind when it was you I gave myself to."

"That's different. You are mine," he grumbled, his jaw clenching.

"Possessive reptile. I would think that you would see the same behavior in Pallas."

He furrowed his eyebrows at me.

"She loves Jun, that I know for certain. And that is enough for me." I would take no more arguments from him, but he pushed on anyway.

"Tori, that's..." He didn't finish his sentence.

"What, stupid? Say what you mean."

His face hardened. "Naïve."

"I've heard it before, hundreds of times, in fact. But this naïve princess and that brave woman are the reason your scaly ass is alive, so perhaps you should show some godsdamned respect."

His face twisted as if in pain. "Tori, no matter what else happens in this world, I will always respect you. You don't need to prove anything to me."

"Then trust me, Abraxas. Pallas... she is hurt, but I know she would do anything to protect Jun. Even if you cannot trust her, trust that."

"It would be foolish for Pallas to so easily turn to our side, but I know better than anyone that love turns us into the greatest fools on the planet." He gave a long sigh. "You also see a part of yourself in her, don't you?" He knew me well.

"Yes, I didn't always know how to fight back for myself. I had to learn that. She can, too."

Abraxas wrapped his arm around me gently and placed a kiss on my forehead. "I will trust your decision, my love." He sighed. "Do I need to go apologize to her?"

"That may do more harm than good right now. I've got to do all I can to repair this."

He nodded. "Yes, you're right, little bird. I will await your command." That grin slid back onto his face, and he released me. But I grabbed the collar of his jacket and pulled him close.

"But you *will* apologize to me, Your Majesty. On your knees."

His grin grew wicked. "Whatever you command, my goddess." He dropped down, burying his face in the folds of my dress. He inhaled deeply before running his hands up my legs and pulling down my panties. I lifted my dress as he traced one hand up the back of my thigh, his fingers setting off every nerve as he wrapped his hand around it and draped it over his shoulder.

"I'll make sure you feel how very, very sorry I am."

Chapter 46

Pallas

Jun settled me on our bed, the soft surface trying to envelop me. I wished it would swallow me whole. I'd always been so weak. I thought I had come so far and claimed something of myself back, but as soon as I met any resistance, I crumbled.

"Pallas, it's alright, I'm here." Jun gently held my hands.

"But you won't always be."

"What—"

"Do you remember when I was first teaching you about your magic? We were in the gardens, and you were singing so beautifully that a flock of birds came to join us, all singing in harmony with you. You smiled so brightly. Even though the night before..." I wouldn't say it. "But still you glowed, your soul beautiful and true. You smiled at me and laughed as the birds landed in my hair. Even though I was worthless."

Jun gave me a very concerned look like I was mad. "Pallas, you're not—"

"I knew then that you were precious. That I need to get you

out of that place. I knew it in the very depths of my heart. But still, I stood by and did nothing.

"You saved me. You helped Tori free me."

"No, don't you see? It was you who saved me."

He gave me a quizzical look but moved closer, laying his hand on my own. It was a gentle encouragement to go on.

"I'm weak. No, don't say anything. I know it's true. For five hundred years, I did nothing. I saw others suffer and did nothing. I saw myself suffer and did nothing. My own pain. It was never enough to make me strong, only enough to break me. But then I met you, and I knew... I knew what I had to do. I'm sorry it took me so long to help you. I could have prevented so much of your pain if I hadn't been such a coward."

Tears were streaming down my face again. Everything that happened to him, I could have stopped. I was pathetic, worthless, and weak.

A warm thumb rubbed across my cheeks, wiping the tears away. I looked up from my lap to see Jun's beautiful slate-colored eyes shimmering with his own tears.

"I love you, Pallas. And I forgive you." That broke something inside me. The walls of ice I'd kept up for centuries cracked and melted, flowing out of me as I sobbed and wheezed. Tears and snot pooled on the shoulder of Jun's fine robes as I pressed my face to him.

"It was me. I made that collar. It was my fault, all my fault."

He gave me that beautiful, soft smile. "Pallas, I knew you made it. Who else could have? I still love you."

"Don't, please don't. Please hate me. I can't stand it."

His hand stroked over my hair softly. "Never. I think you do that enough for the both of us. But you don't have to. It's time to forgive yourself."

I continued to sob into his shoulder. "Why?"

His grip on me tightened. "I saw you claw yourself out of his grasp. It was small at first. You would kiss me so he wouldn't. You moved your body in between mine and his. I saw how he hurt you for it. But I saw you grow bolder. We didn't really know each other then, Pallas, but you did that for me. Not all heroics are grand battles and gestures."

Jun's face grew hard. "I remember the night that I knew..." His hands shook, but he went on. "Hadeon had me performing for his court. Everyone was there, laughing, drinking, and carrying on as if nothing was wrong. As if I and dozens of others weren't enslaved right in front of them."

He paused, swallowing hard. "You stood near him, looking like you were part of it all. But your eyes... your eyes were on me the whole time. When he commanded another song, one that I hated, one that always drove me deeper into the darkness, I almost broke down." Jun's voice dropped to a whisper. "But then, I saw you step forward slightly. It was almost imperceptible to anyone who wasn't watching. But I was. I always was. You caught his arm and whispered something in his ear. I don't know what you said, but he laughed, that cold, hollow laugh. And then, he changed his mind. Just like that. He chose a different song."

"I remember, I told him that the guests would enjoy something livelier, something to lift their spirits. He didn't care about their spirits, of course, but he cared about his image, about appearing magnanimous and benevolent."

Jun nodded slowly, his eyes glistening. "It was a small thing, so you might say it was nothing. But to me, it was everything. You were protecting me, even at the cost of his wrath."

"I had to," I whispered, my voice breaking. "I couldn't stand seeing you in pain, being used like... like I was."

Jun cupped my face gently in his hands, his thumbs wiping

away the tears that spilled down my cheeks. "And that's when I knew, Pallas. Despite everything, in the midst of that darkness, you were my light. I don't hate you." His voice was steady and sincere. "I could never. You are one of the bravest people I know. But he knew it, too. That's why he collared me, you know. It was as much to control me as it was to control you."

"So, I failed you again. I couldn't even protect you. I only made it worse."

"None of this was your fault, Pallas. You were trapped just like I was."

"I love you, Jun." I hadn't said those words to anyone except Hadeon since I was a youngling; with him they had become twisted, a plea from me, and ownership from him. But when I said them to Jun, they felt true again.

He nuzzled his face against mine. "I love you too, Pallas." It was true love, but not like in the stories. I didn't want him. We had never been lovers by choice. I don't think he desired that with anyone. But that didn't make it any less valuable, any less strong.

We cuddled, foreheads pressed together until a soft knock came at the door.

"May I come in?" Tori sounded the most hesitant I had ever heard her.

"That depends. Are you here to convince me that Abraxas is a good man?"

She shook her head. "No, because I won't convince you of that. But I can promise you that will never happen again." I gave a huff but waved my hand, and she closed the door behind her.

"I'm sorry. You are my guest here, and what Abraxas did was inexcusable."

"Shouldn't he be apologizing to me, then?"

She nodded. "Yes, but I wasn't sure if you were ready for that." Maybe this princess *was* starting to understand me.

"Well, I am." I stood swiftly, surprising both her and Jun. "I'm done being a coward."

She looked at where my hand was still entwined with Jun's. A smile lit her face. "I'm happy to hear it."

Chapter 47

Pallas

I strode into the study, poignantly ignoring Abraxas. This wasn't about him. This was about Jun and by extension, Tori. I promised Jun I would be brave and wouldn't let him get hurt again. The only way I could do that was by destroying Hadeon. He would never be satisfied until he controlled Jun's power or killed him.

Avlyn had joined Abraxas and gave me a shy smile. I would be brave; I would.

"What sort of information do you need to fight Hadeon?" I asked the commander.

"Perhaps..." Abraxas said, the arrogant bastard unwilling to be ignored. "...it is time you share what you know about the enchantment on my father's heart?"

Jun and Tori each squeezed one of my hands. I looked across the room at the man I had considered an enemy for centuries. A man who had never actually hurt me, while I stood at the side of one who nearly broke me down into nothing but bones and ash. I couldn't look at Abraxas without seeing the rivers of blood he'd left behind for centuries. So, I didn't.

I locked eyes with Tori. Her deep slate-grey stare held me, and she was fierce. She was reckless and often quite an idiot, but she loved in a way I had forgotten how to. A way I realized I hoped I could again someday.

They were Jun's eyes as well. I looked at him, and he gave me the smallest smile. "You can do this, Pallas," he encouraged gently.

I felt Tori lean in and whisper in my ear, "Remember, you aren't his anymore." She was so quiet I was sure no one else had heard her. The creature inside me responded, rubbing up against my ribs and stretching out, no longer content to lay dormant.

"I'm going to need some paper."

ACROSS THE DESK, TORI HAD ROLLED OUT A LONG SCROLL of paper, and Avlyn handed me a quill. I began drawing a map of Adimos. After a few moments of silence, I heard Tori whistle.

"Wow, I can't believe you drew all this from memory." She ran her fingers over the coastline I had just completed.

"I've always been able to remember things. My mother called it an eidetic memory. Everything sits in my mind like drawings in great detail. It's what she said would make me a great enchantress."

"So, you remember everything..." Her face tightened, her lips pursing into a thin line.

"Yes, everything." A moment passed between us, and her hand twitched before she laid it on top of mine. She gave my fingers the smallest squeeze in understanding. My chest grew tight, and I continued drawing to distract myself from it.

"Indeed, this is impressive," Abraxas admitted, walking around the table. "But what does it have to do with my father's heart?"

Out of the corner of my eye, I saw Tori shoot him a warning look, and the way he yielded to it with a small smile almost made me laugh. Almost. I continued to draw.

"The enchantment around the heart is likely the most complex ever woven. My mother's magnum opus. It not only links the heart irrevocably to Hadeon but protects it." I tapped the map before me, tracing straight lines across the continent.

"The ancient fae knew the power of the earth, if incompletely. They built their cities on these concentrated lines of power. Ley lines. Your castle is built on one, Abraxas. Your magical protections are tied directly into it." I grabbed a well of blue ink and drew a line straight south from Xyr towards Koron.

"There are many of these lines." I drew another between Metlin and the bay between Vath and Oeth. Another crossed Ashenforge Peak, Koron, Manan, and Niata. "Some cross each other, and those are places of concentrated power. But there is nowhere where more of these lines meet than—"

"Koron." Jun uttered the word like a curse. I nodded." That is why the ancient Alderi fae moved the capital from Metlin to its current location in Koron. The palace was built with its keystone tied to the heart of all these ley lines. It makes the entire city nearly indestructible; that is how it has survived through countless ages."

"And the enchantment is tied directly to this power," Abraxas surmised.

I nodded. "Yes, you wouldn't be able to break it even with the strongest of counter enchantments. You would need to destroy the very castle itself to have any chance of undoing the enchantment, which is impossible. I don't know what you intended to do when you came a few weeks ago."

"We had the Diadem of Soraya or at least the most important part of it," Tori stated flatly.

I balked. "That was... what was in the necklace? That's how you freed Jun."

She nodded. "Would it have worked?"

"I am... not sure. But if the gem was as powerful as was rumored... The outer shell of the enchantment is the protection, tied to the castle. If a hole could have been created in that, then a skilled enchanter with strong magic could have undone the heart."

Her face turned grim. "And now it's lost somewhere inside Koron, likely in Hadeon's control." She etched grooves into the table with her nails, and the sound had my nerves on edge. Jun's hand came to rest on his throat, as it often did when he thought I wasn't looking.

I slid my pinky into his. "It still proved its value." I said. Jun gave a hard swallow and Tori gave me a small nod.

"So, what can be done?" Tori asked, her face tight.

I traced my fingers over the lines again. "I have a theory..." Everyone stared at me in silence, and I heard Hadeon's voice in my head, as I had so many times. *No one wants to hear your foolish notions, Pallas.*

I looked up into those four matching slate-grey eyes and saw nothing but encouragement.

"Along these ley lines are nodes. Concentrated points of power. Koron is built on one, but there are many. If these are destroyed, the flow of mana along the line is disrupted."

"If you could destroy the nodes around Koron, it will weaken the flow of mana to the palace, and then the enchantment could be undone."

"And you will be the one creating this counter-spell?" Abraxas inquired; his voice filled with doubt.

"Do you have anyone else who can craft such a thing?" His lips tightened.

Tori interrupted, "So which nodes shall we destroy? How many will be needed?"

"I believe three will be enough, and you have already destroyed one."

Her face twisted in confusion. But realization dawned on her as she followed one of the lines off the map into the Sea of Spirits. "The island?"

"Yes, the spring there was a place where the mana of the earth flowed to the surface. Now, no more."

"World Breaker, indeed." Abraxas gave Tori a long, affectionate glance before turning back to me. "But this is just a theory you have. No one has ever tested such a thing."

I drew one more line on the map. It connected that lone island with Xyr and Tenebrae Forest.

"The island was also connected here to Xyr. Tori, have you felt any difference in the mana below the city?"

Abraxas and her locked gazes. I watched them have an entire conversation with no words when Tori turned back to me. "Yes. During the battle... there was less power to draw on. Much less than when I had tried before our journey."

Jun gave a soft laugh. "I think that is as much proof as we can hope to get."

"What other effects will this have? On the earth?" Abraxas traced the lines on the map with his long fingers.

"Well, the prophecy speaks of the Breaking of the World. That doesn't sound reassuring."

"*Morka Tempeli*. For a new world to be born, the old must die. That is the way things have always been." Abraxas' face was blank.

"And your revenge on Hadeon is worth this, the end of all things?"

"I highly doubt the end of the world is fire and brimstone, as so many fear. It is not my intention to harm the innocent. Do you think humans care which ancient beings rule over them? No, they care where their next meal will come from and if their loved ones can live happy lives. Our struggles are more myth to them than reality."

"Until they are squashed under our armies when they get in the way." Jun's voice was harsh, but he spoke the truth.

"We will avoid casualties where we can, but it would be naïve to think none would suffer," Tori reasoned. "But would you avoid this suffering to preserve the world we live in now?" Jun didn't answer.

"At the island, no one was hurt by the destruction there, well, almost no one." A smile flicked at the corner of her mouth, and a small part of my heart twinged. "So, our best options would be nodes away from populated areas."

I nodded. "Yes, and it would be best to break nodes along the same ley line, one on either side of the city. Our best option would be to target the node rumored to lie outside the city of Manan in the River Kingdom. I believe you have an alliance with the queens there?"

Abraxas nodded. His face grew tight as he traced the line on the map in the opposite direction. His eyes widened in realization, and his face grew hard.

"No." It was a king's rejection with no room for argument.

"It is the best option. It lies within your own Kingdom and will have the greatest impact on—"

"I said no." The air in the room grew boiling hot, and Abraxas' eyes turned that horrible gold. His pupils turned to slits.

"Abraxas, calm down." Tori grabbed his shoulder, but he flinched away, breathing heavily. He held her gaze, and she did not back down. The moment stretched on before he pushed past her and out of the room without saying another word.

"Where is this node?" she asked. I pointed to the location on the map, at the edge of the Cold Mountains, southwest of Xyr. She frowned. "What's there?"

"The place where the dragons made their last stand."

Chapter 48

Abraxas

I retreated to the balcony that overlooked my city. I sat on the stone railing, my legs dangling over the side. I needed to calm down and looking down at everything always helped. My people went about their lives, reminding me there was peace and calm in this world.

The city was still a wreck after the last battle, but I could already see rebuilding efforts. Neighbors and friends came together, stacking bricks and building scaffolds to repair what had been torn down. Everywhere, soldiers in dark attire milled about. Some offered leadership, but others just assisted where needed. It calmed my heart.

I heard her footsteps before she hopped up on the railing beside me, her hand finding mine.

"Tell me about that place." Her voice was soft as she met my gaze.

"That place... Sacrignis Torr. It was the dragon's last stronghold in the War of Flames. A place for families where eggs were laid. King Obion brought his forces there and murdered them all. My aunts, my cousins, my entire people. Gone."

"How? How could he have taken on so many?"

I felt my claws extend from my fingertips, ripping into the stone beneath them. "Treachery. He came, claiming peace, wanting to negotiate a truce. So many dragons had already been killed, but still, we had not learned the wickedness of the fae. He was welcomed in. My father begged them not to, but they wouldn't listen. They thought that logic and the greater good would prevail. Those fools." I shook my head.

"I had always heard there was a great battle and the valor of King Obion. But there was no way he could have taken on a force of dragons like that. What happened?"

"I don't know. They ordered my father away, saying he was too volatile. By the time we heard of the betrayal, it was too late. Me and him were now the last dragons in existence."

Her face was grim. "That's why your father invited Hadeon into the city that day. Retribution."

"I believe he saw it that way. But the cost was too high."

"We will not repeat the mistakes of the past."

"I have lived long enough to know that is never true, little bird. I know I will sacrifice whoever stands in my way to destroy him."

"Abraxas." She held my cheek in her hand, stroking gently with her thumb, "I've seen you choose your people time and time again. Why do you doubt that now?"

"Yes, my people. During the War of Flames, the people of the dragon kingdom remained loyal. Even humans with lives so short, were willing to sacrifice themselves to save my people. It was the same in the River Kingdom to the south. This is why we have always remained allies. The rest of the continent, however, can burn for all I care."

"Abraxas, you said so yourself. The humans and small folk of this world don't care about war. They care about their own daily survival. You cannot blame them for the crimes of generations past." Her eyes hardened. "Let us focus on the destruction of our true enemy."

"Wise words from one so young. But what will happen to this world once Hadeon is gone, I wonder?"

She shrugged. "What always happens when the hydra loses a head? Another grows back in its place."

"You make it sound like killing Hadeon has no merit, my love."

"Oh, it has merit. It will feel damn good to squeeze the life out of him with my own hands. However, I won't pretend it will solve all that ails with this world." She let out a long sigh, then squeezed my hand. "I understand why going to the Torr will be painful for you, my king. But Pallas is right; there is no better place for us to go. It's protected, so we can figure out what needs to be done and how to destroy the node. Besides..." She looked out over the balcony to the west. "I've been dreaming of it."

I raised an eyebrow at her. "What sort of dreams?"

She shook her head. "All the mushrooms I have been taking muddled it, but I can feel it. It feels like..." She pointed to the barren land outside the city, the cursed place where my father had been slain.

"So, you do know it. The curse that the Torr will hold. You felt how it seemed to suck the life from you. It is worse for me. At the Torr, the curse is tenfold. No one can enter and survive."

She looked thoughtful, and then a mischievous smirk entered her eyes. "No fae can enter and survive." She leaned into me and planted a soft kiss on my cheek. "Leave this to me."

She moved to hop down when I snagged her around the waist, pulling her body against mine and pressing my tongue into her mouth. She surrendered immediately, running her fingers through my hair. I felt her grip down, trying to take control as she claimed my mouth with her own. I fought back, and she bit down on my lip hard. I hissed and pulled away.

301

She flashed me that wicked grin. "Not interested in playing a little rough?"

"Princess, it's time I reminded you who the god is here." I wrapped my arms around her waist tightly and shifted our weight over the edge of the balcony.

"Abraxas, what are y—" But her eyes widened, and she screamed as I pushed our weight over the edge, and we plummeted towards the city below.

For a moment longer, I held her in my arms, reveling in her panic as she clung to me, arms around my neck. Then I found that power through her that had been kept away from me for so long. In the space of two heart beats, I changed, my wings stretching out behind me, slowing our descent. She still clung to my neck, but now she rested between my wings, her warm skin pressed against the scales of my back. I stretched my neck and tail as I soared over the city.

Her breathing started to regulate. *Don't you ever fucking do that again!* She screamed at me while she still clung to me with all her strength.

I laughed. *You had it coming, little bird.*

Domineering reptile.

I could still feel her rage, but it slowly faded, and her grip relaxed. She held me with her thighs and released her hands, arms spread wide. The wind surrounded her, and I knew she felt the same joy that the sky brought me.

I've got something to show you, little bird.

Chapter 49

Tori

Ve flew over the city, and I could hear surprised screams from below. We soared over the cliff and the ocean. Goosebumps prickled my skin as the misty sea air clung to me. Abraxas spread his wings, and we took a great, sweeping turn back towards the cliffs. I was so distracted by the sky rushing past me that I didn't notice he flew straight towards the cliff.

Um, Abraxas...

Don't you trust me, Tori? Hold on tight.

I wrapped my arm around the back of his neck as best I could and clamped my legs down, feeling his massive muscles rolling underneath me as his wings beat. The cliff grew alarmingly closer, and then he tucked his wings in as we dove. I screamed and closed my eyes, and I could hear him chuckling, the asshole.

We dove for the cliff, and Abraxas darted behind an outcropping to reveal a perfect dragon-sized cave. It wouldn't have been visible without flying or taking a very dangerous climb down from the back of the castle.

He passed through the rocky opening, and dust tickled my

nose as we landed inside the cavern. Abraxas' ribcage expanded beneath my legs as he inhaled and let loose a spray of dragonfire. Torches along the walls were set ablaze, holding that bright green color for a few moments before settling into the soft orange of natural flames.

I slowly climbed off Abraxas' back, my mouth agape at what I saw before me. The cave was connected to the lower levels of the castle. The torchlight highlighted columns carved directly into the stone. We stood in a giant chamber with soaring ceilings, supported by high arches, holding up the weight of the castle above. I hardly noticed the grand architecture as the room was filled to the brim with gold in every form. Coins, bars, jewelry, plates, and glasses. Scattered throughout the glowing metal were precious gems, some as large as my hand. They were all thrown together in one great pile like... well, like the hoard of a dragon.

Abraxas stretched his wings, nearly filling the entire space before he dove into the pile like it was a warm spring and not a mountain of solid metal. The clatter of coins and jewels rushing every which way as he slithered through the mass was deafening until he finally settled himself. Only a few coins continued to scatter down the pile, unable to find their final resting place.

I hiked up the great mountain of wealth and sat next to his gold eye that just barely emerged from beneath the pile. It was so similar in color that it was almost hard to see. I shifted and pulled a particularly pointy topaz out from underneath my seat before settling back against him.

"You were right," I said. He huffed out of his nostrils in question. "If I had seen this before I knew you, I might not have cared about your personality."

Flaming-hot gusts of air flew from his nostrils as his belly shook with laughter. It destabilized the mountain of treasure, and I stood, trying to get my footing, before I was sucked under the surface, never to be seen again. He calmed himself and stretched his wings up. I covered my head with my arms as more coins came raining down. "It used to be nearly double what it is now. Imagine how you would have felt then."

"Double? What happened?"

His giant slit pupil rolled to stare directly at me. "Well, it's expensive keeping a kingdom fed and an army mobilized for centuries on end, Princess."

I crossed my arms. "I didn't know I was involved with a king who has such poor financial management of his kingdom." I was just teasing. I knew he kept his people happy and his soldiers well paid, and if that meant his personal horde had suffered, well, maybe I loved him all the more for it.

"Well then, you certainly aren't going to like that I haven't collected tithe from anyone but the nobles since I became king."

"What? Why didn't you tell me?"

"Princess." He let his long tongue snake out and wrap around my body, holding me as he shifted and the coins below my feet gave way. "I so enjoyed that delicious fantasy of yours, I didn't want to ruin it with reality." He set me down on the solid stone floor and changed back into his fae self, smirking. Before he could say anymore, I wrapped my arms around him and drew him into a deep kiss.

"So, why did you really want to bring me here?" I questioned, pushing my body into his, but to my surprise, he pulled away slightly.

"It is dragon tradition to present your horde to your mate after they have accepted your mark."

"Your mark?" I asked, but my hand shot up to the wound at my neck that still ached. It was healing slowly, just as it had the first time he had bitten me.

"Yes, this would have shown dragon society that we had

accepted each other. Shown the world that you are mine and mine alone."

"Possessive male."

"You have no idea, little bird."

"You already bit me before on the ship, remember?"

His lips flattened. "That was... reactionary. I couldn't let the mark of that other male stand, even if I knew it would not last."

That had been so long ago, during our journey to Xyr. I had hated him so completely then. A smile twisted my face, and I couldn't resist teasing him. "You truly have been smitten since you first laid eyes upon me, haven't you?"

He growled. "You have always been mine, even if I wasn't sure if I would rather take you or throw you off the side of that ship."

"Sounds awfully monogamous, coming from you, Dragon King," I baited, giving him a cheeky grin. To my surprise, his eyes welled with sadness. "Abraxas?"

"Dragons are monogamous creatures, my love. We know at a very young age who our soul is bonded to, or at least, we are supposed to. I never did. My parents never discussed it, perhaps hoping to spare me. But I knew it was wrong. Many whispered of it, a sign of the end to come for our people. As more of them died around me, I believed it as well. It did not leave me in a good place. And then I became trapped in my fae body, and fae are promiscuous creatures. I had to play the part. After so much time... it was no longer a mask I wore but an escape. I think you know it as well."

I nodded and ran my hand gently over his cheek and laced it through his long, silver hair.

"I would understand if you cannot forgive me for it," he confessed, crestfallen.

"Abraxas, how could I blame you for something like that? You didn't even know I existed."

"But after I did, I still continued..."

"My love, I accept you as you are. And I accept your mark. Thank you for bringing me down here." I smiled at him and ran my hand over his bite again. "I have much to learn about dragon society, don't I? Does this mean all your old scars are from other dragons as well?"

He averted his eyes, and I saw his fingers trace over the scar that ran around his ribs absent-mindedly.

"Abraxas... how did you get that scar on your ribs?"

Color rose into his cheeks. "I don't want to tell you."

"You said no more secrets, Abraxas!"

"It's not a secret, it's... embarrassing."

"Now you have to tell me."

He let out a long sigh. "As I said, when I was young, I assumed I had no mate. This put me in a... *unique* position amongst dragons. When the War of Flames began, dragons were killed, and many lost their mates to the cleanse."

"What does this have to do with your scar?"

"It's important you know the context, impatient one. Dragons are monogamous, but with the cleanse, things changed. Dragons were losing their mates, and I was a young male with no mate who was more than willing to... offer my assistance."

"Are you telling me this really was a sex injury?" I had been joking, but it seemed the joke was on me.

"One dragon, Levania, had just lost her mate in one of the first battles of the war. She was beyond distraught. I went out to comfort her. Don't look at me like that. I really was just trying to help. She was in pain. I did what I could, but she was beyond consolation. So, I did what she needed, and well... a raging dragon isn't gentle, as you know."

"It's a huge scar! She must have nearly killed you."

He let out a soft chuckle. "That she did. But that's in the past now, Tori. She and the others are long gone."

I could feel my face heating. "She's lucky she is." Dragonfire licked at my arms at the thought of *anyone* hurting him like that.

He gave me a sad smile and pulled the dragonfire away from me, toying with it in his hand and staring deeply into its depths, like he might be able to see the past if he looked hard enough.

"I'm sorry. I should not have—"

"It is alright. I actually quite like seeing you this jealous, my love. Fae like yourself are natural wanderers, so knowing you have some loyalty to me is comforting."

I gripped his face in both my hands. "You're mine, Abraxas. You're the only one for me, now and always."

Chapter 50

Abraxas

Tori and I spent the night with my treasure. I stayed in my fae form to hold her through the night, stroking her hair and just reveling in the feeling of her warmth against me. In the morning, she buried her face in my chest, her voice muffled with sleep as she grumbled about needing a mattress if this was to become a regular affair.

I carried her up to our room and made excellent use of the mattress there until late into the morning. As she dozed peacefully after, I traced my fae hands down the beautiful curve of her back, placing small kisses all along her spine.

I had a kingdom to run and couldn't linger with her all day, despite how much I wanted to. I drew the curtains tight to let her rest.

After weeks away, I sat through hours of briefings and updates. My mind continued to wander back to the beautiful woman sleeping in my bed, and maybe I wasn't the only one. Tori's presence dominated the war room even though she was peacefully sleeping elsewhere. My officers spoke of her with the utmost respect. I almost wondered if they had even missed me.

As I strode back to my room, a peculiar sight caught my attention. One of the castle balconies was littered with small songbirds. They hopped on their tiny feet, and sang harmoniously, a sight I had never seen before.

I peered out to see Prince Jun seated near the balcony's edge, even more birds crowded his shoulders and hair. They sang as if encouraging him to do the same, but his mouth stayed closed, and he gave them a sad smile.

I carefully stepped out into the open air, but the birds still rose in a flutter of wings as they fled from my presence. Jun stood.

"To what do I owe the honor, King Abraxas?" If he was surprised to see me, he didn't show it. I waved my hand to dismiss the formality.

"I apologize for scaring away your... friends. I didn't mean to intrude." My voice was so soft it even surprised me.

He offered a small smile, a hint of warmth in his eyes. "No apology necessary. They come and go as they please." I could see how so many had fallen in love with him. He was like the first blossom of spring, gentle and radiant. It would be easy to want to protect him, but I had learned my lesson with Tori. Sometimes, protection was nothing more than a cage; I could see how Jun had suffered for it.

"Just as you can, Your Highness."

He furrowed his brows. "I don't think Tori would like that."

He was correct, but my sweet mate suffered from the same overprotectiveness that I needed to fight as well. "No, I don't think she would, but she would not stop you. She would understand."

Darkness fell over Jun's face. "I doubt that."

The air was quiet, the hush that precedes a storm, and it seemed fitting for our conversation.

"Your sister is like a tempest, violent and seen from miles

around. I love her all the more for it. But you, I think you are more like me. Your rage simmers deep below the surface, a molten pool that will eventually no longer be able to be contained, to disastrous results."

"No, I don't harbor anger. It has just never lingered in my heart. All I feel is sadness, like a great wallowing pit trying to suck me under. It's harder some days than others to tread those waters, but having Pallas and Tori nearby helps." He let out a long sigh. "I never knew how to fight. I'm not like Tori. But that doesn't mean I'm helpless."

"What you did during that battle wasn't the actions of someone who doesn't know how to fight."

"Perhaps I should say I have never *desired* to fight. I don't think she's ever understood that." I saw it there, that space between them.

"Sometimes those who love us most know us the very least, especially when it's family."

At this, Jun said nothing.

"I know there are many who care for you deeply, but sometimes that makes it harder for them to see the wound and bleed with you. Should you need someone who is more removed... I am here."

I thought I pushed too far. I hardly knew this man, even if he was now some of the only family I had. I turned to leave when he spoke again.

"I wish I could talk to her, to Tori. It is what I did for two hundred years. Now...the silence is unbearable, and I know it hurts her. I don't think she will ever forgive me for that."

"I have done more unforgivable things in my life than I can count. Things I know I will not be forgiven for. Your sister knows them, and she loves me still. She accepts me with those scars. She would do the same for you."

"She never knew you without them."

"Do you truly think she would shy away from your scars? You may have no desire to fight, but I know she does, and she would fight for you. She already has, recklessly."

At that, Jun's mouth twitched into the smallest smile. "That sounds like her." He sighed again, but I saw a dam inside him break. "Singing, music, it used to be everything to me. It was my life, my joy. But now, I can't even pick up a harp. Every note is just a reminder of his touch, of the pain. When he collared me, it was like he ripped the music out of me, and I can still feel the scratches where it held on, trying to stay inside. And now it's gone, and there is nothing left but scars."

Jun's voice croaked, and he hid his face in his hands. "What he did to me, that was terrible. But this is worse. It's like he's stolen my very soul. I don't know if I'm even me anymore. Tori can see it. I know she does. I see how she wishes I was just the brother she knew in Niata again. But I don't think I can ever be him again."

Moving closer, I sat down beside him, careful to maintain a respectful distance. "I don't think you will ever be that man again, Jun." He pulled his face up to look at me. "Life's most painful events change us irrevocably. It's natural to grieve for the person you were before, but it's also necessary to let that person go to embrace who you are becoming."

He didn't say anything for a second, letting his gaze drift to the floor again. "And who is that?"

"Perhaps someone who can harbor anger."

He looked at me like I had spoken the impossible.

"For five hundred years, I was stagnant. I let my anger trap me in place. I lived, but I too felt as if it was with my soul ripped out. Then I went to Niata…Your sister, she has changed me completely. She allowed me to be reborn in more ways than one."

"But that's a beautiful thing, what the poets write about in songs that last through time."

"It is, but... there is strength in anger. If I had never met your sister, Hadeon would be dead." Jun's eyes widened. "The man I was before would have never hesitated. He would have ripped Hadeon to shreds, no matter the cost, no matter who I dragged down with me. My journey to Koron might have been my end, but it would have been his as well. I would have taken this entire world with me if I had needed to."

"That's... horrifying," Jun muttered.

"Yes, just as I was. But tell me, have you ever felt the same? Even a spark of that dark desire for retribution?" At this, he remained silent. "Through suffering, you have grown strong. Of that I have no doubt. Lean on your sister, on Pallas if you must, but use that strength. Let that righteous anger guide you. It's the key to your survival."

It may be the key to all our survival. I would not lay that thought on him. Not yet.

"Love can save you, but violence will free you. If you learn to guide that inner anger, Jun, I have no doubt you will shift this world just as much as your sister."

He held my gaze, and I could see the battle being fought inside his mind. He had much to think about; much to learn about himself.

"Sleep on it, Your Highness. Tomorrow, we leave for the Torr."

Chapter 51

Pallas

The overland journey to the Torr was miserable. Every night the soldiers set up a rickety canvas tent for Jun and me, where every insect and miserable creature could come and go freely. I pulled back the coverlet on my cot one night to find a spider the size of my palm happily waiting within. I had screamed so loud that Avlyn had come running, only to meet me with laughter. What was worse, I'd thrown my shoe at the thing, and turned around to see Spinner staring at me with eight big, hurt eyes. I hadn't had time to even try and apologize to him before he sped off into the night. I hadn't seen him since. My sleep had suffered for it.

So, instead, I lay awake listening to Jun's breathing and the rustling of every foul creature of the night scraping at the side of my tent. Somehow, this wasn't drowned out by the rambunctious activities of the soldiers that went on every night, the princess being the loudest and the most obnoxious of them all.

After days of no baths, cold meals, wet feet, and freezing nights I was about ready to end it all. I smelled like horse, dirty bodies, and gods knew what else. I was about ready to rip my own skin off if it meant I might feel clean again.

I rolled over on my cot that was harder than stone, trying to drown out the sounds of braying laughter with my wafer-thin pillow when a loud crash broke through what little calm I had found. Next to me, Jun gave a small snore and rolled over, returning to sleep, but I'd had it.

I scrambled off my cot, the meager blanket getting tangled around my legs in my frustration, and I tumbled onto the dirt floor. I hissed and scrambled out of the tent making for the ring of light surrounding the campfire.

The crash had come from a huge crate that now lay in scattered pieces around the body of Raula, who was laughing jovially. Tori reached down beside her and picked up a wooden tankard, noticeably empty of the ambrosia that leaked from the nearby barrel. She chucked it at Raula with all her strength, and it hit the orcess square in the abdomen. The wooden vessel shattered and Raula let out another booming laugh.

"You're going to need to do better than that. We orc aren't as soft as you fae." Tori lurched around for something else to lob at her when a slurred voice called out from the ground near my feet.

"Don... hic... t encooorage 'er, she'll have yuh gettin' the knives ou... hic... t next."

Raula flashed her tusks with a wicked grin, but Tori's face fell, suddenly very sober. "Who gave Noki ambrosia?" She scrambled over to the prone man.

"Was just a little sip, Princess. Didn't think it would hurt him." A soldier I didn't know chuckled, hitting a comrade on the shoulder. Tori spun on the man and his face went whiter than the snow at the peaks of the Cold Mountains. "I didn't mean any harm by it!"

"That's '*Your Highness*' to you, Captain Lem. Get out of my sight, now." Lem scrambled away without so much as a glance back. Tori heaved a sigh as she moved next to Noki and finally noticed me.

"Oh, Pallas? I'm surprised to see you out here after dark."

"I couldn't sleep with all the noise." I was trying to antagonize her, but she clearly wasn't very interested. She knelt in front of the inebriated man with a worried look. She gently pushed the dark hair back from Noki's sweaty face, placing her hand along his forehead to cool him. He was barely conscious and mumbling some tune I had never heard.

She scooped him up easily despite him being nearly the same size as her. She wrapped his knees over one arm, his shoulders the other, and stood with little effort. "Come on, let's get you to bed before you do something stupid," she tutted gently.

"I think you mean something stupider, Princess," Avlyn called from the other side of the fire.

She gave them a flippant glare before walking off into the dark, the human male snoring gently in her arms. I now stood very alone at the edge of the fire light.

"Hey, *dijurk*, stop skulking and come join us, will you?" I looked up. Raula had found a seat on the ground next to Kaleos and Oryx, the smaller man huddled under the larger one's arm in the brisk night air. Raula patted the ground on her other side, which was directly next to Commander Avlyn. Raula flashed her tusks at me in a wicked grin that very clearly communicated she knew I had been avoiding the commander ever since Xyr.

I shuffled from foot-to-foot, unwilling to decide what to do, when Avlyn did it for me. They stood from their crossed-leg position with an exaggerated stretch. "I'm off to bed; don't get too rowdy out here, younglings." They passed by me, laying a hand on my shoulder for a moment and giving me a soft smile before heading into the dark. I could barely meet their eyes.

"Get over here, *dijurk,*" Raula hollered. I meandered over to her and sat down, only to find six pairs of eyes staring at me.

"What?"

"Don't *what* us. Why are you and the commander acting like this?" She scowled at me.

"I don't know what you are talking about. We aren't acting any different than normal."

Kaleos laughed at that. "Yeah, that's the problem."

Raula's dark green mouth curved into an even deeper frown. "It's bad enough I have to deal with these two." She jerked her thumb over her shoulder at Oryx and Kaleos. "But now I have to smell you and the commander as well."

"What do you mean, smell us? I'm sorry, but it's impossible to bathe out here and trust me when I say—"

But Raula was shaking her head, and then her dark eyes lit up in a way that reminded me of a wolf with a rabbit. "I don't mean you're unclean. You smell like... well if you were orcs, I would say you were about to go into a breeding cycle."

"*What?*" I clutched my hand to my chest, and my mouth hung open.

"No use denying it, my lady. I might not have Raula's sense of smell but it's pretty obvious with the way they look at you," Kaleos commented.

Oryx chuckled, "It's just like the princess all over again, isn't it?" All three of them laughed, and I was sure I was about to melt into the ground with embarrassment. My mind was still clinging to Kaleos' words "*the way they look at you.*"

"What's just like me again?" Tori had come around the nearest tent, arms empty and Noki tucked into bed.

"Oh, we were just asking Pallas why—" I punched Raula hard on the arm. It was like a fly trying to knock over a teapot, but she laughed instead of finishing her sentence. "Hey, look who's got some strength after all?"

"I'm going to bed," I grumbled, starting to stand up when her arm came down over my shoulders.

"Don't run away, my lady. We'll stop teasing. Sometimes, we soldiers forget how to act around the gentry."

Tori sat down beside me, and we sat in silence for some time. I counted, wondering how long it would take for her to break it.

"So, have you seen Spinner lately?" Ten seconds.

"Pardon?"

"I know he likes you, and I haven't seen him in two nights. I was wondering if you had?"

"No, I haven't. We had a bit of a... falling out." I couldn't believe how sad that made me.

"He saw you squish a spider, huh?" Kaleos asked, knowingly.

"I didn't even squish it!"

"Take it from me, check your boots for webs before you put them on next time." He laughed, but Tori looked out along the horizon.

"We aren't far from Tenebrae; I wonder if he went home?" Her mouth twitched in a sad smile before she stood abruptly.

"We should all get to bed. Who knows what we will find tomorrow."

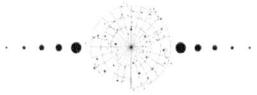

THE TORR ROSE AHEAD OF US, BUT I FELT IT LONG BEFORE we had crested the final rise of hills that preceded it. It wasn't visually different from the Cold Mountains that spanned the horizon behind it. Dark rock jut up into the sky, curious in its solitude. The surrounding, flatter earth quickly shifted into a steep cliff that formed a single tower of rock. It was taller than any palace, at least tenfold, and the top looked as if a great hand had cut it flat. All around the exterior of the natural tower, the dark openings of caves could be seen.

Perhaps that is all it looked like to the humans in our entourage, notably devoid of plant life but not so extraordinary. But I would have known this place was an abomination had I been stripped of all my senses. A terrible wrongness pulsed from it that wrapped its horrible tendrils around the very pit of my stomach and tugged with great force. My breath started coming in shallow pants with each step towards the Torr as if it was trying to squeeze the life directly out of me.

I saw numerous members of our party falter as we drew closer. Most who did were fae, or partially so, but on none was it so obvious as it was with the king.

His skin had grown even more pale, and his entire brow shone with sweat. He pulled up the reigns of his horse and didn't move; his eyes locked on the Torr. Tori rode her horse beside him, somewhat awkwardly, clearly not used to riding. She leaned over and lay her hand on the king's shoulder, whispering something.

Abraxas barely reacted, but she turned her horse away and shouted, "Far enough. Let's set up camp two hundred pace to the east."

She grabbed the reins of his horse with her own, and gently guided them away from the Torr. The king was still locked in a trance.

I looked over to Jun, who rode beside me, and was surprised to see him looking remarkably unperturbed. He saw my gaze and asked, "Are you alright, Pallas?"

"Yes, this place is far more unnerving than I thought it would be." He didn't respond. "Can't you feel it?"

"Yes." A blank answer. I waited to see if he would give me

more, but instead he turned his horse around, following the flow of travelers behind his sister.

We settled at the top of a slight rise as the soldiers began setting up the camp. It was unnaturally silent, especially compared to every night on our journey out here. Everyone moved as if they expected to be attacked at any moment.

No one looked worse than Noki, though. He had huge bags under his eyes, sallow skin, and cracked lips.

"Lem's a right bastard; he was just jealous you chose me to lead this," he mumbled as he helped the princess pull a huge canvas tent up. She saw me walking by and tossed a rope at my face. I barely managed to stop it from making contact before fumbling and dropping it to the ground.

She sighed. "Be useful and hold that tight." I glared at her but obeyed. Everyone was wound tight, and I didn't want them to snap. She ducked behind the other side, and I gripped my rope tight as she tugged in the opposite direction.

"If I may, my lady?" Noki took the rope from me and tied it to a stake he had placed in the ground. He gave me a pained smile as he stood before rubbing his head.

"You know, klaris root would help with that hangover," I advised.

"Yeah, Oryx already brought me some. My head still feels like it's going to split open. I'm gonna kick Lem's ass when I get the chance."

"You're lucky you remember last night at all."

He groaned again. "Wish I could forget right now. I see how it's easy for humans to get addicted to this stuff. Felt amazing last night." He sighed and rubbed his head again. "Not worth it, though." He straightened his shoulders. "The princess has given me the honor of running this operation, and I won't let her down."

I raised an eyebrow at him, examining him from head to toe.

His dark hair was messy and hung in front of his face, and I could see the tremors in his fingers as the ambrosia still lingered in his system. This little, hungover human was who Tori decided to put in charge of the investigation of the Torr?

"How old are you?" I asked.

His face tightened and he straightened a bit more. "Twenty-eight."

I laughed, and his face grew red. Twenty-eight? For the fae, that was practically still a youngling. I didn't know what we would find in this horrible, cursed place, but there was no way a human would be able to handle this.

"Pallas! Stop harassing my men and come help me." The princess had come back around the tent and looked ornery. "Noki, start gathering your cohort for the first scouting mission." Noki snapped into a salute, and she gave him a soft smile. "You've got this under control, Lieutenant." He ran off, and Tori gave me another displeased look.

"A strange leader you have chosen, Princess."

"I didn't see you volunteering to lead the charge."

I shivered. "I don't think I would last very long in there."

She rolled her eyes. "Exactly. Why do you think I put Noki in charge."

"But he's so young and only a human. How do you expect him—?" She gave me a harsh look, like I was missing the very obvious. It turns out, I was. "It's because he's human. He's less affected by the curse."

"I knew you'd get there eventually, Pallas." She wrapped an arm around my shoulder and dragged me away quite aggressively. *She'd been spending too much time with the soldiers; she's forgotten how to be a lady.*

"Didn't forget, just never much cared to lock myself in that particular cage."

Had I said that out loud?

"You still are, Pallas. An effect of the curse, perhaps? Best be careful. You might admit some things you would rather not. I'll warn the camp to be on their best behavior."

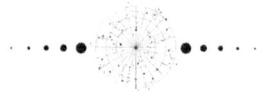

THE NEXT FEW DAYS WERE SPENT WITH Nomi and his cohort of humans and a few orcs investigating the Torr. Tori planned on one scout mission each morning and one in the afternoon, but that had quickly fallen apart. Groups of humans would enter the Torr only to emerge minutes later, claiming they had been lost for days deep within the caves. Others would enter only to emerge days later, claiming they had been inside only a few hours.

The princess had quickly become much more cautious, sending only small groups and waiting for them to emerge before sending others. So far, everyone had come back, eventually. The days ticked by with little progress.

The camp became putrid, and it wasn't just from weeks of waste. The non-consensual honesty that had been placed on those of fae blood had started more than a few fights and ended more than one relationship. Kaleos and Oryx were currently not on speaking terms it seemed, so the healer had been spending more time with Jun, the two of them often foraging together in the surrounding fields.

The reports that came back from the Torr were just as festered. Visions of grand ballrooms and ancient temples. Some said they had seen their childhood homes, complete with the family pet, down to the last detail. Others reported seeing their loved ones torn to shreds, their bodies massacred and feasted upon.

It sounded like classic illusion magic, calling on the memories and fears of the intruders. I made the mistake of mentioning this to the princess and she called me to every debriefing of the scouts since.

I sat in an uncomfortable chair in the corner, mostly ignoring them until one day, something impossible happened.

"It was the emperor; I was sure of it. It was like I had wandered into his war council or something," Noki said. He'd been in the mountain for three days, and for once, his timeline lined up with ours. He had gotten the furthest into the caves, the best we could surmise. Abraxas had drawn a map from what he remembered, but by his own admission, those memories were over six hundred years old and "cloudy."

"But he wasn't the emperor yet. They kept calling him 'Prince Hadeon' and this other guy 'king.' Hadeon was working to strategize an attack on something. I wasn't sure what. All I could think about was how pissed that king guy was as he watched Hadeon. Just fuckin' staring daggers into him. Especially when the commanders were all 'great job, Hadeon' and 'you're a great strategist like your father, Hadeon.' After they all cleared out, the king went up to him, grabbed his collar, and was all, 'remember your place, boy.' The whole thing was weird as hell. No way any of that was real."

It was real. I hadn't been there, but it played like so many similar incidents I had seen in those years before Obion's death, that there was no doubt it had been true. How had Noki seen such a thing? A true vision of the past—that was a magic that could only be woven by the most complex of enchantments... or curses.

The soldiers quickly devolved from any useful topics and I left the tent. This was something that I needed to update the princess about. I walked to her tent but paused outside when I heard lowered voices. I stood outside, listening through the paper-thin walls and peering through a small crack in the canvas.

"It's like Tenebrae, the warping of time. But so far no one has been lost."

"Not yet, but I can feel it. The curse was sleeping, but it slowly awakens." The king shook his head. "It's calling to me, calling for blood. Our people won't be safe in there much longer."

"Then we have no choice, I have to—"

"No! I will not allow it." I saw her expression twist in annoyance, but it softened, and she gripped Abraxas' face gently.

"I can feel it, that well of mana beneath the mountain. But I can't reach it! This damn curse is blocking me."

"Exactly, I won't be able to connect with you, Tori. The curse will warp our bond. I can't stand it. I won't be separated from you again."

"Do you not believe I am strong enough on my own?"

"Of course I do. Don't you see? It is I who isn't strong enough without you."

My heart twinged at how he looked at her, how he held her close, and meant those words. I hated how very jealous it made me. I let out a soft cough and they turned as I entered the tent.

"Pallas, good. Any news from Noki?"

"Yes, everyone came back without injury again, but there was something interesting this time."

"Let us hear it. I have no time for dramatics." The king's face was ashen, with deep bags under his eyes. I almost felt bad for him but couldn't quite find that sympathy. I turned to the princess.

"Noki saw a vision of something that happened in the past."

"Yeah, we've seen that before, people's memories. Was there something else?"

"The past he saw was not his own. It was an event none of

the humans in his party could have known, as it happened four hundred and fifty years ago."

At this, I had both of their attention.

"And you are sure the things that Noki saw were true?"

"Yes." I didn't explain more. I could not lie, but I didn't have to tell the whole truth. Neither of them pressed me. Instead, Tori turned to the king.

"Think of what we might learn, Abraxas. We could destroy the node and perhaps discover something, maybe something that would help us."

"I hate to say it, Your Highness, but for once, I agree with Abraxas." They both looked at me with surprise. "This curse is beyond anything I've ever read about before. It has warped the very fabric of reality. Who knows what you will see? What will you find? You say you will find knowledge, but I say you will find untold danger."

Abraxas nodded. "Even Pallas agrees, Tori, you must—"

"No. I will not put my cohorts at risk, a risk I wouldn't be able to tackle myself. I'm going in there tomorrow morning."

They began to squabble again, and I excused myself before I saw anything I didn't care to witness.

I wandered back to the tent I shared with Jun, and once again found myself listening in on a conversation from the outside.

"He's just always so damn overprotective of me. I'm older than he is! I can take care of myself."

Jun nodded, his face grim. "I know. Tori is the same way. She treats me like I'm still a youngling, and it makes me... beyond frustrated." I froze, unable to believe what I heard. The truth of his heart revealed.

I peered through the gap in the tent and saw Oryx lay his hand gently on Jun's. "Have you talked with her about it?"

"I feel like now may not be the best time. We might end up just fighting over it like you and Kaleos."

Oryx waved his hands. "Yeah, I mean, it was really upsetting what he said, but now we understand each other a bit better. We have to work on his protectiveness, but at least now we are starting from a place of honesty. Maybe this curse really was a blessing in disguise?" He laughed. "I've really already forgiven him."

Jun chuckled, too. "Then why are you here talking to me and not him?"

Oryx twitched his soft, pointed ears. "He can't stand the silent treatment, and he still needs to grovel a bit more for what he said." They both laughed amicably, and I cleared my throat.

"Come on in, Pallas." Jun turned to me with his soft smile.

Oryx rose off the cot. "Guess it's time for me to go and end his suffering."

I sat down. "You two seem to be getting close."

"He's easy to talk to."

"As you predicted, your sister has come up with the reckless idea that she's going to head into the Torr solo."

Jun's face tightened. "When?"

"Tomorrow morning."

"I'm going with her." His response was so fast and cold I thought I misheard him. His mouth was set into a grim line, and I knew that I had not.

"You can't do that. It's too dangerous!"

"Would you keep me caged, too, Pallas?"

"Jun, I don't understand."

"Ever since Koron, you and Tori both; you've doted on me like I'm a youngling. A weakling who needs protecting. But have you ever considered that I don't want that? That I just might be able to take care of myself?" His words were soft, they always were, but they were laced with a venom I've never heard before.

"I'm sorry. I never meant to make you feel that way. I love you. I can't bear the thought of you hurt."

"I know, but that's not your choice to make."

I looked at him and swore I could see those shadows Tori had talked about swirling in his eyes. How many years had I longed for a choice in my own life, no matter what the consequences were? I understood his need completely. And he was strong, not just in magic, but in his heart. That is why I loved him so.

"I'm sorry, Jun. What can I do?"

I saw those shadows fall back, just a little. "You have to let me go, Pallas."

I linked our pinkies together. "Better than that, I'll let you fly."

I thought it might be difficult to find sleep, my mind swirling over what little we knew about the Torr. But sleep found me, like a spectral hand pulled me under into that familiar darkness. I drifted in the space between thought and nothingness until a harsh voice sounded in my ear.

"Hello, thief." Queen Soraya swirled around me, unformed, but I felt the chill of cold fingers sliding around my neck. I wondered if I would ever get a good night's rest again.

"Hello, Your Majesty. I thought that the spiders might have finished you off."

She hissed a laugh, and it sounded like the thick ice over a cracking lake. "You cannot kill what is already dead, child."

"And yet you linger here?"

"Yes, I was never able to master Death, but we came to an arrangement of sorts. Now, where is my gem?"

I shrugged my shoulders and tried for my best impersonation of Avlyn. "Dunno."

Air pushed out of the gaping shadow that was her mouth in a high-pitched whine.

"Foolish girl. How can you expect to slaughter your enemies when you cannot even hold on to the strongest weapon in your arsenal. You will need every tool at your disposal to keep your enemies away once the people turn on you."

I bared my teeth back at her. "I protect my people, care for them. I am not hated as you were."

To my surprise, her wicked grin grew wider. "Your people? And who is that, I wonder? The people of the Dragon Kingdom? Of Niata? So many left out from your protection. So many enemies left to fear you."

I said nothing.

"Don't worry, little beast. They will all come to hate you, friend and foe. There is nothing that this world hates more than a woman who will take what she wants. I did and look what they did to me."

"I think there were a few other things you did that they hated as well."

She gave that grating laugh again. "You will see, child."

She coalesced before me, those depthless shadows forming her face. She was beautiful, but it had been distorted into something beyond softness long ago. She was beautiful, like the endless void that welcomed all things beyond imagining. Her full lips pulled into a frown. "Where is your brother?"

"What do you want with Jun?"

Her brows furrowed. "It was not often that I dreamed without my brother at my side. And yet, you dream without yours. Perhaps, you are not as strong as I thought."

"My *relationship* with my brother is not the same as yours."

Her frown turned wicked. "I wouldn't be so sure, my pet. My brother and I shared a soul, just as you and your brother do. We shared our bodies as well; it was the natural next step."

I gagged. Her frown deepened.

"You were kept apart as younglings?" she asked.

"They tried."

"But something has happened, you are no longer connected."

My fists tightened. Yes, Jun and I were further apart than ever. I didn't let it show on my face, but she saw the truth.

"You must correct this."

"Forgive me if I don't feel like taking advice from you."

Suddenly, I was choking. Shadows flowed down my throat and twisted around my neck. I clawed at them reflexively, but it did nothing.

"Hear me, you impudent child. Should you wish to reshape this world, you will need your brother. Separated, you are weak, but together, you are stronger than you can possibly imagine."

Black stole into my vision, so I fought it. Dragonfire erupted from my skin, and I heard her scream. It was so high-pitched it might have broken glass, and she continued on without breath, but my fire grew and grew until her shadows melted away and there was nothing but the woman left.

My flames swirled around her as she cowered. It was the most human she had ever looked. Her pale skin was tainted with swaths of black and a crown of thorns sat upon her dark, stringy hair.

She looked up at me as I approached her, and her eyes were pitch black. I saw fear, but then I saw elation in them.

"Yes, yes how you've grown. You are nearly there. But you will need him. You will need them all."

"Get out of my head, witch." Her shrieks erupted as I consumed her in flames, and they pierced the very fabric of reality.

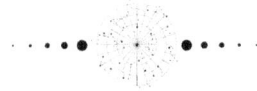

I woke to Abraxas sleeping beside me, his arm wrapped around my waist. Sweat dripped down my neck, but there were no burns or damage. I snapped my fingers, and dragonfire swirled around my hand, controlled and calm. I was getting much better at this.

"Are you trying to excite me, little bird?" Abraxas' voice was rough with sleep, but he rolled his body into mine, and a shiver rolled down my spine. I turned over and placed a kiss on his cheek.

"Go back to sleep, Your Majesty. I have a few things I need to work out." He gave a disappointed groan but relaxed and almost immediately fell back asleep. This place was taking a toll on him, even with him keeping his distance.

My feet silently hit the floor, and I padded barefoot into the light of the early dawn. I found Avlyn at the edge of our encampment, coordinating the switching of the guard.

"Any news from the front?"

They sighed, "Not much, fortunately. The defeat at Xyr has crippled Hadeon's army for now, but he gathers reinforcements at the edge of the kingdom. We should be able to hold them but..." *But at what cost.* How many lives would be lost trying to buy us time? Too many.

I nodded to Avlyn and let them retreat to their tent for some much-needed rest. I let my feet guide me, and soon enough, I found myself at Jun's side, sitting out in the grassy field in front of the Torr.

"What did you dream about?" he asked me right away. No avoiding it.

"Queen Soraya. And you?"

"King Soractes." His eyes were hard.

"What did he say?"

"That I need to fix this rift that has grown between us." Why did Jun voicing this truth, which I knew all too well, make my heart shatter?

"Queen Soraya said the same. Amongst some other things." Silence stretched between us, horrible and infinite.

"You're going into the Torr today?" he questioned, not looking at me.

"Yes."

"I'm going with you."

"Jun, I don't think that's a good—"

"I'm going with you." He could not lie, and so it was true. He stood and walked back into camp. "I'll be ready before the sun hits the Torr."

Chapter 53

Tori

W e met back at the field before the Torr. The whole camp had come out to watch our approach, Pallas and Abraxas at the forefront. Avlyn stood beside Abraxas, and I saw them subtly supporting him. I clenched my fist, but that wasn't something I could focus on now.

I looked over at Jun, and he didn't look back. His eyes were locked on the challenge before us. "Are you ready?" He said nothing but slid his fingers into mine. It eased my aching heart.

"Don't worry. I'll protect you." I squeezed his fingers but was surprised to see his face twist in displeasure, if only for a moment. Then, that hard expression vanished, and his brows relaxed.

"Let's go."

The Torr stretched into the sky before us, its dark, rocky surface was dry and barren of all life. The grass stopped in a perfect line, immediately giving way to nothing but dust and ash. I took a deep breath and stepped over. Immediately, I felt my fingers clench around Jun's, and my legs shook, like a great weight pressed in on me over my whole body. I coughed and tried to keep my feet moving. I heard Jun whimper beside me as his feet faltered.

"Let's go back, we'll find another way."

He staggered, but then straightened his spine and grit his teeth.

"No, this is it." He locked his eyes with mine. "Together?"

I nodded. "One step at a time."

Our pace was slow, but we kept moving. Every step brought that weight down on us more. My chest ached, it felt like my heart was fighting to beat while being strangled.

We reached the lowest cave opening, the darkness surrounding us, but we did not stop. Our steps echoed off the hollow walls until I couldn't see anything. I tried to summon flames using Abraxas' and my bond, but nothing came. The bond remained, but it was muted, the curse of this place sinking its claws into it just like it had my heart.

"Should have brought a torch," I mumbled, and I heard Jun grunt in agreement.

"No fire then?" he asked. I shook my head, not that he could see. I felt him fumbling in his pockets, and he released my hand. I panicked in that moment of darkness until I heard the scratching of flint, and a spark lit the wick of a candle. The tiny flame flickered back and forth; its light caught in Jun's eyes. I gasped.

The Jun before me now wasn't the man I had entered with, but the little boy I had once known. He was smaller, his face and eyes soft with youth. He gave me a quizzical look and spoke with a high-pitched voice. "What's wrong, Tori?"

I reached out and touched his face, my fingers tracing his cheeks that were still chubby and rosy. I didn't know what sort of illusion this could be, but he felt real beneath my touch.

The curse has warped the very fabric of reality. Who knows what you will see?

"Nothing. Let's keep going." I reached for his hand again, and his much smaller fingers slipped into mine.

We continued down what felt like endless tunnels, trying to follow the path I had memorized. The only sound was our breathing until I could hear the faintest trickle of water ahead.

"The spring!" Jun's young voice squeaked, and he dashed off.

"No! Wait!" It was already too late, as I saw the light from his candle disappear around a corner. I ran after him, slipping on the rocky floors as I rounded the corner and nearly lost my footing. I set my hand on the ground to steady myself as I took the turn and stood, only to have my feet freeze in place as I was blinded by light.

I threw my hands up in front of my face, blinking furiously. The cave was filled with jungle plants, and I heard water. Was that the sky? No time to think on it.

"Jun! Jun! Where are you?" I crashed through the plants in front of me to stumble out into a well-manicured garden, the trickling of water from a fountain at its center. It shot a clear stream of water into the sky before it fell back down like rain into a shallow pond filled with large fish in nearly every color.

It was a fountain I had seen nearly every day for two hundred years. "Niata?" How could this be?

I heard a soft laugh and spun to see Jun rolling on the grass on the other side of the pond, trying to hide behind a bush. I sprinted to him and grabbed his shoulders, hauling his small body up.

"Jun, what are you doing? We have to get out of here."

"Ha, you found me!" He giggled again and tried to pull away.

"What are y—"

Jun's face dropped in horror, and a shadow fell over me. Before I could turn, pain laced itself across my face as the back of my father's hand collided with my cheek. I stumbled to the ground.

"Tori, how many times do I need to re-enforce this lesson? Stay away from your brother." I looked up as my father lifted his hand to strike me again. I was the child, small and helpless.

"Father, no!" My brother threw himself between us, but my father's eyes remained hard, and his hand quivered.

"Jun, move, or I will have to—"

"No, not my boy!" My mother wrapped herself around Jun, hauling him away.

"Tori!" He reached back for me, and our fingers met for just a moment before we were wrenched apart.

"Jun!" I tried to crawl after him as he struggled against my mother's iron grasp, but pain laced itself over my face again, and I fell back down into the grass.

It wasn't grass but a rocky cave floor, and the sun winked out, and I was in total darkness again. I scrambled, screaming Jun's name over and over, only to be met with echoes. I stumbled blindly until the sound of water found my ears again. I slipped over the uneven floor as I scrambled towards it.

The day broke through, golden and filled with the smell of ambrosia. I stumbled into the room of a fine palace. The walls shimmered in the early morning sun, and a fae wearing the flaming crown of the Golden Kingdom stood at the window. It wasn't Hadeon. In fact, this man looked nothing like him. The sound of water came from a slave pouring tea into a fine porcelain cup. The man took it from the slave's outstretched hand before slowly spinning towards me. I threw my hands up, ready to fight.

"You certainly enjoy keeping me waiting," the man said.

"Apologies, Your Majesty." I jumped nearly a foot in the air at the familiar voice behind me. I spun around to see Lord Plagis standing next to... Pallas? Lord Plagis was younger, his hair still dark and his face smoother, but still had that same slimy look to him, though.

"As I have said numerous times, this work cannot be rushed, Your Majesty." The woman spoke with no deference to the monarch before her. She certainly sounded like Pallas, but it wasn't her. They were almost twins, but this woman was older and harsher. Her grey eyes were honed like daggers as Plagis shot her a withering look. She ignored him.

"What news do you bring me, Runya?"

"The evidence continues to support my previous conclusions. With every great beast felled, the animavita of our prisoners diminishes. It follows the pattern I have seen in my own magic." She hesitated, then added, "And in yours."

King Obion's mouth was set into a harsh line. "And you have not changed your opinion on the solution to this problem."

Runya stood tall and proud, and I admired her resolve against the male before us. "No. When a dragon is killed, the drop is tenfold than with any other beast. We must call off the attack on Sacrignus Torr. The destruction of the dragons on that scale can only result in one thing, the loss of all magic."

Plagis let out a grunt of disapproval. "As usual, Runya continues to ignore the Great Prophecy. The boy continues to gain power, and he grows more popular among the rabble every year. His latest victory against the dragon Levania has the bard singing songs that will last through the age."

"I base my opinions on facts and alchemy, Plagis, not ancient faetales spun by drug-addled women." I would have cowered from the face that Runya gave the man, but his sleazy smile only grew.

"Yes, but I see how you have let that beautiful daughter of

yours remain plastered to the boy's side. No mere coincidence, I'm sure. Tell me, has Hadeon's power diminished after he killed Levania?"

Runya's face grew ugly, caught in her own logic. "No, but..."

"And there you have it. Proof enough for me, Your Majesty. The boy is destined for greatness."

Plagis' statement did not seem to ease the King's mind. In fact, his face grew even grimmer. He looked between his two advisors. "The attack will continue. Plagis, make sure everything is as it should be."

"Of course, Your Majesty." The man gave a sweeping bow and shot Runya one more satisfied smirk before leaving the room.

"Your Majesty, I must really—" Runya began.

"Do not think I have not also noticed your daughter's position beside my heir." She hesitated but did not cower.

"My Lord, it is simply an affair of youth, youngling love. I'm sure once Hadeon grows into his role as prince, he will leave her behind. I have warned her of this myself many times."

The king's brow rose in thought. "Tell me, have you ever had absolutely nothing?"

"I'm afraid I do not understand, Your Majesty."

Obion let out a chuckle with no humor. "You are a knowledgeable woman, but you have never been burdened by the curse that can be love."

"I knew enough to give him something to fight for, didn't I?" Runya responded, but Obion seemed done with the line of thought.

"No matter. Is everything prepared for after the battle?"

"The enchantment is complete. But as I have stated before, the likelihood of being able to return with a dragon's heart intact is—"

"You have told me the odds, Runya. It is your job to make sure that everything is prepared, nothing more."

"Of course. Then I only need the last component." King Obion nodded as Runya stepped forward with a dagger. He pulled back his sleeve, and the blade flashed as it cut across his fair skin. Runya quickly stowed the weapon and pulled out a small vial. Glyphs flashed a deep grey around the neck of the bottle, and as the blood dripped from Obion's arm, it fell into the vial without a single drop going to waste, guided by the magic.

As I stepped forward for a closer look, the scene dissolved into nothingness. The last thing I saw was Runya's face set in a look I had seen many times on Pallas. Stoney resolve.

I stumbled in the dark again until I heard the rustle of legs, and a familiar chitter in the dark.

"Spinner?" I scrambled after the sound until a soft blue light leaked from around another bend. I ran towards it, and a cavern was revealed.

Water dripped down the walls of the cave, dropping in a steady rhythm off the end of stalactites into the glowing pool below. Wisps danced over the pool's surface, and it felt so familiar. This was where I needed to be, what I needed to destroy. I couldn't do that until I found my brother.

"Over here, Tori." I spun, and in the heart of the cave grew a cherry tree, the twin of the one in the gardens back home. This one blossomed virulently, sending waves of delicate floral aroma towards me. Below its protective branches, little Jun sat holding his youngling-sized harp, strumming a tune and humming. He smiled at me and waved as if this was just another day in the gardens of our marble palace.

"Jun, what are you doing?"

"Shh, just listen." The song he played turned somber, a slow and lilting minor key melody that brought tears to my eyes.

"Why such a sad tune, brother?"

"Well, it is a dirge, sister."

"Who is it for?"

His face was hidden in shadow. "Everyone."

The reality of the chamber shifted, and Jun pulled away from me. "No!" But it was too late. The branches of the cherry tree whipped down and held me like chains. No longer blossoming, they were gnarled and barren. Roots thrashed up from the ground, pinning me down as I fought fruitlessly to escape.

As I was pulled below the earth, my mind was filled with even more visions. The images came at me too quickly; I only caught small glances, but I felt pain, pervasive and inescapable. The pain of an ancient body that fought on despite how Death clawed after her. Battered and broken but unwilling to surrender. With every new image, the pain flared.

Men in golden armor chased down a large, magnificent stag, whiter than freshly fallen snow and with antlers containing hundreds of splits. Arrows flew, piercing that vulnerable flesh, and blood stained the ground. The blood flowed into the Varda River, wider than any castle. But the blood didn't stop until the banks were overflowing and forests and towns were swept away.

Heat from the sun blasted at me as fae surrounded a cave carved in dry sandstone. Inside, a terrible rattling echoed off the walls as a serpent, nearly as large as a dragon, was poised to strike. His giant triangular head split as he flashed his fangs, but the fae shouted, and glyphs flashed, collapsing the cave on top of his head. When his rattle finally ended, sand pelted the fae as the wind whipped up, pulling all life from the sparse surrounding plant life until only heat and the scorched, cracked earth remained.

A massive harpoon flew from the deck of a ship, this time finding its mark in the heart of a Leviathan smaller than the one

I knew. His body flashed a terrified red before turning a ghostly white, and he floated listlessly in the waves. The waves grew, tossed by raging winds and pelting rain until a storm violent enough to rip apart cities swallowed everything. The rain was her tears. The tears of a mother, begging to spare her children. I heard it in my own mother's voice. *Please, don't take my son.*

I felt roots digging into me, wrenching me apart as they split the earth that was my skin. Those roots led to golden flowers, hundreds of thousands in neat rows, waiting for their fae master. They were not kind. It wasn't like the forest, where roots gripped the earth with reverence and danced between tree and fungi, life and death. Here, there was no rot, no rebirth, only death. The roots dug down and stole mana straight from the earth. Mana that had been stolen year after year after year for an age until what should have been rich soil was nothing but dust. The roots grew down, pulling the mana directly from the ley lines that flowed under Koron. They pulled and pulled until the lines barely had anything left to give.

Those roots kept growing until they spread everywhere across the continent, across our entire world. They reached into everything and everywhere, and I saw them climb up into the heart of every man, woman, and child, wrapping and squeezing them tight.

"No!" I tried to scream, but dirt filled my mouth. I thrashed, and I felt the dirt dig under my nails and the roots tightened, threatening to cut off my limbs and crush my heart.

"Tori!" Jun's voice called to me, and my heart flared, but not with green dragonfire, but instead a burning bright white light. It cut through the roots, and my fingers broke through the dirt above me. I gasped, pulling as much air in as I could as I hauled myself out of the hole.

My hands gripped onto huge cobblestones, and I was

standing on the mist district bridge, but it was shrouded in darkness. All I could see was little Jun waiting for me.

I ran towards him, and as I did a shadow swept over him. He was back to himself, tall with his hair cut short.

"We have to fix this rift between us, Tori." An enormous crack formed in the bridge, separating us. He pulled away.

"Jun! What do I do? How do I fix this?" The bridge pulled further apart.

"Trust me," He held out his hand.

I ran to jump across that great divide when erratic violet light flashed off the metal around his neck, and I froze.

Out of the shadows, a hand curled around Jun's neck. Hadeon's wicked face appeared, and his tongue snaked over my brother's jaw.

"He's mine now, Princess. You should have been there to protect him, and now his heart belongs to me." Lightning erupted from Hadeon's fingers, and Jun's skin turned black as his power coursed through flesh. My brother didn't move or cry out. He just stood there, as his heart turned blacker before my eyes.

"No!" I screeched and dove for them. "Jun, please fight!" He let out a horrible scream that wasn't human or fae, and the bridge beneath me shattered. I was falling down into nothing. I tumbled, head-over-foot for what felt like an eternity until I stopped with a bone-crunching thud. My face collided with a dirt floor, and I felt my nose snap on impact.

I got my hands beneath me and rose on shaking arms.

"Jun?" He wasn't there. Something else was. I felt hundreds of eyes latched on me in the dark, the creatures lurking just beyond my sight.

Fae! Traitors! Liars! Murderers! They emerged from the dark, dead, and horrible. They were the vestiges of the dragons who had once called this place home. Some were no more than skeletons given life while others still retained some of their rotting flesh. It hung off their frames in chunks, and every once in a while, a single eye would glow from inside a hollow socket. Talons raked into the earth around me as they came closer, some breaking off the hollow bones. I drew my sword, but it was pointless. There were too many, and in the back of my head, Queen Soraya whispered, *you can't kill what is already dead.*

Shadows slunk between the dragon's legs, and I saw the fledglings. Some were larger than oxen and some were so small I could have held them in my arms. Children, the future of their people, all murdered.

Liars! Liars! Liars! They pounced, ghostly fangs and talons ripping into me. I didn't fight back. They were just babies, babies the fae had destroyed.

No, Jun was still out there. I need to save him. I needed to protect him. As those razor-sharp teeth flashed in the dim light and their tongues wrapped around me, I realized something for the very first time.

I didn't need to save him; he needed to save me.

"Jun! Don't leave me, please!" I reached into my heart, deep into that well that now glowed with brilliant white light. It wasn't just my power but also his.

Jun, I need you.

Tori!

His voice felt far away, but I could hear it coming closer as my body transitioned from pain to bliss. He would be too late, but I would get to see him again. It was selfish, so very selfish. I tried to tell him to run, but I couldn't even think the words.

"**LEAVE!**" The creatures around me retreated, and my body fell to the floor with another horrible crunch. My head throbbed, and my skin burned, but I felt a warm and gentle hand on my face.

"Tori, Tori!"

"I'm still here, Jun."

"We have to get out of here. He's coming."

I wanted to ask who, but again, I couldn't find the words. Jun tried to help me stand, but my legs gave out beneath me. I felt his arms wrap behind my knees and I did my best to hold his neck as he carried me. I lay my head against his chest, and I could hear our hearts beating in sync. He ran in the darkness, but there was nowhere to go.

"Tori, can you call mama? We need to find—" The ground beneath us shook with a deep tremor, then another.

"He's here." Jun's voice shook in a way I had never heard before. The tremors continued until I recognized them for what they were. Great footsteps of a beast beyond my wildest nightmares. Jun's hands clamped around me in a painful vise. I pulled my face away from his chest and wished I hadn't.

From the depths of the cave, all I could see were his eyes, eyes that glowed a red deeper than the heart of the earth. From the shadows, those eyes followed us. As his steps grew closer, I could hear his talons cutting into the rock below with an ear-splitting scratching sound that made my hair stand on end. Below his eyes, his heartfire started to glow, the red was so deep it was almost invisible. It illuminated his pitch-black scales, so dark I could only see the highlights where the red light reflected off them dully. He took a deep breath, and his fire illuminated his mouth and fangs as heat like nothing I'd even felt before scorched my skin.

Leave her and go, little prince. She has already stolen something from me. Do not make the same mistake.

His voice may have been in just our minds, but it was so deep and menacing, I felt it vibrate through my whole body. Jun's grip on me tightened further.

"Never!"

Death gave a deep chuckle, and it reminded me so much of

Abraxas my heart spasmed. There was no mischief here, only destruction.

You cannot escape me. I am everywhere. I am inevitable.

"Jun." My voice was barely a whisper. I saw tears glinting in his eyes as I reached up to cup his face. "I'm sorry. I should have seen... should have seen how strong you are. How strong you have always been. You are soft and kind. I never understood how that took so much bravery. But I see it now."

"Tori, stop. Stop talking like this is the end." He looked up, and I could see the deep red fire reflected in his eyes. I heard Death stalking around us, but I wasn't afraid.

"Go, Jun. It will all be alright."

He looked down at me. "Of course, it will be because we'll be together. Together, we can always face anything."

I put my hand on his chest to feel his heart beating and from beneath my fingers, a white bright light glowed. I pulled my hand away to see the beautiful light of his heart. I saw the shadows there too, still trying to hold his life in their deadly claws. This light wasn't the mana of the earth, but something that was uniquely ours.

It was his heart, but it was also mine. Two bodies, one soul. A soul split into its opposite parts, but fit back together perfectly. And when those two halves collided, we were stronger than even Death himself.

"I love you, Jun. I always have and always will, no matter what. I can't wait to see the man you have become."

He squeezed my hand in his, and I saw some of those entangling shadows burn away. They weren't gone; they never would be, but they didn't hold power over him anymore.

Death spread his wings, and the cave was filled with deep red light. I felt his network of shadows closing in. They were just that, shadows. We were nothing but pure light. It was time to burn it all away.

Just below, I could feel the deep pool of mana, the deepest I had ever felt. Death tried to keep that power from me, his shadows blocking it. It was time to show him just who he was dealing with.

I laced my fingers through Jun's, and he squeezed back until my bones crunched. Death's throat burned as he called his dragonfire.

"Together?" I asked softly.

My brother squeezed my fingers one more time. "Always."

Death's dragonfire swirled, ready to erupt. "Now!"

"BREAK!"

The ground below us split with a great crack, and Death stumbled. Blue-green light shot through the cracks below us, a network of light spilling into the cavern. I didn't hesitate. I pulled all of it into us. Light, pure and white burst from our hearts and the surrounding cave crumbled. As I pulled more and more power from the earth, more and more cracks burst forth until it wasn't mana that flowed from beneath us, but magma.

Death staggered again, trying to find his footing as the ground gave out beneath him, huge chunks of rock sank down and were replaced by pools of glowing, molten rock. Everywhere he moved, his substantial weight would cause more of the floor to give way. He hissed like a giant serpent as the roof caved in.

He spun toward me, and Jun and his eyes widened. Reflected in the darkness of his scales was our burning, white light. I watched in awe as our light spread above our heads, unfurling like a great feathered tail. It wasn't dragonfire, but a light that burned like the sun, and as great wings surrounded us, I felt more and more of the earth's power weaving through my heart and into Jun.

Death gave a tight grin. *So, it was you. I almost didn't recognize you.*

Before I could question this, the floor beneath Jun and I gave out. I snagged him in my arms tight, and the light merged our hearts together. As boiling magma rose and the ceiling came down, our great white wings surrounded us. We shot through the earth and into the sky above as everything around us came crumbling down.

Chapter 54

Abraxas

I hadn't taken my eyes off the Torr since Tori and her brother had entered it that morning. It was nearly nightfall.

"Abraxas, come, have something to eat." Avlyn laid their hand on my shoulder, giving it a gentle squeeze. "You can't glare through solid stone."

I could try. I sharply pulled my shoulder from their grasp, and I heard them release a long sigh. Nothing mattered to me right now, not food, drink, or air. None of it mattered until she was back safe in my arms. I reached down our bond and it felt warped, no doubt by the strange curse of this land. But it was still connected. I tried to see into her mind, but it was clouded to me, as it had been all day.

Then the bond tugged painfully, and I was met with only one feeling. Fear. My claws extended, and I felt my horns rip from my temples. I heard Avlyn gasp behind me at the sudden change. My mate was in trouble. The beast inside me cowered from that place of Death, but the part of me that was fae didn't care. She needed me, and that was all that mattered.

I wanted to shift, but our bond was too distorted. I couldn't pull the power I needed. No matter, nothing would keep me from her. I moved to rush towards the cliffs when strong arms wrapped around me from behind.

"Abraxas, no! You can't go in there."

"Release me now, Commander, if you wish to keep your arms."

"Stubborn asshole! Get a grip on yourself. She's going to be alright."

I flung my arms wide, and Avlyn flew back off me. I spun on them, my fangs extended, and I saw a flash of fear in their eyes, but it was overruled by defiance.

"I said I would always protect you, even if it's from your dumbass self." They drew their sword. "Don't make me hurt you." I felt my lips twitch when the ground beneath shook with a terrible tremor.

We stumbled, and both of us turned to the Torr.

"What was—?" Avlyn's words were cut off as another massive tremor shook us so violently, I fell to my knees. I could hear a commotion from the camp, but none of it mattered.

Tori! Tori... what is going on?! I tried to scream at her through our bond, but there was nothing. I reached further and was blinded by white light hot enough to scorch even me. It raced up the bond, and I covered my eyes as if it would do any good.

Then a crack louder than anything I had ever heard before sounded from the cliffs, and the Torr began to crumble. Fissure after fissure burst through the rock, and a massive landslide cascaded towards us, carrying debris and dust with it. In a matter of moments, the entire cliffside was obliterated.

"Tori!" I tried to rise to standing, but the ground continued to fight me. My eyes widened in fear as more and more of the Torr sunk down into the earth.

"Abraxas, get back!" Avlyn's shouts were barely discernible

over the sounds of destruction. As more cliff disappeared, I felt the heat of molten rock rising out of the earth. A giant wave rose up from the ground, flowing out of any remaining caves and openings.

Anything that remained of the Torr collapsed into that pool of magma. Nothing was left.

"Tori!" It was a bestial roar, her name lost in it. I clamped my hands over my heart until my claws drew blood. That white light still burned inside my heart, and I felt the palms of my hand singe.

Then a cry rent the evening sky. It was a sound so otherworldly that I couldn't place it. A combination of a death throws, and a newborn's cry mixed with the screech of a giant bird of prey.

The pool of lava erupted, two great plumes spreading to either side as a meteor brighter than anything I have ever seen burst forth from the center. Like a newborn star, it shone and rose into the sky.

I shielded my eyes with my fingers but couldn't look away as it rose higher and higher, slowing down.

The light shrank as it rose, until it finally came to a halt. It lost its momentum, and its path shifted as the star fell, straight down to the earth in front of us.

I grabbed Avlyn and leaped down the nearby rise as it crashed, sending shrapnel and dust in all directions.

Avlyn huddled under my arm, but as the dust settled, they raised their head to look at the crater. "What the Huldu-loving fuck was that?"

I didn't wait. I scrambled over the edge of the rise. The star had scarred the earth, leaving a long trail in its wake. The earth there was burning and glowed, but I was a beast of flames and never feared to burn.

Dust and mist still rose around its beating heart. As I

approached, it cleared, and I saw them. Tori and Jun wrapped tight in each other's arms, as if sleeping peacefully.

I shook them both. "Tori, Jun, please wake up."

They stirred, their movements were mirrored as their eyes blinked and limbs stretched. When they finally awoke, their gazes met, and twin smiles broke across their lips. They started laughing. It was the laughter of children, unrestrained and pure. Their arms wrapped around each other, and they kept laughing as their bodies started to glow a beautiful soft white.

Avlyn crested the walls of earth behind me and gave a tight smile. "I told you she'd be alright."

WE MOVED TORI AND JUN BACK TO CAMP, AND THEY immediately passed out on a cot together. I don't know who fussed over them more, me, Pallas, or Oryx. But eventually we all agreed they were in excellent health and just needed some rest.

That didn't mean I would leave them, however. Pallas had the same inclination. We both sat in the dark tent, pointedly not looking at each other as the twins rested peacefully, their breaths coming in slow, steady rolls.

An eternity passed as the silence stretched between Pallas and I. It was so still that I could practically hear the grass growing beneath us.

"So, what happened out there?" she finally asked.

"I don't know." The truth spell had worn off with the destruction of the Torr, but I found no reason to lie.

She scrunched her face unattractively. "They rose into the sky on a beam of starlight. That's magic that this world has never known. You're her mate. Your hearts and souls are linked. You don't know what it is?"

"It seems I may not be the only one who can claim the honor of sharing her soul."

Pallas looked to where the twins still lay, arm in arm.

"It is not the same," Pallas insisted flatly. No room for argument. I didn't intend to. Her eyes lingered on Jun.

"I have no doubt of that. What Tori and I share is not the same as what she and Jun do. I feel it may be something... older."

Pallas flattened her lips until they disappeared, her mind wandering away.

"You said that it was magic the world has never seen, but what if it is just magic the world has forgotten?" I asked.

"When I saw them, I thought it was a star falling from the heavens. What is it the old legends say? Dragons were made by the stars, who had grown lonely in their eternity." She paused, and her eyes met mine without a hint of fear. "What's even older than the gods?"

"*Fenix*," I whispered. A prayer, one I had not spoken since I was a child. This was sacred history; one I had been taught never to share. My people were gone, and our secrets were nearly lost with them. What good did our secrets do if they were dead, along with the rest? Pallas still held my gaze.

"The gods before the gods. *Fenix*, there is no translation. What is the word for the heart of the rising sun and the death of the day that is claimed by night? They were those who burned eternally. When an age came to a close, they would die only to rise again from the stardust and chaos of creation."

"Is it possible that Tori and Jun...?"

"Your estimations are as good as mine, my lady. I think all we can know is that we do not know. Whatever this is, it has never been seen before in all the history the dragons have ever known."

"Something new then," Pallas mused, and I nodded. The silence stretched between us again.

"You love him?" Her eyes sharpened immediately, and I raised an eyebrow at her. "You would hide the best part of yourself from me?"

Her eyes softened, and for the first time in our conversation, she looked away. "Yes, I love him."

"And yet you seek the affections of another. I will never understand the hearts of fae."

Her eyes sharpened, and her claws came out. "My love for Jun is not based on unmitigated desires for another's body, Abraxas. I don't feel the need to keep him trapped within my clutches at all times."

"Then what is it based on?"

Her eyes were unfocused as she shuffled through memories and thoughts. "Mutual understanding and... tenderness."

"Tenderness... from you?"

She hit me with that ferocious glare that I found myself enjoying. It was comforting to see her fighting back.

"And what of Avlyn?"

The corner of her mouth twitched up. "Perhaps that is closer to unmitigated desires."

I huffed a laugh, surprised. The flap of the tent opened like it had been pushed by a ghostly hand, but no one entered. I heard the rustle of feet and Pallas and I peered around the cot.

"Spinner?" She rolled onto her knees next to the ever-growing spider. "Hey, I'm sorry about the shoe. It won't happen again, ok?"

He gave a pleased chirp before turning his attention to me and hissing.

"I missed you as well, spider."

He huffed at me before heading over to the cot, trying to

settle himself between the twins like a massive dog. The twins grumbled and woke.

Pallas and I rose, staring down at them. Tori's eyes opened first, and she rolled over, before freezing when she looked up at us.

"Oh gods, what happened?"

"What happened? *What happened?!*" Pallas was vibrating. "You sank the entire Torr into the earth and shot out of it like a comet. That's what happened!"

"Pallas, too loud," Jun moaned, covering his ears. She ducked down and fussed over him again while Tori sat up. She placed an idle pat on Spinner's head before looking at me. I grabbed her hand and gave it a soft kiss. "And how are you feeling, my World Breaker?"

She gave me a smile that was all teeth. "Ready to take on the Great Hero."

Chapter 55

Pallas

"You can't be serious."

"'Fraid so, my lady," Avlyn said with a massive grin on their face.

"Stop looking so pleased with yourself," I grumbled.

"No can do! Alright, let's load in." They wrapped an arm around my shoulders and dragged me towards the monstrosity.

We had returned to Xyr for a brief respite, but everyone was eager to find the next node in the River Kingdom. Everyone but me. It would be weeks by horse and carriage. We didn't have time for that, even if the entire continent wasn't crawling with soldiers trying to press into the Golden Kingdom. So, we had to find another way.

That other way was a carriage with its wheels removed and replaced by long planks of wood. The entire thing was caged in a huge iron frame that had two massive rings on the top. The princess stood beside it, grinning nearly as broadly as Avlyn.

"What do you think, Pallas?" She slapped the wooden side of the carriage. "We could fit a dozen World Breakers in here."

"I think there is no chance in the hells that I am getting in that thing."

"Why, Pallas, I'm hurt. Do you not trust me?" Abraxas had come around the side of the "carriage" and his look was positively predatory.

"Not even a little," I admitted.

He laughed and slid his arm around the princess's waist. "It was either this or all of you on my back, and I didn't want Tori to get jealous." Tori shoved him playfully, and I rolled my eyes.

Avlyn squeezed my shoulders again reassuringly as the royals squabbled. Jun came up on my other side and grabbed my hand.

"It's this or a much longer version of our journey to the Torr," he said with a gentle smile. "You're willing to face down a dragon but not fly with one?"

I grumbled again, but really, I didn't have a choice. I let them both push me towards our vehicle. Avlyn opened the door, careful to avoid the iron frame. I climbed inside, and the normal benches had been removed. The whole thing was filled with thick fur rugs, blankets, and pillows. The glass of the carriage windows had been taken out and covered, except for two small slits on either side.

"We've got a day's journey ahead of us. I figured it would be better to be comfortable and able to spread out." Avlyn said, before jumping into the pile of pillows and stretching out to occupy half the cabin. Jun climbed in next, seating himself delicately against the back wall. I couldn't quite force myself inside yet, so I turned to see Tori giving Abraxas a gentle kiss as I felt the pull of mana. He shifted before I could even blink. Both he and the princess were getting very good at this. She placed one more kiss on his snout before turning and joining me at the carriage door.

She gave me a kind smile and waved her hand towards the

awaiting space expectantly. I hesitated until Abraxas gave a beat of his wings and the gust of wind nearly took me off my feet.

Tori laughed as my hair flew into my face and mouth, sticking to my lips. I grumbled and finally climbed into the carriage. I sat down next to Jun as the princess kicked Avlyn's legs to make room for herself. Avlyn sat up and pulled the door closed, locking it in place with a latching beam.

The whole carriage shook as I heard the metallic clink of Abraxas' talons against the iron rings, and my stomach dropped out as we lurched away from the ground.

Someone was screaming. Oh, it was me. Muscular arms wrapped around me, and Avlyn whispered in my ear, "I've got you."

I quieted as I felt color rising into my cheeks. This was the closest we had been since that day at the lighthouse. I reflexively wanted to jerk away but I told Jun that I would be brave. Instead, I let myself relax into Avlyn's gentle embrace, at least until Abraxas rose above the castle roof.

"How high will we go?" I was nearly shouting and could barely hear myself over the roar of the wind through the slats in the carriage. My hair whipped around my head again.

"Abraxas said we will stay just below the clouds, so we don't get too wet," Tori responded. Somehow, her short hair managed to whip around her head elegantly, like she was born to ride the wind.

We continued to rise, and I didn't try to wiggle out of Avlyn's grip, especially as the air temperature continued to drop. Tori and Jun were both looking out the small window and pointing.

"Wanna have a look, my lady?" Avlyn asked. I shook my head ferociously. They chuckled and wrapped a fur around me before joining the twins.

My fingers dug into the edges of the soft fur as I pulled it tighter around myself. The trio gave an excited whoop and pointed out the small window. Jun turned back to me. "Pallas, come look."

"I'm fine right here, thanks." Jun gave me a soft smile and turned back to the window. After a few more minutes of excited chatter from the three of them, my jealousy got the better of me. I crawled over beside Jun, and he moved over to let me see out the small window.

We were so high that the trees below us looked smaller than ants. My instinct was to pull away from the window immediately, but Avlyn set a warm hand on my lower back and gave me a gentle smile, and I couldn't seem to pull away. I remembered the top of the lighthouse, and suddenly, looking down at the incredible space between me and the ground seemed less terrifying than holding Avlyn's gaze.

As we flew over the countryside, I saw small lines of people and soldiers traveling along the small brown strips that were the roads, cutting across a sea of grass. The Vitmos river shimmered in the sun like a snake carved from diamonds, and the sea stretched out beyond that, endless.

It truly was an exhilarating sight to see the world so very far away. Suddenly, everything in life felt very small, single threads in a much greater tapestry.

"Not something you see every day, eh, hellcat?" Avlyn gave me a warm smile, and I felt the hand on my back tighten ever so slightly.

"No, it certainly isn't." We stayed at that window for quite some time, until rolling grasslands gave way to snowy peaks, and I felt Abraxas bank to the west.

Best not to fly directly over enemy territory. The king's rumbling voice echoed through my head, answering the question I had only thought.

How do I keep you out of my head, Your Majesty?

Don't think so loud.

I grumbled, and I heard deep rumbling in the sky above. Asshole.

Heard that. Quite a mouth on you, my lady.

I swatted at the air around my head like I could drive him off, and Jun gave me a puzzled look. Tori understood immediately.

"Don't pester her, Abraxas. I need her working." She moved over to the trunk in the corner. Unlatching it, she revealed dozens of scrolls stacked on end.

"I figured we'd have time for a little work on the flight." She pulled out a scroll and revealed the most detailed map I had ever seen of the River Kingdom.

"How funny. I had the same idea," I replied, reaching into the satchel I brought along.

I pulled out a few of my own scrolls and look back to see Tori's face twisted in displeasure.

"Lessons, huh?"

I ignored her. "Jun told me the practice of mindfulness and meditation was common in Niata. Did you ever practice it?"

She shrugged her shoulders, but I saw the tightness in her face. "Occasionally."

"Well, it is the best starting place for controlling your power better."

She tilted her head. "I feel like I've been pretty good thus far without much concentration."

"Obliterating everything in your path isn't going to work every single time, Princess."

She shrugged again, unconvinced.

I sighed. "We don't know what challenges we will face in the River Kingdom, and when we do travel to Koron, brute force won't cut it. My mother made sure of that."

She huffed, but shifted her body so she sat in a crossed-legged position, her back tall and straight. "Alright. Tell me what I need to do."

I unrolled one of my scrolls. It was a simple enchantment, only a few glyphs arranged in a circle. I had once used it to lock the pages in my diary as a youngling; my mother provided the magic to activate it. I spread the paper out before us.

"The enchantment is like a knot, one that has been layered on itself a thousand times over. You will need to tug at the threads of it gently, finding where they move and loosen. Be careful not to weave it tighter." I weighed down the corners of the scroll, so the paper didn't curl back in on itself. "This enchantment is a simple lock. I want you to try and unmake it with mana."

Tori tilted her head at me quizzically. "Don't I need to activate it first?" I shook my head.

"If you activate it, that will make it easier to undo, your magic will know itself even if you didn't create the enchantment. I was hoping that Jun would—"

"Hold on a minute there, Nightingale." Avlyn placed their hand Jun's shoulder as he moved towards us. "I was hoping I could give it a shot."

Jun looked at Avlyn, and something sly slid through his gaze. He nodded. "Go ahead."

Avlyn scooted forward in their crossed-legged position and placed all their fingertips on the paper. They closed their eyes and took several deep, long breaths. A faint amber light crawled across the glyphs I had inked on the page. They opened their eyes and gave a proud smile.

"You've been practicing," I observed.

"I had a good tutor." They gave me a smile that had my stomach writhing.

"Weeelllll, I guess I should try unraveling this thing," Tori said. The twins exchanged one of their looks that I knew meant they were communicating in that way they did without words. "Any pointers, tutor?"

"Visualize your magic, or for you I suppose the flow of mana. Reach out to the enchantment with it. You have already been doing this with your connection to Abraxas. Tell me what you feel."

It was Tori's turn to close her eyes, her breath slowing, and I felt the hairs on my arms stand on end as the air hummed with power.

"You're not having trouble calling the mana, even this far from the earth?" I asked.

"No, I've gotten pretty good at calling it; it's controlling it that's hard." She let out a breath, and I felt the power recede.

"What is it?"

"I'm just thinking about how Father was the one who taught me this. It's strange; he might have given me the key to controlling my power." She laughed but it overflowed with sadness. "It was all he ever wanted from me."

"Some gifts come at a price we would never be willing to pay, but fate gives us no other choice," Jun said. They shared one of their knowing looks again, but this one was much sadder.

"Focus, Tori. Use whatever you can. You'll need it all if you want to fight Hadeon."

Her brow furrowed as she focused, her eyes closing. "I can feel the enchantment. I can taste and smell it, too. It kind of smells like fish." She peeked open her eye to see Avlyn's reaction and was greeted by a splash of water in the face.

"Hey!" She attempted to tackle the Lieutenant.

"Younglings, focus please." I sighed. They scrapped a moment more before both laughed and sat back into position. She closed her eyes again.

"It feels like... you're right, like a knot. But it's moving and changing as I try to get a better idea."

"Yes, it will try to adapt to you. You'll have to outsmart it."

"And how exactly do I do that?"

"That's what you are here to figure out." She frowned but didn't open her eyes to argue. She sat quietly. The only way I knew she was focusing was the very subtle pulse of her power on the page in front of me.

"Well this is about as exciting as watching ink dry. What will we do to pass the time?" Avlyn raised a brow at me.

"Don't worry, I brought some more exercises for you, too." Their face fell. "Gods, it's like basic training all over again."

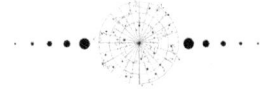

THE HOURS PASSED EASILY. JUN HAD BROUGHT HIS SMALL harp with him. I had found it outside our door a few days prior with nothing but a note that said, "A guide for the storm." I hadn't understood but it had made Jun chuckle. Hearing him play even a few casual tunes on it brought me so much joy I completely ignored the maps I was supposed to be studying to listen. Occasionally, Avlyn would huff as they overextended their well of magic and needed to take a break to recover, but the princess sat in perfect concentration the entire time.

"I've never seen her focus this long. Gods know she couldn't do it during sword training."

"This is different," Tori responded, and we all jumped. "This is like the best puzzle I've ever had. Every move I make causes a reaction, a countermove. It's almost like a sword fight, and I need to learn to read my opponent the same way." There was a soft fizzle and the amber light on the page in front of her winked out of existence as the ink of the page floated away, leaving an unmarred white page behind. She gave me a cocky smile. "Looks like I won this duel."

She looked over at Jun. "You were always better at puzzles than me; you would be great at this."

He strummed his harp, looking thoughtful. "I am good at it. I just didn't want to make you look bad." She crumbled up the paper and threw it at him.

"You did well. But that was a basic enchantment, and it took you over two hours. We won't have that kind of time in Koron."

Her face grew hard, but she nodded. "Then I'll have to get better. Do you have more?"

"Don't worry, Princess; I came prepared." I opened my sack to show her a dozen more scrolls. A deep, rumbling laugh cut through my mind. I had almost forgotten about the dragon carrying us across the continent.

We have a great distance more to travel. Best get to work.

THE SUN WAS HITTING THE HORIZON WHEN I FELT ABRAXAS begin to descend from the sky. The princess had burned through half the scrolls I had prepared. She had gotten a bit faster, but she was sweating, and it was clearly tiring. Her teeth were grinding as she worked on a particularly complex one.

"Give it a rest, Princess. We don't want you burnt out," Avlyn advised. They had stopped practicing hours ago and had been napping beside me, their leg pressed up against mine.

"I've almost got it," she huffed, more sweat appearing on her brow. A look flashed across her face, and I realized she must have been talking with Abraxas. "Focus on flying, domineering reptile."

I heard the deep rumbling I now recognized as Abraxas' draconian laughter. My seat left the floor of the carriage as he took a much more aggressive dive, and I screamed, clinging to Avlyn.

Tori shouted something at him, but I didn't hear it because all I could focus on was Avlyn wrapping their arm around me and pulling me close.

I flushed and looked up to see Jun giving me a very Tori smirk from across the carriage. I did something I hadn't in centuries and stuck my tongue out at him in a rude gesture. He laughed and gave me a soft smile of encouragement.

Only a few moments later, our movement slowed dramatically, and I felt the soft impact of the carriage on the ground. "Oh, thank the gods."

I scrambled towards the door, but it opened before I could reach it. Abraxas stood outside looking disgustingly smug. "You are very welcome, Pallas."

Jun laughed behind me and helped me out of the carriage. I hadn't noticed it as we had descended, but the air here felt sticky and wet, and my neck immediately started sweating. I looked around to see our landing location was a small clearing in a deep jungle. Huge, broad-leafed plants fought against even taller trees that towered over all of us, their canopies blocking the sun. Even without the direct light, it was sweltering, and I found myself panting.

Beside me, Jun took a deep breath, pulling that moist air into his lungs. "Gods, I missed this. It feels almost like—" He paused and looked over at Tori, but she was helping Avlyn unload something off the carriage. "Home."

"We best get a move on before the evening rains hit us," Abraxas said, looking up at the clouded sky.

"It would go faster if you would help us unload, Your Majesty," Avlyn called from the carriage.

"A king does not lower himself to such menial tasks, Commander. That is what I brought you along for."

Avlyn rolled their eyes. "How I always get stuck with all you royals, I'll never know." I walked over to them, the thick layer of leaf litter crunching under my feet.

"How can I help?"

"I've got it. I just like to give him a hard time. No need to strain yourself," they said with a jovial smile.

"I won't break, Avlyn." I held out my hand to take hold of the trunk they held in front of them.

The smile reached their eyes. "No, you certainly won't." They let go of the trunk and bid me to follow the rest of the crew.

My feet sunk further in with the added weight, but I followed after Jun into the thick of the jungle. He grabbed the handle on one side of the trunk, and we swung it between us as we continued to walk in silence. Well, our silence. The forest around us was alive with life, birds in every shade flying from tree to tree, and creatures rustling the leaves unseen.

I soaked it all in and realized in the space of a few weeks I'd travel further from my home than I ever had in the five hundred years before. I opened my mouth to speak when the trees before us parted and I was greeted by an extraordinary sight. The forest had dropped away into a stoney canyon, a great waterfall cascading down into a tranquil pool at the base. Carved into the walls and rising up above the surrounding trees were stone buildings that more resembled temples than homes. Their tiered shape flowed from a square base, and each level was decorated with steps and golden carvings. The images were inlaid with turquoise and red stones, and verdant green plant life sprung from every crack and crevasse as if it couldn't have been stopped had the designers tried.

Flat-bottomed boats floated along the pool below, pushed by

porters with long sticks. Beneath their decks, I could see the shimmer of a magnificent magenta fish that was longer than the boat above it.

More waterfalls flowed from the canyons' side and away from us; the city perfectly existed within its surroundings instead of fighting them. I was so entranced I didn't notice a small group of locals until they were nearly upon us.

They were dressed in boldly colored robes with large, geometric patterns, similar to the carvings on the stone walls. They fell straight from the shoulder to the floor and were relatively plain except for the massive collars that lay across the wearers' neck and shoulders, made from golden cloth and trimmed with a complex pattern made from gems and stones of every color. Two women wore headwear that mimicked these collars, extending above the head like the rising sun.

Jun gave me an apologetic smile before hoisting the weight of the trunk back onto me and walking over to stand beside his sister and the king.

"*Lak'ech Ala K'in*, King Abraxas. It has been too long." One of them greeted him and pressed their two index fingers together, tapping them to their forehead. The woman beside her did the same.

"*Lak'ech Ala K'in*, Queen Xareni, Queen Itzayana," Abraxas greeted, mimicking the gesture. "May I present to you, the Prince and Princess of the Pearl Kingdom, Jun and Tori Khato." The twins both mimicked the gesture as well before Tori spoke.

"Thank you for welcoming us into your home, Queen Xareni and Queen Itzayana."

"We are honored to be received by you," Jun added with a soft smile.

The queens did not return it.

"Come inside. There is much to discuss."

Chapter 56

Tori

We were led through the halls of the River Kingdom palace. It was difficult to think of it as one. Each floor of the palace was open to the outside, and the building seemed to be mostly made of arches and columns, with very few walls. Where walls did block the flow of air from the outside, they were covered in mosaic murals that were absolutely stunning. Artisans had laid out thousands of tiles made of glass, metal, and stone to recreate the beauty of the world outside. Well, at least to pay it homage.

As the Queens led us to the top of the pyramidal building, one in particular caught my eye. Azure glass had been transformed into thousands of scales that flowed along the back of a beast that stretched from one end of the hall to another. A stylized face held golden fangs and horns that looked very similar to the one I now saw every night.

"A cousin of yours?" I asked, looking at Abraxas. He ran his longer fingers over the tiles on the wall thoughtfully.

"No, not a cousin. A lover, perhaps?" He smirked at me, and I slapped his arm. He laughed, but the queens in front of us turned around with a disapproving glare, and we hopped away from each other like younglings caught in the gardens.

The rest of our journey to the top passed in silence except for my embarrassingly loud breathing as we climbed more and more stairs. I felt like my lungs were going to give out when the floor beneath me finally flattened out. We had come to the top of the pyramid, and the square floor had been covered with dark tiles laid out in a circle that touched all four edges. White moonstones had been inlaid to illustrate the constellations that match the sky above.

"What day does this sky represent?" I asked, motioning to the floor.

Queen Itzayana turned to me with a quizzical look. "The winter solstice, our most holy of days," she said simply.

"We have the biggest celebration then!" A small face popped out from behind the queen's skirts. Prince Aapo, the youngest of all fae royals, was born only a decade ago. He was the spitting image of his mother, from his bold eyebrows to the curve of his aquiline nose.

"Oh, and what happens that day?" I questioned. His mother subtly tried to push him away, but he barged forward.

"The sun is reborn, and when his light breaks over the roof of the palace, we offer a sacrifice to honor him!"

"Oh, and what do you sacrifice?"

"Sheep, mostly," his mother answered before he could.

"Sounds very formal."

He screwed up his face at that. "Yeah, it can be boring, but there is always a big party later."

"Aapo, that's enough." Queen Xareni stepped around her wife and gave the boy a stern look, and he looked down at his toes.

Both of his mothers turned and headed towards the altar at

the center of the roof, but I leaned in and whispered to the boy, "Sounds like a lot of fun."

He dared a smile at me. "It is! You should come; we never get any visitors."

"Aapo, to me." Queen Itzayana called. He scuttled away but gave me one last smile first. She pulled him into her lap as she sat down near the altar, and Queen Xareni sighed.

"The boy is right. Our kingdom has both suffered and benefited from its remote location. Our jungle is impossible for outsiders to traverse, and the river is treacherous on her kindest days. King Abraxas is one of the few visitors we ever have."

She looked at me, and I realized she was trying to open up the discussion.

"But your army has joined ours; how did they leave if the jungle is—"

"I said it is impossible to pass for outsiders, Your Highness. Our people know this land, and they have no reason to fear it."

I nodded. I did not mean to offend. The Pearl Kingdom's jungle had not been as dense as this one or as ancient, but the humid air and rich scent of life made my heart ache for a land that held nothing for me anymore. I wanted the queens to understand I saw the beauty of this place, perhaps better than most. Now was not the time.

Queen Itzayana spoke next. "I always did wonder how you managed to visit us so easily, Your Majesty."

Abraxas gave a casual shrug. "Is a man not allowed to have his secrets?"

"It seems you have many of those, old god."

At that, Abraxas' face tightened. "Indeed. But it is a secret no longer. Your Majesties, we have been allies for many centuries. Your kingdom has always kept to the old religions, and I—"

"Spared us from your armies and swords." Queen Xareni's voice was not kind.

"Yes." Abraxas' face turned to that icy mask I hated. "I did spare you; few others received the same kindness."

"And now you have come to collect," Queen Itzayana surmised. She pushed Aapo from her lap and stood tall, not shrinking back at all. "We have sent our armies to your war front despite advice against it. We do not expect to see many of our people again as they will lay dead on a battlefield fighting against an unbeatable opponent. We have done this out of mutual respect and..." she paused for several moments. She locked eyes with her wife, who nodded. "And a desire to see the balance of power in this world shift. But we have done more than any other, and still, you ask more of us?"

I stepped forward. "Your support thus far has been invaluable, and we come here today because of our mutual respect for you and your kingdom. But your kingdom holds something we need. We wish to come to an agreement."

The queens exchanged glances again. "Speak your mind, Princess Tori. What have you and the king come all this way to claim from us?"

Abraxas unrolled the map Pallas had drawn for us. She had added more details to the River Kingdom and marked the assumed location of the node a few leagues outside the city of Manan. The queens' eyes tracked Abraxas' finger as he circled our target.

"Outside your city, there is a spring of wild magic, of mana. We need to destroy it."

The color fled from both the queens' faces. Behind them, their entourage rustled with panic and annoyance. The queens moved away from us, joining them, hushed whispers spreading like wildfire.

This wasn't good. I locked eyes with the young prince, who

remained seated behind the altar, away from his mothers. He held his body tight, clearly upset by the arguing. I gave him a soft smile, and he looked away shyly, but I saw a grin spread on his face. I screwed up my eyes and stuck out my tongue, and he gave a soft laugh. It warmed my heart and calmed me. I needed all the calm I could get.

The queens turned back to us, their posture tall and proud. This definitely wasn't good.

"You speak of the cenote, one of our most ancient and sacred places. And you wish to destroy it? Why would you want to do such a thing?"

Abraxas leaned forward onto the table before us. "As you assumed, that place holds power. Your people's own legends speak of it. That power now feeds directly into Koron, into Hadeon's magic. By destroying it, we weaken him."

"Even if this was true, surely it would weaken our kingdom as well?"

"How much more could it possibly weaken?" Abraxas shot at them.

Queen Xareni shook. "I expected more from you, *kuhul ajaw*. You should know better than any other that while our access to magic has died, the earth's still remains. Our kingdom flourishes as we have protected it for centuries. We are not separate from our earth, as so many others so foolishly believe. She is our mother, the great womb of us all, and you wish to maim her."

"Our power would grow weaker," Queen Itzayana said. "While yours would grow stronger. Do not think we don't see this, King Abraxas. You position yourself well."

At that, Abraxas growled. "Let it be said here and now I have no desire to rule this world."

"Then what is your goal?"

Hadeon's death. That had always been what Abraxas

371

desired, above all else. Revenge for his people. Hadeon's father had started the war against the dragons, and his heir finished it.

I wanted it, too. For my mother, for Jun's suffering, and for Pallas'. For everyone who had suffered under Hadeon's cruelty. It had become more than that. I needed these queens to see it.

"You have seen what the Golden Kingdom has become. Their greed has sucked this earth dry. King Obion started the War of Flames, promising to restore fae to their former glory. But every action he took was for his own gain, and all it did was push us farther away. Magic died as the dragons were killed. He knew this, but he did not stop. He pushed forward, seeking a way to consolidate power for himself. And now Hadeon carries on that legacy. Ambrosia grows and strips the earth where once there were verdant lands full of food. The rivers flood and wash away more and more every year. Storms rage in ways they never had before. This is all connected. Our earth, she is already maimed; she is dying."

I felt it every time I reached for her power. Her pain lingered in every drop. But every time, there had also been hope.

"It is not too late to correct this," I declared.

"You speak beautiful words, Princess Tori. You stand beside the last dragon and speak of the earth as if you know her, have spoken to her, and learned her truth. You may be a twin, but no twin can claim all these things. So, tell me, who are you?" Queen Xareni's words were strong, but underneath them, I heard the plea. The plea for an answer, a solution that she and her people could not find.

I felt a tug on my heart as mana flowed through me. The golden bond between Abraxas and I shimmered and pulsed with it; physical touch was no longer needed between us.

He shifted; the whole plaza shadowed as his great wings ripped out of his back. Dark scales consumed his pale features, and his eyes turned that burning gold as he grew. His massive, scaled form shimmered under the setting sun, hues of deep blues and greens dancing across his hide like the sea under a stormy sky. Screams sounded from around us. People dropped to their knees as the dragon Abraxas formed before us.

"*K'inich Ajaw...*" Queen Xareni whispered the prayer, fear etched into her face. Everyone cowered away from him. Everyone but the small prince Aapo, who stood and approached with awe on his face. I gently grabbed the prince's hand in mine, but he didn't shake as Abraxas let out a deafening cry.

"Aapito, to me," his mother cried, but he was entranced, so I turned him and gently led him back to them. As soon as we were close, they snatched him into their arms.

I stood before them as they cowered. "Who am I? I am Princess Tori Khato, the mate of the last dragon, the twin sister of Jun Khato, and the Breaker of Worlds."

They blanched white, their hands wrapping tighter around the boy in their arms.

"The future may be unknown, Your Majesties, but you can either join it or be left behind. What will you do?" Abraxas let out another roar behind me, and they shook, but they met my stare. "What sort of future do you want for him?" I gestured to Prince Aapo. "One where he will be forced to obey the power that be, those who would destroy this world for their meager gains? Or would you rather have one that is unknown, but he may be able to grow to heights you have never imagined?"

To my surprise, Queen Itzayana stood and approached me.

"Yana..." Xareni whispered behind her, but she did not turn. She stood tall, taller than me even, her gaze fierce as she held mine. She looked up at the dragon behind me, and I saw the shadows of his flames fall across her face.

A moment more, she gazed into the eyes of a god, and then she pressed her two index fingers together and raised them to her forehead. "What's ours is yours. Tell us what we must do."

Chapter 57

Pallas

T he room I had been given was lovely. Everything was a set
that a fine lady would need. Books lined the shelves, most
in the common language, but many were in the ancient tongue
of the region. I flipped through a few, and I felt the old spark
light within me of a challenge. I just needed a few weeks and
some alone time in the library to master it. The language was
highly symbolic; it would be easy to memorize the first one thousand characters or so, and I was sure that I could make my way
through most of it then.

I started to pull the book on translation out, but my hand
shook. Why go through the effort when we would leave soon for
what could easily be the end of us all?

My hand shook again when a tan one landed on the book
instead. "New project of yours?" Jun's warm smile lightened my
heart.

"Is your sister teaching you how to sneak around? I didn't
hear you come in."

He laughed. "We've been sneaking together for over two
hundred years. I'm quite proficient all on my own." He handed

the book to me, and I grasped it in both hands, trying to calm their shaking.

He eyed me curiously. "What's wrong?"

"I'm just worried about finding the mana nodes here. River kingdom architecture is so different from what I've studied before."

"Pallas, come on, talk to me." Jun reached out and set a gentle hand on my cheek.

I shook my head. "I'm just scared. I've always been scared of him. What if he...?" Tears started to flow again. I felt his warm arms wrap around me. I was so shocked by the contact that it stopped my sobs.

"It's alright, Pallas. I'm scared, too." Jun held me tightly, and it felt so right and warm that, for a moment, all those doubts fled.

"How can you be so calm then?" He held me at arm's length so he could look into my eyes.

"Well, having a master glyph expert teaching me how to control my voice magic has helped." He smiled at me, and I smiled back.

A soft knock on the door was followed by Tori popping her head in. "May I come in?"

I nodded, wiping what remained of my tears away.

"Jun, do you mind giving Pallas and me a few minutes? You know, for girl talk?"

He twisted his face. "Girl talk? Who's the girl that's going to join Pallas for this?"

Tori made a rude gesture at her brother. "Fine, stay if you want, ass." Jun smiled, and it was wicked. The princess rolled her eyes and turned to me.

"If we are going cave diving tomorrow, your hair is going to be a problem," she stated flatly.

"What's wrong with my hair?" I combed it nervously.

"It's long and luxurious. It will get in the way." Tori moved to stand behind me. "May I?" I nodded my head.

She guided me to the chair in front of the vanity and gently ran her hands through my hair, softly brushing it and dividing it into sections. Her touch was so light it sent tingles down my spine, and I shivered. I saw a gentle smile in the mirror, and she continued, starting to braid the hair near my temple.

"Is this taught in the barracks?" I asked.

She laughed. "No, I used to force Jun into letting me do this to him. Didn't I?" she called over to him. I saw Jun sit down on the bed and rub his head absentmindedly, perhaps remembering when she wasn't so gentle.

"He didn't complain too much," Tori added with her own wicked grin.

"Yes, I did," her brother retorted, and she just laughed.

"Recently, I've been practicing on Abraxas." The image of the fearsome dragon king with his hair in a long, delicate braid laced with flowers and clips almost had a smile on my face. Almost. She smirked at me again, looking for my reaction. I couldn't smile back.

"I'm scared, too, you know." I stiffened in my seat. "It's good to be scared. It means you know what we face and what our failure will cost us. You've been instrumental in this, Pallas. We couldn't have done this without you."

I didn't say anything. It still felt wrong after all this time. Hadeon haunted my every thought, even now. Going against him felt so unnatural. I looked in the mirror and saw Jun smiling up at me. I would do this for him. I would never let Hadeon get him back.

Tori finished up the braid, which wrapped around my head like a crown, holding the hair tight to my head. She smiled and patted it lightly. "Much better. Shows off your pretty face."

I twisted my face at her, and she laughed again.

"I have one more thing for you." She cupped her hands in front of me, and I watched as shimmering blue mana pooled in her hands. It was like a tiny star, threads of it orbiting the whole as she gathered up the power. I saw her lace it with that white magic that flowed between her and Jun. She compressed it tight, then sent it gently into my chest, where it sat like a warm embrace over my heart.

"What's this?"

"You're not the only one who can run experiments, you know, Pallas. Think of it like a container of mana. I've been practicing making bigger ones for Abraxas so he could transform without me nearby."

"Tori, I don't have any fae magic. This will be useless in me."

Her face lit up with that annoying smirk that was starting to grow on me. "Perhaps. Just consider it good luck, then. Something to remind you that at the end of all of this, you will always have Jun and I, no matter what."

"Jun... and you?" I raised an eyebrow at her.

There was no teasing in her expression. "Yes, and me. Thank you, Pallas. Thank you for everything."

I reached up and grabbed her hand, which lay on my shoulder. She didn't have to say anymore. It seemed she couldn't help herself.

"I also know a certain someone else who would never forgive me if anything happened to you." I scowled, and she chuckled.

"I don't know what you are talking about."

"Birds of a feather, indeed."

Tori and Jun bid me good night, and for the first
time I could remember, Jun left me for his own room. With
them both gone and the sunset, suddenly, the beautiful room I
was in felt like a tomb. I climbed into bed. It was much too large
for just me. I hadn't realized how much I had grown used to
Jun's presence. I hadn't thought about how we had shared a bed
every single night for the last few months, even if that bed was
sometimes a ship's deck or a musty cave.

He'd been smiling and laughing more, and it brought me so
much joy. That dark, selfish part of me longed for him, longed to
keep him in the dark with me. If we were both broken, then at
least we would have each other. I shook my head. No. No, I
would not want that. Even if Jun left me behind, I would be
happy because he deserved that. He deserved to be whole. It
was I who didn't deserve that.

As I tried to make myself comfortable in the cold sheets, a
knock came at my door again.

"Enter."

Avlyn's beautiful face looked around the door to find me on
the bed.

"Oh, I didn't realize..."

"It's alright, Commander. I wasn't ready for bed, anyway." I
threw back the sheets and sat on the end of the bed as they came
in, shutting the door behind them.

"I just wanted to see how you were getting on. We have
quite a trek ahead of us tomorrow."

"The princess did my hair, so you can say I'm very prepared."

They chuckled. "That's good to hear. I didn't need to worry about you at all then." They flashed their teeth at me, and I looked away. "Or maybe I should. Is there anything else you need, Pallas?"

"Nothing I deserve, Commander."

I felt their fingers trace under my chin, and I lifted my eyes to meet theirs.

"How long are you going to go on punishing yourself?" Avlyn asked.

"How long does it take to earn redemption?"

"Dunno." That was all they said.

"Dunno?! Is that all you have?"

"I've never tried to be redeemed before." They shrugged their shoulders. "I've done terrible things in my life, too, Pallas. I know there are those out there who likely wish for my death; pray for it. I could try to justify it, say it was for survival or for some greater good. But that feels cheap like I'm sweeping their pain away. So, I don't try to redeem it; I let it sit with me and shoulder all the pain that I can."

"Doesn't that eat away at you?"

"Some days, yes. Sometimes it's almost too much."

"So, how do you go on?"

To my surprise, a smile spread across their lips. "I use it. All that weight I carry is a reminder of what it costs to have those I care for safe. I never forget what a blessing it is to have my soldiers, my king, or my friends with me. Everything in this life has a price, and if I am to be the one who bears it for them, then I will."

They looked at me with those deep eyes, and their smile grew into something lascivious. "And I must be doing something right because the gods have blessed me with a beautiful and erudite woman waiting for me in bed."

I felt the color rise on my cheeks and couldn't let them win, not yet. "Erudite? Someone's been studying."

"Anything to impress you." They leaned in, and I felt their hand slide up my thigh, sending bolts of pleasure straight between my legs, and my stomach flipped.

"I've been trying to impress you ever since you kissed me. I haven't been able to stop thinking about it." Their other hand came up and gently wrapped around the back of my neck, and I couldn't have escaped even if I wanted to. I didn't want to. I wanted nothing more than the feeling of them on me right now.

"I'm not good, Avlyn. You have to know that."

"Pallas, right now, I really don't fucking care." They closed that final distance, crashing their lips into mine. A soft moan escaped me, and I threw my arms around their neck, pulling them down on top of me as we crashed into the bed.

Avlyn wasn't small, and the feeling of their entire weight pressing into me was divine.

I wrapped my hand around the back of their neck, careful not to snag any braids with my nails, as I twisted their head slightly so I could deepen the kiss. Their mouth opened, and I explored them with my tongue. I was quickly drunk on their taste. Their soft tongue played with mine, and each meeting exploded with long overdue satisfaction.

Their callused fingers moved over my skin with such reverence it felt like worship. They traced the crests on my ribs and across my stomach. I pulled our mouths apart because I needed air, my blood racing so fast that there was nothing left in my lungs. Avlyn moved their lips to my neck, each kiss spreading over my skin like ripples in a pond. Their fingers traced swirls beneath my belly button until they came to my hips, following the shape of it down between my thighs.

As they brushed the sensitive skin of my inner thigh, I shivered, and I heard them elicit a soft moan against my neck. They moved until that venerating touch pressed down on the bundle of nerves that so desired it... and feared it.

My whole body flinched, and my heart stopped. I tried to moan, to move to cover it up as I would have before, but Avlyn knew. They pulled back immediately.

"It's alright. I'm fine!" I tried to grab their neck and pull them back to me, but Avlyn gently grabbed my extended hands, locking our fingers together and holding themselves away.

"Pallas, it's alright. Gods know I would understand after everything you've been through." They pulled further back, and I almost screamed. "This was too soon. I'm sorry."

"Please, Avlyn, please don't go. I'm sorry, I'll do better." Tears rose in my eyes, and I looked down at the floor to hide them.

"Hey." They grabbed my chin gently, tracing a thumb over my cheek. "You don't owe me anything. You understand that, right?"

I grabbed their wrist, leaning into their touch. "I know. I know I don't. Maybe you're right; I'm not ready for more. Not yet. But... will you kiss me, please?"

Their eyes softened. "Is that really what you want? If I leave now, it changes nothing between us. I'm happy to wait as long as you need me to."

They would. It wasn't my body they wanted. It was me. How long had it been since I'd felt anything like that? I leaned forward again so my lips met theirs. They didn't retreat, so I grasped their cheeks in my hands, tracing the high cheekbones with my fingertips. I shifted my weight, so they fell back onto the bed with me. For a moment, our lips parted, and they laughed.

"I told you I was way too lenient with beautiful women."

AFTER WHAT SEEMED LIKE HOURS, I CUDDLED INTO Avlyn's chest and listened to their heart slow down as they fell asleep. The same sleep never claimed me. I traced my fingers over Avlyn's cheekbones and soft skin one more time. They were absolutely beautiful. I pressed my lips softly against their cheek and walked over to start on the book of translation I'd been toying with earlier. Avlyn shifted as I got out of bed but didn't seem to wake. I walked across the room, my feet light on the floor. A hand slammed over my mouth, and another wrapped around my waist.

"Nice to see you, gorgeous," Luxos whispered in my ear. I tried to scream, but his shadows snaked under his hand and gagged me so no sound could emerge. I struggled against his grip and threw an elbow back into his stomach like Tori had shown me.

It wasn't that hard of a hit, but he staggered and hissed loudly. "Pallas, enough."

"Let her go, Shadow Walker." I squeaked as I heard Avlyn behind us.

Luxos spun us around. Avlyn stood mostly undressed, holding a small dagger, poised and ready to strike.

Luxos chuckled, "Up to your old tricks, Pallas? I didn't think they were really your type." He clamped his arm tighter around me but moved his hand so his thumb ran underneath my breast. Avlyn's eyes locked onto it, and they snarled. "Tell me, Commander, she always was so good with her tongue. Did she show you that?" Avlyn lunged, but Luxos anticipated the move and dodged out of the way.

Avlyn spun in a way that almost defied logic and thrust the dagger into Luxos' side. He groaned, and I felt his hot blood spilling down my leg. Before I could even process that, a sword flashed, and more blood sprayed everywhere. My entire night-gown was drenched, and it wasn't only Luxos blood.

Avlyn staggered away, clutching what remained of their arm. Crimson rivulets ran between the fingers that clutched where their other hand had been. I screamed and screamed, but no sound came out. Darkness and cold overtook me with the smell of death and roses. Avlyn's mangled body disappeared as Luxos carried me away.

Part 4

Chapter 58

Tori

"Where were the fucking wards?!" I slammed my fist on the table, and the two queens staggered back.

"Tori, this isn't the place." Abraxas' voice was rough. His face was pale, but he tried to retain his composure.

"Like hell, it's not. They said they had wards in place against magical intrusion. He still got in here. He took Pallas, and Avlyn..." I tried to not cry; I really did. All I could see was their arm wrapped in those blood-stained sheets as they'd run to find me.

"They won't be able to fight again, Abraxas. If we had the rest of their arm, maybe... but..." It had vanished along with Luxos and Pallas.

"Princess Tori, we understand your distress, truly," Queen Xareni said. "Our Xaman have done all they can to maintain our wards these last centuries, but none of us are still blessed with the gift of the earth as you are. Trust me, we have much to lose should Emperor Hadeon's wrath come down upon us as well."

I looked down to see Prince Aapo still lingering amongst the adults of the room, and I saw the fear all mothers share.

"Where are your warding glyphs? I shall restore them." Jun was pale. He hadn't slept at all. He even tried to convince Abraxas to fly him to Koron before daybreak. I don't know what my lover had said to him, but it had calmed him enough so that he merely paced his room all night instead of running off into the jungle. "No one else will come to harm because of him."

A distraction would be good for him. I gave his shoulder a tight squeeze before he walked off with the ancient Xaman fae, heading down the long stone hallway of the river kingdom palace before disappearing from sight.

"What of the cenote, King Abraxas?" Itzayana asked. "Our guides are ready to take you."

Abraxas looked at me, and I squeezed his hand. We had already discussed it during the night.

There wasn't time. It had taken us weeks to enter and destroy the Torr. The cenote wasn't cursed, but who knew what we would find there? The choice was laid before us simply, destroy this site sacred to the River Kingdom to weaken Hadeon's enchantment a fraction, or save Pallas.

Abraxas had let his feelings be known. "We do not know she is in danger. My love, for all we know, she has run to Hadeon with open arms, revealing all she knows to him."

"All the more reason. We cannot wait any longer!"

"Always in such a hurry, my love. You and your brother." He softened his gaze. "She may already be dead."

"She is not. I would know." The ball of magic I had given to her was still tied to me. The bond was nothing like my tie to Abraxas or even Jun, but I would know if it disappeared. She was alive, at least for now.

"There is something else. Something I saw at the Torr. The ley lines under Koron are weaker than we thought. The ambrosia has been pulling mana from the earth without respite for centuries. I talked with Oryx about it. He said he's seen something similar with farmers who don't rotate their crops. The earth below grows weak. This is on another level, centuries of mistreatment. We don't need to destroy the cenote here. It's time, Abraxas."

He gave another long-suffering sigh, but then his roguish grin returned. "I figured as much. I have already sent word to the army. They will mobilize, and we will meet them in the field." His eyes sparkled.

I tackled him to the bed and did not let him get up for quite some time.

"We thank you for your willingness, Queen Itzayana, Queen Xareni. However, as soon as Jun returns, we shall depart these lands."

Both of their eyebrows shot up in surprise. "You're sure?" Prince Aapo called out from behind his mother, looking at me shyly.

I gave him my bravest smile. "Yes. Take good care of this place until we can visit again, little prince." He had given me the brightest smile I had seen in an age.

"I will!"

Chapter 59

Abraxas

I walked down the stone halls of the outbuilding, winding until I found the door to the infirmary. It was hidden behind a waterfall. The flowing water was believed to help with the healing of the patients within. I let my fingers trail through the water's flow, trying to memorize the details of this place that had once been home to a small but significant number of my people. It was so different from my homeland, but something about it had always sparked a familiarity like I knew it in my very blood.

But there was no time for that now. I pressed open the round stone door and saw Avlyn sitting hunched over on one of the cots, facing away from me. A few healers surrounded them, but at my entrance, they scattered like fleas.

Avlyn didn't turn to me as I approached.

"Before you ask, I'm fine. It was just my sword hand. Won't really be needing that in the battles to come, anyway."

"Avlyn... perhaps—"

"If you say I should stay behind, I swear to the gods I will stab you with my other hand. I'm pretty unpracticed, so I'll probably hit something vital in the process."

I sat down next to them on the cot. "Has she really become so important to you?"

They stiffened next to me. I laughed. "If anyone would understand how quickly a beautiful woman can completely undermine your entire life, it would be me."

They sighed, "It's not just her. It's for everyone we have lost for the last five hundred years. Everything we've done because of that fucker."

"The burden of that guilt should not fall on you. It is mine to bear. It was my choice to follow Hadeon."

"I understand why you did; truly, I do. Even before I knew about all this... dragon shit, I understood. It's what kept our people safe. That's what you taught me. But Tori is right."

"Didn't think I would hear you say that. How long was I asleep?"

They gave a soft smile. "Like you said, these women have a way of worming into our hearts, don't they?" Their smile dropped. "It's not just Xyr, not just our kingdom that needs protection. It's everyone. We can't let someone like him have so much power. We have the strength to defend them, so we should."

"And Pallas is one of those people?" I wasn't teasing now.

"We wouldn't be here without her, and I know... Well, I think I know what it costs her to help us. We can't leave her there with him. That's a fate I would not wish on my worst enemy."

I understood that very well. "You really are sounding like Tori." I was teasing again.

Their nose scrunched. "Don't say that. I can't let her head get any bigger."

I nodded and rose off the cot. "Then you better find a way to make yourself useful, Commander."

Avlyn jumped up. "Yes, sir."

I placed a hand on their shoulder. "I'm proud of the fae you have grown into."

They rolled their eyes. "Abraxas, I'm over five hundred years old."

"Still just a fledgling in my eyes, but it's time for me to let you soar."

A faint, dark blush rose in their cheeks, but they controlled it quickly.

"When do we leave?"

"I just received a falcon back. The army has mobilized from their position in the Reach. Reinforcements come from Xyr. At sunset, we will fly."

Avlyn moved awkwardly, and I realized they had intended to smack their chest with their hand, the one that was no longer there. I gripped their shoulder instead. "Let's go kill this bastard."

Chapter 60

Pallas

Luxos abandoned me in an unused room before disappearing. I scrambled to the door and found it locked, of course. I slammed my fists into it and screamed. Long dark tracks of blood followed my fingers down the wood of the door as I slunk to the ground. Avlyn's blood.

I couldn't breathe. With every inhale, that cloying, metallic scent caused me to spiral inward. It's all your fault.

My stomach heaved as the creature inside me yowled, begging me to get out, but I couldn't. Instead, I shoved her away and caged her in the very depths of my soul until I felt absolutely nothing. I'd gotten good at it. My breath steadied, and I thought of nothing. Not Avlyn, not Jun, not Tori, not the pain that was sure to follow. I walked into the void and let it swallow me whole.

As I sat in the corner, knees hugged to my chest, the door swung open. Two guards entered. They grabbed my arms to haul me up. I barely felt their fingers dig into my flesh as they dragged me to another room. I stumbled forward when they pushed me inside, and two slaves greeted me in tattered, grey robes. Their hoods hid their faces, but I wouldn't have seen them anyway. I was pulled towards the round wooden tub that filled most of the space. They yanked off my clothes, and I didn't feel embarrassed or flinch away. I just let it happen like I always did.

I stepped into the tub, and they poured pitchers of water over me; the dark red blood swirled with the bath water in the most interesting of patterns. Was that my blood? I couldn't seem to care. I let my fingers dance through the shifting liquids, and they felt as if they belonged to someone else.

The slaves washed me, scrubbing every inch of my skin with harsh, abrasive sponges. It was as if they tried to wash away any trace of the Dragon Kingdom. As if my taste of freedom could be scrubbed off. In just a few minutes, I was blank and sparkling.

They hauled me out, toweled me dry, and pulled a flowing white gown over my head. The split sleeves were so long they dragged on the floor, and the train of the gown seemed to float behind me. I glanced at myself in the mirror as a human girl braided my hair. I was perfect and pure. The very image of the emperor's consort, ethereal beauty beyond compare. I could hardly see that uncaged beast hiding behind my eyes.

They led me down the halls of the palace that had been my home for centuries, the guards following close behind. They pushed open the door to my room. Hadn't I been sharing it with someone?

I entered, and a man turned around to greet me.

"Pallas, my love!" Hadeon swept over to me, and I felt my whole body flinch, but there was no pain, only his arms wrapping around me. His hand landed on the back of my head, holding me to his chest. His other held my waist tight. He smelled the same, like the golden sun and a warm summer thunderstorm. He smelt like home.

Don't! The creature inside me hissed, but my arms came up and wrapped around his waist, and he let out a long, contented sigh.

"I was so worried about you, my darling. Commander Luxos has been punished for his incompetence in retrieving you sooner." He cupped my face in his hand gently, forcing me to look up into those deep violet eyes.

I couldn't help tears from rising to mine. "Your Eminence..."

He gave me a soft smile. "So formal, Pallas." He pulled me into a soft kiss, his lips moving gently against mine. His hand pressed into my lower back, so our bodies fit together as they always had. The creature in me hissed, but the part of me that was weak always won out. I collapsed into that embrace, into his affection.

He lifted me up and moved us towards the bed, and my heart nearly stopped, but he simply set me down on it and tucked me in. His hands wrapped the blankets around me as if there was nothing more precious to him in the entire world. He sat down beside me and brushed the hair away from my face, his eyes never leaving me.

"You've been through so much, my love. You need some rest. Tomorrow, we can discuss your time away." He ran his finger over my forehead gently again before planting a soft kiss there. "I'm so happy to have you home, Pallas."

He got up and left without another word. My heart fluttered, remembering when he had always been gentle with me.

My creature hissed and clawed, but I slammed the cage shut on her, rolled over, and fell asleep in my own bed.

Chapter 61

Tori

We met the army inside the Golden Kingdom. They had pushed through the last of Hadeon's forces that weren't at Koron. Commander Tulius updated me on casualties and our movements toward the capital over the next few days.

The price had been too high. I sat in the verdant fields outside the camp, staring up at the crescent moon, and prayed for every last soul whose name I had read on that list. To whom I prayed, I wasn't sure. Maybe it was just to myself; a promise that those losses would be repaid in kind and that this world would change.

Despite the recent violence, I could feel the restlessness of the camp. The upcoming battle at Koron was ever looming. Abraxas had ordered everyone to bed, and that had promptly been ignored.

All around me, the sounds of singing, drinking, and fucking filled the air. When death loomed, life always seemed to blossom in its more ferocious form, clinging to this world with every tooth and nail.

I finished my silent requiem and made my way to Avlyn's tent. They sat on a cot with a bucket of water in front of them. Spheres of water leaped from the surface, dancing and orbiting one another. They gave a small grunt, acknowledging my presence, but continued to focus on their magic. I sat down next to them, placing my hand on their back.

Immediately, the small spheres Avlyn controlled grew until the entire contents of the barrel floated in front of us as a massive spinning orb that caught the torchlight.

"You're getting pretty good at this," I complimented.

Avlyn gently channeled all the water back into the barrel without even the smallest splash. "Pallas taught me a few tricks for concentration." Their face went hard.

I grabbed their shoulder and gave it a soft squeeze. "We'll get her back," I vowed.

They shook their head. "It's not that. I just hope... I hope she's alright. Who knows what horrible things Hadeon is doing to her? He has to know she has information on us. If he's hurting her to get it, I won't be able to live with that. I should have kept her safe." They rubbed the end of their injured arm absentmindedly.

"Maybe she'll just give him the information freely. Maybe she was right all along; we shouldn't have trusted her."

"She won't. I know she won't." I didn't argue with them. We would find out in a few days' time, one way or another.

"Get some rest, Avlyn."

"Yes, sir." They gave me a sarcastic salute and turned back to their barrel of water. I rolled my eyes and gave them a gentle kiss on the top of the head before heading out.

I walked to the edge of the camp again, looking out toward Koron. There were a few hundred leagues between us and our destination still, so I couldn't see the city. I sat down in the field of flowers that covered the Golden Kingdom. The sweet scent of the ambrosia flowers stirred in the night wind. Digging my fingers into the ground, I reached for the mana below. I followed the stream to the earth's beating heart, where it sat below Koron. It writhed and pulsed, like it, too, knew the destruction that lay ahead.

The foundation of the palace tied into that immense power, and I followed it higher to where it knotted and flowed in an incredible pattern. Mana was woven into an unbreakable lock. That had to be Malech's heart. I tugged at the threads that were woven around it, but it only pulled them tighter, keeping me away. They were intertwined with exacting precision. It did not surprise me that they had been created by Pallas' mother. I saw the same attention to minute detail and rigid control in her daughter.

Pallas had been right. This was truly a masterwork of enchantment. I didn't need to be any sort of expert to see that. Despite my concentration, trying to unravel it from this great distance was like trying to separate grains of sand blindfolded. I would need to get closer, right up next to it, if I was to have any hope of ever reaching the heart. I sighed, ready to let it all go, when something caught my attention.

A small, floating point of light, separate from the lock, hovered nearby as if observing it. It shone a soft blue, like the color of the noonday sky, and beat like a heart. It felt familiar.

I slowed my breathing, sending all thoughts away so that I might see deeper and observe what the earth was showing me.

A face emerged, and it was Pallas, standing in front of those great doors I had once failed to open. Her hand reached out, and she touched the enchantment there. The lock of mana flared, and she stepped back.

She shook her head and turned away, fleeing the dungeon. I

followed the blue glow beating in her heart, the very magic I had given her. It felt different now; it was no longer just mana of the earth. It felt like Pallas. I observed it and saw that it, too, was composed of threads. They wrapped around something deep within Pallas's heart. A lock, just like the enchantment on the door.

The threads were erratic, like brambles that had grown in every direction, over and through each other. The magic that wove them wasn't fae. The enchantment felt like Runya. These threads felt almost like...roots.

I dared tug at one and felt Pallas falter. The root seemed to swell and grip tighter every time I tried to move it, but if there was one thing I had learned, it was this. Everything burned.

I focused on my dragonfire, but the distance was too great. I couldn't have undone this knot any more than I could the lock.

I let go and came back to my body. I was now lying flat on the ground, looking at the great starry river Maiak. What lay beyond the tangles of Pallas' heart might very well be what changed our days ahead from victory to defeat. We would see whose side she was on soon.

I wandered back to the camp, but my mind lingered on that tangle around Pallas' heart. Something about it felt too familiar. I rubbed my arm at the phantom sensation of tendrils rising from the earth and rooting under my skin. Roots made from mana that not only wrapped around me but also every man, woman, and child in the world.

"You alright, Princess?" I startled. Abraxas had snuck up on me as I wandered, my mind miles away.

"Yes, I... come with me." I grabbed his hand, and he followed without hesitation. I pulled us into our tent and ran my eyes over him from head to toe.

"See something you like, little bird?" he teased, grinning.

"Hush, I'm thinking."

He obeyed, at least until I pulled off his jacket. "Tori, I really am trying not to misread this situation, but—"

"Hush."

I yanked his shirt over his head and lay my hands on his chest. His dragonfire glowed green beneath his skin; the light leaked between my fingers. His heart was mine, but how close had I really looked at it? I pressed my concentration beneath his skin. Emerald green light flowed through him, and in this form, it felt like fae magic.

"You said that in this body, you are bound by the laws of the fae. You cannot conduct mana, only wield magic as a fae would." He nodded. "You said you used to be stronger?"

He gripped my hand in his. "Yes, as magic has faded from this world, it has also faded in me."

"What did that feel like?"

He furrowed his brows. "It was slow, almost unnoticeable, like a pot being slowly brought to a boil. I didn't sense it until it was too late. Now, if I think on it, it feels like... like my magic has been caged inside iron. I can feel it, but I cannot access it."

A cage. I reached back into his heart. It was so bright now, overflowing with fire, life, and, at its core, love. I pushed tendrils of mana inside of it, digging deeper until I heard Abraxas grunt with pain, but he did not stop me.

There! Shadows hiding in the light. Vines made from iron and stone, just like I had felt around Pallas' heart, around almost everyone's heart.

I struck them with mana and fire to no effect. Abraxas grunted again. "This is really starting to become a bit unnerving, Princess."

I didn't answer as I wrapped tendrils of power around each branch and tried to pull them loose, but they wouldn't budge. I snapped at them with dragonfire, but these vines had grown in the flaming heart of a dragon, and no flame would touch them.

I poured more mana into them, more power, and it did nothing.

Abraxas fell to one knee. "Tori, whatever you intend to do here, I don't know how much more I can take." I pulled back on my power.

Finesse and control. That's what Pallas had said. I couldn't just ram my power into this. I needed help.

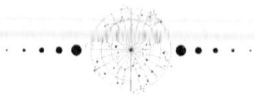

I RETURNED SHORTLY WITH JUN TO FIND ABRAXAS DOZING on the cot, still shirtless. I guess I had worn out the old man.

"Tori, I still don't exactly understand what we need to do."

"You will."

I knelt down beside Abraxas and shook him gently. He groaned. "Whatever you have planned for me, please try not to kill me."

"After I went to all that effort of getting you back? I think not." I gave him a reassuring smile, and he gripped my hand tightly. I placed my hand on Abraxas' chest, but Jun hesitated.

"It is alright, Prince. I consent to this." Jun's lips flattened, but he nodded and placed his hand on mine.

I pulled mana into us. I tried to weave it into a song, a resonance between Jun and me. Our hands glowed, and we sent that light into Abraxas' heart.

"I see them," my brother muttered with a smile on his face. "Time to show you how much better I am at puzzles."

Together, we guided that white light around the entanglement. Seeing it like this pressed against the ancient magic of the earth and the fire of Abraxas' heart, I could see how alien it was. It was the light of a star that had flown across time and space, through the unimaginable distances and emptiness of the universe to find its way here. The magic of the earth was just a blip to it, no more than the plankton of the sea was to the Leviathan. To a magic that had existed since before time even had any meaning. What was the life of one world?

Jun guided it with grace, tugging at each thread as the earth unraveled under his work. I pressed that light into Abraxas' heart, protecting it from all the jagged edges.

Abraxas let out a moan of pain that had my eyes snapping open. Blood flowed from his nostrils, and his jaw was clenched so tight that the muscles popped in his jaw.

"Stop—"

"No!" He slapped his hand down on top of ours. "Don't you dare stop; I can feel it. It's almost done!" His eyes shone bright green, and fire licked all over his skin.

I forced it away from Jun as sweat beaded on his brow. "Almost there..." My brother gritted his teeth, and I felt the last of the vines get swept into the light and dissolve into nothing.

Fire exploded over the tent, and I threw myself and a shield of raw mana over Jun. We scrambled away from Abraxas as the tent above us was incinerated. I heard his maniacal laughter as dragonfire oozed from every pore. It swirled around him blazing-hot, creating a vortex that pulled on the surrounding tents until they threatened to collapse.

Abraxas laughed and laughed. He let his arms be swept up in the dance of the flames, his hair flowing wildly as he shot an enormous green fireball straight into the sky. It exploded like fireworks, and embers rained down, starting small orange flames all over the camp.

"This is it." He was caught in the rapture of the flames. His glowing eyes locked on mine, and he stalked towards me, every inch a predator.

I moved between him and Jun, but he just swept me into his

inferno. My skin sizzled, but the fire no longer burned my skin. He ran his hand up my back and wove it into the hair at the base of my neck, pushing me back as his mouth pressed to mine. I tilted my head and took in all the heat and softness of his tongue and the strength of his grip until I completely melted.

He pulled away, his eyes burning. "My goddess, is there nothing you cannot do?"

Chapter 62

Pallas

The morning sun broke gently through my window—my room, back home. I pushed back the silken sheets of my bed and observed everything. Nothing had been touched. My bookshelves were tidy, and my vanity was organized just as I liked it. I ran my finger over the deeply stained wood, and not a speck of dust was to be found.

My place here had been preserved and cared for. A soft knock came at the door. "Enter." One of the many slaves I had known for most of their human life entered. She gave me a soft smile before depositing a tray of food for me and turning to go.

The tray was laden with my favorite things: scones soaked in thick cream and numerous ramekins of jam set out like little jewels all around. Freshly sliced preserved meats and cheese were accompanied by soft-boiled eggs already cut and salted. I dug in and immediately fell into the familiar flavors and textures.

Home. Was I really home?

The creature inside me hissed, but I drowned her in jam

and tea served with lemon. I leaned back in my plush chair and let my hand gently rub over my very full stomach.

Another knock came at my door, but before I could respond, Lord Plagis pushed inside. Immediately, my hackles raised, and I sat up straight in my chair.

"Ah, my lady, it's so wonderful to see you again."

I said absolutely nothing, but Plagis was used to that. My nails cut into the chair's fabric, but he didn't notice.

He approached me boldly, smoothly setting himself down in the chair opposite me. He let his eyes roam over my nightgown, and I wanted to cross my arms and hide. No, I want to snatch his eyes right out of their sockets. My own thoughts surprised me so much that I missed his attempt to speak to me.

"Did you hear me, my lady?" I shook my head. "Oh my, your ordeal must have been truly gruesome for you to be so divorced from the present. No matter. I said the emperor expects you to join him for dinner tonight."

I didn't move or respond. He didn't care.

"I must say, I look forward to hearing everything you have gleaned during your time in the Dragon Kingdom. Despite my many visits, King Abraxas kept his affairs tightly locked away. Ha! Well, I think we all know why now. The last dragon? I can hardly believe it." He continued for quite some time, and I once again didn't hear a word he said.

This routine was familiar to me as well, as was what came next. I was home, indeed.

"I am so grateful to have you returned to us, my lady. I have missed you dearly."

I didn't even notice him grabbing my hand. His eyes leered at me, and his other hand came up to trace over the curves of my side. He leaned in and placed a sloppy kiss against my knuckles.

When you are ready, I'll be the first in line. The image of Avlyn doing the same thing flashed through my mind. It had been the same action, the same kiss, but somehow, it was completely different.

Plagis' hand roamed under the curve of my breast, his fingers greedy, and my mind tried to flee to anywhere but this room. *Do you want to be rescued, Pallas?* Yes, but Avlyn wasn't here. No one was here for me. I was all alone again, surrounded by monsters. I had never known how to fight.

Not all heroics are grand battles and gestures. Jun was right. I snatched my hand away from Plagis and stood so rapidly that he nearly toppled over.

"My Lady?"

"Lord Plagis, I have just returned from quite the ordeal, as you said. And I have spent no time with our Divine Emperor yet. Wouldn't it be prudent to do so before engaging in any other social calls?"

I saw Plagis' eyes wrinkle in anger, but before he could speak, I added, "Don't you think that is what the Divine Emperor would want?"

Plagis was a vile man, but he wasn't a fool. He would not cross Hadeon, at least not yet. "Of course, my lady. How right you are. Well, I look forward to enjoying your company soon." He spun and exited my room without another word, and I slumped back into my chair. I was home, indeed.

No one stopped me as I wandered the halls of the palace. Few even spared me a greeting or glance. After a few courtiers approached me with casual greetings and idle gossip, I realized many probably didn't even know I had been gone.

I thought about wandering to the gardens to see the flowers

in all their late summer splendor, but my feet took me elsewhere. Slowly, the surrounding air grew colder and more humid, the stench of wet earth leaking from the stone walls as I descended into the bowels of the palace. It was broken briefly by that familiar floral scent, and I could feel the shadows watching me, but he did not approach.

"Lurking, as always, Luxos?" He didn't respond, and I didn't care.

Down in the darkness, it was easy to recall the taste of Avlyn's blood as it splattered over my face. I wasn't sure what I would do if Luxos approached me, but I was sure neither of us would leave unharmed.

I continued to walk until those great wooden double doors stood before me. The last time I had stood before them, I'd been only a youngling, watching my mother work. She had been lecturing me, but I had daydreamed about the kisses Hadeon and I shared the night before. A fool, even then.

I touched the door, and it flared to life. The glyphs were a terrible deep violet. I scanned them, memorizing every inch.

What are you doing? You're not on their side anymore. Do you think they would really save you now, after everything that happened? Avlyn never cared for you; you didn't even give them what they wanted. Jun prefers his sister to you, and Tori only used you. You're still that same fool you always were.

I pulled my hand away from the door, and tears rolled down my face. Alone. I had always been alone, but the defenses I built had eroded over the last few weeks. And now...

My heart pulled, and I thought it just might give out. Then it pulled again, harder this time. The creature inside me purred, and my heart tugged again to the point of pain. It felt like someone was gripping and pulling against it crudely, trying to rip it out of my chest. It felt almost like...

"Tori?" I whispered. Of course, there was no response, and

the tugging stopped. I wiped the tears on my face away and turned my back on the door. I had a dinner to get ready for.

WHEN I RETURNED TO MY ROOM, TWO SLAVES WAITED WITH their grey hoods pulled up over their heads. They silently undressed me. They had gotten out my favorite dress made of gossamer lavender that shimmered silver in the light. The fabric was so thin it floated around me as I walked, with slit sleeves that trailed nearly to the floor. One slave gently brushed my hair and placed a classic silver circlet adorned with moonstones across my brow. They turned me to the mirror, and my reflection was the very vision of a fae princess. I was no such thing.

They led me to the dining hall. I had expected the room to be packed with the denizens of the court as it normally would be, but the long table was completely empty except for Hadeon at his usual spot. As I entered, he rose, waiting for me to approach him.

"Your Eminence." I gave a small curtsy, looking down at his feet.

"Pallas, we discussed this." His hand moved towards me, and I immediately flinched. All he did was gently trace my jaw and raise my chin so I would look at his beautiful face. "No need to be so formal."

His eyes sparkled, and I waited for my punishment, but he planted his lips on mine—a soft, loving kiss. I fell into it immediately before he pulled away, sweeping my chair out for me. I quickly sat down, my dress fluttering around me. "You truly are a beauty beyond compare tonight, my love."

"Thank you, Y... Hadeon." I risked giving him a soft smile,

and he returned it in kind before carefully taking a bite of his dinner.

We ate in silence for a while, and it made me wonder how long it had been since we had done anything like this. Had it been decades? I couldn't be sure. What was I supposed to say? Once, the words between us had flowed like water, ever bubbling up from an eternal spring. We couldn't have stopped them even if we wanted to. Now, there was only silence.

"I hope you have found everything to your liking. I made sure that all of your things were prepared for your return."

"Lord Plagis came to my room this morning." I heard the soft clink of Hadeon's fork as he set it down on his plate. "He seemed to expect—"

His chair slid back, and I finally dared to raise my gaze. He stood beside me and leaned down, gently cupping my face again. "My enchantress." My heart stilled at the nickname he had once lavished on me with abandon. "Your absence has made me realize how very... poorly you have been treated these last decades. I swear to you, this ends now. Should Plagis, no, should any other man ever dare to touch you again, I will make sure that he dies screaming." My eyes widened as he leaned in. "You are mine, Pallas. Mine alone. Let me soothe that long aching heart of yours."

The kiss he gave me was not soft. He laced his fingers through the hair at the back of my neck, pulling me into him. His plush lips met mine, and he pressed his tongue into my mouth, claiming every surface. I opened up to him immediately and tilted my head to give him even more access. I was his in every way. I always had been. I was right back there, in that garden. That place where he loved and cherished me. The place I desired with all my heart.

My inner creature clawed at me, spitting and yowling in a way I had never felt before. She scratched at my heart, trying to destroy the treacherous thing, but Hadeon's hand at my waist and the soft moans I emitted drowned her out.

As quickly as it had started, he released me. He flashed that gorgeous smile that had won him the hearts of Adimos. "Now tell me, what did you learn in the Dragon Kingdom?"

My head was still spinning, so I didn't respond right away, and I saw the corner of his mouth twitch.

"I'm sorry. What do you mean?"

"What I mean..." Hadeon's voice was smooth, but I heard the subtle edge to it now. "...is that you've spent considerable time with the Dragon King and his little princess. You're a smart woman and my greatest love. Surely you used that to your advantage?"

I had learned things. So many things. I'd learned about Tori's magic and how it would all disappear if Abraxas was killed. Their intentions to destroy his heart. The fact I had taught them how. Traitor.

"I know the princess is the king's mate." I dared a small glance at Hadeon and saw the fury crinkling the corners of his eyes. "That's no secret now, my love. But what does it mean?"

It means that she shares his power. It means she can conduct mana, enough to destroy your enchantment. It means that if you kill Abraxas, she'll be too weak to fight you. It means if you hurt her, Abraxas would be destroyed.

"I don't know." My fingers tightened around the stem of my wineglass. "I am no spy. I was lucky to survive my time with them. I have no secrets to share." The lie came surprisingly easy.

His smile faltered, replaced by a flicker of irritation. "Come now, my enchantress, there's no need for games. Luxos informed me you were kept in comfort at the prince's side. His sister is a greater fool than he was. I have no doubt she thought herself a savior to you."

I said nothing, but Hadeon read me like an open book. "Was

she kind to you? Did she pull you to her side and tell you she valued you? Don't be a fool, Pallas. She cares only for herself. They all do. Would you betray me so?"

Voices, so many voices, swirled in my head.

You're acting like a youngling, Pallas.

You've just been caged too long.

All you ever do is embarrass me.

You're not his anymore.

I can't believe how sensitive you've gotten.

I love you, Pallas.

I swallowed hard, my gaze flickering to the ornate ceiling of the dining hall just for a moment. "I assure you, Your Eminence, my loyalty lies with you. I wasn't privy to anything other than the prince's healing."

"It's that boy, isn't it? Do you care for him so much? Do you hope to protect him? Tell me what you know, and I assure you no harm will come to him."

No harm. I caught myself before I laughed at the ridiculousness of that statement. Hadeon had nearly destroyed Jun, and I would not let that happen again. I might be a fool. I might be naïve. I might have fallen right back into his arms, but I would die here before I ever let him touch Jun again.

"Just like before, right, Hadeon?"

His eyes glowed violet. There it was. His true self. The tension in the air between us crackled like lightning. "You forget yourself, Pallas. You belong to me. Now tell me what you know before I—"

"You what? There is nothing you can do to me you have not done a thousand times before." I stood so violently that my chair toppled over.

Before I could move even an inch more, he was on me, his hand gripping my head and arm as his power raced through my body. I screamed.

"I can't believe you have brought me to this, Pallas. I wanted to be kind, to be gentle with you. But look what you have done! You have given me no other choice."

Lightning danced over my body, and I screamed. The pain was so familiar. Tears leaked from my eyes. I had always been too weak to fight him. I'd always been a fool. I sank into that pain and prayed that this time, it would sweep me away into nothing like I truly deserved.

Chapter 63

Tori

I was sitting with Jun, eating our cold camp dinner, when I felt it—cold, wet dread gripping at my stomach. The food turned to ash in my mouth, and I set my bowl down on the ground beside me with a clank.

"Tori?" Jun looked at me with concern. I grabbed his hand and focused on the feeling that was twisting itself around my stomach. It was fear, deep and ingrained, but it wasn't mine. I visualized the mana of the earth and followed it to that floating light I had given to Pallas, and it was beating so fast I thought it might explode.

"Pallas?" My brother felt it, too, and his face blanched. "What's happening? We have to help her." He rose like he was ready to run straight to her across the fields of ambrosia. It was a very me thing to do. I grabbed his hand and pulled him back down.

"Focus. We've got a lock to pick."

He raised his eyebrows but didn't question me as I pulled his forehead to mine. I entwined our fingers and the white light in our hearts. That ancient and foreign magic flowed down the ley line beneath our feet and straight into Pallas' heart.

Those twisted roots remained, just like I had seen in Abraxas. These were stronger and more numerous. Some areas were so thick that they almost completely blocked out the light that was hidden inside. The heart underneath threatened to give out, and as I focused more, I could hear Pallas' screaming. Jun's jaw clenched as he heard it, too. We didn't have time.

Together, we reached out with our magic, probing gently at the shimmering tangle surrounding Pallas's heart. I hesitated, but Jun launched in, tugging at the roots with abandon. The first he pulled on snapped; its loose end was sucked deeper into the writhing mass. I gripped his hand tighter. We had to be careful. He squeezed back and worked slower.

We pulled and worked at the puzzle, and with every bit loosened, I saw more and more of that blue light that was Pallas peeking out. Pain shot over my legs and back, and I knew it was only a shadow of what she was feeling. I couldn't let it break my focus. I ground my teeth until they nearly cracked, and Jun gripped my fingers until I thought they might snap.

We persisted, and more light emerged from the depths of Pallas's heart. Finally, our white magic and her blue light were too much, and the knot disintegrated into ash, the threads of the earth unraveling like strands of silk as they fell away.

Pallas' magic burst forth, and we were both thrown back, landing next to the fire. Numerous worried eyes looked at us, but I only saw Jun.

"She has to do the rest," I whispered, and he nodded.

"We're with you, Pallas," Jun murmured, sending it on the wind to her.

"Fight, Pallas."

Chapter 64

Pallas

I was nearly gone; the edges of my vision were black, and my throat was raw. My screams were silent now, but they still tried to escape. I felt my heart giving out. I wouldn't survive much longer.

Then it tugged, trying to jump out of my chest. The sensation was so similar to the feeling in the hallway before I was able to cling to it.

I felt something unraveling inside me, and then they were there.

We're with you, Pallas.

Fight, Pallas.

The pain ceased for a moment as Hadeon retracted his magic. He threw me onto the floor, and the side of my head cracked against the stone audibly. My vision danced black again, and he stooped over me.

"Tell me what you know, my enchantress."

"I don't know anything!"

His hand snaked around the front of my throat, and he lifted me. My lungs strained, and pain radiated from his tight grip as all my weight was forced into it. I clawed at his hand with my own, but it did nothing.

"Perhaps a night in the dungeon will trigger your memory. No need to worry, my love; the men have been quite without amusement these arduous weeks. I'm sure you won't be alone down there for long."

No. No, no, no, no. Fight Pallas!

I kicked him hard in the stomach, and it stunned him so much that he dropped me and staggered back. I coughed, trying to force air into my head. He didn't move towards me yet, but his eyes burned like the heart of a storm.

"You bastard! I can't believe I..." I wouldn't say it. Not to him. His smile broke into that wicked, knowing grin that haunted me whether I slept or woke.

"What, Pallas? Do you think I loved you? Me, the Divine Emperor, the Great Hero? Like I could love someone like you. You're weak, powerless. Don't insult me." His hand shot out, and I was consumed by lightning again. It always seemed to find those old scars hidden away just below the surface, taking the same path over and over, century after century. The pain was more familiar to me than kindness. My oldest friend. Now, I felt different. That pain made a power inside me swell like something had been unlocked. The creature in my gut roared, no longer willing to be contained. I was scared, but I didn't want to cower.

"I'm going to kill the prince, Pallas. I'm going to make him scream and beg and make you watch. When the light finally dies from his eyes, I want you to know you could have stopped it if only you hadn't been such a naïve little girl. But I won't let you go then. I'll keep you, my little enchantress, forever."

I wanted to fight him. I wanted to kill him.

I called to that animal in me. She was ragged and ferocious, but for the first time, she wasn't starved and broken. She shined with that glowing blue light that Tori gave to me. Just a small seed, something she said I would need to make grow. So, I did.

I called to her, and she purred. That blue magic grew into my claws and skin. For a moment, I was free. Free of Hadeon's magic, free of his hold. I slashed the blue flames of my claws across his face as his eyes grew wide. Red lines blossomed along pale flesh, and I cursed myself for missing his eyes. I slashed again and again. More blood welled up across his chest and arms. He tried to strike me with his magic, but my skin was protected. Protected by my magic.

"Don't you ever dare touch me again!"

His eyes were wild with alarm as he staggered back, trying to protect himself. There was nothing he could do. I could taste his fear now, and I never had anything so delicious. His mouth moved, and he might have been commanding me to stop, but I only heard the blood rushing in my ears and the magic pouring out of every broken piece of me.

I raised my hand, ready to pluck out his heart, when ice shot over my body. The ice cracked and broke every bit of myself. The magic I conjured was snuffed out like a light, and I felt the harsh bite of metal around my neck.

"Seems like these bitches keep surprising us with new tricks." I could barely hear Luxos voice over the ringing in my ears, but I could smell ash and rose, the telltale sign of his magic.

A harsh metallic taste rose in my mouth as my hands clawed at my neck. A collar, he'd collared me!

I didn't know if it was the enslavement magic or my shock, but my body shut down. I collapsed back into the hard wall of Luxos' body, and my vision tunneled as I saw nothing but Hadeon's eyes glowing with rage as he came at me, hands outstretched. I felt Luxos wave his hand, words floating in one ear and out the other, incomprehensible. And then there was nothing. No light, no magic, no hope as I blacked out.

Chapter 65

Hadeon

Why couldn't they see it? Pallas was mine. This whole world was mine. I'd saved it. I'd stopped the World Breaker. My reward had been the return of magic to be mine and mine alone.

I was more god now than those dragons had ever been. They had shared their power with the world. Fools. Look what it brought them, nothing but destruction. I had been weak once but I had killed that pathetic creature long ago. I had molded myself into power, raw and undiluted. I only ever saw shadows of my former self in her eyes.

I had let that shadow linger there too long. I let her linger. I traced my hand over the scab that still refused to heal on my face. I had been lenient with both Pallas and Abraxas. That had been my only flaw. A god did not hold such worldly attachments. It was time to correct this long overdue error.

Pallas was nothing; she could wait, but Abraxas' time had come. I looked out over the golden fields before me, filled with nothing but the bodies soon to be flayed apart on my power.

The city below me was locked tight, every window and shutter closed. I cared not. Every single one of them was in my way.

It was time to remind them of all the power their Divine Emperor wielded.

Chapter 66

Abraxas

Morning broke, and I had been reborn, again. Tori and Jun's magic was unlike anything else in the world. They had broken the chains that restrained my power, and I felt as I had when I was young again. I could hardly contain the flames that had so long been held prisoner. My skin itched to unleash this power, and the time was finally upon us.

After the ordeal, the twins almost immediately passed out; their bodies and magic were exhausted. I let Tori get as many hours of rest as we could spare. It was ironic. I'd been on this earth for over one thousand years, and in these last few weeks, I had no time.

I pressed my lips to her forehead gently to wake her, and she grumbled with annoyance. "It's time, my goddess."

She rubbed her eyes, swung her legs out of the cot, and leaned her forehead against my shoulder.

"Time to end this."

THE COOL MORNING AIR STIRRED AROUND ME; A WHISPER of the chaos that was soon to be unleashed. Tori climbed onto my back, her weight and the grip of her thighs familiar. Her heart was beating wildly, a vibrant pulse that resonated with my own rising bloodlust.

Around us, our assembled forces stood ready. I saw the infantry, their armor catching the first light of dawn, forming a stern sea of iron will. The cavalry's horses snorted and stamped, their breaths puffing clouds into the chilly air. My eyes scanned the horizon, spotting the golden banners of Koron's walls fluttering mockingly in the distance.

Outside the city gates, the Golden Army was a shimmering sea of opposition. They stood along the ramparts with arrowheads flashing in the early morning light. Between us, fields of ambrosia spread, many already trampled. But where one had been pushed down, dozens remained.

Ready? I had sent my thoughts to her.

Always, she replied, her resolve sharp as the edge of her blade strapped to her side. I let out a deep, growling breath, feeling the surge of my heart, and with a powerful thrust of my wings, we ascended.

From that height, it was easy to imagine the troops below as only pieces on a chessboard. Pawns to be sacrificed for the ultimate victory. Before us, the emperor was the only piece that mattered.

Tori lay her hand on the scales of my neck. *He will be ours, but remember our plan, my love.*

Our plan was simple: strike at Koron's defenses from above,

cripple their artillery, and in the process, drive the city into a lockdown.

But there was one thing we had to do first. I dove, and the flames that were so eager for destruction flew before me. I didn't aim at the city, not yet.

Instead, we flew around the fields of Koron, and I incinerated every last ambrosia flower. At first, I had doubts, but as more golden petals rose on the flurries of heat, I could feel it. Mana, more than flowed through the earth below, being released. Tori pulled it out of the earth, blue-green tendrils dancing in the air before me. She shaped and wove together an entire world's worth of power. She split the writhing mass in half and sunk one piece into my chest, where it sat next to my heart.

For later. Her smugness cut through her mental words.

And the rest?

Also, for later. I watched as she wove it into the earth and under the city, where her machinations were lost to me.

Below us, the sounds of battle broke out. Swords and spears flashed in the sunlight as the two great waves of our armies collided. Masses of bodies pressed together in inseparable chaos.

Tori pointed towards a cluster of siege weapons nestled against the eastern wall.

"There, those first," she commanded, her finger steady against the wind.

With an affirmative snarl, I adjusted my wings, diving towards our target. The wind howled in my ears, a fierce symphony that heightened the rush of the descent. Just as the ground loomed close, I pulled up sharply. My shadow swept over the panicked soldiers below. Tori released a blast of dragon-fire, a glittering arc that ended in an explosion of flame and destruction.

Cheering reached my ears, yet the enemy was quick to

respond. Arrows and spears streaked towards us in a desperate attempt to clip my wings. I twisted in the air, and Tori clung tightly as gravity tried to unseat her.

Tori's voice called out again, "Now! The gatehouse!" Her determination was a beacon. I aimed my descent, our combined fury unleashed in another fiery onslaught. The gatehouse became an inferno, its portcullis buckling. A breach was opened wide for our forces to exploit.

Both groups of soldiers moved towards the opening, but that was not what I focused on. The city's outer ring was home to its forgotten humans and the small folk. Many fled towards the safety of the inner ring, but as Tori and I watched, the gate was slammed shut before even a dozen souls could pass through.

Cowards. Tori's rage was evident as the elite locked themselves in their homes, leaving the rest out for destruction.

They will pay. They will all pay.

We swept back around outside the city wall. Multiple legions of enemy soldiers still stood between our troops and the new rift. As I flew over, I felt Tori release her grip on my back.

What are you doing, my love?

Something I learned from you. Don't catch me.

She let herself fall off my back, and I couldn't stop my fear as she plummeted towards the earth. She twisted her body, and I felt her call upon my dragonfire again as she shot powerful jets of flames out of each hand. Below, shrieks came from the enemy lines as flesh was melted off bones and armor turned into nothing but molten puddles.

The flames slowed her descent, so she landed with a soft grace, her hair fluttering around her. She stood in the crater of destruction and pulled out her sword, commanding our troops.

I swooped down and snatched her in one of my claws.

Show off.

She grinned up at me. *I couldn't let you have all the fun now, could I?*

I circled over our troops and out to the safety of the field beyond.

I landed, dropping her gently as I transformed into my fae body. The small group who lingered away from the battle surrounded us. The day had just begun.

Chapter 67

Tori

"I don't like this, Tori." Abraxas wrapped his arms around me in a crushing grip. "Last time I let you out of my sight, I nearly lost you."

"I'm not the same as I was then. None of us are." I gave him a gentle kiss on the cheek before pushing out of his arms.

He chuckled, "You certainly aren't." He ran a hand down my cheek before peering over my shoulder. "And you certainly aren't alone."

In the morning light, I could see all their faces clearly. Avlyn, Jun, Kaleos, Raula, and even Spinner. My friends and family. It was quite the entourage, to be honest. I'd made the mistake of leaving them behind before. I wouldn't do that again.

In the distance, I could still hear the ring of battle. Abraxas would return, our rallying point, but if we wanted to win the day, we couldn't depend on force alone.

The king turned to Avlyn. "Commander, without you..."

"Tulius is in command. He's got this. Now it's my time to be useful." They twisted their injured arm, a phantom movement of a sword. Their gaze was steady as they furrowed their eyebrows. "You know, as a dragon, you could be much more effective."

Abraxas shook his head. "We decided that once we entered the city, I would be too destructive. The battle is only a distraction. I need to lure Hadeon out; the best way to do that will be in this form."

Avlyn nodded. "No time to waste, then."

Abraxas gave me one last lingering look. "Good luck to all of you."

"SLEEP."

The group of soldiers we snuck up on all collapsed into a snoring pile. We hadn't met many on our journey around the battle to the back of the city, but Jun had taken care of them all peacefully.

In the distance, the clash of swords rang out. Each was a potential death. We didn't have time to waste. As if he had read my mind, I felt Spinner speed up until I heard what we were looking for.

The water that splashed out from the grate at the foot of the wall smelled horrendous from the waste of a dozen species mixed with refuse and who knew what else. I tried not to throw my hand over my nose, but it only took a few moments before my eyes were watering like the smell was burning them.

No point in complaining. This was the only way. Luckily, Noki did it for me.

"Is this really our only choice?" Noki whinged.

"Yes," Avlyn and Raula answered in unison. Noki pinched his nose.

"How did you know about this place?" I asked Avlyn.

"Pallas told me. She said Koron was actually built over an ancient river that still flows beneath the city, acting as a sewer. It's connected to the palace directly."

I hummed approvingly. The best chance we had.

The grate that covered the sewer opening was made of iron bars as thick as a man's wrist. Out of the corner of my eye, I saw Kaleos wrapping his hands in linen, and Raula dutifully trudged through the putrid stream to take up her place on the other side. They both grabbed a bar and looked at Jun.

He stepped forward, and I heard him take a deep breath. The world seemed to still as I felt my heartbeat slow along with his as he focused on his power. His face was serene, and it reminded me of how he would look during one of his performances a lifetime ago.

He took one more steadying breath and slowly opened his eyes. In a voice no more than a whisper but sharper than any blade, he said, "**CUT.**"

The spell was beautiful in its precision, truly a work of art. The magic shifted around the grate, and I saw line after line appear through those impenetrable bars, the sound of them cleaving no louder than the wind through the trees.

Jun stepped back, nodding to Raula and Kaleos. They each gave strained groans as they pulled the leaden grate, but it slid out smoothly, each cut perfectly laid. They set it down beside the opening.

"Not bad, Nightingale." Avlyn's teeth flashed in the dim light. "Now it's my turn. Princess, if you don't mind."

I nodded and placed my hands on Avlyn's back, guiding mana through them. They shifted the flow of putrid water against one wall of the tunnel, clearing a drier path for us.

"Not bad, yourself, Commander." Jun quipped.

"Oh, you know me, always trying to make the best of a shitty situation." Avlyn replied with a cocky smile.

I groaned, "Please stop looking so pleased with yourself."

"No can do, Princess. Best to get this over with."

"Could have done that before I had to wade through it," Raula grumbled.

"Gotta preserve my energy, still getting used to this whole magic thing." Avlyn wiggled their eyebrows as they spoke.

"Convenient," Raula huffed, but she was the first to climb into the dank tunnel. Spinner followed.

The darkness beneath Koron carried the echoes of our attempt to muffle our steps. The chill from the sewer's damp walls nipped at my skin, and I shivered, but that wasn't the only reason. This was it, the end, one way or another. This same thought seemed to weigh on everyone as we moved forward in silence.

As we rounded a bend, the narrow tunnel opened into a larger underground chamber, likely a junction for the various sewer paths under the city. Waiting for us was a squadron of palace guards. They stood alert and ready; our intrusion was not as stealthy as we had desired. Their armor clinked menacingly as they arranged themselves into a defensive line, spears pointed outward and a row of archers behind.

Without hesitation, Avlyn stepped forward, their arms raised. The putrid water they had been holding back formed a swirling shield. "Duck!" they yelled, just as a volley of arrows hissed through the air toward us. The water intercepted the arrows, each shaft sinking into the liquid barrier but not passing through.

Raula and Kaleos wasted no time. They met the approaching guards as they darted around the barrier, one on each side, their blades drawn and gleaming even in the scant light offered by the few torches that lined the damp corridor walls. The clang of steel rang out as they met the first of the palace guards, amplified in the tight space.

"Move forward!" Raula's strong and commanding voice echoed back to us.

Jun, his earlier calmness now replaced with a focused determination, nodded at me and followed, his body glowing a soft white. He stepped beside Avlyn. "My turn," he murmured, the air around him shimmering with magical energy.

He wrapped his hand around his mouth to create a channel and let out a piercing shriek. It nearly tore out my ears, but I saw he had aimed it to reflect off the sewer ceiling in a way that focused it at the opposing archers. They clutched their heads, staggering from the disorienting sonic attack; their formation faltered.

Seizing the moment, Kaleos and Raula charged. They moved with lethal precision, and one enemy after another fell. Noki and I followed behind them, finishing any who had escaped their blades.

As the last guard slumped to the ground, the chamber fell silent except for the distant drip of water and our ragged breathing. Raula and Kaleos had taken the brunt of the attack. Raula was uninjured; her orc skin protected her.

Kaleos had a gash across his arm that he waved me away from as I tried to pull bandages from my pack. "No time, Princess, and honestly, I'm used to this after all our dueling. Let's get moving before they hear—"

He froze as Spinner crawled down the wall beside him, grabbing Kaleos' arm and holding it with his front legs. He pushed his abdomen forward, and the man flinched. A stream of ultrafine spider silk shot out over the wound, stanching any bleeding.

"Thanks," Kaleos said with his bright smile, and Spinner returned it with a soft chitter.

"Let's keep moving," I ordered. We had a long way to go.

Chapter 68

Pallas

I woke slowly, my body and mind trapped in thick sludge that held me in unconsciousness. The room, the dungeon cell, slowly came into focus. Light from a few torches bounced off the stone walls as the squalor of long-forgotten prisoners assaulted my nose. That woke me more than anything else. I sat up, my hand instinctively going to my neck, where the metal of my collar sat ice cold despite my skin's attempt to warm it. I tried to pry it off; my fingernails scraped my skin as I tried to wedge them underneath, but pain shot up the back of my neck to my skull, and I didn't persist.

"It's been sealed, you can't get it off." Luxos' dark voice sounded from the corner of the cell, where he sat wrapped in shadows. I snarled at him.

He let out a soft chuckle. "How ferocious you've become, but I like that in a woman." He approached, his shadows slowly curling out to run over my skin before he reached for me. I tried to slap them away.

"Don't fucking touch me!" Pain shot up through my skull again, and I gritted my teeth as tears welled in my eyes.

His shadows recoiled, and a frown flicked at the edges of his mouth. "You're lucky I was there, Pallas. He would have killed you if I hadn't stopped him."

"Or maybe I would have killed him if you hadn't stopped me."

He said nothing, his frown deepening.

"You look awful," I observed.

The deep burn scar Tori had given him was visible on his neck, still a vivid purplish red that I knew still hurt; her dragon-fire left a lasting mark. I eyed him up and down, but he still said nothing. When did I become the talkative one?

"You should have just let me die, Shadow Walker. I'd rather be dead than collared to him." He owned me, but my mind was still my own, at least for the present. I wasn't disobeying, so in truth, I felt fantastic. I knew that would all change quickly.

"Who said you were collared to him?"

I bolted upright. I raised my hand to the metal that I had crafted. My hand drifted over the gem at its center. Magic rushed through my fingertips, but it didn't feel like Hadeon. He always felt electric, the unnerving feeling of your hair standing on end just before the strike. Hot and erratic and loud. This magic was soft, dark, an endless void of shadows. Luxos had bonded the collar to him.

He chuckled at my surprise. "You think I learned nothing from you over all these years?"

"Why?"

"I had to show you were controlled. That was the only way I could get you out alive. Don't act dumb. It doesn't suit you."

"It's not like you to put yourself at risk for someone else, Luxos. Perhaps you can understand my confusion."

Suddenly, he was on his knees before me, his hands on my thighs. The touch was familiar, but the collar amplified it, sending shivers through my skin straight into my lower stomach. Pleasure, to reward my compliance.

"Pallas, I told you I would protect you, even from yourself! How can you still act as if you don't know I would do anything for you?"

We stood still for a moment, my body growing warmer with his touch; the collar's magic begged me to give in. It promised me everything I had ever wanted. Peace, gentleness, pleasure, and most of all, love. Love that so felt like that golden light Tori had once shown me. How I had created such a perfect replication for the magic of this collar, I would never know. But that's all it was, a replication, a glamour, a lie.

"Luxos, if you had really cared for me, you would have never touched me."

His response was immediate. "And I never did, not until you asked me."

"No, you just used to drug me so I would forget."

"No, I drugged you so you wouldn't remember, so you wouldn't tell Hadeon I never touched you. He would have assumed that I just wanted someone else, which I didn't. At least, on those nights, I could look after you. At least I knew that... no one else was hurting you."

My mind was racing. For decades, Hadeon had been sending me to Luxos, just as he had to so many of his other commanders and courtiers. I never remembered Luxos touching me, violating me. It had made it easier. I never dreaded those nights like I did the others. Sometimes, I even welcomed them and the void of being that came with the hot cup of tea he had always served me. I always assumed... but there was no lie in his voice, in his eyes.

"Why? Why did you hide the best part of yourself from me?"

"I'm not a good man, Pallas. Just one fighting to survive, just like you."

"And yet you always stayed. It would have been so easy for you to leave, to disappear. Why didn't you?"

His face turned ugly. "And done what? Be some petty lord's general? I lead the shadow troops of the Divine Emperor. Anything I have suffered has been worth the power I have. For someone like me to be this... I could have anything I wanted, except..."

He closed the space between us, his hand coming to rest on my jaw. I wanted to pull away, but the collar around my neck prevented it.

"Until that night. You took my hand, and you asked me. I could see you were trying to reclaim something, and I'll admit, I'm not a strong man. To have the object of all my desire offer herself to me. I couldn't resist." A smug smile crossed his face. "Besides, I knew you weren't faking how good I made you feel."

"You could have freed me."

His face fell. "Like I said, I'm not a strong man. Nor a brave one. Can you blame me for not wanting to incite Hadeon's wrath?"

"Yes, I can." His eyes were deep pits, and he wouldn't let me drop my gaze.

He ran his fingers over my lips. My body was torn in every direction. I tried to move away, and pain lanced from the center of my head down my spine, my collar willing me to obey his desire. It would be easy to give in. I helped make this collar. I knew what would happen. A deep, satisfying pleasure. The pleasure of submission, of surrender. A reward for a good little captive. I'd been with Luxos before. This wouldn't be any different. He already knew my body, the sounds I made when he entered me. Why fight it now?

A vision of Avlyn's strong arms wrapped around me as they

whispered in my ear that everything would be alright filled my mind. *You're not broken, only caged.* The words jolted my heart. No, I would fight. I had spent too long not fighting. I would not do that again. I shoved him off, even as it sent grating pain through me.

His jaw clenched, but then the ground under our feet roiled. I gripped the cot to stop myself from toppling over. Luxos stood quickly, drawing the sword from his side.

A voice I would recognize anywhere spoke. **"OPEN!"** The wall around the cell door exploded, crumbling to the floor as the door flew off its hinges. As the dust settled, Jun stepped through. "Let her go." His voice was rough, but his face was pure ice as he stared down Luxos.

I heard him chuckle. "Looks like the little prince has come to play. Nice to see you out of bed, Jun."

My fists clenched, but then a smug smile, so like Tori's, spread across Jun's face. "Oh, I can do a lot more than play now, Commander."

I saw Luxos face pale as Jun opened his mouth, but then his eyes fell to my neck. His eyes went wide with fear. "No..."

"Your lot isn't the only one with tricks, little prince. Pallas, come to me." Pain shot through my head, and I stood, my legs wobbling as they tried to walk toward Luxos. I resisted, but a dark hand reached up from the corners of the room and pulled me to him. I saw a flash, and a dagger sat at my throat while Luxos' other hand wrapped itself familiarly around my waist.

I looked at Jun's pained face, and tears rose to my eyes. *It's alright.* I wanted to reassure him, but my jaw was locked. *I'm going to be alright.* I was always such a liar.

Footsteps sounded from the hallway, and Avlyn appeared beside Jun. The prince's eyes were still locked on my neck, but the commander's attention immediately went to where Luxos ran his thumb in a gentle pattern over my ribs.

"Looks like you could use a hand, Commander Avlyn." Their teeth flashed as they snarled at Luxos. "You've amassed yourself quite the set of admirers," Luxos whispered in my ear.

"Release her, or there will be a world of pain waiting for you," Avlyn growled.

"Oh, I haven't feared something as dull as pain in a long time." Luxos' grip on me tightened.

More footsteps crunched across the broken hallway, and Tori charged in, green flames dancing across her body. "I'm sure I could come up with something that will excite you, Luxos."

There they stood, ready to fight for me. They had all come for me. But all Luxos had to do was step into those shadows, and we would be gone. I felt him stiffen, and I tried to look each of them in the eyes. *I'll be alright.*

Shadows curled around us, and Avlyn's body tensed as they made to bolt across the room. The shadows jumped up, holding them back.

Luxos leaned down so that his warm breath danced across my ear. "You said you never had a choice, Pallas. It was all out of your control. So here is your choice. Come with me. We'll be free like you always wanted. No more empires, no more kings, just you and me. Or stay with this rabble as this place comes crumbling down."

I looked deep into Jun's eyes, into Avlyn's. I'd been so afraid for so long, and here it was, my escape. The weight of the collar shifted around my neck as Luxos pressed the knife into my skin, threatening Avlyn as they tried to throw off his shadows.

No, he didn't offer me freedom but another comfortable cage; outside of the cage was dangerous, and I might not survive it. I would suffer, both my body and my heart. I would let that freedom destroy me if that's what was destined. I would pay the price.

"Let me go, Luxos." I expected the collar to hold me, to

punish me for those words. Nothing came. I could feel my heart pounding against my chest when he let out one more sigh.

"It seems our time together has drawn to a close. I may not have done it right, but I cared for you, Pallas, ever since I first laid eyes on you."

I felt the click of metal, and there was a great relief of weight on my neck. The collar fell away, and I felt him place something cold and wrong in my hand. He shoved me forward, so I fell into Avlyn's arms.

I spun to see him one last time as he faded into his shadows. "Maybe in another life, Pallas." And then he stepped into the darkness and was gone.

"Are you alright?" I looked up into Avlyn's eyes, so filled with concern that my heart fluttered.

"Yes." It wasn't a lie. I looked at my hand and a red gem the size of a peach pit glimmered in the torchlight.

"Oh, shit." Tori slowly removed the gem and held it up. The light caught on the shadows that swirled deep inside. She looked over to where Luxos had disappeared. "Like calls to like." She shivered. "I can feel it muting my magic, but..." Her smile was all teeth. "It looks like the good commander helped us find two things we needed tonight."

But then Tori clamped a hand over her heart, and the gem clattered to the floor. I scrambled to grab it, and when I looked back up, she was deadly white as she panted, "We need to hurry."

Chapter 69

Abraxas

The sky was clear; I made sure of it. The clouds had always been my allies, but today, they would only have served Hadeon and his lightning.

I stood before my troops at the entrance to the city. The Golden Army stretched back along the streets inside the outer wall. The fight faltered when we took the gate, and neither side could gain ground. Bodies littered the ground, both dark and golden alike. There would be time later to honor their sacrifice; for now, the crows could have them. I gave one last look at the palace that my companions infiltrated. I had a distraction to cause, alone.

I stood before them, a king. A god. A general stepped forward to meet me.

"Where is Hadeon? My quarrel is with him, not you."

The general laughed. "Our Divine Emperor does not need to sully himself with the likes of you—"

The man was cut off when a great clap of thunder rolled through the empty sky. My hand flew to my sword as the skies darkened, clouds rolling in at an unnatural pace. They swirled and merged over the Golden Palace, dark and filled with power. Purple lightning flashed as they crashed into each other; the sound was monstrous. I called to the wind, trying to disturb them, but it wouldn't listen. I fought, trying to get it under my control, but I wasn't rewarded. The sky belonged to him, at least for now.

A great bolt of lightning struck the palace and then shot straight to where we stood. The ground erupted with flashes of violet light, and stones flew about faster than if launched by a trebuchet. I threw up a wall of flames to block them, but a few of my surrounding soldiers weren't so lucky; the small stones passed straight through their armor.

The dust cleared, and there he stood. His hair floated out as if caught on an invisible wind, and his whole body shimmered with power. He walked out of the crater towards me. "My oldest friend, at last, we face each other as we have always desired."

As I faced Hadeon, a storm brewed between us, crackling with energy. His eyes, dark pools of malice, met mine.

"Surrender, Hadeon. Your forces are no match for mine, as you are no match for me. Surrender and be spared." He never would, and I would never let him, but all of this bought me time.

"Surrender? To you? You're weak, Abraxas; you have always been weak. How quickly you bent the knee to me and my army outside your own home. How very willing you were to please me, to bow to me. How you obeyed my every command like the obedient dog you are, and how I enjoyed holding your leash. Come, beg my forgiveness, and maybe I will let you live."

The beast inside me clawed to come out, to destroy him for that insult. I took a deep breath and fought the urge to give in more than anything. Time, I needed to buy Tori time. I tightened my grip on my sword's hilt, pulling it from its scabbard and holding it aloft between us.

Lightning wreathed his arms as it gathered in his palms, crackling and deadly. "You dare challenge me, Abraxas?" Hadeon's voice echoed across the open space. "You and your pathetic magic are no match for my power."

Who would win this, the fae with the heart of a dragon or a dragon with the heart of a fae?

I ran my hand along the blade of my sword, and viridian flames erupted along its surface. "Once, perhaps. But now... now you will be annihilated." We were surrounded by soldiers on all sides, but there was no one on this earth but him and I.

"That's no way to talk to the Great Hero!" He shaped his power into a blade and launched at me.

I dug my heels into the ground and readied myself. As lightning crashed towards me, I called upon the ancient magic coursing through my veins.

The emerald flames surged around me, forming a protective barrier against the oncoming storm. The clash of elements filled the air with a deafening roar, and sparks flew everywhere.

With a swift movement, I lunged forward, my sword ablaze. Hadeon dodged with a mocking grin; his movements were as swift as the wind. I was relentless, pressing the attack.

Our blades clashed in a symphony of steel; each strike fueled by centuries of animosity. Sparks flew, and the meeting of our power pushed us back repeatedly as it erupted into a miniature supernova.

Hadeon's chilling and manic laughter rang in my ears. His mad grin spread over his face, indicating his ecstasy.

"This world is mine, Abraxas! Magic belongs to me and me alone. I am a god, and no one can stand against me. Not even you."

Maybe once, I had believed that. I had let myself be subjugated, fearing my own weakness, but no more. My mate had saved me, and I was more powerful than I had ever been.

"No." I spun around him, fueled by centuries of rage. "You are a false god, a thief. I am the last dragon, the last veritable god. You will kneel before me and beg for your life."

He was skilled, but I had always been the better swordsman. My sword cut through the armor at his waist, my strength enhanced by the magic that flowed through me. His screams of agony fueled my magic. My flames erupted from the sword, engulfing Hadeon in a blazing inferno.

Yet, even as the flames consumed him, Hadeon's power remained undiminished. With a roar of defiance, he unleashed another barrage of purple lightning, the crackling bolts searing through the air with lethal precision. They cut open my skin, and blood ran down my face, obstructing my vision.

I danced through the storm, my sword weaving a deadly path as I deflected each bolt with precise skill. The ground trembled beneath us, the very earth groaning in protest at the intensity of our clash.

Hadeon threw me back with a burst of power. I gathered dragonfire in my hands and launched a barrage of projectiles at him. He slashed through each one with his sword of lightning, deflecting them past him.

I pulled the flames back to me, and they arched in the air, returning to their maker. They hit him, one after the other, building until they erupted in a percussive explosion. A flash of lightning flew at me as he cut through the fireball and leaped toward me.

I met his assault head-on, our blades colliding with explosive force. The impact sent shockwaves rippling through the air, knocking everyone around us down with raw power.

"I killed him. I will kill you, too, Abraxas!"

He was desperate now, unable to overcome me with raw power. I struck again and again. Hadeon's parries slowed as he was forced back. He stumbled, and I kicked him. He flew back, crashing into the city wall so hard it cracked.

I let the tip of my sword slide along the ground as I approached. The metallic screech caused his eyes to widen as blood leaked from his mouth.

Then he threw himself off the wall with his power, launching himself into the air. He careened across the sky, trying to escape. Fool. The sky was mine. I called down my bond to Tori, but a magical barrier separated us. No matter. I reached into that knot of mana she had stored in my heart. I felt her there with it; it was all her strength, the only strength I needed. Flames pumped from my mouth as I grew, fragile fae skin giving way to impenetrable scales.

I flew after him. He sensed my pursuit and threw his magic back at me. The wind shifted as his power reflected off harmlessly. Two more pumps of my wings, and I was on him. I drank in how his eyes grew wide with fear as I towered over him.

His face was ugly with rage as he continually threw bolts at me. They stung, some even ripped off scales, but the taste of his fear drove away any pain.

I see you, Hadeon, the little boy that you have always been. I see your fears. Deep in the night, when you would call out in terror, it was always me who was watching you from the darkness.

His entire being glowed an erratic violet as his rage consumed him. "This world belongs to me!"

Not while I still breathe. I lunged, ready to swallow him whole. He threw his power wide, holding my jaws open, each of his hands pressed into a fang on opposite sides. He groaned, and his blood ran onto my tongue. Before this moment I'd never wounded him like this, and his blood fueled the revenge that I no longer repressed in my heart.

I chuckled darkly. *You taste delicious, old friend.* His fear spiked, and he threw me back with an outpouring of power.

"Enough! I'm the Great Hero! I'm what the prophecy foretold! You are nothing! NOTHING!" Dark storm clouds swirled between us, and lightning struck me from every direction at once until all I saw was blinding violet light.

Chapter 70

Tori

My chest heaved as my breath left me in violent spurts. Kaleos, Raula, Noki, and I cut through dozens of men on our way through the dungeons while Jun protected Pallas and Avlyn. We were drenched, and I could feel the bloodlust trying to take over my mind. I gripped the pommel of each half of my sword hard, trying to stay grounded. It was all so similar to last time, and I could not fail again.

The halls were deathly quiet, and I stood before those great doors, but this time, I was not alone. I clicked my sword back together and sheathed it. I called a ball of viridian fire into my hand and pulled it back, ready to strike.

"Don't even think about it," Pallas scolded, stepping between me and the door. "Unless you want to kill us all."

She walked up to the door and slowly placed her hand on the wood, and it flared to life with glyphs etched in a deep, violent purple. Her brow furrowed, and I saw a shimmer of light blue magic ghost over the runes. They quickly returned to purple, and she frowned.

"Got some new trick there, huh, hellcat?" Avlyn gave her a proud smile. I saw the faintest blush on Pallas' cheeks.

"Not enough tricks, it seems. Even with Tori, Jun, and I together, this could take hours." We didn't have that kind of time. She held her hand out to me without looking back. "Might as well try out our gift."

I slipped my hand into the pack at my waist and was greeted by a horrible, caustic sensation as the gem touched my fingers. I pulled it out, carefully placed it in Pallas' hand, and saw her flinch. She set the gem against the wood of the door, and the glyphs there sputtered and disappeared.

Pallas' eyes widened. "Could it really be that easy?"

"Don't look a gift Nykur in the mouth." Avlyn placed their hand on her shoulder, and Jun nodded.

"Now, do I get to burn it down?"

I could tell Pallas wanted to object, but she nodded. She had to hold the gem in place, so I couldn't just blast the wood as much fun as that would have been. Instead, I focused my mind as she had taught me and called a single tendril of fire, honing it into an edge like a knife. I sliced a Kaleos-sized hole out of the center of the two doors. I kicked, and the interior pieces fell flat against the stone floor with a loud thud.

I moved to pass through the hole when the violet enchantment flared again, and Pallas hissed.

Underneath her fingers, sparks engulfed the gem, and I could hear cracking. The power laced through Pallas' hand, but she held it there, unwavering. I saw her blue magic flare, and the enchantment on the door faded again.

"Hurry!" I didn't need to be told twice. I ducked through with everyone else following me.

We spilled into the room, and I turned in time to see Pallas sliding past the opening, her hand still pressing the sparking gem into the wood. No sooner had she stepped through when a huge spark flashed, and the gem shattered. Pallas stumbled back, and the enchantment flared to life, trapping us inside. Avlyn rushed to help her up as she cradled her burned hand. They fussed, but Pallas just gave it a gentle shake and moved towards the center of the room.

The space wasn't much larger than any other in the palace, but the floor sloped downward from all the walls like a great weight pressed the stone down. I shielded my eyes from the dark crimson ball of fire that hovered above its center.

Everyone stood beside me, equally entranced. Pallas was the only one to move, carefully walking down the sloped floor. She lifted her hand towards the glowing heart, and the orbiting glyphs sparked and flew around her but did not cause pain. Jun grabbed my hand and walked with me down the slope. "Guess it's our turn."

I don't know how much time passed as Jun and I sat forehead to forehead, that bright white light glowing between us as we slowly worked at untangling the enchantment around the heart. I just knew that my back, ass, and legs ached from sitting, and it was breaking my concentration. I lost focus and pulled the wrong strand, and the whole enchantment tightened again.

"Fuck. Pallas, this is taking too long."

A blue tendril of magic slid in along ours. "All we can do is keep working." She was right. I rolled my shoulders and went back to focusing, probing at a new side of the lock. Pallas was a natural, to my mild annoyance, and soon the lock shifted apart, its outer layer opening.

"Good, now we just need to—" Pallas' voice cut off as the

enchantment started shifting on its own. Layer after layer lurched, just like the tumblers in a lock. More of the enchantment fell away, but as one particularly large portion dropped away, a jet of deep red flames sprayed out. I threw myself over Jun as the flames licked across my back. I yelped as the pain cut through me, even as I felt my skin already regrowing itself.

Malech's heart was fighting back. The flames were cutting through the enchantment, but it didn't care what else was destroyed in the process.

We are not your enemy. I tried to talk to it as I would Abraxas, but now red flames burst across the room, and I could feel the temperature rising. Sweat beaded at my brow, and I summoned flames to combat the heart, but you can't fight fire with fire.

"Tori." Jun's voice was so soft. "Don't fight it. Can't you feel his pain?" My brother was right. Malech had been trapped by Hadeon, just like Jun and Pallas. A cornered beast couldn't be reasoned with, and a fight would only end in death. I held Jun's hand tighter and focused on sending mana through him. White light shimmered around us both.

"**You're going to be alright.**" I heard the words, but they were more, and I felt them deep in my very soul. The heart stopped fighting.

"You're going to be alright." The light between us grew. I chanted it with Jun. "You're going to be alright." I could hear everyone shouting our names, but I didn't dare stop. I felt Jun's fingers cinch mine, and all I saw was white light.

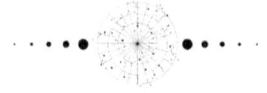

I AWOKE WITH MY FACE PRESSED INTO SOFT GRASS AND THE smell of home. A gentle breeze stirred the blades, so they tickled my nose, and I opened my eyes to see Jun lying next to me. We blinked at each other and pushed up to find ourselves on the cliffs outside Xyr. The sound of the ocean waves crashed far below us, and I dared to lean over the sheer drop. Black sand stretched out below, just as it had before our departure, but the sky beyond was broken. Great cracks cut through the noonday blue, a deep darkness lacing through it like mud baked in the sun. I looked at Jun and he shook his head, when a great rumbling behind us caused us both to spin around.

Curled up like an enormous, sleeping kitten was a dragon. His maroon scales glimmered in the sun, and the rumbling was his great breath, his nose tucked under his tail. His wings rose and fell gently as I stood, the grass compressing beneath my feet as I approached him.

I knelt down beside his long face, placing a hand on his snout, just as I had done with Abraxas. "Malech?"

A great ochre eye snapped open, and I stumbled back as he unfurled himself, nearly knocking me off the cliff. I put myself in between him and Jun as he stretched his wings skyward before locking me in his gaze again.

It seems two little pests have found their way into my prison. How very interesting.

His scaled lips pulled back as he revealed every one of his glimmering fangs, the shortest longer than my hand. *It's been so long since I have had any entertainment.*

He moved towards us, his mouth widening as he approached until I could see straight down his throat. I pushed Jun behind me and wove ribbons of dragonfire around my arms. Malech froze in place.

What blasphemy is this? How is it you control dragonfire?

447

Even in my mind, it was a hiss, his eyes burning an even more heated red as he bore down on me.

I saw his eyes widen, but he still moved closer until his nose nearly pressed against my chest. He inhaled with such force it nearly toppled me.

"They are a gift from my mate."

Lies! All fae do is lie! He inhaled sharply, and a burst of deep red fire shot from his mouth. I threw my flames up between us and over Jun and me. His red flames danced over my shell of green until they merged into sunshine yellow.

"We are not your enemy!" I shouted, but golden claws swiped at us, and I had just enough time to push my brother and me down into the grass.

"I don't think he's listening," Jun stated.

"Then make him listen."

"STOP!"

Malech shuddered as he tried to fight the hold of Jun's magic. Jun coughed beside me. "It won't hold him long."

I flung myself onto the dragon's snout, and immediately, he tried to whip me off, quivering, but the magic still held him.

"King Amaros, listen!" At the use of his fae name, he stopped fighting. "Abraxas, your son, is my mate. We are here to help you."

The dragon below me inhaled so forcefully that my clothes were suctioned to his face. He stopped trying to fight and instead tilted his head so that I slowly slid to the ground, my hands still on his scales.

How can this be?

"I have heard that fate has quite a wicked sense of humor." He bore into me with those huge ochre eyes. The burning orange faded to a soft brown as Malech shrunk, and his scales were replaced by pale skin. My hands now rested on the stern face of the fae man I had only seen in portraits. His long, dark hair gently blew in the wind.

"Show me again."

I snapped my fingers, and a spark of viridian flame hovered over them. King Amaros snatched it out of my control and into his palm, staring intensely into the fire as if it would reveal some great truth.

"My son..." He gazed a moment longer before snuffing the flame out. "All fae do is lie."

"It is no lie." Jun stepped up beside me. "We aren't just fae."

Amaros' gaze drifted between us. Jun opened his mouth, and a sound like I had never heard emerged. It wasn't a song, and it wasn't speech, but the cry of a creature from beyond our world. We began to glow from our toes to the top of our heads, where our hair floated on a phantom wind.

Amaros' eyes went wide. "No, it seems you are not just fae."

At Jun's cry, the sky above us split. The cracks widened to reveal more darkness, but not true darkness. A moonless night with the great celestial river Maiak flowing overhead as the stars moved across the sky.

Amaros gazed upward as the stars swirled overhead, but his eyes fell back to me.

"You have accepted the bond with my son?"

I pulled aside the collar of my armor so he could see the bite mark that Abraxas left on me. The scar was still a fresh pink.

At that, he gave me a wicked smirk that I knew all too well. "Then you have given me the greatest gift I could have ever hoped for in this frozen place." At that, he moved faster than I could see, and he had his arms wrapped around me. For a moment, I struggled, trying to get out of his arms. The arms of a father, arms that could only inflict pain.

I was small again, and I envisioned a hand striking me so hard I thought my teeth would shatter. The pain never came.

Instead, the arms were warm and gentle, rubbing soft circles on my back. That gentle touch broke me in a way that nothing before ever had. I was still that little girl, craving a father's love and gentleness, and I broke down. I sank into the embrace, and tears rolled down my cheeks.

If Amaros was surprised by my reaction, he didn't show it. He only held me tighter, letting me linger in a feeling that I had never had before.

Once my tears had stopped, he gently held me and whispered in my ear, "Thank you. Please tell my son... Ah, I have lingered here for centuries, and now I have no time. There is too much to say. Tell him I am sorry. I am sorry for everything, and I love him." He held me back, and darkness fell over us. "Tell him his mother gave him the dragon name, Astaroth, in the hopes he would find love in a world of violence."

"I will," I promised, nodding. He gave me one more soft look. "She would have been honored to know you."

Malech stepped away, and Jun took his place at my side. The dragon grew again, his scales nearly black in the depths of night. A deep red glow appeared over his heart, and he let out one last sky-shattering roar as he dissolved into embers and floated to the sky.

More tears flowed down my cheeks as I followed those drops of light upward. *I wish you could have seen him, my love.*

Jun wiped away my tears and pressed our foreheads together as the stars above us dimmed. As the darkness grew, our hearts glowed white until it all burned away.

THE ROOM WAS DARK. NO RED GLOW REMAINED.

"You did it," Pallas murmured softly with disbelief.

"Try not to sound so surprised," Jun chuckled.

"It just dissolved and floated away into the air." Avlyn's voice was barely above a whisper. "Does that mean we are done?"

My knees cracked as I lifted myself to standing, extending my hand to pull Jun up. Then the entire room shook so violently that he tumbled into me, causing us to slam back to the floor.

Pallas crashed into Avlyn in much the same way while Kaleos and Raula drew their swords against the unknown foe.

The room had glowed a deep, menacing red before, but now light dead and void of color emerged from glyphs along every wall. It wasn't pure white light, but something that leeched our faces into horrible, desaturated shadows of themselves, even as I was blinded by the brightness.

"Mother, what have you done?" Pallas stumbled over to the wall, running her hands over the glyphs. I saw the sparks of her blue magic again, but they were swallowed into that horrible, grey magic.

"Pallas, what is happening?"

"It's a failsafe of some kind. My mother must have built it into the enchantment. Something to prevent anyone from leaving should something happen to the heart."

Jun lurched to her while everyone else stood back-to-back in the center of the room. A thick black line traced over Kaleos' cheek, and it slowly grew as dark liquid flowed out of it. Blood.

More slashes appeared on Kaleos, and then on Avlyn and Noki. Raula grunted as even her orc skin was cut open by the spell. The only one who seemed unaffected was Spinner, but he was panicked, running between all of us.

I heard Jun screaming in pain and trying to use his magic to stop the spell, but he fell to the floor, coughing. The enchantment did not waver. Pallas threw herself on top of him, and her blood ran down his torn clothes as her arms were ripped open.

I tried to scramble to them as a sharp and inescapable burning cut across my shoulder and leg. I fell to the floor and tried to crawl to them, leaving a gruesome trail behind me. Spinner ran to me and lashed his web around my waist, dragging me towards them, unaffected by the spell.

"Pallas, how do I stop it!" I reached out to the enchantment in my mind, but it wasn't a lock like the others. It was writhing and terrible, unbelievably sharp, so any attempt I made to undo it only opened new wounds along my skin. Whereas the enchantment around the heart had been a study in perfection and complexity, this one was nothing but rage and destruction.

"There is nothing you can do. It's tied to the castle's foundation. There is too much mana left to destroy it."

Tears welled in her eyes, and she clung to Jun, holding him close as they were both torn apart.

I reached down into that pool of mana that was greater than any I had ever seen. I saw it flow into the castle, into the enchantment that was trying to destroy us. Laced along every stone that held the castle together were roots, roots I had grown from the power of the ambrosia fields around the city. It was power that had been stolen from the earth, and I was going to give it all back.

I broke the dam I had built with my brother's and my power, and all the mana rushed back to the source, where it so longed to be. It didn't matter what earth, stone, or foundation was in its way.

"What are you doing?!" Pallas screamed.

"Obliterating everything in my path."

The building gave way around us, the floor crumbling beneath our feet. The ceiling broke apart as the walls snapped.

The enchantment was broken at its very foundation, and I felt it wink out of existence.

Jun and Pallas tried to stand, but more of the floor gave way, and they stumbled, barely avoiding a huge chunk of the ceiling that fell beside them.

"Out of the frying pan and into the fire, huh, Princess?" Avlyn and the others had stumbled over to me. They helped me scramble up, and we all pushed towards Jun and Pallas.

"Any good ideas on how to get out of here before the whole place comes down on us?" I asked everyone and no one.

The floor cracked completely open, and the great river underneath Koron broke through and started flooding what was left of the chamber we were still in. Avlyn's eyes lit up. They grabbed onto my shoulder.

"No, but I do have a stupid one. Hold on tight, everyone."

Chapter 71

Hadeon

My power carried me across the sky. Dark clouds filled with static gathered around me, giving me cover as I felt the dragon follow. His green dragonfire streamed behind me, but he was slower than I was. I darted around him, over and under the clouds following in my wake. I struck out again and again until each landed with the smell of burnt flesh, and the dragon let out a roar that echoed off the earth below us.

"You'll never be able to best me, Abraxas. I'll claim your heart, just like I claimed your father's."

His deep laugh echoed off the clouds around me as his voice penetrated directly into my mind.

Come and try.

His rage was palpable. The surrounding clouds, heavy with the power of the storm, buzzed and sparked with my command. They were mine, just as he would be.

With each beat of his colossal wings, he surged towards me, an avatar of fury bathed in the green glow of his own flames. He was a vision from my nightmares, but he was hopelessly predictable. It would be easy to draw him in.

I summoned a dense vortex of purple electricity around myself, a shield crackling with raw energy. His fire met my storm barrier, exploding in a cacophony of steam and blinding light, turning the dark sky momentarily bright.

Never one to waste an opportunity, I soared above him, my agility in stark contrast to his brute force. Lightning, my only faithful ally, arced from my outstretched fingers, forging bolts of destructive beauty aimed directly at him. The first bolt was a miss, a mere warning shot, but the second seared a path across his underbelly. The smell of scorched scales filled the air. He had grown cocky, and I would remind him who he feared these past centuries.

In response, his massive and deadly tail sliced through the air towards me. I moved, but not fast enough to avoid a glancing blow. The impact sent me reeling, disrupting my rhythm. Pain flared on my shoulder, but it only fueled my resolve.

As I stabilized, he closed in, his massive jaws and sharp claws ready to end this dance we had played for over four hundred years. With a surge of energy, I readied myself, letting the storm's power envelop me, turning my whole being into a conduit of destruction.

We met in the middle, the force of our collision sending shockwaves through the air. Dragon against storm, an ancient battle of raw elements. I surrounded us with a whirlwind of lightning, each one a bit of my wrath made manifest.

The battle was not just a clash of bodies but of wills, the storm against the flame, each feeding off and challenging the other in a spectacle of primal fury. This was what I wanted —Abraxas, powerful and predictable. How easy it would be now to overtake him.

"Where have you left that beautiful princess of yours?" I felt the air shift and dodged out of the way as his jaws snapped closed where I had just been.

Somewhere you will never reach her, Hadeon.

"I doubt that."

His fire shot out at me, but I avoided it easily. I saw it in his eyes then. He was getting sloppy, his rage for me overpowered by worry for her. The fool. He nearly had me. I imagined he would have if he hadn't let that girl crawl into his heart as a fatal weakness.

"After I've claimed your heart, I will not rest until she's mine to play with. I so had fun with her last time." He snapped at me wildly, and I saw my opening. He stretched too far, and I flew around his head with more speed than he could follow.

I shot my power out like a whip, lashing it around his neck. I swung around him until I was between his wings and squeezed it tight until his deep, animalistic cry was choked off.

"I wonder, with your heart tied to mine, will you hear as I pull all those incredible sounds out of her? Will they be sounds of pain or pleasure, though? You always enjoyed mixing the two." He thrashed wildly, but I could taste my victory now. I exploded with every ounce of power I had, and the lightning cut through his wings until they were shredded, and he lost his flight.

The sky ripped past us as we plummeted to the earth. The cloud we fell through struck him with its charged power until thick red blood covered me. We crashed into a small building at the edge of the palace grounds, and the entire thing exploded. Bricks and dust rained down as I was thrown from his back. I scrambled up to see him struggling to lift himself, his limbs quaking as blood pooled out onto the ground below him.

As Abraxas lay broken, the emerald light of his dragonfire dimmed. The taste of victory was on my tongue. I approached, my footsteps echoing with the promise of conquest. He was mighty, but I had seen every last dragon fall, and I was ready to turn this legend into nothing more than a memory.

I wove my magic into the snare that would capture his heart, my greatest treasure. He looked upon me with so much hatred it was like a heady drug, and he summoned the last of his power.

Then my heart vanished. The channel of power that had been mine for centuries just... disappeared. I reached for it, but it was like trying to catch the early morning mist. It slipped from my grasp, and I watched as it winked out of existence.

"It can't be..." There was no way. No way they could have undone the enchantment. It was impossible. IT WAS IMPOSSIBLE!

Missing something, Hadeon? Abraxas chuckled as he tried to raise himself again.

"You will pay for this!" I called to all the magic I still held in my heart and condensed it into a single spark. I had killed Malech like this. I would kill him, too.

Before I could deliver the final strike, the ground beneath my feet trembled violently. My eyes shifted just in time to see the palace quake and groan as if in agony. It sank, slowly at first, then rapidly, into the gaping maw of the earth itself, swallowed whole by a cataclysm of dirt and stone.

From this chaos, a monumental blast of water shot out from the crater where the palace once stood, mist spraying into the surrounding air and soaking me. The water surged like a beast unleashed, its roar drowning out even the echoes of the collapsing palace. An enormous bubble burst forth from that colossal jet, and six bodies tumbled out.

My eyes immediately locked on Pallas and the princess; both sputtered as they coughed water out of their lungs. The princess raised her head, and her gaze immediately locked on me and the dragon.

She scrambled to her feet and drew her sword. "Get away from my mate, Hadeon."

"Gods, what does it take to be rid of you vermin?" They

were a distraction, nothing more. Abraxas was my only focus. I swept a hand out, and lightning danced through the water they had so graciously laid out everywhere. However, blue light surrounded the party, and nothing touched them.

The princess stalked towards me, and beside her, I was surprised to see the prince. His gaze was nothing but infernal fire as he shouted, "**CRUSH!**"

I was forced down into the earth as if by a giant hand, the earth pressing in around me until my arms and legs were immobile. The princess wore a smug smile as she closed the distance between us, but it was Pallas who reached me first.

"It's time for this to end, Hadeon." Her eyes glowed.

"You will pay for this betrayal, whore."

"Oh, I don't think so, old friend." I felt the cold metal of Abraxas' sword as he wrapped it around my neck, back in his fae form.

I threw my power out in an explosion that ripped my skin from my flesh. They all flew back, landing in disarray as I gathered myself, wiping the blood from my nose where it leaked horribly.

Traitors, bastards. I had earned this. I had earned this world. They would never stand in my way.

Chapter 72

Tori

We all flew at Hadeon, swords drawn. Steel flashed against lightning as we surrounded him. We were all worn down, bleeding, and half-drowned. It was too easy for him to parry us. Behind him, Abraxas was more blood than skin at this point.

I wanted to draw my sword and strike him down; the rage in my heart was overwhelming. I took a breath and controlled it. There was something better I could do. I reached down into the well of magic beneath us and sent it to everyone, strengthening them.

Wounds stitched closed faster, and I saw Avlyn surround Hadeon in a massive ball of water. He wasn't contained for long before his lightning cut through, but it was enough time for Abraxas, Kaleos, Raula, and Noki to surround him.

They all swung at once, but Hadeon still contained so much power. It was unfathomable to me. We had cut him off from Malech's heart, but still, he managed to overpower everyone. I tried to send more mana to Abraxas, but I could feel his weariness overpower it.

Four swords struck at Hadeon at once, but he built a shield of lightning that cast them all back.

His eyes locked on me, and he charged. "Time for our dance, Princess." I was too locked into the earth to move.

Jun stepped in front of me. "**SLEEP!**" Hadeon fell to his knees but would not obey, resisting the command. His hand shot out, and lightning lanced over my brother's chest, and he flew back.

"JUN!" Both Pallas and I were at his side in an instant. He groaned; his armor was burned away, and his chest was blackened. White light danced over the wound. I pulled mana to him, and the light burned away the dark.

The sword wielders were on Hadeon again, but he had pulled up a shield of lightning, keeping them all at bay. I sent mana to Abraxas and Avlyn, and their magic swirled over the shell of Hadeon's power.

I had an idea. "Pallas, Jun, help me."

I grabbed each of their hands and pulled as much mana into us as I could. The mana connected us, connected our hearts. Bright white magic swirled with Pallas' soft blue.

"What are we doing, Tori?" she asked.

"Making a lock, master enchanter."

Pure magic shot out of the three of us. It slammed into Hadeon, and he fell to his knees again, clutching his chest. Tendrils of mana rose out of the ground, lashing around his arms and legs. He struggled against them, burning them away with lightning while he kept the swords at bay, but he couldn't keep us out. Jun and I wrapped white light around his heart and squeezed.

The battle raged inside and out. Thunder rolled as his magic met swords, and lightning penetrated our cosmic shield. We struck back, and it was all to give Pallas time.

Her blue light snaked over his heart; I felt it burn in one

glyph after another. His power fought back, sizzling them away, but for every one he destroyed, three more took its place.

"I need more, Tori." Sweat dripped from her hairline as her teeth clenched. That I could do. I let Jun control the shield while I channeled. I dug deeper into the earth, into a pool of mana that felt endless, but it still wasn't enough. I pulled down every ley line that radiated from Koron, gathering every bit of the earth that I could.

It was all mine. I saw the entire world through those lines—every rock, stone, and blade of grass. Mana flowed through every tree and every man, woman, and child—but it was stunted. I saw the roots around their hearts. It was just like Abraxas but stronger.

I felt Kaleos as he fought nearby; the roots wrapped tight, completely trapping what was inside.

Noki's human heart held the most. Around his heart, the threads had woven so tight it appeared more like an impenetrable wall of stone than any sort of knot. I could feel just how fragile his human heart was underneath as well, but magic stirred in it, just like all the rest. It stirred in everyone's heart.

Pallas jolted, her eyes glowed blue, and her skin was covered in a magic shield. Blood trickled from her nose, but she did not stop. Glyph after glyph appeared on Hadeon's heart until I couldn't keep track anymore, and he faltered. He rose but dug his fingers into his chest like he could claw us out.

"How dare you? HOW DARE YOU?!" He ran at us, but Avlyn threw up a wall of water. He crashed into it, lightning turning the water into nothing but steam. He burst out, his hands outstretched, when I felt the last piece of Pallas' lock slide into place.

The lightning vanished from his hands, and his eyes faded to a dull purple. He ran at us, but we were too deep into the magic and could not pull away.

461

Steel erupted from his chest. Abraxas' great sword skewered through him. He coughed; blood and spittle flew from his lips, and he tried to grab the blade extending from his chest.

"For my father," Abraxas whispered into his ear before letting him fall to the ground. He wasn't dead, but I paid it no mind.

I barely saw any of it; I was still within the mana flow. I saw the curse that the earth had placed upon the people of our world, and I knew that I had to break it.

"Help me." My words were barely a whisper, but they heard it since all our magics were linked together. I wove mana from that great pool beneath me with Jun's white light and guided it with Pallas' precision. I slashed it through every root in every heart except for one.

Kaleos and Noki fell to their knees as white light glowed from their chests.

I was everywhere. I was everything. I was this world and I felt the very last of that imprisonment melt away.

"Tori, it's over. Come back to me." Abraxas' voice sounded like it was reaching from the other side of the universe.

I was everywhere, and it was too far. I was everything, and it was too much. I felt it coming. A tidal wave of power. Mana, more than anyone could handle, more than any of us could handle. I snapped my hands free of Jun and Pallas, severing our connection as it crashed over me.

"Tori, what did we just—?" Pallas tried to ask, but the last thing I saw was horror crashing over Jun's face as he screamed, **"STOP!"**

I couldn't stop. I tried to pull back from that river, but I couldn't escape it. The power flow from the earth was too great; it was no longer a river but a flood beyond proportion. The flow wasn't warm and comforting but burning hot; the magma and heat of the earth tore through me.

It wasn't like dragonfire. That pain had been immense, but it had been real. This was a pain no fae, human, or dragon was meant to feel. It burned, and it froze. It sliced, and it crushed. It destroyed, and it created. This was the pain of an entire world, long abused, eras beyond imagination condensed into a single moment, and I felt my body fracturing beneath the weight of it. I tried to see, but there was nothing. I tried to hear, but there was only infinite sound. I tried to move, but my body wasn't mine any longer. I reached for my bond, but there was nothing but the earth and the sky and sea. All tried to speak to me in a language I could never understand.

Suddenly, the pain ended as if it had never been. The noonday sky was filled with stars that rushed for me, and that river I danced at the edge of my entire life finally consumed me. I could hear Abraxas shouting through our bond and feel him tugging my heart back to him. This time, it wasn't enough, and the river swept me away.

Chapter 73

Abraxas

Something was terribly wrong. Instead of the smile of victory that I expected to see on Tori's face, she was locked in place; her expression was contorted with pain.

"Tori, it's over. Come back to me." I reached out to her, but the surrounding air was hot enough to burn even me. I tried to push through, but the flesh of my fingers sizzled away and charred to black. "Tori, you must stop!"

Her only answer was her body convulsing and seizing erratically as the power coursed through her. Her eyes pressed closed and then shot open, the blue light of the earth streaming out like a beacon. She opened her mouth in a silent scream, expelling more blue light.

Power, pure and undiluted, shot up from the ground beneath us. I swept Pallas and Jun away as I grabbed her, my skin sizzling in a sensation I had never felt. Mana flowed through me, but it was useless. Her skin cracked open beneath my hands; her body couldn't contain the power inside. I did the only thing I could, holding her to me and keeping our bond tight. The pain was unspeakable, but I would endure it. I would endure anything for her. Anything but this.

The bond that tied our hearts stretched, and I sobbed. "Tori, you can't. You can't leave me behind."

Death had no pity. The bond stretched until it was no more than the shadow of hope, and she was gone. There was nothing. Only silence. She was gone. I couldn't hear her laugh, her labored breathing, or the beating of her heart. There was nothing. I couldn't even feel her cold body in my hands or see her beautiful face. Her skin cracked like mud baked under the summer sun, the lines filled with the remnants of that glowing power that consumed her. There was nothing because, without her, the world ceased to exist.

Chapter 74

Pallas

Abraxas ran into the eruption of mana that had exploded from the earth below. It swirled like a giant twister, the vortex pulling us in. I grabbed Jun's hand and tried to pull him away from where the earth continued to crumble below our feet.

"I have to help her!" I could barely hear Jun over the thrum of power.

"Jun, there is nothing we can do. Abraxas is with her—"

Hands clutched my arms, and I was being hauled up and away. Kaleos and Raula grabbed me and Jun, pulling us back to the relative safety of the palace wall as we watched the mana rage.

Then, in an instant, it was gone. Some sunk back into the earth while the rest floated away into the sky. At its core, Abraxas knelt with Tori in his arms.

"No...no, no, no." Jun pulled against Raula, but she held him fast.

"It can't be," she murmured.

Abraxas rose and turned, never once taking his eyes off his mate. Tori's head flopped back as her arms hung down, swinging

466

with no control. Her normally tan skin was sickeningly pallid. It was cracked in patches all over like all the moisture had been sucked out, and beneath it glowed a haunting blue-green. Her eyes were open, dull, and unmoving. She was very much dead. No twisting shadows or uncertain fates. She was gone.

Raula's grip faltered, and Jun lunged for his sister.

"Tori, Tori! **WAKE UP!**" He grabbed her face, twisting it towards him. Magic had no effect on the dead.

He screamed, and the entire world shook. Everyone covered their ears, but Abraxas, who just stared at the woman in his arms, almost as lifeless as she.

My ears rang, so I couldn't hear what was said, but Jun shouted at Abraxas. He reached out and grabbed the man's armor around his neck to shake him. Abraxas didn't even react.

Jun said something else, and finally, Abraxas' face changed; something like life returned to his eyes. He nodded and strode off. Jun followed right behind him. I ran to follow when Jun spun around. He locked eyes with me, and I saw the apology.

"**FALL!**"

The archway he passed beneath crumbled to the ground, blocking my way.

"WHERE THE HELL ARE THEY?" AVLYN AND KALEOS HELPED me pull some of the rubble clear so we could follow after Jun and the king, but we had lost time. Raula had hauled Hadeon off to a nearby manor, where a whole cohort guarded him. Right now, I didn't even think about him. All I was thinking about was Jun. What the hell was he going to do?

We scrambled down the crumbling alleyway. Most of the

fine manors were completely destroyed to rubble. Bodies in fine clothes lay crushed beneath stone alongside those who wore nothing but rags. A few still had walls standing, only partially victim to the city's destruction.

"Keep moving," I told Avlyn as they started to pull open a door to a still-standing building. They frowned but followed me.

We kept going until we passed a home with its entire right side destroyed, all the fine trappings covered in a thick layer of dust. The hair on my arms rose, and I felt the air vibrate as magic was used nearby.

I motioned to Avlyn, and they helped me pull open a door in one of the undamaged walls. We stumbled into a library, the shelves lined with deep red oak bookshelves; most of the books were knocked to the floor from the destruction. Jun and Abraxas moved about the space frantically. In the center of the room I saw gashes in the floor where they had hastily pulled a table over; the princess' body rested motionless on top of it.

Jun slashed his arm and let his blood drip into a bowl held out by Abraxas.

"What are you doing?" I scrambled over the prone furniture and books towards him. I reached out for his arm, but he jerked away.

"My blood is Tori's blood. We need it to locate her."

I'd seen spells like that before. Using a person's own living blood to find their location. Tori lay on the slab before us. It was no mystery where she was. I looked at Jun with worried eyes.

Abraxas saw my concern and interrupted before I could speak. "We are using it to locate her spirit."

He had inscribed a glyph circle on the ground, and it pulsed eerily with the faint green glow of his magic. He had healed from the battle, his dragon blood making quick work of any injuries, but his eyes were still hollow, and his skin was almost as sickly as Tori's.

"You may be a God, but even you cannot cheat death."

"I have once, and I will do it again."

I looked over at Tori's body. This wasn't like the cavern. There, I could feel how life had clung to him and how he had clung back. His heart had still beat, if weakly. Tori's heart was empty.

I looked at Avlyn, and tears streamed from their eyes. They reached out for Abraxas cautiously.

"She is gone," Avlyn whispered.

"SHE IS NOT GONE!" he snarled, his eyes turning that blazing yellow.

My heart caught in my throat, and I took a step back, trying to drag Avlyn with me. The king took a deep breath and calmed himself. That gold faded back into a deep green that was drowning in sadness.

"I can still feel her; she still clings to life. Our bond is not broken—not yet." A heartbroken fool.

Jun hit me with a look so unlike him, so menacing and full of warning. It reminded me of Tori. I reached out with the magic I now felt beating within my own heart. Tori had broken the world open, and magic now sprung up from every leaf and stone. It was easy to find and easy to use. Like I had been born with it. I reached out to it. I didn't need much; just a fraction of my energy gone. The magic leaped from my heart to Abraxas', and I felt his bond with Tori. It was weak, stretched tight like Spinner's web, just a moment away from snapping, but it was there.

"You have little time," I stated blankly. He blinked and then nodded, returning to his work.

It was cruel for me to give him hope. Death was the final barrier, the one all magi faced and had tried to overcome. How many stories had my mother recited to me over the years, the moral always the same? Anyone who tried to cheat death failed every time. Any other hope was no more than a faetale.

I saw what he intended to do. He would use Jun's blood to locate Tori's soul and try to summon it back to her body. It wouldn't work. I had read the accounts of numerous attempts over the ages, all of them failures. Death was the greatest force of them all, and it cannot be overcome. At best, the spell simply didn't function. At worst, something much more horrible came back, or the caster themselves were flung directly into the hells. I could see there was no arguing with him. I let him work.

I readied the magic that now blossomed from my heart. Whatever Abraxas did was his own prerogative, but I would not let it harm Jun. I would not let it harm Avlyn, who I knew wouldn't leave his side. I slid my hand into theirs. Their eyes widened for a moment as I slipped my fingers into theirs, but they squeezed my hand gently as we watched Abraxas' manic work. Jun trailed behind him, providing more blood as needed.

Eventually, he finished his preparations and nodded to Jun, who stepped out of the circle. I sighed in relief as he came to stand near Avlyn and me.

Abraxas walked over to the table that held Tori's body and picked her up as if she were the most delicate of flowers. Her head and arms lolled lifelessly, and it brought a wave of nausea to my stomach. He stepped into the circle with her and knelt down in the center.

He tightened his grip on Tori's fractured body. The glyphs at the edge of the ward shifted from green to a glowing bright white; Jun's blood bubbled as it was burned away by Abraxas' magic. I looked over the glyphs again, and I frowned. They weren't right. These weren't the glyphs for a summoning, and he wasn't leaving the circle. He just held Tori with their foreheads pressed together.

"Abraxas, this is wrong..." I said. Avlyn looked at me with

worried eyes, moving closer to the circle, but the power of the spell drove them back. I looked at the glyphs again when I saw it. No, this wasn't a summoning but a sending.

"Abraxas, you can't possibly mean to..."

He didn't look at me, only at Jun. "It's time."

Abraxas looked into Jun's eyes, eyes the perfect mirror of Tori's, and they held all of her ferocity right now. Abraxas relaxed, and I think he took comfort in knowing that they might be the last thing he saw in this life.

He nodded to Jun, and I tried to reach out to stop this. It was madness. Before I could move, a single word fell from Jun's lips, but the entire room shook with it. "**DIE.**"

Chapter 75

Abraxas

You burned for me, now it's my turn to burn for you.
I told her once that I would always find her, and I intended to keep my word. I would have rather died than spend a single moment on this earth without her, so that's just what I did.

I landed in a river, plunging to my stomach. The water was ice cold, and I could feel frost coating my skin. This was no place for a living soul, and I wouldn't be living much longer if I lingered. The sky above was lit by only stars, as dark and endless as a moonless night. Even my vision only allowed me to see a short distance ahead, and all I could see was the endless expanse of the river that separated life and death. I tried to conjure my flames and felt nothing but the unending cold.

I made my way with the current. Even traveling with it, it nearly knocked me off my feet. Fighting our way back against it would be nearly impossible. My wings were useless here. They were soaked in that icy water, frozen and bogged down. I had expected this would not be simple, but I had counted on them.

Dragons weren't meant to walk; they were meant for the sky. But people weren't meant to come back from the dead either.

I would worry about that later. Something smashed into me, and I looked down to see the culprit was a body. It had wrapped itself around my knees from behind, and I carefully extracted myself as the river ripped it away. I had seen the man's face but didn't know him. I was sure his soul was one of the many who had fallen in our battle. Enemy or ally, it didn't matter now. I said a small prayer for him as he drifted down the river.

He had been lifeless as he drifted with no awareness as the river carried him to the end. Was that what Tori had been like? Was this all a farce, and she had already been swept too far for me to follow? No, I would not allow it.

As the thought plagued me, I felt a pull at my heart. Our bond was still present, if only weakened. Now that I was here, it felt stronger. No, she was still here and I would find her. I focused on that golden thread and followed into utter darkness.

Before I could see it, I heard the river change. No longer the forceful but calm flow, it churned. Eddies of current ripped in erratic patterns, battering me this way and that. The bottom of the river became slicker as if it, too, was coated in ice. I sunk my claws in to keep myself above the water, which was growing deeper and deeper as I traveled forward.

Pain lanced through my wing as a sharp rock hidden just below the surface tore through it. I gingerly pulled the wing back, ice cracking along my skin as I did, which was just as painful. The river was becoming more treacherous, but I had spent my youth exploring the Sea of Spirits, and I would not be bested by it. I may not have had my magic, but it still held me. I felt the movement of air over the dark water, sensing the changes in the current around the rocks and obstacles. This was all slowing me down far too much.

That tug came at my heart again. It was no longer forward

but to my side. I made my way towards its source and found her. She was strewn across one of the razor-sharp rocks, and I could see the flesh of her spirit was flayed, even if it did not bleed. But her hands gripped the rock until I could see her nails cutting through the ice. She slowly raised her head, her eyes faded and unfocused.

"So, you have finally found me again, Death. You shall not have me, not yet." She tightened her grip on the sharp surface, but I saw that light return to her eyes, that same burning hatred she had thrown at me so long ago; it focused her.

I brought my nose close to her face, and the wrinkles at the corners of her eyes softened. "Abraxas? Is that you?" She loosened her grip, but then she swiped at me with her fingers clenched like claws, grazing my nose. "No, just another of your tricks. A particularly cruel one." She slashed at me again.

Little bird, it's me. She held her hand aloft, but I saw the division on her face.

"It can't be. That would mean you are..." she trailed off as her hand slipped on the rock. I swung my tail around and used it to hold her before she could float away.

I told you once before, Tori, no force on this earth, or beyond it, could keep me from you. Now that she was held to the rock with my tail, she lifted both hands to my snout and ran her fingers over the scales there.

"I should have known I couldn't escape you, even in death." Despite the cold, imminent danger, and unending darkness, she cracked a smile mischievous enough to deny Death himself.

You remember that next time you pull another stunt like this. As if the river could hear our hope blossoming, it struck. The tide underneath us rose, and the rock she clung to was submerged. I wrapped my tail around her and, with no small effort, lifted her high enough for her to crawl onto my back. I could hear the ice cracking on both her skin and mine as we moved.

She climbed, sitting just in front of the joints of my wings before she collapsed. The bond between us faltered. She had been fighting for so long; I didn't know how much longer she had. I turned upstream and tried to claw us back to wherever in the hells we needed to go.

To my horror, the river kept rising, the water flowing faster and faster. I sunk my claws into the riverbed, but it was useless. Tori clung to my neck as I lost my purchase, and we were swept away.

I slammed into multiple rocks, their surfaces sharper than a newly honed blade. Each broke away scales and cut into the flesh below. I tried to keep Tori protected, but the next crash sent her flying. She reached out and grabbed one of my horns, twisting herself so she landed on my face.

In the pitch black, I could see her face by the golden light that radiated from my eyes. It highlighted her features in stark relief. She looked deep into my soul, and a sad smile crossed her lips. She pressed them into the scales of my forehead, and over the din of the river, I heard her say, "I love you."

I love you, little bird. Until the void takes us.

And it would. I could hear it now. The river crashed over the edge as it fell into that place where nothing could escape. She held me tight as we fell.

I tried to spread my wings, and as I did, I felt not just the ice that clung to me but their very existence crackling and crumbling into nothing. I couldn't slow us, let alone fly. The thin flesh became nothing more than dust on the wind.

As we toppled down into the pit that was the original chaos of all things, I felt Tori clinging to me with all her strength. I reveled in it, that last feeling of her I would ever have. For centuries, I had longed for my dragon form and cursed the fae body I had been trapped in. Now, I wished for nothing more than to wrap her in my arms, holding her tight to my chest with our lips pressed together so that we might enter death together.

I suddenly felt very light and looked back. Had my wings miraculously caught the air? I saw them stretch behind me now, great and black. They were far larger than mine had ever been. That's when I felt the claws clamp around my neck and tail. With a great tug, we were pulled out of our fatal dive. I couldn't twist to see, but I felt Tori lurch at the sight of what held us. I tried to rear back and fight, but it squeezed around my throat, and in a place of unending darkness, I saw nothing but black.

I AWOKE TO A CELESTIAL CONSTELLATION. MORE STARS than I had ever seen coated the sky, somehow closer and brighter. Nebulas of purple and pinks swirled between them, moving slower than time itself. I pushed myself up on four legs and found myself partially submerged in a pool of water that was perfectly still like a mirror, reflecting the sky above.

A small groan came from beside me, and I saw Tori push herself up. She met my gaze, and scrambled over to me, her arms wrapping around my snout.

"Where are we?"

"The edge of everything," a deep voice rang behind us. We spun around, and I beheld them. They were enormous, even compared to me. They were the mother and father of all dragons, the first gods. Life and Death. She was perfectly white, like fresh fallen snow, and he was darker than the void itself. Her eyes shone a deep blue, and his an infernal red. Those eyes bore into us.

"You have caused quite a situation, little beast." I realized Death was talking to Tori.

"I don't know what you mean?" She shrugged her shoulders. Gods, she was bold.

Death sneered, "You know well what I mean. You have broken the earth's curse and released magic back into the world. This will have consequences you cannot imagine."

"Well, I am the World Breaker."

My laugh cut through that infinite place.

"That you are." Life smiled like a mother looking down on a mischievous child.

"And you, last dragon." Death turned his sneering face to me. "You have once again attempted to steal what belongs to me."

It was my turn to be bold. "Tori is my mate, mine and mine alone. You will not have her while I live."

"Yes, but you do not. You are in my realm now, and you would both do well to remember—"

Life pressed her snout to Death's, and he stilled. She ran the scales of her neck along him, and he calmed.

Life turned her sapphire eyes back to me. "A fae mated to a dragon. Such a thing I could have never predicted."

"Ah, but she is not just a fae, is she, my mate?" Death responded.

"No, I am not. I am something new. Me, my brother, Abraxas, this entire world is new, and it deserves a chance." Tori glared at them like she had at me when we had first met.

"You think I should return you?" Death asked.

"I know you should."

He laughed, the rumble of something that could break apart the very cosmos.

"You cannot go backward, only forward. This is the way of all things, little beast."

"The river can cut deeper, but it can also run dry. The forest may burn, but it allows new life to grow. Not everything is so linear in our world," Tori countered.

"It is in death."

"I cannot believe that." Death bared his teeth at her, and I wrapped my tail around her, encircling her with my body.

"Even I cannot change what is done. You are dead, little beast and your mate is not far behind. I would not linger before the price is too high for either of you to pay."

"I will not allow that." I pulled my lips back, revealing all my fangs.

Death only laughed. "Then go through the final gate together. I care not."

At this, Life snorted, a flurry of blue flames ghosting over her mate.

"Our work is not done," Tori declared. "Hadeon is defeated, but there will come another. They always do. He was just a symptom. There will always be those who think of themselves as greater than others and who will try to place themselves above others. Someone has to stop that."

"Ha! And that is to be you?"

"Not just us."

"Very few pass through my gates believing their life is ready to be over, but they pass through all the same. Now, if you do not hurry—"

"I will go."

Before Death could respond, Tori swatted my nose. "Abraxas, I won't let you sacrifice yourself for me. Not again."

"Not all of me, little bird. Just the part of me I no longer need. That part of me that will always burn for destruction and revenge for a people that have long passed beyond the stars. It is easy to fight, to destroy. It is easy to die. I want to live, Tori, with you."

"Abraxas, you can't mean..."

At this, Life roared, "You are the last dragon, the last of our people. You would give that up?"

"I cannot bear the burden of an entire people upon myself, not anymore. I tried, and it brought nothing but more pain. You yourself helped weave the curse upon everyone's hearts. What did it solve?"

Life did not deny my claim. "I had hoped, with magic gone, our people might survive. I might subvert our great prophecy. Even I, after all this time, can make mistakes. I tried to wield the grief of the earth, but I only magnified it."

Death ran his snout along his mate's nose, and they huddled together, purring gently.

All I saw was Tori.

"Abraxas, I cannot ask this of you." In this place, we were nothing more than spirits, and I finally let my spirit be what had always been destined. I shifted down until we were eye to eye, and I kissed her gently with soft, fae lips.

"You will never have to, my love. It is mine to give and to have a chance at a life with you. I would pay this price a thousand times over."

"Your dragon name, it was to be Astaroth."

I paused, stunned. "How do you know this?"

"Your father, I saw him in his last moments. He said your mother had given it to you."

Tori had given me so many gifts. This was just one more. I gave her face a gentle squeeze as tears rose in her eyes.

"You will be weak. You would give up this power you have fought millennia for... for her?" Death's voice carried no malice this time. Only curiosity.

"Yes." A resounding truth.

Death sighed. "It is... noble. But impossible. I cannot

unweave the part of you that is dragon any more than I can turn back time."

"Maybe you can't." Tori's smile was all wicked fae.

"We are not in our world anymore, little beast. You cannot channel mana here," Death stated flatly.

"I don't need to."

She placed her hand on my chest and reached into the well of life at its core. Death was right; the part of me that was dragon and the part of me that was fae were almost inseparable. Almost.

She pulled on the white light in her heart and followed it across the cosmos to Jun. His light was smaller than the furthest star, but it was there.

"One more puzzle, brother?" Her voice rang out across the vast empty space.

The star winked back, but so did the surrounding stars. They shifted across the sky, the dust and clouds of nebulas spinning into new life. They coalesced above us, drawn into each other as I felt the life inside me shift apart, sliding and unlocking as white light unwove the two halves.

Life and Death stood awestruck as the part of me that was dragon died and was reborn. Scales shimmered over my skin before disappearing forever. My claws punched out and retracted, and my horns rose above my head. At that, I felt the smallest tug in my heart, and I didn't feel my horns disappear. The twins pulled, and half of me broke away; a golden light drifted above our heads.

We both watched as my lifeforce was pulled by the gravity of the stars, and a new world was born. White light surrounded us, and we rose into the air to follow it.

Life and Death were silenced, and time stood still. A deep rumble grew in Death's chest. I could see that brilliant red fire glowing around his heart.

"You'll catch me someday, Death."

"I look forward to it, little beast."

Life chuckled, but she called out, "But know this, little beast and the last dragon, the time you will need to rule may be shorter than you imagine. When the time comes to give up that power, you will, or there will be consequences beyond reckoning."

With that, we shot across the universe.

I AWOKE, AND TORI LAY IN MY ARMS, JUST AS SHE HAD before. She looked calm and serene. So unlike herself.

"Tori, open your eyes." Her hair draped over her face, and I gently tucked it behind her ear, my fingers gliding over her soft skin. I leaned over and kissed her. Her lips were warm under my own, and after a few heartbeats, she jerked awake. Her limbs flailed as she sucked in a deep breath and sat up. Her head spun to everyone waiting just outside the enchantment circle. A moment later, a body collided with us.

"It worked; I can't believe it worked! You're both alive!" Jun wrapped his arms so tightly around Tori I thought she might pop, but she hugged him back with equal enthusiasm. Almost immediately, another body hit me.

"You fucking assholes! You need to stop doing this to me," Avlyn sobbed into my shoulder.

"I'll take that into consideration the next time I die, Avlyn." I wrapped my arms around them, enjoying the sensation of being crushed; it reminded me I was very much alive.

"Interesting new crown, Your Majesty," Pallas said dryly. I reached up and felt my horns pulling back from my temple. I gave Tori a puzzled look.

"What, I couldn't let you give it all up, now could I?" She smiled and I felt her tug at our bond.

I snapped my fingers, and dragonfire, raw and true, sprang forth between them.

"Clever little goddess."

Chapter 76

Pallas

"Are you sure, Abraxas?" I heard the princess whisper. "I don't need this, not anymore. She does."

I climbed down the wooden ladder to the basement of the manor house we had taken over. The space had obviously been used for storage. Foodstuff and crates were stacked everywhere. Against the back wall, between two supporting pillars, Hadeon was strung up on gossamer threads of spider silk; the web held his hands spread wide.

His chin drooped, but his head snapped up as he heard me approach. "Come to gloat, whore?"

I ignored him. I turned to the two guards on either side of him; Avlyn had wanted to make sure there wouldn't be any escapes.

"Leave us."

The guards looked at each other but didn't move.

"Do as the lady says," Avlyn called from the room above. The guards snapped to attention and left the basement, closing the trapdoor behind them.

We were alone. Some of his wounds, cuts and burns by

magic and beast, still hadn't healed. It reminded me so much of when I first saw him, a young, injured boy in a cell, that I thought I wouldn't be able to stand it.

"Why have you come, Pallas?" His voice, cracked and weak, still carried the venom of his bitterness.

I stepped closer. "To end it," I breathed, my voice barely a whisper. The words felt heavy in my mouth, laden with a thousand memories and a thousand regrets.

Hadeon laughed, a hollow, rasping sound that echoed against the damp walls. "To end me, you mean. Your heart bleeds for me, Pallas. I can see it in your eyes. You still love me."

I swallowed hard; the truth was like ash in my mouth. "I loved you, yes," I confessed. The bright and beautiful image of him had been shattered by the darkness in him; each piece was a shard that cut deeply into my heart.

"You're a fool," he spat, struggling against the silken threads that bound him. "You should have shown me your power and ruled by my side. We could have been invincible. We still could be. My love, free me. Free me and let us take back this world together."

I flinched, not from fear, but from the pain of hearing my greatest desire and having it feel so hollow. "You chose power over me long ago, Hadeon."

He sneered, his teeth flashing. "And you've chosen what, exactly, Pallas? New monarchs to serve, to bow to? Pathetic. You were always pathetic. You could never hurt me. At least go find me someone worthy."

Maybe if he had felt remorse, maybe if he had even tried to apologize, I wouldn't have been able to do it. I would have left it to someone else.

"I always was a fool, wasn't I, Hadeon? They molded you into their weapon, their Great Hero. Then, I expected you to just be able to come home and find that I was enough. All I ever wanted was to be your peace."

He thrashed against the web that held him like a rabid dog. He looked just like the boy I nursed so long ago. A boy who was so sweet and reverent. That boy had been dead a long time.

Blue light sharpened into claws, and I rammed them into this chest. I felt them penetrate his flesh. The bone and flesh resisted before giving way. He screamed; his eyes were wide with fear as I ripped the heart straight out of his chest.

"Goodbye, Hadeon. It only seems fair I get to keep this." Blood bubbled from between his lips, and he held my stare just a moment longer despite the gaping wound in his chest. He tried to speak, but I didn't care to try to understand what he said. I just stood there and watched until the heart of the man I once loved with all of my own stopped beating.

When there was no doubt he was dead, I dropped his heart, turned, and climbed out of the basement. Jun and Tori were waiting for me, arms outstretched. I collapsed into them and knew nothing but tears.

Epilogue

Pallas

My legs swung over the edge of the balcony overlooking Xyr. The main bridge that separated the mist district from the lower city still wasn't complete, and on any other day, I would have seen bodies swarming over the wood scaffolding still surrounding the half-completed structure.

Today it was empty as every man, woman, and child in Xyr had taken to the streets to celebrate. Every lintel and balcony was decorated with flowers of various colors and types. Music floated up from every direction into some sort of a discordant chorus as it reached me at the castle. Revelers danced hand-in-hand in the great plazas below; giant circles formed as they started a choreographed dance. Others just writhed in masses, letting the joy of the celebration overtake anything else. Wine flowed freely and leaked into the cracks between the cobblestones of the streets, and no one paid any mind.

"I thought I might find you up here." Avlyn's melodious voice sounded from behind me, and I turned to give them a smile.

"I was hoping you would, Commander."

486

Their dark cheeks colored a bit at that, but they played it all in stride. "Not interested in joining the festivities?"

"I can't. Tori has me running around for her all day."

Avlyn lifted an eyebrow. "You don't seem to be running much right now."

I raised my finger to my lips and chuckled, "What she doesn't know doesn't hurt her." I patted the stone railing beside me, and they easily leaped over to sit beside me.

We sat silently as we watched the crowd below for a while, but I noticed that Avlyn's eyes drifted to the sea beyond.

"May I see it, Avlyn?"

"Are you sure you want to?" they asked. I nodded. Avlyn lifted their right arm towards me. A metal hand had been created for them, and it was cool against my fingers as I gripped it. I pushed back the sleeve of the formal tunic to where it was attached to their arm. I raised my eyes in question, and Avlyn gave me a curt nod. I unbuckled the leather straps that held it to them and placed it on the railing between us.

My hand lingered on what remained of their arm. "I'm sorry."

"S'not your fault, Pallas."

"If you hadn't been there with me that night..."

"There are many things I regret in this life. But spending that night with you is not one of them."

I held their intense stare; they deserved that much. They deserved much more than that.

"Thank you, Avlyn." I gave them a gentle kiss on the cheek.

"For what?"

"For seeing something in me I couldn't see in myself."

"I've always been a commander of vision," they said, giving me a snarky smile.

I shoved them playfully. "Smartass."

"Learned it from the best." Their eyes dropped to their prosthesis, and they made to grab it before I snatched it away. They gave me a puzzled look.

"May I try something?" They nodded again.

I pulled a small brush and ink from the deep pocket of my dress. Avlyn raised an eyebrow. "You just carry that around with you? That's the most...*dijurk* thing I have ever seen."

"Shut up and let me focus," I said, without an ounce of venom. I flipped the hand over and painted a series of glyphs on the inside, moving the brush slowly to form the curves so that each was a perfect inscription. I set the brush beside me and steadied my breath, pulling a single spark of magic out of my heart and placing it in the enchantment. It glowed a soft blue before the glyphs faded from sight. I helped attach the prosthesis back onto Avlyn's arm.

"So, what did that do—" Their eyes went wide as I slid my hand into their metal one.

"I can feel you."

"It's just a first attempt. I will have to work directly with the smith to make more involved work. It will be hard to design the metalwork around the structural basis of the enchantment, but I think I've found one who has the—what?"

Avlyn wrapped their arms around me, their left hand coming to the back of my head as they pulled me into a deep kiss to which I immediately surrendered. It didn't last nearly long enough before they pulled back.

"You are amazing, you know that?" I said nothing, just looked into those beautiful, deep eyes as they held my face in their hands.

"Have you been dreaming about the sea again?" Avlyn finally looked away.

"Every night."

"So, what will you do?"

"I'm not sure. I've never...been away from the army. Never

been away from the king. Ha, you would think after five hundred years of living, the thought of something like that wouldn't scare me so much. Maybe I really am more broken than I thought."

"Someone told me that I wasn't broken—only caged. I've finally gotten myself out of captivity, and it's absolutely terrifying. But...maybe it wouldn't be so scary if I wasn't alone."

"Thinking of sailing the high seas, my lady?"

"The world's a big place. Who knows where I might fly? Tori said I could charter a ship to anywhere my heart desired."

"No more dragon rides for you, huh?"

I gave them the best smile I could. "But, Avlyn, I—I don't know what this is between us. I would...be honored if you came with me, but I can't promise anything."

Avlyn's smile grew to stretch nearly across their entire face.

"Just two adventurers sharing a boat on a perilous journey across the high seas, filled with ancient mysteries and reborn magic? Don't go getting the wrong idea about my intentions, Pallas. That doesn't sound romantic at all."

I smacked their shoulder again. "Good, glad you don't have the wrong idea."

"Same to you. I know a few idiots who would love to come along and completely ruin any romantic mood."

I groaned, but my smile grew. That was until a yell sounded from the open balcony doors behind us.

"Our queen calls, but I'll see you this evening for the celebration?"

Avlyn swept my hand up and kissed my knuckles gently. "Wouldn't miss it for the breaking of the world, Pallas."

Epilogue

Abraxas

Tori's gown was almost as gorgeous as her. Layers of lace and gauzy fabric had been draped over her shoulders and gathered below her ribs before flaring out into a train longer than a man was tall. The craftswomen had spent hours on the fabric alone, and I knew Tori had compensated them handsomely. I'd offered her any gems she wanted, but she had used them as payment, except for one emerald she had placed over her heart. It was a far simpler gown than any other queen had ever worn to her coronation, but it suited her perfectly.

She spun around as I entered our room and scrunched her face at me. "I thought in Xyr's traditions it's bad luck to see me before the ceremony begins?"

"What is life without a little risk, little bird?" I swept her up in my arms and kissed her.

An irritated grunt sounded to my left, "Excuse me, but we have a timetable to keep here, Your Majesty," Pallas said, wearing a very unamused expression.

"Oh, let them be, Pallas." Jun wrapped his arm around the irritable woman, and she deferred, her expression still one of annoyance. "We are done anyway. Let's give them a minute." Jun led her out of the room before. Before he closed the door, he stuck his head back in and gave me a poignant stare and instructed, "One minute."

I laughed and waved him off before returning my gaze to my bride. "You are more lovely than Life herself, little bird."

She smiled, her eyes twinkling. "Quite the compliment. She looks like the kind who could leave a few scars."

I chuckled and placed one more kiss on her forehead.

"What's in the box, Abraxas?" She eyed the package I had hidden behind my back.

"You know I always liked you in a crown." I opened it to reveal a dark metal tiara that mimicked the shape of my horns, but I had emeralds and diamonds to compliment the rest of her coronation jewelry. I placed it on her head, the weight pressing into her hair before she gave me a spin.

"So, what do you think?"

"Ravishing. Much more beautiful than mine." She reached up and ran a finger along the length of one of my horns, and I shivered.

She gave a wicked smile. "I liked these from the first time I saw them." She gently tugged on them and pulled me into a deep kiss, but our minute was up.

"Time to go, my Queen."

ALL OF XYR HAD GATHERED ON THE CLIFFS OVERLOOKING the sea. The celebration had begun early in the morning, and the crowd was raucous and mostly drunk. However, as Tori and I stepped up to the edge of that haunted place, silence fell.

Jun stood on Tori's other side, and she took his hand. They glowed a soft white.

For five hundred years, the earth had been scorched and barren here. Tori and Jun's power allowed it to be reborn. Tendrils of white light poked up through the earth, followed by thousands of blades of grass. Their green blades danced in the autumn breeze, reflecting the setting sun's light. Tori released Jun's hand and took mine.

"Ready?"

I took her hand and stepped onto that land that had been nothing but a curse. As my steps left footprints in the fresh grass, I felt nothing but elation.

We walked to the small shrine at the cliff's edge, and the crowd followed behind us. Jun stood above us on the stone landing as Avlyn and Tori's cohort pushed themselves to the front of the crowd. Even Pallas was present, her hand in Avlyn's.

"Oi, shut up!" Avlyn shouted over the crowd, and slowly, the noise died down to a low simmer.

We both looked to Jun, whose eyes were alit with tears but whose smile was as bright as Tori's.

"Tori, do you take Abraxas to be yours until the breaking of the world, or you know, maybe a bit after that?" Jun chuckled.

"I do." She smiled, and it was like the light of a thousand dawns.

"And do you, Abraxas, take Tori to be your queen and wife from now until the end of all things?"

I let my fangs show as I smiled at her. "I do. Not even the end of the world would keep me away from you."

"Just kiss, you idiots!" Avlyn shouted from the crowd, and several agreeable whoops followed behind them.

"You heard them." Tori smirked at me.

I wrapped my arm behind her back and dipped her low as

my lips pressed into hers as the entire crowd erupted into deafening cheers.

I held her there just as long as I dared before standing her back up and facing her towards the crowd.

"Presenting, King Abraxas and Queen Tori Corignus. Long may they reign."

The crowd's din was so loud it shook the very earth. Tankards clashed, and bodies met all throughout the unending horde. Tori leaned into me, and I held her close.

"You really will never be rid of me now, *husband*."

"You are mine, little bird. Mine to cherish, mine to revere and worship, from this day until the end of all things." I kissed her once more.

Over everything, I could just barely hear Jun's soft singing, his voice a celestial bridge between us and the brand-new evening star.

Beneath the amber cascade of setting sun's glow,
At twilight's end and dawn's first show,
Stood Life and Death, a paradox spun,
In an eternal waltz, their dance just begun.

Life, in her gown of blossoming dawn,
Radiant as morning's first golden yawn,
She breathes the promise of springtime leaves,
A renewal dance, where time never grieves.

Death, in his cloak as dark as night's reign,
Guardian of silent realms, peace to sustain,
His touch whispers change, not an end, but anew,
Guiding stars, their path forward and true.

Together, they step to the rhythm of hearts,

Ava Thorne

The horizon blushes as unity starts,
In their eyes, an eternal promise shines bright,
The cosmos watches with ancient light.

As the world turns beneath skies stardust-sown,
They promise in silence where universes are grown,
"To love from this twilight through all ages' turns,
Until all worlds fall apart and the sky burns."

Thank you!

Thank you for reading Rising from Flames and Starlight. If you enjoyed this book, please consider leaving a review on Goodreads or Amazon. This makes a huge difference for a small indie author like me.

I have so loved sharing Tori's and Abraxas' story with you. While this is the end of their story, it is certainly not the end for Adimos. I have many more stories to tell, and I'm sure we will see some old friends as we go along. Please enjoy this **preview** of the next novel in the Songs of Adimos series, *Forged in Stardust*.

Forged in Stardust

"Go ahead, try."

I took the dagger from his hand. He couldn't be serious, could he? I had made these daggers myself. I knew how sharp they were. I reached my hand out for his forearm, feeling the suede soft skin under my fingertips, and lightly dragged the dagger across.

A low chuckle rumbled his chest. "You will need to try harder than that, *koroq-sa*."

He was right, not even a slight mark marred his moss-green skin. I tried again, pressing harder, and then harder still, and still not a scratch.

"See *koroq-sa*, we orc are not so soft as the other people of this world." He gave me a cocky smile, his tusks gleaming in the forge's firelight.

"Why purchase so many daggers and swords if they are useless?"

His smile vanished. "Who said they were for fighting orcs?"

I blinked. After my conversation with my sisters I assumed

that his cohort was fighting with the one he had split from. But that's all it was, an assumption. Hell, who knew if he was even a part of those splintered tribes? *I don't really know much about him at all... Perhaps Father was right about providing them weapons...*

As I thought of all the things I didn't know about Viok and his people, I realized that my hand was still on his forearm, thumb absentmindedly tracing circles, feeling his strange texture. He seemed to notice what I focused on and the smile returned to his face.

"Feeling me out for weaknesses I assume?" His grin was all tusks as my cheeks turned red. I wouldn't let him have the upper hand again.

"Perhaps I am? Perhaps your skin is more vulnerable in... other places?" My boldness shocked him, but memories of the previous nights spurred me.

I lifted the dagger again, gently tracing the tip up his arm now, then over the tight muscles of his chest, then down over the ridges of his abdomen. Lower, and then lower still towards that delicious V at the edge of his pants.

In one swift motion, he had grabbed my wrist and twisted the dagger from my grasp, while pushing me back until my ass hit the workbench. It was strong and commanding, but he didn't cause any pain. He leaned in and the full size of him became very apparent. His chest was less than an inch from mine, his arms braced on either side, locking me in place. He leaned his head down so he could whisper in my ear, the warm air from his words caressing my neck. "It is not polite to tease, *koroq-sa*."

My heart pounded so hard I was sure he could hear it. A fire was growing in my low belly, deeper than any heat from my forge. It completely obliterated any rational thoughts. "Who said I was teasing?"

He leaned back. The look in his dark eyes stopped my breathing. It was the look of a predatory, with prey in his sights, waiting for the moment to pounce. He was completely still, waiting...waiting for me, I realized. To make the first move. *Or the fatal mistake...*I chuckled to myself. There would be no going back after this, no more games of flirting and sarcastic remarks. Whatever this was would be real, and have consequences. *Damn the consequences.*

I reached my hands out, placing them on his chest. Despite his insistence orcs were not soft, there was no other way to describe his skin. The smooth, velvet sensation guide my fingers to trace his muscles again, feeling the ridges on his stomach. I traced around his sides and a low moan vibrated through him. Still, he did not move.

I ran my hands down his back then pulled him close into me, pinning my body between him and my workbench. I was immediately greeted by a swelling hardness beneath his trousers and found this only made the fire in me burn hotter and lower between my thighs. I felt him hiss against my ear as I pressed my hips into him, and felt him throb.

His hands slowly, agonizingly slowly, traced up my sides to the back of my neck where my work apron was hooked. He gently lifted it over my head, then moved his body back so that it could fall to the ground. His fingers traced along the edge of my lined blouse, their calloused texture excruciating as it met my bare skin. He pulled the top off of me, and the hot air of the forge caressed my skin. Sweat pooled in the curves of my breasts, caught in the bandage I used to secure them. Viok stepped back calmly, but his gaze was even darker now, nearly pitch black. Color rose to my cheeks as that gaze raked over my body slowly, from my face, to my breasts, to the place between my legs.

"So kind of you to wrap yourself as a present for me, *koroq-*

sa." He grinned, and let his fingers trace the bottom curve of my breast, tugging on the wrappings. I bit my lip, trying to contain myself. In the firelight he looked every bit the snarling wolf closing in on his next meal. "But I think there are other parts of you I would like to unwrap first." And then he pounced.

Glossary

People and Places

Aapo Atotoztli - Prince of the River Kingdom.

Abraxas Corignus - King of the Dragon Kingdom.

Adimos - Name of the continent our story takes place on.

Amaros Corignus - former King of the Dragon kingdom, Abraxas' father. Killed during the final battle at Xyr during the War of Flames. Also known as the dragon Malech.

Avlyn Unditem - Commander of the Dragon Army, Abraxas' long time companion.

Bogata Gunnarsdóttir - Lady of the Dragon Kingdom. Owns large swaths of agricultural land outside the city of Xyr.

Bolon Tutulis - High Lord of the City of Metlin.

Ciara - Handmaiden of Princess Tori in the Dragon Kingdom.

Hadeon Aurelius - Emperor of Adimos, the Great Hero and slayer of the World Breaker.

Itzayana Atotoztli - Queen of the River Kingdom.

Jun Khato - Prince of the Pearl Kingdom, Tori's twin brother.

Kaleos - Half-fae soldier in the Dragon army, companion of Princess Tori.

Koron - Capital of Adimos, and Center of the Golden Kingdom.

Lavania - A dragon who fought in the War of Flames.

Luxos Umbratis - Commander of Hadeon's notorious Shadow Troops.

Malech - The Last dragon, known as the World Breaker from the Great Prophecy. He is also secretly King Amurot Curlgnus, and Abraxas' father.

Manan - Capital of the River Kingdom.

Metlin - Largest port city in Adimos.

Niata - Capital of the Pearl Kingdom.

Noki - Human soldier in the Dragon army, companion of Princess Tori.

Obion Aurelius - King of the Golden Kingdom until the end of the War of Flames when Hadeon became Emperor of all of Adimos. Hadeon's adoptive father.

Oryx - Half-fae healer for the Dragon Kingdom.

Pallas Morvavare - Long time consort of Emperor Hadeon.

Plagis Agora - Long time advisor to both King Obion and Emperor Hadeon. Nearly 2000 years old.

Raula - Orc soldier in the Dragon Army, companion of Princess Tori.

Runya Morvavare - Held as the greatest enchanter of the age who worked for King Obion mother of Pallas.

Sea of Spirits - An ocean and collection of islands to the north of Adimos near the Dragon Kingdom. Legend says these islands were once part of the original home of the fae, before disaster struck.

Soraya Lathiel - The last known fae fraternal twin before

Tori and Jun. Ancient fae Queen, was murdered by her people for marrying her brother, King Soractes.

Soractes Lathiel - Last known fae fraternal twin before Tori and Jun. Ancient fae King, was murdered by his people for marrying his sister, Queen Soraya.

Spinner - Baby Giant spider who joined Tori after her time in Tenebrae Forest.

Talius - Commander of the Dragon Army.

Tenebrae Forest - A cursed forest at the edge of the continent. Was once the home of Queen Soraya and King Socrates before their murder. It is believed they cursed the forest after their deaths.

Tezca - The mate of Malech, and the first dragon killed in the War of Flames. Abraxas' mother.

Tori Khato - Princess of the Pearl Kingdom.

Xareni Atotoztli - Queen of the River Kingdom.

Xyr - Capital of the Dragon Kingdom

Terms

Animavita, fae magic - magical energy that sleeps within the hearts of fae, as well as some humans.

Dijurk - term in the orc language for 'one who is studious'... nerd, it means nerd.

Enchantment - a physical glyph based design that when infused with magical energy, works like a spell and allows the control of magic.

Faruk - an orc term used to refer to the matriarchal leader of a clan.

Heartfire - the fire that burns within a dragon's heart, the source of their magic and life.

Huldu - A lesser fae people who have strong animavita naturally. They tend to be lean with blue skin.

K'inich Ajaw - Yucatec name for the mayan sun god.

k'uhul ajaw - Yucatec term for a divine lord or leader.

Lak'ech Ala K'in - a greeting used in various mayan languages that carries many translations, but one is 'I am you, and you are me.'

Mana - magical energy that flows through the earth.

Morka Tempeli - 'Death is the Beginning' in the old dragon language.

War of Flames - a conflict 500 years ago between the fae and dragons. Fae believed that destroying the dragons and the World Breaker would return magic that was fading from the world.

War of Magic - a conflict 700 years ago that started when wide spread panic due to the fading of magic had people desperate for a solution.

Acknowledgments

First and foremost, I would like to thank my husband. He has been my biggest supporter and champion through not only my writing, but my whole life. I love you dearly and look forward to following you around for the rest of this life and all the ones to follow.

A special shout out to my MIL and Mom who helped watch my kids so that I could write this book! I would not have gotten it done without you.

I must thank my beta readers who gave me so much valuable feedback and did it all on a crazy timeline because I am a diva. Thank you Taylor, Jess, Jessica, Alex, Sierra, Antonina, Caroline, Devin, Vanessa, and Poppy. You guys are the real MVP's.

I would be amiss to not include Nobuo Uematsu and Daniel Deluxe, whose music got me into the hyperfocus zone and I played it heavily on repeat for the months of writing this book.

About the Author

Ava has been writing stories since she was a child and has the handwritten notebooks filled with (terrible) stories to prove it. A shocking number contain morally grey love interests and badass women.

When she isn't writing, she can be found spending time with her husband and her two small children in the American Southwest, where she will talk your ear off about water conservation and sustainable living if you will let her.

Printed in Great Britain
by Amazon

43733213R00294